15th IADIS International Conference WWW/Internet 2016

Mannheim, Germany
28-30 October 2016

Editor:

Pedro Isaias

ISBN: 978-1-5108-3297-8

Printed from e-media with permission by:

Curran Associates, Inc.
57 Morehouse Lane
Red Hook, NY 12571

Some format issues inherent in the e-media version may also appear in this print version.

Printed by Curran Associates, Inc. (2017)

For permission requests, please contact International Association for Development of the Information Society (IADIS) at the address below.

International Association for Development of the Information Society (IADIS)
Rua Sao Sebastiao Da Pedreira
No. 100, 30, 1050-209
Lisbon, Portugal

Phone: 351 21 3151373
Fax: 351 21 3151244

secretariat@iadis.org

Additional copies of this publication are available from:

Curran Associates, Inc.
57 Morehouse Lane
Red Hook, NY 12571 USA
Phone: 845-758-0400
Fax: 845-758-2633
Email: curran@proceedings.com
Web: www.proceedings.com

15th INTERNATIONAL CONFERENCE

WWW/INTERNET 2016

PROCEEDINGS OF THE
15th INTERNATIONAL CONFERENCE
WWW/INTERNET 2016

MANNHEIM, GERMANY

OCTOBER 28-30, 2016

Organised by
IADIS
International Association for Development of the Information Society

Co-Organized by

UNIVERSITY OF
MANNHEIM

TABLE OF CONTENTS

FULL PAPERS

SHORT PAPERS

REFLECTION PAPERS

POSTERS

FOREWORD

These proceedings contain the papers and posters of the 15th International Conference WWW/Internet 2016, which was organised by the International Association for Development of the Information Society and co-organized by University of Mannheim, Germany, 28-30 October 2016.

The WWW/Internet 2016 Conference aims to address the main issues of concern within WWW/Internet. WWW and Internet had a huge development in recent years. Aspects of concern are no longer just technical anymore but other aspects have arisen. This conference aims to cover both technological as well as non-technological issues related to these developments.

Submissions were accepted under the following main tracks and topics:

- Web 2.0
  - Collaborative Systems
  - Social Networks
  - Folksonomies
  - Enterprise Wikis and Blogging
  - Mashups and Web Programming
  - Tagging and User Rating Systems
  - Citizen Journalism

- Semantic Web and XML
  - Semantics Web Architectures
  - Semantic Web Middleware
  - Semantic Web Services
  - Semantic Web Agents
  - Ontologies
  - Applications of Semantic Web
  - Semantic Web Data Management
  - Information Retrieval in Semantic Web

- Applications and Uses
  - e-Learning
  - e-Commerce / e-Business
  - e-Government
  - e-Health
  - e-Procurement
  - e-Society
  - Digital Libraries
  - Web Services/SaaS
  - Application Interoperability
  - Web-based multimedia technologies

- Services, Architectures and Web Development
    - Wireless Web
    - Mobile Web
    - Cloud/Grid Computing
    - Web Metrics
    - Web Standards
    - Internet Architectures
    - Network Algorithms
    - Network Architectures
    - Network Computing
    - Network Management
    - Network Performance
    - Content Delivery Technologies
    - Protocols and Standards
    - Traffic Models

- Research Issues
    - Web Science
    - Digital Rights Management
    - Bioinformatics
    - Human Computer Interaction and Usability
    - Web Security and Privacy
    - Online Trust and Reputation Systems
    - Data Mining
    - Information Retrieval
    - Search Engine Optimization

The WWW/Internet 2016 Conference had 97 submissions from more than 23 countries. Each submission has been anonymously reviewed by an average of four independent reviewers, to ensure the final high standard of the accepted submissions. The final result was the approval of 27 full papers, which means that the acceptance rate was 28%. A few more papers have been accepted as short and reflection papers, posters/demonstrations and panel presentation. Best papers will be selected for publishing as extended versions in the IADIS International Journal on WWW/Internet (IJWI) (ISSN 1645-7641) and other selected journals.

The conference, besides the presentation of full papers, short papers, reflection papers and poster presentations also features one keynote presentation from internationally distinguished researcher. We therefore would like also to express our gratitude to Prof. Miriam Foeller-Nord, Hochschule Mannheim, Germany.

The conference also includes a panel entitled "Health services on the Net - What's good for me? What's bad? And how do I tell the difference?" by Thomas Wetter, Célia Boyer, Tobias Neisecke, Jonas Pendzialek and Monika Pobiruchin.

As we all know, organising a conference requires the effort of many individuals. We would like to thank all members of the Program Committee for their hard work in reviewing and selecting the papers that appear in the proceedings.

We are especially grateful to the authors who submitted their papers to this conference and to the presenters who provided the substance of the meeting.

This Proceedings book contains a rich experience of the academic & research institutions and the industry on diverse themes related to the Internet and Web. We do hope that researchers, knowledge workers and innovators both in academia and the industry will find it a valuable reference material.

Last but not the least, we hope that everybody will have a good time in Mannheim and we invite all participants for the next year's edition of the International Conference WWW/Internet.

Pedro Isaías, The University of Queensland, Australia
Conference & Program Chair

Mannheim, Germany
October 2016

PROGRAM COMMITTEE

CONFERENCE & PROGRAM CHAIR
Pedro Isaías, The University of Queensland, Australia

COMMITTEE MEMBERS

Abdolhossein Sarrafzadeh, UNITEC New Zealand, New Zealand
Agostino Poggi, Università degli Studi di Parma, Italy
Alexander Troussov, Russian Academy of National Economy, Ireland
Alexiei Dingli, University of Malta, Malta
Amaury Trujillo, IIT-CNR, Italy
Ananya S. Guha, Indira Gandhi National Open University, India
Andrea Kienle, University of Applied Sciences, Dortmund, Germany
Andreas Papasalouros, University of the Aegean, Greece
Andreas Schrader, Insitute of Telematics, University of Luebeck, Germany
Anirban Kundu, Netaji Subhash Engineering College, India
Asadullah Shaikh, Najran University, Saudi Arabia
Bo Hu, Universität der Bundeswehr München, Germany
Christos Bouras, University of Patras, Greece
Clodoveu Davis, Universidade Federal de Minas Gerais, Brazil
Costas Yialouris, Agricultural University of Athens, Greece
Cristiano Costa, Universidade do Vale do Rio dos Sinos (UNISINOS), Brazil
Damian Bulira, Wroclaw University of Technology, Poland
Davide Careglio, Universitat Politecnica de Catalunya, Spain
Debajyoti Mukhopadhyay, Maharashtra Institute of Technology Pune, India
Demetrios Sampson, Curtin University, Australia
Diana Andone, Politehnica University of Timisoara, Romania
Dickson Lukose, GCS Agile Pty. Ltd., Malaysia
Dirk Bade, University of Hamburg, Germany
Dirk Thissen, Rwth Aachen, Germany
Dongqiang Yang, Shandong Jianzhu University, China
Elias Kirche, Florida Gulf Coast University, USA
Erick López Ornelas, Universidad Autónoma Metropolitana - Cuajimalpa, Mexico
Evangelos Sakkopoulos, University of Patras, Greece
Fatos Xhafa, Universitat Politècnica de Catalunya, Spain
Fernanda Lima, UNB, Brazil
Florence Sedes, Universite Paul Sabatier of Toulouse, France
Frantisek Darena, Mendel University, Czech Republic
Giuseppe Patane, CNR-IMATI, Italy
Gustavo Rossi, Universidad Nacional de la Plata, Argentina
Hector Migallon Gomis, University Miguel Hernandez, Spain

KEYNOTE LECTURE

THE INTERNET OF THINGS – BOON AND BANE OF THE MODERN WORLD?

By Prof. Miriam Foeller-Nord,
Hochschule Mannheim,
Germany

Abstract

The Internet of Things (IoT) is currently all around. It finds its way in nearly all areas of life. But what does it exactly mean, what stands behind this name? Is it a brand-new technology, a business case or a mere buzzword? What is the difference or the addition to the "normal" Internet, so what is necessary to go for IoT?

Seems, we need "things". But what kind of things, and what must be their features? In fact, they need to be connected to Internet and for that, they need to transform from simple (stupid) objects to "smart" objects. So, regarding IoT everything has to become connected and "smart". In private we use smart watches to track our activities and even our home is no longer a simple housing, but will become a smart home. In business and industry smart production, smart factory and smart retail are the upcoming keywords, in healthcare smart health and in traffic smart mobility.

The keynote highlights some answers to the questions above and describes main challenges from technical, social and security side. It gives an overview over the technical aspects and requirements. It shows typical scenarios, the architecture and the components of IoT applications and relations to other current trends like cloud computing and big data. But also a look to the social aspects is necessary. How will the Internet of Things influence our life, will it lead to more freedom and enrichment or to technical dependency? Last but not least, strongly related to the brave new IoT-World and leading us far beyond pure technical issues we have to face a new dimension of security risks.

PANEL

HEALTH SERVICES ON THE NET - WHAT'S GOOD FOR ME? WHAT'S BAD? AND HOW DO I TELL THE DIFFERENCE?

By Thomas Wetter[1], Célia Boyer[2], Tobias Neisecke[3], Jonas Pendzialek[4] and Monika Pobiruchin[5]

[1]Heidelberg University, IMBI, Im Neuenheimer Feld 130.3, D-69120 Heidelberg, Germany and University of Washington, Dept. BIME, South Lake Union, Seattle, WA 98195, USA

[2]Health On the Net Foundation and Kconnect European Union Project, 2 chemin du Petit Bel-Air, 1225 Chêne-Bourg, Switzerland

[3]Medizin und Neue Medien, Schönebergerstr. 17a, 10963 Berlin, Germany

[4]Techniker Krankenkasse, Bramfelder Straße 140, D-22305 Hamburg, Germany and University Hospital Cologne, IGKE, Gleueler Str. 176-178, D-50935 Cologne, Germany

[5]Heilbronn University, GECKO Institute for Medicine, Informatics and Economics, Max-Planck-Str. 39, 74081 Heilbronn, Germany

Abstract

Many medical applications for citizens are conveyed through the Internet or mobile net (subseq.: Net): health information, search for physicians, calendar apps for diabetics, etc. To become regular health care, paid through health insurance and ushered through trusted channels, Net health services need scrutinized proof of effect and minimal risk. By contrast, services in the so called second health market, where customers choose and (sometimes) pay, are found through search, with results as unpredictable as when searching for games, restaurants, or merchandise. While in the former ethics and legislation widely curb the patient against harmful advice, he operates at his own benefit/risk in the latter. Free customer choice is not bad per se; it rather fosters patient empowerment in a traditionally paternalistic medicine. However, limited health literacy often precludes the patient from rationally and effectively selecting from overwhelming supply.

In the panel we will sketch how wide the field is and how fast and erratically it evolves. We will juxtapose the potential seen by providers of all kinds with risks of harm through patients' irrational use of information, plus physicians' take of the intrusion of the Net into their domain. We will explore the role of Net services as an asset in health insurance competition, how Net services undergo clinical trials, are approved and launched as well as how Medical Informatics based efforts strive for indicators of trustworthiness in the market approach [Boyer et al 1998 and 2015]. We will conclude with the challenge of a dwindling clinical workforce in most industrial economies and discuss with the audience how health care systems can evolve for the full potential of Net medicine to be unleashed and the gaps to be closed [Wetter 2016].

The panel will include five short, introductory speeches given by the authors (5 x 10min). During the speeches controversial conjectures – e.g., "Net services widen the digital divide!", "The app market will regulate itself!" – are presented which should fuel the following discussion phase. Participants are polled whether they confirm or reject these conjectures. Afterwards panelists and participants discuss the statements and respective voting results. Before closing the panel, participants vote for a second time to determine if their attitude towards the presented hypotheses has changed.

REFERENCES

Boyer, C., M. Selby, J. R. Scherrer, and R. D. Appel. 1998. The Health On the Net Code of Conduct for Medical and Health Websites. *Computers in Biology and Medicine 28*, no. 5 (September 1998): 603–10.

Boyer, C. and L. Dolamic. 2015 Automated Detection of HONcode Website Conformity Compared to Manual Detection: An Evaluation. *J Med Internet Res, 2015*; 17(6):e135. doi: 10.2196/jmir.3831.

Wetter, T, 2016; *Consumer Health Informatics. New Services, Roles, and Responsibilities.* Springer, Cham, Switzerland

Full Papers

INTENSIFYING THE DEVELOPMENT OF WEB-BASED VIRTUAL MUSEUMS FOR E-LEARNING DOMAIN

Luciana A. M. Zaina[1], Eline F. de A. Welter[1], Guilherme J. de C. Góis[1] and Andréia D. Leles[2]
[1]*Federal University of São Carlos – campus Sorocaba, Rdv João Leme dos Santos, Km 110 -Sorocaba - SP - Brazil*
[2]*Engineering College of Sorocaba, Rdv Senador José Ermírio de Moraes, 1425 - Sorocaba – SP - Brazil*

ABSTRACT

Museums are a large repository of memories of History, Art and Humanity that may become an important teaching-learning tool on the Web. Although there are many museums on the Web, the effort for building and maintaining them can directly impact the adopting for learning purposes. This article presents an approach to intensify the building of web-based virtual museums to be used as an e-learning tool. Regarding that the web-based virtual museums are a specific domain, we have developed the e-MuseumSPL - a software product line to support the building of virtual museums based on software reuse principles. To validate the proposal was implemented - by two groups of developers - two versions of museums. Based on the outcomes, we outlined some reflections about: (i) the advantages and disadvantages of using the approach in the developers' point of view; and (ii) the feedback of ten end-users (students) about their satisfaction on interacting with the museums.

KEYWORDS

Web-based virtual museum; e-learning; software reuse; web software architecture

1. INTRODUCTION

The virtual museums can be considered an important tool in different degrees of education process: (1) formal - following the school curriculum guidelines, (2) informal - based on the parents' and society's interventions, and (3) non-formal - occurs outside of the school, but it is directly related to it (Smith, 2002). When a person visits a museum (real or virtual), s/he deeps into the historical facts and can link them to the present, developing meaningful experiences with significant contribution in all the perspectives: formal, informal, and non-formal. In the e-learning perspective, the virtual museums bring the flexibility to extend and construct tools to meeting different features of educational context. Besides this, an e-learning tool allows the teacher to build learning scenarios to enrich his/her classes.

The exhibitions of museums artworks supply directly to the development of culture and education, justifying its importance for the education and culture of humanity. Some works report reviews and experiences that highlight the importance of museums in the teaching-learning process (Sarah, Prihatmanto and Rusmin, 2012; Berry, Sheard and Quartly, 2011). Vavoula et al (2009) addresses an experiment in the MyArtSpace project in which mobile devices are used by children during a museum visit. An application on the smartphone guided children with multimedia presentations related to exhibits. During the visit children could upload photos and videos that were recorded into a website. When they returned to the classroom they were able to share and exchange the acquired knowledge and the photos and videos with one another. On the other side, Arends et al. (2009) presents an exploratory study of art museum websites and their web 2.0 features. In the work, the authors state the characteristics on the dimensions of exploring artwork, using for educative purposes, and announcement of events and discussions. For educative purposes the study points out the use of sharing and annotations about artworks and the games to motivate the visitors in testing their knowledge.

Although making available the virtual museums as web-based tools improve the access for them, it is necessary to offer approaches for enhancing the development and maintenance of these tools. Despite of the Web technologies, as HTML, could be enough for constructing virtual museums, the implementation of reuse and maintenance of coding will demand arduous efforts on the designing of them. Concerning the focus on (1) the effort to developing and maintenance of virtual museums as a web-based tool; and (2) that the virtual museums represents a specific domain of product families, the Software Product Lines (SPL) may be an alternative to promote the quality, productivity, and the reuse of the applications developed for specific domains (Chimalakonda, and K. Nori, 2012; Falvo et al 2014). A SPL may supply the process of software construction with concepts and technical tools for developing products in a systematic way in order to generate a family of products. The main proposition is the building of products based on the reuse of an infrastructure that includes: software architecture, components, design patterns and planning methods. Differently of an oriented-object reuse in which the reuse of components are the main point, an SPL approach is driven by a development oriented by the software architecture; and the structure are composed by unit tests and documentations that easily promote the reuse and the automatically generation of code.

To the effectiveness of the reuse, the software components are developed concerning the similarities (common or generic points), called core assets, and the variabilities (which must be defined and managed by a specific instance) in a family of products. The traditional methodology for SPL construction is divided into two steps: Domain Engineering (DE) - activities to provide that solution driven by systematic tasks for the identification and organization of the knowledge domain; Application Engineering (AE) in which the applications are built based on the reuse of the core artifacts previously developed in DE (Clements and Northrop, 2002). Within the advantages of adopting SPL to developing web-based e-learning tools, some works explore different approaches: the use of Model-Driven Development (MDD) (Zhou et al., 2008; Cong et al., 2010), m-learning applications (Falvo et al, 2014), interactive applications (Dalmon et al, 2012), and a SPL for teaching dialects in India (Chimalakonda and Nori, 2012). All the authors of these works highlighted that the SPL adoption was important not only to improving the productivity, reuse and quality of the product, but also the satisfaction of developers and end-users with products generated by the respective SPL.

Based on two statements – (i) the value that web-based virtual museums can bring for e-learning area, and (ii) the use of SPL fundamentals to support the creation of virtual museums - this paper has the goal to present an approach that aims to intensify the building of web-based virtual museums for the e-learning domain. Regarding that we were dealing with a specific domain, we have developed the e-MuseumSPL - a software product line to support the construction of web-based virtual museums based on strong software reuse principles. The approach supplies the developers with a web-oriented architecture solution which focus on the reuse, quality and productivity of software development. The 3D environments are out of the scope of the e-MuseumSPL whose focuses on the museum artwork and not on the immersion in historical surrounding (Karoulis, Sylaiou and White, 2006; Marty and Twidale, 2004).

The remainder of this paper is organized as follows: Section 2 presents the approach e-MuseumSPL and outlines on how the domain of virtual museums was explored for the conception of it; Section 3 reports the conduction and the outcomes of the approach experimentation in both viewpoints: by the developers and by the students (end-users); and finally Section 4 summarizes the conclusions and the directions for further works.

2. THE APPROACH: CONCEPTION, DESIGN AND IMPLEMENTATION

The development of a SPL starts in the DE step aiming at the identification and investigation of specific domain aspects in order to produce the SPL based on their similarities and variabilities. In this work, we followed the traditional activities of DE: (i) study and analysis of the domain aspects; (ii) the specification of the web-based and domain-based architecture; and (iii) the development of the core assets of the SPL (Clements and Northrop, 2002). First, two sub-activities were carried out to support the activity (i): (a) a comparative study of six web-based virtual museums, and (b) an exploratory activity with potential end-users for checking the acceptance of the features of the museum gathered from sub-activity (a).

The comparative study (a) aimed to raise the key features usually found in virtual museums that go beyond the artwork exposition, and to verify aspects related to user interaction (interaction channels). Driving by the statements of Karoulis, Sylaiou and White (2006) and Marty and Twidale (2004) - who report that the use of excessive elements of interaction may cause troubles into the end-users attention on the artworks - the study was carried out in six famous web-based virtual museums (Van Gogh, Louvre, British, Egyptian, Salvador Dali, and Minas Conspiracy); five of them were selected because of their popularity and of their free access; and the Minas Conspiracy Museum was included for its relevance to the History of our country. The study revealed to us the common features (present in most of the products of the family) and the variabilities (found in one or in some products of the family) which restate the viability of developing the SPL in virtual museum domain.

In order to verify the acceptance of the features and the potential of the web-based virtual museum for teaching and learning purposes, an exploratory activity (b) was conducted in two steps. First, with the participation of two museum experts and four History teachers, a brainstorming was carried out, allowing the identification of the museum system actors and their respective educational activities into the virtual museum. The museum expert actor has basic activities the construction of the museum: (i) the cataloging and the publishing of the artworks and the scenarios of visitation, and (ii) the building of a specific museum. In the teaching perspective, the *teacher* (i) uses the scenarios of visitation and (ii) can create learning challenges in order to motivate the students on testing their learning. And in the learning perspective, the *students* (i) navigate in the tool exploring the scenarios and (ii) answering the challenges. Adding the (b) brainstorming outcomes to the (a) comparative study allowed us to set up the main domain elements. Based on this, we developed a functional prototype to be run in both, web and Android platform, in order to validate the domain elements in the end-users' viewpoint. The activity was carried out in Brazilian's Elementary schools and museums with the participation of 174 students, 3 History teachers and one museum expert; the validation details are found in Welter et. al. (2014). The results of the activity reinforced that the domain elements found in the previous sub-activity (a) could be inserted into the core assets of the SPL and into its variability list. During the collection of the audiences opinion, both - the teachers and the museum expert - outlined that to the development of the students' skills it would be important to provide a feature which allows the students to understand the historical event by making the relationship between past (from the museum artwork) and the facts of the present moment. This feature was added as variability in the SPL. For concluding the domain analysis step (i), the model of features (see Figure 1) - outlined the common features and the variabilities - was designed following the FODA (Feature-Oriented Domain Analysis) method (Kang et al., 1990).

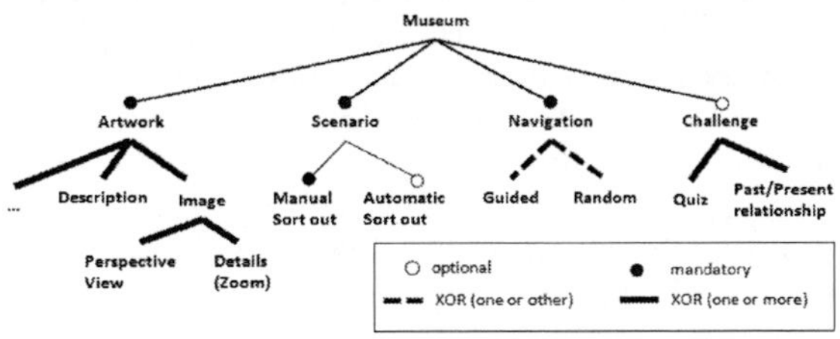

Figure 1. Model of features of e-MuseumSPL

Based on the step (i) outcomes, the next DE step was the SPL architecture specification (ii) which must be figured out by meeting the attributes of being flexible and extensible, and according to the model of features. Since the architecture foundations of our approach were Web platform the architectural pattern MVC (Model View Controller) was adopted, mainly because this pattern naturally defines the responsibilities of each element of architecture. Allowing for the flexibility for dealing with the issues of end-user interface and interaction, the architecture specification was concentrated on the functional requirements. Additionally, the focus on functional requirements brings up a flexible interface to be run in different platforms. In the SPL conception, the architecture elements have to be adherence to the domain features. In this direction, the Domain-Driven Design approach (DDD) states principles that drive the SPL architecture have to be aligned to the business rules, simplify the reuse, reduce the coupling, and allow the use of independent technology product (Vernon, 2013). Following the DDD approach and the model of features (Figure 1), we proceeded with the identification of the objects on which the business rules were reflected: *Museum*, *Scenery* and *Artwork* - main similarities, and being the *Challenge* element classified as a variability.

Driving by the principle of independent layers (MVC pattern), the architecture of the individual domain object (DDD approach) was drawn and splitted into different layers (see Figure 2). The *Model* layer deals with the persistence requirements and is supported by the components: *Entity*, object of value (*DTO*), and Data Access Object (*DAO*) pattern. Aiming to provide the proper service to the *Application* layer, the *Controller* layer deliveries from the *Service component* (Facade pattern) the functional system behavior to the control of the application (*Application* layer), that are represented by the product that is built from the SPL. In the same layer, the *Constructor* (Builder pattern) enables the creation of a complex domain object (objects that are composed by other objects) - in the museum domain are: artworks, scenarios and museum - which is used by the *Service component*. The proposed architecture reduces the complexity of the objects creation by invoking a single method. A Behavior element was added to the architecture - Dynamic layer - whose purpose is to handle the components which implement behavior to the museum as guided navigation (core asset), or random (variability), or even the insertion of variabilities for sharing on social networks or other repositories. The non-dependence of technological tools and flexibility of the structure allows the developers to work with frameworks such as Spring, Java Server Faces among others in the Application layer for integration of their own components to the SPL architecture proposed in this work.

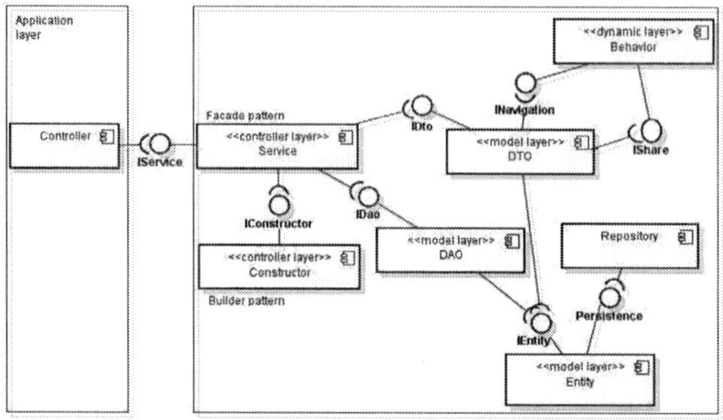

Figure 2. Architecture of individual SPL components

Regarding the architectural foundation of the individual component and the model of feature, the e-MuseumSPL was designed by providing the core assets and the respective points of variability. The core assets of a SPL are composed not only by components, but also by documentations and other artifacts. In this sense, the core assets of the e-MuseumSPL also provide templates and documents, and automated unit tests that were developed for each of the mandatory components of the SPL (artwork, scenario and museum). The implementation of the e-MuseumSPL used the following web technologies: Java, Eclipse Link JPA (provides developers with a standards based in object-relational persistence), and Apache Maven1. Figure 3 illustrates the core assets in what are indicating the mandatory and the variable elements. The first version of e-MuseumSPL presents three types of components (in Figure 3 – the status of the elements were illustrated): (white) is a part of the core assets and was implemented; (gray) is a variability available; and (**) is a variability prepared to be implemented by extension. All the main components (classes) have extension points that can be identified by the stereotypes labeled as mandatory and variability. Taking into account the rules of object-oriented development that induces reuse (programming for super type and abstraction) and the behavior changing by extension, the *Strategy* design pattern was adopted in the model allowing for the adding of new behavior requirements as variability points.

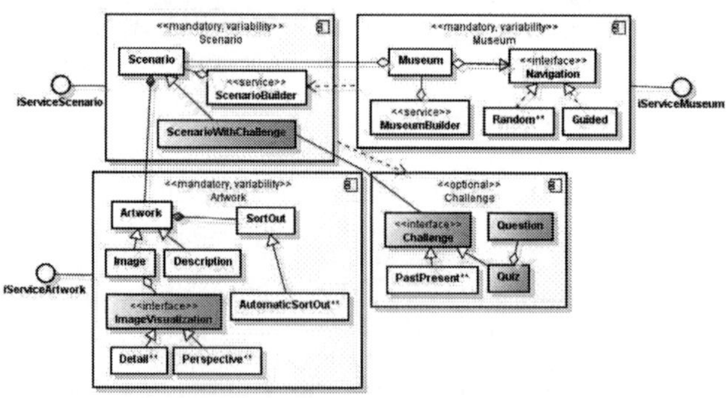

Figure 3. Core assets of e-MuseumSPL

---

[1]Apache Maven allows describes how software is built, and its dependencies (https://maven.apache.org/).

Comparing our proposal with the works presented in Section 1 (Zhou et al., 2008; Cong et al., 2010; Falvo et al, 2014; Dalmon et al, 2012; Chimalakonda and Nori, 2012) on the perspective of reusing, the e-MuseumSPL promotes the intersection of elements inserted into the people's culture to the e-learning context. The development driven by domain oriented allows the specification of system elements closer to the elements of real world. In the perspective of using museums for e-learning, the works, Vavoula et al (2009) reported experiments with real museums, but not with a virtual platform. And Arends et al. (2009) discussed trends without concrete results.

2.1 First Experimentation: Application Engineering

The AE was driven by the fundamentals of SPL and of Empirical Software Engineering (Wohlin et al, 2012). Two groups of undergraduate students (6 participants divided into groups of three members) who belonged to the sixth semester of Computer Science course at University of São Carlos were invited to develop two different virtual museums by using the e-MuseumSPL. All participants signed a consent form for participation in the experiment. The profile of the participants - collected in a pre-interview - was: (a) They had consistent knowledge in the Web technologies that are a requirement to use the SPL; (b) only two participants - one in each group - have heard about the use of SPL and Apache Maven concepts - that is important to automatically generation of the museum instances from the SPL; and (c) only one of the members has had experience in software development in companies; the others had applied their developer's skills only for academic purposes. Given that the participants' profile was characterized by little experience on software development, a warming up - 4 hours splitted into two days - was carried out in order to leveling the participants knowledge about development of products by using a SPL: the architectural models (Figure 2 and 3) and all core assets (models, unit tests, etc) were presented to the participants. The participants implemented some examples using the e-MuseumSPL.

The minimum requirements requested for the participants were focused on the using of the web-based virtual museum by the students and not on the creation of the museum by the museum expert. The mandatory functional requirements were: the random and guided navigation and the offering of challenges for the students; the groups had freedom to include new requirements. As non-functional requirements were stated: the access should be via web and mobile devices (by responsive web interfaces); and the groups should use artworks of real museums. Considering the audiences and the museum theme, the groups had different targets: (i) Group 1 (G1) a museum for teaching Brazilian History (Museum of the Republic) to elementary school; and (ii) Group 2 (G2) a museum for education of Arts (Artworks Museum) to the high school.

As the participants of G1 and G2 had attended the HCI (Human Computer Interaction) course before the experimentation, they decided to build low fidelity prototypes to validate their ideas with potential end-users using POP tool (POP, 2016) based on low fidelity prototypes. Each group proceeded with prototypes evaluation with the participation of 3 end-users each one. After the evaluation, the groups developed the museum instances by using e-MuseumSPL and adopting SpringMVC, Bootstrap and AngularJS to implement the controller and application layers. The groups took different projects decisions: while G1 has developed a responsive web product that could be used in both PC and mobile platform; G2 followed the mobile first principles delivering a version produced by using web technologies. Figure 4 illustrates the museum instances (I – produced by G1 and II – produced by G2). Similarities and differences of each instance are highlighted: (A) the application's homepage; (B) the challenges - for G1 a scenario challenge: past-present relationship, for G2 a quiz; (C) guided navigation; and (D) extra requirement – in G1 the students can make annotations about a given scenario, and in G2 the image may be viewed in original size. The annotation feature was an important extension stating the Web 2.0 principle of collective construction of data; the students could exchange their ideas sharing the annotations in social network. After the implementation, the groups conducted tests with end-users whose results will be reported in next subsection 3.2. An important finding during AE is that it was not necessary to fix anything or add any modifications into the e-MuseumSPL to meet the requirements and to produce the instances. The developers validated all the elements of the core assets (tests, components, and documentation). Then we can conclude that the Goal 1 was achieved: the AE was successfully performed based on the DE outcomes.

To support the conclusions the *Goal 2*, we asked the groups before starting the product implementation, an estimation of time (number of hours and days) for the web-based virtual museum implementation (based on the mandatory requirement: functional and non-functional) considering they would not use a SPL. For the delivering of the final product version, we set a deadline of one month. The groups reported similar time predictions for the implementation of both - functional and the interface/interaction requirements - a total: G1 - 24 days, and G2 - 26 days, with a dedication of around 6 hours/day. Taking into account their time prediction, the groups planned to use the remaining days for testing the museums with the end-users (G1 - 6 days; and G2 4 days). However, the real time spent was better than the prediction (around 32% less): G1 - 18 days and G2 - 17 days, maintaining the dedication of 6 hours/day. Within this achievement, the groups had time to conduct end-users tests - planning, conduction and analysis - and subsequently make some adjustments into the products according to users' feedback.

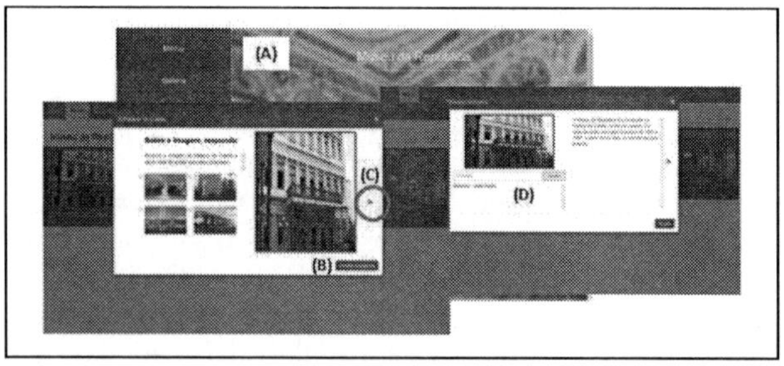

I - Museum of the Republic

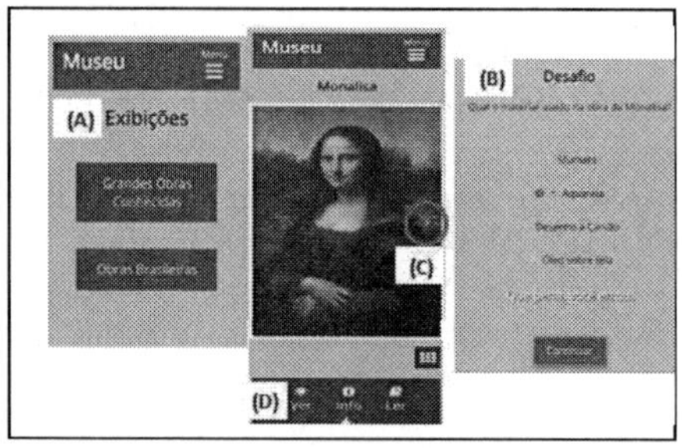

II - Artworks Museum

Figure 4. Core assets of e-MuseumSPL

In addition to the aspect of time spent during the museums development, we conducted a post-interview with the developers who had participated in AE, driving by two questions: (1a) state the positive and (1b) negative aspects of using the e-MuseumSPL; (2) if they agree they could build the same product, spending the same time without using the e-MuseumSPL. Regarding the question (1a), G1 highlighted as positive that they had *"more time to focus on the front-end of the project, building an attractive interface; and the back-end coding and/or structure were totally supplied by the SPL"*; G2 emphasized that *"the controllers codification were easily built by the calling of SPL services"*; and both groups pointed out as negative aspect (1b) *"the initial time spent understanding how to use the SPL"*. For the question (2), G1 reported that *" I think that we could not developed it spending the same time; we would have spent a long time in idealize the architecture - database, entities, and DAO – and in performing the tests, in writing the documentation..."*; and G2 stated that *"without the SPL, they had to track more carefully the requirements... the SPL forced them to follow an architecture, and then the requirements were fulfilled naturally..."*. Taking into account the answers, we can conclude that *Goal 2* was successfully achieved. Even though the participants outlined the difficulties on the learning of how to use the SPL, they stated that the SPL brought advantages in saving time of the development. Concerning this, we can conclude that the groups could develop the products in a shorter time (less than 18 days) if they had previous experience the using of SPL concepts. The post-interview reinforced the conclusions of the *Goal 1*, thus the participants reported the widespread use of the core assets and the acceptance of the architecture.

2.2 End-users Feedback

As the groups (G1 and G2) had more time until the deadline, they decided to adopt the end-user testing based on the SUS (System Usability Scale) questionnaire, improving the products analysis over the usability point of view. Proposed by John Brooke in 1986, SUS states the product usability in five dimensions: ease of learning (D1), efficiency (D2), ease of memorization (D3), minimization of mistakes (D4), and user satisfaction (D5). Each dimension consists of one or more questions and the answers are requested in the Likert scale ranging from *"strongly disagree"* to *"completely agree"* (Bangor, Kortum and Miller, 2009). The set of ten questions must be presented in a prescribed sequence, because each one represents a specific SUS dimension. The user satisfaction index (ranging from 0 to 100) of SUS is calculated by the rules: for questions in the odd position, we subtract 1 to the user's response, and the questions in the even position the score is 5 minus the user's response. The minimum SUS factor is 70 for a product with a good usability. After getting the score of each question, add up the scores and multiply the result by 2.5. More information about SUS factor may be found in Bangor, Kortum and Miller (2009). Although SUS focuses on usability aspects, they can have a high impact on the software functional aspects. The usability problems can be caused not only by interface and interaction aspects; functional requirements may interfere in the usability quality, especially in SPL that is driven by the architecture structure and the domain elements (Juristo, Moreno and Sanchez-Segura, 2007). Besides, Kang et al (1990) state that a feature is a user-visible aspect and a SPL focuses on features of the products, then the usability tests can reveal issues which impact in SPL funcionalities.

The groups planned the tasks to be performed by the users during the usability testing, and recruited 10 end-users (5 of elementary school - G1 product, and 5 of high school - G2 product). All end-users – who had never had contact with the products - signed a consent term for participation in the tests. The tests – planning, conduction and analysis – were led in four days. At the end, the users should answer the SUS questionnaire individually. For the 5 users of the elementary school, G1 adapted the SUS questions in order to use a vocabulary closer to the participants' age. Besides the SUS, the groups tracked the users' actions performed during the tests by annotation observations of difficulties and doubt. The methodology used by the groups for the analysis was: review the notes gathered during the observation to identify problems of interaction and calculation of SUS factor.

In the tests carried out with G1 product, 3 of 5 users performed the tasks on tablets and the others on PC. On the other hand, in the G2 tests, 5 users executed the tasks exclusively on smartphones. The usability tests did not reveal serious shortcomings of interface and interaction, and none of functional error arose. Only two observations were written down by the groups which reported: G1 - some end-users have doubts about the challenge tasks during few seconds, but quickly overcome it; and G2 - the end-users tried to use some interaction patterns (pitch and spread movement to zoom, for example) that the product did not implement them in the first version.

After the tests, the developers groups calculated the SUS factor based on the students' answers. The media of SUS factor was considered satisfactory for both products, 87,5 and 83,5, for G1 and G2 respectively – being 70 the minimum SUS factor for a product with a good usability. Table 1 reports the SUS factor and the media per SUS dimension of each product by end-user. The numbers revealed to the developers the potential of the products in the end-users viewpoint (*Goal 3*). In addition, based on the SUS factor results and on the observations of the users' interaction, we could infer that the e-MuseumSPL is a flexible product that can meet the needs of different audiences. Additionally, the end-users did not reported misunderstandings about the elements used the museums instances, restating that the domain analysis could catch elements that represents the museums domain.

Table 1. SUS factor details by end-user and by product

	Users						SUS Dimension				
Product	**U1**	**U2**	**U3**	**U4**	**U5**	**SUS factor (media)**	**D1**	**D2**	**D3**	**D4**	**D5**
G1	97,5	100	85	92,5	62,5	87,5	83	90	85	80	80
G2	77,5	75	87,5	95	82,5	83,5	87,5	83,33	80	90	80

3. CONCLUSIONS AND FUTURE WORK

The contributions of this work can be highlighted in four aspects: (i) proposes the e-MuseumSPL to step the development of virtual museums up on the e-learning context providing the students of different levels of school with an open access tool; (ii) offers to the society the benefit of visiting museums on the web, reducing the geography distances; (iii) reports an empirical analysis that demonstrates the gain in productivity during the building of museums by allowing the developer to focus on the creation of different front-ends and on the performing of end-user tests; and (iv) states the evaluation on two viewpoints: developer and end-user. Tangentially, we could highlight an important contribution: demonstrates the feasibility of using reuse techniques for building e-learning tools by introducing good practices of software development into the process. Others exploratory works have to be conducted to obtain a deep study about the software development issues.

Besides the technical contributions, the development of virtual museums on the web also overcomes the problem of geographical distances, promoting social and educational gains. Addressing the proposal evaluation, two versions of museums - for teaching History and Arts - were built by two different groups of developers in order to meet two audiences: elementary school and high school. The evaluation results stated some reflections of the developers about the advantages and disadvantages of using the approach. In another direction, we also reported the end-users' feedback – students of elementary and high school - about their satisfaction on interacting with the museums. As future work we have planned to test other features of SPL, and developed a complete version of a virtual museum - features for museum experts, teacher, and students, through a partnership with a Brazilian Museum.

ACKNOWLEDGEMENT

We thank the financial support – grant #2013/25572-7, São Paulo Research Foundation (FAPESP).

REFERENCES

Arends, M., Goldfarb, D., Merkl, D., Weingartner, M., 2009. Interaction with Art Museums on the Web. *In: Proceedings of the IADIS Int'l Conference WWW/Internet*, Rome, Italy, pp 117-125.Bangor,

Bangor, A., Kortum, P., Miller, J., 2009. Determining what individual SUS scores mean: adding an adjective rating scale, *J. Usability Studies*, vol. 4, n.3, pp. 114-123.

Berry, G., Sheard, J., Quartly, M., 2011. A Virtual Museum of Computing History: an educational resource bringing the relationship between people and computers to life. *In: Proceedings of 13th Australasian Computer Education Conference.*

Chimalakonda, S., Nori, K., 2012. Accelerating educational technologies using software product lines. IEEE Int. Conf. on Tech. Enhanced Education (ICTEE), pp. 1-4.

Clements, P., Northrop, L., 2002. *Software Product Lines: Practices and Patterns. Addison-Wesley Longman Publishing Co*: Boston, MA, USA, 2002.

Cong, X., Zhang, H., Zhou, D., Lu, P., Qin, L., 2010. A Model-Driven Architecture Approach for Developing E-Learning Platform. *Edutainment*, pp. 111-122.

Dalmon, D. L., Brandão, L. O., Brandão, A. A. F., Isotani, S., 2012. A Domain Engineering for Interactive Learning Modules. *Journal of Research and Practice in Information Technology*, vol. 44, n. 3, pp. 309-330.

Falvo, V., Duarte Filho, N. F., Oliveira, E., Barbosa, E. F., 2014. A contribution to the adoption of software product lines in the development of mobile learning applications. *IEEE Frontiers in Education Conference*, pp. 1-8, 2014.

Juristo, N., Moreno, A. M., Sanchez-Segura, M.-I., 2007b. Guidelines for eliciting usability functionalities. IEEE Transactions on Software Engineering, vol. 33, n. 11, pp. 744–758.

Kang, K. C., Cohen, S. G., Hess, J. A., Novak, W. E., Peterson, A. S., 1990. Feature-oriented domain analysis (FODA) feasibility study, *Technical report CMU/SEI-90-TR-21*, Software Engineering Institute.

Karoulis, A., Sylaiou, S., White, M., 2006. Usability Evaluation of a Virtual Museum Interface. *INFORMATICA*, vol. 17, n. 3, pp. 363–380.

Marty, P., Twidale, M., 2004. Lost in gallery space: a conceptual framework for analyzing the usability flaws of museum web sites. *First Monday*, vol. 9, n. 9.

POP. Prototyping on Paper. Available at: https://popapp.in/. Accessed in September, 2015.

Sarah, L.L., Prihatmanto, A.S.,Rusmin, P.H., 2012. The design and implementation discovery learning method on virtual museum of Indonesia: A case study museum of geology for rock materials. *In: Proceedings of 2012 International Conference on Digital Object*, pp. 1-5.

Smith, M. K., 2002. Informal, non-formal and formal education: a brief overview of different approaches. The Encyclopedia of Informal Education. Available at: http://www.infed.org/foundations/informal_nonformal.htm. Accessed in February, 2016.

Trias, F., 2012. Building cms-based web applications using a model-driven approach. *In: Sixth International Conference on Research Challenges in Information Science* (RCIS), p. 1-6.

Vavoula, G. et al., 2009. Myartspace: Design and evaluation of support for learning with multimedia phones between classrooms and museums. *Computers & Education*, vol. 53, no. 2, pp. 286–299, 2009. Vernon, V., 2013. *Implementing Domain-Driven Design*, Pearson, 2013.

Welter, E. F. A.; Zaina, L. A. M.; Leles, A. D.; Ribeiro, M. S., 2014. Learning History through Virtual Museums: a partnership between teachers and museum experts. *In: 20th Workshop of Informatics in the school, 3th Brazilian Conference of Informatics in the Education*, Dourados, Brazil, pp. 76-85 (*in portuguese*).

Wohlin, C. et al., 2012. Experimentation in software engineering, Springer.

Zhou, D., Zhuo, Z., Zhong, S., Pan, X., 2008. The Design of Software Architecture for E-Learning Platforms. *Edutainment*, pp. 32-40.

GAME ELEMENTS IN "LABOURS OF HERCULES"

Selay Arkün Kocadere, Fatma Bayrak, Pınar Nuhoğlu Kibar, Şeyma Çağlar and Zehra Sayın
Hacettepe University, Department of Computer Education and Instructional Technology
Ankara, Turkey

ABSTRACT

The use of Information and Communication Technologies (ICTs) has been shown to engage 21st century learners in the learning and education process. One such ICT product is the educational 3D mobile game "Labours of Hercules" (LOH), an output of the European Union Erasmus+ project developed to teach the myth of the Twelve Labours of Hercules to students. The player takes the avatar of Hercules, whose goal is to complete the 12 labours. The game is structured in 12 levels of increasing difficulty, each featuring the two phases of running and boss fights. The educational components of the game include the visualization of Hercules' journey to different locations in Europe and the labours themselves as well as player interaction in order to complete the labours. The current study analyses the game in terms of its key game elements: Story, Goals, Rules, Challenges, Interaction, and Feedback. The Story element of LOH determined the structure of all other game elements, in particular the elements of Goals, Rules, and Challenges. Detailed review of the 6 components revealed that the design of one element affected all other elements. It can be concluded therefore that games cannot be designed element by element due to their interconnecting relations and thus necessitate a holistic review.

KEYWORDS

Mobile game, educational game, game elements

1. INTRODUCTION

Myths are ancient stories and tales that account for aspects of nature or for a historical event (Öztürk, 2009). Mythology is the discipline that interprets and reviews the birth of myths and its meanings (TDK, 2015). In general, mythology is considered to be the collection of myths and legends that belong to a nation or religion, and to Greek and Latin civilizations in particular (Öztürk, 2009).

Mythology aims to create a perception of the real world through symbols (Alizade, 2013) and can be considered an ancient education system. Although mythology's origins lie in prehistoric periods, their study has become more widespread as mythological theories were documented and mythological systems studied in the 20th century. It is possible to say that the study of mythology became popular in the science community thereby (Alizade, 2013). The integration of mythology into the education systems in various forms can be seen in countries such as the United States, Greece, and the United Kingdom (GES, 2012; IUM, 2014; SWSC, 2015).

In the study "Teaching Mythology Creatively", Linksman (1983) suggested classroom activities such as writing letters to Greek gods and preparing mythological newspapers to learn about mythology, as well as using games. Linksman reported that students love to play games based on mythological stories and characters and that developing and playing games based on the mythology are effective methods for learning mythology.

Currently, while mythology-based video games such as "Age of Mythology" were not developed with educational purposes in mind, such games contribute to learning mythology. Gee (2003) reported that children who play "Age of Mythology" read and research mythology and create pictures and stories both within the context of the game and outside of the learning environment and concluded that such self-initiated engagement with mythology was an especially effective form of learning.

Described as 'digital natives' by Prensky (2001a), students in the 21st century differ greatly from those of previous generations in both characteristics and learning needs. Today's students require successful acquisition of the skills and tools necessary in the modern world. (Prensky, 2012). According to Prensky (2001a), digital games are one of the best ways to reach out to digital natives and communicate with them in their own language.

Games present a learning incentive and an opportunity for individuals to develop quick decision making skills and strategies to overcome problems, join new groups and work in collaboration, and obtain information from different areas (Prensky, 2003; Gee, 2014) by providing active experiences in meaningful and real-life like settings (Malone & Lepper 1987). Due to the high entertainment value of games, students' motivation and attention increase and learning outputs are resultantly enhanced (Huizenga, Admiraal, Akkerman, & Dam, 2009; Liao Chen, Cheng, Chen, & Chan, 2011; Gee, 2014). It is possible to achieve cognitive, motivational, emotional, and social development with the use of games (Lee & Hammer, 2011). For these reasons, educators have attempted to incorporate games in the teaching environment (Tüzün, Akıncı, Yıldırım, Sırakaya, 2013).

The Labours of Hercules (LOH) mobile game is one of 6 intellectual outputs of the "Searching for the Labours of Hercules" (SFTLOH) project (www.laboursofhercules.com) supported by the European Union Erasmus+ Program Key Action 2, Mixed Strategic Partnership for School Education. The SFTLOH's main goal was to give educators examples of and opportunities for the use of Information and Communication Technologies (ICT) in order to improve and facilitate learning and teaching for students and teachers. A total of 8 institutions, including 2 universities, 5 high schools, and 1 non-governmental organization from 6 different countries collaborated in order to enrich this process by incorporating academic and socio-cultural differences.

The project was based on the mythological story of Hercules' Twelve Labours, which were said to have occurred throughout Europe. The 12th labour, the Entrance of Hell (Cehennemağzı) Caves, was located in the current Turkish city of Zonguldak. LOH was developed with the aim of creating a qualitative example of technologically-supported learning and to teach the story of the Twelve Labours of Hercules to students, principally those in high schools takin part in the project.

Game development is a complicated process and challenges increase in educational games in order to make them not only fun, but also informative and educational. Unfortunately, there is no perfect recipe for the development process nor a set list of characteristics that a game should have. For this reason, educators and academics have attempted to create various frameworks using sets of game elements, the building blocks that make up a game. The aim of the current study was to examine the educational 3D mobile game "Labours of Hercules" with regards to its game elements. LOH was developed for both iOS and Android devices using the game engine Unity under the European Union Erasmus+ project 2014-1-TR01-KA201-012990 with the support of the Hacettepe University Scientific Research Coordination Unit as part of the "Development of an Educational 3D Mobile Game" (SUA-2016-9609) project.

2. GAME ELEMENTS

Prensky (2001b) reported ta 6 elements are prominent in games: (a) Representation/Story, (b) Goals and Objectives, (c) Rules, (d) Conflict/Competition/Challenges/Opposition, (e) Interaction, and (f) Outcomes and Feedback. According to Vandercruysse, Vandewaetere and Clarebout (2012), game elements contribute to the game in different ways; rules determine the game's structure, goals provide motivation and stimulation, interaction makes sure the user is active and socializing, outcomes inform about progress, challenges contribute to excitement, and story contributes to emotion and stimulation. In other words, games provide players with goals, establish rules in order to create a challenge, and stimulate curiosity with sound and visual effects and constantly changing dynamics (Malone, 1980). All of the above occur in games in which the user is actively experiencing and controlling the game and identifies with the character they are representing (Malone & Lepper 1987).

2.1 Story

The story is one of the most important characteristic of an effective video game (Dondlinger, 2007). Prensky (2001b) reported that the story element often includes a fantasy element as well. Malone & Lepper (1987) described fantasy as physical and social situations that do not exist in real life.

As the game is about Greek mythology, fantastic components were included in the story. Told to the player through animation at the beginning of the game, the game's story follows Hercules as he goes mad at the hands of his stepmother Hera and kill his own wife and children and then seeks redemption. Feeling great sorrow when he comes to his senses, Hercules consults with an oracle. With the oracle's guidance, Hercules puts himself under the command of King Eurystheus who gives Hercules 12 labours. Hercules travels around Europe to complete the 12 labours and thus obtains immortality (Cömert,1999). In the LOH game, each of Hercules' labours corresponds to one level.

Hercules' labours are: (1) Slay the Nemean Lion, (2) Slay the nine-headed Lernaean Hydra, (3) Capture the Ceryneian Hind, (4) Capture the Erymanthian Boar, (5) Clean the Augean stables in a single day, (6) Slay the Stymphalian Birds, (7) Capture the Cretan Bull, (8) Steal the Mares of Diomedes, (9) Obtain the girdle of Hippolyta, Queen of the Amazons, (10) Obtain the cattle of the monster Geryon, (11) Steal the apples of the Hesperides, and (12) Capture and bring back Cerberus.

In the game, he locations of the 12 labours are shown on a map with every level marked on a certain point of the map, so that his journey across Europe can be visualized (Figure 1). Hercules, the player's avatar, travels to the locations in the manner of a "jump and run" game by avoiding obstacles and collecting certain objects (Figure 1). At the end of each level, Hercules reaches the boss fight phase (Figure 2).

Figure 1. Screenshots of the game

Figure 2. Screenshots of the game

Boss fights are designed to reflect Hercules' labours as much as possible, with fights against an object in the 5th and 11th labours and against a character in the others. Boss fights are conducted through double tap or flick gesture interactions. The opponent is rendered ineffective with the player double tapping as many times as possible in a certain period when the Hercules character is in a close quarter fight, or by shooting the opponent with the relevant tool (net/arrow) at a certain angle and speed in fights at a distance.

The myth was taken into consideration in designing the game's environment. Levels were designed in accordance with the locations of Hercules' labours. For instance, the 4th level (Capture the Erymanthian Boar) takes places in a snowy environment and the 12th level (Capture and bring back Cerberus) in hell. In addition to environmental conditions, visual feedback is given after completion of every level, clearly visualizing Hercules' success in order to relay the story.

2.2 Goals

Goals are one of the most important elements affecting the player's motivation and games that do not include goals and objectives are considered mere toys (Presky, 2001). In LOH, goals are based on Hercules' story. Swartout and van Lent (2003) categorized goals as short term, medium term, and long term. LOH's short term goals are 1) avoiding obstacles and collecting gold and potions in the runner phase, 2) earning the highest score, and 3) winning the boss fight. Medium term goals are passing each level by completing the relevant labour and unlocking the next level and obtaining stars (1, 2 or 3) at the end of every level corresponding to that level's scores. Although personal choice, completing a level with 3 stars can be considered as a medium term goal. The long term goal is completing all 12 levels and obtaining immortality for Hercules.

2.3 Rules

Rules are what make a game a game. Without rules, one can only speak of 'play'. Rules set the limits of the game, force people to make choices (Prensky, 2001b), and comprise the game's overall structure (Vandercruysse et al., 2012) and shape up the process of goals being completed (Prensky, 2001b). In this context, there are 3 types of rules: system, procedural, and imported (Garris, Ahlers, Driskel, 2002). System rules are those that are determined depending on the designed world of the game. Procedural rules are those regulating the player's actions, such as how a player can spend the gold they earn or how they level up. Imported rules are those made by bringing rules of natural life into the game, such as being unable to move through walls.

2.3.1 System Rules

In the runner phase of each level, Hercules goes to the location at which he will carry out his labour by running constantly forward. The player sees all of Hercules' body from his back. It is not possible for Hercules to go beyond the lanes or places provided for him in the environment. In the boss fight phase, the camera angle changes and the factor is shown to the player from Hercules' point of view. In this phase, Hercules can only see the challenge factor (creature, object) and the tool he is using to fight against it (fist, sword, net, arrow etc.). In this screen, movements to right/left are limited and only the tool provided can be used.

2.3.2 Procedural Rules

Procedural rules vary in the runner and boss fight phases of the levels. Rules for the runner phases are the same at all 12 levels, while those of the boss fight phases are different depending on the fight type. In the runner phase, Hercules avoids obstacles by jumping over, dodging, or ducking under obstacles in order to reach the boss fight. He collects gold, potions, magnets, and golden shoes to obtain points. Potions allow Hercules to resume the game from whichever point he was at when the game finished. Potions can also be bought with the collected gold. When the game finishes without any available potion, Hercules returns to the beginning of the level. In addition, magnets and golden shoes can be used as facilitating items. Magnets allow Hercules to collect all the gold on the road regardless of which lane he is in and golden shoes allow him to run faster without crashing into obstacles, earn additional points, and reach the boss fight location faster.

In the boss fight phase of the levels, Hercules fights against different factors in different ways to complete the labour. In boss fights in which the double tap gesture is in play, the player is required to double tap a certain number of times, filling the progress bar within a certain time period. With every unsuccessful move, Hercules' energy bar, which is limited, drains. In boss fights in which the flick gesture is in play, Hercules tries to neutralise flying or running living creatures by shooting arrows and running ones by throwing nets. The player needs to perform a flick gesture to use the relevant tool considering the distance and angle between the creature and Hercules in order to hit it. The player needs to hit the creature as many times as the number of tools they have.

2.3.3 Imported Rules

In the runner phase, imported rules include the need to jump over low obstacles, duck under high obstacles, jump to collect high items, change lanes to avoid obstacles, and fall over when running into an obstacle. In the boss fight phase, throwing the tool in consideration with angle and distance are also imported rules.

2.4 Challenge

Rouse (2005) stated that one of the greatest reasons for players to keep playing a game is the challenge element. Challenges increase the player's adrenaline and make them excited to play the game (Prensky, 2001b). Garris et al. (2002) reported that goals that become increasingly difficult as the game progresses through the levels increase the player's motivation and performance. It is recommended that early levels are easier in order to allow the player to learn about the game (Adams, 2009).

In LOH, labours should be completed in accordance with the story. As the sequencing of labours is one of the key elements, levelling up is only possible if the previous level is completed. Every level's challenge is more difficult than the previous one and the player faces more obstacles, requiring faster and more precise reactions. In this context, in the running phases, Hercules runs faster towards the end of the level with each level. In addition, he must run farther with each level in order to reach the boss fight phase. Boss fights in which Hercules takes on a factor are harder than the previous one and require Hercules to fill the progress bar by double tapping at greater speeds in a shorter period of time. In boss fights in which Hercules needs to capture a creature, the number of relevant tools (net/arrow) decreases at every level, thus ensuring that the challenges progressively become more difficult.

Although designed as a single player game, when connected to the Game Center and Google Play Games the player may participate in a leader board. Reaching a higher rank on the leader board can be considered an additional challenge for the players.

2.5 Interaction

Another game element that increases the player's motivation is interaction. Interaction is classified under two types: the player's interaction with the game and the player's social interaction with other players (Prensky, 2001b). The interaction between the player and the media takes form in accordance with the game's goals and the story's context (Donglinger, 2007). In the LOH game, interaction makes use of the touchscreen and gyro features designed for mobile devices such as smartphones and tablets. The player uses the swipe gesture to move in 4 directions in the runner phases and either the double tap or flick gesture in the boss fight phases. After certain parts of the game, the gyro feature is activated in order to increase the challenge. In these parts, the player plays the game by tilting the device to the left and right. Additional standard interfaces such as play, pause, replay, resume, info, game center, volume, Facebook, use potion, next labour, and main menu buttons are also included. In terms of social interaction, the game can be connected to Facebook and Game Center/Google Play Games. This creates an environment where the players can interact with others.

2.6 Feedback

Feedback notifies the player of their current situation in the game (Prensky, 2001b). As in every learning process, feedback is quite important for game based learning (Prensky, 2001b). In this context, feedback must be given after every user behavior (Garris, Ahlers and Driskel, 2002).

One of the most basic feedback is the notification of win/lose situation. Feedback can be given by notification of numerical score or can be presented in visual, audio, or animation forms (Prensky, 2001b). In LOH, feedback is provided in different forms that are consistent with each other and the game's environment. Feedback can be classified under 3 types: pre-level, in-level, and end-level.

In pre-level feedback, the location of the labour, whether the level is locked or unlocked, and the number of stars awarded for the achieved score are given visually; the level's rank and loading of the game is given in text form; and whether the music is on or off is given in audio and visual forms.

In-level feedback varies in the runner and boss fight phases. In the runner phase, feedback on the outcomes of Hercules' actions such as collecting magnets, golden shoes, and gold, and running or hitting an obstacle etc. are given with audio and animation. The runner screen is designed in a way that the player can see the number of gold and potions they have collected. The blackout of the screen tells the player that the boss fight is about to commence.

In the boss fight phase, feedback changes in accordance with the factor Hercules is up against. If Hercules is trying to neutralise a factor with the double tap gesture, the feedback is provided by a bar which indicates how sufficient his hits are. If it is a living creature, both Hercules' and the creature's energy levels are shown in the interface visualised as a power bar. In tasks that must be completed within a certain timeframe, the player is informed of the time in seconds. The situation after every hit attempt is reported visually. Hercules' action is visualised by animation in accordance with the story. For example, in the 1st level, every time Hercules attacks the lion, his fists are shown on the screen. The feedback for neutralization of factors is given by a "win situation" screen and the feedback for the failure at it is given by a "game over" screen.

In boss fights based on throwing objects, the number of tools Hercules has is shown with text and visual elements, and the number decreases after every use. When the net or arrow hits the target, the player can see the situation through animation.

Two separate screens containing information are designed to provide end-level feedback. This feedback is shaped depending on whether the player has won or lost. When the player completes the level, the visualised information regarding the story is shown on the screen and a briefing screen appears providing "level completed" information in text form, the score, and the number of collected gold, potions, magnets, and shoes visually and in text form, and the number of stars won visually. In addition, when a labour is completed, the unlocking of the new labour is shown visually. If the player cannot complete the labour, the "game over" screen appears, providing the score and the number of collected gold, potion, magnets, and shoes in a visual and text form and the number of stars visually.

3. CONCLUSION

The literature reports the positive effects of game-based learning and that of game-based mythology learning in particular. The mobile game aiming to teach the story of the "Twelve Labours of Hercules" focuses on Europe's common cultural heritage and the integration of technology into the learning-teaching processes. The game was developed as part of the SFTLOH project. In this study, LOH was reviewed in terms of the key elements of story, goal, rules, challenge, interaction, and feedback.

Rouse (2005) reported that games take their origins from the 3 basic points of story, gameplay, or technology and that a choice between these three points limits the choices in other two. The LOH game aims to teach a mythological story. Accordingly, it is possible to say that this game's origins come from the story, leading it to be the most dominant game element.

In this context, the story element determined the structure of all the other game elements. As can be seen in the previous chapter, the aim, rules, and challenges of this game in particular are determined based on the story.

On the other hand, arrangements made about a certain element affected others. As can be understood from our explanations of the game's elements, they do not diverge sharply. For example, the Nemean Lion is an evil character that Hercules needs to neutralise as the 1st level's goal. The rule "Nemean Lion gets neutralized after 3 accurate hits by Hercules" also determines the difficulty of this level. As can be seen in this example, an arrangement in an element affects another element's structure. This also shows that games cannot be designed element by element because of the interlaced relations between them, necessitating a holistic review of the game and its design process.

Because the game design process requires detailed study, it was not possible to delve into much detail while reviewing and reporting the game elements. For example, feedback of some kind is necessary for every button pressed during game play. On the other hand, an analysis this detailed would mean losing the focus of the whole picture and was thus not performed in the current study.

This study reviewed the Labours of Hercules game based on the most accentuated game elements in the literature. Further studies considering different elements and approaches to game design outlined in the literature would allow for analysis from different perspectives. In addition, modelling LOH's development process would further contribute to the literature.

ACKNOWLEDGEMENT

"Labours of Hercules" mobile game is funded by the Erasmus+ Program of the European Union as apart of project "Searching for the Labours of Hercules" (2014-1-TR01-KA201-012990) and Hacettepe University Scientific Research Coordination Unit with the project titled "Development of an Educational 3D Mobile Game" (SUA-2016-9609)". This educational game is designed and developed in cooperation with Pixega Game Studio. This publication reflects the views only of the authors, and neither the Commission nor Hacettepe University cannot be held responsible for any use which may be made of the information contained therein.

REFERENCES

Adams, E., 2009. *Fundamentals of game design (second edition)*. Pearson Education.

Alizade, R., 2013. Türk Mitolojisi ve Eğitim. *The Journal of Academic Social Science Studies,* Vol. 6, No. 2, pp 31-35.

Botte, B., Matera, C., Sponsiello, M., 2009. Serious Game, between simulation and game: A proposal of taxonomy. *Journal of e-Learning and Knowledge Society*, Vol. 5, No. 2, pp 11–21.

Cömert. B., 1999. Mitoloji ve İkonografi. *Ayraç Yayınları.* ISBN 975-8087-26-6.

Dondlinger, M. J., 2007. Educational video game design: A review of the literature. *Journal of Applied Educational Technology*, Vol. 4, No. 1, pp 21-31.

Garris, R., Ahlers, R., & Driskell, J. E., 2002. Games, motivation, and learning: A research and practice model. *Simulation & Gaming*, Vol. 33, No. 4, pp 441-467.

Prensky, M., 2003. Digital game-based learning. *Computers in Entertainment (CIE)*, Vol. 1, No. 1, pp 21-21.

Gee, J. P., 2014. *What video games have to teach us about learning and literacy*. Macmillan.

GES, 2012. Greece Education System. http://www.etwinning.net/shared/data/etwinning/country_focus/greece_education_system_en.pdf [accessed 14 July 2015].

Huizenga, J. et al, 2009. Mobile game-based learning in secondary education: engagement, motivation and learning in a mobile city game. *Journal of Computer Assisted Learning*, Vol. 25, No. 4, pp 332-344.

IUM, 2014. National Curriculum for England. https://www.gov.uk/government/collections/national-curriculum [accessed 14 July 2015].

Lee, J. J., & Hammer, J., 2011. Gamification in education: What, how, why bother?. *Academic exchange quarterly*, Vol. 15, No. 2, pp 146.

Liao, C. C., et. al, 2011. My-Mini-Pet: a handheld pet-nurturing game to engage students in arithmetic practices. *Journal of Computer Assisted Learning*, Vol. 27, No. 1, pp 76-89.

Linksman, J., 1983. Teaching Mythology Creatively. *The English Journal*, Vol. 72, No. 3, pp 46-47.

Malone, T. W., 1980. What makes things fun to learn? Heuristics for designing instructional computer games. *Proceedings of the 3rd ACM SIGSMALL symposium*, pp. 162-169.

Malone, T. W., & Lepper, M. R., 1987. Making learning fun: A taxonomy of intrinsic motivations for learning. *Aptitude, learning, and instruction*, Vol. 3, pp 223-253.

Meyer, B., 2009. Learning English through serious games–reflections on teacher and learner performance. *In Transactions on Edutainment III* . Springer Berlin Heidelberg.

Tüzün, H., et al, 2013. Bilgisayar oyunları ve öğrenme. *Öğretim teknolojilerinin temelleri: Teoriler, araştırmalar, eğilimler*. Pegem Akademi, Ankara, Turkey.

Öztürk, O., 2009. *Folklar ve Mitoloji Sözlüğü*. Phoenix Yayınları, Ankara, Turkey.
Prensky, M., 2001a. Digital Natives, Digital Immigrants. *On the Horizon*, Vol. 9, No.5, pp 1–6.
Prensky, M., 2001b. Fun, play and games: What makes games engaging. *Digital game-based learning*, McGraw-Hill, New York.
Prensky, M., 2003. Digital game-based learning. *Computers in Entertainment (CIE)*, Vol. 1, No. 1, pp 21.
Prensky, M., 2012. *From digital natives to digital wisdom: Hopeful essays for 21st century learning.* Corwin Press.
Rouse III, R., 2005. *Game design: Theory and practice*. Wordware Publishing, Texas, USA.
Rosenberg, D., 1998. *Dünya Mitolojisi, Büyük Destan ve Söylenler Antolojisi*. İmge Yayın Evi, Ankara, Turkey.
Swartout, W., & van Lent, M., 2003. Making a game of system design. *Communications of the ACM*, Vol. 46, No. 7,pp 32-39.
SWSC, 2015. Sacramento Waldorf School Curriculum. http://www.sacwaldorf.org/sacramento-waldorf-school-curriculum.html [accessed 14 July 2015].
TDK, 2015. Türk Dil Kurumu Türkçe Büyük Sözlük, http://www.tdk.gov.tr/ [accessed 14 July 2015].
Vandercruysse, S. et al, 2012. Game-based learning: A review on the effectiveness of educational games. *Handbook of Research on Serious Games as Educational, Business, and Research Tools*. PA: IGI Global, Hershey.
Yıllar, Ö., 2005. Mit-Efsane ve Eğitim. *Kazım Karabekir Eğitim Fakültesi Dergisi*, Vol. 11,pp 383-392.

AN ONTOLOGY-BASED CLASSIFICATION OF LEARNING MATERIALS IN SOFTWARE ENGINEERING AREA

Joselaine Valaski, Sheila Reinehr and Andreia Malucelli
PPGIa – Pontifical Catholic University of Paraná (PUCPR)
Imaculada Conceição Street, 1155, Curitiba – PR – Brazil

ABSTRACT

Organizations need to adopt practices in order to provide training of their employees and thus keep themselves competitive. However, not always corporations provide physical environment training programs to their employees. Collaborative and autonomous virtual environments that promote learning material sharing have been an option for professionals to keep up to date. Nevertheless, learning material sharing is not enough by itself. This needs to be of easy and accurate access. Thus, it is necessary to use mechanisms that aid knowledge structure, facilitating the future retrieval of these learning materials. Ontologies may be used to structure knowledge and enable automatic processing by computers. In such context, this research had the goal of analyzing whether an ontology integrated in an organizational learning environment may support the automatic learning material classification in the Software Engineering area.

KEYWORDS

Software Engineering, Organizational Learning, Ontology, Learning Material, Learning Organization

1. INTRODUCTION

Learning in organizations is seen as a prerequisite for any organization survival (Lahteenmaki et al, 2001). Organizations from many different areas have been investing in learning. The application of organizational learning may occur in several ways, such as, analysis of previous experiments (Zhang, 2006), identification of skills (Nevo and Wand, 2005) and learning environments (Wang, 2011). Learning environments are applied in order to provide virtual training to organization employees. The trainings may occur in physical environments (classrooms, auditoriums etc.) or virtual ones (Web). The Web environment has the advantage of providing remote corporate training (Rosemberg, 2001). However, regardless of whether the environment is physical or virtual, there is usually the role of the tutor responsible for planning the content to be taught. Nevertheless, the availability of tutors to prepare learning materials in various knowledge areas may be financially unviable. A virtual environment that enables the sharing of learning materials may be a means to minimize this problem. Whenever professionals use a learning material and consider it useful, they can share it with their colleagues. Thus, it is created a collaborative learning process.

Nevertheless, special resources must be applied in this environment in order to promote the retrieval of appropriate learning materials according to the learners needs. One important aspect of knowledge management is to create a system that is capable of providing mechanisms allowing the right knowledge to be at the right place and at the right person as well as at the right time within an enterprise (Oztemel and Arslankaya, 2012). The challenge is not only to make information available to people at any time, at any place and in any form, but to reduce information overload by making information relevant to the task-at-hand (Fischer, 2001). One way to reduce the search time for the desired learning materials is classifying them according to knowledge areas. Thus, it is necessary to have mechanisms to support the automatic classification of learning materials. Ontologies may be applied to represent recommendations and knowledge areas and thus, provide the automatic classification of learning materials.

Ontology is a type of formalism used for knowledge representation. It is applied to enable common and shared comprehension of information (Noy and McGuinness, 2001). In this context, this research had the goal to analyze whether an integrated ontology in an organizational learning environment, may support the classification of learning materials. An ontology in the Software Engineering knowledge area was defined, based on the Software Engineering Body of Knowledge (SWEBOK) (Abran and Moore, 2004). The following section presents the main concepts and the related works. Section 3 describes the method. Section 4 presents the developed organizational learning environment. Section 5 describes and discusses the results. Finally, Section 6 concludes this research.

2. LITERATURE REVIEW

2.1 Learning in Organizations

It is through learning that organizations achieve a culture favorable to innovation and improvement (Murray and Donegan, 2003). In literature it is possible to find some concepts related to learning in organizations, such as, organizational learning, learning organization and corporate university. Organizational learning is an adaptive process of change influenced by past experiences, focused on development or in the modification of routines and supported by organizational memory (Nonaka and Takeuchi, 1995). Learning organizations are organizations that facilitate learning, enabling their members to continually expand their capacity to create the results they truly desire. New broad thinking patterns are encouraged, collective aspiration are set free and people learn to continuously learn together (Senge, 2000; Sicilia and Lytras, 2005). The corporate university concept is more related to the organizational interest in developing skills, ways of thinking, attitudes and habits, giving people the mental tools in order to improve their work (Meister, 1998).

Virtual learning environments are more focused on developing the people's kills. In this environment, the training occurs through the availability and use of learning resources, such as learning materials. However, it is important that these materials are organized according to knowledge areas, so that their retrieval is facilitated. In an autonomous learning environment, where there is no tutor to organize these materials, there is a need for computational mechanisms to help this organization. The formalization is necessary so that computers can manipulate these symbols in a meaningful way. This can occurs through formal ontologies.

2.2 Ontology

In the computing area, one of the best-known definitions of ontology has been presented by Gruber (1995), an "ontology is an explicit specification of a conceptualization". Gruber (1995) points out that some of the benefits of applying ontologies are: enabling the use of knowledge in computers applications; allowing many computers to share knowledge; helping individuals to better understand a knowledge area and supporting individuals to build consensus on a knowledge area. Ontologies application in learning environment has been identified in two contexts: organizational and educational. In an organizational context, Wang (2011) describes a collaborative learning environment in order to integrate organizational, social and individual aspects. An ontology was developed to specify the required skills for a specific position in an organization. In an educational context, Gamelel-Din (2010) proposes a learning environment based on three components: learner, tutor and learning materials. An ontology was proposed to represent course content, presentation sequence and its prerequisites. Yaghmaie and Bahreininejad (2010) propose an adaptative learning environment using agents. In this environment, an ontology is used to represent course topics, topics sequence, learner model and learner interactions with the system. According to the presented researches, it is possible to observe that ontologies have been integrated into learning environments and can facilitate the structuring of knowledge by means of automatic processing by computers.

3. METHODOLOGY

3.1 Ontology Development

The Ontology for Recommending Learning Materials (ORLM) allows the classification of learning materials according to the Software Engineering knowledge area. The ORLM has been developed using the 101 methodology [9] and the ontology editor Protégé. The terms to represent the Software Engineering knowledge areas have been extracted from the SWEBOK. However, the SWEBOK does not present an approach to define their areas using relationships among concepts and explicit properties. Thus, some RUP elements have been added into the ORLM. The Rational Unified Process (RUP) is a model for software development process that presents well defined relationships among its elements: artifact, role, task and discipline. Although the RUP goal is not to represent knowledge areas, the concept of discipline may be mapped among some SWEBOK knowledge area as showed in Table 1. The RUP elements were used to add recommendations to the learning materials. Through these recommendations, the ORLM infers the knowledge area which the learning material is related to.

3.2 Environment Development and Ontology Integration

The Organizational Learning Environment based on Ontology (OLEO) was implemented including the following functionalities: user identification; addition of learning materials in several formats, such as, video, audio, text, etc; learning material recommendation; automatic classification of learning materials; and material search according to the Software Engineering knowledge areas. The ORLM was integrated to the OLEO in order to provide the automatic classification of learning materials.

Table 1. Mapping between SWEBOK areas and RUP disciplines

SWEBOK area	RUP discipline	SWEBOK area	RUP discipline
Software Engineering Management	Project Management	Software Maintenance	
Software Engineering Process		Software Quality	
Software Engineering Tools and Methods		Software Requirements	Business Modeling; Requirements
Software Configuration Management	Configuration and Change	Software Testing	Test
Software Construction	Implementation		Deployment
Software Design	Analysis and Design		Environment

3.3 Experiment Execution

Whenever the ORLM was integrated to the OLEO, an experiment was performed in order to analyze the ontology performance related to the learning materials classification. This performance was evaluated comparing the results obtained by the ontology and the specialists. A comparison by the learners has also been made in order to evaluate whether the ontology reached better results or not.

3.3.1 Manual Classification of Learning Materials by Experts

Learning materials using Google search mechanisms were manually selected. Materials with content related to only one predominant knowledge area have been preferably selected. In this selection, six Software Engineering knowledge areas (Software Configuration Management, Software Engineering Management, Software Construction, Software Design, Software Requirements and Software Testing) represented by the ORLM were considered, because these areas have direct relation with the RUP disciplines (Table 1). The ORLM enables automatic classification into these six Software Engineering knowledge areas.

Fifteen experts were selected in order to manually classify these learning materials. It was considered experts, the professionals with PhD degree and working as professor in the Software Engineering area. It was defined that each expert would receive a list of ten learning materials to perform the manual classification. The learning materials were divided into three groups, providing five evaluations related to a same material. After selection, the learning materials were provided in the Google Docs tool, divided into three folders: group 1, group 2 and group 3, with ten learning materials in each folder. In each folder, at least one learning material related to each one of the six Software Engineering areas was added. The experts were also divided into three groups with five participants in each one. The classification performed by the experts aimed to identify which knowledge area the learning material was related to. Subsequently, the result was compared to the manual classification performed by the learners and also to the automatic classification performed by the ORLM. In order to facilitate this comparison, it has been asked to the experts to select only one predominant area.

3.3.2 Manual Classification of Learning Materials by Learners

Eighty-four learners were selected to perform the manual classification of learning materials related to the Software Engineering knowledge area. In this group, undergraduate students from Computer Science and

Information Systems majors were selected. These students had already attended or had been attending the Software Engineering subject. Using the same learning materials selected in the previous substep, six groups of learning materials were created. Each group was composed by five learning materials to be classified by the learners. Each participant received a document with the steps to be performed, along with the corresponding number of the group attached to it. The participants performed the manual classification of five learning materials according to the Software Engineering area by filling out a form. This form was prepared through the Google Docs tool. Six different forms were prepared corresponding to each of the six groups of learning materials. The classification performed by the learners aimed to identify which knowledge area the learner would classify the learning material to. Subsequently, the result was compared to the manual classification performed by the experts and also to the automatic classification performed by the ORLM. In order to facilitate this comparison, it has been asked to the students to select only one predominant area.

3.3.3 Automatic Classification of Learning Materials by Ontology

The same groups of learners and learning materials from the previous substep were also used in this one. After manual classification of learning materials, the learners accessed the organizational learning environment developed with the integrated ORLM and executed the following operations: creation of a login ID for identification in the environment and addition of learning materials. For each learning material added in the learning environment, learners made recommendations related to the following RUP elements: role, task and artifact. With this information, the ORLM performed the automatic classification of learning materials, according to the Software Engineering knowledge area. The results of automatic classification by the ORLM were then compared to the manual classification performed by the experts and also to the manual classification performed by the learners. There was no limit on the number of recommendations that the learners were allowed to make.

4. ORLM AND OLEO

4.1 ORLM

As described in Section 3.1, the ORLM was developed based on the SWEBOK knowledge area and the RUP elements. The main RUP elements represented in the ORLM are as follows: Artifact, Role, Task and RupDiscipline. As showed in Figure 1, the elements are related through two properties: "modifies" and "hasDomain". These relationships allow identifying the discipline that an artifact, a role or a task is related to. The following is an example: one role is related to one or many artifacts through the property "modifies", while the artifact is related to one discipline through the property "hasDomain". The definition of each subclass has been established using the relationship showed in Figure 1.

An element artifact or task is related to only one discipline, whereas an element role is related to one or more disciplines. The Software Architect role can modify the Design Model artifact and also the Implementation Model artifact, for instance. The Design Model artifact has the property "hasDomain" equal to Analysis and Design discipline while de Implementation Model artifact has the property "hasDomain" equal to Implementation. In this case, the Software Architect role is related to Analysis and Design and Implementation disciplines. After the representation of the RUP elements, the relationship between the RUP elements and the learning materials was established. The "orlm:LearningMaterial" class was created and the relationship was defined through the property "isRecommendTo". The relationship between RUP elements and learning materials helped to establish the relationship between the learning materials and the SWEBOK knowledge area. The subclasses related to each one of the six areas of SWEBOK were created in the class "orlmLearningMaterial". It is important to emphasize that the ORLM provides the automatic classification in the six SWEBOK knowledge areas. It has been chosen to represent in the ORLM only the SWEBOK knowledge areas which have direct relation with the RUP disciplines (Table 1).

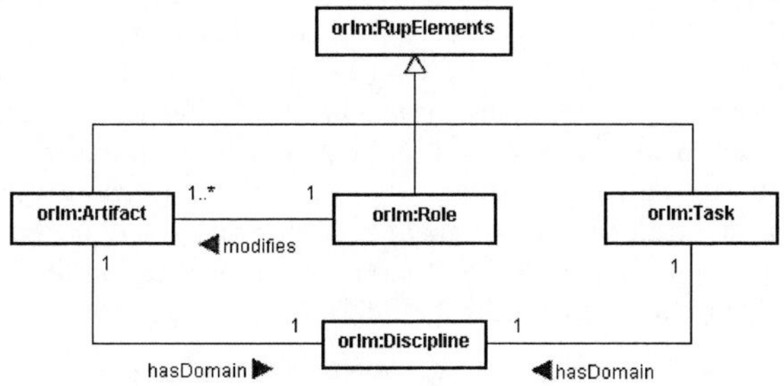

Figure 1. RUP elements and their relationships

4.2 OLEO

The environment was developed using the Java platform, the JBoss application server, the DB2 Express DBMS (Database Management System) for data persistence, which was integrated through the DAO (Data Access Object) component, and finally, the Jena API was used in order to integrate the ORLM. The Jena API is a Java framework used to develop semantic applications. The Jena framework provides an environment for the manipulation of RDF and OWL files, SPARQL language and inference machine. It is through the Jena API that the interface of the learning environment handles the OWL file, which contains the ontology.

In order to add a learning material, it is necessary to select the file related to the material and make recommendations by role, artifact and task. In the ORLM, the Software Engineering area is defined through these three elements. Once the learning material is added, the data related to the recommendations are then loaded into ORLM. The ORLM, through the Pellet inference engine, makes the classification of the learning material according to the knowledge area.

5. RESULTS/DISCUSSION

5.1 Manual Classification of Learning Materials by Experts

The Software Engineering experts classified the learning materials according to the knowledge areas proposed in the SWEBOK. Fifteen previously selected experts made the classification of materials. Each one of them classified ten learning materials. An identifier was arbitrarily defined for each one of the ten areas of SWEBOK in order to facilitate the presentation of the results: SC (Software Construction), SD (Software Design), TM (Software Engineering Tools and Methods), SCM (Software Configuration Management), SEM (Software Engineering Management), SM (Software Maintenance), SEP (Software Engineering Process), SQ (Software Quality), SR (Software Requirements) e ST (Software Testing). The classification results manually performed by the experts are shown in Table 2. The votes were transformed into percentages and distributed into columns in Table 2 in order to demonstrate the ranking among the most voted areas and the corresponding percentage of votes. The ranking represents the percentage up to the second most voted area, since only three learning materials (MAT008, MAT009, MAT030) obtained distributed votes in more than two areas.

This distribution of votes allows us to observe if there was consensus among the experts in choosing the Software Engineering area which the learning material belongs to. The highlighted cases refer to the percentage of votes equal or inferior to 60% in the first most voted area. Thus, one can observe that only materials MAT008, MAT009, MAT029 and MAT030 presented to the first most voted area, a percentage of classification equal or lower to 60%. For MAT009 for instance, out of the 5 five votes received by the experts, 2 of them (40%) were given to the Tools and Methods (TM) area. All the other areas received one vote each: Construction Software (SC) (20%), Software Engineering Process (SEP) (20%) and Software Requirements (SR) (20%). As far as these 4 materials, there was not a consensus among the experts regarding the Software Engineering area the learning materials belong to. However, among the thirty learning materials classified, twenty-six of them obtained a percentage of classification above 60% in the first most voted area. MAT003, for instance, received 5 votes (100%) in the Software Engineering Management (SEM) area; MAT004 received 4 votes (80%) in the Software Construction (SC) area and received 1 vote (20%) in the Software Design (SD) area. By these results, it has been concluded that, for the most part of the materials classified by the experts, there was a consensus to which Software Engineering knowledge area the learning material belongs. Thus, it may be stated that the majority of the learning materials used to perform these classifications have a clear definition to which main area of Software Engineering they belong to, at least to the experts. Although, one may question whether people with expertise in the Software Engineering area and who are not experts, could correctly classify these materials.

Table 2. Percentage of experts 'votes for each learning material

ID	1st most	%	2nd most	%	Material	1st most	%	2nd most	%
MAT001	SC	80.00	TM	20.00	**MAT016**	SCM	100.00		
MAT002	ST	80.00	TM	20.00	**MAT017**	SC	100.00		
MAT003	SEM	100.00			**MAT018**	SC	100.00		
MAT004	SC	80.00	SD	20.00	**MAT019**	SCM	100.00		
MAT005	SC	100.00			**MAT020**	SR	80.00	SCM	20.00
MAT006	SR	100.00			**MAT021**	SD	100.00		
MAT007	SEM	80.00	SEP	20.00	**MAT022**	SR	80.00	SEP	20.00
MAT008	SQ	40.00	SR	40.00	**MAT023**	SEM	80.00	TM	20.00
MAT009	TM	40.00	SC	20.00	**MAT024**	SR	100.00		
MAT010	ST	100.00			**MAT025**	ST	100.00		
MAT011	SEM	80.00	SQ	20.00	**MAT026**	SD	80.00	TM	20.00
MAT012	SCM	100.00			**MAT027**	SD	80.00	SR	20.00
MAT013	SEM	100.00			**MAT028**	SR	80.00	SEP	20.00
MAT014	SCM	100.00			**MAT029**	SEM	60.00	ST	40.00
MAT015	SCM	80.00	SC	20.00	**MAT030**	SD	60.00	SEP	20.00

5.2 Manual Classification of Learning Material by Learners

Eighty-four students manually classified five learning materials, i.e., each material was classified by fourteen learners. Fifty-five percent of these students have already been working professionally in some Software Engineering area and have two years of experience in the area on average. The results of this classification are shown in Table 3.

Table 3. Percentage of learners 'votes for each learning material

ID	1st	%	2nd	%	3rd	%	O.%	ID	1st	%	2nd	%	3rd	%	O.%
MAT001	SC	71.43	TM	14.29	SCM	7.14	7.14	**MAT016**	SCM	64.29	SEM	21.43	SC	7.14	7.14
MAT002	ST	85.71	SQ	7.14	SR	7.14		**MAT017**	SC	64.29	TM	14.29	SCM	14.29	7.14
MAT003	SEM	57.14	SCM	14.29	SEP	14.29	14.29	**MAT018**	SC	50.00	TM	21.43	SCM	7.14	21.43
MAT004	SC	57.14	TM	21.43		14.29	7.14	**MAT019**	TM	28.57	SCM	28.57	SC	21.43	21.43
MAT005	SC	64.29	TM	35.71				**MAT020**	SQ	64.29	SM	14.29	TM	7.14	14.29
MAT006	SR	100.00						**MAT021**	SD	35.71	SEP	28.57	SC	14.29	21.43
MAT007	SEM	35.71	SEP	28.57	TM	14.29	21.43	**MAT022**	SQ	42.86	SEP	21.43	SC	14.29	21.43
MAT008	SQ	42.86	SD	21.43	SC	7.14	28.57	**MAT023**	SEM	42.86	SEP	28.57	SC	14.29	14.29
MAT009	SC	28.57	SD	21.43	ST	21.43	28.57	**MAT024**	SQ	85.71	SCM	7.14	SEP	7.14	
MAT010	ST	71.43	SC	14.29	TM	14.29		**MAT025**	ST	92.86	TM	7.14			
MAT011	SEM	28.57	SC	21.43	SR	21.43	28.57	**MAT026**	SD	57.14	TM	21.43	SQ	14.29	7.14
MAT012	SCM	50.00	TM	14.29	SC	7.14	28.57	**MAT027**	SC	57.14	SD	28.57	TM	7.14	7.14
MAT013	SEM	21.43	SR	21.43	SC	14.29	42.86	**MAT028**	SEP	28.57	SR	28.57	TM	21.43	21.43
MAT014	SCM	50.00	SEP	14.29	SC	7.14	28.57	**MAT029**	ST	35.71	SEM	21.43	TM	14.29	28.57
MAT015	SCM	35.71	TM	28.57	MT	21.43	14.29	**MAT030**	SD	78.57	TM	14.29	SEP	7.14	

The votes were converted into percentages and distributed in Table 3 as columns in order to show the ranking among the most voted areas and the percentage corresponding votes. The percentages obtained from the fourth most voted areas downwards, have been concentrated in the column "Other Voted Areas". This distribution allows us to analyze if there was consensus among the learners in choosing the area to which the learning material belongs. The cases with the first most voted area equal or inferior to 60% have been highlighted.

Through the results presented in Table 3 it can be observed that, on the contrary to the classification performed by the experts, there was no consensus related to what knowledge area the learning materials belong. Among the thirty materials that have been classified, only eleven learning materials obtained a percentage of classification on the first most voted area, superior or equal to 60%. As far as MAT011, for instance, it received 4 votes (28.57%) on the Software Engineering Management (SEM) area, 3 votes (21.43%) were given to the Software Construction (SC) area, 3 votes (21.43%) to the Software Requirements (SR) area and 4 votes (28.57%) were distributed among the Software Configuration Management (SCM), the Software Engineering Process (SEP) and the Software Quality (SQ) areas. Based on these results it is possible to conclude that even people with a moderate Software Engineering knowledge degree have difficulty in identifying the specific knowledge areas. In this context, in an organizational environment, where people are searching for knowledge and also sharing their knowledge, a learner who has no advanced knowledge in specific and specialized areas may have difficulty in classifying learning materials.

5.3 Automatic Classification of Learning Materials by Ontology

The same eighty-four learners from the previous substep were also involved in this substep. Through the learning environment developed, each learner added five learning materials, which were the same materials manually classified by the experts and the learners. During the addition of each material, the learners made their recommendations based on three elements of RUP (paper, artifact, and task) and through to these recommendations, the ontology automatically classified the learning materials according to the SWEBOK knowledge areas. Due to limited space it was not possible to insert the entire results. But, it is possible to affirm that recommendations lead ontology to classify the learning materials in different knowledge areas. For example, in the material MAT001, Software Design (SD) area was in the first place with 57.14% of the learners, Software Engineering Management (SEM) and Software Requirements (SR) areas were in the second and third place with 42.86% of the learners, Software Construction (SC) and Software Test (ST) areas were in the fourth and fifth place with 35.71% of the learners and Software Configuration Management (SCM) area was in the sixth place with 28.57% of learners. Table 4 compares the percentage of classification obtained by the learners and the ontology in the same areas identified by the experts as predominant.

Table 4. Comparison among percentage obtained by the learners and the ORLM in the area identified by the experts

ID	Area	Expert %	Learner %	Ontology %	ID	Area	Expert %	Learner %	Ontology %
MAT001	SC	80.00	71.43	35.71	**MAT017**	SC	100.00	69.23	71.43
MAT002	ST	80.00	85.71	78.57	**MAT018**	SC	100.00	50.00	71.43
MAT003	SEM	100.00	57.14	85.71	**MAT019**	SCM	100.00	28.57	71.43
MAT004	SC	80.00	57.14	21.43	**MAT020**	SR	80.00	64.29	78.60
MAT005	SC	100.00	64.29	78.60	**MAT021**	SD	100.00	30.77	85.71
MAT006	SR	100.00	100.00	100.00	**MAT022**	SR	80.00	42.86	78.57
MAT007	SEM	80.00	35.71	50.00	**MAT023**	SEM	80.00	42.86	71.43
MAT010	ST	100.00	71.43	85.70	**MAT024**	SR	100.00	85.71	100.00
MAT011	SEM	80.00	23,08	64.29	**MAT025**	ST	100.00	92.86	92.86
MAT012	SCM	100.00	46.15	64.29	**MAT026**	SD	80.00	57.14	100.00
MAT013	SEM	100.00	21.43	85.71	**MAT027**	SD	80.00	28.57	92.86
MAT014	SCM	100.00	50.00	92.86	**MAT028**	SR	80.00	28.57	92.86
MAT015	SCM	80.00	35.71	85.71	**MAT029**	SEM	60.00	21.43	64.29
MAT016	SCM	100.00	69.23	85.71	**MAT030**	SD	60.00	78.57	78.57

The materials MAT008 and MAT009 were removed from the comparative table because the area identified as predominant by the experts do not belong to one of the six areas represented in the ontology. Among the thirty learning materials compared, three of these learning materials classified by the learners (MAT001, MAT002 and MAT004, orange color) obtained a percentage of classification closer to the one made by the experts, than the classification achieved by the ORLM. It is also observed that three materials (MAT006, MAT025 and MAT030, yellow color) obtained similar percentages when classified by the learners and by the ontology. Nevertheless, twenty-four materials (green color), representing 80% of the classified learning materials, obtained a percentage of classification closer to the experts' classification using the ontology, than the results achieved by the learners. The ORLM integrated into the learning environment allows the learner to search the learning materials according to a specific knowledge area and also according to recommendations made by learners. These search options may aid the learner to find the learning materials needed more easily. This functionality is essential in an autonomous environment where there is no tutor to indicate the more adequate learning materials to the learner.

6. CONCLUSION

In this paper an ontology for the Software Engineering knowledge area was developed and integrated in an organizational learning environment, which was also developed in this work. The ontology was integrated into the environment with the goal of enabling the automatic classification of learning materials. An experiment was conducted in order to examine whether the ontology would aid the automatic classification of learning materials. In the experiment, experts, learners and ontology classified a group of learning materials. When comparing the classifications, the results achieved by the ontology got closer to the ones performed by the specialists. It was also observed that the learners, despite the fact that they have worked in the area and have attended subjects related to the Software Engineering area, they presented difficulties to manually classify the learning materials. Therefore, it is evident the need for mechanisms to aid solving this issue. The experiment was conducted only in the Software Engineering context. However, ontologies from other knowledge areas could be integrated into the environment in order to support the classification of learning materials according to specific areas.

REFERENCES

Abran, A. and Moore, J.W., 2004. Guide to the Software Engineering Body of Knowledge. Society. IEEE Press.

Fischer, G., 2001. User modeling in human-computer interaction. User Modeling and User Adapted Interaction. 11, pp 65-86.

Gamalel-Din, S., 2010. Smart e-Learning: A greater perspective; from the fourth to the fifth generation e-learning. Egyptian Informatics Journal.11(1), pp 39-48.

Gruber, T.R., 1995. Toward Principles for the Design of Ontologies Used for Knowledge Sharing, International Journal of Human and Computer Studies, 43(5-6), pp 907-928.

Lahteenmaki, S., Toivonen, J. and Mattila, M., 2001. Critical Aspects of Organizational Learning Research and Proposals for Its Measurement, British Journal of Management, 12, pp 113-129.

Meister, J.C., 1998. Corporate Universities: Lessons in Building a World-class Work Force. McGraw-Hill.

Murray, P. and Donegan, K., 2003. Empirical linkages between firm competencies and organisational learning, Learning Organization, 10 (1), pp 51–62.

Nevo, D. and Wand, Y., 2005. Organizational memory information systems: a transactive memory approach, Decision Support Systems, 39 (4), pp 549–562.

Nonaka, I. and Takeuchi, H., 1995. The Knowledge Creating Company: How Japanese Companies Create the Dynamics of Innovation. New York: Oxford University Press.

Noy, N.F. and McGuinness, D.L., 2001. Ontology Development 101: A Guide to Creating your First Ontology, Stanford Knowledge Systems Laboratory Technical Report KSL-01-05 and Stanford Medical Informatics Technical Report SMI-2001-0880, March, 2001.

Oztemel, E. and Arslankaya, S., 2012. Enterprise knowledge management model: a knowledge tower. Knowledge and Information Systems, 31(1), pp 171-192.

Rosemberg, M. J., 2001. E-Learning – Strategies for delivering knowledge in the Digital Age. New York: McGraw-Hill.

Senge, P.M. The fifth discipline: The art & practice of the learning organization. São Paulo: Best Seller, p. 352, 2000.

Sicilia, M. and Lytras M.D., 2005. The semantic learning organization, The Learning Organization, 12 (5), pp 402-410.

Yaghmaie, M. and Bahreininejad, A. 2010. A context-aware adaptive learning system using agents, Expert Systems with Applications, 38 (4), pp 3280–3286.

Wang, M., 2011. Integrating organizational, social, and individual perspectives in Web 2.0-based workplace e-learning, Information Systems Frontiers, pp 191–205.

Zhang, J., 2006. A semantic framework to support corporate memory management in building construction, Automation in Construction, 15, pp 504-521.

ASSISTING USERS IN OPEN DATA INFRASTRUCTURES: A MANAGEMENT PERSPECTIVE

Hashim Iqbal Chunpir[1, 2] and Luciana A. M. Zaina[2]
[1]*The German Climate Computing Centre (DKRZ), Scientific Computing, University of Hamburg*
Bundesstraße 45a, 20146, Hamburg, Germany
[2]*Federal University of São Carlos – campus Sorocaba , Rdv João Leme dos Santos, Km 110 -Sorocaba - SP - Brazil*

ABSTRACT

Utilizing user support is an essential activity in e-Science to maintain and strengthen the research activities via an e-Science infrastructure to benefit science as well as our society. User support process is present in almost each and every e-Science infrastructure to support the users. However, there are fewer studies conducted that empirically evaluate the user support process in federated open data e-Science infrastructures and highlight major problems in the user support process. In this paper, a popular climate data e-infrastructure; Earth System Grid Federation (ESGF) is chosen as a case-study. This paper expounds a study conducted using interviews with the major stakeholders of ESGF. Based on the analysis of the interviews, a central problem in the current user support practices in ESGF is identified. In this paper, a solution to this central problem is recommended that can not only enhance the user support process in federated e-Science infrastructures like ESGF from the management perspective but also can improve the user experience and usability of federated e-Science and IT infrastructures.

KEYWORDS

Open Data; e-Science; Information Technology Information Library (ITIL); user support; FeUSE framework; service desk

1. INTRODUCTION AND BACKGROUND

Nowadays, e-Science infrastructures[1] are quite mature, as far as their underlying technology is concerned, to deliver the open science data to users (Buyya & Murshed, 2002). These infrastructures facilitate e-Research, also known as e-Science[2] to the industrial and scientific communities worldwide. Subsequently, the users of these infrastructures discover new scientific phenomenon by performing research through them (Hashim Iqbal Chunpir, Ludwig, & Williams, 2015). Amongst other challenges that include scientific data collection, data licensing and copy right issues, data connectivity and replication, persistency of data, data archival, data governance, data access and data visualization (H. Chunpir & Moll, 2015; Hey & Trefethen, 2003; Karasti, Baker, & Halkola, 2006; Rudolph, Thoring, & Vogl, 2015; Schulte, Chunpir, & Voß, 2016); we focus on the managerial issues to support users to access data resources.

An interesting quote from a popular article goes like; *"to promote data-intensive, multi-disciplinary research, we will need to integrate e-Science, utilize it within the various scientific and scholarly domains, and generate value for society"* (Bohle, 2013). But how the integration and utilization of e-Science facilities is possible and how value for a society can be generated are two important research questions. One side of the coin is to develop and facilitate developers, designers, data managers to collaborate amongst each other to establish and maintain operations of e-Science infrastructures (Hashim Iqbal Chunpir, Badewi, & Ludwig, 2014; Karasti et al., 2006). Another side of the coin is to attract users to use the e-Science infrastructure by offering them adequate user support and better user experience (Hashim Iqbal Chunpir, Curri, Zaina, & Ludwig, 2016; Hashim Iqbal Chunpir, Rathmann, & Ludwig, 2015). Consequently, looking at the both sides

---

[1] The term "Cyber-infrastructures" is a synonym of e-Science infrastructures used often in USA.
[2] E-Science is "the application of computer technology to the undertaking of modern scientific investigation, including the preparation, experimentation, data collection, results dissemination, and long-term storage and accessibility of all materials generated through the scientific process." (Bohle, 2013)

of the coin, the value for the society and particularly for scientific communities can be generated if the user support process and usability of systems are made valuable to the users. This can fulfil users research needs, promote collaboration amongst them as well as facilitate e-learning in multi-disciplinary research fields.

With this paper, the aim is to contribute to the discussion of enhancing organization and management of e-Science that governs the user support process in order to create a value for e-Science infrastructure users. This study aims to analyze the supporters[3], users and other stake-holders; empirically in climate science domain, with ESGF taken as a case-study of Earth Science Modeling (ESM). Moreover, this paper focuses on a major problem that ESGF e-Science infrastructure is facing i.e. unclear role definitions amongst the management and the employees of e-Science infrastructure who can contribute in supporting users. This problem is identified and derived from the qualitative empirical study conducted via interviews to find out the problems within the current state of the user support process in ESGF. The identified problem demonstrates the need for establishing a comprehensive and well-defined user support management process in e-Science. Moreover, the guidelines from IT Service Management (ITSM) frameworks such as IT Infrastructure Library (ITIL) based Federated User Support Enhancement (FeUSE) framework can help to overcome the identified problem (Hashim Iqbal Chunpir, 2015). The research methodology used in this paper is based on Design Science Research (DSR) paradigm (Hevner & Chatterjee, 2010).

The organization of this paper is as follows: The reasons why ESGF was taken as a use case for this study are given in Section 2. The research method is explained in Section 3. The problem that was found after analyzing the interviews is elaborated in Section 4. Section 5 provides the rationale of using ITIL and FeUSE framework guidelines that are helpful in solving the problem. The suggestions in the form of the treatment of the problem are elucidated in Section 6. Finally, future work and conclusion is given in Section 7.

2. OUR USE CASE: EARTH SYSTEM GRID FEDERATION (ESGF)

The case chosen for our research is ESGF. ESGF is a prominent e-Science infrastructure in climate science (Hashim Iqbal Chunpir, Ludwig, et al., 2015; Cinquini et al., 2012). ESGF hosts numerous data models and data projects (Hashim Iqbal Chunpir, Ludwig, et al., 2015). ESGF hosts Coupled-Model Inter-comparison Project Phase 5 (CMIP5[4]) data-sets via its e-Science infrastructure that is significant in generating the Inter-governmental Panel for Climate Change (IPCC) reports on the global climate change (Hashim Iqbal Chunpir, Ludwig, et al., 2015). The last report generated by IPCC was Assessment Report 5 (AR5) that presents an up to date view of the current scientific knowledge about climate change (World Meteorological Organization & UNEP, 2015). The political decisions about climate change and conservation of environment taken at the global conferences such as the UN Climate Change Conference, Paris, 2015 are based on IPCC reports. It has more than 27,000 users from all over the world, mainly climate scientists (Hashim Iqbal Chunpir, Ludwig, & Badewi, 2014b). Out of 27,000 users, several hundred are active users. The people who are responsible for the operation of ESGF infrastructure as whole are more or less 50. These are the active staffs from different data centers in the participating organisations in ESGF such as German Climate Computing Centre (DKRZ), Lawrence Livermore National Laboratory (LLNL) and others.

The governance structure of ESGF comprises of steering, executive and technical committees namely: SC, EC and TC that form ESGF Review Board (ERB). The technical committee (TC) and executive committee (EC) participate in the decision and policy making of ESGF. Each decision has an impact on the overall service delivery of ESGF. In the current governance policy, concrete user support policies are not well defined as far as the function, boundary and interfaces of user support process and user relation is concerned (Hashim Iqbal Chunpir, Ludwig, & Badewi, 2014a, 2014b; Hashim Iqbal Chunpir & Ludwig, 2014). The forthcoming section illustrates the results of a qualitative empirical study to identify a major problem in the current user support practice in ESGF.

---

[3] Supporters or human support agents are usually the employees who support users of an e-Science infrastructure.

[4] "CMIP5 is meant to provide a framework for coordinated climate change experiments for the next five years."(PCMDI, 2013; Taylor, Stouffer, & Meehl, 2012)

3. METHODOLOGY: A QUALITATIVE EMPIRICAL STUDY

In this qualitative empirical study is based on DSR (Hevner & Chatterjee, 2010); we investigated the current user support process and identified a major problem that is faced by the stakeholders when they practice the function of a service desk[5] in ESGF. For this study, 12 semi-structured narrative interviews of 70 minutes of duration on the average were conducted, in-person and online via teleconferencing tools (see Table 1). Interviewees from Germany, USA, Australia and Spain participated in this study. The interview guidelines were divided into three parts: introduction/ entry questions, story like narration of situation guided by directional questions and reflection. The interviews were digitally recorded, fully transcribed and analyzed with regard to categories used in guidelines according to methods of qualitative content analysis with application of deductive categories (Mayring, 2000).

The interviewees were stakeholders of ESGF comprising mainly: climate scientists; i.e. the researchers who are the users of the ESGF e-Science infrastructure, technical staff members and executive staff members of the ESGF e-Science infrastructure (as shown in Table 1). From the total of almost of 50 active employees of ESGF, interviewing eight prominent members of ESGF and four active users is a good sample to extract relevant knowledge about the current problems in the current user support process of ESGF. Furthermore, the composition of the sample of the interviewees allows us to gain an insight into the matter with different perspectives. The interviewees were a rich source of information as the employees of the ESGF were experienced. In addition, they had an overview of different situations in the current user support process as well as the over-all management of ESGF. The interviewees who were users of ESGF had experience in conducting their climate research activities using ESGF and other e-Science infrastructures. They had been using ESGF for a minimum of 6 months. Furthermore, the users knew well about the usability part of the ESGF. The subsequent paragraphs present the brief outcome of the interviews i.e. the major problem.

Table 1. The table demonstrates the interviewees, their roles, their location of job and the mode the interview was conducted

Interviewee	**Interviewee's Attributes**		
	Role	***Location***	***Mode***
A	Social Scientist [a]	Germany	In person
B	Climate Scientist, contact of ESGF to Data Modelling institutes, Member of Executive Committee of ESGF	USA	Online
C	Developer, Member of Technical Committee ESGF	USA	In person
D	System Administrator, Member of Technical Committee ESGF	USA	Online
E	Principal Investigator, Member of Executive Committee	Australia	Online
F	Master user [b] at COLA	USA	Online
G	Developer of C3Grid web services and web portal	Germany	In person
H	Climate Researcher Scientist at the Spanish institute / User of ESGF	Spain	Online
I	Climate Researcher Scientist at MPI-M / User of ESGF	Germany	In person
J	Climate Researcher Scientist at MPI-M / User of ESGF	Germany	In person
K	Climate Researcher Scientist at MPI-M / User of ESGF	Germany	In person
L	Chair of Executive Committee - ESGF	USA	Online

a. Social Scientist was observing ESGF and related projects for three years.

b. Master user is the one who collects data-sets from ESGSF at a particular research institute so that the researchers can access the data-sets locally.

[5] A service desk is a functional unit staff involved in servicing user requests. The primary purpose of the service desk is to "restore normal service" to users as quickly as possible. (Office of Government Commerce, 2011)

4. THE PROBLEM

From the interviews it was found out that *the role of managing user support activities is not defined exclusively* and these activities are being performed by the employees of ESGF in addition to the core activities of their job description. This observation is also supported by the previous studies conducted to find out the current user support scenario in ESGF (Hashim Iqbal Chunpir, Ludwig, & Badewi, 2014a, 2014b). For instance; there is no designation of user support manager who is exclusively responsible and accountable for performing user support activities. As a result, the user support activities are performed by the top computer scientists and climate scientists, in particular servicing simple and routine user queries. Henceforth, this is mainly misappropriation of their creative skills. Moreover, the additional responsibility on the shoulders of the technical staff does not reward them in monetary terms, promote them or bring them some form of recognition. Thus, the user support requests are not serviced by the employees on regular basis resulting in overlooking of some user requests (Hashim Iqbal Chunpir, Ludwig, & Badewi, 2014a). All interviewees are of the opinion to assign user support responsibility to someone who is a structurally anchored person with the ESGF dealing with the user support process.

5. REASONS TO APPLY ITIL AND FEUSE FRAMEWORK GUIDELINES IN FEDERATED IT INFRASTRUCTURES

Authors have pointed out relationship between ITIL and the service desk in the non-commercial environment (Arora & Bandara, 2006; Jäntti, 2012). ITIL is suitable in any organization whose goal is to deliver IT services that meet the need and requirements in user or consumer oriented set-ups (Potgieter, Botha, & Lew, 2005). ITIL is flexible and embraces a practical approach to service management. One can apply whatever works and leave whatever does not work within an organization. Moreover, ITIL is vendor neutral i.e. any organization irrespective of the platform it uses, can utilize ITIL practices to add value to its business. ITIL is generic i.e. it offers robust, mature and time-tested practices applicable to all sorts of organisations. Furthermore, ITIL recommendations are based on best and successful service providers around the world (Office of Government Commerce, 2011).

Likewise, ITIL reduces costs for the organization providing the service to customers, thus optimizing costs (Office of Government Commerce, 2011; Potgieter et al., 2005). Consequently, for the enhancement of the user support situation in ESGF e-Science infrastructure of climate domain, ITIL guidelines can be applied. A tailored version of ITIL framework to enhance the user support process in federated e-infrastructures was recommended in FeUSE framework (Hashim Iqbal Chunpir, 2015). In FeUSE framework, the ITIL recommendations are adapted to suite the dynamic and ever changing environment of e-Science infrastructure such as ESGF. In the forthcoming section the earlier identified problem (detailed in the previous section) is handled in the light of ITIL V3 from 2011 and FeUSE framework recommendations.

6. TREATING THE PROBLEM

In this section we focus on the problem: "*Unclear role definitions for performing user support in federated e-Science infrastructures.*" The suggestions in the light of FeUSE framework to solve the problem are explained as follows: In ESGF, the roles for performing user support are not assigned in particular to any employee exclusively (Hashim Iqbal Chunpir, Ludwig, & Badewi, 2014a). Therefore, no reward, responsibilities and accountability are agreed upon for the employees of the ESGF by ESGF committees. Due to this fact, the user support queries are handled on voluntarily basis by the ESGF employees (Hashim Iqbal Chunpir, Ludwig, & Curri, 2014). Although efforts have been made to attract employees and other volunteers to support users (H. I Chunpir, 2016; Hashim Iqbal Chunpir et al., 2016), however, the unclear role definition impacts the whole user support process as some of the user requests are overlooked and for some solution is not provided. Consequently, it is vital to assign responsibilities and accountabilities in the form of roles. In order to assign responsibilities and accountabilities in ESGF, roles of user support process owner, user support services owner, user support practitioner and user support coordinator need to be introduced, as depicted in Figure 1.

The role of user support services owner is responsible for the delivery of the support services to the users according to service level agreements (SLA) set between the service provider i.e. ESGF and the users of ESGF. The result of the user support services must meet the expectations of users therefore providing them satisfaction. Currently, there is no such SLA defined, implemented and known to the employees of ESGF who provide support to the users. SLA can be defined in this regard.

The user support process owner is the person accountable for the working of the whole user support process. The main task of user support owner is to ensure that the whole process remains effective, efficient with in the ESGF and is providing value to the users and other stakeholders. The user support owner has an obligation to get connected with-in and outside of e-Science infrastructure stakeholders. Through his/her connection with other colleagues belonging to the executive and the technical committee, the user support manager permanently encourages enhancement of user support and collects support requirements. In addition, the user support manager detects new ideas, trends and collaboration possibilities to improve the user support process. S/he also undertakes research to improve intangible assets such as knowledge management, knowledge transfer, training and innovation which can be outcomes of user support process in e-Science. Moreover, the user support process owner analyses the impact of technology used in the user support process and assesses whether the development of new technology to automate the process is needed.

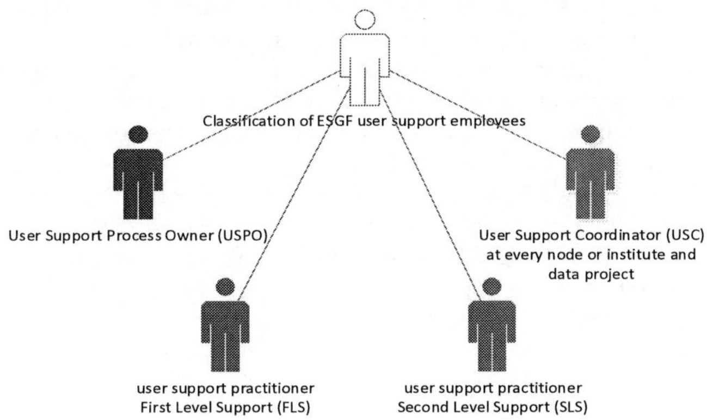

Figure 1. The figure shows ESGF user support employee roles

In ESGF, role of user support services owner and process owner can be merged and one fulltime position may be assigned to a qualified person. In other e-Science infrastructure role of user support services owner and process owner may be created and practiced either solely or also merged together according to the needs, budget constraints and the overall situation.

Another important role is the role of user support coordinator (also known as user support manager) who is responsible that the user support process within a participating organization remains transparent. Furthermore, s/he ensures that within a particular organization the tools, techniques, human resources used to service user requests are known and confirm to the standards set by the ESGF central governance committee. User support coordinators should have a complete knowledge of the experts available in a particular organization who may process a user request of their specialized as well as generalized area. The user support coordinators must be attached at least one person per participating organization in the ESGF. The user support coordinators must be attached to the partner institutions who are participating in ESGF by providing technical services such as maintaining a node via which the data can be hosted. In addition, the data modelling centers which are offering their data sets to be delivered via ESGF to the climate-researchers world-wide. Therefore, there are two types of the user support coordinators one working with the organisations having employees focused on the technical know-how and other having scientific know-how as shown in Figure 2. The user support coordination role can be either made exclusive or assigned to someone with part of his or her job description, in addition to other activities that one carries out.

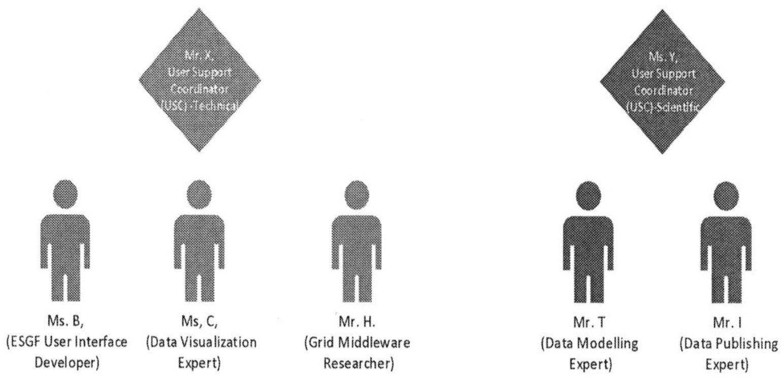

Figure 2. The diamond shapes show the user support coordinators who maintain the directory of the user support specialists (SLS) at their respective institution, participating in ESGF. User support coordinators are present in both technical as well scientific organizations

The user support practitioners, who actually process user requests can comprise of the first level support and the second level. These user support escalation levels are not defined so far in the ESGF, as evident from another study (Hashim Iqbal Chunpir, Ludwig, & Badewi, 2014a). It is suggested in ESGF to introduce two-level of user support escalation levels, also known as tiers that constitute the user support (help-desk) structure. The first level support practitioners handle the user requests exclusively or develop techniques in guidance with their user support coordinator and user support process owner. If the first level support cannot solve an issue, they may escalate it to the second-level support practitioners. Second-level support practitioners are the specialists of their particular domain such as a particular component, for instance UV-CDAT visualization tool. The user support practitioners may include system administrators, data managers, software developers, climate and computer scientists who process the user requests in addition to their own activity. The roles and responsibilities should be assigned so that there is no confusion and delay in processing user requests.

7. CONCLUSIONS AND FUTURE WORK

The necessity to establish a systematic user support process is widely accepted in practice and literature. However, a concept to establish such a process is lacking in federated e-Science infrastructures. In this study, the user support process is analyzed empirically, by interviewing stakeholders with different roles in a case study of climate e-infrastructure. After analyzing the current user support process in ESGF, we have identified one of the major problems in the user support process i.e. the roles of people, including employees involved in the user support process in e-Science infrastructure, are needed to be introduced to provide reliable user support. Furthermore, amendments in the user support process have been suggested by following FeUSE framework recommendations to enhance user support practices. Currently, user support management approaches are needed to be integrated with the main governance and management of e-Science infrastructures.

The recommendations suggested in this paper to improve user support process is the first step to integrate user support sub-processes in the overall governance structure of e-Science. For future research, user support services are needed to be elaborated in a greater detail. For instance: taking a multi-case study comprising of e-Science infrastructures of various domains. It is imperative to identify and describe patterns if handling user support process. These patterns may be different for certain organisations collaborating together to form e-Science infrastructures. Since ESGF is concerned with delivering data to the consumers who are users, therefore it is important to investigate that to what extent the ITIL as well as FeUSE guidelines have been applied and can be applied in e-Science infrastructures to improve the user support process. Moreover, the user interfaces provided by an e-infrastructure must also be investigated i.e. to what extent the users' needs are being met while the users use the interfaces to perform their research.

ACKNOWLEDGEMENT

We thank the financial contribution of CAPES and FAPESP.

REFERENCES

Arora, A., & Bandara, W. (2006). IT Service Desk Process Improvement – A Narrative Style Case Study. In H. Lee & B. Tan (Eds.), *The Tenth Pacific Asia Conference on Information Systems (PACIS 2006)* (pp. 1274–1285). Kuala Lumpur, Malaysia. Retrieved from http://www.pacis-net.org/file/2006/1178.pdf

Bohle, S. (2013). *What is E-science and How Should it be Managed? Nature.com, Spektrum der Wissenschaft (Scientific American)*. Retrieved from http://www.scilogs.com/scientific_and_medical_libraries/what-is-e-science-and-how-should-it-be-managed/

Buyya, R., & Murshed. (2002). GridSim: A toolkit for the modeling and simulation of distributed resource management and scheduling for grid computing concurrency and computation practice and experience. *Concurrency and Computation: Practice and Experience (CCPE)*, *14*(13), 1175–1220. Retrieved from http://citeseerx.ist.psu.edu/viewdoc/summary?doi=10.1.1.12.4262

Chunpir, H. I. (2015). *Enhancing User Support Process in Federated E-Science*. University of Hamburg.

Chunpir, H. I. (2016). Prioritizing Tasks using User-Support-Worker's Activity Model. In S. Yamamoto (Ed.), *Lecture Notes of Computer Science (LNCS), Human Computer Interaction International (HCI) Proceedings* (pp. 379–390). Toronto: Springer International Publishing. doi:10.1007/978-3-319-40397-7_36

Chunpir, H. I., Badewi, A., & Ludwig, T. (2014). User support in the complex environment. In A. Marcus (Ed.), *Design, User Experience, and Usability. Lecture Notes in Computer Science Volume 8520, Proceedings of HCI* (Vol. 8520, pp. 392–402). Heraklion, Crete, Greece: Springer International Publishing. doi:10.1007/978-3-319-07638-6

Chunpir, H. I., Curri, E., Zaina, L., & Ludwig, T. (2016). Improving User Interfaces for a Request Tracking System: Best Practical RT. In S. Yamamoto (Ed.), *Lecture Notes of Computer Science (LNCS), Human Computer Interaction International (HCI) Proceedings* (pp. 391–401). Toronto: Springer International Publishing. doi:10.1007/978-3-319-40397-7_37

Chunpir, H. I., & Ludwig, T. (2014). Reviewing the governance structure of end-user support in e-Science infrastructures. In E. Plödereder, L. Grunske, E. Schneider, & D. Ull (Eds.), *Lecture Notes in Informatics (LNI), Volume 232, Mastering Big Data Complexity, Informatik 2014 Proceedings.*

Chunpir, H. I., Ludwig, T., & Badewi, A. (2014a). A snap-shot of user support services in Earth System Grid Federation (ESGF): A use case of climate cyber-infrastructures. In L. Freund & W. Cellary (Eds.), *Proceedings of the 5th Applied Human Factors and Ergonomics (AHFE) Conference*. Krakow, Poland: AHFE Conference, CRC.

Chunpir, H. I., Ludwig, T., & Badewi, A. A. (2014b). Using soft systems methodology (SSM) in understanding current user-support scenario in the climate science domain of cyber-infrastructures. In A. Marcus (Ed.), *Design, User Experience, and Usability. Lecture Notes in Computer Science, Volume 8519, Proceedings of HCI, Part III* (pp. 495–506). Heraklion, Crete, Greece: Springer International Publishing.

Chunpir, H. I., Ludwig, T., & Curri, E. (2014). Improving Processes for User Support in e-Science. In *IEEE 10th International Conference on e-Science (e-Science), Volume 2* (pp. 87–90). IEEE.

Chunpir, H. I., Ludwig, T., & Williams, D. N. (2015). Evolution of e-Research : From Infrastructure Development to Service Orientation. In A. Marcus (Ed.), *DUXU 2015, Part III, LNCS 9188* (Vol. 20, pp. 25–35). Springer International Publishing. doi:10.1007/978-3-319-20889-3

Chunpir, H. I., Rathmann, T., & Ludwig, T. (2015). The Need for a Tool to Support Users of e-Science Infrastructures in a Virtual Laboratory Environment. *Procedia Manufacturing*, *3*, 3375–3382. doi:10.1016/j.promfg.2015.07.527

Chunpir, H., & Moll, A. (2015). Analysis of Marine Ecosystems: Usability, Visualization and Community Collaboration Challenges. *Procedia Manufacturing*, *3*, 3262–3265. doi:10.1016/j.promfg.2015.07.878

Cinquini, L., Crichton, D., Mattmann, C., Bell, G. M., Drach, B., Williams, D., … Schweitzer, R. (2012). The Earth System Grid Federation (ESGF): An open infrastructure for access to distributed geospatial data. In *8th IEEE International Conference on E-Science* (pp. 1–10). Chicago, Illinois, USA: IEEE. doi:10.1109/eScience.2012.6404471

Hevner, A., & Chatterjee, S. (2010). Design Research in Information Systems, *22*, 9–23. doi:10.1007/978-1-4419-5653-8

Hey, A., & Trefethen, A. (2003). The data deluge: An e-science perspective, (January 2003), 1–17. Retrieved from http://eprints.soton.ac.uk/257648/1/The_Data_Deluge.pdf

Jäntti, M. (2012). Improving IT service desk and service management processes in Finnish tax administration: A case study on service engineering. In D. Oscar, J. Andreas, & J. Natalia (Eds.), *Proceedings of the 13th International Conference on Product-Focused Software Process Improvement, PROFES 2012* (pp. 218–232). Madrid, Spain: Springer Berlin Heidelberg.

Karasti, H., Baker, K. S., & Halkola, E. (2006). Enriching the Notion of Data Curation in E-Science: Data Managing and Information Infrastructuring in the Long Term Ecological Research (LTER) Network. *Computer Supported Cooperative Work (CSCW)*, *15*(4), 321–358. doi:10.1007/s10606-006-9023-2

Mayring, P. (2000). Qualitative Content Analysis, *1*(2). Retrieved from http://www.utsc.utoronto.ca/~kmacd/IDSC10/Readings/text analysis/CA.pdf

Office of Government Commerce. (2011). *ITIL V3 2011: Service Operation*.

PCMDI. (2013). *Overview of coupled model intercomparison project phase 5 - CMIP5. LLNL-WEB*. Retrieved May 24, 2014, from http://cmip-pcmdi.llnl.gov/cmip5

Potgieter, B. C., Botha, J. H., & Lew, C. (2005). Evidence that use of the ITIL framework is effective. In *18th Annual Conference of the National Advisory Committee on Computing Qualifications*.

Rudolph, D., Thoring, A., & Vogl, R. (2015). Research Data Management: Wishful Thinking or Reality? *PIK - Praxis Der Informationsverarbeitung Und Kommunikation*, *38*(3-4), 113–120. doi:doi:10.1515/pik-2015-0009

Schulte, F., Chunpir, H. I., & Voß, S. (2016). Open Data Evolution in Information Systems Research: Considering Cases of Data-Intensive Transportation and Grid Systems. In A. Marcus (Ed.), *5th International Conference, DUXU 2016, Held as Part of HCI International 2016, Toronto, Canada, July 17–22, 2016, Proceedings, Part III* (pp. 193–201). Berlin, Heidelberg: Springer Berlin Heidelberg. doi:10.1007/978-3-319-40406-6_18

Taylor, K. E., Stouffer, R. J., & Meehl, G. a. (2012). An overview of CMIP5 and the experiment design. *Bulletin of the American Meteorological Society*, *93*(4), 485–498. doi:10.1175/BAMS-D-11-00094.1

World Meteorological Organization, & UNEP. (2015). *Inter-governmental panel on climate change. IPCC*. Retrieved January 10, 2015, from http://www.ipcc.ch/organization/

MORE THAN CONTENT CLASSIFICATION: SELF-EXPRESSION THROUGH IMAGE TAGGING

Angelina Ziesemer, Luana Müller and Milene Silveira
Faculdade de Informática – Pontifical Catholic University of Rio Grande do Sul
Avenida Ipiranga, 6681, 90619-900, Porto Alegre, Brazil

ABSTRACT

Tagging has the potential to improve information retrieval. Although its primary purpose is description and categorization of content, the tagging task has evolved and now users express more than the explicit content presented on the resources being tagged. However, tagging is a repetitive work and, due to this fact, tag recommender systems were developed to support this task by suggesting tags based on similarity. Although these types of systems improve the quality and homogeneity of tags, users have distinct criteria, motivation and style for tagging. In this work we conducted two studies to investigate how users express themselves using tags on images. Results show that tags' language and structure are a matter of personal style and users want to express the context that an image represents through tags. Despite the fact that users want to express themselves by using personal tags, when recommendation is involved they change their tagging style and assume the collective tag expression.

KEYWORDS

Self-expression, tagging, recommendation, image-sharing.

1. INTRODUCTION

As technology evolves, sharing digital-images has become a common practice among users, increasing the amount of content available online. Although some systems allow users to organize images into albums, it is common for users to publish images individually on social networks, which makes future retrieval difficult. Tagging has become a popular approach to freely classify content by regular users on the web. It allows resource classification by subject or content, and it is pretty helpful for indexing non-textual content such as images and videos. However, this freedom to classify content using any word or phrase may require a significant amount of work whenever there are too many resources to be tagged. Thereby, tag recommender systems were created to aid users in the tagging task (Song 2011).

The recommendation of [hash]tags aims to improve tags' reuse, making the tagging task easier and helping users choose among similar tags based on the image context, for instance. Yet, tagging is not just a matter of preference, it is also a task performed by users that involves the language (Stiller et al. 2011) chosen for tagging and the content (Klavans et al. 2014) being tagged. Even though tags were created to help the content description/classification task, users have distinct motivation (Strohmaier et al. 2010) for tagging and, consequently, new types of tags have emerged (Manish et al. 2010). Some researchers have reported users' distinct motivations for tagging as self-presentation, opinion expression, social signaling, among others. Tags have become a socialization tool and communication is now involved, since users have expanded tags to express their opinion and emotions (Manish et al. 2010) about the content presented on images.

Self-expression is a phenomenon related to individuality, personality and idiosyncrasies of the self and it is connected with human communication (Johnstone 1996), through which we can manifest our point of view (Green 2008). We can express ourselves in several ways, not only through our voice tone, body language, and arts, but also through our interaction with computers (Monteiro and De Souza 2012).

There are studies indicating that recommender systems can change users' choices (Zhu et al 2012)(Cosley et al 2003). In an initial study (Ziesemer et al 2016), we found out that recommender systems play a role in the language users choose for tagging. The results we found leveraged our research to investigate users' behavior from the point of view of self-expression. We investigated not only the motivation and criteria for tagging but mainly *"How do users use tags to express themselves?"*.

In order to answer this research question we reported the results from two studies we conducted. In the first study we asked participants to assign tags to four digital-images in two different conditions (with and without a recommendation support). After that, in a second study we conducted a new set of tagging tasks followed by an individual interview to answer open-ended questions so that an in-depth understanding about participants' self-expression on tagging systems could be achieved.

In this work, instead of solving recommendation algorithm issues, we are trying to raise designers' awareness about the implications of "one-size-fits-all" approaches for tagging on users' self-expression. The obtained results show that language and structure of tags are personal styles. Both image context (where, when, how, who/what) and its audience influence the users' decision on the type of tag assigned for expressing themselves. Moreover, although users want to express themselves through personal tags, when recommendation is involved they change their tagging style and assume the collective tag expression.

In the next section we present the Background used in our research: Tagging, Self-Expression and Recommender Systems. After that, we report the Research Method used, followed by our Findings, presenting the concepts found by the analysis of the data gathered. Next we present the Discussion about the results found in both studies and finally our Final Considerations.

2. BACKGROUND

Tagging is a crowd-sourcing task that was first adopted for content description. Its main goal is to add text to sources as digital images and videos that have lack of textual information associated, which makes the indexing task made by search engines difficult (Dattolo 2010). One of the biggest problem of tagging systems is that most tags are used only once and several of them are not related to the context of the resource being tagged (Stromaier 2010). However, the textual information associated to images and videos increases and helps recommender systems (Siersdorfer and Sizov 2009) (Gemmell et al. 2009) to model users' profiles and preferences. These systems are based on the idea that similar users share similar tags (Dattolo 2010).

In order to ease the tagging task, designers have developed the recommendation of tags (Sigurbjörnsson and Zwol 2008)(Ziesemer and Oliveira 2013). It aims at helping users to choose among a set of similar tags those that could improve the content indexing from the content available on social media networks, such as Flickr, Instagram and Youtube. **Recommender systems** were created based on the idea that those who shared similar preferences in the past, shall have the same interest in the future (Adomavicius and Tuzhilin 2005). It aims to help users to find relevant content based on users' rating, feedback, profile or friendship on social networks (Ziesemer and Oliveira 2011). This kind of system can suggest several types of items, such as documents, movies, music, tags, products and even people (also known as social matching).

On the other hand, Turkle (2005) believes that in certain ways computers can reflect people's mind, because *"the machine can act as a projection of part of the self, a mirror of the mind"* (p. 20). According to her, when different people sit down in front of computers, even when they are executing the "same" job, their interacting styles with the machine are very different from each other.

From the linguistics perspective, Johnstone's (1996) view about **self-expression** is: *"people express themselves with everything they do, whether or not self-expression is at the moment or in the context particularly valued or even though relevant at all"*. Individuality is a prerequisite for humanity and *"a sense of oneself as separate, autonomous, and temporally continuous, is functionally important in the maintenance of social life"*. Self-socialization becomes socially evident only through self-expression and this is the reason why tags become a way of communication inside social networks. Users started to express their feelings or opinions regarding a resource using terms that express more than the explicit content present in an image.

3. RESEARCH METHOD

We used a set of four digital-images (*A, B, C, D*) to perform the tagging task in the first study and the same images in the second study to understand users' self-expression from one study to another. All images were publicly available on Google Images and, as it is common in this kind of research, we classified the images by their content (Klavans et al. 2014). In this work we focus on the level of context/situation presented on the image content. This information was classified by fourteen individuals that did not take part in any other study reported here. Individuals were asked to classify the content of each image by how much information the images conveyed about their context. Figure 1 shows the level of context present in each image as a result of individuals' vote.

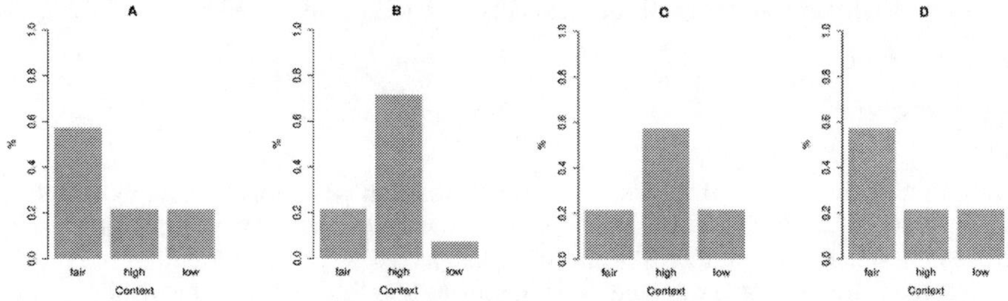

Figure 1. Images' context classification

3.1 First Study - Tagging and Recommendation

A total of 57 participants (26 female and 31 male, with a mean age of 26) took part in the first study we have conducted (Ziesemer et al 2016). All of them were residents of a Portuguese-speaking country and any previous definition was given regarding the language or structure they must have adopted during the tagging task.

We asked participants to assign tags in two distinct conditions (two browser-based interfaces for assigning tags - one with the support of the recommender system and the other without it). We conducted this experiment using a counterbalancing design approach, in which participants received the conditions in a different order. Participants received four images (A, B, C, D) and were asked to assign tags to these four images in both conditions of the experiment. We explained them that they should assign tags as if the images were from themselves. As a design platform for recommendation we used a model (Ziesemer and Oliveira 2013) that has as primary purpose the recommendation of tags. This approach recommends a ranking of similar tags based on co-occurrence (Sigurbjörnsson and Zwol 2008).

3.2 Second Study - User Expression through Tags

About six months after we conducted the first study we contacted the same individuals who took part in this previous study to participate in the second stage of our research to address answers related to the results we have found. At this stage a total of six participants (three females and three males, with ages from 21 to 35) agreed to participate by performing a tagging task and answering a set of questions during an interview.

We showed participants the same four images presented in the first study and asked them to choose among three sets of tags those which they thought would be more accurate with the tags that they would have assigned. We randomly presented each image with three sets of tags following these three criteria: (1) the set of tags the target participant has assigned in the previous study without recommendation for the same image; (2) the set of tags the target participant have assigned in the previous study supported by the recommendation for the same image and; (3) a set of tags that was not assigned by the target participant but by other participant(s) for the same image in the stage without recommendation.

We moved on our investigation by conducting a semi-structured interview using open-ended questions that have emerged from the analysis and observations of the data collected during the first study. The interview was structured in six guiding questions through which we investigated aspects about tagging criteria, motivation, language and style. The final question of the interview was related to the participants' perceptions about the set of tags they have chosen in the previous step. This task aimed to investigate whether users would start taking on the recommended tags as part of their self-expression after using the tags' recommender system.

In order to analyze the data obtained in this study, we used the Grounded Theory version (Corbin and Strauss 2008). Three researchers led this work, in which each one of them conducted their own open and axial coding in order to define concepts about the data. In the open coding step we focused on the analysis of the transcribed interviews to identify some categories that could help us answer our research question. Thereon, during the axial coding step we identified relationships among the categories generated by the previous step (open coding). Based on this analysis each researcher generated their own concepts about the participants' answers. Thereafter, a triangulation was conducted among the concepts found by each researcher, resulting in main concepts and sub-concepts that will be discussed in the following section.

4. FINDINGS

As we analyzed the tags, the first behavior we noticed was that participants changed the language used to assign tags (Ziesemer et al 2016). In the stage without recommendation, images had tags assigned mainly in Portuguese. As they started to assign tags in the stage supported by recommendation, this behavior changed. Participants switched the language adopted for tagging to English and the set of tags assigned started to become more homogeneous.

Since the recommendation approach is based on co-occurrence, even if participants assigned reference tags in Portuguese, they received recommendations in English. This behavior occurs because the English language works as a hub to other languages due to its high dissemination on the Web (Ronen et al 2014), also representing how tags that co-occur are connected in the training dataset gathered for recommendation.

Moreover, regarding image *B,* which was classified with the highest level of context in its content, we observed that participants assigned tags composed by more than one word and it was the image which presented the highest heterogeneity of tags. For example, in the set of tags participants assigned for image *A,* the tags described mainly the content through the use of single words (*"cat", "gato*[1]*", "kitten"*), while for image *B*, among the tags for content description, participants assigned a variety of tags to express the context the image represents *("dontFallAsleepInPublicPlaces", "megaCansada*[2]*").* This behavior has also changed during the stage supported by recommendation. Participants started assigning tags with a unique word not only for images with low level of context, but also for those classified as having high level of context.

At this stage we found two main concepts to represent users' behavior in this study: *language* and *structure*. Based on these concepts, we had some insights about how users express themselves through tags, thus leading us to prepare a set of questions aimed at conducting interviews with participants that have taken part in this first experiment in order to address questions related to users' self-expression on tagging systems.

4.1 Ascertaining Tags and Self-Expression

At this point we report the results from the second study we have conducted with participants who also took part in the first study previously reported. The concepts found during the axial coding and some participants' sentences spoken during the semi-structured interview are reported in the next sections.

4.1.1 Criteria to Assign Tags

Regarding tagging criteria, the main concepts we have found were *description* and *context*. Participants indicated their goals while tagging content: they want to describe the items or even their feelings about the situation presented in the image. More than a simple description, they also want to express the context of the image, by composing tags with their perceptions about the moment pictured by that.

One of the biggest insights reported by participants during interviews was that whenever tagging they try to describe more than isolated objects presented on the image. They want to compose tags based on the image's scenario. This was particularly observed on the images previously classified by their high level of context (*B* and *C*). We present as follows some sentences spoken by the participants regarding these concepts. All sentences were originally spoken in Portuguese and translated by the researchers:

P1: *"I try to compose things. I don't try mentioning only one specific thing."*

P2: *"I imagine myself at the moment of the image: in that place, with those people, and I say (using tags) what that image represents for me."*

---

[1] This tag was assigned in Portuguese and it means *cat* in English.

[2] This tag was assigned in Portuguese and it means *veryTired* in English.

P4: *"(...) I express the feeling that the actual image represents for me."*

When users are assigning tags to images, they express more than the explicit content this resource brings. They try to assign tags based on the set of objects that together compose a situation/scenario full of implicit and explicit context presented on it.

4.1.2 Motivation for Tagging

Related to the reasons users assign tags to images and other contents, we could define two concepts, namely *visibility* and *personalization*, which were generated based on participants' answers to two questions. In the first question we directly questioned why they use tags. The main concept we extracted from their reports was *visibility*, and we can split this concept in two sub-concepts: *indexing* and *message*.

Regarding the *visibility-indexing* concept, participants reported that they use tags in order to help the system to index the content of the image. One participant highlighted that even though she does not frequently assign tags, she understands that tagging is important to content indexing. She stated:

P5: *"I understand that it is interesting to a search engine (...) if you search for a specific [hash]tag/word, you can find them (the contents)."*

Participants also reported they use tags in order to deliver a *message* or opinion to a specific public, such as their families or friends. They want to emphasize something to their audience, making clear how they think or feel about a resource/image/content. Regarding the *visibility-message* concept, they reported:

P2: *"... when I assign tags I aim to say something about the moment I was living, to express an opinion."*

In the second question we sought to understand how the participants would feel if they were invited to use a hypothetical system, which automatically proceeds content tagging. The suggested system would assign the tags related to the image, only describing punctual items presented on it (e.g., if the image is picturing a beach, the system would only use tags as *"beach"*, *"sea"*, *"sky"*, and *"blue"*) and the user would not be allowed to interfere or add tags. The main concept emerged from their reports was *personalization*:

P3: *"(...) as many other automatic systems, it would be good to do 80% of the work, which would be the boring part of the task. However, the other 20%, which is the interesting part, I mean, the personalization, the creativity, the edition... that part should be done by me."*

P4: *"It depends on which type of information I want to index. Sometimes I want to index my feelings, the place I am, (...) So, this type of things, you know, feelings... the system has no way to know what I was thinking at that time, at that moment I was sharing something."*

Although tags were first introduced as a tool for indexing content, users expand the tagging functionality to express feelings, opinions and messages, and these are tags they consider too personal to be performed by a system. P4, who uses tags for content indexing, reported that tagging depends on the moment and sometimes he just wants to "index" feelings. It depends on the image context and the situation it represents.

4.1.3 Tagging Style

As we have previously reported, language and structure were the concepts we found in our first study and, from them, new insights have emerged, helping us to move forward to this second study. During the interview we asked questions about the participants' choice for tagging regarding language and structure. About language we could define two main concepts: *routine* and *propagation*.

In the first question we asked participants whether they used to assign tags written in other languages and why they did so. They reported that the decision about which language choose is associated with their *every day life*:

P2: *"The English language, for example, is part of my daily life. I read a lot of articles in English... it is not a matter of preference. I think it is now part of my personality."*

For these participants this type of behavior is guided by their routine. The daily contact with resources from foreign languages seems to be the main influence on their tagging language choices:

P1: *"(...) I add tags in Portuguese, this is my personal insight. I do not feel creative to assign tags (...) So, when I assign them, I use Portuguese."*

Although he does not feel confident to assign tags in another language, during the first study in the recommendation step, the system helped him to choose tags that could match with the tag he had assigned in Portuguese. In fact, this participant assigned all tags in Portuguese in the stage without recommendation support, but he has completely changed in the stage with the recommendation aid, assigning tags in English.

The second concept we found regarding language aspects is *propagation*. Tags can help the categorization and organization of content on the Internet and the use of some tags can help to spread this content on the web. Depending on the set of tags assigned to an image, it can reach distinct audiences. Our participants reported this factor as a reason to use tags written in different languages:

P4: *"(...) for example, on Instagram, tags reach more people. Besides that, I do not like to write a lot. It is easier to express myself when I use tags."*

P5: *"(...) in English, for example, you can reach a higher number of people, because English is one of the most spoken languages."*

We could observe that, to P4, assigning tags seems to be a safe way for self-expression and spreading content even using another language. Although he is not an English native speaker, he can express himself by tags and increase his content visibility among people that use tags in English for searching content online.

The second question was related to the use of composed tags and the reasons why users opt for this kind of structure. At this point, the concept we found was that they use this type of tagging in order to express a *concept* or the *context* present on the image. This concept can be a combination of tags to describe a scenario, the image context, a message that cannot be expressed by a single word, an opinion, or even a "meme"[3]. Regarding this question, participants reported:

P1: "(...) if an image has a set of things like a "campsite", you know, a "tent", a "campfire", "people having fun", so you may think this is maybe a barbecue (like a party). In my point of view, a tag should describe the scene, not just the objects one at a time."

This participant uses composed tags and single words aiming to express - what we call Conceptual tags - the mental combination of the photo characteristics, which results in tags such as *vacation*, *cold*, *party*, etc.

P3: *"My personal insight is that a tag is an expression, not just a word."*

P5: *"(...) most of my tags are single words, sometimes I use more than a word to write a place's name - if it is composed - maybe I can combine words with a verb or something else."*

Moreover, the context of the image plays a role on the tags users choose to express themselves. On the other hand, P5 expressed that she used tags to describe the content, as she had said before. Differently from other participants, she uses tags for content indexing. For example, she kept the same tagging behavior from one stage to another in the first study. In the stage without recommendation support, her tags were all assigned using English and most of her tags were single words. The only behavior affected by the recommender system was the number of tags assigned by her. She assigned 20% more tags in the stage supported by recommendation than in the stage without such system.

4.2 Identifying Personal Tags

All participants reported somehow that they recognized their tags among the sets presented to them. However, by analyzing the participants' answers and the set of tags assigned during the tagging task at this stage, an unexpected concept emerged: *occasion*.

Although one of the participants (P1) has correctly "recognized" himself in all the chosen sets, participants P3, P5 and P6 have chosen sets of tags that were not from themselves to all four pictures. Participants P2 and P4 have chosen their set of tags (assigned in the stage without recommendation) for only one of their four pictures. In fact, all participants have completely ignored the set of tags that resulted from the stage with recommendation. According to P1, the language was a factor that helped him during this step:

P1: *"(...) in the first image it was very easy to recognize myself, because all my tags were in Portuguese. It has gotten my attention right away! Also, when I looked at the image, and if I had to assign tags again, I would do it again in a very similar way."*

Participant P4 expressed that he saw himself represented by the chosen set:

P4: *"Those tags can express what I would assign to those pictures. (...) I felt myself well represented."*

Despite the fact that tags were not originally written by the participants, the set they chose were representing the things they wanted to express about the picture at that *occasion*. We observed that some participants, as P5, only used tags in order to describe some objects presented in the image during the previous experiment. However, this participant chose the set of tags in which the image context was highlighted. These tags featured a combination of words, with traces of humor and feelings. Even in this case the participant told us she recognized the tags as a set she had assigned in the past.

[3] A "meme" is an idea, behavior, or style that spreads from person to person within a culture.

5. DISCUSSION AND FINAL CONSIDERATIONS

When posting resources such as texts, videos and images on social networks (which was the case covered by this work), users can freely add tags on them in order to categorize their content. In some cases, these resources are produced by the user himself, and, due to this fact, users may have intrinsic motivations for tagging.

During the first study in the stage without recommendation, we could observe that users tagged images using words or sentences that describe more than only their content (e.g. *"energy", "peace", "animalLover", "withFriendsIsBetter"*). By analyzing the tags resulted from the first study, we observed that participants have changed their tagging behavior while supported by recommendation. When using the tag recommender system, participants used more tags in English and tags assigned mainly as single words, differently from the tags assigned without any recommendation support.

From this observation, our research question emerged (*how do users use tags to express themselves?*) and a new study was conducted in order to understand how the phenomenon of self-expression through tagging images occurs. The concepts we found during the axial coding show that participants assign tags not only motivated by content description but also by sharing feelings, perceptions of the image context or concept, and expressing opinions and messages. These motivations have an impact in the tagging style used by participants for self-expression. They understand that tagging is a powerful tool for indexing content that can support search engines on information retrieval. However, they made it clear that the description of the content is not their main reason for assigning tags. They want to use personalized terms, messages and words to describe the situation "taking place" at that moment, which we called Conceptual tags.

Furthermore, in addition to sharing personal tags, they try to reach distinct audiences through the content (as well as their tags) they share using tags in different languages, or some popular/funny expression (e.g. "memes"). Assigning tags in other languages can reach distinct audiences without the need to write a long description of an image (which requires some knowledge about grammar) to express a situation, opinion, etc. The user may only use some "isolated words" or "common sense words" written in a foreign language to improve the spreading of his image. For this reason, tags are now used as a tool for communication among cultures by requiring just few words to express the image's content and context.

Another factor that caught our attention was their answers related to the use of a hypothetical system that could automatically proceed with the image tagging. Their answers showed that they were aware of the use of tags to express more than just the content. Even though the offered system has the ability of tagging images using sets of words that describe only the content presented by them (that is, the main role of tags), they answered that taking control of the content being shared is important and they want to interfere and personalize the tags. This need to reflect themselves in the tags is clearly an aspect of *self-expression*. However, although they want to assigned tags to express themselves, they assumed a collective self-expression that changed their language and the structure used for tagging, while recommendation was involved. We found that recommendation had main impact on the self-expression of participants motivated by social communication, opinion and feeling. The tags created with these motivations present a high potential to be composed by more than one word, and, in this case, the recommendation approach has completely changed P1's set of tags, for example - who used conceptual and composed tags - whereas it did not affect P5's set of tags - a participant that used tags motivated by describing and indexing content.

Moreover, although the language and structure used for tagging were reported by participants as a personal insight, they did not follow a pattern for tagging in all tagging tasks, specially in the last one when they should choose a set of tags based on their previous tagging task. It seems that tagging is a matter of moment and occasion. While they know what type of tag they use for self-expression, they are open to choose distinct tags if they feel that another set is more appropriate for the image and can represent what they want to express at that moment.

These findings have relevant implications that should be taken into account during the designing of a tagging system supported by recommendation: *where, when, who is portrayed in the image, who its audience is*, and so on. These are just few examples of relevant questions regarding an image context that can support designers to understand the sense of users' self-expression during the tagging task.

This viewpoint - that tags are used for self-expression - can support designers to generate users' model based on tagging behavior to support their decision making process on what type of approach would suit better for each user. As a next step, we aim to investigate the tagging expression in a long-term view to understand how users change their set of tags over time.

ACKNOWLEDGEMENT

CNPq (National Council for Scientific and Technological Development of the Brazilian government).

REFERENCES

Adomavicius, G. and Tuzhilin, A., 2005. Toward the next generation of recommender systems: A survey of the state-of-the-art and possible extensions. *In IEEE Transactions on Knowledge and Data Engineering*, Vol. 17, No. 6, pp. 734-749.

Corbin, J. and Strauss, A., 2008. *Basics of qualitative research: Techniques and procedures for developing grounded theory*. SAGE Publications, Thousand Oaks, USA.

Cosley, D. et al, 2003. Is Seeing Believing?: How Recommender System Interfaces Affect Users' Opinions. *Proceedings of the SIGCHI Conference on Human Factors in Computing Systems*. Ft. Lauderdale, USA, pp. 585-592.

Dattolo, A. et al, 2010. The role of tags for recommendation: A survey. *Proceedings of 3rd International Conference on Human System Interaction*. Rzeszow, Poland, pp. 548-555.

Gemmell, J. et al, 2009. Adapting K-Nearest Neighbor for Tag Recommendation in Folksonomies. *Proceedings of the 7th International Conference on Intelligent Techniques for Web Personalization & Recommender Systems*. Pasadena, USA, pp. 253-265.

Green, M., 2008. *Self-expression*. Oxford University Press, Oxford, United Kingdom.

Johnstone, B. 1996. *The Linguistic Individual: Self-Expression in Language and Linguistics*. Oxford University Press, Oxford, United Kingdom.

Klavans, J. L. et al, 2014. Subject matter categorization of tags applied to digital images from art museums. *In Journal of the Association for Information Science and Technology*, Vol. 65, No. 1, pp. 3-12.

Manish, G. et al, 2010. Survey on Social Tagging Techniques. *In ACM SIGKDD Explorations Newsletter*, Vol. 12, No. 1,pp 58-72.

Monteiro, I. T. and De Souza, C. S., 2012. The representation of self in mediated interaction with computers. *Proceedings of the 11th Brazilian Symposium on Human Factors in Computing Systems*. Cuiabá, Brazil, pp. 219-228.

Ronen, S. et al, 2014. Links that speak: The global language network and its association with global fame. *In Proceedings of the National Academy of Sciences*, Vol. 111, No. 52, pp. [NI].

Siersdorfer, S. and Sizov, S., 2009. Social Recommender Systems for Web 2.0 Folksonomies. *Proceedings of the 20th ACM Conference on Hypertext and Hypermedia*. Torino, Italy, pp. 261-270.

Sigurbjörnsson, B. and Zwol, R., 2008. Flickr Tag Recommendation Based on Collective Knowledge. *Proceedings of the 17th International Conference on World Wide Web*. Beijing, China, pp. 327-336.

Song, Y., 2011. Automatic Tag Recommendation Algorithms for Social Recommender Systems. *In ACM Transactions on Computational Logic*, Vol. 5, No. 1, pp.1-31.

Stiller, J. et al, 2011. Is Tagging Multilingual?: A Case Study with BibSonomy. *Proceedings of the 11th annual international ACM/IEEE joint conference on Digital libraries*. Ottawa, Canada, pp. 421-422.

Strohmaier, M. et al, 2010. Why do Users Tag? Detecting Users' Motivation for Tagging in Social Tagging Systems. *Proceedings of the Fourth International Conference on Weblogs and Social Media*. Washington, USA, pp. [NI].

Turkle, S., 2005. *The Second Self*. The MIT Press, Massachusetts, USA.

Zhu, H. et al, 2012. To Switch or Not to Switch: Understanding Social Influence in Online Choices. *Proceedings of the SIGCHI Conference on Human Factors in Computing Systems*. Austin, USA, pp. 2257-2266.

Ziesemer, A. and Oliveira, J. B. S., 2011. How to know what do you want? a survey of recommender systems and the next generation. *Proceedings of the 8th Brazilian Symposium on Collaborative Systems*. Parati, Brazil, pp. 104-111.

Ziesemer, A. and Oliveira, J. B. S., 2013. Keep Querying and Tag on: collaborative folksonomy using model-based recommendation. *Proceedings of the 19th International Conference CRIWG*. Wellington, New Zealand, pp. 10-17.

Ziesemer, A. et al., 2016. Multilingual Tagging Behavior: The role of recommender systems. *Extended Proceedings of the 24th Conference on User Modeling Adaptation and Personalization*. Halifax, Canada, pp. [NI].

QUALITY MODEL FOR INTERNAL SECURITY FEATURES OF SOFTWARE COMPONENTS

Everson Mauda[1], André Menolli[2], Andreia Malucelli[3], Altair Santin[3] and Sheila Reinehr[3]
[1]Pontifícia Universidade Católica do Paraná – PUCPR, Curitiba, Brazil
[2]Computer Science Department, Universidade Estadual do Norte do Paraná, Bandeirantes (UENP), Brazil
[3]Graduate Program in Computer Science (PPGIa) - Polytechnic School Pontifícia Universidade Católica do Paraná (PUCPR), Brazil

ABSTRACT

Software components are a means of achieving software reuse, aiming at improvements in the quality and productivity of the development team. One of the main concerns of component development is related to information security. One way to make a component more secure is to improve the security of its internal characteristics. Software quality models describe the quality characteristics for software-based systems; however, most of these models do not focus on security-specific issues. The main goal of this paper is to present a component quality model, focusing on their internal security aspects. This research was developed in four phases: analyzing the component-quality model scenario, analyzing the security characteristics of the components, defining a quality model, and assessing the model. The proposed model was assessed by a specialist and the suggested improvements were incorporated to the final version of the model.

KEYWORDS

Quality Models, Component-based Software Development, Component Security, Quality Characteristics

1. INTRODUCTION

The development of reuse-based software systems has become an economically sound alternative, mainly through the "use of existing software rather than building systems from scratch, thus reducing the build time and improving the quality of the final product" (Krueger, 1992). However, when the reuse is not properly planned, the time and resources within the organization are wasted. Moreover, if the reuse culture fails, senior managers may become wary of attempting to develop new applications (Alvaro, 2009).

There is no standardization of a reuse application, and the form of application depends on the company culture (Frakes and Isoda, 1994). Regardless of the application form, the main objective is to prevent the redevelopment of a given artifact by seeking ready-made solutions within the organization or market.

One way to implement software reuse is through component-based development (CBD), which makes use of software components to carry out development projects. According to Capretz (2001), a software component is a block of something, and the software is obtained by connecting such blocks.

There are many factors that hinder the extensive use of components by developers and organizations. Bass (2001) refers to them as: (i) lack of available components; (ii) lack of stable patterns for the component technology; (iii) lack of certified components; and, (iv) lack of an engineering method for consistently producing high-quality systems from the components.

As observed, one of the issues is the lack of certified components, meaning there is a question regarding the quality. A way to promote better quality lies in the planning of the software project. According to Kalaimagal and Srinivasan (2009), a project's planning team must be able to identify damage to a system by inserting new components.

Shin and Williams (2008) define vulnerability as a lack of specifications in the development or configuration of a piece of software such that its implementation may violate an implicit or explicit security policy of the system. Thus, several models have been used to assess the different quality characteristics of the components and analyze them. The standardization and most software quality models are hierarchical, that is, they define features by integrating subfeatures. These subfeatures define attributes that are used to evaluate the software.

One important feature of some of these models is related to security. This area, which had always been considered a risk-management strategy, is now being viewed as a competitive advantage, especially in the areas of finance and business (Shin and Williams, 2008). According to NIST (2009), some approaches have yet to be studied in the area of security metrics, such as the definition of formal security metric models, the analysis of historical data, evaluation techniques using artificial intelligence, concrete and practical measurement methods, and inherently measurable components.

The quality models for the current software components do not deal with the security features of a component at a suitable depth. Consequently, the development of a quality model capable of assisting developers and architects in defining such aspects of a software component is of great importance. Therefore, to develop state-of-the-art software, this study aims to assist in improving the quality of the software components in terms of their security, to contribute to an enhancement in the development and quality of the components, and to propose a quality model for the internal security features of such components.

2. BACKGROUND

2.1 Quality Models for Software Components

Software reuse is the process of creating software using existing artifacts rather than building them from scratch (Krueger, 1992). A reuse-based development focuses on the strategies, techniques, and principles that enable developers to create new systems in an effective manner. One of the best-known strategies with the highest level of abstraction is the reuse of components. A component is a unit of composition that contractually specifies the documented interfaces based only on the explicit context dependencies. A component can be delivered independently and is subject to a third-party composition (Szyperski, 2002).

With the increased use of components, component-based software engineering (CBSE) has emerged to include specific activities (Brown and Short, 1997), such as the gathering of the components, and qualifying, adapting, composing, and upgrading them. One of these activities, a quality check, may be inaccurate because there is no consensus regarding which features are the most relevant for measuring the quality.

To evaluate the software quality, various quality feature models have been developed. The organization of these models is typically performed hierarchically, following international standards. These standards include the international standards ISO/IEC 9126 (ISO, 2001), which features a general-purpose quality model for software products, and ISO/IEC 25000 (ISO, 2005), which features the software quality model under the name Product Quality Model, as an update to the model defined in the ISO/IEC 9126 standard. However, despite defining quality models for use in software, these standards are not focused on software components and can become starting points for researchers to define their models and make adjustments according to the universe of components.

The literature includes various quality models for different components, with very few reports focusing on practical experience with the applications of the proposed models. Most existing component quality models are based on ISO/IEC 9126, as described follow:

- Bertoa and Vallecillo (2002) developed one of the first component-specific models, which was adapted to ISO/IEC 9126, with a focus on COTS components.
- Rawashdeh and Matalkah (2006) adapted several models to standards such as ISO/IEC 9126 and ISO/IEC 15504-2, also with a focus on COTS components.
- Andreou and Tziakouris (2006) developed an adaptation based on ISO/IEC 9126, which focuses on original components.
- Choi et al. (2008) described their model adapted to ISO/IEC 9126, which can be applied to any type of component.
- Sharma et al. (2008) adapted a model to ISO/IEC 9126, along with other model types, also with a focus on any type of component.

2.2 Security of Software Components

The quality models presented herein aim to ensure the overall quality of the components in the absence of any other specific model for the quality of the security component. When proposing a security model for a software component, certain software evaluation features have to be observed.

Among the existing software security evaluation proposals, Bayuk (2000) indicate that such an evaluation of the features can be divided into five categories: i) an evaluation from market best practices (external audit), ii) an evaluation from internal security practices (internal audit), iii) a capacity-building maturity model, iv) a risk analysis, and v) the elimination of defects.

In addition to the described features, a software component evaluation has to consider other security software aspects, such as data encryption, identification or authentication, log file, auditing of threats (which can be classified into three main classes, i.e., i) failure, ii) error, and iii) fault (Avizienis et al., 2004)), integrity checks, and validation.

Any model proposed for the security components must take into account the presented features so as to include clear documentation on the security applied. A minimum set of features for mobile is described by Campadello et al. (2004): (i) Authentication: A relationship between user devices and service providers can be established only if the proper identification is provided by all; (ii) Integrity: Each component must maintain its integrity throughout its life cycle; (iii) Confidentiality: The information stored within the component, and the component itself, must remain confidential to third parties.

One aspect of security lies in component monitoring. Lenzini et al. (2007) define a metric framework for a real-time component evaluation. Depending on the measurements gathered, this framework may restart or stop a component that is being monitored. Another aspect is related to the certification of the security features of a component. An early study in this area (Ghosh and Mcgraw, 1998) describes the use of a security certification, and divides a certification into two types: component-level and system-level certification. Furthermore, some forms of whitebox and blackbox certification were presented.

Khan and Han (2008) created a process framework to characterize the security of software components and their compositions, namely, the integration between the two. This framework was designed for developing components following a policy of specifying the security features, any existing component that do not follow this framework cannot be evaluated without creating new documentation.

3. RESEARCH METHOD

To conduct the research four stages were carried out:

i) **Analyzing the model scenario**: consists of searching the literature for studies proposing new quality models for software components. These models were used to create a knowledge base for the development of a new model within the software engineering standards. A systematic review was used to achieve this goal. The searches carried out provided a total of 375 articles. After conducting the systematic review phases, nine quality models for software components were found.

ii) **Analyzing the security features**: the focus at this stage was searching for software component security features from two main perspectives: a search for security features based on the quality models, and a search for security features focusing primarily on the area of security. Based on the literature review, the most important topics were defined and put into context within the scope of the components, thus composing the new quality model features. The security area topics reserved at this stage were data encryption, authenticity and identification, auditability and system log, threats and vulnerabilities, and data manipulation.

iii) **Defining the model**: this stage defines the quality model for the internal security features of software components. Three tasks were conducted: defining the features, defining the sub features, and defining the attributes and types.

iv) **Evaluating the proposed model**: this final stage consisted of evaluating the quality model proposed I was made through an expert evaluation using a survey.

4. PROPOSED MODEL

The visions of the user, producer, and product were considered in the proposed quality model for the internal security features of the software components. Based on a study of the main quality features, the first question is "What does one need to enumerate within a component so that its quality meets the user's expectations?" This question gives rise to the task of searching a database for studies on component quality models. The models defined as of 2002 through a systematic review. This is the year after the latest version of ISO/IEC

9126 was published. Most models found in the systematic review are based on ISO/IEC 9126 (ISO, 2001), and only the model of Kalaimagal and Srinivasan is based on ISO/IEC 25000 (ISO, 2005). As a result, they all use the hierarchical standard defined by the ISO/IEC models, which includes features and sub features; additionally, some models include attributes and metrics. The metrics were defined very broadly, which did not help the developer in defining the steps required to obtain consistent values for a good analysis. After identifying the existing software component quality models, two other stages were completed: (1) Analysis of software component security features; (2) Definition of the quality model for the internal security features of the software components. Each of these stages is described in the following sections.

4.1 Analysis of Software Component Security Features

This stage deals with in-depth studies of the quality models found. At this stage, the features and subcategories pertaining to the security of each model identified in the systematic review were analyzed along with the ISO/IEC 9126 standard (ISO, 2001). Published studies of the four models described in (ISO, 2001), (Rawashdeh and Matalkah, 2006), (Choi et al., 2008), and (Sharma et al., 2008) showed no attributes. A total of 15 attributes were cited in the quality models. Table 1 presents a summary of the models, and contrasts their security features and subfeatures.

Most of the models identified showed the security subfeature as a subitem of functionality. The ISO/IEC 25010 quality model (ISO, 2005) defines the security feature through five subfeatures: confidentiality, integrity, non-repudiation, accountability, and authenticity. The model of Kalaimagal and Srinivasan (2010) creates two features for the security area, security and security in use. The first has two subfeatures, authentication and data encryption. The second has four subfeatures, software risk, commercial risk in use, operator risk in use, and risk of public use.

Table 1. Comparison of security features and subfeatures among quality models

Features	Subfeatures	(ISO, 2001)	(ISO, 2005)	(Bertoa and Vallecillo,2002)	(Rawashdeh and Matalkah, 2006)	(Andreou and Tziakouris, 2006)	(Choi et al., 2008)	(Sharma et al., 2008)	(Kalaimagal and Srinivasan, 2010)
Functionality	Security	x		x	X	x	x	x	
Security	Confidentiality		x						
Security	Integrity		x						
Security	Non-Repudiation		x						
Security	Accountability		x						
Security	Authenticity		x						
Security	Authentication	x							x
Security	Data Encryption								x
Security in Use	Software Risk								x
Security in Use	Commercial Risks in Use								x
Security in Use	Operator Risk in Use								x
Security in Use	Risk of Public Use								x

Table 2 provides a summary of the model attributes and identifies three attributes, auditability, data encryption, and authentication, which appear the most in the models. All of the studies reviewed failed to evaluate these attributes in depth. After the initial analysis, five important features were surveyed for the proposed quality model: data encryption, authentication, auditability, control of vulnerabilities, and data manipulation. These categories enabled the development of the proposed model.

Table 2. Comparison of attributes among quality models

Security Attributes	(ISO, 2001)	(ISO, 2005)	(Bertoa and Vallecillo,2002)	(Rawashdeh and Matalkah, 2006)	(Andreou and Tziakouris, 2006)	(Choi et al., 2008)	Sharma et al., 2008)	(Kalaimagal and Srinivasan, 2010)
Auditability			x		x			
Authenticity		x						
Authentication	x		x		x			x
Confidentiality		x						
Data Encryption			x		x			x
Integrity		x						
Non-Repudiation		x						
Privacy								
Resistance to Scalability of Privileges					x			
Accountability		x						
Commercial Risks in Use								x
Risk of Public Use								x
Software Risk								x
Operator Risk in Use								x
Vulnerability								

4.2 Definition of the Quality Model for the Internal Security Features of Software Components

This stage describes the features and subfeatures found in the proposed model. This study is not intended to generate a complete model of the features of the software components, but to build a submodel of the security portion by stressing the important aspects related to information security within the context of software components.

- **Data Encryption Feature**: Data encryption is the study of mathematical techniques related to information security aspects, such as confidentiality, integrity, authentica-tion of the entities, and data origin authentication (Menezes et al., 1996).
- **Authentication Feature:** Identification of the entity during a process in which one party is ensured of the identity of a second party involved in the protocol through the acquisition of corroborating evidence, and the second party participates, i.e., is active at the time the evidence is acquired (Menezes et al., 1996).
- **Auditability Feature**: The process of preserving the qualities of non-repudiation and accountability through an audit mechanism capable of system recording and data access.
- **Control of Vulnerability Feature**: Vulnerabilities pose a risk to a component when its proper operation fails to be preserved, and thus verifying the instances of failures in the specifications, development, or configuration of the component may allow the execution of one such instance, thereby violating the company's security policy (Shin and Williams, 2008).
- **Data Manipulation Feature**: The data manipulation feature is the process of validating the data provided by other entities within a set of predefined rules (Netland et al., 2006).

5. MODEL EVALUATION

The main goal of the expert evaluation was to assess the distribution of features, sub features, and attributes of the quality model, and whether or not they are relevant to the model. Likert scale was used to achieve this evaluation by measuring the level of agreement/disagreement with each statement provided. To evaluate the features, sub features, and attributes, a scale with the following options was used: not important, slightly important, moderately important, very important, and essential. To aggregate the values obtained and interpret the results, a summary was chosen, as illustrated in Figure 1.

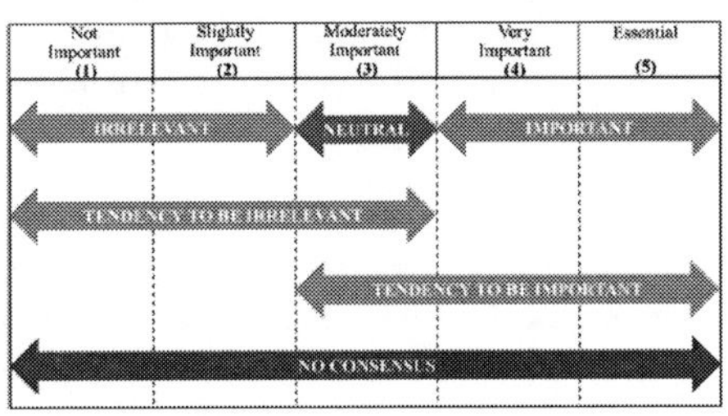

Figure 1. Scale for an interpretation of the results

The evaluation was conducted by five experts with two to eight years of experience in areas such as requirements engineering, systems analysis and design, software component development, systems architecture, software testing and deployment, and security architecture and deployment.

A given item was considered important if rated by all evaluators as being either very important or essential. This meant that they agreed that the item is relevant for the model and should be kept. A given item was considered irrelevant if rated by all evaluating experts as being either not important or slightly important. This meant that the experts agreed that the item is irrelevant for the model and should be removed. When the expert evaluations included opinions classified as moderately important, yet still focused on one of two extremes, it was understood that they were classified with a tendency to be important or irrelevant, as illustrated in Figure 1. This interpretation was also used when all votes but one were concentrated on one opinion, with the other vote being of the opposite opinion (outlier). For all other cases, it was understood that no consensus was reached and that the item requires further assessment.

This research consists of evaluating several security concepts related to the quality model, such as the features, sub features, and attributes included in the proposed model. Initially, the quality model itself was not mentioned, but the security items making up the model were mentioned. The first points evaluated were the features or large areas of information security. The sub items of each area were evaluated using five other questions, which ended with an evaluation of the authentication of the security items. The first evaluation is related to the importance of large information security areas and applies the following question: "In your opinion, what is the importance of the following security areas?" This question evaluates the importance of the features defined in the model by considering the perception and experience of the respondents. Table 3 shows the answers. This question was followed by a question of whether any other area of security not mentioned in the question exists. The comments are transcribed in Table 4.

Table 3. Importance of security areas

Area	Not important	Import. Low	Imp. Interm.	Import. High	Essential	Analysis
Auditability	-	-	-	2	3	Important
Authentication	-	-	1	1	3	Tendency to be Important
Data encryption	-	-	1	2	2	Tendency to be Important
Control of vulnerabilities	-	-	-	3	2	Important
Data Manipulation	-	-	1	3	1	Tendency to be Important

Table 4. Expert analysis on security areas

Expert Commentary on Security Areas	
Identification	**Comment**
Expert 1	"There is no mention of the security issue in the software development process, for instance, the classification and secrecy of information from the developers or internal threats relating to individuals."
Expert 4	"Treatment of people, I see that the areas above only mentioned the technology, but individuals play a key role in information security. How does the company treat its employees? Are there contracts signed regarding information theft? Is training people with respect to company data exposure worthwhile? Also, how the company deals with its assets was not mentioned. Is the process being applied correct? Is there continuous improvement? ISO standards? Is auditing occurring often?"

As observed, the comments questioned the role of the individual in information security and the role of the development process used in the production/maintenance of a software component. Experts 1 and 4 made some observations regarding the people involved in the software development process. The focus of this model is more technical, in other words, it aids in the development of new software components with greater security in their internal features. The secrecy of an information item is more related to the important aspects of the corporate software development process, which is not the focus here. Expert 4 made another observation related to the assets and processes applied within a corporation. This observation is again related to a corporation's development process and is not discussed in the present study.

After analyzing the different areas, an analysis of each of the five features was conducted. Based on the individual analyses of the questions, a general framework was created to summarize the expert opinions on the evaluated model. To do so, the general tendency of the model was calculated by including all of the questions, as shown in Table 5.

According to Table 5, it is worth noting that many attributes were considered as having a tendency to be irrelevant by the experts. These can be characterized as ancillary operations and should not be removed from the model. These attributes are as follows: log file rotation, log file compression, event aggregation of a log file, log file conversion, log file normalization, computational cost required to produce an encryption key, computational cost for the use of the encryption key, use of regular expressions, and data format.

Table 5. Overall research results

Item	No Consensus	Irrelevant	Tendency to be Irrelevant	Neutral	Tendency to be Import.	Important	Analysis
Security Areas	-	-	-	-	3	2	Important
Auditability	1	-	5	1	6	1	No Consensus
Authentication	-	-	-	-	5	1	Important
Data Encryption	1	-	2	-	3	2	No Consensus
Control of Vulnerabilities	-	-	-	-	3	2	Important
Manipulation	-	-	2	-	3	1	No Consensus

As can be seen, 32 items were considered as *important* or *having a tendency to be important*, which characterized a good number of items as being very important. Some observations made by the experts were taken into account for addition into the model. Another positive aspect appeared in the overall evaluation of the proposed model items in that none were rated as irrelevant. Only a few items were classified with a tendency to be irrelevant. Table 6 shows the quality model along with the new attributes, as suggested by the experts. These updated items appear in bold-underline.

Table 6. Security features model for software components

Feature	Subfeature	Attribute	Type	Value
Data Encryption	Algorithm	Name	String	AES, 3DES, blowfish, Elgamal, RSA, Diffie-Hellman
		Algorithm Type	String	symmetric and asymmetric
		Key Size	Integer	positive in bits
		Lifespan	Integer/String	time/unit of time
		Computational Cost Production	Integer/String	time/unit of time
		Computational Cost Operation	Integer/String	time/unit of time
	Key Storage	Form	String	SiRiUS, Cepheus, SNAD, EFS
		Key Management	**String**	**Key management frameworks**
Authentication	IdentificationClass	Something Known	String	passwords, PINs, challenges-responses
		Something Owned	String	magnetic cards, chip cards, tokens
		Something Inherent	String	biometrics, written form
	Combination of Forms	List of Forms	String	combination of items from the three classes
		Robustness	String	low, intermediate, high, very high
	Cryptographic Hash Function Algorithms	Name	String	MD5, SHA1, SHA2
		Hash Code Size	Integer	positive in bits
		Block Size	Integer	positive in bits
		Computational Cost Production	Integer/String	time/unit of time
Control of Vulnerabilities	Classification	Type	String	error, fault, failure
		Origin of Faults	String	creation phase, system boundaries, phenomenological cause
		Failure Domain	String	content, time, content and time
	Handling	Detection	String	competing, preemptive, **whitebox test, blackbox test**
		Handling Errors	String	rollback, rollforward, compensation
		Handling Faults	String	diagnosis, isolation, reconfiguration, reboot
	Monitoring	Vulnerability Modeling Process	String	STRIDE/DREAD, TRIKE, CVSS, OCTAVE
Data Manipulation	Data	Format	String	ISO 8601, ISO 19794, language APIs
		Internationalization	String	ISO-8859-1
	Validation	Defense Strategy	String	Confidence threshold and bottlenecks
		Validation Strategy	String	whitelists, blacklists, data cleaning
		Hash Algorithm	String	MD5, SHA1, SHA2
		Regular Expressions	Boolean	true, false
Auditability	Log Format	Event Class	String	emergency, alert, information, debug
		Format	String	Syslog
	Storage	Form	String	printed, WORM device, storage
		Classification	**String**	**Public, Private**
	Storage Operation	Hash Algorithm	String	MD5, SHA1, SHA2
		Log File Archiving	Boolean	true, false
		Log File Rotation	Boolean	true, false
		Log File Compression	Boolean	true, false
		Log File Reduction	Boolean	true, false
		Viewing Log File	Boolean	true, false
	Parsing Operation	Event Filtering	Boolean	true, false
		Event Aggregation	Boolean	true, false
		Event Correlation	Boolean	true, false
		Log File Conversion	Boolean	true, false
		Log File Normalization	Boolean	true, false
		Log File Report	Boolean	true, false

6. FINAL CONSIDERATIONS

This study proposed a quality model for the internal features of software components to be used by software developers and architects as a means to improve the component and software security. Some models presented in the literature have provided proposals on how to improve the overall quality of the software components, but they lack in-depth knowledge on software security, which is proposed here.

The proposed model synthesizes the knowledge in the areas of security, which is often restricted to a small portion of developers working with or specialized in soft-ware security. The scope of this research was to describe the most important features of software security. In this manner, although new details regarding the model areas described herein, and even new areas themselves, may appear, they will not change the basic structure of the quality model proposed in this study.

Future studies are needed to stress the application of the proposed quality model in software component projects, aiming to fine tuning the model attributes and evaluate them.

REFERENCES

Alvaro A., 2009. A Software Component Quality Framework, *Doctoral Thesis*. Pós-Graduação em Ciência da Computação, Universidade Federal de Pernambuco, 2009.

Andreou A. S. and Tziakouris, M., 2006. A quality framework for developing and evaluating original software components. *In Information and Software Technology*, Vol. 49, No. 2, pp. 122-141

Avizienis A. et al., 2004. Basic Concepts and Taxonomy of Dependable and Secure Computing. *IEEE Transactions on Dependable and Secure Computing*; Vol. 1, No. 1, pp. 11-33.

Bass L., et al. 2001. Market Assessment of Component-Based Software Engineering (CMU/SEI-2001-TN-007). Pittsburgh: Software Engineering Institute, 41.

Bayuk J. L., 2000. Information Security Metrics: An Audited-based Approach. *Proceedings of: National Institute Of Standards And Technology (Nist) And Computer System Security And Privacy Advisory Board (Csspab) Workshop*, Washington, DC.

Bertoa M. F. and Vallecillo, A., 2002. Quality Attributes for COTS Components . *Proceedings of* 6th *International Workshop on Quantitative Approaches in Object-Oriented Software Engineering*, Malaga, ES, 1-11.

Brown A. W. and Short, K.; 1997. On components and objects the foundations of component-based development. *Proceedings of: 5th International Symposium On Assessment Of Software Tools*, 1, Washington, DC,112-121.

Campadello S. et al., 2004. Security and Reliability Challenges in Component-Based Software for Consumer Devices. . *Proceedings of International Conference On Software Engineering And Applications* (IASTED), Innsbruck, Austria, 692-700.

Capretz L.F. et al., 2001. Component-Based Software Development.. *Proceedings of the Annual Conference Of The Ieee Industrial Electronics Society (IECON)*, Denver, CO, pp.1834-1837.

Choi, Y. et al., 2008. Practical S/W Component Quality Evaluation Model. *Proceedings of 10th Ieee International Conference On Advanced Communication Technology* (ICACT 2008New York, NY, 259-264.

Frakes W. and Isoda S., 1994. Success Factors of Systematic Reuse. *In IEEE Software*, Vol 12, No 1, pp 15-19

Ghosh A. K. and Mcgraw G. 1998. An Approach for Certifying Security in Software Components. *Proceedings of 21st National Information Systems Security Conference*, 1., 1998, Arlington, VA, 1-7.

ISO, International Organization For Standardization. 2001. *International Electrotechnical Comission ISO/IEC 9126: parts 1-4*. Software Engineering-Product Quality. ISO/IEC.

ISO, International Organization For Standardization. 2005. *International Electrotechnical Comission ISO/IEC 25000*: Systems and software Quality Requirements and Evaluation (SQuaRE) – Guide to SQuaRE. ISO/IEC.

Kalaimagal S. and Srinivasan, R., 2010. Q'Facto 10 – A Commercial Off-the-Shelf Component Quality Model Proposal. *Journal of Software Engineering*, Vol. 4, No. 1, pp. 1-15.

Kalaimagal, S., and Srinivasan, R. 2009. The need for transforming the COTS component quality evaluation standard mirage to reality. *ACM SIGSOFT Software Engineering Notes*, Vol. 34, No. 5, pp. 1-4.

Khan K. and, Han J. 2008. Specifying Security Goals of Component Based Systems - An End-User. *Proceedings of Seventh International Conference on Composition-Based Software Systems (ICCBSS)*, Madrid, Espanha, 101-109.

Krueger C., 1992. Software Reuse. *In ACM Computing Surveys,* Vol. 24, No. 2, pp.131-183.

Lenzini, G. et al., 2007. Managing Trustworthiness in Component-based Embedded Systems. *Electronic Notes in Theoretical Computer Science*, Vol. 179, pp. 143-155.

Menezes A. J et al., 1996. *Handbook of Applied Cryptography*. 1. ed. CRC Press, 780.

National Inst of Stand and Technology (NIST). 2009. Directions in Security Metrics Research, NISTIR 7564, 1ed, 26.

Netland, L. H. et al., 2006. Security Pattern for Input Validation. *Proceedings of 5th Nordic Conference On Pattern Languages Of Programs (VikingPLoP)*, Helsingør, Denmark, 71-79.

Rawashdeh, A. and Matalkah, B., 2006. A New Software Quality Model for Evaluating COTS Components. *In Journal of Computer Science*, Vol, 2, No. 3, pp.73-381.

Sharma, A. et al., 2008.. Estimation of Quality for Software Components – an Empirical Approach. 2008. *ACM SIGSOFT Software Engineering Notes*, Vol. 33, pp. 1-10.

Shin Y., and Williams L., 2008. Is Complexity Really the Enemy of Software Security? *Proceedings Of The 4th Acm Workshop On Quality Of Protection*, Alexandria, VA, , 47-50.

Szyperski C., 2002. *Component Software - Beyond Object-Oriented Programming*. 2. ed. Londres: Addision-Wesley Publishing Company, 589.

FAME.Q - A FORMAL APPROACH TO MASTER QUALITY IN ENTERPRISE LINKED DATA

André Langer and Martin Gaedke
Technische Universität Chemnitz

ABSTRACT

Whereas in the past, research and industry mainly focused on technological aspects related to the exposure of data and its processing from remote sources, the concern in Semantic Web Data Management started to shift over to other non-technical challenges when dealing with so called Linked Enterprise Data. Information Quality is such an aspect that plays an important role in the process of selecting the best available data source in the Web, consolidating it with already existing information and thereby improving the business value of the own data stock. Throughout the last decades, research has already comprehensively dealt with the question of what quality is and how it can be interpreted through different approaches. Surprisingly, it is all the more astounding that there are only vague and no concise and formal definitions of the quality concept so far, especially in the Semantic Web context. A formalization would help to make quality calculations more comparable and implementable. The paper addresses this challenge and raises the question on how to compute the quality of a particular data source by combining different aspects from existing approaches resulting in a more concise model. As a finding, data quality is expressed as the percentage to which degree a particular data source fulfills a set of specified requirements in a certain context. The formalized definition of data quality helps to discuss specific assessment aspects, and is exemplarily applied to a scenario from the CRM application domain.

KEYWORDS

Data Quality; Formal Model; Semantic Web; Linked Data; Enterprise Data Management

1. INTRODUCTION

It is assumed that the management of knowledge will be one of the most crucial aspects for business success in the twenty-first century. Although the problem domain itself is yet well-understood because lots of research has been done throughout the last four decades in different communities such as database management and information retrieval systems, its deliberate application will be of increasing importance in the future. Additionally, it still faces unsolved problems, especially in its adoption to distributed, heterogeneous, semantically-annotated data sources and in the selection process of a permanently increasing amount and variety of available information sources within the World Wide Web.

(Stvilia et al. 2007) already gave a comprehensive overview on miscellaneous definition approaches for the concepts *data*, *information* and *knowledge* from different authors in the past. We will base our current work on the definition of (Taylor 1986), where *data* is seen as a "sequence of symbols" representing *information*, which itself "is data plus relations" and references to a scheme in a certain context, in which it needs to be interpreted. The term *knowledge* then incorporates information that "is selected, analyzed, judged and organized in a stock" and "can be used for informing and decision making" relatively stable by a certain community. Following an Entity-attribute-value (EAV) model, data is a physical representation to store and transfer information.

Quality is a term originating from lat. *qualitas* for characteristic. From a neutral perspective, it is first of all a perceivable state of a system based on its measurable attributes on a certain point of time. IEC 2371 defined quality as "the agreement between the determined properties and the previously defined requirements of an observation unit". (Crosby 1979) described quality as "conformance to requirements, meaning both the product and the customer's requirements". (Wang, R. Y., and Strong 1996) provided another, well-accepted definition that quality is "data that is fit for use". So the term quality itself is a characterization of a system and states the degree of fulfillment of a target requirement specification. The perception of a systems quality can be subjective because the requirements and use context vary from person to person. Thus, it makes a difference if data quality from a data source shall be assessed from a consumer point of view with a focus on information completeness and other intrinsic criteria, from a data provider view, or from a more technical perspective where performance and delivery aspects play a more important role (Kahn et al. 2002). More than a hundred *quality dimensions* have been defined that represent assessment criteria which are relevant for the customer, starting with an empirical classification of the 15 most relevant dimensions from a consumer point of view by (Wang, R. Y., and Strong 1996) and not ending with (Zaveri et al. 2015) who presented an extensive survey and systematic classification in 18 quality dimensions based on 118 related papers published throughout the last years. Therefore, we will not concentrate on a discussion or formalization of certain specific quality dimensions in this paper, but rather on a more generic calculation model on top.

To objectively measure certain quality dimensions and make them comparable among different data sources, several *metrics* can be used that we exemplarily discuss as part of our formalization model in Section 4. The overall data quality (DQ) of a considered data set is then an aggregation of all these relevant dimensions and metrics. A vast number of definitions exists of what data quality actually includes. However, the most of them are either textual definitions based on natural language or deal with certain data quality issues that are formally expressed for algorithmic purposes. Although the quality concept is an abstract term and highly dependent on the operation area, information domain, underlying data and context, it would be great, if we can express the general understanding in a more concise way than in an ambiguous, excessive textual representation. Our main contribution of this paper is

- a basic theoretical model with preliminary character for the definition of data quality in a unified, more formal way that is generally applicable in current Semantic Web scenarios in Section 3
- a common scenario relevant for industrial customers where data quality can be exemplarily investigated based on certain metrics in Section 4
- a brief overview with respect to the validity of our measurement methodology based on existing Quality assessment frameworks in Section 5

At first we introduce in Section 2 a general setting which we use as an example to discuss existing challenges, independent from the actual underlying data representation. Then we apply this scenario specifically to distributed, RDF enabled data sets with knowledge graphs in the following sections.

2. CHALLENGES IN DESCRIBING DATA QUALITY

In the following, we focus on the definition and assessment of data quality, that means the basis is a persistent set of items with specific characteristics described through attributes and values of a certain domain. This data represents objects from the real world and can be interpreted by the consumer after putting it in a certain context.

In a first example, we investigate data items representing existing persons. We are interested in several *attributes* describing each person, e.g., *gender, prename, surname, date of birth, email address*, and so on. The list of possible attributes and their allowed values from a given *domain* is called a *scheme*. These attributes have a certain *value* for each concrete person they describe – that is called a data *instance*. Each data instance consists out of a set of tuples, that is a concrete attribute – value combination related to the described *entity*. Figure 1 illustrates an example for several instances.

e_1		e_2		e_3	
Gender:	male	Gender:		Gender:	femael
Prename:	John	Prename:	Bob	Prename:	Jane
Surname:	Doe	Surname:	Smith	Surname:	Doe
Birth date:	1980/01/01	Birth date:	1977/11/05	Birth date:	1982/02/10
Email:	john.doe@example.com	Email:	bob.smith@mail.com	Email:	none

Figure 1. Example data instances

The main challenge is, that the content of concrete instance tuples is often error prone ((Dasu et al. 2003) state that more than 60% of data in a common Enterprise data stock are likely to contain errors). The provided values can be syntactically wrong, semantically false or missing at all. Additionally, they sometimes do not fulfill functional requirements or certain business rules. Or the instances provide tons of attributes that are not needed at all but do not mention aspects we are interested it. Some of these aspects are intrinsic properties of the data itself, other requirements are task-dependent contextual requirements and have to be predefined.

If we define such a requirement e.g., that each data item shall contain a gender attribute that corresponds to the real-world situation, the assessment step can map each data entry to a Boolean value, representing if the requirement is fulfilled or not. The statement can be false if the stated (literal) value is not part of the attribute domain (or if it is misspelled, cf. e_3), if it is contradictory (the attribute value would be female although John is obviously a male person) or if the attribute is mandatory but no value is specified (cf. e_2). Otherwise it is regarded as free of defect.

If the entire data item for an entity is examined, the complete list of provided assertions has to be taken into consideration for quality detection. In the example from Figure 1, each of the data items contains data values for the attributes *{gender, prename, surname, birth date, email}*, and we naturally expect for any other data item to provide also data values from this attribute space. Though, it does not state anything about data quality so far. Therefore, requirements onto the data set have to be first defined that have to be fulfilled best possible by every data item. One of these requirements could be that each entity has to provide the just mentioned attributes (schema completeness). Other requirements could be, that the values of these attributes have to be valid, or the restriction that each of these attributes is mentioned only once. If this requirement is fulfilled by an entire data item we can also map it to a Boolean representation, stating if it fulfills the specific requirement or not. Authors like (Kano et al. 1984) have discussed in more detail aspects, how implicit assumed requirements will affect quality perception and customer satisfaction.

A Linked Data approach in the Semantic Web allows customers to access and process distributed data in a more homogeneous fashion. With RDF graphs as an underlying data representation in a data set and a semantic typification, it becomes possible to map concepts between heterogeneous data providers and even perform inference operations on them. New quality dimensions arise that ask for the correctness and semantic accuracy of facts, coherence between links to external data sets, or the adequacy of the semantic representation. On the other hand, quality assessment operations face new challenges such as completeness checks in an open-world data scenario assumption where not all existing data has to be entirely provided by one data source, or the occurrence of blank nodes that are not referenceable by external data sources at all.

3. FAME.Q AS A FORMALIZATION TO REPRESENT DATA QUALITY

In this section we present the main contribution of the paper. Our objective is a concise definition of the general concept *data quality*. The resulting model should be usable for implementation purposes and autonomous quality measurement. Crowd-based reviews and quality assessments that involve human interaction will not be taken into consideration.

We see Data Quality as a multi-dimensional criteria construct that characterizes a system how well it corresponds to certain requirements. Therefore, it can be mapped to a numeric value representing the degree to which the provided data fulfills all predefined target requirements, or not. The objective is to obtain a summarizing indicator that allows a context-specific, multi-criteria comparison among multiple data stocks.

The following assumptions are made:

a) A data source *DS* exists that provides relevant data whose quality *DQ* should be assessed
b) The data source is based on a (maybe distributed) data *scheme* which defines a list of attributes *A* and an allowed range of values from a related domain for each attribute *Dom(A)*
c) Multiple data instances are supplied in form of data items that shall correspond to this data scheme.
d) An *application context* exists in which the data content should be used
e) A list of requirements *reqs* exists within this context so that the data set can be defined as perfectly applicable if it fulfills all the requirements

Data Quality can then be defined as

$$DQ_{context} = DQ_{context}^{objective} + DQ_{context}^{subjective} \tag{1}$$

The calculation should obviously primarily focus on objective measurable means to gain the DQ value for a given data source, however, in reality it can also be influenced by subjective perceptions of individual users although we want to minimize the influence of the second term. The components can be extended to

$$DQ_{context} = \langle \sum_{Levels} DQ_{context}^{Level} \rangle + \varphi \quad (2)$$

where

- $DQ_{context}$ is a quality value stating a percentage between 0.0 and 1.0. how good the assessed data fits to the given context
- The first term is a normalized representation of DQ deviated from concrete characteristics on levels such as *instance* level, data *scheme* level or *service* level, see below
- φ is an adjustment value to optionally represent not-directly-measurable influences on data quality in the computation result

As an example., if we solely concentrate on data quality requirements on instance level, the formula can be further extended to

$$DQ_{context} = \langle \sum_{reqs} \omega_{req} \cdot fulfill(req, data\ instances) \rangle + \varphi \quad (3)$$

where

- ω_{req} are factors to weight the importance of a certain requirement for the final result with $0 \leq \omega \leq 1$
- *fulfill* is a function stat states to which extend the requirement is fulfilled by the considered object

It is important to point out, that this formulation is independent from the view of granularity we are interested in. The fulfillment function can be calculated on a single metric (that is a criterion, that means a measurement), on a quality dimension consisting out of multiple metrics, on a clustering of several quality dimensions or on all available dimensions that represent the customer requirements. Additionally, the formulation leaves open the amount of data that is being assessed; it is also possible in a Big Data context to only check a sample set of data against the specified requirements.

In the following, some details of the definition are emphasized and compared with the example from the previous section. In Section 2, the basis for quality investigation was the description of a specific entity from the real world through attributes and corresponding values out of a certain domain for that object instance. Let A be a list of these attributes $A = a_1\ a_2\ a_3\ \ldots\ a_n$ and $dom(a_i)$ an allowed range or set of values that an instance can take for that criteria. An instance then consists out of a set *of tuples* $t_e = \langle e, a_i, val(a_i) \rangle$ with $val(a_i) \in dom(a_i)$. In our provided example from Figure 1, A would consist out of the attributes {*gender, prename, surname, birth date, email*} and *dom(gender)* = {*male, female*}, *dom(prename)* = $\{str = c_1c_2\ldots c_n \mid c \in [a\text{-}z],\ str \text{ is valid name for a person}\}$; and $val(e_1, gender) = male$, $val(e_1, prename) = John$, and so on.

A simple requirement *req* would then be a logical statement that each entity provides a set of tuples supplying a value for all the necessary attributes, we are interested in.

$$req: \forall obj, obj = \{ t \mid t = < e, a_i, v >, v \in dom(a_i), a_i \neq a_j, i \neq j \},$$
$$a_i \in \{gender, prename, surname, birth\ date, email\}$$

We then want to define a function *classify* that is able to map the entity representation of an object (a set of assertions in form of tuples) to a conclusion weather it fulfills the requirement or not (that is, if the contemplated data value is good or bad). The result is a Boolean value.

$$classify(req, obj) \rightarrow \{0,1\} \quad (a)$$

The fulfillment function from (3) on the instance level is then the application of the classification step onto all considered elements

$$fulfill(req, data\ instances) = \frac{\sum_{data\ instances} classify\ (req, data\ instance)}{count(data\ instances)} \quad (b)$$

If each item in the data set fulfills the specified requirement, we will state the entire data collection as of very good quality. If none of the requirements is fulfilled, the entire data set will be of poor quality irrelevant from all the other data it might provide. The result will be a value in $\mathbb{R}^+$ between $0 \leq DQ_{req} \leq 1$.

This formalization of data quality is based on the general assumption, that we are able to measure some certain characteristics in a data source. This does not necessarily have to be a characteristic on instance level, it can also be a requirement on scheme level such as ontological validation or including dependencies, or on service level as a characteristic for the entire data source endpoint. Very often, quantifiable quality indicators are used to measure a more complex characteristic as a floating value or any other datatype, e.g., a performance metric on service level. This computed metric expresses a particular trait but is neutral for the assessment of quality at first. Only the definition of a task-specific requirement will set it in relation to the quality of the entire data set. Therefore, a more universal way to compute these metrics on the given object in a numeric data type or requirement specific classification is

$$compute(req, obj) \rightarrow \mathbb{R} \tag{a*}$$

and then check it for fulfillment of a certain requirement as the degree to which it fulfills the initial requirement.

$$fulfill(req, obj) = \left|\frac{compute(req, obj)}{val(req)}\right| \tag{b*}$$

The formulas *(a)* and *(b)* are a special case of *(a*)* and (b*) above with *val(req)=1* and *compute(req,obj)=* $\sum$ *classify(req, instance)* / *count(instances)*. *Val(req)* is the expected value to which a *req* should be fulfilled, e.g., an answer time of less than 2 seconds.

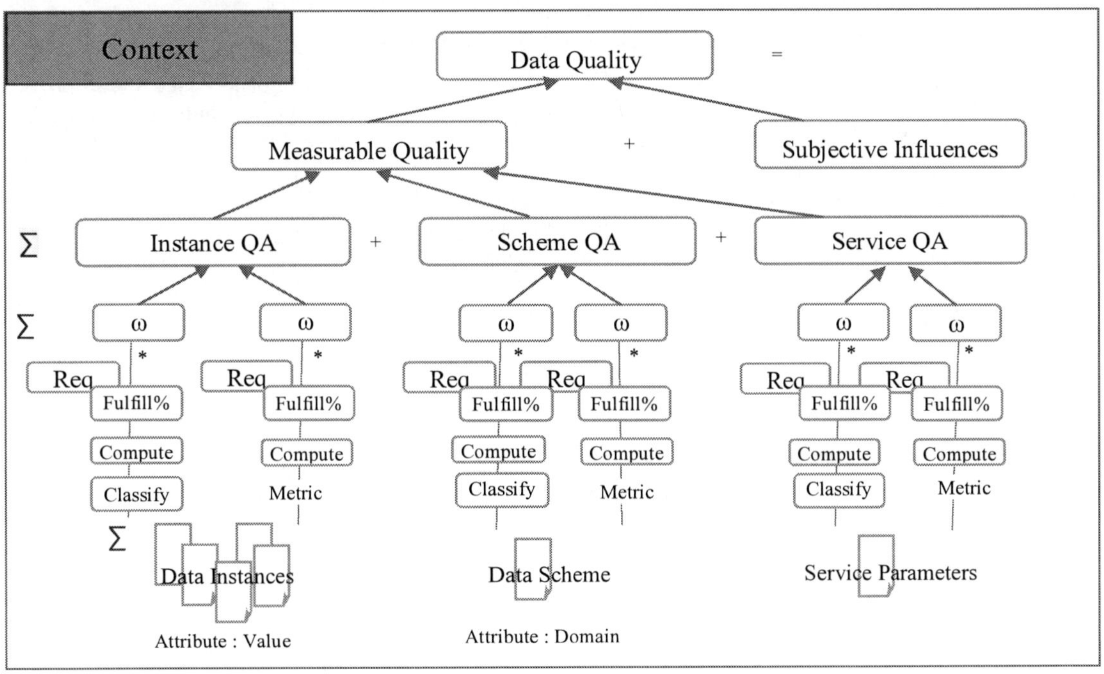

Figure 2. The FAME.Q approach to formal describe Data Quality assessment

The formalization in *(3)* allows several interpretations. First of all, it represents the degree (a percentage) how the underlying data meets the actual requirements. It is a continuous function with a value between *0.0* for *fatal* and *1.0* for *perfect* which means that all requirements are fulfilled by all data instances. A computed data quality value is dependent from the data itself and from a specific context in which requirements are defined on the data that can be assessed independently. So, data quality is in the end a cost function that can be improved by optimizing the calculation result, either by optimizing the underlying data set or adopting the preferences and criteria on that data in a certain context.

This also means, that data quality cannot be stated absolutely and be perfect because the requirement definitions are relative to the use context and can therefore be also contradictive for different use case scenarios. A huge set of qualitative high data can be poor for a certain use case, and vice versa excellent for another scenario although its data sets incomplete or lacking any other typical characteristic.

4. QUALITY CALCULATION ON SEMANTIC DATA SETS

The provided introductory example from Section 2 was kept very simple so far. Nevertheless, it becomes immediately relevant if we extend it to a Use Case scenario known from the Customer Relationship Management where business institutions maintain data stocks of enterprise customers with thousands of instances and tuples. The provided contact information should be as complete, consistent and up-to-date as possible which is sometimes tricky because the meta data of a contact can change over time or even another person can succeed a former contact. If a company possesses corporate data that is already semantically enabled, business decisions are thereby no longer limited to the own data stock because additional information from external data providers can be taken into consideration. Other appropriate data providers can be queries within legal boundaries, for example Linked Open Data providers in a customer data domain or also platform APIs exposing user profile information from the Social Web, such as Facebook, LinkedIn or Xing, as long as it works to transform their provided semi-structured data with proprietary attributes in a semantic-enabled RDF representation. Purposes that motivate the usage of external data sets are:

1. Use it as trusted data to check quality of own corporate data stock
2. Extend own knowledge base with additional data items or attributes
3. Entirely use external Linked Data service for own needs

Figure 3 shows an example of case 2 how the quality of existing data could be assessed and improved by using external data sources. If we define a fine-granular requirement for our special context, we can calculate data quality estimations with our formalization in a more appropriate way than simply relying on general quality dimensions. In the mentioned example, a requirement could be "all data instances shall contain a *gender*, *telephone* and *image* property with a non-blank value". Obviously, this is not the case in the provided data instance, so the computation of the *classify* function would assign a 0 to it. If this computation is done over all existing data items in the data set, the *fulfillment* rate states how many instances violate the requirement. Assuming only one single quality criterion, this will correspond the perceived quality of the current data stock.

<u>Local Corporate Data</u>

```
{
  "@context": "http://schema.org/",
  "@type": "Person",
  "@id": "http://example.com/e2",
  "gender": "",
  "givenName": "Bob",
  "familyName": "Smith",
  "birthDate": "1977-11-05",
  "email": "bob.smith@mail.com"
}
```

\+

<u>Linked Open Data</u>

```
{
  "@context": "http://schema.org/",
  "@type": "Person",
  "@id": "http://example.com/e2",
  "gender": "Male",
  "Name": "Bob Smith",
  "image": "http://avatar.com/bob.png",
  "birthDate": "1978-11-05",
  "telephone": "+1 805 12345",
}
```

=

<u>Improved Data Instance</u>

```
{
  "@context": "http://schema.org/",
  "@type": "Person",
  "@id": "http://example.com/e2",
  "gender": "Male",
  "givenName": "Bob",
  "familyName": "Smith",
  "image": "http://avatar.com/bob.png",
  "birthDate": "1978-11-05",
  "telephone": "+1 805 12345",
  "email": "bob.smith@mail.com"
}
```

Figure 3. Fusion of Local Enterprise Data and Linked Open Data in JSON-LD

It is then possible to perform a similar calculation on other available Linked Open Data providers and compare their quality score among each other. Additionally, it is possible to use the pre-calculated metrics and classifications to only manipulate affected data instances. Data Fusion and Co-evolution are disciplines that explicitly deal with this topic, therefore wo do not further extend the topic within this paper.

5. RELATED WORK

Data Quality concerns have already been widely discussed in several research areas such as Database Management, Information Retrieval and also the Semantic Web community, but many publications dealt with the concept of what data quality involves and less with the theoretical foundation how it can be generally formalized and implemented.

Already twenty years ago, (Wang, R. Y., and Strong 1996) provided appropriate definitions in textual form of what data quality actually is and which quality dimensions exist that are relevant for a customer, which was later refined in (Kahn et al. 2002). Recently, (Zaveri et al. 2015) presented an updated excellent, overall survey about quality dimensions and appropriate metrics that can be used for quality assessment of Linked Data sources.

Concerning a formalization of quality concepts, (Oliveira et al. 2005) presented formal definitions for several issues that arise during the assessment of data quality, however, the term quality itself was not defined in a concise way and the findings were solely applied on classical relational data models and no Semantic Web scenario. (Knight & Burn 2005) presented the IQIP model, a framework aimed on determining quality aspects that are relevant for a user when performing a search, with the focus on how to measure data quality.

Knight also summarized the 12 most relevant quality assessment frameworks of that time which were able to calculate quality appraisals on a given data source. Since then, a lot of other quality assessment frameworks were developed to calculate and interpret the data quality for a particular data source. (Stvilia et al. 2007) or (Cappiello et al. 2016) first identified appropriate quality dimensions, then developed an own IQ measurement model, and afterwards implemented the calculation of several quality metrics in an own Information Quality assessment framework. Multiple approaches are used how these assessment frameworks output and visualize miscellaneous quality dimensions or data quality calculation results. Common approaches are:

- simply state the value of measured indicators as metrics and leave the interpretation open to the user (e.g.: number of properties: *5*, number of data items: *9805*)
- state a percentage as an overall mean for data quality assessment (e.g.: Overall Quality: *73%*)
- state an individual, proprietary quality score, e.g.: *4.2*

The existing assessment frameworks differ on various characteristics such as functionality, processable data format, implementation language, user interface or result output manner. Whereas the IQ assessment framework from (Stvilia et al. 2007) followed a general approach and did not specifically focus on Linked Data Quality assessment, other implementations exist like *SWIQA* (Fürber & Hepp 2011a), *Luzzu* (Debattista et al. 2015), *KBMetrics* (Ruan et al. 2015) or the *Roomba OpenData Checker* (Assaf et al. 2015) that were specifically designed to assess Data quality on Semantic Web related data sources. For instance, the *OpenData Checker* (Assaf et al. 2015) calculated metrics from data quality indicators specifically for CKAN data stores and simply outputted them in percent. *KBMetrics* (Ruan et al. 2015) used a scoring system to make different data sources comparable. *SWIQA* (Fürber & Hepp 2011a) calculated a quality score based on the percentage how many instances violate given data quality rules. Other publications contributed propositions for the calculation of specific quality metrics, for example (Fürber & Hepp 2010) used SPARQL queries and SPIN to define requirements on particular data sets.

Other publications deal with the question, how to provide quality assessment measurements in a machine-readable fashion and how to make them comparable to each other going further than simple statistic statements with vocabularies such as SKOS or DataCube. (Fürber & Hepp 2011b) proposed with DQM a first generic vocabulary based on quality requirement rules. (Debattista et al. 2014) independently developed with daQ another ontology to express data quality concerns. Currently, a W3C working group extends these propositions to a promising DQV data quality vocabulary (Debattista et al. 2016).

6. CONCLUSION AND FUTURE WORK

The objective of this paper was to outline existing definitions for the concept of quality and to develop this general understanding further to a more concise formal model of what quality actually is and dependent on which characteristics it can be computed. We showed aside of generally accepted definitions that a formalization can be designed that interprets the quality of a data source in a certain context based on several levels of observation. On each level of the presented quality assessment model, it is checked among all existing entities to which degree they fulfill specified requirements that are either directly derivable from entity descriptions or by calculating particular metrics based on common quality indicators.

Our suggested definition allows all output types known from existing practical implementations. The most important requirement is that the expressiveness of such a data quality assessment value must be clear because only then the provided information is useful. On the other hand, quality assessment results between separate measurement methodologies should be comparable or even translatable.

So far, the presented solution lays only the theoretical foundation for our future research. We will use the concept to implement an own demonstrator on which an evaluation of this quality approach can be done. We will re-use existing DQ vocabularies for this prototype, contribute to their enhancements. Additionally, we want to discuss in more detail appropriate bounds for metrics in the assessment step and plan to further investigate quality influences in the process of combining data from multiple, distributed data sources.

ACKNOWLEDGEMENT

This work was supported by the grant from the German Federal Ministry of Education and Research (BMBF) for the LEDS Project under grant agreement No 03WKCG11D.

REFERENCES

Assaf, A., Troncy, R. & Senart, A., 2015. Roomba: An Extensible Framework to Validate and Build Dataset Profiles.

Cappiello, C. et al., 2016. A Quality Model for Linked Data Exploration.

Crosby, P.B., 1979. *Quality is free: the art of making quality certain*, McGraw-Hill.

Dasu, T., Vesonder, G.T. & Wright, J.R., 2003. Data quality through knowledge engineering. In *Proceedings of the ninth ACM SIGKDD international conference on Knowledge discovery and data mining - KDD '03*. p. 705.

Debattista, J. et al., 2016. Data on the Web Best Practices: Data Quality Vocabulary.

Debattista, J., Lange, C. & Auer, S., 2014. Daq, an ontology for dataset quality information.

Debattista, J., Lange, C. & Auer, S., 2015. Luzzu - A Framework for Linked Data Quality Assessment. *ISWC 2015*

Fürber, C. & Hepp, M., 2011a. SWIQA – a Semantic Web Information Quality Assessment Framework.

Fürber, C. & Hepp, M., 2011b. Towards a vocabulary for data quality management in semantic web architectures. *Proceedings of the 1st International Workshop on Linked Web Data Management - LWDM '11*, p.1.

Fürber, C. & Hepp, M., 2010. Using SPARQL and SPIN for data quality management on the Semantic Web.

Kahn, B., Strong, D. & Wang, R., 2002. Information quality benchmarks: product and service performance. *Communications of the ACM*, 45(4), pp.184–192. Available at: http://dx.doi.org/10.1145/505248.506007.

Kano, N. et al., 1984. Attractive Quality and Must-Be Quality. *Journal of the Japanese Society for Quality Control*,

Knight, S.-A. & Burn, J., 2005. Developing a framework for assessing information quality on the World Wide Web. *Informing Science Journal*, 8(3), pp.159–172.

Oliveira, P., Henriques, F. & Henriques, P., 2005. A formal definition of data quality problems. *2005*

Tong Ruan et al., 2015. KBMetrics – A Multi-purpose Tool for Measuring the Quality of Linked Open Data Sets.

Stvilia, B. et al., 2007. A framework for information quality assessment.

Taylor, R.S., 1986. *Value-added processes in information systems*, Greenwood Publishing Group.

Wang, R. Y., and Strong, D.M., 1996. Beyond accuracy: What data quality means to data consumers. Journal of Management Information Systems. *Journal of Management Information Systems*, 12(4), pp.5–33.

Zaveri, A. et al., 2015. Quality Assessment for Linked Data: A Survey. *Semantic Web Journal*, 1(2012), pp.1–5.

MAPPING RDB TO RDF WITH HIGHER SEMANTIC ABSTRACTION

[1,2]Dewi Wisnu Wardani and [2]Josef Küng
[1]Informatics Department, Sebelas Maret University, Surakarta, Central Java, Indonesia
[2]FAW Institute, Johannes Kepler University, Linz, Austria

ABSTRACT

We propose mapping relational databases (RDB) to Resource Description Framework (RDF) which considers the higher semantic abstraction of the real world. Whereas the previous works focused on the direct mapping, our approach maintains semantic of the schema and data, particularly for the high-order relationships. Our approach adopts the graph model where edges may have properties. Therefore, in our RDF model, predicates may have attributes as well. Finally, the model can be retrieved naturally by SPARQL.

KEYWORDS

Converting, relational model, graph, semantics, RDF

1. INTRODUCTION

Data is abundant, yet it is not semantic web friendly. Either structured data, semi-structured data or unstructured data. The structured data is dominated by relational databases (RDB). RDB has wide-area domain users and has high-quality information, in the sense that it does not contain much noise information (Cafarella et al., 2011). This kind of data cannot be ignored to populate the semantic web. Therefore, some approaches have proposed the mapping RDB to RDF, which mostly refer to the direct mapping approach. Some tools have been developed (Bizer, 2003) (Thuy et al., 2014) based on the direct mapping approach and its variations. W3C recommendation also provides the language mapping (Das et al., 2012) for the direct mapping approach (Arenas et al., n.d.). The other methods directly map to OWL (de Laborda and Conrad, 2005) (Būmans and Čerāns, 2010, p. 2). We also investigate the direct mapping which is a part of the W3C Recommendation (Arenas et al., n.d.) that has a rule to map a table which does not have a primary key. If this condition occurs, it means the relational model is not valid enough, because it is not possible that a logical table does not have a primary key. The other rule, the *m:n relationships* is mapped as a resource instead as properties. Briefly, in our opinion, the direct mapping cannot always maintain the original semantic of data. Considering the semantic abstraction in the mapping RDB to RDF is an important issue. It's known that RDB is obtained by implementing semantic abstraction steps of the real world. In the other side, the RDF needs to maintain the semantic of the real world. Therefore, the mapping RDB to RDF also needs to consider the semantic abstraction. The other side, it's been known that knowledge in the real world is closer to graph model. Nodes represent entities and edges represent relationships among entities. The number of entities which are involved in a relationship may be more than two entities.

The limitations of direct mapping and its variation influence our idea that the mapping should consider a higher semantic abstraction. This work is more related on composing RDF data model than providing a semantic schema of RDF like in the direct mapping approach and its variation. Those works related to finding the fittest vocabulary terms (RDFS or OWL). This issue is not the concern in our work. We constrain the mapping result is RDF instead of OWL, but later on, we will show that the result of our approach can be extended easily to OWL format.

The goal of the semantic web is to create the web of data (Berners-Lee et al., 2001) which can process information automatically. The web of data has a meaning that data are connected each other. Intuitively we see that data in the semantic web as a graph model. Graph models themselves are known more expressive to represent the data and knowledge (Chein and Mugnier, 2008) (Aggarwal and Wang, 2010) which may be complex and heterogeneous. One work mentioned (De Abreu et al., 2013) that RDF stores have a limitation in managing the graph-oriented data. To adopt the expressiveness of graph models and to maintain the semantics is a challenge not only for RDF stores but also the data model of the semantic web. The existing RDB to RDF mapping approaches ignore those issues.

Those above explanations are the motivations of our work. The aim of this work is **to propose mapping RDB to RDF with considering a higher semantic abstraction of RDB**. The remaining sections are organized as follows: we summarize the related work in Section 2. Section 3 explains the idea of our approach. Section 4 discusses the experimental result then finally conclusion and possible the near future works in section 5.

2. RELATED WORK

In general, the existing approach RDB to RDF is a direct mapping. This method directly converts RDB to RDF by following some rules. The rules define direct transformation and provide the fundamental steps for mapping RDB to RDF. Some approaches and tools have been introduced (Bizer and Seaborne, 2004) (Das et al., 2012) (Thuy et al., 2014) (Hert et al., 2010) (Arenas et al., n.d.). Some works map directly to OWL (de Laborda and Conrad, 2005) (Laclavık, 2007) (Būmans and Čerāns, 2010, p. 2) (Čerāns and Būmans, 2011). In general, the direct mapping to OWL maps properties and classes to new or existing ontologies. In brief, the rules are the mapping logical table to class, mapping many-to-many relationship, mapping attributes, mapping to URI, mapping data types, dealing with blank nodes and mapping the integrity constraints (Hert et al., 2011). The mappings to OWL have additional features specifically to map to object properties or data properties (Spanos et al., 2012).

The other authors proposed two steps mapping with considering the semantic of the relational model in a direct style. It defines semantic (vocabulary) of RDF from the features of the relational model (Lv and Ma, 2008). Another work proposes bi-directional mapping RDB to RDF which focused on creating a bridge between RDB and RDF (Ramanujam et al., 2010). The other work also tries to maintain consistency between RDB and RDF (Zhou, 2010). The higher abstraction is used in one work, but it uses to create the schema of RDF (RDFS) (Xu et al., 2010). This work is similar to the earlier works which try to find the fittest vocabularies for RDB.

3. THE MAPPING APPROACH

The idea of our approach is that the mapping RDB to RDF needs to consider a higher semantic abstraction which has a format as like a graph model. We emphasize on the mapping of edges. Two possible formats of relationship in relational model are: (i) naturally as foreign key(*FK*); (ii) relations but conceptually as a relationship. Some approaches map an *n-ary relationship* as an OWL class (Astrova, 2009) (Li et al., 2005). The other methods map it to simple triples (Bizer and Seaborne, 2004) (Arenas et al., n.d.), but they map it as a resource instead of a property. One work shows to map it as a property but only the join between two logical tables (Hert et al., 2010). In the real world, often we find that an edge is a hyperedge which connects more than two nodes. The edges themselves may have properties as well. In higher semantic abstraction, only entities shall be formed as nodes. In glance within RDF concept, nodes are resources either subjects or objects and edges are properties or predicates. The other issue in graph/ hypergraph is how to determine the direction of an edge. This issue is ignored by the previous mapping approaches since they do not consider the graph of a higher semantic abstraction.

We define how to capture the higher abstraction of the relational model (Definition 1-3) then we define its graph including the direction issue (Definition 4-5) and finally define how to obtain the RDF dataset (Definition 6).

DEFINITION 1 (The relational model). Let $S\ (R_1, R_2 \dots R_i)$ be a relational model which consists of a set of relations, a set of primary keys $\{PK_1, PK_2 \dots Pk_{iPK}\}$ and a set of foreign keys $\{FK_1, FK_2 \dots FK_{iFK}\}$. Each relation schema consists of a set of attributes, $R_i\ (A_1, A_2 \dots A_p)$, p is a degree of attributes and a set of domain integrity constraint $DI\ (DI_1, DI_2 \dots DI_p)$. t is an instance relation of R, a set of tuples $t\ (t_1, t_2, \dots, t_n)$. For each tuple, v is an ordered list of t values, $v=(v_1, v_2, ..., v_{np})$, each t is a value of attribute A_p.

DEFINITION 2 (The link structure of RDB). Let $FK_{i \to j}$ be a foreign key which connects relation R_i to relation R_j. x_i is the number of in-link and y_i is the number of out-link of the relation R_i.

x and y are calculated on the assumption that all relations are connected.

DEFINITION 3 (The Relation Type Set). Let L be a set of link structure information of relation $L=L_1, L_2 ... L_i$, each L_i is a list of value $L_i=(x_i, y_i)$ and let *RSink*, *RSource* and *RHub* are a list of a relation R_i which satisfies L information. If in the relation R_i, $y_i=0$ then R_i is an *RSink*. If in the relation R_i, $x_i=0$ then R_i is a *RSource*, otherwise the relation R_i is a *RHub*. Each relation type set (*RSink, RSource, RHub*) is a set of Relation R_i

DEFINITION 4 (The graph model). Let G be a graph model of a relational model S, is a set of nodes N and a set of edges E, a directed property graph $G(N,E)$ where N is a set of nodes $N=\{N_1, N_2 ... N_i\}$ and $N \in (RHub \cup RSink)$. Each N_i is a set of attribute and its value $N_i = (A_{ip}, V_{ip})$. The edges are defined as (i) $(N_i, \overrightarrow{N_j}) \in E$ if there is a FK between two relations $R_i - FK - \overrightarrow{R_j}$. The label of the edge is *"hasR$_i$"*. (ii) $N_r \in E$ where $R_r - FK - (\overrightarrow{R_i, R_j})$ and $R_r \in (RSource)$ hence the form of the subgraph is $N_i - N_r - \overrightarrow{N_j}$. Each edge N_r has a set of attribute and its value $N_r=(A_{rp}, V_{rp})$. The label of the edge is the name of hub relation N_r. (iii) $N_r \in HE$ where *HE is Hyperedge* and where $R_r - FK - (\overrightarrow{R_1, R_2 ... R_i})$ and $R_r \in (RSource)$ hence the form of the subgraph is $(N_1, N_2 ... N_i) - N_r - \overrightarrow{N_j}$. N_r has a set of attribute and its value $N_r=(A_{rp}, V_{rp})$. The label of the hyperedge is the name of the relation N_r.

We need to determine the direction of edges in point (ii) and (iii). We calculate the weight of authority of each node. N_i^A is the authority node and N_j^H is the hub node. The weight of authority A_i means how famous node N_i is referenced by the other nodes. The weight of hub H_i means how often node N_i refers to the other nodes. We calculate which node has the greatest weight of authority $WA_i = A_i - H_i$. In point (ii) N_i^A is the node which has greater WA_i and N_j^H is the other one node in a subgraph. In point (iii) N_i^A is the node which has greatest WA_i and N_j^H is the node which has the least WA_i. All the other nodes follow the obtained direction. In case we obtain the same number of weight then to choose any direction will be accepted, e.g., we can choose *"Jolie"* or *"Yogyakarta"* as the hub node because they have the same weight of authority. The formulas to calculate the weight of authority and the hub are as below:

$$A_{Ri} = \sum_{j \to i} hub_{Rj} \text{(i)} \qquad H_{Ri} = \sum_{i \to j} auth_{Rj} \text{(ii)}$$

g is a graph data, $g=(n,e)$ which following $G=(N, E)$ as a graph model.

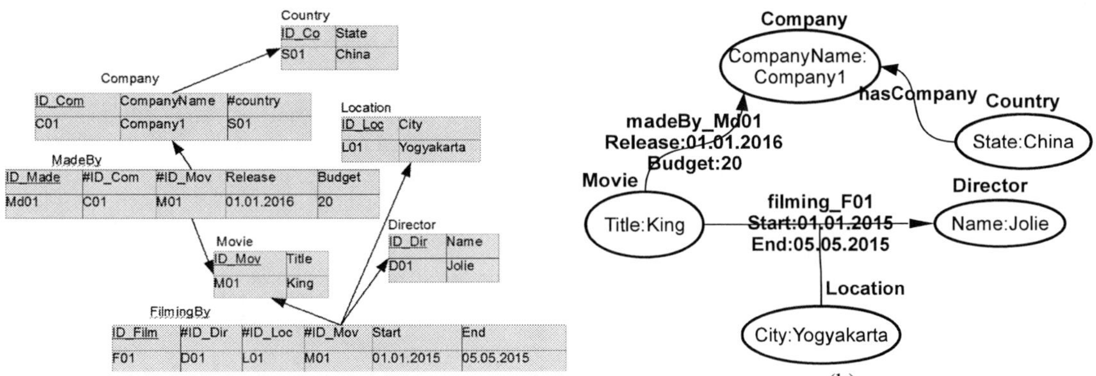

(a) (b)

Figure 1. (a) The example of a relational model, (b) The obtained graph data of the example in Figure 1.a included the direction of edges based on our approach

Figure 1.b shows that two types of edges: (i) the edge *"hasCompany"* which is created from *FK* as a labeled graph. (ii) The edge *"madeBy"* which is created from relation *"MadeBy"* is a directed property digraph and the edge *"filming"* which is created from relation *"Filming"* is a directed property hypergraph. The obtained graph model influences our approach to composing RDF. We see that *"MadeBy"* is not an entity but relationship between *"Company"* and *"Movie"* and *"filming"* is the relationship between *"Director"*, *"Location"* and *"Movie"* instead of an entity.

Intuitively, we can see nodes are resources (subject, object) and edges are properties (predicates) in RDF point of view. Figure 1.b shows that both resources and edges may have attributes. Our RDF model will maintain the semantics as well.

DEFINITION 5. (The graph of RDF). Let H be a hypergraph of RDF, $H = (V,E)$ which consists of a set of vertices $V=(v_1, v_2 \dots v_m)$ and a set of non-empty edges/ hyperedges $E=(e_1, e_2 \dots e_n)$.

We obtain five types of RDF subgraph: (i) $hv_m=(A_{mp}, T_{mp}, D_{mp}, R_m)$ is a set of attributes (A_{mp}), its value (T_{mp}), its domain integrity (D_{mp}) and its relation name (R_m). (ii) $he_n=(FK_m, T_{mFK}, R_m, R_{mj})$ is a set consists of a foreign key (FK_m), its value (T_{mFK}), its relation (R_m) and its referenced relation(R_{mj}). It is a labeled edge from relation-node, named by "$hasR_m$". (iii) $he_n=(R_{mi}, R_{mj}, R_{Hn})$ is a set consists of the relation (R_{mi}), its referenced relation (R_{mj}) and their edge relation (R_{hn}). (iv) $he_n=(A_{np}, T_{np}, D_{np}, R_{nj})$ is a set of attributes (A_{np}), its value (T_{np}), its domain integrity (D_{np}) and its relation (R_{nj}). (v) $he_n=(A_{np}, T_{np}, D_{np}, R_n)$ is a set of attributes (A_{np}), its value (T_{np}), its domain integrity (D_{np}) and its relation (R_n). The example is illustrated in Figure 2.a.

DEFINITION 6. (The triple RDF). Let r be URI prefix and S, P, O be a triple RDF. They are terms which hold the following conditions:

(i) For a subgraph $hv_m=(A_{mp}, T_{mp}, D_{mp}, R_m)$: (a) S-P-O is $r{:}PK_{mp}$-$r{:}A_{mp}$-V_{mp} .V_{mp} can be formed as a URI or a literal. (b) Entail the semantic of S to R_m.

(ii) For subgraph $he_n=(FK_m, T_{mFK}, R_m, R_{mj})$: S-P-O is $r{:}PK_{mi}$-"$hasR_{mi}$-$r{:}PK_{mj}$

(iii) For a subgraph $he_n=(R_{mi}, R_{mj}, R_{Hn})$: (a) S-P-O is $r{:}PK_{mi}$-$r{:}R_{Hn}\_PK_{Hn}$-$r{:}PK_{mj}$ (b) Entail the semantic of S to R_{mi}, the semantic of O to R_{mj} and the semantic of P to R_{Hn}.

(iv) For a set subgraph $he_n=(A_{np}, T_{np}, D_{np}, R_{nj})$: S-P-O is $r{:}\ R_n\_PK_n$-R_{nj}-$r{:}PK_{nj}$.

(v) For a set subgraph $he_n=(A_{np}, T_{np}, D_{np}, R_n)$: (a) S-P-O is $r{:}R_n\_PK_n$-$r{:}A_{np}$-V_{nj}. (b) Entail the semantic of S to R_n.

The example is illustrated in Figure 2.b.

The mapping RDF data types follow the domain integrity constraints. For each value V (in subgraph (i) and (v)) add the prefix or xsd type based on their domain integrity. E.g., if V_m is a string/ varchar/ char/ non-numeric/ non-date/ non-time then format O as $r{:}V_m$ or "V_m"^^`xsd:string`. If V_m is integer/byte/bigint, then add format O as "V_m"^^`xsd:integer`. If V_m is decimal, then add format O as "V_m"^^`xsd:float`. If V_m has type date, then add format O as "V_m"^^`xsd:date`. If V_m has type time, then add format O as "V_m"^^`xsd:time`, etc.

Definition 6 is the direct mapping in our approach under the assumption that the relational database is valid. Further, it can be augmented with more rules. This step is derived after some steps which consider the higher abstraction and the expressiveness of graph model. The prefix r is reserved URI. Based on the DEFINITION 6, we obtain RDF from the example RDB as below; (the example of the composed RDF from the five subgraph types are marked in enclosed brackets)

```
@prefix r: <http://example/#> .
@prefix rdf: <http://www.w3.org/1999/02/22-rdf-syntax-ns#> .
@prefix xsd: <http://www.w3.org/2001/XMLSchema#> .

r:M01 r:title "King" .                                  (i)
r:M01 rdf:type r:Movie .
r:C01 r:companyName r:Company1 .
r:C01 rdf:type r:Company .
r:M01 r:madeBy_Md01 r:C01 .
r:S01 r:hasCompany r:C01 .                              (ii)
r:S01 r:state r:China .                                 (i)
r:S01 rdf:type r:Country .
```

```
r:madeBy_Md01 r:release "2016-01-01"^^xsd:date .
r:madeBy_Md01 r:budget "20"^^xsd:integer .
r:madeBy_Md01 rdf:type r:madeBy .
r:D01 r:name r:Jolie .
r:D01 rdf:type r:Director .
r:M01 r:filming_F01 r:D01 .                                    (iii)
r:filming_F01 r:location r:L01 .                               (iv)
r:filming_F01 r:start "2015-01-01"^^xsd:date .                 (v)
r:filming_F01 r:end "2015-05-05"^^xsd:date .
r:filming_F01 rdf:type r:filming .
r:L01 r:city r:Yogyakarta .
r:L01 rdf:type r:Location .
```

We augment the role of the predicates *"madeBy_Md01"* and *"filming_F01"* to handle the information as attributes. It is generated from subgraph type (v), and they are formed as property graphs/ hypergraphs. A predicate which has attributes is formed as a predicate instance, then entail their semantic to the predicate type. The predicate *"filming_F01"* connects three type nodes (movie, director, and city) and the other several data properties. Our approach creates a hypergraph where *Movie* as a domain node, *Director* as a range node and put the rest nodes and data types as attributes. As the comparison, for the underlined snippet given above, based on the earlier approaches we will obtain as below:

```
r:F01 rdf:type r:Filming .
r:F01 r:movie r:M01 .
r:F01 r:location r:L01 .
r:F01 r:director r:D01 .
r:F01 r:start "2015-01-01"^^xsd:date .
r:F01 r:end "2015-05-05"^^xsd:date .
```

They map *"madeBy"* and *"filming"* as resources instead properties. Thus, the semantic is lost.

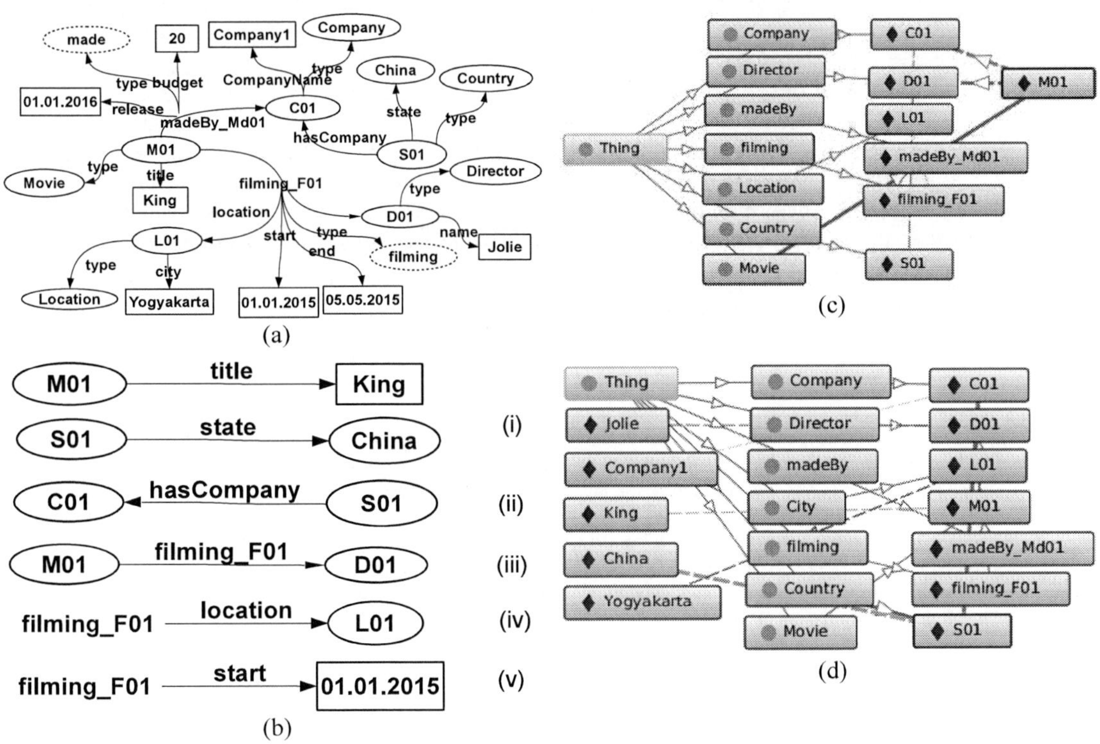

Figure 2. (a) The RDF graphs of the example (b) the examples of five types the possible subgraphs. (c) the obtained RDF within OWL format type 1 (literal type as string) and (d) in OWL format type 2 (literal type as URI)

In summary, our approach and the result RDF are both different comparing all earlier works. The previous works are the direct mapping, and our approach considers the higher semantic abstraction of RDB. The previous works compose within the standard RDF, and our approach proposes a new model of RDF.

The obtained above RDF and Figure 2.a show that we use class approach. There are classes for resources and properties. The only one purpose in using a class of property is for entailing the semantic of predicate types. Therefore, predicate instances can entail their semantic to predicate types. The rest of RDF is formed as simple triples. Figure 2.c and 2.d illustrate that the obtained RDF can be formed easily as OWL, even though it is not the concern in this work. The main important on this part is mapping the semantic of properties (predicates) in more detail ways to fit the expressiveness of OWL, e.g., *owl: ObjectProperty*, *owl: DatatypeProperty*, *rdfs: domain*, *rdfs: range*, etc., and the set of vocabularies from various external ontologies. The comparison of the obtained OWL for the underlined snippet based on our approach and earlier approaches are as below:

The obtained OWL based on our approach.

```
r:M01 r:filming_F01 r:D01 .
r:filming_F01 rdf:type r:filming .
r:filming_F01 rdf:type owl:ObjectProperty .
r:M01 rdf:type r:Movie .
r:D01 rdf:type r:Director .
r:filming_F01 r:location r:L01 .
r:location rdf:type owl:ObjectProperty .
r:filming_F01 r:start "2015-01-01"^^xsd:date .
r:filming_F01 r:end "2015-05-05"^^xsd:date .
r:start rdf:type owl:DatatypeProperty .
r:end rdf:type owl:DatatypeProperty .
```

The obtained OWL based on earlier approaches.

```
r:F01 rdf:type r:filming .
r:F01 r:movie r:M01 .
r:movie rdf:type owl:ObjectProperty .
r:F01 r:location r:L01 .
r:location rdf:type owl:ObjectProperty .
r:F01 r:director r:D01 .
r:director rdf:type owl:ObjectProperty .
r:F01 r:start "2015-01-01"^^xsd:date .
r:F01 r:end "2015-05-05"^^xsd:date .
r:M01 rdf:type r:Movie .
r:D01 rdf:type r:Director .
r:start rdf:type owl:DatatypeProperty .
r:end rdf:type owl:DatatypeProperty .
```

The previous approaches map an edge *"filming"* a resource. Thus the semantic is lost.

4. THE EXPERIMENT

We conducted experiments for two real datasets, World Bank[1] and Mondial[2]. World Bank has four relations, and Mondial has 30 relations. We utilize RDF store Jena[3] without any new indexing system. Table 1 shows the schema mapping which describes that our approach maintains the higher abstraction through graph approach. We obtain the storage size is ***19.3 Mb***, ***475660 number of triple*** and the storage size is ***3.5 Mb***, ***97833 number of triple*** for World Bank and Mondial datasets respectively.

Table 1. The schema mapping relational to a group of resource and property graph

Dataset	Relations	Graph Schema Mapping
World Bank	Country, Data, Indicators, Topic	Nodes: Country, Indicators, Topic (3); Edges: Data (1)
Mondial	Borders, City, Continent, Country, Desert, Economy, Encompasses, EthnicGroup, Geo_Desert, Geo_Estuary, Geo_Island, Geo_Lake, Geo_River, Geo_Sea, Geo_Source, Island, IslandIn, IsMember, Lake, Language, Located, locatedFor, MergesWith, Organization, Politics, Population, Province, Religion, River, Sea	Nodes: City, Continent, Country, Desert, Economy, EthnicGroup, Island, Lake, Language, Mountain, Organization, Politics, Population, Province, Religion, River, Sea (17); Edges: Borders, Encompasses, Geo_Desert, Geo_Estuary, Geo_Island, Geo_Lake, Geo_River, Geo_Sea, Geo_Source, IslandIn, IsMember, locatedFor, MergesWith (13)

As the approach is based on native triple RDF, it can be naturally retrieved by SPARQL. We provide ten queries for each dataset to evaluate the retrieval process of the new RDF model. Without any difficulties, SPARQL naturally handles the queries. The main difference is that it uses predicate instance to reify the

1 http://data.worldbank.org/
2 http://www.dbis.informatik.uni-goettingen.de/Mondial/
3 https://jena.apache.org/

needed attributes of queries. The results are all corrects. The example queries, Q1 for World Bank dataset and Q2 for Mondial dataset.

Q1: Show the countries and indicator name in topic (T20), where for the same indicators, in one country has been decreased for four years until 2012 but in the other countries has been increased for four years until 2012

SELECT DISTINCT ?ic ?in
WHERE {{ ?ic rdf:type :Indicators . ?ic :hasINDICATOR_TOPIC :T20 . ?ic :hasINDICATOR_CODE ?ic . ?ic :hasINDICATOR_NAME ?in . ?ct ?hasDataic ?ic .?hasDataic rdf:type :hasData . {{ ?hasDataic :hasYR2012 ?a . ?hasDataic :hasYR2011 ?b . FILTER (?a < ?b) } UNION { ?hasDataic :hasYR2011 ?b . ?hasDataic :hasYR2010 ?c . FILTER (?b < ?c) } UNION { ?hasDataic :hasYR2010 ?c . ?hasDataic :hasYR2009 ?d . FILTER (?c < ?d)}}} { ?ic rdf:type :Indicators . ?ic :hasINDICATOR_TOPIC :T20 . ?ic :hasINDICATOR_CODE ?ic . ?ic :hasINDICATOR_NAME ?in . ?ct ?hasDataic2 ?ic . ?hasDataic2 rdf:type :hasData . {{ ?hasDataic2 :hasYR2012 ?a2 . ?hasDataic2 :hasYR2011 ?b2 . FILTER (?a2 > ?b2) } UNION { ?hasDataic2 :hasYR2011 ?b2 . ?hasDataic2 :hasYR2010 ?c2 . FILTER (?b2 > ?c2) } UNION { ?hasDataic2 :hasYR2010 ?c2 . ?hasDataic2 :hasYR2009 ?d2 . FILTER (?c2 > ?d2) }}} }

Result: The needed time is 4.928s

```
|ic                          | in                                                  |
======================================================================================
|:SP_URB_TOTL_IN_ZS          | "Urban population (% of total)"^^xsd:string          |
|:EN_URB_MCTY_TL_ZS          | "Population in urban agglomerations of more than 1 million (% of total
population)"^^xsd:string |
|:EN_POP_DNST                | "Population density (people per sq_ km of land area)"^^xsd:string |
|:EN_URB_LCTY_UR_ZS          | "Population in the largest city (% of urban population)"^^xsd:string |
|:SP_URB_GROW                | "Urban population growth (annual %)"^^xsd:string     |
--------------------------------------------------------------------------------------
```

Q2: List of countries which located in continent Africa, has relation with organizations, has inflation more than 60 in number and infant mortality less than 100

SELECT DISTINCT ?coname
WHERE {{ ?country rdf:type :Country . ?country :hasName ?coname . ?coeco rdf:type :Economy . ?coeco :hasCountry ?country . ?coeco :hasInflation ?i . FILTER (?i > "60"^^xsd:float) ?p rdf:type :Population . ?p :hasCountry ?country . ?p :hasInfant_Mortality ?im . FILTER (?im < "100"^^xsd:float) :Africa ?encom1 ?country . ?encom1 rdf:type :hasencompasses . ?country ?isM ?o . ?isM rdf:type :hasisMember . }

Result: (not all result). The needed time is 6.612s

```
| coname                        |
=================================
| "Sudan"^^xsd: string          |
| "Cape_Verde"^^xsd: string     |
| "Guinea-Bissau"^^xsd: string  |
| "Ethiopia"^^xsd: string       |
| "Ghana"^^xsd: string          |
| "Niger"^^xsd: string          |
| "Nigeria"^^xsd: string        |
| "Cote_dIvoire"^^xsd: string   |
| "Mali"^^xsd: string           |
---------------------------------
```

5. CONCLUSIONS AND FUTURE WORK

We propose a new mapping approach RDB to RDF, which considers its higher abstraction and its graph expressiveness. Our approach novelty is to map the complex relationships in a relational model which refers to an attributed hypergraphs. Our approach combines the class approach and the simple triple approach. Our approach also manages the direction of hypergraph which determines the role of resources whether as a subject or an object. To make the RDF follows the higher semantic abstraction, the RDF model augments the function of a predicate to handle the complexity of the relationship. Even though the obtained RDF has different model comparing the native RDF, it can be naturally retrieved by SPARQL. The reasoning issue of the obtained RDF in OWL format will be our near future work.

REFERENCES

Aggarwal, C.C., Wang, H., 2010. *Managing and mining graph data*. Springer.

Arenas, M., Prud'hommeaux, E., Sequeda, J., n.d. *Direct mapping of relational data to RDF.* W3C Working Draft 24 March 2011.

Astrova, I., 2009. Rules for *Mapping SQL Relational Databases to OWL Ontologies*, in: Sicilia, M.-A., Lytras, M.D. (Eds.), Metadata and Semantics. Springer US, Boston, MA, pp. 415–424.

Berners-Lee, T., Hendler, J., Lassila, O., others, 2001. *The semantic web*. Sci. Am. 284, 28–37.

Bizer, C., 2003. *D2R MAP - A Database to RDF Mapping Language*, in: World Wide Web Conference Series.

Bizer, C., Seaborne, A., 2004. *D2RQ-treating non-RDF databases as virtual RDF graphs*, in: Proceedings of the 3rd International Semantic Web Conference (ISWC2004). Springer.

Būmans, G., Čerāns, K., 2010. *RDB2OWL: a practical approach for transforming RDB data into RDF/OWL*, in: Proceedings of the 6th International Conference on Semantic Systems. ACM, p. 25.

Cafarella, M.J., Halevy, A., Madhavan, J., 2011. *Structured data on the web*. Commun. ACM 54, 72–79.

Čerāns, K., Būmans, G., 2011. *RDB2OWL: a RDB-to-RDF/OWL Mapping Specification Language.* Databases Inf. Syst. VI 139–152.

Chein, M., Mugnier, M.-L., 2008. *Graph-based knowledge representation: computational foundations of conceptual graphs*. Springer Science & Business Media.

Das, S., Sundara, S., Cyganiak, R., 2012. *R2RML: RDB to RDF Mapping Language*.

De Abreu, D., Flores, A., Palma, G., Pestana, V., Pinero, J., Queipo, J., Sánchez, J., Vidal, M.-E., 2013. *Choosing Between Graph Databases and RDF Engines for Consuming and Mining Linked Data*., in: COLD. Citeseer.

de Laborda, C.P., Conrad, S., 2005. *Relational. OWL: a data and schema representation format based on OWL*, in: Proceedings of the 2nd Asia-Pacific Conference on Conceptual Modelling-Volume 43. Australian Computer Society, Inc., pp. 89–96.

Hert, M., Reif, G., Gall, H.C., 2011. *A Comparison of RDB-to-RDF Mapping Languages*, in: Proceedings of the 7th International Conference on Semantic Systems, I-Semantics '11. ACM, New York, NY, USA, pp. 25–32.

Hert, M., Reif, G., Gall, H.C., 2010. *Updating relational data via SPARQL/update, i*n: Proceedings of the 2010 EDBT/ICDT Workshops. ACM, p. 24.

Laclavık, M., 2007. RDB2Onto: *Relational database data to ontology individuals mapping*, in: Proceeding of Ninth International Conference of Informatics.

Li, M., Du, X., Wang, S., 2005. *A Semi-automatic Ontology Acquisition Method for the Semantic Web*, in: Fan, W., Wu, Z., Yang, J. (Eds.), Advances in Web-Age Information Management: 6th International Conference, WAIM 2005, Hangzhou, China, October 11 – 13, 2005. Proceedings. Springer Berlin Heidelberg, Berlin, Heidelberg, pp. 209–220.

Lv, Y., Ma, Z.M., 2008. *Transformation of relational model to RDF model*, in: Systems, Man and Cybernetics, 2008. SMC 2008. IEEE International Conference on. pp. 506–511.

Ramanujam, S., Khadilkar, V., Khan, L., Seida, S., Kantarcioglu, M., Thuraisingham, B., 2010. Bi-directional Translation of *Relational Data into Virtual RDF Stores, in: Semantic* Computing (ICSC), 2010 IEEE Fourth International Conference on. pp. 268–276. doi:10.1109/ICSC.2010.61

Spanos, D.-E., Stavrou, P., Mitrou, N., 2012. *Bringing relational databases into the semantic web: A survey. Semantic Web* 3, 169–209.

Thuy, P.T.T., Thuan, N.D., Han, Y., Park, K., Lee, Y.-K., 2014. *RDB2RDF: completed transformation from relational database into RDF ontology*, in: Proceedings of the 8th International Conference on Ubiquitous Information Management and Communication. ACM, p. 88.

Xu, L., Lee, S., Kim, S., 2010. *E-R model based RDF data storage in RDB*, in: Computer Science and Information Technology (ICCSIT), 2010 3rd IEEE International Conference on. pp. 258–262.

Zhou, S., 2010. *Exposing relational database as RDF, in: Industrial and Information Systems (IIS)*, 2010 2nd International Conference on. pp. 237–240.

A SYSTEMATIC LITERATURE REVIEW OF OWL ONTOLOGY EVALUATION

Alex Mateus Porn, Cristiane Aparecida Gonçalves Huve, Leticia Mara Peres
and Alexandre Ibrahim Direne
Federal University of Parana

ABSTRACT

We present in this paper a systematic literature review, using Kitchenham approach [24], of methods, techniques and tools to evaluate OWL ontologies. We identify methods, techniques, and tools for OWL ontology evaluation, and we classify them based on quality criteria. We conclude that although there is a large number of related studies on ontology evaluation, there are quality criteria which were still unexplored. At the same time, the evaluation process needs computational advances related to tools and processing power.

KEYWORDS

OWL Ontology, Ontology Evaluation, Quality Criteria

1. INTRODUCTION

Ontologies are formal representations of concepts and relationships, which enable sharing and reuse of knowledge [20, 37]. They establish a common vocabulary and semantic interpretation of their terms by describing classes, attributes, individuals, and relationships in a machine and human readable structure [1, 37].

OWL is a computer language standardized by W3C (World Wide Web Consortium) [27] to define and instantiate Web ontologies. OWL ontologies specify how to derive logical consequences through OWL formal semantic, clarifying facts which are not explicitly presented in ontology but are linked through semantics [35].

Ontology evaluation encompass methods, techniques and tools which assist to understand, refine and decide the issues to be revised or improved [29]. In Ontology Engineering, ontology adequacy is associated with quality features or criteria [39]. In light of this, our research question is: which methods and techniques exist to evaluate OWL ontologies in the context of validation and verification, considering ontology quality criteria?

We performed a systematic literature review to answer this question and identified existing papers which reflect OWL ontology evaluation related to research efforts. We studied and classified methods, techniques and tools for OWL ontology evaluation according to quality criteria.

This paper is organized as follows: section 2 briefly presents ontology evaluation definitions and quality criteria. Section 3 presents the systematic literature review methodology and synthesis of obtained data. Following, we present in section 4 the result analysis, and in section 5 our final considerations about OWL ontology evaluation.

2. ONTOLOGY EVALUATION AND QUALITY CRITERIA

Ontologies are developed to specify standard procedures to extract and share knowledge among different systems. They are used to ensure the consistency of system extracted data and the sharing of data among computers and computers, and computers and humans [39].

It is important to perform an ontology evaluation process [16] to identify whether an ontology meet its goals. Since mid-1995, ontology evaluation is object of study [15, 18, 19, 31]. The OWL ontology evaluation process can be conducted in different ways, as manually, where the knowledge domain specialist participation is needed, or automatically, through criteria and specific techniques types, such as comparing the ontology being evaluated with a standard ontology. Evaluation has a number of challenges, for example [39] due the ontology declarative nature becomes difficult its compilation and execution during its evaluation; ontologies tend to be shared among different contexts and used in different tasks; and also, ontologies are reused or integrated with other ontologies.

Gómez-Pérez [17] defines that the evaluation activity consists in two distinct processes: verification, which addresses methods and techniques to evaluate whether the ontology was correctly built, and validation, which evaluates concepts in ontology to conclude the modeling closeness with real-world definitions.

Several authors proposed quality criteria to conduct an ontology evaluation process. Vrandečić [39] asserts a quality criterion is a quality characteristic made as an agreement during ontology conceptualization. Quality criteria try to reflect the correct representation of real-world definitions, the ability to reuse and share knowledge, the clarity understanding or its completeness [39]. Table 1 presents a summary of quality criteria proposed by several authors.

Table 1. Ontology quality criteria

Criterion	Initials	Definition
Accuracy [30] / Correctness [21]	ACR	It evaluates whether concepts, relationships and instances of an ontology modeling and represent correctly the real-world definitions.
Adaptability [30] / Extendibility [18] / Expandability [17]	AEE	It evaluates the ontology flexibility of new terms definitions, without impacting its current definition, aiming to expand to the accurate domain representation.
Clarity [18]	CLA	It evaluates whether ontology definitions are objective and independent of context, whether they expressed in an efficient and understandable way the concepts, whether there are partial definitions or descriptions, whether all definitions are documented and whether the ontology is understandable.
Completeness [17] / Competency [19]	CCP	It evaluates whether ontology is complete, in other words, whether all alleged definitions should be included in the ontology are explicitly defined informally and formally.
Computational Efficiency [30]	CEF	It analyzes the facility with which reasoners processes the ontology and the computational cost required to perform tasks such as queries and instances rating.
Conciseness [17]	CSN	It evaluates whether information addressed in ontology is useful and accurate, aim to find occurrence of irrelevant and redundant axioms.
Consistency [30] / Coherence [18]	CCH	It evaluates the possibility of exist contradictory conclusions in an ontology, from valid input data.
Organizational fitness [13]	OGF	It evaluates ontology implementation issues, checking whether ontology was developed in accordance with organization processes, whether it is aligned with other existing ontologies, among others.
Sensitiveness [17]	SST	It evaluates how small changes in an ontology definition change the set of defined properties. This criterion should ensure that completeness, conciseness and consistency definitions are strongly connected.
Minimal encoding bias [18]	MEB	It evaluates whether ontology concepts are encoded in knowledge level, without relying of a particular coding type, and whether they are independent of notation and implementation.
Minimal ontological commitment [18]	MOC	It is aligned with conciseness criterion; it has the purpose of determining whether the ontology address the minimum activities for sharing and knowledge representation.

Some of those criteria such as consistency [30] and conciseness [17] can be determined with a high confidence level using ontology tools, such as FaCT[1] and RACER[2] reasoners. These tools provide means for checking errors in ontologies, such as redundant terms and inconsistencies among definitions.

On the other hand, there are other criteria, such as clarity [18] and expandability [17] which may be difficult to evaluate, due to require manual help of domain experts. This result in the absence of automated ways to apply these criteria in an ontology evaluation. By the same way, the correctness criterion [21] requires participation of expert or ontology engineer to verify whether ontology definitions are correct according to the real world [42].

Guarino [21] proposed the precision and recall measures, which can satisfy correctness and completeness criteria, respectively. These measures are used to consider whether ontology definitions cover the represented domain and whether all concepts were defined, allowing it to examine which definitions are not clear in the ontology and the lack of domain concepts representation.

All criteria considered in Table 1, can be used in OWL ontology evaluation process, during construction or selection of OWL ontology. For this, methods and techniques were proposed in different studies. However, they still were not defined as standards to be used in evaluation. Following, a systematic literature review is presented focused on helping developers and knowledge engineers to select existing methods and techniques for OWL ontology evaluation.

3. METHODOLOGY OF SYSTEMATIC LITERATURE REVIEW

A systematic literature review (SLR) process, based on Kitchenham and Mulrow [24, 25, 28] was performed to identify proposals in the OWL ontology evaluation context. The SLR provides a comprehensive view of applied studies in this area, by allowing papers identification which present relevant considerations, practical suggestions, open questions, and issues to be explored.

Since we had not found any systematic literature review with the same proposed objective, we identified the need for a SLR to search studies which define and apply OWL ontology evaluation according to quality criteria. In essence, our aim is to provide an understanding of existing methods, techniques and tools, and which quality criteria they correspond.

We elaborated a review protocol to conduct the SLR process, based on Kitchenham approach [24]. Objectives, search criteria, and sources were defined to search, select, validate, and after to include or exclude papers. The SLR was conducted by four researchers, from February to May 2016.

For search, five electronic sources to research were consulted to identify primary studies: ACM Digital Library (ACM DL)[3], Engineering Village[4], IEEE Xplore Digital Library (IEEE Xplore DL)[5], Science Direct[6] and Scopus[7]. In addition, we also conducted searches in Google[8] search engine, and in Philosophy Department website at State University of New York at Buffalo (PD-SUNYB)[9]. There were no restrictions on publication year and were considered only English material.

The following search strings were used: "*Owl Ontology Validation*", "*Owl Ontology Verification*", "*Owl Ontology Evaluation*", "*Owl Ontology Test*", "*Owl Ontology Testing*", "*Test for Owl Ontology*" and "*Owl Ontology Quality Assurance*". Each search string was used separately in advanced search filtered by abstract, title and keywords, in each digital library. Although the search strings were very specific, we still found a large number of false positives, i.e, papers which do not make reference to OWL ontology evaluation.

We selected 233 papers from search process and we discarded repeated papers. According to SLR [24], we created a quality questionnaire presented below, and based on Question 1 (Q1), we performed a validation

1 http://owl.cs.manchester.ac.uk/tools/fact/
2 http://www.ifis.uni-luebeck.de/index.php?id=385
3 http://dl.acm.org/
4 http://www.engineeringvillage.com/
5 http://ieeexplore.ieee.org
6 http://www.sciencedirect.com/
7 http://www.scopus.com/
8 https://www.google.com.br
9 http://ontology.buffalo.edu/evaluation.html

of 233 papers in the selected paper. At first, we read each title, keywords, abstract, and introduction section of selected papers, to classify them as included or excluded.

Following we present the quality questionnaire: We included 98 papers from validate process. We full read the included papers. Each paper which presents method, technique or tool was classified as "extracted paper".

- Q1 – Is there a clear statement of goals of study towards OWL ontology evaluation?
- Q2 – Does the paper report methods, techniques or present tools for OWL ontology evaluation?
- Q3 – Is there a clear statement of proposals techniques?
- Q4 – Are there experiments conducted to prove the effectiveness of methods and techniques to OWL ontology evaluation?
  - ✓ Is there an automated tool developed?
  - ✓ Is there a tool available?
  - ✓ Is there a manual evaluation carried out?
  - ✓ Is there a clear statement of experiment results?
  - ✓ Are there problems or difficulties reported?
- Q5 – What suggestions for future works are indicated on OWL ontology evaluation?

In the case of papers which did not satisfy the first two questions (Q1 and Q2), the last question (Q5) was considered before the paper was classified as excluded, to analyze whether there are some future proposal of evaluation method or technique. Table 2 shows the number of papers by step of SLR.

Table 2. Number of papers by step of SLR

Eletronic sources	Selected papers	Included papers	Extracted papers
ACM DL	21	03	0
Engineering Village	57	07	2
IEEE Xplore DL	86	44	9
Science Direct	07	05	4
Scopus	21	08	3
Google	25	16	2
PD-SUNYB	16	15	4
TOTAL	233	98	24

After reading included papers, we identified 24 [1, 2, 3, 4, 5, 6, 7, 8, 9, 10, 11, 12, 14, 22, 23, 26, 29, 32, 33, 34, 36, 38, 40, 41] which addresses OWL ontology evaluation techniques or tools development. In the extracted papers 7 techniques types and 67 techniques were cataloged to evaluate OWL ontology.

4. RESULT ANALYSIS

Kitchenham approach [24] suggests to catalog the data analysis of results. Reading the extracted papers, we identified 67 techniques to evaluate ontologies. These techniques are presented in Table 3 and from them, 07 papers [4, 7, 8, 14, 23, 33, 40,] have proposed to automate the ontology evaluation process and one paper [10] proposes to adapt the ISO 25000 standard model to evaluate ontology quality.

We observed that different researches addresses similar aspects in the ontology evaluation process. With this in mind, we performed a sensitivity analysis, as shown in Table 4, whereby each technique was classified under quality criteria for OWL ontology evaluation: Clarity (CLA), Minimal encoding bias (MEB), Completeness/Competency (CPP), Conciseness (CSN), Adaptability/Extendibility/Expandability (AEE), Consistency/Coherence (CCH), Sensitiveness (SST), and Accuracy/Correctness (ACR).

We identified 7 techniques types for OWL ontology evaluation, also presented in Table 4. We classified these techniques types in: GSE - when an ontology evaluation is done from a model ontology, technique type defined as "gold-standard ontology" [9]; EOE – when an ontology evaluation is done with the aid of knowledge domain experts; QOE – when an ontology evaluation is done with questionnaires help; MOE – when an ontology evaluation is done using quality models features, criteria, and ontologies metrics; SOE – ontology evaluation semantics; TOE - task-based ontology evaluation, and DOE - data driven ontology evaluation.

Table 3. Ontology evaluation techniques

Paper	Amount of techniques	Application
[1]	01	This technique evaluates the standard deviations among concepts represented in the ontology.
[26]	02	These techniques remove redundancies and evaluate the satisfaction degree of defined concepts.
[5]	02	These techniques evaluate whether the ontology represents all domain concepts.
[22]	09	They evaluate the pragmatic and semantic quality through the Precision, Recall, and Coverage metrics and apply the coupling and cohesion metrics to analyze the external referenced classes.
[33]	05	They evaluate the pragmatic quality through the concepts accuracy; existence of inconsistencies; whether the language primitives and syntax were defined correctly and understandability.
[40]	04	These techniques apply unit test to check for errors; assess whether addressed domain definitions are all represented and the ontology behavior after making changes.
[4]	02	These techniques evaluate the inferences based on competency questions and results.
[32]	01	This technique evaluates the ontology efficiency to perform a determined task.
[11]	01	This technique evaluates the query reasoning time among modules of a modular ontology.
[7]	11	These techniques evaluate the ontology pragmatic, semantic, syntactic, and social quality through Precision, Recall, and Coverage metrics, as well as, the existence of inconsistencies.
[3]	01	This technique evaluates the existence of possible anomalies in the ontology.
[14]	05	These techniques evaluate instances of classes.
[12]	01	This technique evaluates the ontology cognitive quality.
[41]	01	This technique evaluates the ontology complexity according to its development.
[36]	01	It evaluates the ontology completeness and correctness through queries integrity constraints.
[38]	05	They evaluate open world assumptions, competency questions coverage, consistency after reasoner perform, knowledge coverage and range and domain definitions analysis.
[2]	01	It evaluates the existence of inconsistencies through FNQuery queries based on Prolog.
[29]	01	It evaluates the ontology structure, based on the width and depth of the classes and relationships.
[9]	01	It evaluates the hierarchy and lexical terms through Precision, Recall, and F-measure metrics.
[6]	02	They evaluate ontology utility and veracity in specific tasks through the use of questionnaires.
[23]	05	They evaluate pragmatic and semantic quality through Precision, Recall, and Coverage metrics.
[34]	04	They evaluate incorrect nodes definitions, disjunctions, redundancy, and disjunction omission.

Each quality criterion was classified according to their applicability under a validation perspective (CLA, MEB, CCP, CSN, AEE and MOC) and/or verification (CCH, SST, ACR, CEF and OGF). This classification is shown in Table 4. Coincidentally quality criteria to conduct OWL ontology validation or verification process have a similar number of techniques. In this analysis, comparing criteria presented in Table 1 with related papers presented in Table 4, just one paper was found to the criterion minimal encoding bias (MEB) [7] and computational efficiency (CEF) [22]. Non-research work was identified to the criterion organizational fitness (OGF) and minimal ontological commitment (MOC). However, the MOC criterion depicts a similar manner of conciseness criterion (CSN) definitions, thus, the used techniques in this last one can be also adapted to MOC criterion to evaluate OWL ontology.

On the other hand, to completeness (CCP), consistency (CCH), and accuracy (ACR) criteria, a considerable amount of papers was found addressing techniques to this subject. This is justified due the most presented techniques to evaluate OWL ontology towards these criteria corresponding a reasoner-based execution, such as FaCT, RACER or Pellet[10], or made available by ontology building tools, such as Protégé[11] or Tawny[12].

With regard to techniques types for OWL ontology evaluation, the gold-standard technique showed large number of studies [5, 22, 26, 40, 41]. This technique type is widely used to validate whether the ontology structure is aligned with concepts underlying the respective domain, which assist the ontologies maintenance process. However, gold-standard is not applied in domains which do not have a previous representation model.

To the expert evaluation technique type [6, 7, 23, 26, 33] and the technique type using questionnaires [4, 6, 14, 26, 33, 38, 40], there was also significant amount of studies, as in the case whereby Jianliang [23] proposes an evaluation technique which includes philosophy and computer science experts. Both techniques

10 https://www.w3.org/2001/sw/wiki/Pellet
11 http://protege.stanford.edu
12 http://arxiv.org/abs/1303.0213

types, expert evaluation and using questionnaires requires a high involvement of a domain specialist. These techniques types are not automated, however, they have good results when used in ontology building process [6, 26, 33].

The applied techniques types exclusively for ontology test are rarely explored in the literature, some authors propose specific solutions for ontology test [2, 3, 4, 7, 14, 22, 26, 33, 34, 38, 40], compared to tests applied in software engineering.

We found expressive studies of evaluation metrics and which present techniques to quantify ontology validation measures, such as techniques using precision and recall [1, 7, 9, 20, 22, 23, 29]. Regarding to ontologies semantic evaluation [1, 7, 38], few papers were found.

In this analysis, some papers techniques [1, 7, 10, 11, 12, 14, 29, 34] are not classified in any quality criteria in Table 4, because they do not fit in these criteria. Some examples are: measuring the standard deviation among ontology concepts [1]; evaluation of computational reasoning time to answer queries among ontology modules [11]; and also, measuring the number of times which an ontology is accessed [7].

Table 4. Related papers of ontology quality criteria and techniques types for OWL ontology evaluation

Related	Validation					Verification				Techniques types for OWL ontology evaluation						
papers	CLA	MEB	CCP	CSN	AEE	CCH	SST	ACR	CEF	GSE	EOE	QOE	MOE	SOE	TOE	DOE
[26]				X						X	X	X				
[5]			X							X						X
[8]								X								
[22]	X		X	X	X	X		X	X	X			X			X
[7]	X	X	X		X	X		X			X		X	X		
[41]	X									X			X			
[23]	X		X			X		X			X		X			
[33]			X		X	X		X			X	X				
[40]			X				X	X		X		X				
[4]			X			X						X				
[32]			X												X	
[36]			X													
[38]			X			X		X				X				
[2]			X													
[6]			X	X							X	X				
[3]						X										
[9]								X					X			

Some studies presented tools to automate the implementation and execution of techniques [4, 7, 8, 14, 23, 33, 40,]. The evaluation techniques types based on gold-standard ontology and semantic evaluation presented only one tool [40]. To the expert evaluation technique type was found three tools [7, 23, 33] and two tools were found to the evaluation metrics technique type [7, 23]. In relation to the questionnaires evaluation, 5 papers present a proposal [4, 8, 14 33, 40], in which the first one of these presents a tool for taxonomy errors evaluation.

5. CONCLUSION

Whereby systematic literature review, 24 related papers which addresses OWL ontology evaluation techniques or tools development were found in 7 electronic sources. We identified 11 quality criteria in literature, as show in Table 1, which we classify in ontology validation and verification: 6 of them applied for ontology validation and 5 for verification. We extract 7 techniques types and 67 techniques for OWL ontology evaluation. As presented in Table 4, we organized 17 papers according techniques, which were classified in 9 quality criteria categories and techniques types.

This research focused efforts on more comprehensive evaluation activities, involving quality criteria for validation and verification process. Validation, to evaluate OWL ontology concepts, with the aim to analyze the proximity of model to the real-world definitions; and the verification criteria, which proposing analyze whether the OWL ontology was built correctly.

Through the systematic literature review, we could identify a deficiency related to amount of automated tools in face of the large number of proposed techniques to conduct the OWL ontology evaluation. However, we also observed which exist effective manual processes available.

Advances in OWL ontology issues was possible observe, once this subject is object of study since mid-1995, being related to OWL ontology accuracy, consistency, and comprehensiveness, especially when it comes of techniques based on reasoners made available by OWL ontologies implementation tools.

Finally, we could detect a lack of research in computational implementation and automated tools development of ontology semantic evaluation.

ACKNOWLEDGEMENT

We thank the support from CAPES and Federal University of Paraná.

REFERENCES

[1] Batet, M. and Sanchez, D., 2014. A Semantic Approach for Ontology Evaluation. 26th International Conference on Tools with Artificial Intelligence. Limassol, Cyprus, pp. 138-145.

[2] Baumeister, J. and Seipel, D., 2005. Smelly Owls-Design Anomalies in Ontologies, Proceedings of 18

th International Florida Artificial Intelligence Research Society Conference. AAAI Press, pp. 215-220.

[3] Baumeister, J. and Seipel, D., 2010. Anomalies in ontologies with rules, Web Semantics: Science, Services and Agents on the World Wide Web, Vol. 8, No. 1, pp. 55-68.

[4] Blomqvist, E. et al, 2012. Ontology testing-methodology and tool, 18th International Conference in Knowledge Engineering and Knowledge Management. Galway City, Ireland, pp. 216-226.

[5] Brewster, C. et al, 2004. Data driven ontology evaluation, International Conference on Language Resources and Evaluation. Lisbon, Portugal.

[6] Bright, T. J. et al, 2012. Development and evaluation of an ontology for guiding appropriate antibiotic prescribing, Journal of biomedical informatics, Vol. 45, No. 1, pp. 120-128.

[7] Burton-Jones, A. et al, 2005. A semiotic metrics suite for assessing the quality of ontologies, Data & Knowledge Engineering, Vol. 55, No. 1, pp. 84-102.

[8] Corcho, O. et al, 2004. ODEval: a tool for evaluating RDF (S), DAML+ OIL, and OWL concept taxonomies, 1st IFIP Conference on Artificial Intelligence Applications and Innovations. Toulouse, France, pp. 9-382.

[9] Dellschaft, K. and Staab, S., 2006. On how to perform a gold standard based evaluation of ontology learning, 5th International Semantic Web Conference. Athens, USA, pp. 228-241.

[10] Duque-Ramos, A. et al, 2011. OQuaRE: A SQuaRE-based approach for evaluating the quality of ontologies, Journal of Research and Practice in Information Technology, Vol. 43, No. 2, pp. 159-173.

[11] Ensan, F. and Weichang, D., 2013. A semantic metrics suite for evaluating modular ontologies, Information Systems, Vol. 38, No. 5, pp. 745-770.

[12] Evermann, J. and Fang, J., 2010. Evaluating ontologies: Towards a cognitive measure of quality, Information Systems, Vol. 35, No. 4, pp. 391-403.

[13] Gangemi, A. et al, 2006. Modelling Ontology Evaluation and Validation. 3rd European Semantic Semantic Web Conference. Budva, Montenegro, pp. 140-154.

[14] García-Ramos, S. et al, 2009. OntologyTest: A Tool to Evaluate Ontologies through Tests Defined by the User. 10th International Work-Conference on Artificial Neural Networks. Salamanca, Spain, pp. 91-98.

[15] Gómez-Pérez, A., 1996. Towards a framework to verify knowledge sharing technology, Expert Systems with Applications, Vol 11, No. 4, pp. 519-529.

[16] Gómez-Pérez, A., 2001. Evaluation of ontologies. International Journal of intelligent systems, Vol. 16, No. 3, pp. 391-409.

[17] Gómez-Pérez, A., 2004. Ontologies Evaluation. Handbook on Ontologies. Springer, pp. 251-273.

[18] Gruber, T. R., 1995. Toward principles for the design of ontologies used for knowledge sharing. International journal of human-computer studies, Vol. 43, No. 5-6, pp. 907-928.

[19] Grüninger, M. and Fox, M. S., 1995. Methodology for the Design and Evaluation of Ontologies. Workshop on Basic Ontological Issues in Knowledge Sharing in International Joint Conference on Artificial Intelligence. Toronto, Canada.

[20] Guarino, N., 1998. Formal ontology in information systems. Proceedings of the 1st International Conference. Trento, Italy, pp. 3-15.

[21] Guarino, N., 2004. Toward a formal evaluation of ontology quality. IEEE intelligent Systems, Vol. 19, No. 4, pp. 78-79.

[22] Hlomani, H. and Stacey, D., 2014. An extension to the data-driven ontology evaluation, 15th International Conference on Information Reuse and Integration. Redwood City, USA, pp. 845-849.

[23] Jianliang, X. and Xiaowei, M., 2008. A web-based ontology evaluation system, 7th International Conference on Advanced Language Processing and Web Information Technology. Liaoning, China, pp. 104-107.

[24] Kitchenham, B., 2004. Procedures for performing systematic reviews. Technical Report, Keele, UK, Keele University, pp. 1-26.

[25] Kitchenham, B., 2007. Guidelines for performing systematic literature reviews in software engineering, EBSE Technical Report, Ver. 2.3.

[26] Köhler, J. et al, 2006. Quality control for terms and definitions in ontologies and taxonomies, BMC bioinformatics, Vol. 7, No. 1, pp. 212-224.

[27] McGuinness, D. L. and Harmelen, F. V., 2004. OWL Web Ontology Language Overview, On-line: http://www.w3.org/TR/owl-features/, july of 2004.

[28] Mulrow, C. D., 1994. Rationale for systematic reviews. British Medical Journal, Vol. 309, No. 9, pp. 597-599.

[29] Ning, H. and Shihan, D. I. A. O., 2006. Structure-based ontology evaluation, IEEE International Conference on e-Business Engineering. Shanghai, China, pp. 132-137.

[30] Obrst, L. et al, 2007. The evaluation of ontologies: Toward Improved Semantic Interoperability. Semantic Web: Revolutionizing Knowledge Discovery in the Life Sciences. Springer US, pp. 139-158.

[31] Porn, A. M. and Peres, L. M., 2014. Mutation Test to OWL Ontologies, 13th International Conference on WWW/Internet. Porto, Portugal, pp. 123-130.

[32] Porzel, R. and Malaka, R., 2004. A task-based approach for ontology evaluation, Proceedings of the Workshop on Ontology Learning and Population at the 16th European Conference on Artificial Intelligence. Valencia, Spain.

[33] Poveda-Villalón, M. et al, 2012. Validating ontologies with OOPS!, 18th International Conference in Knowledge Engineering and Knowledge Management. Galway City, Ireland, pp. 267-281.

[34] Qazi, N. I. and Qadir, M. A., 2010. Algorithms to evaluate ontologies based on extended error taxonomy, International Conference on Information and Emerging Technologies. Karachi, Pakistan, pp. 1-6.

[35] Smith, M. K. et al, 2004. OWL Web Ontology Language Guide, On-line: http://www.w3.org/TR/owl-guide/, july of 2004.

[36] Rieckhof, F. et al, 2011. Formal validation techniques for Ontology-based Device Descriptions, 16th Conference on Emerging Technologies & Factory Automation. Toulouse, France, pp. 1-8.

[37] Suárez-Figueroa, M. C., 2010. NeOn Methodology for building ontology networks: specification, scheduling and reuse. Doctoral Thesis, Madrid, Spain.

[38] Vrandečić, D. and Gangemi, A., 2006. Unit tests for ontologies, On the Move to Meaningful Internet Systems. Montpellier, France, pp. 1012-1020.

[39] Vrandečić, D., 2009. Ontology evaluation. Handbook on Ontologies. Springer, 2nd Edition, pp. 293-313.

[40] Warrender, J. D. and Lord, P., 2015. How, What and Why to test an ontology, The 18th Annual Bio-Ontologies Meeting. Dublin, Ireland.

[41] Yang, Z. et al, 2006. Evaluation metrics for ontology complexity and evolution analysis, IEEE International Conference on e-Business Engineering. Shanghai, China, pp. 162-170.

[42] Yu, J. et al, 2009. Requirements-oriented methodology for evaluating ontologies, Sixteenth ACM Conference on Information Knowledge and Management. Information Systems, Vol. 34, No. 8, pp. 766-791.

AN AGENT-BASED COMPOSITION MODEL FOR SEMANTIC MICROSERVICES

Ivan Salvadori, Alexis Huf and Frank Siqueira
Department of Informatics and Statistics, Federal University of Santa Catarina, Brazil

ABSTRACT

Microservices are replacing the traditional monolithic Web applications by splitting them into multiple small and independent services that work together. Focused on doing one thing with excellence, microservices may be composed to provide more complex capabilities upon a given domain. This paper presents a composition model, aimed at composing semantic microservices for achieving more valuable outcomes. The proposed model is aligned with microservices architectural principles, such as independence of development, high cohesion, loose coupling, organizational alignment, composability, and so on. This paper also presents a reference architecture and a case study for the proposed model.

KEYWORDS

Semantic Web Services; Agents; Microservices; Composition

1. INTRODUCTION

The adoption of microservices is in continued expansion, and traditional monolithic applications are giving way to highly cohesive and loosely coupled sets of services (Newman, 2015). Microservices are designed to provide solutions upon a bounded context within a well-defined domain, resulting in multiple components that communicate and operate together. While some concepts are similar to SOA (Service Oriented Architecture), the focus on loose coupling precludes integration approaches based on central architectural entities, such as the service bus approach, where business logic may be concentrated on a single not cohesive component and highly coupled component. Despite the advantages such as technological decoupling, scaling, easier deployment, and better reuse, the adoption of microservices results in a more complex ecosystem with fragmented functionality, which requires additional communication and cooperation efforts.

Several service composition approaches can be found in the literature. However, there are few proposals that primarily address the microservices architecture. Stubbs et al. (2015) and Florio (2015) have proposed solutions that are specifically focused on microservices. However, their main goal is service monitoring, instead of service composition. Charif and Sabouret (2013) and Kumar (2012) adopt a multi-agent approach for service composition. These solutions could be applied to microservices, however composition does not take into account semantic descriptions neither aspects specific to microservices architecture, such as the distribution of functionality previously present on a single service.

This work presents a composition model for semantic microservices. In this model, microservices functionalities are modeled in terms of concrete desires, in which a given microservice is responsible for implementing operations that result in an outcome aligned with a predefined concept in a domain ontology. The proposed model makes use of agents capable of establishing a communication and negotiation process fulfilling abstract and more expressive desires using the simple concrete desires provided by microservices. This work also presents a reference architecture for the proposed model, which is defined at a higher level and independent from the technological stack employed to develop microservices.

The remainder of this paper is organized as follows: Section 2 summarizes the main concepts related to semantic microservices composition. Section 3 describes related research efforts found in the literature. Section 4 presents the proposed composition model for semantic microservices. A reference architecture is presented in Section 5. An illustrative case study is presented in Section 6. Finally, the conclusions and future work are presented in Section 7.

2. BACKGROUND

According to Newman (2015), microservices are small independent services. These services must be deployed as different artifacts, ideally on different machines and must work together by communicating across a network. There is no widely accepted measure of how small a microservice should be, however some rules of thumb are listed by Newman, such as keeping things that change for the same reason together, and separating things that change for different reasons. By splitting up a monolithic application into several microservices, deployment and maintenance are facilitated. It also makes easier to reach resilience and scalability, since there is no central point of failure, and due to the possibility of scaling only the more demanded microservices. According to Newman (2015), each microservice should be developed and maintained by a single team. This is an important characteristic that makes microservices independent from one another and from developers as well.

Considering that all microservices implement simple tasks, in order to execute more complex tasks, with more valuable outcome, microservices must be composed. According to McIlraith et al. (2001), automatic Web service composition involves the automatic selection, composition and interoperation of services to perform a given task that none of the available services is able to entirely perform. To allow such composition, a richer description of the services is necessary. Semantic Web Services are described with the use of semantic web technologies, allowing the development of complex composition algorithms that take into account the functionalities of services.

Multi-agent systems have a similar definition. Horling and Lesser (2004) define such systems as an aggregation of agents that perform simple tasks in order to fulfill more complex ones. Therefore, multi-agent systems provide a useful paradigm for splitting complex problems into sub-problems that can be solved by the computational elements of the system. In addition, Wooldridge (2009) highlight the potential of such systems for dealing with distributed issues. When a monolithic application is refactored into microservices, the goal is that each microservice implements only a set of highly cohesive simple tasks and is able to operate independently from other microservices, both characteristics also present in agents.

3. RELATED WORK

Stubbs et al. (2015) present a decentralized solution for communication and service discovery in Docker containers with embedded agents. These agents are able to monitor child containers and to emit custom events, in addition to membership messages to inform that containers joined or left the system or suffered a failure. With respect to discovery, membership events allow only simple tagging of services, therefore they do not provide all the required information for service composition.

Florio (2015) proposes a self-adaptive infrastructure based on multi-agent systems for managing multiple microservices deployed into Docker containers. In order to allow the system to scale up, and to improve availability and performance, agents that run a self-adaptive loop are attached to each Docker manager, and coordinate their actions through communication.

Charif and Sabouret (2013) propose a dynamic, decentralized and autonomous approach with four steps for service composition. The first step consists in the service consumer defining its needs, which may be a request for data or for an action to be executed. The second step consists in extracting keywords from the consumer request and in selecting a service based on these keywords. In the third step, services establish a communication process to undertake the consumer request. In this step, agents decompose the request into several feasible sub-tasks. Finally, in the fourth step, the selected services are activated and their responses are forwarded to a mediator capable of verifying that the result is correct. A drawback is that all communication is performed through synchronous messages, therefore the consumer has to wait for the answer, otherwise the process is lost.

Kumar (2012) presents an approach for service selection and composition based on multi-agent systems that adopts the Foundation for Intelligent Physical Agents (FIPA) communication model. In this approach, agents establish a negotiation based on multiple attributes. A dedicated coordinator agent is responsible for service composition. Multiple attributes, such as time consumption, reputation, among others, are combined into a utility value. Negotiation terminates when this utility value reaches a predefined threshold.

Only the first two of these works Stubbs et al. (2015), Florio (2015) have microservices as their primary target architecture, but they do not tackle the service composition problem. On the other hand, the works that leverage multi-agent systems for service composition, while applicable, do not target microservices architectures. These works also do not perform functional composition based on semantic description of services.

4. A COMPOSITION MODEL FOR SEMANTIC MICROSERVICES

Semantic microservices provide semantic descriptions of their capabilities and also manipulate data enriched semantically. In both cases, a RDF syntax such as RDF XML, Turtle, or JSON-LD, among others, is used. The proposed model is based on agents that are able to fulfill one or more desires, each one is applied to a single information element. To fulfill such desires, an agent may directly use a microservice, whose implementation is aligned with the desires and information elements, or it may coordinate other agents in order to fulfill his assigned desire, therefore composing the functionality of the available microservices.

Desires are used to represent a consistent unit of functionality applied to a domain information element. Such functionality is modeled by the application and may be modeled as fine-grained CRUD (Create, Read, Update and Delete) operations on specific domain classes, or as coarse-grained domain processes to be dynamically orchestrated. The granularity and number of desires to be provided by a single microservice is largely determined by the application domain. The goal in designing microservices, however, should be on minimizing both of these aspects while respecting the Single Responsibility Principle and taking into consideration the business boundaries as explained in (Newman, 2015).

In this model, desires are ontology individuals of a desire class, applied to an information element, which is also a class. A summarization of the ontology used to describe desires is shown in Figure 1. For example, suppose that in a public security domain, a client has the desire to obtain the criminal record of a person. In this case "get" would be modeled as a desire, and microservices providing the *GetInformation* (*CriminalRecord*) desire would provide functionality to this end. Desires document both customer needs and microservices, and are used to govern the microservice composition approach as described in this section.

```
usa:Desire a owl:Class .
usa:CompositeDesire a owl:Class.
usa:InformationElement a owl:Class .

usa:informationElement
    a owl:ObjecProperty;    rdfs:domain usa:Desire;           rdfs:range usa:informationElement.
usa:relatedDesire
    a owl:ObjecProperty;    rdfs:domain usa:CompositeDesire;  rdfs:range usa:Desire .
```

Figure 1. Summarized μSA (μService Agents) ontology, in Turtle syntax

There are three types of agents in this model: service, composing and client agents. A service agent is associated with a single microservice and has the purpose of representing the microservice in bidding processes. The service agent extracts all *concrete desires* from the microservice semantic description and registers them as provided desires. The composing agent, on the other hand, provides a single desire, which is described by an ontology as a *composite desire*. Composite desires are satisfied by fulfilling all documented related desires, in an order determined by the inputs and outputs of the selected agents and by the data provided to the composing agent. The third type of agent, a *client agent*, represents the client and coordinates the bidding process. This type of agent does not fulfill any desire directly.

Desires can be classified as either *concrete* or *abstract*, the former being a desire that can be completely fulfilled by a single microservice, and the later are those that cannot. In addition to composite desires, abstract desires include those for which only desires involving subclasses of the information element are offered by agents in the system. For this type of abstract desire, the information element hierarchy provides the information necessary for composing the available microservices. Both composition types are non-exclusive and may be combined in any order.

Since abstract desires provide more valuable results to service consumers, they demand more implementation effort in terms of functionality, development and time. Concrete desires, however, are easier to implement, require less code and may be developed and maintained by a single team. The characteristics of concrete desires are similar to the microservices principles, which make microservices suitable for developing this type of desire. However, it is important to provide to service consumers more valuable results that can be achieved by combining concrete desires. In terms of services, the process of combining desires is referred to as microservices composition. Hence, the proposed model aims to produce a microservices composition method capable of producing more valuable results that were not available previously.

Hierarchical composition is performed as part of the bidding process, where the client agent broadcasts the bidding of the target desire to all desire-providing agents. Each agent replies with a bid specifying how it participates in fulfilling the desire and a set of non-functional parameters. In order to fulfill a desire $d(e)$, the set of desires offered during the bidding that are to be fulfilled is given by $\{d(e_i\ )$ s.t. $e_i \in E\}$, where $E = \{e_1,e_2,...,e_n\}$ and for all $e_i \in E$, e_i is equivalent to or subclass of e, and there is no $e_j \in E$ s.t. e_j is a subclass of e_i . For each $d(e_i)$ to be fulfilled, there may be more than one agent providing the desire, and in such situation, the agents are considered to be in competition. Competition is solved by using non-functional parameters of the providing agents, prevailing only the agent with the best parameters.

Considering the second type of composition, from the composite desire definition the agent knows that fulfilling the set of related desires, in any order, is both necessary and sufficient to fulfill the composite desire. Knowing this, the composing agent is responsible for bidding the fulfillment of each related desire, as previously described, and for selecting providers for each of them. Given all selected providers, the agent must then compute a possible workflow, taking into consideration the input/output descriptions provided by the selected agents. If, given the input data provided by the client, the workflow cannot be built, the failure is forwarded to the client with an explanation of the missing data.

In both composition types, the data produced by selected agents must be combined by the coordinating agent before it is returned to its client (another agent or the end user). Such combination is also necessary when a workflow computed by a composing agent is executed, and outputs obtained in previous steps need to be used as inputs on the next steps. If RDF is used ubiquitously by the semantic microservices, the underlying data model allows such combination to be trivially performed as a union of the RDF graphs. In fact, if the microservice architecture is obtained by decomposing a monolith that happens to consume and produce RDF, the only change on the client would be the need to specify his desire.

An application of the desire metaphor and this composition model is offering action-driven services on top of data-driven microservices. Data-driven microservices manage information elements and allow only basic operations, such as those specified by the HTTP *GET*, *PUT*, *POST* and *DELETE* verbs. These basic operations enforce basic business rules related to data validation and resources state. Domain specific actions can be defined as combinations of these domain-independent operations on information elements, and the complexity of combining these operations to achieve a business goal can be abstracted. Furthermore, the workflow for accomplishing the business goals is dynamically constructed from the current available microservices.

5. REFERENCE ARCHITECTURE

A reference architecture for the application of the composition model previously presented is shown in Figure 2. The architecture includes two infrastructural (Richards, 2015) microservices and the three previously mentioned agent types. The infrastructural Common Knowledge microservice stores all the information necessary for reasoning about desires and information elements, as well as the definition of the composite desires. The conversation repository acts as a bridge between the consumers from the external environment and the agents, by providing an HTTP interface to a message-based bidirectional channel between the consumer and a Client Agent allocated for that conversation. Conversations allow a prompt response to the client, which must not remain blocked while the desire is fulfilled.

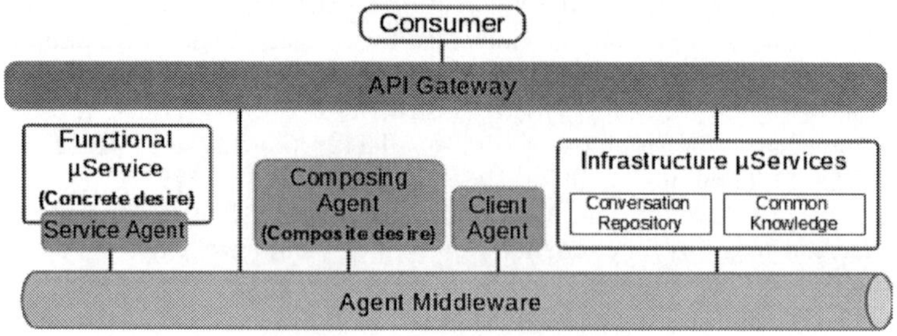

Figure 2. The reference architecture

The API Gateway assigns an idle client agent selected from a pool for each conversation. Both the desire and the provided input data given by the external consumer are forwarded to the client agent, which starts the bidding process (see section 4). Once the bidding process is complete, the client agent requests the fulfillment of the desire to all selected agents. Finally, the client agent combines the outputs received from the selected agents and forwards them to the client through the conversation repository.

It is mandatory that a service agent be able to understand the functionality exposed by the service it represents. While high-level functionality is modeled by desires and information elements, invocation details are also necessary, and can be described using existing service description languages. In the same way that microservices can be implemented using different technologies, no particular description language is recommended for use with the reference architecture. One example of such language is WSMO-Lite, which can be used to describe both SOAP and REST services (Roman et al., 2014).

Microservice environments also have the characteristic of high dynamism, with new microservices being made available and in some cases even competing with existing services. An agent middleware provides infrastructural support for agent discovery and for the implementation of negotiation protocols such as the one proposed in Section 4.

6. CASE STUDY

This section describes the application of the proposed composition model through a simplified case study based on an a system managing criminal, financial and immigration information about persons. This example demonstrates the details on how the composition model can be applied to a microservice architecture. It also shows how microservices are selected, composed and activated in order to fulfill a given desire.

Composition is driven by an ontology that describes the domain elements and desires that can be fulfilled in such domain. Figure 3 shows the domain ontology modeled for the case study. The entities on the left define the information elements managed by the system, while the entities to the right are desire classes that could be satisfied by microservices. Instances of the desire classes must be applied to information elements. For example, to register a criminal record, the desire instance would be *Register(CriminalRecord)*.

Microservices implementations are aligned with the desires defined in the domain ontology, which means that a microservice should implement one or more functions that lead to the complete fulfillment of a desire. Note that the desire abstraction need not be present in the microservice implementation, but the service agent must be able to map a desire to a set of operations on the microservice.

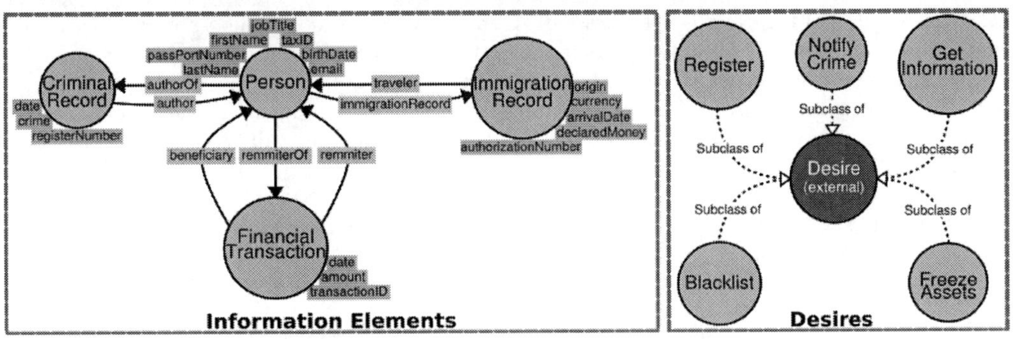

Figure 3. The case study domain ontology

The components of the case study are shown in Figure 4. The criminal records, immigration (travel) records, financial transactions and personal data were generated using the Mockaroo tool. In this example, for all information elements but Person, data is fragmented. This fragmentation simulates the fact that as actual data would be under responsibility of different organizations, different structures and technologies would be required to access this data, therefore different teams would each develop a different microservice for each data source. To avoid unnecessary complexity, instead of countries, only four regions (South America, North America, Asia and Europe), and two law enforcement agencies (Interpol and FBI) were considered. The symbol * beside information elements of the provided desires in Figure 4 represents that the microservice provides the desire not on the listed information element, but on a subclass of it.

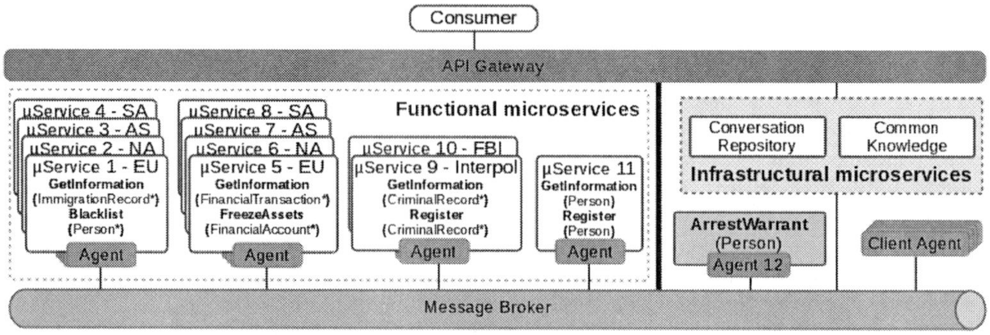

Figure 4. The use case components in the reference architecture

Figure 5 shows what a consumer would send to his client agent through the conversation repository in order to fulfill the *GetInformation*(*CriminalRecord*) desire on a person with a given tax ID. During the bidding process, only the agents associated with microservices 9 and 10 will place bids. Since there is no bid of greater value than these two, and these microservices are not in a competition state (as both offered subclasses of *CriminalRecord*), both will be invoked in order to fulfill the desire. The client agent that coordinated the bidding process will receive the output from both microservices and combine the two RDF graphs into a single graph that constitutes the response for the desire.

```
[ a secd:GetInformation; usa:informationElement sec:CriminalRecord ].
[ sec:taxID "733-11716-531-23" ].
```

Figure 5. Example of a desire to get Criminal Records from a person's tax ID

```
[    a secd:NotifyCrime
     usa:informationElement sec:CriminalRecord ;
     usa:relatedDesire
          [ a sec:Register; usa:informationElement sec:CriminalRecord ] ,
          [ a sec:GetInformation; usa:informationElement sec:Person ] ,
          [ a secd:Blacklist; usa:informationElement sec:Person ] ,
          [ a secd:FreezeAssets; usa:informationElement sec:Person ]        ] .
```

Figure 6. Example definition of a composite desire.

An example of a composite desire is *NotifyCrime*(*CriminalRecord*), defined in Figure 6. During the bidding process, the only agent to place a bid will be Agent 12. From the definition, the agent knows it has to fulfill four desires, but the order is not specified. Agent 12 coordinates a bidding process for each of the four related desires, and with all selected agents in hand, it must match the documented inputs and outputs with the agent input in order to establish a workflow.

During the negotiation that leads to the workflow definition, the agents do not exchange input/output documentations, but instead negotiate by exchanging sample data and validation results. The workflow is assembled as a sequence of layers, where the outputs of a layer are combined with the inputs to form the inputs of the next layer. The first layer includes all selected agents that accepted the data provided by the client as valid input. The i-th layer is composed by all agents that were not chosen for previous layers that accepted the merged inputs and outputs of the $(i-1)$-th layer as their input. Execution of the workflow follows the same logic as the workflow definition, except that actual data from the fulfillment of desires is used.

In this prototype, the input and output documentation of the agents for fulfilling a desire is given by SPIN (http://spinrdf.org/) constraints. Inputs are documented with either ASK or CONSTRUCT rules, while outputs are documented with ASK queries. This restriction on the output documentation is necessary so that the service agents are able to produce example output data. Service agents must extract the desires and construct the associated SPIN documentation from the microservices semantic description.

The adopted agent middleware was JADE (Java Agent Development Framework) and the microservices were implemented using Spring Boot. Due to the small scale of the environment, a single agent platform was sufficient to host all agents. The processing overhead, not including communication overhead introduced by the composition algorithm, was evaluated for both desires discussed in this section on an Intel i5 with 3.10GHz and OpenJDK 1.8.0_02-b14. The execution details and results are available in a public repository at https://dx.doi.org/10.6084/m9.figshare.3856155. Each test sample involves configuring the whole environment, but the same JVM instance is reused. In the following conclusions, the first sample is discarded due to lazy initializations.

For the desire shown in Figure 5, the average overhead is 2.016 ± 0.109 milliseconds at 99% confidence. The desire shown in Figure 6 requires the evaluation of SPIN input constraints 16 times and the results for 200 runs is shown in Figure 7. The jitter in the first samples is due to the JVM Just-in-time compiler and such effects are not observed if the JVM is set to interpret-only mode (-Xint). The coefficient of variation (σ/μ) for total time in Figure 7 is 0.360 ms, however, with -Xint JVM option, it is only 0.0219 even with an average of 249.183 ± 0.729 milliseconds. For both desires, SPIN constraints checking is the most expensive operation, amounting to 62.188% ± 0.409% for the desire in Figure 5 and 61.702% ± 0.169% for the desire in Figure 6, both at 99% confidence.

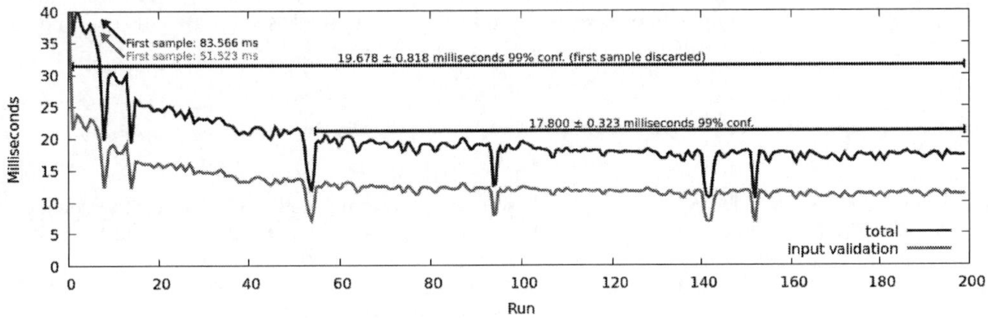

Figure 7. Processing overhead times for fulfilling a *NotifyCrime* desire

7. DISCUSSION

Similar to Kumar (2012), the service composition model described in Section 4 relies on a coordinator. However, instead of minimizing a utility value, agents cooperate to directly decompose a task identified by a desire applied to an information element. In comparison with Charif and Sabouret (2013), the proposed composition model defines user requests using the same modeling as is used to document the microservices, and does not relies on keyword extraction nor on a mediator to verify results.

With respect to how the composition is achieved, there is a distinction between planning techniques that consider pre- and post-conditions, such as Klusch et al. (2005), and the more numerous techniques that use a graph of services connected by their I/O parameters, such as Rodrigez-Mier et al. (2016). The abstraction of an *information element* corresponds to an input and a *desire*, at a large granularity, corresponds to a combination of outputs, pre- and post-conditions. This large granularity has two features that justify its adoption for microservice architectures. (1) It documents functionality at suitable level for decomposition into microservices. (2) Composite desires can be defined from other desires, which is a middle ground between common planning-based service composition and process templates. Therefore the composition model fits better for microservice architectures than traditional composition methods.

The main difference of the proposed composition model from existing service composition techniques is the direct targeting of the approach to microservice architectures. The fragmentation of functionality previously present on a monolithic application into several cohesive and decoupled microservices naturally creates the need for composition of services. The abstraction of a *desire* applied to an *information element* is intended to describe units of functionality offered by the microservices. It is also used for specification of composition requests eases evolution of the architecture by allowing microservices to be replaced by agents.

8. CONCLUSIONS AND FUTURE WORK

This paper presented a composition model and a reference architecture for discovering and composing microservices, supported by a multi-agent system. In our proposal, microservices can be easily and dynamically added to the system, as the agents that are associated to them have no distinctive traits when started. Composition is guided by agents that fulfill a desire, as would a microservice. The adopted metaphor of desires is strongly related to the microservices architecture and also serves as a guideline during decomposition of a monolith into microservices.

Microservices are a recent architectural model that aims to reduce coupling and to build highly scalable and reliable systems. While container technologies, such as Docker, provide rudimentary service discovery capabilities, bridging customer needs to the offered microservices is still a problem to be solved. In our work we address this problem with service composition. Unlike BPEL engines, common in more traditional SOA environments, the process to fulfill the user needs is dynamically discovered and executed by agents.

More complex compositions are likely to arise when the available services are not described by a single ontology. Third party services and ontologies introduce not only heterogeneity, but also bring numerous additional possibilities for composite processes. In future work, the proposed architecture will be adapted and applied to such more complex and heterogeneous environment.

REFERENCES

Yasmine Charif and Nicolas Sabouret, 2013. Dynamic service composition enabled by introspective agent coordination. *Autonomous Agents and Multi-Agent Systems*, vol. 26 issue 1 pp. 54–85. ISSN 1387-2532. doi: 10.1007/s10458-011-9182-5.

Luca Florio, 2015. Decentralized self-adaptation in large-scale distributed systems. *Proceedings of the 2015 10th Joint Meeting on Foundations of Software Engineering - ESEC/FSE 2015*, pp. 1022–1025, New York, New York, USA, 2015. ACM Press. ISBN 9781450336758. doi: 10.1145/2786805.2803192

Bryan Horling and Victor Lesser, 2004. A survey of multi-agent organizational paradigms. *The Knowledge Engineering Review*, vol. 19 issue 4, pp. 281–316. ISSN 1469-8005. doi: 10.1017/S0269888905000317.

Sandeep Kumar, 2012. Agent-based semantic web service selection and composition. *Agent-Based Semantic Web Service Composition*, SpringerBriefs in Electrical and Computer Engineering, pp. 15–25. Springer New York, 2012. ISBN 978-1-4614-4662-0. doi: 10.1007/978-1-4614-4663-7_3.

Karl Matthias and Sean P Kane, 2015. *Docker: Up and Running*. O'Reilly Media, Inc., Gravenstein Highway North, Sebastopol, CA 95472, USA.. ISBN 9781491917572.

Matthias Klusch et al, 2005. Semantic web service composition planning with OWLS-Xplan *AAAI Fall Symposium on Semantic Web and Agents*, Vol. 5.

S.a. McIlraith, et al, 2001. Semantic Web services. *IEEE Intelligent Systems*, vol. 16 issue 2 pp. 46–53. ISSN 1541-1672. doi: 10.1109/5254.920599.

Sam Newman, 2015. *Building Microservices*. O'Reilly Media, Gravenstein Highway North, Sebastopol, CA. USA. ISBN 9781491950357.

Rodriguez-Mier P, 2016. An Integrated Semantic Web Service Discovery and Composition Framework. *IEEE Transactions on Services Computing*, vol. 9 issue 4 pp. 537-550. ISSN 1939-1374. doi: 10.1109/TSC.2015.2402679.

Mark Richards, 2015. *Microservices vs. Service-Oriented Architecture*. O'Reilly Media, Inc., 1005 Gravenstein Highway North, Sebastopol, CA 95472. O'Reilly. ISBN 9781491952429.

Dumitru Roman, et al,2014. WSMO-Lite and hRESTS: Lightweight semantic annotations for Web services and RESTful APIs. *Web Semantics: Science, Services and Agents on the World Wide Web*, vol. 31: pp. 39–58. ISSN 15708268.

Joe Stubbs, et al, 2015. Distributed Systems of Microservices Using Docker and Serfnode. *7th International Workshop on Science Gateways*, Budapest, Hungary, pp. 34–39. ISBN 978-1-4673-7459-0. doi: 10.1109/IWSG.2015.16.

Michael Wooldridge, 2009. *An Introduction to MultiAgent Systems*. Wiley Publishing, 2nd edition. ISBN 0470519460, 9780470519462.

SEMANTIC PUBLISHING AS A TOOL IN SMART, SELF-PROTECTIVE CRITICAL INFRASTRUCTURE

Anastasiia Girka
University of Jyväskylä, the Faculty of Information technology
P.O. Box 35 (Agora) FI-40014 Jyväskylä, Finland

ABSTRACT

Semantic publishing as a semantic representation of publications makes articles machine-readable. It involves linking an article with another articles and external sources. Also, data provided along with the publication can be made machine-readable, which allows visualizing the data in different ways according to a reader's needs. This kind of semantic technology deployed on physics domain can serve for improving interoperability in critical infrastructure as far as it includes such facilities as atomic power stations, atomic plants and local experimental atomic devices, experimental fusion reactors and demonstration fusion reactors among others. Having shared terminology and data represented in different ways, services and units of critical infrastructure may communicate more effectively. At first, it may help staff members of the critical infrastructure facilities in making decisions, but since information becomes machine-readable this approach may exclude the human factor from the issue of the security of the critical infrastructure at all. This paper gives proposition for improvement of the current state of semantic publishing in physics domain, particularly, utilizing SPAR suit of ontologies that is designed for semantic publishing, and open problem ontology that was developed within the work on this paper.

KEYWORDS

Semantic publishing, semantic representation of documents, ontology in physics

1. INTRODUCTION

Instrumentation and control systems at nuclear facilities, related to critical infrastructure, are intended for secure control of complex processes, which may cause harm for people and/or the environment. Among such facilities, one can distinguish [Foundations, 1997] foremost, atomic power stations, atomic plants and local experimental atomic devices, experimental fusion reactors and demonstration fusion reactors. Undoubtedly, the mentioned control systems require protection, whilst nowadays the security function can be a part of the system as a self-protective feature of the autonomic system [Hinchey, 2006].

There are two main reasons for the accidents at nuclear facilities: one of them is external attacks, and another one is software failures, the latter are often compounded by human error [Byres-2004]. Thus, the improvement of control systems is an important issue for the industry, which can be solved only with a joint effort of physicists and computer scientists.

Hence, the purpose of the present research, a part of which is the current paper, is to find a more efficient way of personnel and units intercommunication within a critical infrastructure by using a formal and shared knowledge of the infrastructure. In other words, the objective is to improve interoperability between different services, tools and systems for better understanding among each other, and to become more efficient and enhanced in the sense of cyber security consequently.

Nowadays, searching the Web is inefficient because the search engine is looking for text or picture matches, but very often generalizations are used as search words, which leads to insufficient searching results. Especially it matters when Web is used for scientific research [Hendler, 2003]. Thus, Artificial Intelligence (AI) presents with a new generation of Web technology, namely the Semantic Web that implements machine-readable descriptions (annotations) of Web resources and machine-readable thesauruses (ontologies). This approach will help to establish links between generalizations and specific concepts, moreover, the links may appear where relationships are currently unsuspected, and in other words, it will make the web-search smart.

This paper includes an overview of the semantic publishing state-of-art and ontologies in physics that exist at the present time. The paper makes a proposition to apply an approach of semantic publishing in documents representation in critical infrastructure.

2. SEMANTIC ANNOTATION AND PUBLISHING OF ARTICLES IN PHYSICS

2.1 Demand for Semantic Publishing

Scientists write articles and publish them for a number of reasons such as to secure intellectual property, to share results in the community as well as their job is evaluated by a number of the articles and their quality. The shared results imply a wide accessibility to materials; however, the current format of scientific journals, even though most of them are nowadays online, does not meet the requirement of accessibility. This happens because of search on the Web is processed in an ineffective manner, because there are no semantic technologies utilized in the Web as well as there is no semantic annotation of sites. The most popular format of scientific report files is PDF and it is perhaps convenient for readers, but a PDF file is not machine-readable in the current form in a sense that search engines are not able to "understand" the content of the files. Hence, the semantic annotation and publishing of scientific reports will bring a significant improvement in accessibility to scientific results and, thus, will make sharing more effective.

Another important point is disambiguation in using terms. Although, authors of scientific articles aim to be precise in wording, the disambiguation still may come from using terms in different sub-communities, moreover, different mother tongues may introduce even more misunderstanding. These problems are addressed by semantic technologies.

The semantic annotation approach for scientific purposes arose in 2005 with a YeastHub web-based application [Cheung, 2005], which is, in a nutshell, a biology data warehouse based on RDF technology. Then, the term semantic publishing appeared in 2009 by virtue of D. Shotton. In his article [Shotton, 2009b] he described how authors, publishers, and readers would benefit from semantic publishing and what it would cost them. Nevertheless, his conclusion is univocal: "publishers, who continue to offer traditional 'text' journals, whether these are in print or online, will lose out" [Shotton, 2009b]. Confirmation for his claim might be seen by a fact that one of the major academic publishers, Elsevier, conducted so called Elsevier Grand Challenge contest (www.elseviergrandchallenge.com), which was intended to find the best solutions in semantic publishing in the domain of life sciences.

In the same article [Shotton, 2009b], D. Shotton said that some Scientific, Technical, and Medical Publishers (STM publishers) and software companies (for example, Microsoft) have already demonstrated a number of advantages provided by semantic technologies, when utilized XML markups in all software systems. However, XML does reveal the full power of semantic technologies, because there is still place for the disambiguity, since the nesting structure in XML document can be interpreted in many ways. Thereafter, D. Shotton claims that more effort should be made for developing approaches in the semantic publishing.

2.2 State of Art in Semantic Publishing

In another article [Shotton, 2009a] David Shotton gives the determination of term semantic publishing as the following: "to include anything that enhances the meaning of the published journal article, facilitates its automated discovery, enables its linking to semantically related articles, provides access to data within the article in actionable form, or facilitates integration of data between articles". There is another definition from the main page of David Shotton's web-blog about semantic publishing [Semantic publishing]: "Semantic publishing is the enhancement of scholarly publications by the use of modern web standards to improve interactivity, openness, and usability, including the use of ontologies to encode rich semantics in the form of machine-readable RDF metadata".

In the same article, D. Shotton describes an example of semantically published article in biology. The example includes "semantic markup of textual terms, which links to relevant third-party information resources", which is RDFa and means HTML pages enriched with RDF, machine-readable reference list as separate RDF file and machine-readable self-referencing metadata in separate RDF file. Some useful enrichment has been done manually such as tag cloud and tag tree.

It is worth to say, that progress in developing ontologies and using semantic technologies in the domain of biology, in general, is much higher than in physics. For instance, there is the Semantic Biochemical Journal experiment where the Utopia Documents software suit was exploited [Attwood, 2010].

In simple words, Utopia Documents is a PDF processor, but it makes articles semantically enriched. Utopia Documents software connects terms from an article with an external online resources such as Wikipedia, UniProtKB, PDB, etc., it links references to their online versions. Utopia Documents using Bio2RDF project, which has SPARQL and REST interfaces, and DBPedia. It is based on Utopia toolkit [Pettifer, 2009], which has an exemplary architecture (Figure 1).

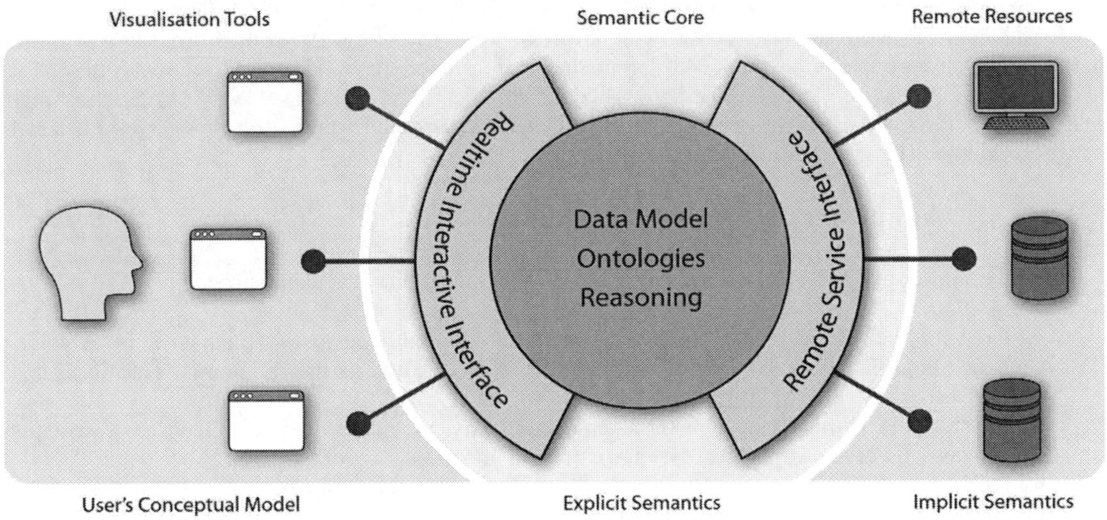

Figure 1. The semantic architecture of Utopia toolkit. (credits: Pettifer, Steve, et al., 2009 Visualising biological data: a semantic approach to tool and database integration. *BMC bioinformatics* 10.Suppl 6: S19). "The Utopia architecture consists broadly of three layers: the visualization tools, which encapsulate the User's Conceptual Model; the core, which encodes and reasons over explicit semantics in its data model; and finally, the remote resources and third-party tools with their implicit semantics"

In addition to representation the text of an article by power of semantic technology, the semantic publishing implies access to data used in the article. The approach implies embedded tools to work with data, for example plotting graphs. The approach of interactive publishing is very attractive and plays a big role in semantic publishing, but it diverts away from the topic of semantic technologies. Visualization tools are desirable, but they are on the second place after the knowledge engineering conception.

Here were mentioned a couple of examples of the semantic publishing efforts in the biology domain, but even more of such examples can be still given. There is a Semantic Scholar web-service (https://www.semanticscholar.org/) for searching scientific articles, which uses semantic technologies approach. Its approach is slightly different from the semantic publishing, because it is based on using machine learning techniques, methods from data mining, natural language processing, and computer vision. The algorithm analyzes an article as a PDF file and extracts keywords, phrases, and important features as figures, tables, and citations, so that originally articles do not have any semantic annotation or metadata. However, this search engine deals only with articles in computer sciences.

Semantic publishing and processing of articles is a growing branch, but in the physics domain it is not developed so far as in biology or computer sciences, for instance.

3. ONTOLOGY OF PHYSICS

3.1 The Need of Ontology of Physics

The need of ontology in the physics domain for semantic publishing was discusses in the Introduction, but there are more other important applications in the physics domain. The Department of Defense Modeling and Simulation community (USA) is interested in ontology of physics for describing physical-based models in order to provide an interoperability of the simulation modules [Collins, 2004a]. When scientists build a simulation model, many assumptions stay hidden even from other experts in the field, despite of the experts in the field may have a common understanding of the background concepts. Therefore, this problem can be addressed by semantic technology, since a comprehensive description of the model is required. Another application for the ontology is to create electronic repositories of scientific papers and provide a shared use of them. This is very similar to semantic publishing in a sense of semantic annotation of articles, but these applications are organized differently.

The applications mentioned above were expressed by Dr. Josef B. Collins from Naval Research Laboratory in his paper [Collins, 2004b], particularly, he claimed that he communicated with the following organizations: American Physical Society (APS), the American Astronomical Society (AAS), the American Institute of Physics (AIP), and the International Union of Pure and Applied Physics (IUPAP), that have expressed interest in electronic document repositories.

3.2 XML Approach for Ontology of Physics

There are number of XML applications that are applicable for physics text annotation:

- Content MathML [Collins, 2005] - Mathematics Markup Language (MathML), namely its part Content MathML allows to annotate complex equation, such as partial differential equations, that are widely utilized for representing physical dynamics.
- PhysML - a markup language for documenting physics knowledge; it includes representation of natural laws, observables, physical systems and experiments.
- OpenMath provides content dictionaries for operations on quantities (namely SI quantities and units [Collins, 2009]), numerical representation of quantities, the concept of standard error, but it does not provide proper treatment of uncertainties. There is a content dictionary for tensor concepts [Collins, 2010], additionally.
- OMDoc (Open Mathematical Documents) [Collins, 2008] - a markup format for annotating mathematical and physical knowledge, which uses Content MathML, OpenMath, and PhysML. There is also an RDFa extension of OMDoc [Lange, 2011].

According to W3 consortium, XML and its applications are part of the semantic web technologies [W3C-FAQ], but it has different from RDF and OWL area of usage. RDF is more robust against changing of Schemas and Ontologies, when XML is versus Schemas, as it is stated by W3C [W3C-FAQ]. Unlike to markup languages, OWL ontologies allow reasoning on themselves; SPARQL queries are applicable to RDF annotations. The drawback of XML is that the structure of the document does not provide an explicit interpretation of data and nesting can be interpreted in many ways. Nevertheless, those XML vocabularies and content dictionaries may serve as a base for future work of developing OWL ontologies.

3.3 OWL/RDF Approach for Ontology of Physics

There are also achievements in RDF-OWL, for example, there is sedOnto (**S**ynthetic **E**nvironment **D**ata Representation **Onto**logy) [Bhatt, 2004]. The term "synthetic environment" means the depiction of the environment in a digital form (http://www.sedris.org/definition.htm). It is based on **S**ynthetic **E**nvironment **D**ata **R**epresentation and **I**nterchange **S**pecification Data Representation Model (SEDRIS DRM) and is designed to be used within the modeling and simulation domain for representation of data related to Synthetic Environment. One of the functions of SEDRIS is a representation of environmental data with help of DRM, which consists of a bunch of object-oriented classes represented in UML. In other words, DRM was mapped into OWL ontology utilizing Protégé development environment (http://protege.stanford.edu). Another achievement is QUDT ontologies (http://www.qudt.org/), which are combination of ontologies of **Q**uantities, **U**nits, **D**imensions and Data **T**ypes, and were developed for the NASA Exploration Initiatives Ontology Models project.

4. SEMANTIC PUBLISHING IN THE DOMAIN OF PHYSICS

4.1 Common Features of a Content of an Article in Physics

Any published scientific article has a title, author(s), bibliographic properties, sections, citations, and a list of references. In addition, any article refers to some opened problem in the field and usually, but not always, it has annotation and list of keywords. Besides the content of articles, there is a structure of articles, which also may carry essential information. It concerns to rhetorical components (abstract, introduction, discussion, methods, and conclusion) rather than to structural components (paragraph, section, and chapter).

Semantic Publishing and Referencing (SPAR) Ontologies are suit of OWL2 ontologies encoded using RDF [Peroni, 2014]. They cover the whole publishing domain. One example among SPAR ontologies, the Citation Typing Ontology (CiTO), was developed by D. Shotton et al. during the work on the example of semantically published article [Shotton, 2009a]. The alternative Bibliographic Ontology (http://bibliontology.com/) is an application of RDF to describe basic concepts and properties of citations and references. Scholarly Article Ontology (http://ns.science.ai/) is another possibility to describe a publication with terms defined in RDF Schema. However, it is more reasonable to use SPAR Ontologies, since they are designed for semantic publishing and referencing purposes and have the biggest scope.

The typical scientific article consists of a narrative part and some kind of data regardless whether it is qualitative research or quantitative; most of the scientific articles in natural sciences may include plots, schemes, tables. A narrative part is typically full of terms and concepts. The data content of scientific articles in physics is different, depending on theoretical or experimental origin of the article. A theoretical article typically includes complex and sophisticated equations and numerical methods of solving equations. Whereas, the experimental article includes numbers, units, errors, data performing methods, and equations are needed sometimes in an experimental article as well, at least fundamental physical laws and, for example, an approximation functions.

Representation of mathematical equations is a nontrivial problem for semantic technologies. There are examples of XML applications presented in Section 2.2 that address this problem, but these applications are not the same as semantic ontologies. However, there are some ontologies that address representation of mathematical equations. For example, there is an extension to OWL for defining data ranges in terms of linear (in)equalities with rational coefficients solved over the algebraic reals [Data range extension, 2012]. However, transcendental functions are not permitted as well as non-linear polynomials. Withal, there is no strong need for the tools for annotation of mathematical equations in the case of the annotation of a scientific article, because the ontologies of the equation types, fundamental physical laws, and named formulae would be enough.

4.2 The ScienceWISE System

Although, there is no strong need for annotation of mathematical equations, there is a need in ontology of physics in every specific subfield. Fortunately, there is a ScienceWISE web-service (http://sciencewise.info/), which is a platform for semantical annotation of the research articles. WISE in the name stands for **W**eb-based **I**nteractive **S**emantic **E**nvironment. The ScienceWISE project was established by the group of physicists from Ecole Polytecnique Federale de Lausanne (EPFL), Switzerland, and CERN in collaboration with computer scientists from EPFL, the University of Fribourg and Vrije Universiteit Amsterdam, Netherlands. The goal of the project is to organize the scientific knowledge in the domain of physics, however, the ScienceWISE is designed in such a way that it can be used by scientists from any field: nowadays they have Life Sciences, Digital Humanities, and Information Technologies sections under construction. The project has a connection to ArXiv.org, the CERN Document Server and also Inspire (comprehensive bibliographic database in high-energy).

The basic principal of the project implies that scientists create and edit their specific ontologies within the framework of the project by the instrumentality of the ScienceWISE portal. The scientific article can be annotated with the number of concepts that consist in ontologies, alternatively the article from the ArXiv.org archive may be bookmarked automatically, and afterward, a user can edit this annotation. As a result, article or author can be searched by one or more concepts. Currently, the ScienceWISE ontology contents more than 60 000 unique entries, each with its own definitions, alternative forms, and semantic relations to other entries [Aberer, 2011; Boyarsky, 2013]. There are several hundreds of active users. The users of the project were and are mostly physicists [Boyarsky, 2015], thus the most described ontology is in physics. Particularly, there are subcategories of astrophysics and cosmology, atomic, molecular and condensed matter physics, nuclear physics, particle physics, plasma physics and a number of others and each of them has thousands of articles related and allocated on the ScienceWISE.

The project has been started using Semantic Web technologies some time ago, performing the "RDFization" of the ontology, as they called it [Boyarsky, 2015], and now it is available in RDF format. ScienceWISE ontology has links to DBpedia, Wikipedia and SKOS ontology through the RDF property "sameAs".

Uniqueness and merit of this project are that it involves specific-domain scientists into the process of ontology developing, providing them convenient interface. As a result, ScienceWISE includes the biggest ontology of physics, which is continually growing.

4.3 The Proposition of Semantic Annotation of an Article in Physics

Taking to account a current state-of-art in semantic publishing and physics, the need of semantic processing of scientific articles in physics is evident. The needed result is a possibility of efficient browsing through the scientific articles in physics with semantically rich querying, for example, "*Find all articles which have particular subject terms*". Thus, the demanded end-product is a combination of search engine and representation system for scientific articles in physics.

The semantic enrichment of articles is a key task here, since semantic querying can be applied only on machine-readable documents. This can be done automatically utilizing Natural Language Processing and Linked Open Data-based entity detection as claimed by Bahar Sateli and René Witte [Sateli, 2015]. This means that no manual effort in annotating from publishers or authors is not required. Semantic vocabularies (ontologies) are the last element needed. There are several public ontologies for semantic publishing as it was stated in Section 3.1. and there is a big ontology of physics terms and concepts namely ScienceWISE (Section 3.2.), but it is not in public access.

The following example of annotating a scientific article was designed based on examples given for SPAR suit of ontologies [Peroni, 2015]. In the example, the FaBiO ontology from the SPAR suit was used and the ScienceWISE ontology (a version of 2014 year). FRBR, DC Terms, and PRISM ontologies were used too, since they are used in FaBiO. In addition, the FOAF ontology was used to annotate persons and XML Schema ontology since it contains basic data types.

```
@prefix : <http://www.example-site.net/example_ontology> .
@prefix fabio: <http://purl.org/spar/fabio/> .
@prefix dcterms: <http://purl.org/dc/terms/> .
@prefix frbr: <http://purl.org/vocab/frbr/core#> .
@prefix xsd: <http://www.w3.org/2001/XMLSchema#> .
@prefix prism: <http://prismstandart.org/namespaces/basic/2.0/> .
@prefix application: <http://purl.org/NET/mediatypes/application/> .
@prefix foaf: <http://xmlns.com/foaf/0.1/> .
@prefix swconcept: <http://data.sciencewise.info/concept/> .
#
#:param_o-modes a fabio:ResearchPaper ;
        dcterms:creator :vogirka , :avgirka , :vvyarko ;
        frbr:realization :published_item ;
        fabio:hasSubjectTerm swconcept:Plasma ,
```

```
            swconcept: Plasma_physics ,
            swconcept: Maxwell's_equations ,
            swconcept: Surface_wave ,
            swconcept: Controlled_fusion,
            swconcept: Nuclear_fusion ;
        prism:keywords  "Vlasov-Boltzmann equation"  ,
               "surface electron O-modes"  ,
               "SECOM"  ,
               "parametric instability"  ,
               "electron cyclotron frequency" ,
               "electron cyclotron waves" ,
               "surface cyclotron wave propagation"  .
#
#:published_item a fabio:JournalArticle ;
        dcterms:title  "Parametric excitation of surface electron cyclotron O-modes by an
        external alternating electric field"  ;
        fabio:hasPublicationYear  "2011" ^^xsd:gYear ;
        prism:doi  "10.1088/0031-8949/84/04/045503"  ;
        frbr:embodiment :pdf ;
        frbr:partOf :phys_scripta-84-045503 .
#
#:phys_scripta-84-045509 a fabio:JournalIssue ;
        prism:issueIdentifier  "84"  ;
        frbr:embodiment :printed_issue;
        frbr:partOf :phys_scripta .
#
#:phys_scripta a fabio:Journal ;
        dcterms:title  "Physica Scripta"  .
#
#:printed_issue dcterms:publisher :iopscience ;
        frbr:part :printed .
#
#:pdf a fabio:DigitalManifestation ;
        prism:publicationDate  "2011-09-20" ^^xsd:date ;
        dcterms:format application:pdf ;
        dcterms:publisher :iopscience .
#
#:vogirka a foaf:Person ;
        foaf:givenName  "Volodymyr"  ;
        foaf:familyName  "Girka"  .
#
#:avgirka a foaf:Person ;
        foaf:givenName  "Anastasiia"  ;
        foaf:familyName  "Girka"  .
#
#:vvyarko a foaf:Person ;
        foaf:givenName  "Vitalii"  ;
        foaf:familyName  "Yarko"  .
#
#:iopscience a foaf:Organization ;
        foaf:name  "IOP Science"  .
```

This fragment of semantic annotation describes the published article: Girka, V. O., A. V. Girka, and V. V. Yarko. "Parametric excitation of surface electron cyclotron O-modes by an external alternating electric field." *Physica Scripta* 84.4 (2011): 045503, available online at stacks.iop.org/PhysScr/84/045503. The annotation contains the following information: this is a research paper written by 3 persons (lines 13, 14) and it is a printed item (line 15); it has a number of subject terms (lines 16-21) and keywords (lines 22-28); it was published as a journal article with corresponding title (lines 30-33); the publication year and DOI are stated then (lines 34, 35); its embodiment is a PDF file (line 36) and it is a part of journal issue #84, journal title is "Physica Scripta" and publisher is IOP Science (lines 37-48); it was published online on 20th of September 2011. There is also information about the date of publication, a format of publication and a publisher (lines 50-53). Authors are described in lines 55-65 and the publisher is described in lines 67-68. The subject terms and keywords are picked up from the ScinceWISE ontology, version of 2014, but the ontology is growing up every day, users can add new terms in it according to their needs in annotating. *Theoretical physics* could be added into ScienceWISE ontology in order to describe this particular article and the term would be used for many of publications. Also, such a concepts as *wave generation*, *modes conversion*, and *plasma instabilities* describe the article but are not in the ScienceWISE ontology.

Ontology of open problems could be the third component in annotating a scientific article in physics in addition to publishing ontology and physics ontology. There is proposition of ontology of open problems below:

```
@prefix : <http://www.example-site.net/OpenProblemsOnto#> .
@prefix owl: <http://www.w3.org/2002/07/owl#> .
@prefix rdf: <http://www.w3.org/1999/02/22-rdf-syntax-ns#> .
@prefix xml: <http://www.w3.org/XML/1998/namespace> .
@prefix xsd: <http://www.w3.org/2001/XMLSchema#> .
@prefix rdfs: <http://www.w3.org/2000/01/rdf-schema#> .

<http://www.example-site.net/OpenProblemsOnto> a owl:Ontology .
##################################################################
# #    Classes
##################################################################

# http://www.example-site.net/OpenProblemsOnto#FieldOfScience

:FieldOfScience a owl:Class .
#
# http://www.example-site.net/OpenProblemsOnto#OpenProblem

:OpenProblem a owl:Class .
#
# http://www.example-site.net/OpenProblemsOnto# SubfieldOfScience

:SubfieldOfScience a owl:Class .

##################################################################
# #    Object Properties
##################################################################
# http://www.example-site.net/OpenProblemsOnto#concernTo

:concernTo a owl:ObjectProperty ;
        rdfs:domain :OpenProblem ;
        rdfs:range :SubfieldOfScience .
#
# http://www.example-site.net/OpenProblemsOnto#containSubfield

:containSubfield a owl:ObjectProperty ;
```

```
        owl:inverseOf :isSubfieldOf ;
        rdfs:domain :FieldOfScience ;
        rdfs:range :SubfieldOfScience .
#
# http://www.example-site.net/OpenProblemsOnto#inFieldOf

:inFieldOf a owl:ObjectProperty ;
        rdfs:domain :OpenProblem ;
        rdfs:range :FieldOfScience .
#
# http://www.example-site.net/OpenProblemsOnto#isSubfieldOf

:isSubfieldOf a owl:ObjectProperty , owl:FunctionalProperty ;
        rdfs:domain :SubfieldOfScience ;
        rdfs:range :FieldOfScience .
```

The aforecited example of open problems ontology includes three classes: *FieldOfScience*, *SubfieldOfScience,* and *OpenProblem.* Classes are connected by four properties: *isSubfieldOf* property links *FieldOfScience* with *SubfieldOfScienced*, there is a reverse connection, namely *ContainSubfield*, *OpenProblem* class is linked with *FieldOfScience* class by *inFieldOf* property and with *SubfieldOfScience* class by *concernTo* property.

Thus, the example of annotation of the article may be added with mentioning that the article contributes to the open problem of *Plasma Physics* and *Fusion Power*, which concerns to such a subfield of *Physics* as *Nuclear Physics*. The following segment of code illustrates it:

```
#################################################################
# #    Individuals
# #################################################################

#http://www.example-site.net/OpenProblemsOnto#physics

:physics a owl:NamedIndividual , :FieldOfScience ;
        :containSubfield :astronomyAstrophysics ,
        :atomicMolecularPhysics , :biophysics , :condensedMatterPhysics , :cosmology ,
        :generalPhysics , :generalRelativity , :highEnergyAndParticlePhysics , :nuclearPhysics ,
        :opticalPhysics , :quantumGravity , :quantumPhysics .
#
## http://users.jyu.fi/~angirka/OpenProblemsOnto#nuclearPhysics

:nuclearPhysics a owl:NamedIndividual , :SubfieldOfScience ;
        :isSubfieldOf :physics .

http://users.jyu.fi/~angirka/OpenProblemsOnto#plasmaPhysicsAnd
                                                                    FusionPower

:plasmaPhysicsAndFusionPower a owl:NamedIndividual , :OpenProblem ;
        :concernTo :nuclearPhysics ;
        :inFieldOf :physics .
```

Thereby, the annotated scientific article could be found by querying the article, which has subject terms such as *controlled fusion*, *nuclear fusion*, *wave generation*, *modes conversion*, *plasma instabilities* and contributes to the *physics* open problem of *plasma physics* and *fusion power*. These phrases are not a part of the text, thus the regular search engine, which is based on text matching, would fail while searching this article with these keywords. Here is the SPARQL query composed basing on the requirements stated above:

```
PREFIX fabio: <http://purl.org/spar/fabio/>
PREFIX exmp: <http://www.example-site.net/example_ontology>
PREFIX opprph: http://www.example-
                                                                site.net/OpenProblemsOnto#physics
SELECT ?paper
WHERE {
        ?paper
              a fabio:ResearchPaper ;
              fabio:hasSubjectTerm
                            swconcept: Controlled_fusion,
                            swconcept: Nuclear_fusion,
                            swconcept: Wave_generation,
                            swconcept: Modes_conversion,
                            swconcept: Plasma_instabilities ;
              exmp:contributeTo
                            opprph:plasmaPhysicsAndFusionPower .
}
```

5. SUMMARY

Search engines are used by scientists all over the world in everyday work. There are specialized databases that contain different kinds of data on specific topics, which are established in order to help people to find what they need. Some of databases have an atypical search engine as, for example, Semantic Scholar web-service. These tools are created because the ordinary searching in the WWW, which is based on text matching, is not efficient in that cases when the searcher does not know what exactly he or she is searching for, despite of some particular web page or article. Thus, there is a need for the application of semantic technologies. Particularly, Semantic Web would allow users to perform a search in a smart way, in simple words, it would allow to get shorter and more precise lists of searching results.

The lion's share of searching activity, performing by scientists, is devoted to browsing for research articles. Hence, semantic publishing would be useful for every scientist. A number of corporations, including Microsoft and Elsevier academic publisher, are already involved in developing approaches and tools for semantic publishing. Semantic publishing and processing of articles is a growing branch but in physics domain it is not developed enough as in biology or computer sciences, for instance.

There is a set of public ontologies for the domain of publishing: SPAR suit of ontologies and some alternatives for it can be found. However, there is no public ontology in physics which could be used for semantic publishing. However, the ScienceWISE project is continuously working on developing such ontology, particularly in the physics domain. The ScienceWISE ontology of physics has a large scope and its feature is that the contributors are physicists. It is the most suitable ontology for semantic publishing in physics nowadays, but it is not in public access.

Physicists are in great need of the possibility of searching among scientific reports and data in a more efficient way by utilizing semantic technologies. An example of semantic annotation and querying of the article in plasma physics is presented in this paper. The ontology of open problems is proposed as the improvement to the ontology of physics.

6. CONCLUSION

Semantic technology, as a tool to formalize a domain of knowledge, and ontology, as an essential part of it, can provide shared knowledge and data in the domain of physics, including nuclear and plasma physics for critical infrastructure [Cardoso, 2007].

With this paper, the solution for the problem of intercommunication between researchers in physics has been proposed, namely, a semantic publishing in physics as an approach for documents representation, which gives possibility for more effective searching and browsing. An improvement for the existing ScienceWISE system is proposed, namely the ontology of open problems. In addition, ScienceWISE system does not offer the possibility of adding to annotation concepts that are not written down in the text. This limitation needs to be removed in the future. Moreover, semantic publishing includes visualization features of the annotated articles that will be useful for browsing the articles. The current research is a contribution to the building of the smart, self-protective infrastructure. Semantic publishing in physics may serve as a basis for a document flow in the critical infrastructure, which may decrease a human factor in critical infrastructure protection.

REFERENCES

Aberer, Karl, et al., 2011 ScienceWISE: a Web-based Interactive Semantic Platform for scientific collaboration. *ISWC (Demonstration Track).*

Attwood, Teresa K., 2010. Utopia Documents and The Semantic Biochemical Journal experiment. *EMBnet. news* 15.4: pp-3.

Bhatt, Mehul et al., 2004. sedOnto: A web enabled ontology for synthetic environment representation based on the SEDRIS specification. *Fall Simulation Interoperability Workshop.*

Boyarsky, A., et al., 2013. From scientific papers to the scientific ontology: dynamical clustering of heterogeneous graphs and ontology crowdsourcing. *Joint Workshop on Large and Heterogeneous Data and Quantitative Formalization in the Semantic Web (LHD+ SemQuant 2012).*

Boyarsky, Alexey, and Oleg Ruchayskiy, 2015. ScienceWISE: A Web-Based Interactive Semantic Platform for Paper Annotation and Ontology Editing. *The Semantic Web: ESWC 2012 Satellite Events: ESWC 2012 Satellite Events, Heraklion, Crete, Greece, May 27-31, 2012. Revised Selected Papers* 7540: 392.

Byres, Eric, and Justin Lowe. "The myths and facts behind cyber security risks for industrial control systems." *Proceedings of the VDE Kongress*. Vol. 116. 2004.

Cardoso, J., Hepp, M. and Lytras, M.D. eds., 2007. The semantic web: real-world applications from industry (Vol. 6). *Springer Science & Business Media.*

Cheung, Kei-Hoi, et al., 2005. YeastHub: a semantic web use case for integrating data in the life sciences domain. *Bioinformatics* 21.suppl 1: i85-i96.

Collins, Joseph B., 2004. Standardizing an ontology of physics for modeling and simulation. *NAVAL RESEARCH LAB* WASHINGTON DC.

Collins, Joseph B., and Doug C., 2004. Towards an Ontology of Physics. *NAVAL RESEARCH LAB* WASHINGTON DC.

Collins, Joseph B., 2005. Mathematical Representations for Web Services. Conference paper (*Simulation Interoperability Workshop (SIW)*), Available at: http://www.nrl.navy.mil/itd/imda/collins-mathematical-representations-web-services

Collins, Joseph B., 2008. Using Mathematical and Scientific Markup as an Approach to Model Specification. *Proceedings of the Society for Modeling and Simulation International [SCS]: Grand Challenges in Modeling & Simulation (GCMS 08).*

Collins, Joseph B., 2009. OpenMath content dictionaries for SI quantities and units. *Intelligent Computer Mathematics*. Springer Berlin Heidelberg. 247-262.

Collins, Joseph B., 2010. An OpenMath content dictionary for tensor concepts. *Intelligent Computer Mathematics*. Springer Berlin Heidelberg. 293-299.

Data range extension : Linear Equations. 2012 Available at: https://www.w3.org/2007/OWL/wiki/Data_Range_Extension:_Linear_Equations

Foundations, C., 1997. Protecting America's Infrastructures: The Report of the President's Commission on Critical Infrastructure Protection.

Hendler, James, 2003. Science and the Semantic Web. *SCIENCE*: Vol 299, 520-521. Available at: http://science.sciencemag.org/content/299/5606/520.full

Hinchey, M.G. and Sterritt, R., 2006. Self-managing software. *Computer,39*(2), pp.107-109.

Lange, Christoph.2011. Enabling Collaboration on Semiformal Mathematical Knowledge by Semantic Web Integration. PhD thesis, *Jacobs University Bremen, number 11 in Studies on the Semantic Web. AKA Verlag and IOS Press, Heidelberg and Amsterdam*, Chapter 5.

Peroni, S. 2014. The Semantic Publishing and Referencing Ontologies. *In Semantic Web Technologies and Legal Scholarly Publishing*: 121-193. Cham, Switzerland: Springer.

Peroni, Silvio, 2015: Example of use of FaBiO #1. Describing a bibliographic entity. Available at: http://www.sparontologies.net/ontologies/fabio

Pettifer, Steve, et al., 2009. Visualising biological data: a semantic approach to tool and database integration. *BMC bioinformatics* 10.Suppl 6: S19.

Sateli, B. and Witte, R., 2015. Semantic representation of scientific literature: bringing claims, contributions and named entities onto the Linked Open Data cloud. *PeerJ Computer Science*, *1*, p.e37.

Shotton, David, and Peroni, Silvio. The Semantic Publishing Blog

Available at: https://semanticpublishing.wordpress.com/_(Accessed: April 2016)

Shotton, David, et al., 2009. Adventures in semantic publishing: exemplar semantic enhancements of a research article. *PLoS Comput Biol* 5.4: e1000361.

Shotton, David, 2009. Semantic publishing: the coming revolution in scientific journal publishing. *Learned Publishing* 22.2: 85-94.

W3C Semantic Web Frequently Asked Questions. [online] How does the Semantic Web relate to XML?

Available at: https://www.w3.org/RDF/FAQ

AUTOMATIC DETERMINATION OF SIMILARITY THRESHOLD FOR FOCUSED CRAWLING PROCESSES ON WEB PAGES

Gustavo Oliveira de Siqueira[1], Guilherme Tavares de Assis[1],
Anderson Almeida Ferreira[1], Amanda Sávio Nascimento e Silva[1],
Vítor Mangaravite[2] and Flávio Luis Cardeal Pádua[3]
[1]*Department of Computing – Universidade Federal de Ouro Preto – Ouro Preto, MG, Brazil*
[2]*Department of Computing – Universidade Federal de Minas Gerais – Belo Horizonte, MG, Brazil*
[3]*Department of Computing – Centro Federal de Educação Tecnológica de Minas Gerais – Belo Horizonte, MG, Brazil*

ABSTRACT

The great popularity and, specially, the fast Web growth have led to the proposal and analysis of new techniques for helping users to locate effectively the needed information in a satisfactory time, without much difficulty. Traditional crawlers are not capable to identify relevant sub-spaces on Web related to a specific theme; however, focused crawlers are capable to solve, effectively and efficiently, the mentioned problem. Usually, a focused crawler process requires a specific value, called similarity threshold value, for determining whether a crawled Web page is relevant or not according to a topic of interest; such value is distinct for each specific topic. In order to determine automatically such a value for focused crawlers related to a genre-aware approach, we propose three strategies in this work. Our experimental evaluation achieved, as the best result, 100% of precision and 98% of F1, considering a specific crawling process for which it was determined automatically a similarity threshold value: a great result compared with the baseline.

KEYWORDS

Similarity threshold, web crawling, focused crawling

1. INTRODUCTION

Web's intense growth due its great popularity have led to new techniques proposal and analysis in order to help users locating the needed information effectively in a satisfactory time, without greater difficulties. Information access on Web is basically made through search engines that exploit the Web's graph structure in order to locate relevant pages to a specific search (Menczer et al. 2004). To allow this, a typical search engine uses a specific program, named crawler, which crawls the largest possible number of Web pages, generating an indexed pages collection. In this case, a traditional crawler crawls Web pages starting by seed-pages set and following the links on it, visiting other pages. Such a process continues with new pages, whose new links are followed until get a sufficient number of pages or reach some specific goal. Another program, named indexer, reads the collected pages and create an index based on the words on the pages. Each search engine uses its own algorithm to create its index aiming to return relevant results for user's searches.

The challenge of identifying specific and relevant Web sub-spaces, according to a theme, is typically referred to intelligent construction in a crawling strategy (Pant and Srinivasan, 2005). This intelligence is usually achieved by the use of appropriated heuristics, which guide the crawling process and aim at determining whether a page is relevant or not to a specific topic of interest. In this case, the crawlers are named focused or topical crawlers. Many focused crawler strategies (Almpanidis et al., 2007; Chakrabarti et al., 1999; Johnson et al. 2003; Pant & Srinivasan, 2005, 2006) make use of text classifiers to determine such relevance with additional cost of having to train the classifiers. Furthermore, due to generality of the situations where these strategies are applied, the crawlers reach low recall and precision levels: generally between 40% and 70%.

On focused crawler context, the work presented in Assis et al. (2009) (see Subsection 2.1) had, as main goal, propose a framework that allows the construction of effective, efficient and scalable focused crawlers, requiring no training or any kind of preprocessing. Specifically, the proposed approach to focused crawling in Assis et al. (2009) is useful in situations where the topic of interest can be expressed by two distinct set of terms: the first set describing genre aspects of the desired page's genre[1] and the second related to the subject or content of these pages. Therefore, following this approach, a specialist must specify sets of content and genre terms to represent the topic of interest and also a similarity threshold value that defines whether a visited page by the crawler is relevant or not to a specific topic. Depending on the similarity threshold value, the effectiveness of a crawling process may not be satisfactory. In order to validate the proposed approach, the authors defined empirically a similarity threshold value for each desired topic. Thus, to become the approach less user dependent, it is necessary to determine automatically the similarity threshold value to be used in a crawling process, according to a specific topic of interest, in order to ensure the effectiveness of such crawling process.

The solution for the mentioned problem is not trivial, once the similarity threshold value for a focused crawling process depends directly on the topic of interest. To achieve this goal, we propose different strategies to automatically determine the similarity threshold, based on statistical data summarizing techniques, traditional clustering methods and the silhouette coefficient metric (Pant et al., 2004).

The rest of this paper is organized as follows. Section 2 addresses related work. Section 3 presents the proposed strategies for automatic determination of similarity threshold values to be used in focused crawling processes. Section 4 describes the experimental evaluation on the defined strategies and the results obtained. Finally, Section 5 concludes the paper and gives some directions for future work.

2. RELATED WORK

Our proposed strategies, in this work, aims to determine automatically similarity threshold values to be used on focused crawling processes following a genre-aware approach. Therefore, works related to this paper are divided in two subsections: the genre-aware approach to focused crawling and automatic threshold estimation for data matching applications.

2.1 Genre-aware Approach to Focused Crawling

The genre-aware approach to focused crawling presented in (Assis et al. 2009; Assis et al. 2007), used as base for this work, considers a set of heuristics to guide a crawler, in such way that it allows the separate analysis of the genre and the content of a Web page. The set of heuristics has been designed with two main objectives: improving the level of F1 of the crawling process (effectiveness) and speeding up the crawling of relevant pages (efficiency).

The Figure 1 illustrates, according to (Assis et al. 2009; Assis et al. 2007), the functioning model of the genre-aware approach to focused crawling. As we can see, firstly (step 01), a priority queue called Frontier is [1]initialized with the URLs of the seed pages (a set of pages from which to start the crawling), setting the URL scores to 1. For each URL in Frontier (step 02), the corresponding page is visited (step 04) and its content analyzed (steps 05 to 09). It has used the cosine measure (Baeza-Yates & Ribeiro-Neto, 1999) to determine the similarity between the current page and the set of terms that represent the pages of interest. This measure is calculated separately to each set of terms (steps 05, 06 and 08), generating a specific similarity score between the current page and the sets of terms that represent, respectively, the genre, the content and the URL string of the desired pages. Each URL string term is related to the page genre or to the desired content. Then, these scores are combined into a final single one (steps 07 and 09) and compared with a given threshold defined by an expert. If this final score is greater or equal to this threshold (step 10), the visited page is included in the set of relevant pages. Next, if the current page is considered relevant, the scores of URLs in Frontier that correspond to pages siblings of the current page are changed to final score (step 11). Finally, the links previously extracted from the current page are inserted into Frontier (step 12) having their scores set to 0.

---

[1]By genre, according to Assis et al. (2007), it is meant to be the kind, the specie or the style of the specific documents.

Two important improvements were proposed for the genre-aware approach. The first one (Mangaravite et al., 2012) proposes the use of link-context (more precisely, anchor text, link title and URL) of the Web pages, that will be visited by the crawler, in order to define their priorities (initial scores) in the Frontier, allowing the crawler to visit the relevant pages as soon as possible; such improvement generated 100% of efficiency increase. The second one (Mangaravite et al. 2014) proposes several heuristics to semi-automatically generate seed-pages for a specific topic based on its genre and content terms (see Figure 2); results showed that the efficiency of the genre-aware approach improves to 53%.

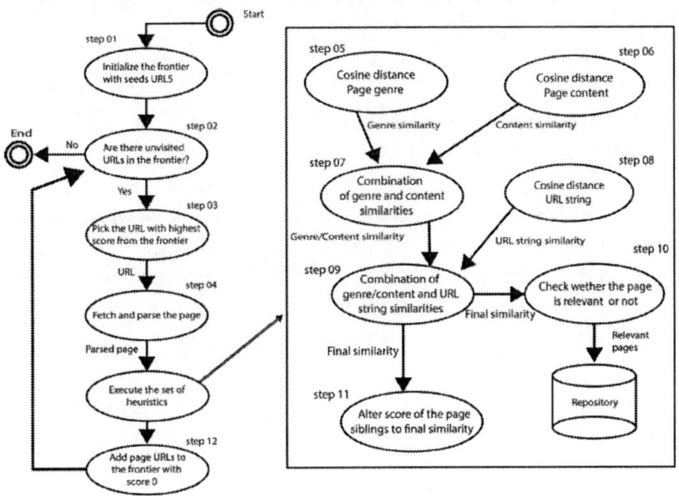

Figure 1. Functioning model of the genre-aware approach to focused crawling

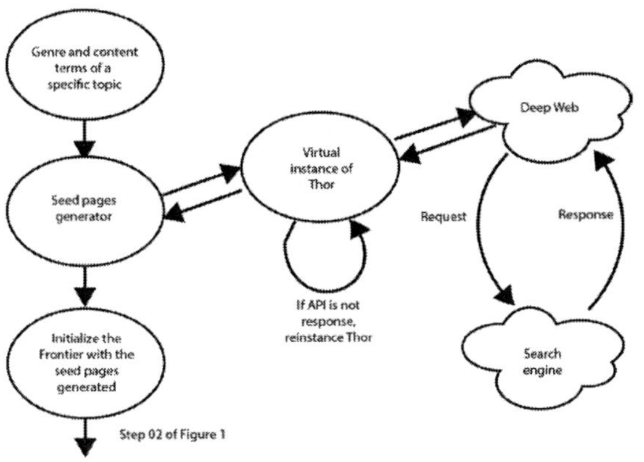

Figure 2. Functioning model of the strategy for generating seed-pages

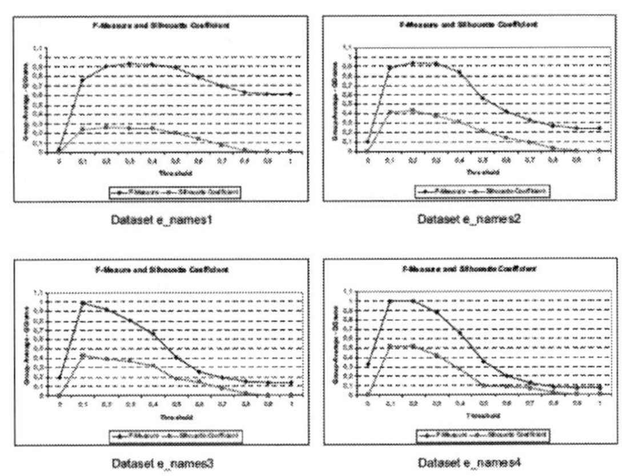

Figure 3. Results obtained by Santos et al. (2008)

2.2 Automatic Threshold Estimation for Data Matching Applications

According to Santos et al. (2008), many data integration processes, such data deduplication and similarity querying, rely on the application of similarity functions. Similarity functions usually require setting a threshold value to evaluate whether a particular object is similar or not.

In order to eliminate human intervention and being capable of estimating precision and recall values for a data set, it is possible to determine similarity threshold values that tend to get the maximum F1 value. Therefore, the approach proposed in in Santos et al. (2008) performs a data clustering process aiming to, ideally, each cluster contains only instances from the same class. The main idea is trying to maximize a metric named silhouette coefficient. According to (Kaufman & Rousseeuw, 2009), the silhouette coefficient is a dimensionless quantitative metric, which can be used to determine the quality obtained by a clustering process, i.e., the similarity between elements from the same cluster and the dissimilarity between elements from different clusters.

The experiments performed in Santos et al. (2008) showed that, in 9 of 16 cases covered by the work, the curve generated by the F1 values followed the same behavior as the curved generated by the silhouette coefficient values. That is, the best silhouette coefficient value, related to a determined similarity threshold value, tends to indicate the best F1 for a given data set, as it can be seen on Figure 3. Thus, we propose a strategy based on this approach (see Subsection 3.3).

3. STRATEGIES FOR DETERMINING AUTOMATICALLY SIMILARITY THRESHOLD VALUES

As already mentioned, this work has, as main goal, proposes strategies to automatically determine similarity threshold values to be used on distinct focused crawling processes based on genre-aware approach (Assis et at., 2009). The following subsections present three proposed strategies to achieve this end.

3.1 Strategy based on Seed-Pages Summarization

This strategy (see Algorithm 1) aims to determine the similarity threshold value, for a specific topic of interest, by the arithmetic or weighted mean of the seed-pages similarities according to genre and content terms from the specified topic. These pages are automatically generated by the strategy illustrated by Figure 2 also using genre and content terms from the specified topic.

```
Algorithm 1: Strategy based on seed-pages summarization pseudo-code
1: function GETTHRESHOLD(S, genre, content)
2:    threshold ← 0
3:    similarities ← Ø
4:    for each seed s ∈ S do
5:       similarities ← similarities ∪ {similarity (s, genre, content)}
6:    end for
7:    similarities ← similarities – outliers (similarities)
8:    threshold ← mean (similarities)
9:    return threshold
10: end function
```

Algorithm 1. Strategy based on seed-pages summarization pseudo-code

According to Algorithm 1, initially (steps 04, 05 and 06), for each seed-page *s* from set *S*, a similarity value is calculated between such seed-page and the genre and content terms specified, being stored in the *similarities* set. Following (step 07), the outliers similarity values are removed of the *similarities* set and, finally (step 08), the arithmetic or weighted mean between the remaining similarities is calculated. Then, the function returns (step 09) the calculated mean (a value in the range [0; 1.0]), representing the similarity threshold value to be used in a focused crawling process of the topic of interest.

3.2 Strategy based on Clustering Methods

This strategy (see Algorithm 2) aims to determine the similarity threshold value, for a specific topic of interest, using a clustering method on the seed-pages similarities. For such strategy, we defined two distinct and classical clustering methods : K-Means (partitioning category) and BIRCH (hierarchical category).

K-Means (Hartigan & Wong, 1979) is a clustering method that requires an input parameter; in our strategy, we defined the *K* value equals to 2: one of the clusters represents the relevant pages' similarity values according to a desired topic, and the other one represents non-relevant pages' similarity values, which are disregarded because they are considered as outliers on the seed-pages' similarity values set.

BIRCH (Zhang et al., 1996) is a clustering method that requires a data instance considered in the clustering process; this data instance corresponds to the similarity value obtained between a seed-page terms and genre and content terms of the desired topic.

```
Algorithm 2: Strategy based on clustering methods pseudo-code
1: function GETTHRESHOLD(S, genre, content)
2:    threshold ← 0
3:    similarities ← Ø
4:    for each seed s ∈ S do
5:       similarities ← similarities ∪ {similarity (s, genre, content)}
6:    end for
7:    clusters ← clustering (similarities)
8:    threshold ← centroid (clusters)
9:    return threshold
10: end function
```

Algorithm 2. Strategy based on clustering methods pseudo-code

According to Algorithm 2, initially (steps 04, 05 and 06), for each seed-page *s* from set *S*, a similarity value is calculated between such seed-page and the genre and content terms specified, being stored in the *similarities* set. Following (step 07), the clusters are generated according to the used clustering method and, finally (step 08), the similarity threshold value receives the centroid value of the relevant cluster generated. Then, the function returns (step 09) such centroid value (a value in the range [0; 1.0]), representing the similarity threshold value to be used in a focused crawling process of the topic of interest.

3.3 Strategy based on Silhouette Coefficient

This strategy (see Algorithm 3) aims to determine the similarity threshold value, for a specific topic of interest, by the maximization of the silhouette coefficient metric on clusters, dynamically generated, which contain relevant and non-relevant pages according to the seed-pages similarities of the desired topic. This is due to the fact that silhouette coefficient values follows the same structural behavior as the metric F1, as presented on Figure 3.

```
Algorithm 3: Strategy based on silhouette coefficient pseudo-code
1: function GETTHRESHOLD(S, genre, content)
2:    threshold ← 0
3:    similarities ← Ø
4:    for each seed s ∈ S do
5:       similarities ← similarities ∪ {similarity (s, genre, content)}
6:    end for
7:    threshold ← ASTS (similarities, 0, 1.0, 0.01)
8:    return threshold
9: end function
```

Algorithm 3. Strategy based on silhouette coefficient pseudo-code

According to Algorithm 3, initially (steps 04, 05 and 06), for each seed-page *s* from set *S*, a similarity value is calculated between such seed-page and the genre and content terms specified, being stored in the *similarities* set. Following (step 07), the threshold receives the return value from the function *ASTS*[2]. Then, the function returns (step 08) such calculated value by function *ASTS* (a value in the range [0; 1.0]), representing the similarity threshold value to be used in a focused crawling process of the topic of interest.

[2] An adaptation from the function proposed by Bessas et al. (2016), which computes a set of similarity threshold values and select the best one associated to the maximum silhouette coefficient value, also calculated by the function.

4. EXPERIMENTAL EVALUATION

In order to validate the strategies proposed on subsections 3.1, 3.2 and 3.3, we performed an experimental evaluation described on Subsection 4.1; the obtained results are described and analyzed on Subsection 4.2.

4.1 Experimental Setup

The experiments were conducted on the Brazilian Web, in order to crawl pages related to three topics: (1) syllabi of database courses, (2) job offers on the computing area and (3) trip to Paris. The first and the second topics were used on the practical validation experiments on the genre-aware approach to focused crawling (Mangaravite et al. 2014, Mangaravite et al. 2012, Assis et al. 2009; Assis et al. 2007), also used as basis for this paper's experimental evaluation. The third topic was defined in order to evaluate the proposed strategies on execution time.

For each topic, an expert manually specifies the set of terms required to represent the genre and the content of the desired pages. The expert also specifies the answer set containing the relevant pages among those visited by the crawler in order to allow us to assess the efficiency of the crawling processes. Table 1 shows the genre and content terms specified for each topic. We used 5 content terms and 7 genre terms for database syllabi, 6 content terms and 13 genre terms for job offers, and 10 content terms and 12 genre terms for trip to Paris.

Table 1. Genre and content terms specified for each topic

Topic	Genre terms	Content terms
Database syllabi	syllabus, course, tentative schedule, class, works, required text, textbooks	data model, relational model, entity-relationship, relational algebra, relational calculus
Job offers	jobs, job offer, vacancies, company, requirements, contact, responsibilities, location, city, description, salary, benefits, career	programmer, developer, system analyst, software, database, internet
Trip to Paris	trip, travel, accommodation, host, stay, passage, package, tour, tourist, air, land, guide	Paris, Arc de Triomphe, Eiffel Tower, Louvre, Notre-Dame Cathedral, Seine River, Musée d'Orsay, Disneyland Resort Paris, Basilica of Sacré Cœur, Panthéon

For the generation of the seed pages to be used in a crawling process related to a given topic, the best heuristic, proposed by Mangaravite et al. (2014), generated 20 seed-pages for database syllabi, 16 seed-pages for job offers and 15 seed-pages for trip to Paris.

For the topics database syllabi and job offers, we used the logs generated in Mangaravite et al. (2014), which include the pages visited by the crawler (45226 and 97636 for syllabi database and job offers, respectively) and the best empirical similarity threshold values (0.21 for both topics). For the topic trip to Paris, a new crawling process was performed, generating a log with 12743 pages (considered a satisfactory number to stop the crawling process); thus, we estimate the best empirical similarity threshold in order to achieve the highest F1 value (in this case, 0.502). The results obtained for each crawling process (see Table 2) were used as the baseline for this work.

Table 2. Baseline used for each topic

Topic	Similarity Threshold Value	Relevant pages	Precision[3]	Recall	F1
Database syllabi	0.210	1684	1.0	0.979	0.989
Job offers	0.210	60201	1.0	1.0	1.0
Trip to Paris	0.502	1970	0.452	0.715	0.554

[3] According to Manning and Schütze (1999), precision is a measure of the number of items selected correctly by a system, recall is the proportion of target items selected by a system and, finally, F1 is the harmonic mean between precision and recall.

4.2 Experimental Results

The proposed strategies, to automatically determine similarity threshold values, were applied to the focused crawling processes described on Subsection 4.1. The results obtained are described on Table 3.

Table 3. Results obtained by the proposed strategies for each topic

Topic	Strategy applied	Similarity threshold Value	Precision	Recall	F1
Database syllabi	Arithmetic mean	0.214	1.0	0.879	0.935
	Weighted mean	0.195	0.427	1.0	0.598
	K-means	0.214	1.0	0.879	0.935
	BIRCH	0.175	0.377	1.0	0.547
	Silhouette coefficient	0.270	1.0	0.038	0.073
Job offers	Arithmetic mean	0.277	1.0	0.055	0.010
	Weighted mean	0.278	1.0	0.054	0.102
	K-means	0.229	1.0	0.965	0.982
	BIRCH	0.310	1.0	0.008	0.102
	Silhouette coefficient	0.390	1.0	0.166×10^{-3}	0.332×10^{-3}
Trip to Paris	Arithmetic mean	0.491	0.329	0.849	0.475
	Weighted mean	0.499	0.248	0.943	0.393
	K-means	0.579	0.690	0.130	0.219
	BIRCH	1.0	0.0	0.0	0.0
	Silhouette coefficient	0.590	0.698	0.078	0.141

As one can note from Table 3, the strategy that presented the best F1 values for the most topics is the strategy based on the clustering method K-Means. This occurs because K-Means achieved a similarity threshold value that is near to the empirical optimal value defined by the baseline (see Table 2). Other strategies presented satisfactory values, in some specific cases, as we can see for the strategy based on summarization using arithmetic mean for the topic database syllabi, which achieved the same best F1 value obtained by the strategy based on the clustering method K-Means.

Especially, for the topic trip to Paris, the strategies are better analyzed using precision value, once the recall value was estimated on the number of pages visited by the crawler when the crawling process were stopped manually. Therefore, the recall value obtained is an estimation of the possible final recall value for this specific topic. Consequently, the F1 value is also an estimation. For this topic, the strategy based on the coefficient silhouette obtained the best precision value. However, the precision value for K-Means is also a satisfactory value once it is better than the precision value of the baseline.

We can also verify that the similarity threshold value is directly proportional to the precision value and inversely proportional to the recall value. Thus it is possible to verify the importance to automatically determine similarity threshold values used by distinct topics on focused crawling processes.

5. CONCLUSION

As presented in Section 4, evaluation experiments for the proposed strategies for automatic determination of similarity threshold values to be used in focused crawling processes, based on genre-aware approach, were realized obtaining, as the best result, 100% of precision and 98% of F1 considering the topic job offers (see Subsection 4.1). This strategy also achieved the best results for the other topics in analysis, which make it the best strategy proposed in this work.

As future work, we intent to: (1) propose a new architecture for the crawler where it is possible to perform a distributed focused crawling process; (2) use natural language processing to improve the genre and content terms defined for the desired topic of interest and, thus, to improve the vector model evaluation of the crawling approach; (3) evaluate proposed strategies on different focused crawling approaches.

ACKNOWLEDGEMENT

This research was partially funded by research grants from PIP/UFOP and by project MASWeb (grant FAPEMIG/PRONEX APQ-01400-14). Furthermore, it was carried out on the GAID/UFOP Laboratory.

REFERENCES

Almpanidis, George, and Constantine Kotropoulos. "Combining text and link analysis for focused crawling." Pattern Recognition and Data Mining. Springer Berlin Heidelberg, 2005. 278-287.

Assis, G.T. de et al., 2009. A Genre-Aware Approach to Focused Crawling. World Wide Web, 12(3), pp.285–319. Available at: http://www.springerlink.com/index/10.1007/s11280-009-0063-7 [Accessed January 4, 2013].

Assis, G.T. de et al., 2007. Exploiting genre in focused crawling. In Proceedings of the 14th International String Processing and Information Retrieval. Santiago, Chile, pp. 62–73.

Baeza-Yates, Ricardo, and Berthier Ribeiro-Neto. Modern information retrieval. Vol. 463. New York: ACM press, 1999.

Bessas, Izaquiel L., et al. "Automatic and online setting of similarity thresholds in content-based visual information retrieval problems." EURASIP Journal on Advances in Signal Processing 2016.1 (2016): 1-16.

Chakrabarti, Soumen, Martin Van den Berg, and Byron Dom. "Focused crawling: a new approach to topic-specific Web resource discovery."Computer Networks 31.11 (1999): 1623-1640.

Hartigan, John A., and Manchek A. Wong. "Algorithm AS 136: A k-means clustering algorithm." Journal of the Royal Statistical Society. Series C (Applied Statistics) 28.1 (1979): 100-108.

Santos, Juliana Bonato, et al. "Automatic threshold estimation for data matching applications." Proceedings of the 23rd Brazilian symposium on Databases. Sociedade Brasileira de Computação, 2008.

Johnson, Judy, Kostas Tsioutsiouliklis, and C. Lee Giles. "Evolving strategies for focused web crawling." ICML. 2003.

Kaufman, L., & Rousseeuw, P. J. (2009). Finding groups in data: an introduction to cluster analysis (Vol. 344). John Wiley & Sons.

Mangaravite, V., Assis, G.T. De & Ferreira, A.A., 2012. Improving the Efficiency of a Genre-aware Approach to Focused Crawling Based on Link Context. In 8th Latin American Web Congress. pp. 17–23.

Mangaravite, V., Assis, G.T. De & Ferreira, A.A., 2014. Semi-automatic generation of seed pages in genre-aware focused crawling. In Proceedings of the 13th International Conference WWW/Internet (ICWI). pp. 51-58.

Manning, C. D., & Schütze, H. (1999). Foundations of statistical natural language processing (Vol. 999). Cambridge: MIT press.

Menczer, F., Pant, G. & Srinivasan, P., 2004. Topical Web Crawlers: Evaluating Adaptive Algorithms. ACM Transactions on Internet Technology, 4(4), pp.378–419.

Pant, G. & Srinivasan, P., 2005. Learning to Crawl: Comparing Classification Schemes. ACM Transactions on Information Systems, 23(4), pp.430–462.

Pant, G., & Srinivasan, P. (2006). Link contexts in classifier-guided topical crawlers. Knowledge and Data Engineering, IEEE Transactions on, 18(1), 107-122.

Pant, Gautam, et al. "Panorama: extending digital libraries with topical crawlers."Proceedings of the 4th ACM/IEEE-CS joint conference on Digital libraries. ACM, 2004.

Zhang, Tian, Raghu Ramakrishnan, and Miron Livny. "BIRCH: an efficient data clustering method for very large databases." ACM Sigmod Record. Vol. 25. No. 2. ACM, 1996.

EXTRACTING DOMAIN-INDEPENDENT INFORMATION FROM THE WEB FOR PORTUGUESE USING REVERB

Julio Cesar Batista Pires and Cedric Luiz de Carvalho
Instituto de Informática – Universidade Federal de Goiás - Campus Samambaia – Goiânia – GO – Brasil

ABSTRACT

Nowadays people are increasingly connected to the web, looking for all kinds of things. The web is a huge source of information. So, they can find almost anything they want. However, web information is not well organized and has little formal structure. This hampers machine processing and consequently makes information access more difficult. Bringing structure to the web is a key point for facilitating user searching and navigation. A recent technique, Open Information Extraction, has been successfully applied to extracting structured information from the web. This technique has been applied mostly to web pages in English. This paper presents a work focused on information extraction for Portuguese.

KEYWORDS

IE, Open IE, Semantic Web, Information Extraction, Natural Language Processing

1. INTRODUCTION

Web documents are not well structured and most of their information content is in natural language. Since natural language "understanding"[1] by machines is a challenging problem, user search for information content is limited on the web. To find information, users use search engines such as *Google*, *Bing*, *Yahoo*, and others. These tools treat user queries as lists of keywords, search for relevant keywords in web pages, and filter the most relevant pages for queries using various algorithms. They are very good at finding potential documents quickly. However, generally, the information the user is looking for must be retrieved manually from search results. Users need to browse through a long list of pages and look what they need (Etzioni et al, 2008). All this suggests that these tools are not powerful enough.

To improve search, it is necessary for computers to better understand the meaning of documents (Madhu et al, 2011). This requires structuring, standardizing, and organizing web content (Hassanzadeth and Keyvanpour, 2012) to facilitate processing by machines. One approach to solve this problem is to define a machine interpretable semantics (Babu et al, 2012) that is appropriate for describing the contents of web pages. Semantic Web technologies attempt to provide such a semantics for web pages. With such descriptions attached to web pages, search effectiveness would be improved. However, even with a language for describing semantics, how will all the semantic attachments be generated?

Currently, there is not much semantic information on the web and it is unlikely that people will provide this information. Hence, it is necessary to automate the process of generating this information. A recent technique, Open Information Extraction (Open IE), examines natural language text and produces triples that have the entity-relation-entity structure. Triples extracted can be indexed and retrieved. Answers can be found quickly and accurately (Savage, 2010). The tedious and error prone task of navigating through documents can be automated (Etzioni et al, 2008). There are some Open IE systems that can extract information from web pages. Among them, we can highlight ReVerb[2]. It is a system developed by Fader and other people at the University of Washington's Turing Center. It automatically identifies and extracts arguments and relations expressed by verbs in English sentences. "ReVerb is designed for web-scale information extraction, where the target relations cannot be specified in advance and speed is important". In

1 Any part of this article that associates the capacity of understanding, comprehension, legibility or interpretation to a computer or to a machine, it means processing power of such computer.
2 http://reverb.cs.washington.edu/

addition to correcting some problems with the Open IE systems developed before (TextRunner and WOE) and having better performance, ReVerb more than doubles the area under the precision-recall curve relative to these systems (Fader et al, 2011).

ReVerb, like most of these systems, works on English text. This paper focuses on information extraction from documents in Portuguese using ReVerb. The rest of this paper is organized in six sections. In Section 2, Information Extraction (IE), a framework for a sub-area of Natural Language Processing is presented. In Section 3, Open IE, a new paradigm of Web Information Extraction, is presented. In Section 4, the most recent and relevant work on Open Information Extraction is discussed. Section 5 presents the extensions that we have made to ReVerb to handle the Portuguese language. In Section 6, the results produced by the extended ReVerb are compared with the results produced by the original ReVerb. Section 7 presents conclusions and some possible future work.

2. INFORMATION EXTRACTION

Information Extraction is a field of Natural Language Processing (NLP), that maps text in natural language to structured information (Etzioni et al, 2008). The emphasis of this technique is to extract entities and relations between entities from text (Chiticariu et al, 2010). Entities and relations or arguments and predicates, are the basic elements which are extracted from text. Entities represent objects of the real world, such as people, organizations, places, products, etc. Relations express relationships between entities, for example, a person (*married to*) another person, or even a person (*born in*) a city (Balke, 2012). Relations are usually expressed by verbs or verb phrases and entities are expressed by nouns or noun phrases.

There are two important quality metrics to evaluate information extraction. The first one is Recall, which is measured by dividing the number of the correctly extracted triples by the total of the extracted triples. The other metric is Precision, which is measured by dividing the correctly extracted triples by the existing triples in a created pattern (Piskorski and Yangarber, 2013), (Soderland et al, 2010). A pattern is created from text. Initially, text phrases are manually identified. Next, for each phrase in text, triples are manually identified. These triples identified by a human being form a pattern. Thereafter, the manually generated triples are compared with those extracted by the system. Triples extracted by the system and existing in the pattern are considered correct. Triples extracted by the system and not existing in the pattern are considered incorrect. These metrics are best defined by the formulas:

$$Recall = \frac{Correct}{Correct + Incorrect} \qquad Precision = \frac{Correct}{Pattern}$$

Another measure is F-Measure, a combination of Precision with Recall:

$$F = \frac{2 * Precision * Recall}{Precision + Recall}$$

IE is focused on small, homogeneous and prespecified domains. Each domain requires that the user manually names relations and creates new rules or new extraction examples labeled by hand. The manual work grows linearly with the number of relations (Banko et al, 2007). This technique is not scalable or portable across domains (Etzioni et al, 2008). Thus, IE has several limitations for extracting information from the web. The web is very large and the relations it contains are not known in advance. The web extraction challenge has led to Open IE, which aims to adapt the methods of IE for the size and diversity of the web corpus (Etzioni et al, 2008).

3. OPEN INFORMATION EXTRACTION

Open IE addresses unlimited relations, does not require specific training examples of the domain, and runs fast enough for the web scale. In opposition to IE systems that require manual work to build relations, Open

IE systems learn a model of how relations are expressed in general and do not require human input (Etzioni et al, 2008). Most current Open IE systems deal only with English.

The only input to an Open IE system is a text corpus and its output is a set of triples (entities and simple relations). A triple or relational tuple model has the format: $rt = (e_1, r, e_2)$ where e_1 and e_2 denote entities and r denotes the relation between them (Banko et al, 2007). The extracted tuples attempt to capture the important relations in the text. The extraction model uses features such as verb identification or nouns in text together with regular expressions (Etzioni et al, 2008). Throughout this process, a predetermined vocabulary is not required (Mausam et al, 2012).

Traditional information extraction is more suitable for extractions where the number of relations is small and the cost to label training data is low (Banko and Etzioni, 2008). When the number of relations is massive and relations can not be prespecified, Open IE is superior. However, Open IE's recall is lower than traditional IE (Banko and Etzioni, 2008).

4. RELATED WORK

This section shows some works on Open IE. The vast majority of these works, described in literature, address this task for English and just few of them have been applied to other languages. Several challenges arise when applying these systems to other languages. Chinese, for example, has grammatical functions quite different from English and there are no limits in separation of sentences.

According to its authors, CORE (Tseng et al, 2014) is the first Open IE system implemented for Chinese. This language is quite different from English. Its grammatical functions are very different and there are no limits in sentence separation. CORE uses NLP techniques to extract information from sentences in Chinese. Given an input Chinese text, CORE extracts words from sentences, labels each of them with their grammatical types, makes an analysis (parsing) of their syntactic structure and groups the words according to their grammatical types. After all this, triples are extracted (Tseng et al, 2014). CORE extraction techniques are quite similar with the ReVerb's extraction techniques. The difference is that CORE uses dependence analysis while ReVerb uses shallow text processing.

DepOE is a multilingual system based on dependence analysis (Gamallo et al, 2012). The system uses a rule-based analyzer to perform extractions in English, Spanish, Portuguese and Galician. For this, it analyzes dependencies of each sentence using a multilingual parser. This parser takes a sentence already labeled, according to its grammatical types, as input. From this, verbal phrases are discovered. For each phrase, subjects, direct objects, attributes, and prepositional complements are identified. Then, many rules are applied to extract triples. CORE, as well as DepOE, uses dependency analysis features.

There are several Open IE systems such as TextRunner (Banko et al, 2007), (Etzioni et al, 2008), Wanderlust (Akbik and Broß, 2009), WOE (Wu and Weld, 2010), R2A2 (Etzioni et al, 2011), OLLIE (Mausam et al, 2012), Kraken (Akbik and Löser, 2012) and ClausIE (Del Corro and Gemulla, 2013). All of these systems can process only English texts and will not be described here.

Table 1 shows the Open IE systems described. Besides the language, the main difference between the systems is the processing type used.

Table 1. Open IE systems

System	NLP	Language
ReVerb	Shallow	English
Core	Deep	Chinese
Third level heading	Deep	Multilingual

5. THE REVERB FOR PORTUGUESE

In this section, the changes we made in ReVerb are presented. With these modifications ReVerb can handle texts in Portuguese. ReVerb was chosen in this work because it is ease to use and has been proven robust and fast enough (low computational cost) for information extraction on the web scale. In addition, the system is licensed for academic[3] use and is written in Java[4] programming language. In Figure 1, the ReVerb architecture model, modified to work with Portuguese texts, can be seen. The numbered texts (from 1 to 6) in figure represent the processing results of each architecture step. The input of a step is the output of the previous one.

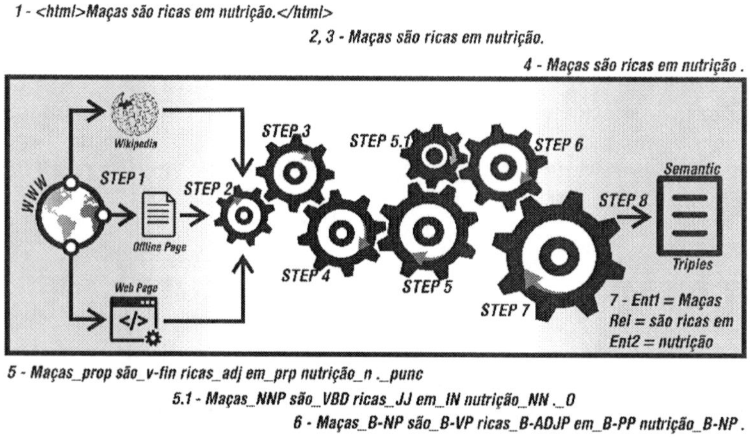

Figure 1. ReVerb for Portuguese Architecture

Eight steps are performed in the system. The first step ReVerb performs is to get the *input*. Originally, the system only accepted offline files. The new modified version has an extractor to online real-time page recovery, i.e., the system does not need a preset corpus. Thus, the entry process is automated and there is no longer need to download pages manually. This makes it possible to save time in getting the input. For experimental purposes, the modified ReVerb also takes as input Wikipedia random pages, in Portuguese or in English. The system can handle several type of input files, such as textual documents, web pages and plain text. After getting input document, they are prepared for the extraction process.

The second step (*preprocessor*) is to remove all markups and HTML tags from web pages. Here, pages are converted into plain text for extractions. After this step, there were only sentences. The ReVerb preprocessor has not been changed. Preprocessor stage is so simple that most of Open IE studies described in literature do not address it. However, there are some works focused only in web content recovery (Negm et al, 2012). After reducing web pages to text only, the next step is to identify sentences.

The third step is *sentence detector***.** ReVerb uses several stages of NLP (Fader et al, 2011). To generate semantic triples, the system requires only shallow syntactic processing and, therefore, uses the Open Natural Language Processor - OpenNLP[5]. This library supports several word processing tasks, such as sentence segmentation, tokenization, part-of-speech (POS) tagging, chunking and other (The Apache Software Foundation, 2010). Sentence detection is to identify if a punctuation character marks the end of a sentence. Thus, a sentence is the longest sequence between two punctuation markers. Only the first and the last sentence are exceptions. In short, a Sentence Detector segments the sentences of a text. Sentence segmentation is the first part of natural language processing. The task here is to receive the plain text from the previous step and separate it into sentences. In the modified ReVerb, it was only necessary to replace the English sentence segmentation module by the Portuguese sentence segmentation module.

The fourth step (*tokenization*) consists in segmenting a character sequence into tokens (words, punctuation, numbers, etc.) Each token is individually separated by a white space. This task is important because the part-of-speech tagger works with texts separated into tokens. In this step, the sentences received from the previous steps are separated in tokens. After this separation, each token is labeled later in another step. A version of the Tokenizer for Portuguese replaces the ReVerb original Tokenizer.

---

3 ReVerb License (http://reverb.cs.washington.edu/LICENSE.txt)
4 Oracle Java Home Page (http://www.oracle.com/technetwork/java/index.html)
5 OpenNLP (https://opennlp.apache.org/)

The fifth step is *POS Tagger.* This process (tagging) is to assign labels to tokens according to their corresponding grammatical types, based on the token itself and in its context. Each token has a label (tag) indicating its grammatical role in the sentence (token_tag). With this process, the sentence parts can be identified. This is important to find the triples later. For example, verbs represent relations and nouns represent entities. A tagger version for Portuguese replaces the ReVerb original tagger. The tools for Portuguese were trained using the same data of the project "Projeto Floresta Sintá(c)tica da Linguateca"[6]. So, it is natural that the tags used by them follow the pattern of this project.

Step 5.1 is the *tag converter.* The tag set used by the model for English follows a different tag set used by the model for Portuguese. Due to this characteristic, it was necessary to create a simple tag converter. The converter runs easily just translating the tag. For instance, in the model for Portuguese, an adjective is represented by "adj", while in the model for English, it is represented by "JJ". This conversion was necessary to be done because ReVerb works internally with these tags. It is noteworthy that for some tags there is no match in the other model. Thus, these tags have been translated into more general tags. The conversion is made soon after all tools handle the texts.

Step 6 is the *chunker.* The text chunking consists only of segmenting text in parts of syntactically relevant words, such as nominal and verbal groups. As seen before, each of these tasks is done one after the other and each subsequent entry depends on the previous output. ReVerb incorporates all of these tasks. Just chunking is not made available[7] for Portuguese or another language by OpenNLP. Due to the lack of this component it is necessary to build it from examples. OpenNLP provides the means for chunker construction in its documentation[8]. The construction steps are detailed in the following.

In the same way as the other tools, the chunker was trained using the file Bosque_CF_8.0.ad, a corpus formed by 9.368 sentences taken from two corpora, a Brazilian Portuguese corpora and other European Portuguese corpora, both in journalistic generic domain. The "bosque"[9] do not have lot of examples, but has a great quality because it was fully reviewed by linguists and thus offers better precision of results. This corpus is stored in the "Arvores Deitadas"[10] format, and thus it is necessary to perform conversion to the OpenNLP native format, which is based on CoNLL 2000[11].

After running the conversion procedure, the training content is ready. The next step is the chunker training. After training the chunker, it is necessary to evaluate its performance. Results of such evaluation are shown in Table 2. In this table, the performance results of the new Portuguese chunker and the original English OpenNLP chunker are shown[8].

Table 2. Performance Results

	Chunker for Enghish	Chunker for Portuguese
Average (sentences per seconds)	161.6	342.0
Total of sentences	2013	4213
Runtime (in seconds)	12.457	12.318
Precision	0.9244	0.9943
Recall	0.9217	0.9944
F-Measure	0.9230	0.9944

Each chunker was evaluated with different texts, according to their languages. As the chunker for Portuguese also showed good results[12], it means that it can achieve good performance in conjunction with ReVerb. After trained, the chunker can be used together with other tools for Portuguese in ReVerb. All detailed steps for the chunker construction can be found in the OpenNLP documentation.

The next step is *extraction, constrains and dictionary.* First, a relation is extracted from a given sentence. This first part consists of using a syntactic constraint, that is to find relations corresponding to the pattern "verb + preposition + nouns or adjectives or adverbs". Lexical constraint should also be considered, i.e., the

6 Distributed Resource Center for Computational Processing of Portuguese Language (http://www.linguateca.pt/floresta/corpus.html)
7 OpenNLP Tools Models (http://opennlp.sourceforge.net/models-1.5/)
8 OpenNLP Documentation (https://opennlp.apache.org/documentation/1.6.0/manual/opennlp.html)
9 "bosque" is a treebank wholly reviewed by linguists
10 Sentences stored in tree structure (http://www.linguateca.pt/floresta/BibliaFlorestal/completa.html)
11 Conference on Computational Natural Language Learning - a conference on NLP (http://www.clips.uantwerpen.be/conll2000/chunking/)
12 Compared with the original chunker.

found relations must have matches in a previously created dictionary. ReVerb's dictionary has 1.717.539 English relations. This dictionary was built using syntactic constraints and a large set of web pages. The relations that often appeared in the corpus were added to the dictionary. Dictionary relations where translated into Portuguese using Google Translator[13]. Due to the large amount of relations, it was not feasible to carry out all translations manually. The translations were simple and some of them were revised.

Finally, there is the *output* step. After the dictionary is replaced and new natural language processors are added, the modified ReVerb is ready to perform extractions in Portuguese. At the end of the process, the output is a set of semantic triples in the model previously presented.

6. EXPERIMENTAL RESULTS

ReVerb uses relations based on verb. It also imposes some constraints on these relations in order to overcome problems of previous systems (TextRunner and WOE), that is, incoherent extraction and uninformative extraction. The system also uses natural language processing and regular expressions to split a sentence into an Entity-Relation-Entity pattern. Using shallow syntactic processing ensures robustness, speed, and efficiency to operate in the web scale. The results of using the modified ReVerb to operate in Portuguese are described in the following.

We conducted experiments on a data set with approximately 60 sentences used to evaluate the system performance. These sentences were taken from examples extracted from the works presented in Section 4. Although the set of sentences is small, we believe they are sufficient to show that Open IE can be applied also to Portuguese. For getting good results, each sentence was manually translated from English to Portuguese by one of the authors. In addition, these translations were verified by another author. Thus, two text corpora were created with the same sentences, one corpora in English and another in Portuguese. After the translation process, each sentence was independently examined by the authors to identify triples present in sentences. In total, they both identified 69 triples simultaneously. These triples represent the pattern to be reached. This pattern is used in metrics showed in Section 2.

The evaluation of the modified ReVerb was based on the exact correspondence, that is, each part of the triple extracted must be identical to the pattern created. The original ReVerb and the modified ReVerb were compared using the patterns created, each in its specific language. For each system, it is given a set of sentences as input. After processing, the output produced is several relational triples. ReVerb for Portuguese remained almost the same as ReVerb for English, only a new dictionary, natural language processors and the tag converter were added. The Reverb inner workings remains the same. We do not modify the way ReVerb works. The modified ReVerb remains doing the same steps the original ReVerb does. We have not made changes in steps. We have just changed what these steps use as input. To measure precision and recall, extractions labeled as correct by the authors (pattern) were used. In Table 3, it is shown the results of precision, recall and F-Measure.

Table 3. Evaluation of ReVerb: English vs. Portuguese

	Precision	Recall	F-Measure
English	0.6508	0.5942	0.6212
Portuguese	0.5272	0.4203	0.4677

It can be seen in Table 3 that the number of triples extracted by the modified ReVerb is smaller than those obtained by the original ReVerb. Some factors could have influenced on this. The first one is that the dictionary was automatically translated from English to Portuguese. So, it is very likely that there are translation errors. A better dictionary probably will produce a better result. Another factor that can influence the results is the label translation. Some labels did not have exact matching for conversion. So, these tags were translated according to the authors judgment. Also, it must be noted that Portuguese and English are quite different languages. These characteristics were not considered in this work. Furthermore, Portuguese OpenNLP processing and English OpenNLP processing have many differences too. Another point to be considered is the chuker construction. The other tools were available, only the chunker was not. So, we

13 Google Translator (https://translate.google.com.br/)

trained the chunker. This training can be improved. We trained it with the available data. The chunker could be trained with other data. Maybe if we had used other data the chunker would be better.

The ease of using ReVerb to work with texts in Portuguese is that its internal operations need not be changed. What changes is only the natural language processors it uses. As there was not a chunker available for Portuguese we had to build one. For this, we used a corpus in Portuguese. The format of this corpus was converted. The chunker was trained and evaluated. After that, it was necessary just to replace the sentence detector, the tokenizer, the POS tagger and the chunker, all for Portuguese. A simple label converter was created and the dictionary was translated. Even if the results achieved with the modified ReVerb are slightly below the original ReVerb it becomes clear that it is suitable for extracting information in Portuguese. To use ReVerb in other languages, it is necessary just to follow these simple instructions. Of course, when one of the natural language processors is not available, it will be necessary to create it.

7. CONCLUSIONS AND FUTURE WORK

Open IE is an automatic method for information extracting from large text sets. The basic idea is simple: most sentences contain reliable syntactic clues to its meaning. Often it is quite simple for computer to find verbs in a sentence, to identify entities related by verb and to use this to create facts (triples) (Etzioni, 2011). The goal of this work was to extract facts from text that are consistent with entities and relations for semantic representation construction. This work dealt with a means for supporting Semantic Web development, specifically facilitating construction of triples in Portuguese. Semantic triples generated by the extraction developed in this work can help web resources to be used more effective.

The main contribution of this work is the use of Open IE for texts in Portuguese. Semantic triples have several applications, like in question/answer systems, in ontology learning, in semantic annotation and semantic base, all linked to the Semantic Web principles. This demonstrates this paper can provide some means to boost Semantic Web construction. Even though simple, semantic triples enable computers to improve results and find answers to users. Finally, we provide a model for a multilingual Open IE system construction, namely a model to modify ReVerb in order to get it working with Spanish, Danish, Dutch, Swedish, among others, for instance.

The original ReVerb got more triples than the modified Reverb. This is due to several factors. The first reason is that the system was not created specifically for Portuguese, but it was adjusted from an English version. Second, there are some divergences in outputs of the OpenNLP tools for each type of language. As an example, there are irregularities in labeling some tokens. Third is the dictionary that was translated automatically. The use of manually translated dictionary could improve results. Besides, internal operation has not changed. So, the modified ReVerb can only find sentences in Portuguese that have the same structure as the corresponding sentence in English. The two languages have its own characteristics that were not treated in this work.

In future work one can explore some solutions to the problems pointed here. First, it can be used other NLP tools to replace OpenNLP. OpenNLP tools can also be trained again. An important issue is the ReVerb's dictionary, which could generate better results if it had been created directly for Portuguese rather than translated from English. To create this dictionary, a huge number of pages in Portuguese is necessary. A question and answer system can be created from this work. This system would be fed by the found triples. Furthermore, these triples could be placed in a graph-driven database. Entities would be represented by nodes and relations by the edges. Thus, all triples could be connected forming a richer semantic representation.

ACKNOWLEDGEMENT

To Coordenação de Aperfeiçoamento de Pessoal de Nível Superior (CAPES) for supporting this work.
To Freepik and Flaticon by the architecture icons.

REFERENCES

Akbik, A. and Broß, J., 2009. Wanderlust: Extracting semantic relations from natural language text using dependency grammar patterns. *Proceedings of the Workshop on Semantic Search (SemSearch 2009) at the 18th International World Wide Web Conference (WWW 2009)*. Madrid, Spain, pp. 6-15.

Akbik, A. and Löser, A., 2012. Kraken: N-ary facts in open information extraction. *Proceedings of the Joint Workshop on Automatic Knowledge Base Construction & Web-scale Knowledge Extraction (AKBC-WEKEX)*. Montreal, Canada, pp. 52-56.

Babu, K. G. et al, 2012. Web mining using semantic data mining techniques. *In International Journal of Soft Computing and Engineering (IJSCE)*, Volume 2, No. 3, pp. 168–171.

Balke, W.-T., 2012. Introduction to information extraction: Basic notions and current trends. *In Datenbank-Spektrum*, Volume 12, No. 2, pp. 81–88.

Banko, M. et al, 2007. Open information extraction from the web. *IJCAI'07 Proceedings of the 20th international joint conference on Artificial intelligence*, Hyderabad, India, pp. 2670-2676.

Banko, M. and Etzioni, O., 2008. The tradeoffs between open and traditional relation extraction. *ACL 2008, Proceedings of the 46th Annual Meeting of the Association for Computational Linguistics*, Columbus, USA, pp. 28–36.

Chiticariu, L. et al, 2010. Enterprise information extraction: recent developments and open challenges. *2010 ACM SIGMOD/PODS Conference*, Indianapolis, USA, pp. 1257–1258.

Del Corro, L. and Gemulla, R, 2013. Clausie: Clause-based open information extraction. WWW'13 Proceedings of the 22nd international conference on World Wide Web, Republic and Canton of Geneva, Switzerland, pp. 355–366.

Etzioni, O., 2011. Search needs a shake-up. *Nature*, Volume 476, No. 7358, pp. 25–26.

Etzioni, O. et al, 2008. Open information extraction from the web. *In Communications of the ACM - Surviving the data deluge*, Volume 51, No. 12, pp. 68–74.

Etzioni, O. et al, 2011. Open Information Extraction: The Second Generation. *IJCAI'11 Proceedings of the Twenty-Second international joint conference on Artificial Intelligence*. Barcelona, Spain, pp. 3-10.

Fader, A. et al, 2011. Identifying relations for open information extraction. *EMNLP'11 Proceedings of the Conference on Empirical Methods in Natural Language Processing*, Edinburgh, UK, pp. 1535-1545.

The Apache Software Foundation (2010) Apache OpenNLP Documentation. Available at: http://opennlp.apache.org/documentation.html (Accessed: 2 September 2016).

Gamallo, P., et al 2012. Dependency-based open information extraction. *ROBUS-UNSUP '12 Proceedings of the Joint Workshop on Unsupervised and Semi-Supervised Learning in NLP*, pp. 10–18.

Hassanzadeh, H. and Keyvanpour, M. R., 2012. Semantic Web Requirements Through Web Mining Techniques. *In International Journal of Computer Theory and Engineering*, Volume 4, No. 4, pp. 616-620.

M, B. (2014) Total number of Websites & size of the Internet as of 2013. Available at: http://www.factshunt.com/2014/01/total-number-of-websites-size-of.html (Accessed: 2 September 2016).

Madhu, G. et al, 2011. Intelligent semantic web search engines: A brief survey. *In International journal of Web & Semantic Technology (IJWesT)*, Volume 2, No. 1, pp. 34-42.

Mausam. et al, 2012. Open language learning for information extraction. *EMNLP-CoNLL'12 Proceedings of the 2012 Joint Conference on Empirical Methods in Natural Language Processing and Computational Natural Language Learning*, Jeju Island, Korea, pp. 523–534.

Negm, N. et al, 2012. A survey of web information extraction tools. *In International Journal of Computer Applications*, Volume 43, No. 7, pp. 19–27.

Piskorski, J. and Yangarber, R., 2013. *Information Extraction: Past, Present and Future*. Springer Berlin Heidelberg, Heildelberg, Germany pp. 23–49.

Savage, N., 2010. New search challenges and opportunities. *In Communications of the ACM*, Volume 53, No. 1, pp. 27–28.

Soderland, S. et al, 2010. Adapting open information extraction to domain-specific relations. *In AI Magazine*, Volume 31, No. 3, pp. 93–102.

Tseng, Y. et al, 2014. Chinese open relation extraction for knowledge acquisition. *Proceedings of the 14th Conference of the European Chapter of the Association for Computational Linguistics – EACL*, Gothenburg, Sweden, pp. 12–16.

Wu, F. and Weld, D. S., 2010. Open information extraction using wikipedia. *Proceedings of the 48th Annual Meeting of the Association for Computational Linguistics, ACL'10*, Stroudsburg, USA, pp. 118–127.

A PLATFORM TO ENRICH, EXPAND AND PUBLISH LINKED DATA OF POLICE REPORTS

Bruno C. N. Oliveira, Ivan Salvadori, Alexis Huf and Frank Siqueira
Department of Informatics and Statistics
Federal University of Santa Catarina, Florianópolis, Brazil

ABSTRACT

Motivated by transparency policies, government agencies have been publishing more valuable data. In order to take advantage of this initiative, data must be published in accordance with Linked Open Data principles. This work proposes a platform capable of enriching police reports with data available on the Web. This work also presents an evaluation tool, which consumes the linked data provided by a Web API, expands it with data extracted from other sources and provides an interface to assess the relevance of the expansions. Results show that the proposed expansion method might be useful for discovery and evaluation of related information, supporting richer analysis of the published data.

KEYWORDS

Linked Data, Web API, Semantic Web

1. INTRODUCTION

Government data have been published due to the growth of public transparency initiatives. The availability of this data is crucial to provide information to society as well as to encourage the framing of new action plans focused on improving the living conditions of citizens. However, it is essential to publish government data according to certain guidelines in order to allow its proper use. Among these guidelines, we highlight the principles that encompass the Linked Data publication, which seek to semantically connect and enrich information. Furthermore, the Linked Open Data (LOD) publication allows underlying datasets to be easily queried, combined, analyzed and reused.

Currently, researchers have been interested in exploring the challenges and possibilities of providing linked data in view of the increasingly relevant movement to publish government data. Authors as Kalampokis et al. (2013) and Chan (2013) show how to reuse published government data and perform mashups to provide deeper and detailed analysis. Lebo and Williams (2010) present a conversion technique of structured open data into linked data. Entity expansion approaches from heterogeneous sources and semantic similarity between resources are covered by Pereira Nunes et al. (2012).

The main contribution of this work is to propose a platform for enrichment, expansion and publishing of linked data, as well as an evaluation tool to assess the relevance degree of expansions. The platform comprises a data retrieval tool, which obtains non-structured data and converts it into structured data, a semantic Web API to enrich these dataset and publish linked data, and a tool that combines different data sources in order to expand the entities with additional related information. The evaluation tool enables the user to assess the expansions in order to enrich the entities. In this paper, we use data published by the Public Security Secretariat of the state of São Paulo (SSP/SP)[1], in Brazil, which discloses police reports information in a non-structured format. The data sources adopted for enriching information contained in the police reports are the Google search engine, which provides all sorts of information available on the Web, and the Court of Justice of São Paulo (TJSP)[2], which provides data on criminal and civil lawsuits in the same region where the police reports were filed. The results of this study point out that the enrichment, expansion and provisioning

[1] http://www.ssp.sp.gov.br/transparenciassp/
[2] http://tjsp.jus.br/

of linked data can assist the discovery and analysis of new relevant information. Moreover, it allows the effective reusing of data.

The remainder of this paper is organized as follows. Section 2 presents the required background for the understanding of this work. Section 3 describes some related work found in the literature. The semantic Web API for enrichment and publishing of linked data relating to police reports is described in section 4. Section 5 presents a tool to assess the police reports expansions. The assessment method is presented in section 6 while section 7 shows the results of the evaluation study. Finally, section 8 draws some conclusions regarding the results obtained with this work and discusses some foreseen improvements.

2. BACKGROUND

According to Bizer et al. (2009), the web has a huge potential to be a global space of linked data. In this view, not only the documents are available and linked to other documents, but also their content. Thus, data is structured in the form of subject-predicate-object triples in which the subject represents the described resource, the predicate represents a feature of the subject, and the object is the value assigned to this feature. Triples are described based on the RDF (Resource Description Framework) standard, which defines a model to describe the semantics of resources and associate them in order to enable that other information be linked to them (Gandon and Schreiber, 2014).

The concept of linked data is defined by Berners-Lee (2006), who presents a set of best practices for publishing structured data on the Web. These principles seek to establish links amongst different sets of data to form a single global data repository, leading to a powerful integration and reusing of data. Among the principles that conduct linked data publishing, HTTP URIs are used to identify and locate resources, which should be structured in the form of RDF triples. In addition, published datasets should include links to extra information. By sharing the same semantic definition base, through maximum reuse of predicates coupled with URIs, it can be created a network of connections that forms the basis of a novel Web.

Another important concept in the context of Linked Data is the Mashup approach, which combines content from different data sources aiming at engendering new resources. However, the lack of a high-level language to describe queries in heterogeneous sources is one of the issues faced in the development of mashup applications (Magalhães et al., 2013). According to Di Lorenzo et al. (2009), building mashups is often accomplished through several invocations to Web APIs, which do not follow a pattern. In addition, the information retrieved from each API is not linked with the remainder of the data involved in the mashup. This characteristic results in isolated data that hinders the integration process.

Another key concept for the understanding of our proposal is the REST architectural style (Fielding, 2000), which is a collection of principles and architectural constraints concerning the development of distributed web applications. One of the core concepts of REST relies on the resources, which can be addressed by a unique identifier (URI) and available to remote clients through representations. A resource can be a list of films showing in a cinema, user comments in a blog or a profile on a social network, for example. In addition, there are different ways to represent a resource. A representation is a sample of the state of a resource at a given moment of time, which can be described using a variety of formats such as HTML, XML, JSON, and so on.

3. RELATED WORK

Kalampokis et al. (2013) and Chan (2013) show the possibilities of information analysis and data integration due to the growth of open government data available on the Web. A mechanism to convert government data published in CSV format into linked data is suggested by Lebo and Williams (2010). The authors developed a tool with RDF vocabulary to describe how CSV datasets should be transformed into linked data. Apart from CSV, this tool neither addresses other dataset formats nor non-structured data.

In the field of mashups, DiFranzo et al. (2011) proposed an approach to create mashups from linked open government data. The work of Minhas et al. (2012) presents a framework driven to the study and evaluation of mashup tools. The authors sought to improve the current mashup development projects with approaches more focused on the users. They have performed an exploratory and qualitative analysis to study the strategies of mashup development tools, the technical resources adopted in its implementation, the graphical resources and the support offered to users. Our goal, on the other hand, is to perform a mashup presented by an evaluation tool, so that users can assess the relevance of the enriched content.

Regarding expansion, Pereira Nunes et al. (2012) present an approach to identify relationships between entities in different datasets. The degree of similarity among entities is measured according to the number of paths and the distance between the entities in a graph. Their approach utilizes social networking algorithms to analyze the graphs of datasets. Thus, the similarity between the different resources based on existing semantic connections is explored. In addition, expansion approach using the Bing search engine was employed to identify the correlation between entities based on co-occurrence of terms on the web. Similarly, our platform uses the concept of entities expansion in order to retrieve additional relevant information from different resources and utilizes the Google web search engine to perform one of the expansions.

The approaches proposed by Lebo and Williams (2010) and DiFranzo et al. (2011) consider only structured data as input parameter for mashups generation, whilst our proposal also takes into account non-structured data. The framework proposed by Minhas et al. (2012) allows assess the usability of and supports of mashup tools to guide new development strategies, although disregards the mashup's content relevance assessment. Pereira Nunes et al. (2012) evaluate, by means of algorithms, the connectivity degree between entities. The documents relatedness is measured based on the co-occurence of terms, yet a real checking if the content is indeed about the same object under study is not applied. On the other hand, the purpose of our study is to publish linked data retrieved from non-structured data sources without semantic annotation. In addition, our goal focuses on the assessment, carried out by humans, of entity expansions to properly enrich the published linked data with additional relevant information gathered from other resources.

4. WEB API FOR ENRICHMENT AND PUBLISHING LINKED DATA

The main component of the proposed platform is a REST Web API that offers data from police reports extracted from the website of the SSP/SP system. The Web API provides the information from the reports in a structured form and semantically annotated with terms of vocabularies and ontologies used in linked open data. In addition, police reports are enriched with geographic coordinates of the incident site.

4.1 Data Retrieval and Structuring

The SSP/SP system classifies the police reports according to their category (suspicious death, intentional homicide, robbery followed by murder, among others). Information about the report such as location, category, police station and date of the incident are available. Also, information of those involved (victims and perpetrators) are also provided, such as name, document number, gender, occupation, skin color, marital status, among others. However, detailed description of the fact is not disclosed, narrowing the accurate understanding of the incident.

In spite of being a substantial initiative of information transparency to society, the SSP/SP system does not publish information in a suitable format to be reused by other systems or even analyzed by researchers. The reports are published in a non-structured format in HTML pages created dynamically and with no semantic enrichment, disregarding basic principles of linked data, necessary to achieve an appropriate level of public transparency. Furthermore, a search mechanism to retrieve available data is not supplied, so it becomes unfeasible to fetch police reports based on certain desired features.

We have developed a tool, available at *Figshare* (https://dx.doi.org/10.6084/m9.figshare.3856074), that is able to retrieve police reports from the SSP/SP system and store data into a structured format. As a result, for each report that is processed, the tool generates a document in JSON format, which is more suitable to be consumed by other systems. In addition, the tool also generates documents in CSV format with all the information obtained from police reports, becoming suitable to be processed by data analysis mechanisms.

4.2 Data Publishing

Access to information obtained from police reports retrieved from the SSP/SP website is provided through a semantic RESTful Web API. As depicted in Figure 1, by means of JSON documents generated previously as well as Google Maps API, the Web API of police reports provides semantic representations enriched with geographical data. Two representations are provided: police reports in JSON-LD (JSON for Linked Data) format (Lanthaler and Gütl, 2012) and maps in HTML format. These outputs are consumed by the evaluation tool described in section 5, and afterwards will be enriched with additional information. Some instructions of how to access and manipulate the APIs are also available in the *Figshare* repository.

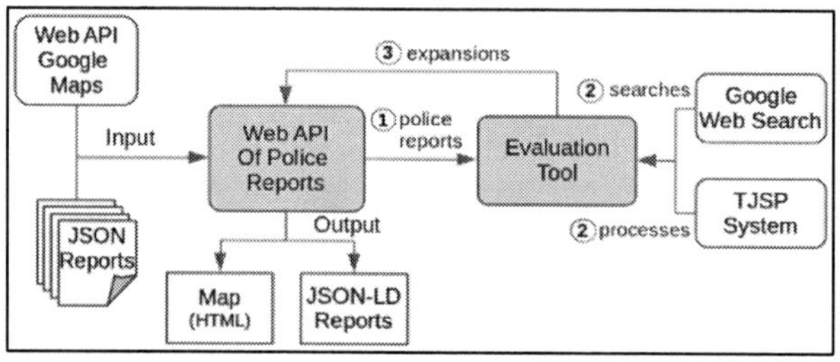

Figure 1. Architecture of the Web API of police reports and Evaluation Tool

The semantic enrichment of provided representations adds semantic annotations to JSON documents, generating JSON-LD representations, which associate objects and properties in the document to classes and properties defined in ontologies. JSON-LD representations are compatible with the RDF data model and can be converted to triples by several existing libraries, for instance, JSON-LD-Java (https://github.com/jsonld-java/jsonld-java). On the other hand, the location pointed out in a police report is enriched by invoking the Google Maps API to convert addresses into geographic coordinates, which can be used to place markers on a map.

Figure 2 (a) shows an example of a police report, categorized as suspicious suicide, represented in JSON-LD. This representation is associated with four ontologies and the entity attributes are related to entities and terms of these ontologies. This example also illustrates the enrichment of a report with its address set as geographic coordinates and with other details about the location, such as the city, state and postal code. Finally, “rdfs:seeAlso” properties are used as expansions to link the report with other related entities. In contrast, Figure 2 (b) depicts the original non structured police report, provided by the SSP/SP system, which has no semantic embedded and none mechanism of LOD to be reused by other resources.

(a)

```
{ "@context": {
   "foaf": "http://xmlns.com/foaf/0.1/",
   "dbo": "http://dbpedia.org/ontology/",
   "schema": "https://schema.org/",
   "ssp": "http://exemplo.com.br/ssp-ontology/",
   "rdfs": "http://www.w3.org/2000/01/rdf-schema#" },
  "ssp:reportNumber": "6923",
  "ssp:dateOfIncident": "16/12/2015",
   ...
  "dbo:victim": [ {
    "@type": ["foaf:Person", "schema:Person"],
    "foaf:name": "JACQUELINE DO CARMO LIMA LEONE",
    "ssp:personId": "OMMITED-INFORMATION",
    "dbo:nationality": "dbpedia.org/resource/Brazil",
    "foaf:gender": "Female",
    "dbo:birthDay": "OMMITED-INFORMATION",
    "dbo:occupation": "Cashier",
    "dbo:skinColor": "Brown",
    "dbo:deathCause": "dbpedia.org/resource/Category:Unsolved_deaths",
     ... }   ],
  "schema:location": {
   "@type": "Place",
   "schema:address": {
    "@type": "schema:PostalAddress",
    "schema:addressLocality": "Santo Andre",
    "schema:addressRegion": "SP",
    "schema:postalCode": "09190-615",
    "schema:streetAddress": "Rua Doutor Henrique..." },
   "schema:geo": {
    "@type": "schema:GeoCoordinates",
    "schema:latitude": "-23.670621",
    "schema:longitude": "-46.533615" }
  },
  "rdfs:seeAlso": "http://.../mulher-baleada-por-ladroes",
  "rdfs:seeAlso": "http://tjsp.jus.br/..."
}
```

(b)

SECRETARIA DE ESTADO DA SEGURANÇA PÚBLICA
POLICIA CIVIL DO ESTADO DE SÃO PAULO

Dependência: 01° D.P. SANTO ANDRÉ **Folha: 1**

Boletim No.: 6923/2015 **Iniciado:** 16/12/2015 10:38hs e **Emitido:** 16/12/2015 10:38hs

Boletim de Ocorrencia de Autoria Conhecida

Natureza(s):

Espécie: Óbito
Natureza: Morte suspeita
Consumado

Local: RUA DOUTOR HENRIQUE CALDERAZO, 321 - PARQUE CENTRAL
CEP: 09190615 - S.ANDRE - SP
Tipo de Local: Saúde
Circunscrição: 01° D.P. SANTO ANDRÉ
Ocorrência: 16/12/2015 PELA MANHÃ
Comunicação: 16/12/2015 às 22:34 horas
Elaboração: 16/12/2015 às 22:38 horas
Flagrante: Não

Vítima(s) e Autor(es)/Vítima(s):

JACQUELINE DO CARMO LIMA LEONE (Vítima) - Vítima Fatal - RG: [redacted] Natural de: MAUA -SP - Nacionalidade: BRASILEIRA - Sexo: Feminino - Nascimento: [redacted] 23 anos - Estado Civil: Casado - Profissão: CAIXA - Instrução: 1 Grau completo - Cutis: Parda - Naturezas Envolvidas: Morte suspeita

Histórico:

"Os históricos dos boletins de ocorrência são públicos. Em regra, serão fornecidos mediante solicitação ao SIC (Serviço de Informação ao Cidadão), excepcionando-se somente os dados necessários a preservação da intimidade, vida privada, honra e imagem das pessoas, nos termos da Lei nº 12.527 de 18 de novembro de 2011."

Exames requisitados: IML

Solução: ENCAMINHAMENTO DP ÁREA DO FATO

01° D.P. SANTO ANDRÉ

15/06/2016 10:38:07

Figure 2. (a) Example of police report provided by the: (a) Web API in JSON-LD and (b) SSP/SP in a Web page

The proposed Web API allows querying data by using search filters, such as the category of police reports, its year or identification number, as well as filters applied to those who were involved in the incident, such as gender, education level and age. Additionally, the Web API provides map representations with markers locating all police reports selected from the filters mentioned above. For instance, it is possible to position markers in a precise place on a map where crime against women were committed in the year of 2015, as depicted in Figure 3. In this way, the Web API provides custom geographic views of police reports. The representations available in JSON-LD are suitable to be consumed by other systems, allowing such information to be used in different ways and for different purposes. Moreover, HTML representations accurately show the location of incidents on a map, thereby providing a geographic view over a set of reports.

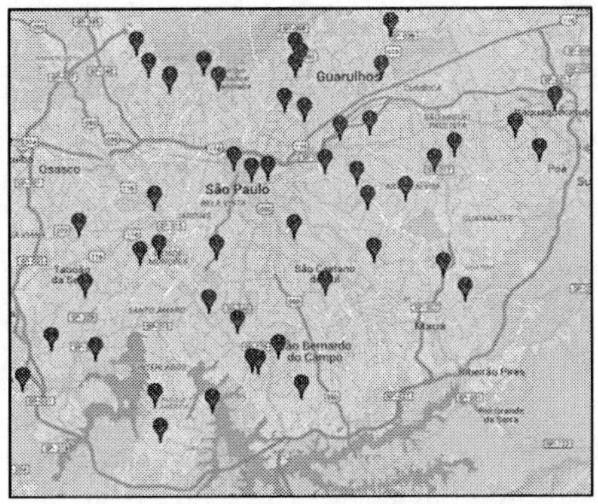

Figure 3. Locations of homicide against women

5. EVALUATION TOOL

The platform proposed in this paper includes a tool that performs a mashup to evaluate the expansion of entities that represent a police report. This tool uses data provided by the Web API of police reports and comprises a web application as an interface for end users and a REST API to manipulate a) the expansions of reports and b) the assessment regarding the relevance of an expansion. Two kinds of expansions are supported: the results from Google web search and the results of lawsuits registered in TJSP. Based on the identification number (available in the report) of those who were involved in the reported incident, the tool performs the expansion of judicial data from TJSP which offers data on lawsuits related to the victims or authors of the crime. Similarly, it retrieves the first result from Google web search based on the category of the police report and the name of those who have been involved in it. Issues of homonyms in the later expansion can be dealt with, since the user can analyze the whole content of the result, namely features of the incident (location, date, time), characteristics of the person (gender, age, skin color, occupation) and the type of crime. This may rule out homonyms who are unrelated to the incident, leading to a more accurate assessment.

Primarily, an assessment is started with the creation of a sample of police reports. The user must inform to the tool a category (homicide, robbery, suspicious suicide, etc.), a year and a desired amount of police reports to be assessed. From the reports provided by the Web API, as depicted in Figure 1 (1), the evaluation tool selects a simple random sample without replacement of police reports that fit the filters passed by the user. Afterwards, both expansions - Google and TJSP (2) - are performed and the obtained data is stored. At the end of evaluation, the result is submitted to the Web API (3), in order to enrich the corresponding entity.

Figure 4 illustrates the user interface of the evaluation tool showing a police report categorized as a suspicious suicide. At the top of the tool, the main information about the report and the parties involved are displayed. Below that, expansions from Google search engine and results of lawsuits obtained from TJSP are presented to the user. Finally, the relevance options for each expansion are provided, so that users can choose the best option according to their analysis. The button "Assess and Continue" submits the assessment result and displays the next enriched police report for evaluation.

Figure 4. User Interface of the Evaluation Tool

6. ASSESSMENT METHODOLOGY

Effectiveness of entity expansions was conducted through qualitative experiments over the dataset under study. We performed the assessment in a manual procedure assisted by the evaluation tool presented in the previous section. As the expansion process seldom fails, the failure cases were disregarded. In the expansion by the Google search engine, failure is defined as a lack of results. On the other hand, if the search engine has at least one result, relevant or not, the result is assessed. In the TJSP expansion, failures are not recorded, since the lack of results is indeed considered as a result, when a person has never been involved in a criminal or civil lawsuit in TJSP.

The population parameters under study are the proportions of police reports, whose expansions were classified by the evaluation tool based on three different ratings, which are mutually exclusive, for each expansion. The expansions from TJSP system are classified as *CRIMINAL* when at least one of those who were involved in the incident was a party to any criminal process. Similarly, when at least one civil lawsuit was found for any of those involved in the incident, yet no criminal process was returned, the expansion is then classified as *CIVIL*. Finally, if no lawsuit was found for any of the parties involved in the incident, the expansion is classified as *NO_PROCESS*. Concerning Google expansions, classifications are ordered in accordance with new relevant information retrieved. The most relevant classification, *WITH_HISTORY*, comprises the police reports for which expansion has gathered the incident detailed description - unpublished by the SSP/SP official system - corresponding to the report. The second classification, *RELEVANT*, covers cases where the expansion has gathered additional information relating to victims and/or perpetrator, though it does not describe the incident in detail. All other cases - when it is not possible to determine with reasonable accuracy whether the incident or parties involved are the same as in the report - are classified as *UNDETERMINED*.

Two categories of police reports were selected to assess the expansions: "intentional homicide" and a sub-category of "Suspicious Death" called "Reasonable questions about suicide or unnatural death". The motivation for the choice of homicides is the large attention given to this type of crime by the media and public opinion, whereas in cases of suicides it is expected a more limited coverage by the media. The experiment covers police reports filed in the year of 2015.

Faced with the extensive process of assessing the high volume of reports, we have estimated, for each selected category, confidence intervals for the classification of expansions, using samples generated by the tool. In order to figure out the sample size required for 95% confidence level and a sampling error of 3%, a pilot study with one hundred police reports for each category was executed. In reference to the estimation of confidence intervals for each category of police reports, we have used a sample sized according to the classification parameter which has required a larger sample. For both categories, the *NO_PROCESS* classification of TJSP expansion determined the sample size. Hence, 748 reports were randomly picked amongst 4.485 murder reports, whereas 334 reports from 1.274 suspicious suicides were picked likewise.

7. RESULTS

Confidence intervals that generalize the proportions measured in the experiments for the entire population of police reports are shown in Table 1 and Table 2. The results of expansions, especially those based on Google, are interesting because, although the detailed description had not been provided by the official SSP/SP system, the history of some crimes was found in 17,78% of the police reports, with a margin of error of 2,74% at 95% confidence. In many cases, the expansions with history brought, besides the description of the incident, the full names of suspects and information about the personal life of victims and authors of the crime. It is worth mentioning that, in these experiments, Google expansion considered only the first result available. Moreover, we measured at 95% confidence and 3,248% margin of error, that parties involved in 28,877% of police reports categorized as homicide had already been involved in lawsuit(criminal and/or civil) registered in TJSP. The qualitative assessment of the expansions reveals a significant proportion of police reports that have been enriched with relevant information obtained from Google search engine and from the TJSP system. It is also expected that higher rates of relevant expansions can be obtained by applying heuristics, including other search engines as well as expanding the scope of expansion beyond the first result.

Table 1. Confidence interval at 95% for assessments of Google expansions

Classification	Homicide	Suicide
WITH_HISTORY	17,78 ± 2,740	6,287 ± 2,603
RELEVANT	8,824 ± 2,033	0,8982 ± 0,869
UNDETERMINED	73,396 ± 3,167	92,81 ± 2,770

Table 2. Confidence interval at 95% for assessments of TJSP expansions

Classification	Homicide	Suicide
CRIMINAL	22,460 ± 2,991	10,479 ± 3,285
CIVIL	6,417 ± 1,756	5,090 ± 2,357
NO_PROCESS	71,123 ± 3,248	84,431 ± 3,888

These statistics paint a quite interesting view of a predilection of homicide cases by the media: among 21 expansions with the history of reports categorized as suicide, 7 of these expansions brought descriptions of homicides, 3 about accidental deaths and 2 described murders in robbery cases. These results have been found even with the search query including the string "suicide". Applying the confidence interval for these 12 cases, we can estimate for suicide reports with 95% confidence that Google expansion brings a detailed description apparently divergent of the original category of the report for between 1,597% and 5,589% of cases.

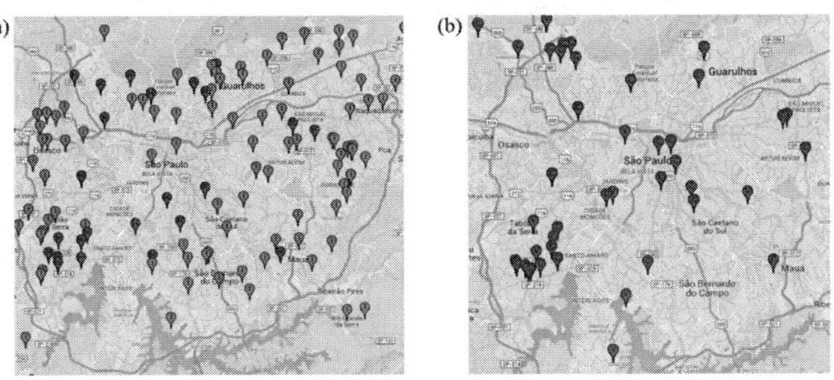

Figure 5. Geographical relevance of (a) Google expansion, and (b) TJSP expansion

Figure 5 shows the geographic coordinates of homicides from the sample concerning both Google expansion (a) and TJSP expansion (b). The expansions which were assessed as *UNDETERMINED* are identified with gray markers and the letter "I". Green ("R") and red ("H") markers indicate the geographic coordinates of homicides assessed as *RELEVANT* and *WITH_HISTORY*, respectively. Red markers identified by the letter "C" represent police reports which have at least one party involved in the incident with criminal lawsuit in TJSP. Green ("V") markers represent instances in which some of those who have been involved in the incident have only civil lawsuits. Thus, the representations on a map for a set of expanded police reports can aid new exploratory analysis.

8. CONCLUSIONS AND FUTURE WORK

In this paper, we have introduced a platform for the enrichment, expansion and publishing of linked data, starting from a non-structured public dataset of police reports. Up to the writing of this paper, 28.992 reports have been extracted, structured and published in a public repository available at *Figshare* (https://dx.doi.org/10.6084/m9.figshare.3856074). The structured information is semantically enriched and provided by a Web API. Then, the content of each police report is expanded to retrieve other similar web documents with relevant information. In addition, an evaluation tool is presented in order to show how we assess the expansions and combine them with the resources.

Some outcomes of the assessment for entity expansions are also presented in this paper. During the evaluation process, we could identify some police reports registered in a category incompatible with the fact described in the expanded results. We have also found criminal and/or civil lawsuits relating to those who have been involved in the report, especially victims of homicide. These findings are only viable due to the content gathered from Google and TJSP expansions and can be important to work on deeper analysis and further investigation about the incidents.

Although the platform was developed in the domain of police reports, we intend to build a generic platform to expand and publish enriched data. Additionally, future work can also include additional data sources into the platform, for instance, new web search engines, social networks as well as other governmental systems. Instead of manually assess the quality of expansions, we might also apply techniques for named entity recognition, enabling the evaluation, in an unsupervised manner, of the relationship between expansions and the original entity.

REFERENCES

Berners-Lee, T., 2006. *Linked Data*. [Online] Available at: http://www.w3.org/DesignIssues/LinkedData.htm.

Bizer, C., Heath, T. & Berners-Lee, T., 2009. Linked Data - The Story So Far. *International Journal on Semantic Web and Information Systems*, pp.1-22.

Chan, C.M.L., 2013. From Open Data to Open Innovation Strategies: Creating E-Services Using Open Government Data. *46th Hawaii International Conference on System Sciences (HICSS)*, pp.1890-99.

Di Lorenzo, G., Hacid, H., Paik, H.-y. & Benatallah, B., 2009. Data integration in mashups. *ACM SIGMOD Record*, p.59.

DiFranzo, D. et al., 2011. The Web is My Back-end: Creating Mashups with Linked Open Government Data. In *Linking Government Data*. New York. pp.205-19.

Gandon, F. & Schreiber, G., 2014. *Resource Description Framework (RDF) Model and Syntax Specification*. [Online] Available at: http://www.w3.org/TR/rdf-syntax-grammar/.

Kalampokis, E., Tambouris, E. & Tarabanis, K., 2013. On Publishing Linked Open Government Data. *Proceedings of the 17th Panhellenic Conference on Informatics*, pp.25-32.

Lanthaler, M. & Gütl, C., 2012. On using JSON-LD to create evolvable RESTful services. In *Proceedings of the Third International Workshop on RESTful Design - WS-REST '12*. New York. p.25.

Lebo, T. & Williams, G.T., 2010. Converting Governmental Datasets into Linked Data. *Proceedings of the 6th International Conference on Semantic Systems*, pp.1-3.

Magalhães, R.P. et al., 2013. QEF-LD - A Query Engine for Distributed Query Processing on Linked Data. In *Proceedings of the 15th International Conference on Enterprise Information Systems*. pp.185-92.

Minhas, S.S., Sampaio, P. & Mehandjiev, N., 2012. A Framework for the Evaluation of Mashup Tools. In *Proceedings of the 2012 IEEE Ninth International Conference on Services Computing*. Washington. p.8.

Pereira Nunes, B. et al., 2012. Can Entities be Friends? *Proceedings of the Web of Linked Entities Workshop in conjuction with the 11th International Semantic Web Conference*, pp.45-57.

SEMANTIC INTERPRETATION AND FORMAL GRAPH MODEL OF AN ATTRIBUTED PREDICATE RDF

[1,2]Dewi Wisnu Wardani and [2]Josef Küng
[1]*Informatics Department, Sebelas Maret University, Surakarta, Central Java, Indonesia*
[2]*FAW Institute, Johannes Kepler University, Linz, Austria*

ABSTRACT

In the semantic web point of view, a complex knowledge cannot be represented naturally by standard triple RDF. Therefore, an attributed predicate RDF (AP-RDF) has been proposed as a new alternative model to represent complex knowledge. AP-RDF augments the role of a predicate to handle attributes to represent any additional statements of the main statement. In this work, we focus on proving whether AP-RDF satisfies the standard semantic interpretation of W3C Recommendation and providing its formal graph model. In the end, we can show that AP-RDF satisfies the standard semantic interpretation by extending the interpretation of property with the interpretation of predicate type. We also define that the formal graph model is the combination between digraph and hypergraph.

KEYWORDS

Knowledge management, AP-RDF, semantic interpretation, graph model

1. INTRODUCTION

RDF (Resource Description Framework) is the standard data model of the semantic web (Consortium and others, 2014a) (Chen et al., 2006) (Consortium and others, 2014b). It naturally represents a triple S-P-O such as *"NaCl consists of Sodium"*. The subject (S) is *"NaCl"*, the predicate (P) is *"consist_of"* and the object (O) is *"Sodium"*. Any additional information on the statement makes knowledge becominng complex such as *"NaCl consists of one portion of Sodium"* or *"NaCl consists of one portion of Sodium and one portion of Chloride"*. Knowledge in the real world could be more complex than those examples.

The prominent approach, N-Quads (Carothers, 2014) has been introduced to represent a complex knowledge as an RDF which has four elements. The fourth element manages the context issue. Named Graph (Carroll et al., 2005) introduced the name of a triple statement as like as the fourth element in N-Quads. The name of a graph manages the provenance, trust and authority issues. Additional information on the main triple statement either as a context, provenance or other types of statements makes the knowledge becoming complex. In this paper, we see that the predicate has a more important role than it's usually seen. The idea of AP-RDF is to extend the role of a predicate. A predicate also can handle other additional information on the main statement. Additional information increases the complexity of the knowledge. The previous works show that the model has promising performance results concerning its retrieval process (D. W. Wardani and Küng, 2015) (D. Wardani and Küng, 2015).

Having a new performed model for representing knowledge in semantic web is not enough. We need to evaluate whether the AP-RDF satisfies the standard semantic interpretation of the W3C Recommendation. Answering the question, whether a model which satisfies semantic interpretation has no influence on the performances but will influence the extended processes e.g. reasoning process for automatically finding a new knowledge. Therefore, making sure a new model satisfies the standard semantic interpretation of W3C Recommendation is an elementary issue. AP-RDF extends the role of a predicate to handle information which adds the complexity of knowledge. It means predicates in AP-RDF have an additional semantics comparing normal predicates in standard RDF. The other fundamental issue is to formalize the formal graph model of AP-RDF. The formal graph model of AP-RDF will be useful in supporting some works which need graph theoretical issues such as data integration and graph mining. The advantage in using graph approach in composing AP-RDF was useful in the earlier work (D. W. Wardani and Küng, 2015). The formalizing graph model of AP-RDF is a reverse idea of this work. In brief, our goals and as well as our contributions in this work are as below:

- Proving that AP-RDF satisfies the standard semantic interpretation of the W3C Recommendation.
- Providing the formal graph model of AP-RDF.

The remaining sections are organized as follows: we summarize the related work in Section 2. We briefly summarize the idea of AP-RDF in Section 3. Section 4 discusses that AP-RDF satisfies the standard semantic interpretation of the W3C Recommendation. Section 5 explains the formal graph model of AP-RDF and finally the conclusion and future works in Section 6.

2. RELATED WORK

Previous works have proposed some methods which emphasized in representing complex knowledge in semantic web technology (Manola et al., 2004) (Carothers, 2014) (Carroll et al., 2005). The recent work (D. W. Wardani and Küng, 2015) shows that AP-RDF has better performance (query times) than the other models. Reification, Named Graph, and N-Quads are all W3C recommendation models in representing knowledge in the semantic web. They are assumed already satisfy the standard semantic interpretation due they are all a part of the W3C Recommendation. The other recent model (Das et al., 2014) did not try to prove whether their model satisfies the standard semantic interpretation of the W3C Recommendation.

The latest document which explains the standard semantic interpretation of W3C Recommendation (Hayes and Patel-Schneider, 2014) formalized precisely several interpretations, which divided into the normative and the non-normative interpretations. The earlier documents (Arenas et al., 2009) (Gutierrez et al., 2004) had introduced several explanations before they became the standard of the W3C recommendation. The main interpretation is a normative interpretation which consists of a simple interpretation (included datatype), RDF interpretation and RDFS interpretation. Each interpretation explains its distinct entailment regimes and its corresponding patterns of entailment. The entailment maps between syntaxes and their semantic interpretations. As the standard of W3C Recommendation, all new models should satisfy this standard. An AP-RDF has a different approach comparing the other models. It creates instances of predicate type as a new concept in representing knowledge. Hence, the modified concept of syntaxes must be evaluated whether it satisfies the standard semantic interpretation.

One work (Hayes and Gutierrez, 2004) has started in defining a formal graph model of RDF. The authors define the most suitable fundamental graph theory for RDF, which eventually turns out derived from the hypergraph. The earlier work also has shown the advantage in using the concept of hypergraph for representing a complex knowledge (D. W. Wardani and Küng, 2015). This work considers that the graph model is more expressive and has some advantages in representing knowledge in the real world (Chein and Mugnier, 2008) (Aggarwal and Wang, 2010) (Deng et al., 2012). The other work shows that a directed property hypergraph which defines a complex knowledge in the real world can be represented as AP-RDF (D. Wardani and Küng, 2015). All the previous works which related in providing the formal graph model use standard triple RDF as the main object. Our work will focus on providing the graph model of AP-RDF.

3. AN ATTRIBUTED PREDICATE RDF (AP-RDF)

Firstly, we are going to explain AP-RDF, which has been proposed in these works (D. W. Wardani and Küng, 2015) (D. Wardani and Küng, 2015). An RDF triple consists of a triple subject (S), predicate (P) and object (O). Each element is a statement, therefore, naturally RDF can be managed freely. The explanations are as below:

- There are no exact criteria for the type and its instances. A node can be a type and the same time can be an instance of the other type. An example below:
  ex:Dahlia rdf:type ex:Flower .
  ex:Waterlily_Dahlias rdf:type ex:Dahlia .
- Properties also can have properties. An example below:
  ex:own rdf:type ex:personAbility .
  ex:hasVehicle rdf:type ex:own .

ex:Dina ex:own ex:Dahlia .

Authors of RDF are conceptually free in composing RDF. We can see from the given above example, *"ex:Dahlia"* can be functioned as S or as O. The term *"ex:own"* can be functioned as S, P and O. The term *"ex:personAbility"* is a property, but it has a role as O in the RDF. *"ex:own"* itself is a property. Therefore, it means properties can themselves have properties. This flexibility influences the approach of AP-RDF that an element of triples may have multiple roles.

The main idea of AP-RDF is to extend the role of predicates. A predicate connects the subject, and the object also connects to additional statements of the main RDF triple. All additional statements are formulated as attributes of a predicate (D. W. Wardani and Küng, 2015). For managing attributes of a predicate, the predicate itself has roles as the standard predicate and as the subject in a different triple statement. In this work, for the clearer explanation, we add a few definitions for AP-RDF as below:

DEFINITION 1. (A predicate type and instances of predicate)
Let PT be predicate type and let PIT be an instance of predicate type $PT.PIT = \{p_{IT} | p_{IT} \in (S \cap P)\}$ and $(PT \cup PIT) \subseteq P$.

Definition 1 defines predicate instances of a predicate type, as a new feature in AP-RDF.
DEFINITION 2. (An Attributed Predicate RDF)
Let T be an AP-RDF triple. T consists of a set of Subject (S), Predicate (P) and Object (O).$T = \{S, P, O\}$ where $S = \{s | s \in (S \cup PIT)\}$,$P = \{p | p \in P\}$,$O = \{o | o \in (O \cup PT)\}$.

Definition 2 defines that an element of triples may have multiple roles.

An example: *"A company Mossack created a new company, named Shell with budged US$990M. Dezeitung wrote that the creating process was in Panama. This statement was inserted by Jürgen. The creating process was led by Leon, started from 2013-01-01 ended on 2013-02-01. Mossack also created another company named GrandShell "*.

Based on the above definitions, we obtain the AP-RDF of the example (*example.ttl*) as below:

@PREFIX ex: <http://example.org/ex1> .
@PREFIX rdf: <http://www.w3.org/1999/02/22-rdf-syntax-ns#> .

ex:Mossack	*ex:creates_A*	*ex:Shell .*
ex:creates_A	*ex:hasBudget*	*"US$990M" .*
ex:creates_A	*ex:location_A*	*ex:Panama .*
ex:creates_A	*ex:leader_A*	*ex:Leon .*
ex:leader_A	*ex:startDate*	*"2013-01-01"^^xsd:date .*
ex:leader_A	*ex:endDate*	*"2013-02-01"^^xsd:date .*
ex:location_A	*ex:source_A*	*ex:Dezeitung .*
ex:source_A	*ex:insertedBy*	*ex:Jürgen .*
ex:creates_A	*rdf:type*	*ex:creates .*
ex:location_A	*rdf:type*	*ex:location .*
ex:leader_A	*rdf:type*	*ex:leader .*
ex:source_A	*rdf:type*	*ex:source .*
ex:Mossack	*ex:creates*	*ex:GrandShell .*

4. THE SEMANTIC INTERPRETATION OF AP-RDF

As a new model of knowledge representation, having good performances in the retrieving process is not enough (D. W. Wardani and Küng, 2015) (D. Wardani and Küng, 2015). It needs to evaluate whether AP-RDF satisfies the standard semantic interpretation of W3C Recommendation. We consider the standard semantic interpretation of the W3C Recommendation (Hayes and Patel-Schneider, 2014). There are three normative semantic interpretations. They are the simple interpretation, RDF interpretation, and RDFS interpretation. The simple interpretation is the minimal truth conditions. The extended interpretation cannot negate the simpler semantic interpretation. It means if it satisfies the truth conditions in RDFS interpretation, it also satisfies truth conditions in RDF interpretation and the simple interpretations. If it satisfies the RDF interpretation, it also satisfies the simple interpretation, but not always satisfies the truth conditions in RDFS interpretation. All interpretations only can be examined over ground triples.

The main idea of AP-RDF is to create the instances of predicate type. The instances of predicate type are allowed to have attribute-statements. This form is a modification of standard triple RDF. Therefore, it must be evaluated that the modification has an entailment regime to normative semantic interpretation. In this work, we show our proving process for the given example, but it can be implemented all cases. From the given *example.ttl*, the first line, and second lines are examples of the main extension of AP-RDF. In the first line "*ex:create_A*" is the instance of predicate type "*ex:creates*" as the substitute of the predicate type itself, then we use the instance of the predicate type to reify meta information on the main triple statements such has shown in line two. Normally, RDF will use the predicate type, "*ex:creates*". Semantically the predicate instances entail to their predicate type, and the predicates are semantically a part of the properties.

As the summary, in AP-RDF, the default predicates are the predicate instances *IPIT*. Therefore, we extend the interpretation of properties *IP* by adding the interpretation of the predicate type *IPT*. Automatically $IPT \subseteq IP$. It purposes to define that the syntax of the predicate instances and the predicate type has the same semantic interpretation. The rest, we follow the W3C standard semantic interpretation (Hayes and Patel-Schneider, 2014). In further explanation in this paper, we name it as the default semantic interpretation.

CONJECTURE 1.

A simple interpretation of AP-RDF follows all default features of the simple semantic interpretation except the mapping function of property (*IEXT*). *IEXT* of AP-RDF is$IP \rightarrow IRxIR$. *IS* is a mapping of IRIs. $IS: V \rightarrow IR \cup IP$

A simple interpretation *I* of the example AP-RDF is defined as follows:

- We obtain IRIs:
  ex:Mossack→a ; ex:Shell→b; ex:Panama→c; ex:Leon→d; ex:Dezeitung→e; ex:Jürgen→f; ex:creates→g; ex:location→h; ex:leader→i; ex:source→j; ex:GrandShell→k; ex:creates_A→l; ex:hasBudget→m; ex:location_A→n; ex:leader_A→o; ex:startDate→p; ex:endDate→ q; ex:source_A→r; ex:insertedBy→s;
- *IL* is a function from typed literal.
  We obtain: *"2013-01-01"^^xsd:date* → L_0;*"2013-02-01"^^xsd:date* → L_1 . $IL = \{L_0, L_1\}$
- *LV* is a partial mapping from untyped literal. We obtain: *"US$990M"* → L_2,. $LV = \{L_2\}$
- *IR* is a non-empty set of resources, the universe of *I*. We obtain:
  $IR=\{(a, b, c, d, e, f, g, h, i, j, k, l, m, n, o, p, q, r, s) \cup IL \cup LV\}$
- *IP* is a set of properties, which may overlap with *IR*. We obtain: $IP = \{g, l, m, n, o, p, q, r, s\}$
- *IEXT* is a mapping function of each property. In the original simple interpretation, the function maps *IP* to the power set of *IRxIR*. Additionally, in AP-RDF the special property which is formed from the instance of predicate type maps a pair resources, *IEXT* is a functional map
  $IP \rightarrow IRxIR$. We obtain:
  IEXT =
  $g \rightarrow \{\langle a,k\rangle\};l \rightarrow \{\langle a,b\rangle\};m \rightarrow \{\langle l,L_3\rangle\};n \rightarrow \{\langle l,c\rangle\};o \rightarrow \{\langle l,d\rangle\};p \rightarrow \{\langle o,L_0\rangle\};q \rightarrow \{\langle o,L_1\rangle\};r \rightarrow \{\langle n,e\rangle\};s \rightarrow \{\langle r,f\rangle\}$

The simple interpretation *I* treats all URIs equally. There are few issues after the evaluation of the simple interpretation: (i) There are properties which are formulated from the instance of predicate type, e.g. *ex:location_A, location_B*. They are formulated from predicate type *ex:location*. The instance of the predicate type is a property, and then the predicate type is a property as well. (ii) The predicate type is a part of the properties. As an extension of the property, it should be defined as a property too. Therefore, AP-RDF needs further semantic interpretation. The next extension is RDF Interpretation. RDF Interpretation contains a simple interpretation and the extra interpretations from the vocabularies of RDF, which have a namespace with prefix *rdf:* (Hayes and Patel-Schneider, 2014).

CONJECTURE 2.

An RDF interpretation of AP-RDF follows all default features of RDF semantic interpretation as an extension of an AP-RDF simple interpretation and adds the mapping function of property *rdf:type* to *IPT*. $XIP \in IPT$if$IP(rdf{:}type) \rightarrow \{\langle X, XIP\rangle\}andX \in IPIT$.

RDF Interpretation *IRDF* of the example AP-RDF is defined below: (excluded the interpretations which have described earlier)

- Add *IR* from the AP-RDF simple interpretation with RDF vocabulary and should satisfy RDF axiom as well. The list of RDF axiom: *rdf:type rdf:type rdf:Property .; rdf:subject rdf:type rdf:Property .; rdf:predicate rdf:type rdf:Property .; rdf:object rdf:type rdf:Property .; rdf:first rdf:type rdf:Property .; rdf:rest rdf:type rdf:Property .; rdf:value rdf:type rdf:Property .; rdf:nil rdf:type rdf:List .; rdf:_1 rdf:type rdf:Property .; rdf:_2 rdf:type rdf:Property .; ...etc.* Therefore, we obtain: *ex:Mossack→a ; ex:Shell→b; ex:Panama→c; ex:Leon→d; ex:Dezeitung→e; ex:Jürgen→f; ex:creates→g; ex:location→h; ex:leader→i; ex:source→j; ex:GrandShell→k; ex:creates_A→l; ex:hasBudget→m; ex:location_A→n; ex:leader_A→o; ex:startDate→p; ex:endDate→ q; ex:source_A→r; ex:insertedBy→s;*
  rdf:type→A; rdf:Property→B; rdf:XMLLiteral→C_0*; rdf:Statement→*C_1*; rdf:Subject→*C_2 *; rdf:Predicate→* C_3*: rdf:Object→*C_4*; rdf:nil→* C_5*; rdf:List→* C_6*; rdf:First→* C_7 *; rdf:rest→* C_8*; rdf:Alt→* C_9*; rdf:Bag→* C_{10}*; rdf:Seq→* C_{11}*; rdf:value→* C_{12} *; rdf:_1 ... rdf:_y→* D_y, $y \in \mathbb{N}$
  $IR=\{a, b, c, d, e, f, g, h, i, j, k, l, m, n, o, p, q, r, s, A, C_x, D_y \mid x \in \{0,\ldots,12\}, y \in \mathbb{N}\}$
- $IL = \{L_0, L_1, L_2\}$
- *IR* is a non-empty set of resources, the universe of *I*. We obtain:
  $IR=\{(a, b, c, d, e, f, g, h, i, j, k, l, m, n, o, p, q, r, s, A, C_x, D_y \mid x \in \{0,\ldots,12\}, y \in \mathbb{N}) \cup IL\}$.
- Add *IP* with RDF semantic conditions.$X \in IP$if only if$\langle X, I(rdf{:}Property)\rangle \in IEXT\big(I(rdf{:}type)\big)$. *rdf:Property* denotes any possible predicate in RDF dataset. Additionally, we define *IPT* to denote all the predicate type also define *IRT* to denote all resource types. Hence, automatically$IPT \subseteq IP$,$XIP \in IPT$ and$YIR \in IRT$, $IRT \subseteq IR$.
  $IP(rdf{:}type) \rightarrow \{\langle X, XIP\rangle\}$where$X \in IPIT$, thus we obtain$IPT = \{g, h, i, j\}$
  $IR(rdf{:}type) \rightarrow \{\langle Y, YIR\rangle\}$where$Y \in IR$, thus we obtain$IRT = \emptyset$.
  We obtain $IP=\{g, l, m, n, o, p, q, r, s, A, C_2, C_3, C_4, C_7, C_8, C_{12}, D_y \mid y \in \mathbb{N}\}$
- The *IEXT(IPT)* is the extension of *IPT* and $IEXT(IPT) \subseteq IEXT$. The *IEXT(IRT)* is the extension of *IRT* and $IEXT(IRT) \subseteq IEXT$. Therefore, $\big((IEXT(IPT) \cup IEXT(IRT)) \subseteq IEXT\big)$
  $\{IEXT(IPT) \mid IP(rdf{:}type) \rightarrow \{\langle X, XIP\rangle\} \wedge X \in IPIT\}$ and $\{IEXT(IRT) \mid IR(rdf{:}type) \rightarrow \{\langle Y, YIR\rangle\} \wedge Y \in IR\}$
  For *IL*, all are ill-typed XMLLiteral, therefore,$IEXT(IL) \notin IEXT\big(I(rdf{:}type)\big)$
  As far, some *IP* in RDF vocabularies do not exist in the example, then $IEXT(C_2)$=$IEXT(C_3)$=$IEXT(C_4)$=$IEXT(C_7)$=$IEXT(C_8)$=$IEXT(C_{12})$=$IEXT(D_y)$for$y \in \mathbb{N}$
  We obtain,$IEXT$ =
  $g \rightarrow \{\langle a,k\rangle\}$;$l \rightarrow \{\langle a,b\rangle\}$;$m \rightarrow \{\langle l,L_3\rangle\}$;$n \rightarrow \{\langle l,c\rangle\}$;$o \rightarrow \{\langle l,d\rangle\}$;$p \rightarrow \{\langle o,L_0\rangle\}$;$q \rightarrow \{\langle o,L_1\rangle\}$;$r \rightarrow \{\langle n,e\rangle\}$;$s \rightarrow \{\langle r,f\rangle\}$;$A \rightarrow \{\langle l,g\rangle, \langle n,h\rangle, \langle o,i\rangle, \langle r,j\rangle\}$;$C_2 = C_3 = C_4 = C_7 = C_8 = C_{12} = D_y \rightarrow \emptyset$, for $y \in \mathbb{N}$

We can see that the property in AP-RDF consists of default property and property type. Default property consists of property instances and property types which do not have instances. All properties are subsets of *IP* and *IP* are a part of *IR*. The above explanation shows that AP-RDF satisfies the standard semantic interpretation of the W3C Recommendation. Therefore, the least semantic interpretation of AP-RDF is RDF Interpretation.

CONJECTURE 3.

An RDFS (RDF Schema) interpretation of AP-RDF follows all features of RDFS default semantic interpretation as an extension of AP-RDF RDF interpretation and adds the mapping function of property *rdfs:*. The class extension *ICEXT(Z)* is defined to be$\{T{:}\langle T, Z\rangle \in IEXT\big(I(rdf{:}type)\big)\}$. It's called the class extension of Z. (Trivial)

The RDFS Interpretation is needed only in case there is a triple element of AP-RDF dataset which use the prefix-based *rdfs:*. Since the modification is based on an extension of *rdf:type*, then the RDFS Interpretation will just follow the default RDFS semantic interpretation without any further extension mapping. The AP-RDF example does not have any *rdfs:* vocabulary, therefore, it does not need RDFS semantic interpretation for the *example.ttl*.

5. THE FORMAL GRAPH MODEL OF AP-RDF

Graph models are more expressive and have some advantages in representing knowledge in the real world (Chein and Mugnier, 2008) (Aggarwal and Wang, 2010) (Deng et al., 2012). Some forms of graph model are a directed graph (Satuluri and Parthasarathy, 2011), a labeled graph (Yang et al., 2011), a property graph (Dai et al., 2014) and a hypergraph (Bu et al., 2010). It's a challenge for RDF as the standard data model of the semantic web considering that RDF is a very simple data model to represent knowledge in the real world, which could be complex. This issue motivated the prior work, and it showed that a directed property hypergraph which defines a complex knowledge of the real world also can be represented as AP-RDF (D. Wardani and Küng, 2015).

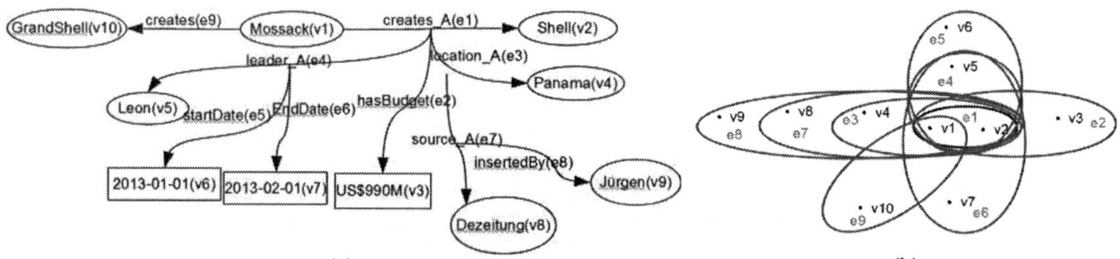

(a) (b)

Figure 1. (a). The graph illustration of the example without the vocabulary *rdf:type*. (b) The hypergraph of the example in Figure (a)

From the graph in Figure 1.b, we obtain the hypergraph as below: (the arrow determines the destination node or the object of a triple)
$H = \{(e1,\overrightarrow{v3}),(e1,\overrightarrow{v4}),(e1,\overrightarrow{v5}),(e4,\overrightarrow{v6}),(e4,\overrightarrow{v7}),(e3,\overrightarrow{v8}),(e7,\overrightarrow{v9})\}$, where $e1=(v1,\overrightarrow{v2})$.
We also obtain the digraph $D = \{(v1,\overrightarrow{v10})\}$.

From the illustration in Figure 1 and the above explanation, it's shown that AP-RDF can be represented as a directed property hypergraph and vice versa. Whereas, a normal RDF triple in AP-RDF, can be represented as a directed digraph. This fact describes that AP-RDF may contain hypergraphs and digraphs. This condition will influence our perspective in defining the formal graph model of AP-RDF.

Our definition tries to formalize the graph model which is closer to its illustration, either as a digraph or as a hypergraph. Our definition uses both edges and nodes to represent a predicate, but each predicate has a single form of representation in a whole dataset. An example: a predicate *"hasBudget"* will be represented as an edge and every occurrence will be represented as an edge as well and a predicate *"create_A"* will be represented as a node in each its occurrence. Hayes et.al (Hayes and Gutierrez, 2004) define representation inconsistency when a predicate is represented twice as a node and an edge in the same RDF dataset. Later, we will elaborate that our idea is excluded from this inconsistent definition.

CONJECTURE 4
Statements of AP-RDF are interpreted as digraphs or hypergraphs. Predicate instances and their predicate types of AP-RDF are interpreted as hypergraphs. Predicate types which do not have instances are interpreted as digraphs.

Short preliminaries; let G be a graph of AP-RDF. G has digraphs D and hypergraphs H. $(D \cup H) \subseteq G$. Digraphs$D = (V, E_D)$ where E_D is an edge of a digraph $E_D \in (V_i \times V_j)$. Hypergraphs $H = (V, E_H)$ where E_H

is a hyperedge of a hypergraph $E_H \in (V_1 \times \ldots V_x), x = 1, \ldots, n$. The vertices in E_H can be formed as a E_D. Therefore, E_H may consist of E_D too.

DEFINITION 3. (A directed digraph of AP-RDF)
Let D be digraphs in AP-RDF and T_{RDF} be set of RDF triples. $D(T_{RDF}) = \{V, E_D, \wp\}$ where nodes $V = \{S, O\}$ and edge $E_D = \{P_t\}$. $\wp: VxE_D \rightarrow \{s, p, o\}$ is a role function of nodes which holds:
$(\wp(V, E_D) = s) \Leftrightarrow (V \in orig(E_D)); E_D = p; (\wp(V, E_D) = o) \Leftrightarrow (V \in dest(E_D))$.

DEFINITION 4. (A directed hypergraph of AP-RDF)
Let H be hypergraphs in AP-RDF and T_{APRDF} be set of AP_RDF triples. $H(T_{APRDF}) = \{V, E_H, \wp\}$ where nodes $V = \{S, P, O\}$ and $P = \{P_t, P_t^i\}$. $\wp: VxE_H \rightarrow \{s, p, o\}$ is a role function of nodes which holds:
$(\wp(V, E_H) = s) \Leftrightarrow (V \in orig(E_H) \wedge (V \in S)); (\wp(V, E_H) = p) \Leftrightarrow (V \in orig(E_H) \wedge (V \in P));$
$(\wp(V, E_H) = o) \Leftrightarrow (V \in dest(E_H) \wedge (V \in O))$.

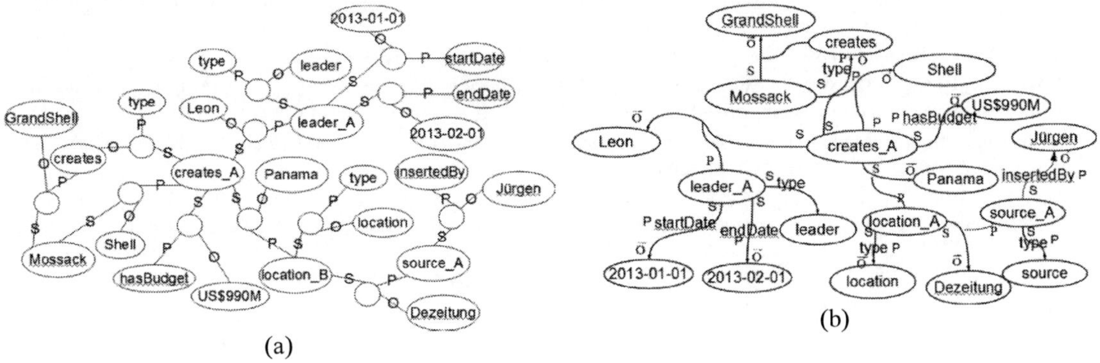

Figure 2. (a) The graph of AP-RDF based on (Hayes and Gutierrez, 2004), (b) the graph of AP-RDF based on our definition

The result of our definition is illustrated in Figure 2.b. It's shown that the graph of AP-RDF has digraphs and hypergraphs. In the real condition, AP-RDF also has both digraphs and hypergraphs. Whereas, the work (Hayes and Gutierrez, 2004), treats all triple as a hypergraph, even though they are a digraph which is shown in Figure 2.a.

We can see, predicates *"startDate"*, *"endDate"*, *"type"* and *"source"* are predicate types and are represented as a digraph. They are predicate types which do not have predicate instances. Predicates *"creates"* and *"location"* are predicate type and are represented as hypergraphs because they have predicate instances which semantically refer to them. Predicate *"creates_A"* is an instance of predicate type *"creates"* and *"location_A"* is an instance of predicate type predicate type *"location"* and are also represented as hypergraphs. Predicate *"startDate"*, *"endDate"*, *"type"* and *"source"* are formed as an edge in a whole AP-RDF graph. Whereas, predicate *"creates"*, *"location"*, *"source"*, *"creates_A"*, *"location_A"* and *"source_A"* are formed as a node in a whole AP-RDF graph. Therefore, our definition of consistency is that a predicate can be represented as a node or an edge, but this format is consistent for a whole AP-RDF graph. A predicate is represented as an edge for the edge of digraph E_D and is represented as a node for hyperedge of hypergraph E_H.

6. CONCLUSIONS AND FUTURE WORK

We have shown the evaluation that AP-RDF satisfies the standard semantic interpretation of the W3C Recommendation. The minimum normative semantic interpretation is the RDF Interpretation. We also provide the formal graph of AP-RDF, which is a combination of digraphs and hypergraphs. Normal RDF in AP-RDF dataset are represented as digraphs and predicates are formed as an edge. Whereas AP-RDF triples are represented as hypergraphs and predicates are represented as a node. The near future work is to study whether this model is useful in driving a new direction of information retrieval. The predicate in triples AP-RDF should be given more attention in the retrieval process. Next, we will evaluate the usefulness of all we have proposed especially in the reasoning process within some real applications. How the proposed concepts influence extended tasks, e.g., graph mining or linked data mining should be studied further.

REFERENCES

Aggarwal, C.C., Wang, H., 2010. *Managing and mining graph data.* Springer.

Arenas, M., Gutierrez, C., Pérez, J., 2009. *Foundations of RDF Databases*, in: Tessaris, S., Franconi, E., Eiter, T., Gutierrez, C., Handschuh, S., Rousset, M.-C., Schmidt, R. (Eds.), Reasoning Web. Semantic Technologies for Information Systems, Lecture Notes in Computer Science. Springer Berlin Heidelberg, pp. 158–204.

Bu, J., Tan, S., Chen, C., Wang, C., Wu, H., Zhang, L., He, X., 2010. *Music Recommendation by Unified Hypergraph: Combining Social Media Information and Music Content*, in: Proceedings of the International Conference on Multimedia, MM '10. ACM, Firenze, Italy, pp. 391–400.

Carothers, G., 2014. *RDF 1.1 N-Quads: A line-based syntax for RDF datasets.* W3C Recomm.

Carroll, J.J., Bizer, C., Hayes, P., Stickler, P., 2005. *Named Graphs, Provenance and Trust*, in: Proceedings of the 14th International Conference on World Wide Web, WWW '05. ACM, New York, NY, USA, pp. 613–622.

Chein, M., Mugnier, M.-L., 2008. *Graph-based knowledge representation: computational foundations of conceptual graphs.* Springer Science & Business Media.

Chen, H., Wang, Y., Wang, H., Mao, Y., Tang, J., Zhou, C., Yin, A., Wu, Z., 2006. *Towards a Semantic Web of Relational Databases: A Practical Semantic Toolkit and an In-Use Case from Traditional Chinese Medicine*, in: Cruz, I., Decker, S., Allemang, D., Preist, C., Schwabe, D., Mika, P., Uschold, M., Aroyo, L. (Eds.), The Semantic Web - ISWC 2006, Lecture Notes in Computer Science. Springer Berlin Heidelberg, pp. 750–763.

Consortium, W.W.W., others, 2014a. *RDF 1.1 Primer.* World Wide Web Consort.

Consortium, W.W.W., others, 2014b. *RDF 1.1 Concepts and Abstract Syntax.*

Dai, D., Ross, R.B., Carns, P., Kimpe, D., Chen, Y., 2014. *Using Property Graphs for Rich Metadata Management in HPC Systems*, in: Proceedings of the 9th Parallel Data Storage Workshop, PDSW '14. IEEE Press, Piscataway, NJ, USA, pp. 7–12.

Das, S., Srinivasan, J., Perry, M., Chong, E.I., Banerjee, J., 2014. *A Tale of Two Graphs: Property Graphs as RDF in Oracle.*, in: EDBT. pp. 762–773.

Deng, Z.-H., Lai, B.-Y., Wang, Z.-H., Fang, G.-D., 2012. *PAV: A Novel Model for Ranking Heterogeneous Objects in Bibliographic Information Networks.* Expert Syst Appl 39, 9788–9796.

Gutierrez, C., Hurtado, C., Mendelzon, A.O., 2004. *Foundations of Semantic Web Databases*, in: Proceedings of the Twenty-Third ACM SIGMOD-SIGACT-SIGART Symposium on Principles of Database Systems, PODS '04. ACM, New York, NY, USA, pp. 95–106.

Hayes, J., Gutierrez, C., 2004. *Bipartite Graphs as Intermediate Model for RDF*, in: McIlraith, S., Plexousakis, D., van Harmelen, F. (Eds.), The Semantic Web – ISWC 2004, Lecture Notes in Computer Science. Springer Berlin Heidelberg, pp. 47–61.

Hayes, P., Patel-Schneider, P.F., 2014. *RDF 1.1 Semantics.* W3C Recomm. 25.

Manola, F., Miller, E., McBride, B., 2004. *RDF primer.* W3C Recomm. 10.

Satuluri, V., Parthasarathy, S., 2011. *Symmetrizations for Clustering Directed Graphs*, in: Proceedings of the 14th International Conference on Extending Database Technology, EDBT/ICDT '11. ACM, New York, NY, USA, pp. 343–354.

Wardani, D., Küng, J., 2015. *Property Hypergraphs as an Attributed Predicate RDF*, in: Debruyne, C., Panetto, H., Meersman, R., Dillon, T., Weichhart, G., An, Y., Ardagna, C.A. (Eds.), On the Move to Meaningful Internet Systems: OTM 2015 Conferences, Lecture Notes in Computer Science. Springer International Publishing, pp. 329–336.

Wardani, D.W., Küng, J., 2015. *An Attributed Predicate RDF*, in: Computer and Information Technology; Ubiquitous Computing and Communications; Dependable, Autonomic and Secure Computing; Pervasive Intelligence and Computing (CIT/IUCC/DASC/PICOM), 2015 IEEE International Conference on. pp. 410–416. doi:

Yang, J., Zhang, S., Jin, W., 2011. *DELTA: Indexing and Querying Multi-labeled Graphs*, in: Proceedings of the 20th ACM International Conference on Information and Knowledge Management, CIKM '11. ACM, New York, NY, USA, pp. 1765–1774.

A SEMANTIC SEARCH ENGINE FOR SOFTWARE COMPONENTS

Bernhard G. Humm[1] and Hesam Ossanloo[2]
[1]*Hochschule Darmstadt – University of Applied Sciences, Haardtring 100, 64295 Darmstadt, Germany*
[2]*Object ECM GmbH, Grimm 3, 20457 Hamburg, Germany*

ABSTRACT

Software development today means, to a large extend, integrating existing software components. An important task of the architect of a software solution is to identify suitable software components. Whereas semantic search engines have gained popularity in the last decade, semantic search engines for finding software components are not yet in widespread use.
The paper presents the concept for a semantic search engine for software components called "SoftwareFinder". SoftwareFinder uses a simple ontology for normalizing the tag sets of various software hosting sites, for providing a semantic AutoSuggest service and a semantic faceted search, and for recommending similar software components. SoftwareFinder has been implemented prototypically and exhibits a good user experience as well as a good run-time performance.

KEYWORDS

Semantic search, ontology, software components

1. INTRODUCTION

Software development today means, to a large extend, integrating existing software components. A component is a well-defined unit of software that has a published interface and can be used in conjunction with other components to form larger units (Hopkins, 2000): libraries, frameworks, web services, and entire applications. Examples are database management systems, middleware components, and GUI libraries. An important task of the architect of a software solution is to identify suitable software components – commercial, free or open source. An application which takes advantage of reusable components has been argued to be more reliable (Vitharana & Jain, 2000), increase productivity of developers (Pearson, 1999) (Lim, 1994), reduce skill requirements (Kiely, 1998), shorten the development lifecycle (Due, 2000), reduce time-to market (Kim & Stohr, 1998) (Patrizio, 2000), increase quality (Sprott, 2000), and decrease development costs (Due, 2000) (Patrizio, 2000).

As the number of components grows rapidly, a major problem in software reuse is the lack of efficient means to search and retrieve reusable components (Spinellis & Raptis, 2000). Usually, software architects rely on software components they have had experience with. Faced with new problem domains, they are left alone to asking colleagues or consulting general-purpose search engines like Google. Alternatively, they consult various sites for hosting software components like GitHub, Apache.org or Sourceforge.net.

Wouldn't it be advantageous to use a semantic search engine for software components? For example, by asking "free Java library for machine learning" it will return a list of suitable software components like Weka and RapidMiner.

Semantic search engines have gained popularity in the last decade (Sirisha, et al., 2015). They have been established in a variety of application domains, including hotel portals, patent retrieval, dating sites etc. Surprisingly enough, semantic search engines in the computer science field, and in particular for software components, are not yet in widespread use.

This paper presents the concept for a semantic search engine for software components which we call "SoftwareFinder", as well as a prototypical implementation. The remainder of this paper is structured as follows. Section 2 details the problem by means of requirements. Sections 3, 4 and 5 are the core of the paper presenting the concept, system architecture, and prototypical implementation of SoftwareFinder. Section 6 evaluates our approach. Section 7 compares related work. Section 8 concludes the paper and outlines future work.

2. PROBLEM STATEMENT

In this section, we detail the problem by means of end-users' and developers' requirements for the semantic search engine SoftwareFinder.

2.1 End-Users' Requirements

1. SoftwareFinder shall facilitate software architects finding *relevant* software components for a particular need.
2. SoftwareFinder shall include information about a *sufficiently large* set of software components so that for most cases, software architects will not need to consult other information sources.
3. SoftwareFinder shall provide best *user experience*. This shall include at least the following features and properties:
    a. An easy-to use *search box* as known from popular search engines like Google.
    b. A *relevance-based ranking* of search results.
    c. Semantic search facilities based on an *ontology* for software components. The ontology shall unify the terminology used in various software hosting sites for describing software components ("tags"). It shall be sufficiently comprehensive, thus facilitating uniform search and comparison of software components hosted on different sites.
    The ontology shall at least contain the following information: preferred tag label, category, synonyms, and acronyms.
    d. A *semantic AutoSuggest* service that supports users in formulating search terms, based on the ontology.
    e. A *faceted semantic search* service that allows users to refine and narrow down search results, based on the ontology.
    f. An overview of the *search history,* which allows navigating in the search space by modifying individual search terms.
    g. Provision of *sufficient information* about a selected software component, including description, semantic tags, and links to project website and download site.
    h. A facility for recommending *semantically similar software components* of interest compared with a particular software component selected.
    i. *Responsive design*, i.e., ability for using SoftwareFinder on various electronic devices in a user-friendly way.
    j. *Response time* of less than 1 s for most searches.

2.2 Developers' Requirements

1. The ontology shall be *easily extensible.*
2. New relevant software hosting sites can be *integrated* with moderate effort.

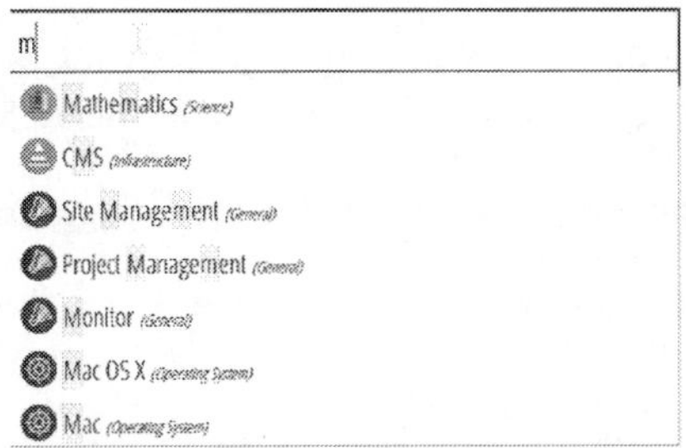

Figure 1. Semantic AutoSuggest example after entering the letter "m"

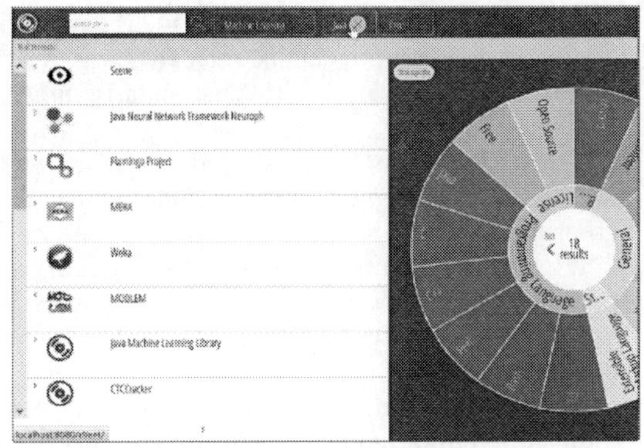

Figure 2. Topic pie, navigation bar and result set in SoftwareFinder

3. SOFTWAREFINDER: A SEMANTIC SEARCH ENGINE FOR SOFTWARE COMPONENTS

In this section, we describe the concept of the SoftwareFinder application by means of the example "free Java library for machine learning". While the user starts typing "machine learning" in the search box, the most relevant matching search terms are suggested to the user. See Figure 1.

All suggested terms are semantically categorized, according to the ontology. In total, 16 categories are used, including "development", "communication", "business", "engineering", "humanities", and "science". The categories have been specifically designed for the SoftwareFinder application using classification techniques as in (Lucredio, et al., 2004).

The user may, of course, also use any other search term as well as wildcards, e.g., "mach*".

After choosing "Machine learning" from the AutoSuggest service, a list of software components is displayed which contain the tag "Machine learning". The list is sorted according to the rating of the software components. The rating (1 star to 5 stars) is a normalization of different rating schemes of the various hosting sites.

In order to narrow down the search result, there is an interaction element which is called "topic pie" (Deuschel, et al., 2014) (Figure 2). In the topic pie, relevant search terms are displayed on the outer ring. The semantic categories of the terms are displayed in the inner ring and discriminated using a color coding. By selecting a search term, the search will be refined, resulting in a smaller search result set. Also, the topic pie will be adapted accordingly.

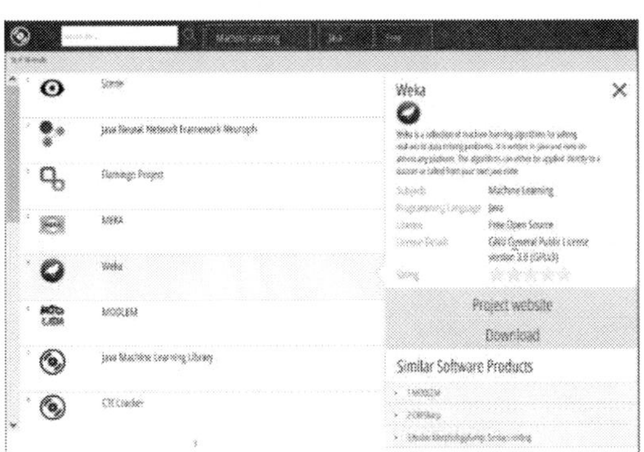

Figure 3. Detail page of a software component

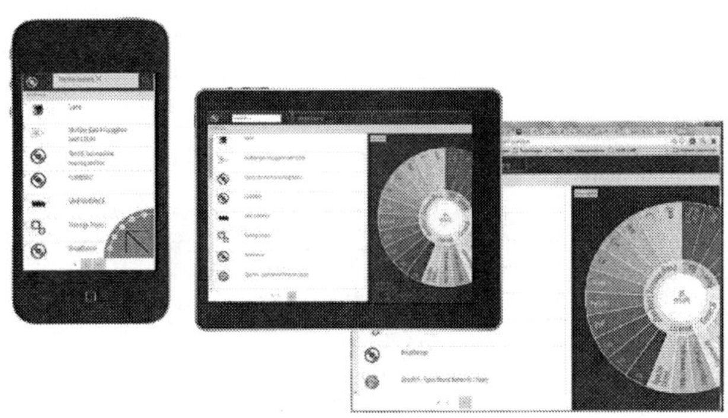

Figure 4. Responsive design of SoftwareFinder

The terms displayed in the topic pie are identified according to a heuristic approach balancing relevance and diversity. For more details, refer to (Deuschel, et al., 2014). Semantic AutoSuggest and topic pie support users in specifying search terms particularly in areas where they are novices and do not yet know the expert vocabulary.

The back button in the navigation bar allows the user to go one step backwards in his search history. Additionally, the navigation bar enables the user to delete or replace one of the search terms thus allowing for exploring the search space.

If a software component is selected, a detail page is displayed (Figure 3). On the detail page, users find a short description of the software component, subjects (a.k.a. tags or keywords), programming language, license type and license details, rating, the home page of the component and, the link to download the component.

Additionally, similar software components are displayed. This feature fosters serendipity and is inspired by the option in e-commerce applications: "people who bought this product also bought...".

SoftwareFinder has a responsive design which adapts according to the resolution of the device being used. See Figure 4 for screenshots of the same application state on a smartphone, a tablet, and a desktop. The smartphone offers the smallest display size. Therefore, the topic pie is minimized. By clicking on the arrow on the right bottom side, the topic pie will be enlarged and can be used as in the tablet or desktop version.

4. SOFTWARE ARCHITECTURE

Figure 5 gives an overview of the software architecture of SoftwareFinder. The software architecture is separated into an online and an offline subsystem. The *offline subsystem* manages the crawling of the software hosting sites, regularly updating the SoftwareFinder data store as a batch process. The *online subsystem* performs the semantic search.

4.1 The SoftwareFinder Offline Subsystem

The SoftwareFinder offline subsystem follows the software pipeline architectural style. The crawler visits software hosting sites and saves the HTML pages for the individual software components hosted. Afterwards, a *semantic ETL (Extract, Transform, Load)* process starts extracting metadata of the software components from the HTML pages, transferring them into a uniform format, preprocessing them semantically and loading them into the data store.

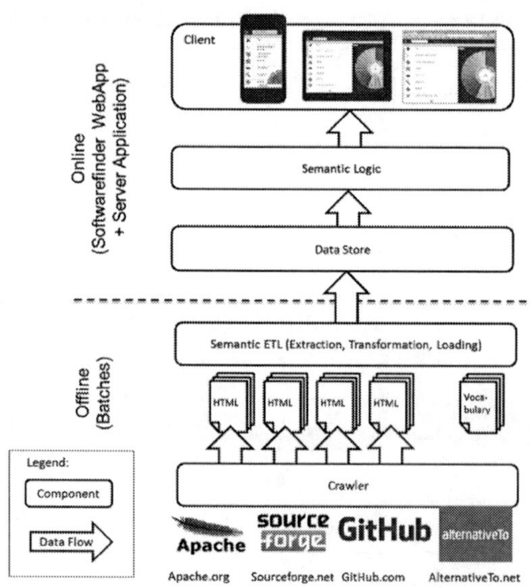

Figure 5. SoftwareFinder architecture

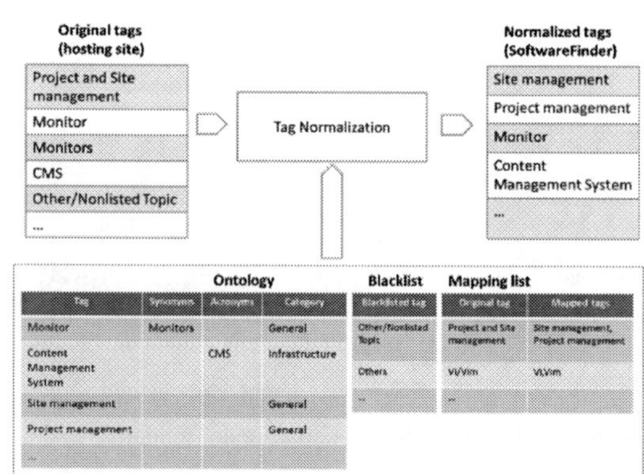

Figure 6. Tag normalization

4.1.1 Tag Normalization

The ontology is used for automatically *normalizing tags* of software components from different hosting sites (Figure 6). For example, the synonym tags "Monitor" and "Monitors" are unified to the preferred tag "Monitor". Acronyms are handled, e.g., "CMS" is replaced by "Content Management System". Blacklisted tags such as "Other/Nonlisted Topic" are omitted and compound tags such as "Project and Site Management" are split up.

4.2 The SoftwareFinder Online Subsystem

The online subsystem is designed as a classical three-layer-architecture, consisting of client, semantic logic, and data store. The data store contains metadata about software components and the ontology. It is indexed for high-performance access. The client implements the SoftwareFinder GUI including the responsive design. It accesses the semantic logic via an API. The semantic logic covers the various aspects: *semantic AutoSuggest, topic pie,* and *similar software components.*

4.2.1 Semantic AutoSuggest

For the semantic AutoSuggest service, all tags in the ontology are indexed, as well as all programming languages, operating systems, license types, and software product names. Initially, the tags matching a user input are ordered according to a heuristics-based relevance ranking. The heuristic used is as follows: the more often a tag is used in the software product metadata, the higher its relevance.

Only the top 7 tags out of potentially hundreds of matching tags will be displayed to the user. Using the relevance-based ranking only has a disadvantage: in many cases, tags of just one category will be displayed. In order to increase the category diversity, the initial, solely relevance-based ranking result is reordered. By omitting excess terms of the same category, it is ensured that the user has tags from at least three different categories to choose from.

4.2.2 Topic Pie Generation

The topic pie is generated in several steps (Figure 7).

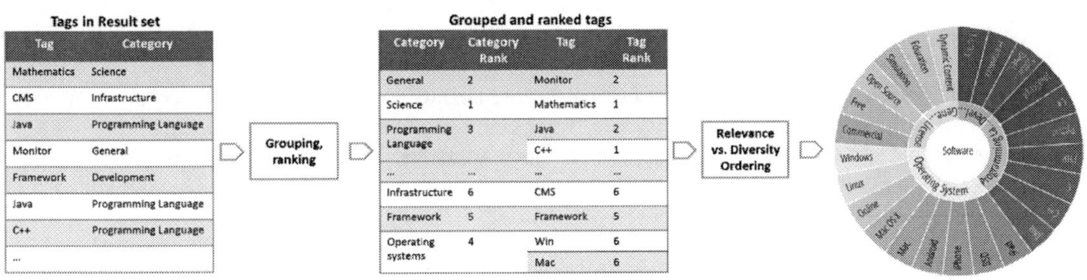

Figure 7. Topic pie generation

Input to the topic pie generator is the result set of the current search, i.e., a list of software product metadata. First, the tags are extracted from the metadata. The extracted tags are then grouped according to their categories and ordered using a heuristics-based relevance ranking. The heuristic used is: the more often a tag is used in the result set, the more relevant it is. So, the rank of an individual tag is the number of its occurrences in the result set. The categories are ranked as well, based on the ranks of their individual tags: the more often a category is used in the result set, the more relevant it is. So, the rank of a category is the sum of the ranks of its tags.

The topic pie accommodates for up to 25 tags, out of potentially hundreds of selected tags. Selecting just the 25 top-ranked tags often results in only one or two categories being shown to the user. Therefore, as in the semantic AutoSuggest, relevance is traded with diversity in order to display a well-balanced topic pie. By omitting excess tags of each category, it is ensured that the user has tags from potentially five different categories to choose from.

4.2.3 Similar Software Components

For displaying software components that are similar to the one currently selected by the user, a similarity metrics is used: the more tags two software components have in common, the more similar they are. Since all tags have been normalized during the semantic ETL process, issues of synonyms, acronyms, etc. need not be considered here. From the list of similar software components ordered according to the similarity metrics, the first three will be displayed to the user.

The ontology is the core of SoftwareFinder as it is used in all semantic functionalities in the offline and online subsystems.

5. PROTOTYPE IMPLEMENTATION

We have successfully implemented a SoftwareFinder prototype. The server is implemented in Java 8 involving a number of third-party libraries: For crawling, the library cawl4j is used; The data store is implemented with Apache Lucene. Semantic search is implemented via Lucene's document fields. Ranking strategies are implemented using Lucene's custom boosting. Indexing for semantic AutoSuggest uses Lucene's suggester based on infix matches called "AnalyzingInfixSuggester".

The client / server communication is via HTTP using JSON as data format.

The client web app is implemented in HTML5 / CSS3 / JavaScript using various JavaScript libraries: Knockout.js is used for implementing the MVVM architecture. JQuery, jQuery UI and jQuery-touchSwipe are used for widgets and the client-server communication.

The server and the web app are deployed in an Apache Tomcat servlet container.

6. EVALUATION

In this section, we compare the SoftwareFinder concept and prototypical implementation with the requirements specified in Section 2.

6.1 End-Users' Requirements

1. As demonstrated via the prototypical implementation, the SoftwareFinder concept facilitates software architects finding relevant software components for a particular need.
2. The current prototype implementation only includes software components from Apache.org, Sourceforge.net and Alternativeto.net. A number of important hosting sites like GitHub are not yet included. Therefore, the prototype does not yet satisfy the requirement that for most cases, software architects will not need to consult other information sources. The SoftwareFinder concept allows integrating other software hosting sites with moderate effort and the integration of prominent hosting sites like GitHub are planned. However, it will be interesting to see whether, after integration of about a dozen of the most prominent hosting sites, this requirement can, indeed, be achieved. A sound evaluation of this requirement is subject to future work.
3. SoftwareFinder has been designed and implemented with a particular focus on user experience. In particular:
   a. The search box is well-known from prominent search engines like Google and is intuitively to use as it provides a clear information structure (Petrie & Power, 2012).
   b. All search results are ranked by the ratings of the various software components on their hosting sites. Since different sites use different rating schemes and some sites use no rating scheme at all, a heuristic approach is used for harmonizing ratings.
   c. A simple ontology containing about 25,000 tags is the core of SoftwareFinder. It is used for automatically normalizing the terminology of various hosting sites, thus facilitating semantic search and comparison of software components hosted on different sites.
   d. The semantic AutoSuggest service based on the ontology extends the functionality of a simple, text-based autocomplete service. For a detailed discussion see (Beez, et al., 2015).

e. The topic pie provides a faceted semantic search service, based on the ontology. For a detailed discussion see (Deuschel, et al., 2014).
f. The navigation bar allows navigating in the search space by removing individual search terms and adding new ones.
g. For each selected software component, sufficient information is displayed: name, description, semantic tags, programming language, operating system, license details, ranking, link to project website and download site.
h. The facility for recommending semantically similar software components supports serendipity. A common use case is that a software architect already knows one software component implementing a certain feature and is interested in alternatives.
i. Responsive design has been implemented allowing SoftwareFinder to be used on various electronic devices in a user-friendly way.
j. We have measured the performance of the SoftwareFinder prototype implementation on a cloud-based virtual server with 4GB RAM and 2.0GHz to 3GHz GHz processor (depends on the traffic of the virtual server service). For random access requests the average response time is 400 ms, which is way below the required 1s.

6.2 Developers' Requirements

1. It is of utmost importance that the ontology is always up-to-date. The ontology can conveniently be edited as a spreadsheet before being imported into the SoftwareFinder application. A number of utilities support the editor in maintaining the ontology. When new tags are identified while crawling software hosting sites, they are presented to the editor. Similarities to existing terms are displayed.
2. The integration of a new hosting site into SoftwareFinder requires implementing a new crawler. Due to predefined facilities in the SoftwareFinder application, this requires about 200 lines of Java code. The implementation effort is moderate.

7. RELATED WORK

During the last decade, a lot of work has been done in introducing semantics and ontologies in a number of application domains (Ege, et al., 2015). However, relatively few applications are in the application domain of software engineering. (Happel & Seedorf, 2006) describe a number of potential application areas of ontologies in software engineering, including component reuse.

(Yanes, et al., 2012) provide a theoretical and empirical evaluation of software component search engines for COTS (commercial off the shelf) products. They compare 18 search engines, some for finding software components, some general-purpose: 8 software component search engines, 9 semantic search engines, and Google as a traditional search engine. For our purpose, we chose the 6 top-ranked search engines according to (Yanes, et al., 2012) which were accessible at the time of writing this paper. We also added alternativeTo.net since it has gained popularity in recent years. The comparison with SoftwareFinder is illustrated in Table 1.

Table 1. Feature comparison between different semantic search engines

Search engine	Semantic search	Semantic AutoSuggest	Faceted search	Similar product suggester	Search refinement	Specialized for software components	Ranking
SoftwareFinder	✓	✓	✓	✓	✓	✓	✓
Sensebot	✓	-	✓	-	-	-	-
Factbites	✓	-	✓	-	-	-	-
Exalead	✓	-	✓	-	-	-	-
Capterra	-	✓	✓	-	-	✓	-
AlternativeTo	-	-	✓	✓	-	✓	✓
Download.cnet	-	-	✓	✓	-	✓	-
Google	✓	-	-	-	✓	-	✓

(Sugumaran & Storey, 2003) describes an early semantic-based approach to component retrieval. Their approach includes natural language processing (NLP), a domain model, and an ontology for querying a component repository. One limitation of their work is the high cost for maintaining the component repository which is necessary for making sophisticated queries. The SoftwareFinder architecture, in contrast, makes little assumptions about the hosting sites being crawled. This is a pre-requisite for the scalability of our approach at moderate cost.

The concept of the topic pie has been introduced in (Deuschel, et al., 2014). It serves as a faceted search service which helps users to refine their search queries in areas where they are not familiar with the domain-specific vocabulary. The difference between both implementations is the underlying ontologies being used. In (Deuschel, et al., 2014), the GND integrated authoring file of the German National Library which is used for finding books in a library. SoftwareFinder uses a simple custom-developed ontology for software components.

The concept of Semantic AutoSuggest and its use in personalized medicine has been described in (Beez, et al., 2015). Whereas the concept of balancing relevance and diversity is used in both approaches, the specific implementation has been customized for the use case of component search.

8. CONCLUSIONS AND FUTURE WORK

"The shoemaker's son always goes barefoot." Whereas semantic search engines are commonplace in domains like hotel search etc., you can hardly find any in the software engineering application domain. In this paper, we have presented the concept and prototypical implementation of SoftwareFinder, a semantic search engine for software components. The core of SoftwareFinder is a simple ontology for terminology describing software products.

SoftwareFinder has the potential of substantially improving the process of identifying suitable software components for a new software solution. The efficiency of this process may be improved by finding components faster; the effectiveness may be improved by getting a better overview of a large set of software components and thus selecting a most suitable component.

A lot needs to be done. The prototype implementation needs a number of improvements, e.g., in the implementation of the heuristics-based ranking. Most importantly, prominent software hosting sites like GitHub need to be integrated. Subsequently, SoftwareFinder shall be thoroughly evaluated for precision and recall, as well as for user experience while being used in real software development projects.

REFERENCES

Beez, U., Humm, B. G. & Walsh, P., 2015. Semantic AutoSuggest for Electronic Health Records. Las Vegas, Nevada, USA, IEEE Conference Publishing Services.

Deuschel, T., Greppmeier, C., Humm, B. G. & Stille, W., 2014. Semantically Faceted Navigation with Topic Pies. Leipzig, Germany, ACM Press New York, USA.

Due, R., 2000. The Economics of Component-Based Development. Information Systems Management, 17(1), pp. 92-95.

Ege, B., Humm, B. & Reibold, A. Hrsg., 2015. Corporate Semantic Web – Wie semantische Anwendungen in Unternehmen Nutzen stiften. Heidelberg: Springer-Verlag.

Happel, H.-J. & Seedorf, S., 2006. Applications of Ontologies in Software Engineering. Athens, GA, USA, Springer.

Hopkins, J., 2000. Component primer. Communications of the ACM, 43(10), pp. 27-30.

Kiely, D., 1998. The Component Edge. Informationweek, Issue 677, pp. 1A-6A.

Kim, Y. & Stohr, E., 1998. Directions, Software Reuse: Survey and Research. Journal of Management Information Systems, 14(4), pp. 113-147.

Lim, W., 1994. Effects of reuse on quality, productivity, and economics. IEEE Software, 11(5), pp. 23-30.

Lucredio, D., de Almeida, . E. S. & Prado, A. F., 2004. A survey on software components search and retrieval. Rennes, s.n., pp. 152-159.

Patrizio, A., 2000. The new developer portals. Informationweek, Issue 799, pp. 81-86.

Pearson, C., 1999. Software development using component technology delivers productivity. Health Management Technology, 20(9), pp. 34-35.

Petrie, H. & Power, C., 2012. What do users really care about?: a comparison of usability problems found by users and experts on highly interactive websites. Austin, Texas, ACM New York, NY, USA, pp. 2107-2116.

Sirisha, J., SubbaRao, B. & Kavitha, D., 2015. A Cram on Semantic Web Components. International Journal of Advanced Research in Computer Science, Vol.6 Issue3, pp. 62-67, 6p.

Spinellis, D. & Raptis, K., 2000. Component mining: A process and its pattern language. Information and Software Technology, 42(9), pp. 609-617.

Sprott, D., 2000. Componentizing the enterprise application packages. Communications of the ACM, 43(4), pp. 63-69.

Sugumaran, V. & Storey, V., 2003. A semantic-based approach to component retrieval. ACM SIGMIS Database, 34(3), pp. 8-24.

Vitharana, P. & Jain, H., 2000. Research issues in testing business components. Information & Management,, 37(6), pp. 297-309.

Yanes, N., Sassi, S. B. & Ghezala, H. H. B., 2012. A Theoretical and Empirical Evaluation of Software Component Search Engines, Semantic Search Engines and Google Search Engine in the Context of COTS-Based Development, s.l.: arXiv preprint arXiv:1204.2079.

THE EVALUATION OF NODE'S POWER IN THE SOCIAL NETWORK SPHERE

Radek Malinský and Ivan Jelínek
Department of Computer Science and Engineering, Faculty of Electrical Engineering
Czech Technical University in Prague, Karlovo náměstí 13, 121 35 Prague, Czech Republic

ABSTRACT

In recent years, the Internet has been experiencing a huge boom in social networking, blogging and discussing on online forums. With the growing popularity of these communication channels, there have been arising a large number of comments on various topics from many different types of users. Such information source is not only useful for academic research, but also for commercial companies that would like to gain a direct user feedback on price, quality, and other factors of their products. However, obtaining comprehensive information from such a source is a challenging task nowadays. Our research is focused on the evaluation of the Internet trends, where the trend may be defined as anything from an event, product name, name of a person or any expression, which is mentioned online. The main emphasis of this study has been placed on the evaluation of trend in the social network sphere.

KEYWORDS

Webometrics, Social Network Analysis, Sentiment Analysis, Web 2.0

1. INTRODUCTION

In recent years, the Internet has been experiencing a huge boom in social networking, blogging and discussing on online forums. With the growing popularity of these communication channels, there have been arising a large number of comments on various topics from many different types of users. Such information source is not only useful for academic researchers, but also for commercial companies that would like to gain a direct user feedback on price, quality, and other factors of their products. However, obtaining comprehensive information from such a source is a challenging task nowadays.

Several models have been proposed for the social media analysis on the Web. However, many of these solutions are usually tailored to a specific purpose or data type, and there is still a lack of generality and unclear approach to handling the data. Moreover, a web content diversity, a variety of technologies along with the website structure differences, all of these make the Web a network of heterogeneous data, where things are difficult to find. It is, therefore, necessary to design a suitable metric that would reflect a semantic content of single pages in a better way.

Our research is focused on the evaluation of the Internet trends, where the trend may be defined as anything from an event, product name, name of a person or any expression, which is mentioned online. The main emphasis of this study has been placed on the evaluation of trend in the social network sphere. Power Degree and Power Threshold have been defined to propose a new evaluation methodology. Power Degree represents a prestige of individual actors. Power Threshold is the smallest value of the power degree that specifies the high-quality actors. This study deals with the influence of the threshold changes on the evaluation in the network of trends.

2. RELATED WORK

Our work is related to three main research topics: sentiment analysis; social network analysis; evaluation of the Internet trends.

2.1 Sentiment Analysis

Sentiment Analysis or Opinion Mining (Pang and Lee, 2008) enables us to automatically detect opinions from structured but also unstructured data. That involves several research areas such as natural language processing, computational linguistic and text mining. The main goal of sentiment analysis is to identify a positive/negative polarity of the text and recognise a subjective/objective impression of the text (Prabowo and Thelwall, 2009).

One of the problems of Sentiment Analysis is a sentiment classification (Liu, 2011; Ohana and Tierney, 2009), which classifies text, sentences or words as positive, negative, or neutral, and determines their strength. Sentiment analysis research involves three main approaches to determine sentiment classification, full-text machine learning, lexicon-based method and linguistic analysis, although many algorithms have elements of all. Our research utilises the lexicon-based method.

Lexicon-based methods use a list of words, where each word is associated with its polarity and sometimes also its strength. These lists are along with a set of rules used to predict sentiment of analysed text (Malinský and Jelínek, 2014; Ohana and Tierney, 2009). Many existing lexicons can be utilised for this kind of lexicon-based analysis: SentiWordNet (Baccianella et al., 2010), Linguistic Inquiry and Word Count (LIWC) (Pennebaker, 2011), The Affective Norms for English Words (ANEW) (Lang et al., 2016). Lexicons are usually built manually for some specific corpus (Taboada et al., 2011) or semi-automatically starting with several annotated word and using heuristics to predict the sentiment of another word.

2.2 Social Network Analysis

A social network is a structure made up of social entities (people or organisations), and their relationships. A social network analysis represents a set of techniques for the analysis of interactions and relationships between actors in a social network. An analysis output can be, just as in the Web link analysis, reported as a network diagram with nodes and links. The nodes, people or groups of people, are called *actors*; and the links, social interaction (such as friendship) between actors, are called *ties*. The ties are divided into directed and undirected. The directed ties are further divided into unidirectional and bidirectional. The bidirectional ties occur for example on Facebook (Viswanath et al., 2009), where two users have each other as a Friend. On the contrary, the unidirectional ties occur for instance on Twitter (Graham et al., 2013), where one user follows the second.

A lot of earlier researches have focused on the position of the individual node in the network and its interaction with adjacent entities. There has been introduced many network measures that help researchers to quantifies the importance of individual node and explain its position in a network. Some of these measures are focused on the node interaction with adjacent entities (Guns et al., 2011; Lee and Bonk, 2016), and others deal with a credibility of the node (Bross et al., 2012; Li et, al., 2012). Centrality and prestige are the most used measures in the social network analysis (Liu, 2011).

2.3 Evaluation of the Internet Trends

The trend may be defined as anything from an event, product name, name of a person or any expression, which is mentioned online. Several studies have been proposed to analyse and evaluate trends on the Internet. Some of those studies are focused on the web mention analysis (Han et al., 2009; Thelwall, 2009) where the trend's popularity is calculated based on the counting how often the trend is mentioned online. Another study deals with the number of the searches in Google search engine for a specific trend (Liu et al., 2015). Different research is based on the Sentiment Analysis and utilises SentiWordNet lexicon for the evaluation of the Internet trends (Malinský and Jelínek, 2014). This approach evaluates trends (Equation 2) according to the evaluation of sentences that mention the trend (Equation 1). The evaluation is based on the sum of words' positive and negative sentiments that are obtained from the SentiWordNet.

$$sentence_{eval} = \frac{\sum pos - \sum neg}{\#pos + \#neg} \quad (1)$$

$$trend_{eval} = \frac{\sum sentence_{eval}}{|sentence_{eval}|} \quad (2)$$

3. EVALUATION OF TRENDS IN SOCIAL NETWORKS

We have defined a new metric for the evaluation of trends in the social network sphere. The metric is a combination of Social Network Analysis and Sentiment Analysis techniques. Social Network Analysis is used to determine the most active actor who has written about a specific trend. Sentiment Analysis is used to determine the actors' evaluation of the trend. Figure 1 shows an example of the social network where it is possible to evaluate Internet trends.

Definition 3.1 (**directed graph**):
A directed graph $G = (N, E)$ *consists of a nonempty set of nodes* N *and a set of directed edges* E*. Each edge* $e \in E$ *is specified by an ordered pair of nodes* $u, v \in N$.

Definition 3.2 (**actor**):
An actor $a \in N$ *is the node of a directed graph* $G = (N, E)$ *for which it holds that every edge* $a, v \in N$ *is pointing out of the node.*

Definition 3.3 (**comment**):
A comment $c \in N$ *is the node of a directed graph* $G = (N, E)$ *for which it holds that every edge* $a, c \in N$ *is pointing the node.*

Definition 3.4 (**network of trends**):
Let T *be a set of trends,* A *be a set of actors, and* C *be a set of comments. A network of trends* $N = (T, A, C)$ *is defined as a directed graph* G*, where* $N = (T \cup A)$ *and* $T = \{C\}$.

The entire evaluation process in the network of trends is defined in several steps. In the first step, an adjacency matrix is constructed from the sets of actors and trends. Table 1 reports an example of the matrix, where columns represent the trends, rows show the actors, and elements indicate whether the actor has written any comment about the trend. An actor-actor relationship might also be defined in the matrix, but then one of the actors would become a trend. A directed graph, a network of trends, can be created from the adjacency matrix to better illustrate the relationships (Figure 1).

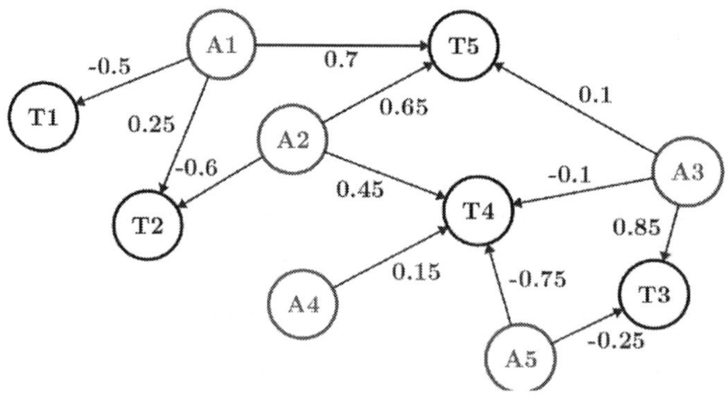

Figure 1. An example of the network of trends where it is possible to evaluate Internet trends. Red nodes represent the actors; blue nodes represent the trends. Edges indicate the actor has commented the trend. The number on the edge represents the actor's evaluation of the comment

Table 1. Adjacency matrix between trend and actor nodes. Columns represent the trends, rows show the actors, and elements indicate whether the actor has written any comment about the trend

Node	T1	T2	T3	T4	T5
A1	1	1	0	0	1
A2	0	1	0	1	1
A3	0	0	1	1	1
A4	0	0	0	1	0
A5	0	0	1	1	0

In the second step, a centrality measure (see Section 2.2 "Social Network Analysis") is used to calculate a degree power for each of actors' nodes. The degree power for each node represents the result of the degree centrality calculation for the node's out-links. Degree power is very similar to the degree prestige (Liu, 2011). However, it calculates with the out-links in contrast to the prestige that counts with in-links. Degree power defines a prestige of individual actors depending on the number of comments they have made; i.e. an actor is prestigious if he has commented many trends. A greater number of out-links indicates a greater power of an actor. The value of degree power is necessary to normalise between 0 (minimum degree) and 1 (maximum degree) to be able to compare the nodes of different networks of trends.

Definition 3.5 (**degree power**):
Let $d_o(a)$ be a number of comments $c \in C$ the actor $a \in A$ has written about the all trends from T. Degree Power of the actor a is then in the network of trends $N = (T, A, C)$ defined as $d_o(a)$ divided by the maximum possible comments $n = |C|$ the actor may have made.

$$PW_D(\mathrm{a}) = \frac{d_o(a)}{n}; \quad \mathrm{a} \in \mathrm{A}, \mathrm{n} = |C| \qquad (3)$$

In the third step, a power threshold is defined to ensure that the evaluation of trends depends only on high-quality sources, i.e. on comments from the actors that have a high power degree. The power threshold can be defined in the range from 0 to 1 to cover the whole scope of the degree power. The lower value of the power threshold implies the use of more sources from which the trend can be evaluated. On the other hand, it may also mean lower-quality sources. All sources are used when the threshold is equal to one.

Definition 3.6 (**power threshold**):
The power threshold is the smallest value of the degree power $PW_D(a)$ that specifies the actor a is a high-quality source.

In the fourth step, Sentiment Analysis approach described in the previous section is used to evaluate all comments of the actors whose degree power is above the threshold. The calculated evaluation is then assigned to each directed edge between actor and trend. All edges are evaluated by the normalised polarity in the range from -1 to 1. The trend node positive/negative strength is then calculated as the sum of positive/negative evaluation of edges that are directed to the node (Equations 4 and 5). The overall trend evaluation is calculated as the difference between positive and negative strengths.

$$pos(t) = \frac{\sum_{a=1}^{n_a} d(a;t)}{|n_a|}; \quad \mathrm{n}_a > 0 \wedge d > 0 \qquad (4)$$

$$neg(t) = \frac{\sum_{a=1}^{n_a} d(a;t)}{|n_a|}; \quad \mathrm{n}_a < 0 \wedge d < 0 \qquad (5)$$

4. METHODOLOGY OF STUDY

A new methodology has been proposed for the evaluation in the network of trends. The method is based on the Social Network Analysis and enhanced by the Sentiment Analysis. Social Network Analysis determines the most active actor who has written about a specific trend. Sentiment Analysis determines the actors' evaluation of the trend. The study described in the previous section uses a newly proposed methodology to determine the most prestigious authors who have written reviews about the trend. In this study, different variants of the Power Threshold are chosen to distinguish prestigious authors. Sentiment Analysis is utilised to determine the authors' evaluation for the specific trend.

The newly proposed approach has been examined over the data from the film industry. User reviews published in 2012-2013 on IMDb[1] serves as the source for this research. Five the best-rated and five the average-rated movies which premiered in the United States in 2012 have been chosen as the trends for the evaluation. The movies have been selected according to the IMDb Charts (IMDb, 2014) at the beginning of January 2014. The IMDb Charts contain the list of movies based on the rating of the website visitors.

Like the first, the adjacency matrix has been created between nodes of the movies and reviewers. Ten columns represent the films, 7,838 rows show the authors and 10,160 edges indicate whether the author has written a review about the trend. Power degree has been calculated to determine the author's prestige. Table 2 reports how many authors have assigned a given value of the power degree. The first row represents the scale of the reviewers' power degree. Values are not normalised, and thus they directly indicate how many reviews must be written for a given degree. The second row shows the number of authors who have assigned the degree, and the third row indicates how many reviews have been written by the authors. For instance, the first degree is assigned to 6,697 authors since each of them has created just the one review. On the other end of the scale, there are 13 reviewers and each of them has commented all of the evaluated movies. Thus it can be stated that these ten reviewers are the most prestigious from all the rest.

Table 2. The distribution of the authors according to their Power Degree and the number of reviews they have written

Power Degree	1	2	3	4	5	6	7	8	9	10
# authors	6697	692	187	85	57	41	28	21	17	13
# reviews	6697	1384	561	340	285	246	196	168	153	130

5. RESULTS

Tables 3 and 4 report the result of the evaluation of movies based on the corpus of reviews. The resulting values are split into the two parts for each column in both tables. The value on the left side is the result of sentiment analysis based on the proposed Node Power evaluation. The values are normalised in the range from -1 to 1. However, these extreme values are a special case when all the reviews consist of negative or positive sentiment only. Therefore, most of the results are rather in the range from -0.1 to 0.1 and the evaluation scale must be adjusted for a larger number of trends. The second resulting value on the right side represents the number of people who have written the movie reviews. The entire corpus of reviews has no more than one review for one movie from a single author. So the value on the right side also represents the number of reviews that have been written about the film.

The individual cells are tinged with a linear gradient of blue, white, and red colours. The shade of the colours represents the value in the cell. The blue colour indicates a higher value, the red colour a lower value, and the white represents the midpoint between the minimum and maximum values in the table.

Table 3. Evaluation results of the selected movies[2] according to the individual Power Threshold

Movie	Threshold 1	Threshold 2	Threshold 3	Threshold 4	Threshold 5	Threshold 6	Threshold 7	Threshold 8	Threshold 9	Threshold 10
1	0.0589 (952)	0.0567 (327)	0.0551 (214)	0.0559 (161)	0.0552 (124)	0.0568 (88)	0.0515 (60)	0.0585 (44)	0.0649 (27)	0.0768 (13)
2	0.0620 (665)	0.0660 (273)	0.0690 (177)	0.0714 (138)	0.0721 (109)	0.0740 (87)	0.0712 (65)	0.0626 (43)	0.0627 (26)	0.0719 (13)
3	0.0821 (1488)	0.0828 (526)	0.0884 (291)	0.0873 (192)	0.0874 (148)	0.0983 (101)	0.0996 (73)	0.0931 (50)	0.0995 (30)	0.1017 (13)
4	0.0614 (2491)	0.0633 (677)	0.0680 (339)	0.0668 (221)	0.0628 (155)	0.0712 (114)	0.0693 (78)	0.0771 (50)	0.0832 (30)	0.0917 (13)
5	0.0569 (1243)	0.0587 (373)	0.0574 (214)	0.0562 (152)	0.0561 (120)	0.0574 (92)	0.0555 (65)	0.0484 (47)	0.0500 (28)	0.0612 (13)
6	0.0346 (1092)	0.0350 (430)	0.0349 (250)	0.0394 (183)	0.0424 (140)	0.0469 (103)	0.0506 (71)	0.0463 (46)	0.0488 (27)	0.0295 (13)
7	0.0523 (465)	0.0504 (199)	0.0568 (142)	0.0541 (116)	0.0496 (89)	0.0513 (77)	0.0509 (60)	0.0560 (42)	0.0618 (28)	0.0736 (13)
8	0.0500 (440)	0.0515 (193)	0.0546 (149)	0.0523 (118)	0.0545 (98)	0.0513 (74)	0.0497 (57)	0.0487 (43)	0.0525 (30)	0.0552 (13)
9	0.0819 (650)	0.0876 (238)	0.0869 (162)	0.0865 (131)	0.0869 (109)	0.0903 (90)	0.0930 (67)	0.1004 (47)	0.1027 (29)	0.1059 (13)
10	0.0547 (674)	0.0627 (227)	0.0626 (141)	0.0593 (106)	0.0601 (86)	0.0621 (67)	0.0667 (51)	0.0669 (39)	0.0633 (28)	0.0724 (13)

Table 3 shows the results according to the specific threshold. The lower value of the threshold implies the use of a larger amount of reviews for the evaluation process; a higher number within the brackets in the left-hand columns. On the contrary, it may also mean lower-quality reviews. The higher number of the

[1] IMDb (Internet Movie Database) - an online database of information related to movies, http://www.imdb.com.

[2] 1 - Django Unchained, 2 - Life of Pi, 3 - The Avengers, 4 - The Dark Knight Rises, 5 - The Hobbit: An Unexpected Journey, 6 - Battleship, 7 - Dark Shadows, 8 - Snow White and the Huntsman, 9 - The Amazing Spider-Man, 10 - Total Recall.

threshold means the evaluation to be processed using the high-quality reviews. However, that also means a smaller amount of reviews for the evaluation; a lower number within the brackets in the right-hand columns.

The values in brackets represent the number of authors whose power degree is equal or above the threshold in the corresponding column. Thus, for instance, the number in the first column "Threshold 1" is the sum of same numbers from the other columns; i.e. the evaluation on the left side reflects the reviews from all authors. The values in the first column also represent the state where no threshold has been applied since the review corpus does not contain any author who has made no comment.

Table 4. Evaluation results of the selected movies[2] based on the reviews by authors with a given Power Degree

Movie	Group 1	Group 2	Group 3	Group 4	Group 5	Group 6	Group 7	Group 8	Group 9	Group 10
1	0.0601 (625)	0.0597 (113)	0.0527 (53)	0.0584 (37)	0.0515 (36)	0.0681 (28)	0.0321 (16)	0.0484 (17)	0.0540 (14)	0.0768 (13)
2	0.0592 (392)	0.0605 (96)	0.0606 (39)	0.0686 (29)	0.0646 (22)	0.0823 (22)	0.0881 (22)	0.0623 (17)	0.0535 (13)	0.0719 (13)
3	0.0817 (962)	0.0758 (235)	0.0905 (99)	0.0872 (44)	0.0640 (47)	0.0948 (28)	0.1137 (23)	0.0835 (20)	0.0978 (17)	0.1017 (13)
4	0.0606 (1814)	0.0586 (338)	0.0702 (118)	0.0762 (66)	0.0395 (41)	0.0752 (36)	0.0555 (28)	0.0680 (20)	0.0767 (17)	0.0917 (13)
5	0.0561 (870)	0.0604 (159)	0.0603 (62)	0.0565 (32)	0.0520 (28)	0.0618 (27)	0.0740 (18)	0.0462 (19)	0.0402 (15)	0.0612 (13)
6	0.0345 (662)	0.0350 (180)	0.0216 (67)	0.0264 (43)	0.0266 (37)	0.0351 (32)	0.0643 (25)	0.0400 (19)	0.0656 (14)	0.0295 (13)
7	0.0538 (266)	0.0288 (57)	0.0670 (26)	0.0764 (27)	0.0442 (12)	0.0526 (17)	0.0353 (18)	0.0427 (14)	0.0528 (15)	0.0736 (13)
8	0.0492 (247)	0.0447 (44)	0.0644 (31)	0.0413 (20)	0.0695 (24)	0.0560 (17)	0.0521 (14)	0.0427 (13)	0.0503 (17)	0.0552 (13)
9	0.0782 (412)	0.0885 (76)	0.0882 (31)	0.0850 (22)	0.0775 (19)	0.0842 (23)	0.0794 (20)	0.0972 (18)	0.0996 (16)	0.1059 (13)
10	0.0487 (447)	0.0629 (86)	0.0771 (35)	0.0567 (20)	0.0477 (19)	0.0457 (16)	0.0662 (12)	0.0741 (11)	0.0554 (15)	0.0724 (13)

Table 4 shows the evaluation results of only those reviews that have been written by the authors whose power degree is equal the threshold in the corresponding column. For instance, the first column "Group 1" represents the evaluation of 625 reviewers whose power degree is equal to one; so each of them has written only the one review.

The results, for instance, show that the movie 6 - *Battleship* reaches the lowest of all the values in both tables. The Threshold 7 is the only exception, where the film is slightly better than 8 - *Snow White and the Huntsman*. However, the value in the corresponding columns Group 7, 8, 9, and 10 in the second table explain this exemption. There are 39 people in the Group 7 and 9 who like the movie more than people from the other groups. It is 39 people from 71 who like the movie more, therefore the exception in the Threshold 7. There is no exception for Threshold 9 even though the rating by Group 9 is almost double in comparison to the other groups. That is because the evaluation by the Group 10 is much lower, and people from that group meet the Threshold 9 together with Group 9.

Overall, the movie 6 is popular only for a very narrow group of people. There is a huge difference in the evaluation of 39 individuals in comparison to 1,053. The prestigious reviewers who meet the Threshold 10 evaluate the movie by the lowest value 0.0295. For comparison, a film with the second lowest value has received the rating 0.0552 from the same group, i.e. 43% difference. Compared to the best movie, the difference is even 73%.

There can be found another discrepancy in the evaluation by the Group 7. The movie 1 - *Django Unchained* has an excellent rating from almost all reviewers. However, the assessment of the Group 7 is nearly half that of the others. It is 16 people from 936 who do not like the move as the others. That shows once again that this is a very narrow group of individuals having a different requirement on a movie genre.

A different example can be seen in the evaluation of movies 3 - *The Avengers* and 9 - *The Amazing Spider-Man* which is rated as the best by the all the all reviewers. These movies are popular both for the general public and also for prestigious film reviewers.

6. CONCLUSION

The newly proposed approach for the evaluation in the network of trends has been examined over the data from the film industry. The network of trend has been represented by the movie titles and the reviewers who have written any comment about the movie. Power degree has been determined for each reviewer to recognise his prestige. Power threshold has been used to divide the reviewers into several groups according to their prestige. The lower value of the threshold implies the use of a larger amount of reviews for the evaluation. On the contrary, it may also mean lower-quality reviews. The higher number of the threshold means the evaluation to be processed using the high-quality reviews. However, that also means a smaller amount of reviews for the evaluation. The data from each group has been used to evaluate the movie titles.

The comparison of the results across the groups may help to identify trends in extreme, i.e. very popular and unpopular trends. Evaluation for this type of trends is usually identical for all groups. On the contrary, there can be found a trend that is popular only for a particular group. It can be helpful to identify the characteristics of different groups and determine their specific requirements.

In this study, the threshold has been used to ascertain the prestige of the author by the comments he wrote. However, the threshold value might also be utilised for the dividing into the groups according to the different parameters. That might help to identify more various groups of people and to determine their requirements better.

ACKNOWLEDGEMENT

The research has been taking place under the aegis of the research group Webing (http://webing.felk.cvut.cz) and has been supported by the Grant Agency of the Czech Technical University in Prague, Grant No. SGS16/092/OHK3/1T/13.

REFERENCES

Baccianella, S., Esuli, A., and Sebastiani, F. (2010). SentiWordNet 3.0: An Enhanced Lexical Resource for Sentiment Analysis and Opinion Mining. LREC '10, pages 2200–2204.

Bross, J., Richly, K., Kohnen, M., and Meinel, C. (2012). Identifying the Top-Dogs of the Blogosphere. *Social Network Analysis and Mining*, 2(1):53–67.

Graham, T., Broersma, M., Hazelhoff, K., and van't Haar, G. (2013). Between Broadcasting Messages and Interacting with Voters: The Use of Twitter During the 2010 UK General Election Campaign. *Information, Communication & Society*, 16(5):692–716.

Guns, R., Liu, Y., and Mahbuba, D. (2011). Q-Measures and Betweenness Centrality in a Collaboration Network: A Case Study of the Field of Informetrics. *Scientometrics*, 87(1):133–147.

Han, S. K., Shin, D., Jung, J. Y., and Park, J. (2009). Exploring the Relationship Between Keywords and Feed Elements in Blog Post Search. *World Wide Web*, 12(4):381–398.

IMDb (2014). IMDb Charts. *IMDb*. Retrieved 8 January 2014, from http://www.imdb.com/chart.

Lee, J. and Bonk, C. J. (2016). Social Network Analysis of Peer Relationships and Online Interactions in a Blended Class Using Blogs. *Internet and Higher Education*, 28:35–44.

Li, R. H., Yu, J. X., Huang, X., and Cheng, H. (2012). A Framework of Algorithms: Computing the Bias and Prestige of Nodes in Trust Networks. *PLoS ONE*, 7(12).

Liu, B. (2011). *Web Data Mining: Exploring Hyperlinks, Contents, and Usage Data*. Springer-Verlag Berlin Heidelberg.

Liu, D. R., Omar, H., Liou, C. H., Chi, H. C., and Hsu, C. H. (2015). Recommending blog articles based on popular event trend analysis. *Information Sciences*, *305*:302-319.

Malinský, R. and Jelínek, I. (2014). Comparing Methods of Trend Assessment. In Casteleyn, S., Rossi, G., and Winckler, M., editors, *Web Engineering*, volume 8541, pages 554–557. Springer International Publishing, Cham.

Ohana, B. and Tierney, B. (2009). Sentiment Classification of Reviews Using SentiWordNet. In *School of Computing 9th IT & T Conference*, page 13.

Pang, B. and Lee, L. (2008). Opinion Mining and Sentiment Analysis. *Foundations and Trends in Information Retrieval*, 2(1–2):1–135.

Pennebaker, J. W. (2011). *The Secret Life of Pronouns: What Our Words Say About Us*, Volume 1890. Bloomsbury Press.

Prabowo, R. and Thelwall, M. (2009). Sentiment Analysis: A Combined Approach. *Journal of Informetrics*, 3(2): 143–157.

Taboada, M., Brooke, J., Tofiloski, M., Voll, K., and Stede, M. (2011). Lexicon-Based Methods for Sentiment Analysis. *Computational Linguistics*, 37(2):267–307.

Thelwall, M. (2009). *Introduction to Webometrics: Quantitative Web Research for the Social Sciences*, Volume 1.

Viswanath, B., Mislove, A., Cha, M., and Gummadi, K. P. (2009). On the Evolution of User Interaction in Facebook. In *Proceedings of the 2nd ACM Workshop on Online Social Networks*, WOSN '09, pages 37–42, New York, NY, USA. ACM.

IDENTIFYING IMPORTANT LIFE EVENTS FROM TWITTER USING SEMANTIC AND SYNTACTIC PATTERNS

Thomas Dickinson[1], Miriam Fernandez[1], Lisa A Thomas[2], Paul Mulholland[1],
Pam Briggs[2] and Harith Alani[1]
[1]*KMI Open University*
[2]*Northumbria University*

ABSTRACT

Identifying global events from social media has been the focus of much research in recent years. However, the identification of personal life events poses new requirements and challenges that have received relatively little research attention. In this paper we explore a new approach for life event identification, where we expand social media posts into both semantic, and syntactic networks of content. Frequent graph patterns are mined from these networks and used as features to enrich life-event classifiers. Results show that our approach significantly outperforms the best performing baseline in accuracy (by 4.48% points) and F-measure (by 4.54% points) when used to identify five major life events identified from the psychology literature: Getting Married, Having Children, Death of a Parent, Starting School, and Falling in Love. In addition, our results show that, while semantic graphs are effective at discriminating the theme of the post (e.g. the topic of marriage), syntactic graphs help identify whether the post describes a personal event (e.g. someone getting married).

KEYWORDS

Semantic Networks, Event Detection, Frequent Pattern Mining, Classification, Social Media

1. INTRODUCTION

Social media platforms are not only the online spaces where billions of people connect and socialise, they are also where much of their prominent life events are captured, shared, and reflected on. Most of these platforms are exploring methods that make use of this content for the purpose of profiling, marketing, and product recommendation, which constitutes a really valuable resource for governments and organisations. More recently, several initiatives are also focusing on exploring the value that this content has for the individuals as a means of self-reflection. Services such as Museum of Me, Facebook Look Back, and Google Creations aim to generate brief automated biographies for the users based on their generated content. Although these services and technologies are still in their infancy, they raise the need for a more accurate identification of personal life events.

However, as opposed to the identification of large-scale events from social media (e.g., detection of news stories (Wayne, 2000), natural disasters (Sakaki, et al., 2010), music events (Liu, et al., 2011), etc.), which has gained much interest in recent years, the identification of personal life events (e.g. getting married, having a child, starting school) is still largely unexplored. This problem poses new requirements and challenges, since these events do not receive the same amount of coverage as large-scale events (unless they involve celebrities (Choudhury & Alani, 2014)), and do not show similar geographical or temporal distributions. In addition, the accurate identification of life events in social media requires distinguishing between posts that mention a life event (e.g., I'm getting married in the church today) and posts about the same theme that do not mention a life event (e.g., check out my wedding photography business). While previous works have found that uni-grams are one of the best features for thematically classifying posts in terms of whether or not they mention the topic of a life event (Di Eugenio, et al., 2013) (Dickinson, et al.,

2015), current methods cannot adequately distinguish posts describing life events from posts of the same theme that do not.

In our work, we focus on identifying events from Twitter data that are regarded as some of the most significant life events in the psychology literature (Janssen & Rubin, 2011): Getting Married, Having Children, Starting School, Death of a Parent, and Falling in Love. To address the above mentioned challenges we propose a novel approach based on the representation of posts as syntactic and semantic graphs. Our hypothesis is that, by considering the conceptualisations that emerge from social media posts (mined in our work by using WordNet and ConceptNet), as well their syntactic structures (extracted by applying dependency parsing), we can obtain relevant insights for a more accurate detection of personal life events. These insights are extracted by performing frequent pattern mining over the generated graphs and used as features to generate life event classifiers. Our results show that our approach significantly outperforms the state of the art baseline in accuracy (by 4.48% points) and F-measure (by 4.54% points). In addition, we can observe from our results that, while semantic graphs are effective at discriminating the theme of the post, syntactic graphs help identifying whether the personal event is present in the post or not. The main contributions of this paper are:

1. Introduce a semantic and syntactic graph-based approach for identifying five personal-life events using ConceptNet, WordNet, and Dependency Parsing
2. Mine frequent graph patterns, and serialise them as features, in a LibLINEAR classification algorithm
3. Compare several feature reduction techniques to elicit the best performance
4. Construct tri-class classifiers to categorise posts into those about an event, those about the theme of an event, and those that are neither
5. Compare results to the state of the art baseline, showing an average increase of 4.48% points in accuracy, 4.54% points in F-measure
6. Discuss the advantages of using syntactic and semantic graphs for personal life event identification

2. STATE OF THE ART

As mentioned earlier, much work has been done on detecting global and/or famous events, such as natural disasters (Sakaki, et al., 2010), music events (Liu, et al., 2011), and prominent news stories (Wayne, 2000). However, detecting life events differs from the detection of such global events. Life events tend to focus on one particular individual, and only very few posts from a user's history are likely to refer to a particular life event. Few works in the literature have attempted to address this problem. Di Eugenio et al (Di Eugenio, et al., 2013) have investigated the identification of life events related to employment, and marriage. Their approach compared several different classifiers trained with different subsets of linguistic features, concluding that uni-grams are the best features to automatically identify these types of event. Li et al (Li, et al., 2014) took a slightly different approach. Rather than trying to identify a set of pre-defined life events, this approach focused on detecting life events mentioned on Twitter by clustering posts based on congratulatory and condolence replies such as "Congratulations", and "Sorry to hear that". Their approach is also based on the use of linguistic features including sequences of words within the tweets, named entities, and topic models for different life event categories. Choudhury and Alani (Choudhury & Alani, 2014) studied the use of interaction features to identify several events: marriage, graduation, new job, new born, and surgery. Their approach aggregates linguistic features with interaction features (i.e, features based on the interactions of users with their social network - comments, replies, etc.).

Our work extends the above approaches by representing social media posts as graphs, to capture the interdependencies of linguistic, semantic and interaction features. Although using graphs for finding similar concepts is not a new idea (e.g., (Resnik, 1999) and (Rada, et al., 1989)), applying it for identifying life events is vastly under researched. Sayyadi et al (Sayyadi, et al., 2009) used graphs for news-event identification, by creating a "key graph" of key words co-occurring within a document, where nodes represent individual keywords and edges represent their co-occurrence. To the best of our knowledge, our work is the first one which uses a combination of syntactic, and semantic graphs for personal life event identification.

3. APPROACH

3.1 Representing Posts as Feature Graphs

Before we can extract frequent patterns from social media, we first need to represent our posts as graph structures. An example of a full feature graph for the tweet "**I had a baby**" is displayed in Figure 1**.** Our graphs can be placed into two specific groups: Semantic, and Syntactic.

We construct semantic graphs by extracting concepts and synsets from the posts, then expanding into two popular semantic networks: ConceptNet, and WordNet. Our hypothesis is that, after expansion, posts may have related nodes amongst one another. For example, the concepts "mother" and "father" are related by the concept "parent" within ConceptNet. By extending these two posts into ConceptNet, /c/en/parent would then become a feature, appearing in two posts. In this work, we only expand 1 hop into both ConceptNet and WordNet, to limit the size of the graphs we create. In the case of WordNet, we extend one hop using both hypernyms, and hyponyms with an "IS_A" relationship, whereas for ConceptNet, we include all relationship types. As concepts in ConceptNet are normalised WordNet URIs, we extract N-grams from each post, and use ConceptNet's URI standardisation API.[1]

Syntactic graphs can be divided into two areas: dependency graphs, and token graphs. Dependency graphs can be constructed using dependency parsing (Covington, 2001), which are the syntactic dependencies between words within a sentence. Dependency parsers represent these dependencies as acyclic directed trees with a word, generally the main verb, representing the main node, root, of the tree, and the rest of the words being dependants of the head or other governor nodes. These trees constitute a graph, where words and their associated part of speech (POS) are the nodes, and the edges are the syntactic dependencies between these nodes. Our hypothesis is that posts about the same life events may share similar syntactic structures. In this work, we use the Stanford Neural Network Dependency parser (Chen & Manning, 2014) to obtain these dependency trees from which syntactic graphs are generated. Use of dependency graphs and n-grams within event detection is not uncommon (Li, et al., 2014). However, we have not seen another approach that mines frequent sub-graphs from syntactic graphs, in order to create feature sets for life event classifiers. With token graphs we represent the different tokens (words) that emerge from social media posts, with their associated POS, as nodes, and the sequence in which they appear within the posts (i.e., one token before/after another token) as the edges. This is very similar to n-grams. Our hypothesis is that posts about a particular life event may share common sequences of either tokens or POS tags. We use TweetNLP (Owoputi, et al., 2013) to extract both tokens and POS tags from the text of each post.

3.2 Mining Frequent Patterns

Once the previously described graphs have been generated from the social media posts, we apply frequent pattern mining to the graphs associated with each type of life event. By frequent, we mean a sub-graph appearing more than n times within a set of graphs. As the size of our training sets are not very large (table 1), we set n to 2. This allows us to identify as many sub-graphs as possible, without returning a posts entire graph. As this will return a very large set of graphs, with many sharing the same information, we only search for closed subgraphs, where a closed subgraph has no parent with the same frequency.

To mine these frequent sub-graphs, we use CloseGraph, which can perform an exhaustive frequent sub-graph search over our graph data sets, returning all frequent closed graphs. We use the Parallel and Sequential Mining Suites (ParSeMiS[2]) implementation of this algorithm. As this type of mining has a high memory cost, we represent our graph as a cyclic structure, collapsing nodes. In addition, we also limit the maximum number of edges allowed in a sub-graph, reducing the search space.

---

[1] https://github.com/commonsense/conceptnet5/wiki/API#uri-standardization

[2] https://www2.informatik.uni-erlangen.de/EN/research/zold/ParSeMiS/index.html

4. EXPERIMENT SETUP

4.1 Dataset

Our dataset was collected back in December 2014, by mining Twitter's advanced search features, using query expansion into WordNet with several key concepts for each type of life event. More information can be found in our previous paper (Dickinson, et al., 2015) This dataset is composed of 12,241 tweets manually annotated through CrowdFlower. Five relevant life events, common across age and culture (Janssen & Rubin, 2011), are represented in this dataset: **Starting School; Falling in Love; Getting Married; Having Children; and Death of a Parent**.

For each tweet, annotations contain answers to two questions: (i) Is this tweet about an important life event? and (ii) Is this tweet related to a particular event theme? - where event theme refers to one of the previously mentioned types of life events. Additionally, we introduce a random sample of tweets collected (2000) and internally annotated from a Twitter sample endpoint to generate a "not about event or theme" class. This represents a class where neither category of theme or event exists. The CrowdFlower annotations for this dataset are publicly available[3].

4.2 Training Set Selection

We use the posts of the previously described dataset to generate the feature graphs (see Section 3.1). These feature graphs are then mined, and the extracted patterns are used as features to train classifiers for each type of life event (Death of a Parent, Having Children, Falling in Love, Getting Married, and Starting School). For each life event, we construct a tri-class classifier with the following labels: About Event and About Theme (+E+T), Not About Event and About Theme (-E+T), Not About Event and Not About Theme (-E-T).

As named, +E+T contains those posts that are both about a particular event, and its given theme, while those in -E+T contain posts that are thematically similar, but do not indicate an event has happened. Our third class, -E-T, contains tweets extracted from Twitter's random sample endpoint. In each case, we balance the training set against the size of the smallest class, with the following distributions: Getting Married (706 per class), Starting School (419 per class), Having Children (387 per class), Death of a Parent (116 per class), and Falling in Love (114 per class). To consider if our approach is statistically significant, we generate our dataset 10 times for each life event, so that we can perform t-tests against our baseline.

4.3 Classifier Generation and Evaluation

Each training dataset, and combination of features (semantic ConceptNet, semantic WordNet, syntactic), is used as input to a LibLINEAR classifier. LibLINEAR works particularly well with very large feature sets. We also independently tested several other classifiers (J48, Naive Bayes, and SVMS with linear, polynomial, sigmoid, and radial bias kernels), but in all cases, LibLINEAR outperformed each in both F-Measure, time performance, and accuracy. The generated classifier is tested using 10-fold cross validation considering Precision, Recall and F1-measure as evaluation metrics. In section 5, we report some of our best performing feature sets using this classification and evaluation set-up.

4.4 Baseline Selection

For our baseline, we implement the features outlined in Li et al. These included **N-grams**, **topic dictionaries**, and **entities**. Entities are extracted using TextRazor[4], and for the case of topic dictionaries, our topic models are generated slightly differently to Li et al, where we discover 5 topics (representing our five chosen life events) across our total annotated dataset. The top 40 words for each topic are used as our topic dictionaries, as outlined in Li et al. Rather than treat n-grams, topics, and entities as a single baseline, for each experiment, we run our classifiers against every permutation of the baseline features, and select the best one to compare against our graph approach.

---

[3] Link removed for blind submission

[4] https://www.textrazor.com/

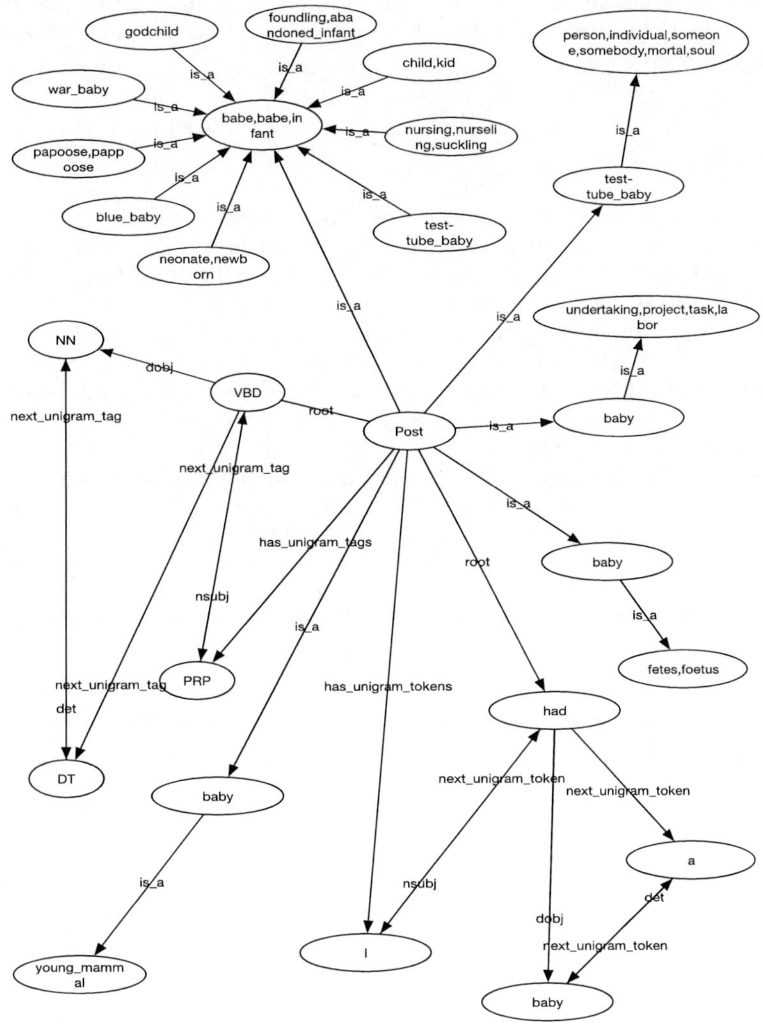

Figure 1. Example Graph of "I had a baby"

4.5 T-Tests

For our T-Tests, we generate 10 samples for each type of event. We create permutations of all possible feature combinations (**N-Grams**, **Entities**, **Topics**, **Syntactic**, **Semantic ConceptNet**, and **Semantic WordNet**), and compare against the best performing baseline combination (mentioned in section 4.4).

Thus, the hypotheses for our t-tests are:

- H0: Graph features do not help improve the f-measure over our baseline.
- H1: By introducing our graph features, we improve our f-measure.

4.6 Feature Reduction

Due to the large number of features extracted from our pattern mining approach, we also consider several feature reduction techniques within Weka. Our approach uses a ranker method, where we filter our attributes via a chosen metric. Initially we remove any feature whose rank is 0, then gradually reduce the number of features over 20 even intervals over the remaining attributes. In order to choose the best suitable attribute metric, we compared the results of several attribute selection algorithms over our Death of a Parent training set: Information Gain, Gain Ratio, Correlation, and Symmetrical Uncertainty. We found that Gain Ratio gave a significant improvement of 13 points.

5. RESULTS

Our results are displayed in Table 1 for all of our events: Getting Married, Death of a Parent, Having Children, Starting School, and Falling in Love. We compare the performance of the best baseline (B) against the best feature combination. We report: F1, change in F1 to baseline (Δ F1), Accuracy (A), Precision (P), Recall (R), P-Value (P-Val). We observe statistical significance when p-val < 0.05.

As can be seen from table 1, in all cases, our graph-based methodology merged with some of the baseline features produces a significant improvement in all measures (F1, Accuracy, Precision, and Recall), across each of our events. Our biggest improvement is in Falling in Love, with a 6.8% percentage point increase, while our smallest is in Having Children, with only 1.1%. However, the improvements over the baseline are all statistically significant (p < 0.01).

Overall our improvements show a 4.54% point increase in F-Measure over our baselines. For each classifier, the best performing baseline combination remains constant (N-Grams, Topics, Entities), which is the full methodology outlined in Li et al. The best performing feature combination is also the same (N-grams, Topics, Entities + WordNet and Syntactic patterns). One explanation for concepts not always appearing in our best classifiers might be that ConceptNet and WordNet have a very similar feature distribution. By adding both, the available features are increased, thus making it more difficult to perform feature selection. Another could be that Concepts may not be effective discriminators.

Table 1. Results Table

Theme	Feature Set	F1	Δ F1	A	P	R	P-Val
Getting Married	Best Baseline: Ent,Ngrm,Tpc	85.9%		86.0%	86.1%	86.0%	
	Con	66.5%	-19.4%	67.8%	67.6%	67.8%	<0.01
	Ent	45.4%	-40.4%	51.4%	63.1%	51.4%	<0.01
	Ngrm	83.7%	-2.2%	84.0%	83.8%	84.0%	<0.01
	Syn	79.0%	-6.9%	79.7%	80.8%	79.7%	<0.01
	Tpc	71.0%	-14.9%	72.3%	71.9%	72.3%	<0.01
	WN	70.6%	-15.3%	71.7%	71.4%	71.7%	<0.01
	Best Graph Only: Con, Syn, Wn	86.3%	0.4%	86.5%	86.5%	86.5%	0.04
	Con,Ent,Ngram,Syn,Tpc,Wn	**90.7%**	**4.8%**	**90.8%**	**90.7%**	**90.8%**	**<0.01**
Death of a Parent	Best Baseline: Ent,Ngrm,Tpc	86.2%		86.2%	86.7%	86.2%	
	Con	71.0%	-15.2%	71.6%	71.5%	71.6%	<0.01
	Ent						
	Ngrm	85.4%	-0.8%	85.5%	86.0%	85.5%	0.02
	Syn	82.2%	-4.0%	82.4%	83.9%	82.4%	<0.01
	Tpc	61.1%	-25.1%	60.4%	67.7%	60.4%	<0.01
	WN	79.4%	-6.7%	79.7%	79.7%	79.7%	<0.01
	Best Graph Only: Con,Syn,WN	87.8%	1.6%	87.9%	88.8%	87.9%	0.06
	Ent,Ngrm,Syn,Tpc,WN	**90.7%**	**4.5%**	**90.7%**	**91.1%**	**90.7%**	**<0.01**
Having Children	Best Baseline: Ent,Ngrm,Tpc	89.8%		89.9%	90.2%	89.9%	
	Con	6.7%	-23.1%	67.7%	67.9%	67.7%	<0.01
	Ent	35.5%	-54.3%	41.4%	59.4%	41.4%	<0.01
	Ngrm	87.9%	-1.9%	88.0%	88.3%	88.0%	<0.01
	Syn	79.7%	-10.1%	80.2%	82.9%	80.2%	<0.01
	Tpc	72.4%	-17.4%	73.1%	72.2%	73.1%	<0.01
	WN	73.8%	-16.0%	74.7%	74.8%	74.7%	<0.01
	Best Graph Only:Con,Syn,WN	86.2%	-3.5%	86.5%	88.0%	86.5%	<0.01
	Ent,Ngrm,Syn,Tpc,WN	**90.9%**	**1.1%**	**91.0%**	**91.7%**	**91.0%**	**<0.01**

Starting School	Best Baseline: Ent,Ngrm,Tpc	87.7%		87.8%	88.3%	87.8%	
	Con	64.9%	-22.8%	66.1%	64.9%	66.1%	<0.01
	Ent	32.1%	-55.6%	37.4%	53.4%	37.4%	<0.01
	Ngrm	85.0%	-2.7%	85.2%	85.2%	85.2%	<0.01
	Syn	86.3%	-1.4%	86.6%	87.9%	86.6%	<0.01
	Tpc	72.4%	-15.3%	72.6%	72.4%	72.6%	<0.01
	WN	66.1%	-21.6%	68.0%	67.0%	68.0%	<0.01
	Best Graph Only:Syn,WN	88.9%	1.2%	89.1%	90.1%	89.1%	0.025
	Ent,Ngrm,Syn,Tpc,WN	**93.0%**	**5.5%**	**93.0%**	**93.5%**	**93.0%**	**<0.01**
Falling in Love	Best Baseline: Ent,Ngrm,Tpc	83.7%		83.9%	84.2%	83.9%	
	Con	68.4%	-15.4%	68.9%	69.4%	68.9%	<0.01
	Ent	29.5%	-54.2%	34.6%	53.3%	34.6%	<0.01
	Ngrm	80.4%	-3.3%	80.6%	81.1%	80.6%	<0.01
	Syn	82.1%	-1.6%	82.3%	84.4%	82.3%	<0.01
	Tpc	62.3%	-21.5%	65.1%	65.3%	65.1%	<0.01
	WN	70.3%	-13.5%	71.3%	71.7%	71.3%	0.103
	Best Graph Only:Con,Syn,WN	86.8%	3.0%	86.9%	87.3%	86.9%	0.03
	Ent,Ngrm,Syn,Tpc,WN	**90.5%**	**6.8%**	**90.6%**	**91.2%**	**90.6%**	**<0.01**

6. DISCUSSION

Our results show that some interesting observations can be made. When combined with our baseline features, our graph F1 scores are consistently and significantly higher. When looking at our top performing features, we found that patterns extracted from ConceptNet and WordNet were regularly at the top, and tended to help discriminate between our negative class, and our two thematic classes. However, when attempting to discriminate theme from event, these types of patterns were less useful as each will tend to use similar languages and concepts. Instead, we found our syntactical patterns helped to discriminate between events and non-events.

While we have successfully identified a number of interesting frequent graph patterns, there is much improvement that can still be made on this. Our choice of algorithm does not scale well, thus we have had to perform some optimization steps that might limit our results. Newer state of the art algorithms (e.g., (Pan, et al., 2015)) also consider the feature selection problem as being part of the pattern mining discovery phase, reducing memory and time cost. An alternative might be to consider using a more distributed pattern mining approach, such as outlined in (Bhuiyan & Hasan, 2014). In addition to this, our assumption that two concepts that are close together in ConceptNet are similar is not always valid. For example, the relationship "IsAntonym" in ConceptNet is the opposite of similar in terms of linking two concepts together. When not taking this into account, concepts such as "life" and "death" might be considered semantically similar. Thus a better approach would be to either filter out all negating relationships like this one, or to add a weighting system where a heuristic function could possibly be used to calculate how close two concepts are together in the graph (Rada, et al., 1989). Future work can also consider expanding our semantic graphs into other networks, such as DBpedia. We could also consider other types of semantic features such as semantic frames using FrameNet (Baker, et al., 1998).

In this work, we focused on the identification of only five of the most common life events. A natural next step is to expand to the full set of life events listed in (Janssen & Rubin, 2011). This would help test the consistency of our results across other types of event. A broader goal would be to consider the detection of life events in general. In addition to this, we construct a classifier for each individual life event. As Li et al (Li, et al., 2014) point out in their work, a single large multi classifier is a more complex task compared to individual theme detection, due to the overlap of n-grams in certain topics. Given our observation of how our semantic patterns work, it would be interesting to see if they can help boost the results in such a classifier.

We opted to serialize our frequent patterns into a key/map pair so that we can represent our training set as a vector of binary values. However, there exist a number of alternative classification algorithms that are designed specifically for graphs; some reliant on frequent patterns themselves, others taking into account the structure of the graph. In terms of our frequent patterns, we also see a number of weak infrequent ones. However, rather than representing these patterns as independent of each other, we could consider a methodology such as COM (Jin, et al., 2009), where co-occurrence of disconnected low frequency patterns is considered instead, converting them into higher frequency ones.

7. CONCLUSION

We have presented a new approach for the problem of life event detection that focusses on five major life events identified by psychologists: Getting Married, Having Children, Death of a Parent, Starting School, and Falling in Love. Our approach expands a Twitter post into both a syntactic and semantic graph. This network is then mined for frequent sub patterns that can be used as features within a classifier, filtered via their gain ratio. Our results showed consistent and significant improvement over baselines from other work, that consider only features extracted directly from the post (i.e., no graphs). We showed that our graph-based approach achieves significantly better accuracy and F1 scores than our selected baseline.

REFERENCES

Baker, C. F., Fillmore, C. J. & Lowe, J. B., 1998. *The berkeley framenet project.* s.l., s.n.

Bhuiyan, M. A. & Hasan, M. A., 2014. *FSM-H: Frequent Subgraph Mining Algorithm in Hadoop.* s.l., s.n., pp. 9-16.

Cao, B. et al., 2015. Mining brain networks using multiple side views for neurological disorder identification. *arXiv preprint arXiv:1508.04554.*

Chen, D. & Manning, C. D., 2014. *A Fast and Accurate Dependency Parser using Neural Networks..* s.l., s.n., pp. 740-750.

Choudhury, S. & Alani, H., 2014. *Personal life event detection from social media.* s.l., CEUR.

Covington, M. A., 2001. *A fundamental algorithm for dependency parsing.* Athens, s.n.

Di Eugenio, B., Green, N. & Subba, R., 2013. *Detecting life events in feeds from twitter.* s.l., s.n.

Dickinson, T. et al., 2015. *Identifying Prominent Life Events on Twitter.* s.l., s.n.

Holder, L. B., Cook, D. J., Djoko, S. & others, 1994. *Substucture Discovery in the SUBDUE System..* s.l., s.n., pp. 169-180.

Janssen, S. M. J. & Rubin, D. C., 2011. Age Effects in Cultural Life Scripts. *Applied Cognitive Psychology,* 25(2), pp. 291-298.

Jin, N., Young, C. & Wang, W., 2009. Graph classification based on pattern co-occurrence. *Proc. Conf. on Info. and Knowledge Man. - CIKM '09.*

Kong, L. et al., 2014. *A dependency parser for tweets.* s.l., s.n.

Li, J., Ritter, A., Cardie, C. & Hovy, E., 2014. *Major Life Event Extraction from Twitter based on Congratulations/Condolences Speech Acts.* Doha, s.n.

Liu, X., Troncy, R. & Huet, B., 2011. *Using social media to identify events.* s.l., s.n.

Ohara, K. et al., 2008. *Pruning Strategies Based on the Upper Bound of Information Gain for Discriminative Subgraph Mining..* Vietn, s.n.

Owoputi, O. et al., 2013. *Improved part-of-speech tagging for online conversational text with word clusters.* s.l., s.n.

Pan, S. et al., 2015. Finding the best not the most: regularized loss minimization subgraph selection for graph classification. *Pattern Recognition,* Volume 48, pp. 3783-3796.

Parameswaran, A., Rajaraman, A. & Garcia-Molina, H., 2010. Towards the web of concepts: Extracting concepts from large datasets. *Proceedings of the Very Large Data Bases Conference (VLDB)* , 3((1-2)).

Philippsen, M., Worlein, M., Dreweke, A. & Werth, T., 2011. Parsemis: the parallel and sequential mining suite. *Available at www2. informatik. uni-erlangen. de/EN/research/ParSeMiS.*

Rada, R., Mili, H., Bicknell, E. & Blettner, M., 1989. *Development and application of a metric on semantic nets.* s.l., s.n., pp. 17-30.

Resnik, P., 1999. Semantic Similarity in a Taxonomy: An Information-Based Measure and its Application to Problems of Ambiguity in Natural Language. *Journal of Artificial Intelligence Research,* Volume 11, pp. 95-130.

Sakaki, T., Okazaki, M. & Matsuo, Y., 2010. *Earthquake Shakes Twitter Users: Real-time Event Detection by Social Sensors.* Raleigh, North Carolina USA, s.n.

Sayyadi, H., Hurst, M. & Maykov, A., 2009. *Event detection and tracking in social streams.* San Jose, {CA}, s.n.

Wayne, C. L., 2000. *Topic detection and tracking in English and Chinese.* NY, s.n.

Yan, X. & Han, J., 2002. *gspan: Graph-based substructure pattern mining.* s.l., s.n., pp. 721-724.

Yan, X. & Han, J., 2003. *CloseGraph: mining closed frequent graph patterns.* Washington, s.n.

DEVELOPING A NEW MODEL FOR THE AVOIDANCE OF MALWARE THREATS THROUGH ONLINE SOCIAL NETWORKS

Ehinome Ikhalia and Dr Alan Serrano
Department of Computer Science, Brunel University
London, Uxbridge

ABSTRACT

The growth of online social networks (OSNs) has revolutionized the way social relationships and businesses are conducted, with dynamic functionalities to connect with friends and family as well as meeting new customers. There has also been a rapid increase in the success of malicious attacks targeting users of OSNs. Malware attackers always find a way to bypass automated security measures to employ social engineering techniques in tricking users to download malware on their computer systems. In this paper, we explore the technology threat avoidance theory (TTAT) for the avoidance of malware threats. We identify potential drawbacks of this model in the context of its application for online social networking, and we propose a malware threat avoidance theory (MTAT) that will help to persuade users to avoid social-engineering-based malware attacks carried out through online social networks.

KEYWORDS

Social networks, malware attacks, mass interpersonal persuasion, threat avoidance, social engineering, human vulnerability

1. INTRODUCTION

The biggest security challenge associated with the use of online social networks is malware distribution through social engineering (Faghani *et al*, 2012; Fire *et al*, 2013). Social engineering is a persuasive technique malware attackers often utilize because it relies mainly on human vulnerability. Basically, social engineering often involves tricking users into executing tasks that they normally would not (e.g. downloading malware on their computer systems unknowingly) (Algarni *et al*, 2013). On social networks, social engineering has become very pervasive and prevalent and has been used continuously to propagate malware attacks (Ikhalia & Arreymbi 2014).

Within online social network settings, a common social engineering technique employed is; persuading users to click on malicious video links which often redirects them into a replica of a legitimate website with a prompt to update a 'software' needed to watch the video (Thomas & Nicol, 2010). The 'software' is essentially a malware which enables the attacker to remotely control the victim's computing system. When the malware is installed, it posts the malicious link to the victim's personal social network space (for example Facebook timeline), and tags his/her social connections (often called, friends/followers), thereby infecting every user that clicks it. The malware is also able to send private messages to victims' connections, spreading the infection even further (Baltazar et al, 2009; Gao et al., 2011; Palmer, 2013).

Attackers are always finding new ways to take advantage of the ignorance, curiosities, trust and fears of users' in order to lure them to download and install malware on their computing systems (Faghani et al., 2012). Efforts by security practitioners to combat these adverse trends have mostly been unsuccessful because more often, they have ignored the biggest security challenge – the human factors. Moreover, online social network ecosystems have introduced new vectors for viral malware propagation which many security awareness systems have not been designed to effectively address (Braun & Esswein, 2013, Ikhalia & Arreymbi, 2014).

1.1 Related Work

Previous researches have been conducted towards the development of effective end-user security awareness systems to mitigate the impact of malicious attacks. Abrams et al., 2013; Aggarwal, 2012; Doostari et al, 2013, focused on developing software to detect malicious attacks. However, their proposed system is mainly reactive in nature; implying that, the implications of attacks may occur before remediation measures are applied. There is evidence in literature (Tidwell, 2011) which suggests that more research work needs to focus on proactive security awareness systems tailored to address the threats faced by users in the technological setting through which malware attacks are being executed.

Wilson et al, (2003) suggests that numerous security awareness frameworks exist which prescribes the required steps to design and implement an efficient and effective security awareness system. A thorough understanding of the steps is compulsory to develop and tailor such an awareness program for a specific technological setting. Some of the methods that have been used include professional training, newsletters, and websites to deliver security awareness information to users. Unfortunately, the nature of these methods could be relatively daunting, costly and strenuous to the end-users who have no technical background in information technology.

In the context of online social networks, an effective and proactive security awareness system that could be useful in avoiding malware attacks must adopt some of the features and characteristics that define users' engagement on the platform. Features such as; video embedding capabilities, social interaction, and active user participation. Ikhalia & Serrano (2015) proposed a novel framework for the development of security awareness systems for OSN users; five components were deduced and proposed; ***Timeboxing, End-User Engagement, Platform Integration, Activity Specific and Knowledge Testing.*** In addition to these factors, this paper supports the theory that motivation is also a key theoretical component for OSN users to avoid malware attacks based on the research conducted by Liang & Xue (2009). Hence, we explore the technology threat avoidance theory (TTAT) through avoidance motivation. We have also included a new construct – mass interpersonal persuasion (MIP) to the TTAT model to motivate OSN users to avoid malware attacks. A security awareness system driven by MIP involves creating persuasive experiences deployed using automated software tools within a small amount of time in a highly socially distributed technological platform embedded with capabilities to measure its impact (Fogg & Hall, 2008). MIP focuses on changing users' thoughts and behaviors and not just informing them. This factor could be extremely useful for deploying security awareness in a setting were security compliance is non-mandatory. The next section describes the TTAT model and a few limitations on its practical application within OSNs.

This work will attempt to improve upon existing research efforts towards security awareness by proposing a malware threat avoidance theory (MTAT) that will help to persuade users to avoid social-engineering-based malware attacks carried out through OSNs. The paper is structured thus; section 2 presents a review of TTAT and identified gaps. Section 3 reviews the newly added construct to TTAT; section 4 presents the research hypothesis and the theoretical justifications.

2. TECHNOLOGY THREAT AVOIDANCE THEORY (TTAT)

The development of this research is based on the technology threat avoidance theory (TTAT) proposed by Liang and Xue (2009) which explains the motivation for technology threat avoidance by users of computer systems. The fundamental principle of TTAT is that when computer users perceive a malware threat they are motivated to use a safeguarding measure to avoid the threat if they perceive that it would be effective for threat avoidance. In the process of avoiding malware threats by users of computer systems, Liang and Xue (2009) proposed a set of key factors that demonstrates the perceptions, motivations, and behavior of users. According to their proposed model, users' malware threat perceptions are affected by the perceived likelihood of the threat's occurrence as well as the perceived severity of its negative consequences. By drawing from previous studies on health protective behaviour (Janz and Becker, 1984; Rosenstock, 1974), Liang and Xue (2009) argue that there are three main factors considered by computer users when evaluating the degree of avoidance of a malware threat – the effectiveness of the safeguard, the self-confidence in applying the safeguard and the costs of applying the safeguard.

TTAT also suggests that users normally perform emotion-focused coping to passively avoid the malware threat. Emotion-focused coping creates a false sense of the situation without essentially modifying one's needs or importance of needs so that negative emotions connected to malware threat are avoided. Thus, it reduces perceived threat or motivation of coping with the threat without altering the reality of the threat (Liang & Xue, 2009).

Liang and Xue (2009) conducted their survey on 152 US college students within the business department and found out that users' malware threat avoidance behavior is predicted by their motivation to avoid the threat. Additionally, they argue that avoidance motivation of malware threat is determined by perceived threat, safeguard effectiveness, safeguard cost and self-efficacy or self-confidence. Therefore, their findings suggest that users develop a perception of malware threat when they feel that a malware has the possibility of attacking them (perceived susceptibility or perceived vulnerability) and the corresponding consequences would be severe (perceived severity).

Furthermore, when faced with a malware threat, they suggest that users are motivated to use a safeguard measure if they perceive the degree of its effectiveness; the inexpensiveness and convenience of using it (safeguard cost); and their confidence in using it (self-efficacy). They identified that perceived threat and safeguard effectiveness have a negative interactive effect on the motivation for malware threat avoidance. This implies that an increase in users' perception of malware threat is correlated with a decrease in the relationship between safeguard effectiveness and avoidance motivation. Also, their findings suggest that an increase in users' perception of a safeguarding measure is correlated with a decrease in the relationship between perceived threat and avoidance motivation. Their research model developed and tested is shown in figure 1.

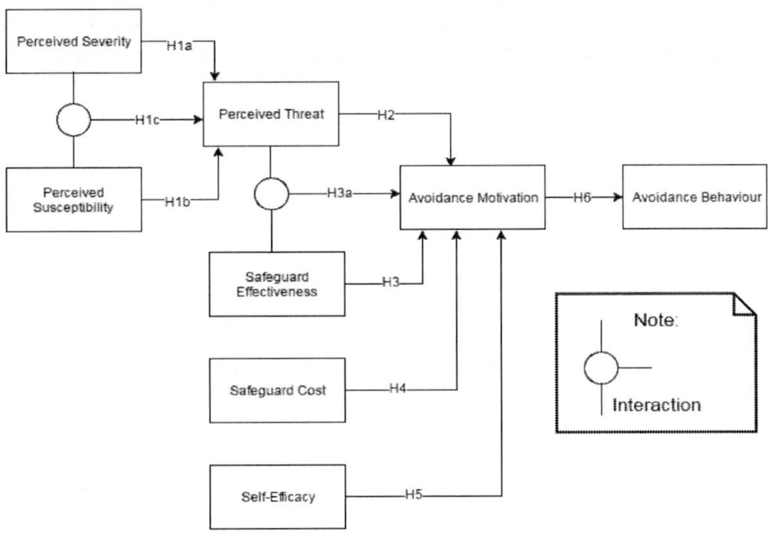

Figure 1. Research model developed and tested by Liang & Xue (2009)

2.1 Limitations of Technology Threat Avoidance Theory

Firstly, their findings cannot be generalized to a larger population of computer users due to the niche convenience sample of Business College Students used for their study. Business College Students do not adequately represent the population of general computer users and as such including other students in various academic departments may have produced more demographically diverse views and understanding on the perception of malware threats by computer users.

Secondly, the use of general computer users to explain the security behaviours of IT users regarding a complex issue as malware threats may not provide in-depth information that can be representative of diverse computer users who normally utilise some specific technological platforms more than the others and thus may encounter varied forms and techniques of malware threats (Bayuk et al., 2011; Reavis, 2012; Sophos, 2014).

A study conducted by Hampton *et al,* (2011) found that the typical internet user is more than twice as likely as others to feel that people can be trusted. The research found that Facebook users are even more likely to be trusting and engage in using the platform multiple times per day; precisely 43% more likely than other internet users and more than three times as likely as non-internet users to feel that most people can be trusted. More enriched information on the IT security behavior of computer users would have been identified if the narrative of their study was focused on the use of a more specified information technology platform (e.g. online social networks, electronic banking, and aviation industries). This idea is also due to the fact that previous studies have shown that the degree of malware threat varies from platform to platform (Bayuk et al., 2011; Reavis, 2012;). For instance, the core computing practices and behaviors' of traffic air controllers would be entirely different from that of online social media marketers.

3. MODIFYING THE TECHNOLOGY THREAT AVOIDANCE THEORY FOR OSN USERS

3.1 Mass Interpersonal Persuasion (MIP)

Fogg & Hall (2008), highlighted a distinct characteristic of online social network termed – Mass Interpersonal Persuasion (MIP). MIP is the biggest factor that influences users of online social networks to perform certain behaviors on a massive scale. According to Fogg & Hall (2008), MIP is a unique characteristic of online social networks which makes it possible for users to reach and influence millions of their direct and indirect connections (friends/followers and friends of friends) within the shortest possible time. MIP is focused on changing users' behaviors and not simply disseminating information to them. A systematic review by (Ikhalia & Serrano, 2015), highlighted some of the challenges faced by IT practitioners in developing effective security awareness systems to assist users in avoiding malware attacks. One of the significant issues identified was the lack of a contextual knowledge whilst deploying security awareness. For OSN users, having a security awareness system deployed through MIP could be very effective in presenting contextual security awareness information because of their tendency to trust content from their interpersonal social network connections.

Based on the unique characteristic – MIP, of online social networks; we argue that the mass interpersonal persuasive (MIP) attribute of a malware safeguarding measure would likely be a key factor that may influence the coping appraisal process of users when evaluating a potential malware threat. This implies that users of online social networks are more likely to use a safeguard measure to identity a malicious threat if they are motivated through interpersonal persuasions on a massive scale. Consequently, in modifying the TTAT model for OSN users, this research posits that MIP positively affects avoidance motivation. In addition, we posit that MIP positively moderates the relationship between safeguard effectiveness and avoidance motivation, further theoretical justification for this argument is presented in the hypothesis section of this paper. Figure 2 shows our proposed research model.

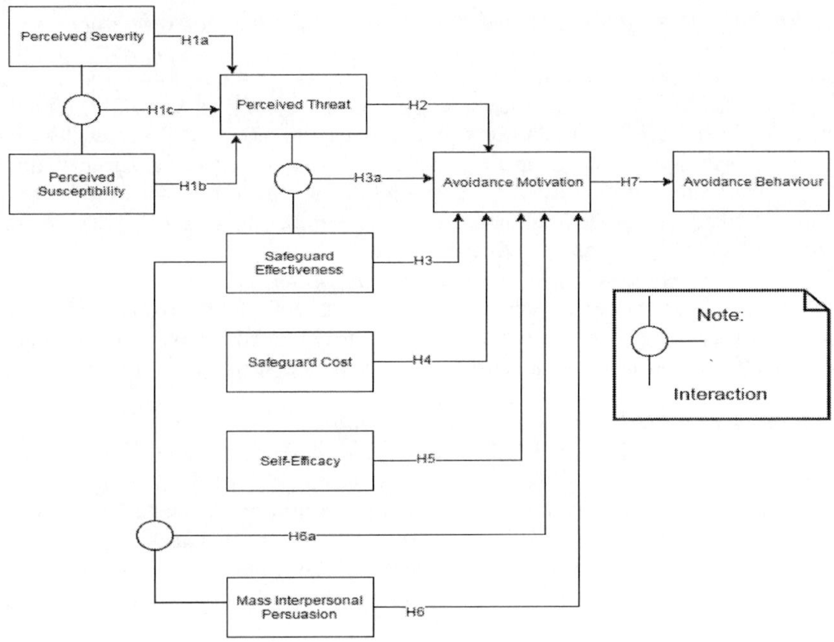

Figure 2. The proposed new model - TTAT-MIP (Liang & Xue 2009; Fogg & Hall 2008)

4. RESEARCH HYPOTHESIS

'Perceived threat' can be defined as, the degree to which a user perceives that a malware threat can be dangerous. According to TTAT, threat perception is developed by perceived susceptibility and perceived severity. Perceived susceptibility is simply defined as, the subjective belief that a user will be negatively affected by malware threat. Meanwhile, perceived severity is the degree to which a user perceives that the negative consequences of a threat will be severe (McClendon, 2012; Stretcher & Rosenstock, 1997). For this reason, this research posits that the combination of perceived susceptibility and severity positively affects threat perception.

H1a: Perceived susceptibility of being attacked by malware positively affects perceived threat.

H1b: Perceived severity of being attacked by malware positively affects perceived threat.

When users' perceived susceptibility of a threat increase, the relationship between perceived severity and perceived threat will consequently increase in strength.

H1c: Perceived susceptibility and perceived severity have a positive interaction effect on perceived threat.

When social network users perceive a malware threat, they are usually motivated to avoid it. Avoidance motivation is defined as the degree to which computer users are motivated to avoid malware threats using safeguarding measures (Rippetoe *et al,* 1987; Weinstein, 1993).

H2: Perceived threat positively affects avoidance motivation.

The effectiveness of a safeguard is defined as the subjective assessment of a safeguarding measure on how effective it can be applied to avoid the malware threat. This theory was drawn from the concept of perceived benefits of health belief model as postulated by Janz & Becker (1984) and the concept of response efficacy in protection motivation theory (Rogers, 1997), which predicts behavior motivation.

H3: Safeguard effectiveness positively affects avoidance motivation

This paper proposes a new safeguard measure based on video animation system that provides useful guidelines through dramatized storytelling on how social network users can avoid malware attack. Therefore, based on the context of our proposed safeguard this research posits that safeguard effectiveness positively moderates the relationship between perceived threat and avoidance motivation. As a result, when the level of safeguard effectiveness increases social network users will feel more motivated to avoid the threat.

H3a: Perceived threat and Safeguard effectiveness have a positive interaction effect on avoidance motivation.

Safeguard cost is defined as the physical and cognitive efforts – such as money, time, comprehension and inconvenience needed to make use of given safeguard measure (Lang & Xue 2009). This means that users are more likely to use a safeguard if it takes less time, money and effort to adopt. Earlier research by Ikhalia & Serrano (2015) identified a key element needed for creating effective security awareness systems – ***Timeboxing***. This means that security awareness solutions for users must ensure strict time boundaries when disseminating instructional guidelines to the user. Therefore the cost of using the safeguard would be relatively less and then the avoidance motivation would increase.

H4: Safeguard cost negatively affects avoidance motivation

Self-efficacy has been studied in previous research (Ng et al., 2009; Woon et al., 2005; Workman et al., 2008) and found to have a positive influence on IT security related behaviors of computer users. Hence, the higher the self-efficacy on using a safeguarding measure the stronger the motivation to avoid a malware threat.

H5: Self-efficacy positively affects avoidance motivation

In order to comprehend the social influence on persuasive experience, it is important to consider how social media such as Facebook, LinkedIn, and WhatsApp or Twitter invitations are modelled. When a Facebook user is invited by his/her friend to use a third party application (e.g. a malware threat awareness video system), Facebook sends an invitation request with messages such as;

"Here is Joseph's IT security awareness score on this Video APP, you can get your score too by viewing the Video APP and together we can become aware on how to stop the spread of malware on Facebook".

MIP as the process of creating persuasive experiences deployed using automated software tools within a small amount of time in a highly socially distributed technological platform embedded with capabilities to measure its impact. MIP focuses on changing users' thoughts and behaviors and only informing them. Foster et al, (2009) carried out research that focused on determining peoples' attitudes on domestic electricity usage, through a Facebook application termed 'Watts Up'. Their application presented visualizations of users' own electricity consumption as well as that of their friends; which positively affected their energy consumption leading to reduced energy consumption by users of the application. This work argues that the motivation to avoid malware threats by OSN users would be positively and significantly affected by the mass interpersonal persuasiveness of a given safeguard.

H6: MIP positively affects avoidance motivation

MIP can positively moderate the relationship between safeguard effectiveness and avoidance motivation. Interpersonal influence theory and research postulates that individuals are normally inclined to conform to the expectations of others regarding purchase decisions (Bearden *et al*, 1989). Oftentimes users demonstrate the tendency to learn about products and services by observing or seeking information from others (Bearden *et al*, 1989). Empirical studies by (Bullee *et al*, 2015; Hutter *et al*, 2013; Lee *et al*, 2014) suggest that online social influence not only can affect consumer perception of quality of a sports brand but also consumer buying intention. Therefore MIP positively moderates the relationship between safeguard effectiveness and avoidance motivation. This implies that the higher the mass interpersonal persuasive attribute of the safeguard, the higher the motivation to avoid malware threats by OSN users.

H6a: MIP and safeguard effectiveness have a positive interaction effect on avoidance motivation

5. CONCLUSION & FURTHER WORK

This paper explored the technology threat avoidance theory (TTAT) proposed by Liang & Xue (2009), in order to study the motivating factors needed for users to avoid IT malicious threats. The TTAT model is relatively useful in helping general computer users understand and avoid malware threats; however, some obvious gaps have been highlighted in its application within online social networking contexts. Online social networks have unique attributes in terms of user behavior and structural design which should be carefully considered when developing a model for malware threat avoidance for its users.

Due to the complexities of IT security, there exists no single solution that can effectively address all the unique threats faced by various technological platforms, and especially its users. Our work is a hypothetical model drawn from TTAT and a unique attribute of online social networks – Mass interpersonal persuasion

(MIP). Similar to the works of Liang & Xue (2009), we suggest the elements that need to be considered in order to motivate users of OSNs to avoid malware attacks. By synthesizing previous works on social influence theory, the theory of persuasion and consumer buying decisions, we rationalize the argument that the mass interpersonal persuasive attribute of a safeguarding measure can effectively affect the avoidance motivation of social network users against IT malicious threats.

In order to empirically validate our theory, we recommend a robust questionnaire survey to gather quantitative data about the security threat perception of online social network users and a potential safeguarding measure designed as a Facebook video animation APP. The measured items of each constructs in the model should reflect the context of online social networks and then a rigorous multiple regression data analysis technique such as – structural equation modelling (SEM) could be utilized for exploratory and confirmatory factor analysis in order to explore the relationship amongst the constructs.

REFERENCES

Abdullah Algarni, Yue Xu, Taizan Chan, Y.-C. T. (2013). Social Engineering in Social Networking Sites: Affect-Based Model. International Journal of E-Education, E-Business, E-Management and E-Learning, 3(6), 456–463. http://doi.org/10.7763/IJEEEE.2013.V3.278

Abrams, R., Pathak, J., & Barrera, O. (2013). Socially Engineered Malware Blocking, 1–18.

Aggarwal, A. (2012). Detection of Spam Tipping Behaviour on Foursquare.

Balasubramaniyan, V. A., Maheswaran, A., Mahalingam, V., Ahamad, M., & Venkateswaran, H. (n.d.). A Crow or a Blackbird ?: Using True Social Network and Tweeting Behavior to Detect Malicious Entities in Twitter.

Baltazar, J., Costoya, J., & Flores, R. (2009). The real face of Koobface: The largest web 2.0 botnet explained. Trend Micro Research, 5(9), 10.

Bayuk, J., Cavit, D., Guerrino, E., Mahony, J., McDowell, B., Nelson, W., … Staarfanger, P. (2011). Malware Risks and Mitigation Report. Bits a Division of the Financial Services Roundtable, (June).

Bearden, W. O., Netemeyer, R. G., & Teel, J. E. (1989). Measurement of consumer susceptibility to interpersonal influence. Journal of consumer research, 473-481.

Benevenuto, F., & Rodrigues, T. (2009). Characterizing user behavior in online social networks. Proceedings of the 9th ACM SIGCOMM Conference on Internet Measurement Conference, 49–62. http://doi.org/10.1145/1644893.1644900

Biswajit Das, J. S. S. (2011). Social Networking Sites – A Critical Analysis of Its Impact on Personal and Social Life, 2(14), 222–228.

Braun, R., & Esswein, W. (2013). Towards a Conceptualization of Corporate Risks in Online Social Networks: A Literature-Based Overview of Risks. Proceedings of the 2013 17th IEEE International Enterprise Distributed Object Computing Conference. Retrieved from http://www.deepdyve.com/lp/institute-of-electrical-and-electronics-engineers/towards-a-conceptualization-of-corporate-risks-in-online-social-4hHWhdNOCE

Bullee, J. W. H., Montoya, L., Pieters, W., Junger, M., & Hartel, P. H. (2015). The persuasion and security awareness experiment: reducing the success of social engineering attacks. Journal of Experimental Criminology, 11(1), 97–115. http://doi.org/10.1007/s11292-014-9222-7

Carver, C. S. and M. F. Scheier (1982) "Control theory: A useful conceptual framework for personality social, clinical, and health psychology," Psychological Bulletin (92) 1, pp. 111-135.

Doostari, M. A., Zeinali, R., Lashkari, H., & Ajamzamani, M. (2013). Anomaly Detection in Cliques of Online Social Networks Using Fuzzy Node-Fuzzy Graph, 3(8), 614–626.

Faghani, M. R., Matrawy, A., & Lung, C. H. (2012). A study of Trojan propagation in online social networks. 2012 5th International Conference on New Technologies, Mobility and Security - Proceedings of NTMS 2012 Conference and Workshops, 6–10. http://doi.org/10.1109/NTMS.2012.6208767

Fire, M., Goldschmidt, R., & Elovici, Y. (2013). Online Social Networks: Threats and Solutions Survey, 16(4), 1–20.

Fogg, B. (2009). A behavior model for persuasive design. Proceedings of the 4th International Conference on Persuasive Technology - Persuasive '09, 1. http://doi.org/10.1145/1541948.1541999

Fogg, B. J., & Hall, C. (2008). Mass Interpersonal Persuasion : An Early View of a New Phenomenon 2 Facebook Makes a New Form of Persuasion Possible 3 A Stanford Course Leverages Mass Interpersonal Persuasion. Persuasive Technology, (2008), 23–34. http://doi.org/10.1007/978-3-540-68504-3-3

Foster, D., Blythe, M., Lawson, S., & Doughty, M. (2009). Social networking sites as platforms to persuade behavior change in domestic energy consumption. Communication. Retrieved from http://eprints.lincoln.ac.uk/2326/

Gao, H., Hu, J., Huang, T., Wang, J., & Chen, Y. (2011). Security issues in online social networks. IEEE Internet Computing, 15(4), 56–63. http://doi.org/10.1109/MIC.2011.50

Gulati, R. (2003). The Threat of Social Engineering and Your Defense Against it.

Hampton, K. N., Goulet, L. S., Rainie, L., & Purcell, K. (2011). Social networking sites and our lives. Pew Research Center's Internet & American Life Project, 47(9), 85. Retrieved from http://www.pewinternet.org/2011/06/16/social-networking-sites-and-our-lives/

Hutter, K., Hautz, J., Dennhardt, S., & Füller, J. (2013). The impact of user interactions in social media on brand awareness and purchase intention: The case of MINI on Facebook. Journal of Product and Brand Management, 22(5), 342–351. http://doi.org/10.1108/JPBM-05-2013-0299

Ikhalia, E., & Arreymbi, J. (2014). Online Social Networks: A Vehicle for Malware Propagation. In Proceedings of the 13th European Conference on Cyber warfare and Security: ECCWS (p. 95).

Janz, N. K. and M. H. Becker (1984) "The health belief model: a decade later," Health Education Quarterly (11) 1, pp. 1-45.

Janz, N. K. and M. H. Becker (1984) "The health belief model: a decade later," Health Education Quarterly (11) 1, pp. 1-45.

Lee, D., Hosanagar, K., & Nair, H. S. (2014). The Effect of Social Media Marketing Content on Consumer Engagement: Evidence from Facebook. Working Papers (Faculty) -- Stanford Graduate School of Business, (Summer 2013), 1–51. Retrieved from http://search.ebscohost.com/login.aspx?direct=true&db=buh&AN=98717234&site=ehost-live

Liang, H., & Xue, Y. (2009). Avoidance of Information Technology Threats A Theoretical Perspective. MIS Quarterly, 33(1), 71–90. http://doi.org/Article

Liang, Huigang, X. Y. (2010). Understanding Security Behaviors in Personal Computer Usage : A Threat Avoidance Perspective. Journal of the Association for Information Systems, 11(7), 394–413.

McClendon, D. (2012). Perceived susceptibility to cardiovascular disease as a moderator of relationships between perceived severity and cardiovascular health promoting behaviors among female registered nurses. Dissertation Abstracts International: Section B: The Sciences and Engineering, 72(7-B), 3955. Retrieved from http://search.ebscohost.com/login.aspx?direct=true&db=psyh&AN=2012-99020-236&site=ehost-live

Ng, B.-Y., A. Kankanhalli, and Y. C. Xu (2009) "Studying users' computer security behavior: A health belief perspective," Decision Support System (46) 4, pp. 815-825.

Palmer, D. (2013). Social media malware rising significantly, says McAfee report - 03 Jun 2013 - Computing News.

Reavis, J. (2012). The Ongoing Malware Threat: How Malware Infects Websites and Harms Businesses — and What You Can Do to Stop It. Symantec, 11. Retrieved from https://www.geotrust.com/anti-malware-scan/malware-threat-white-paper.pdf

Rippetoe, P. A., & Rogers, R. W. (1987). Effects of components of protection-motivation theory on adaptive and maladaptive coping with a health threat. Journal of personality and social psychology, 52(3), 596.

Rogers, R. W., & Prentice-Dunn, S. (1997). Protection motivation theory.

Rosenstock, I. M. (1974) "The health belief model and preventive health behavior," Health Education Monographs (2pp. 354-386.

Silic, M., & Back, A. (2016). The dark side of social networking sites:Understanding phishing risks. Computers in Human Behavior, 60, 35–43. http://doi.org/10.1016/j.chb.2016.02.050

Sophos. (2014). Internet Security Threat Report , SOPHOS. Sophos, 1–34. Retrieved from http://www.sophos.com/threatreport

Stretcher, V., & Rosenstock, I. M. (1997). The Health Belief Model. Health Behavior and Health Education: Theory, Research, and Practice, 31–36. http://doi.org/10.1111/j.1365-2648.2010.05450.x

Thomas, K., & Nicol, D. M. (2010). The Koobface botnet and the rise of social malware? Proceedings of the 5th IEEE International Conference on Malicious and Unwanted Software, Malware 2010, 63–70. http://doi.org/10.1109/MALWARE.2010.5665793

Tidwell, C. L. (2011). Testing The Impact Of Training With Simulated Scenarios For Information Security Awareness On Virtual Community Of Practice Members.

Turkanović, M., & Polančič, G. (2013). On the security of certain e-communication types: Risks, user awareness, and recommendations. Journal of Information Security and Applications, 18(4), 193–205. http://doi.org/10.1016/j.jisa.2013.07.003

Weinstein, N. D. (1993). Testing four competing theories of health-protective behavior. Health psychology, 12(4), 324.

Wilson, M., Hash, J., & Division, C. S. (2003). Building an Information Technology Security Awareness and Training Program. National Institute of Standards and Technology, (October).

Woon, I., G. W. Tan, and R. Low (2005) A Protection Motivation Theory Approach to Home Wireless Security, in International Conference on Information Systems, pp. 367-380. Las Vegas, NV.

Workman, M., W. H. Bommer, and D. Straub (2008) "Security Lapses and the Omission of Information Security Measures: A Threat Control Model and Empirical Test," Computers in Human Behaviour (24) 6, pp. 2799-2816

QRM: A QR-CODE BASED MHEALTH INFORMATION SYSTEM FOR PATIENT-CENTERED CARE

Dongsong Zhang[1], Yueyang Jiang[1], Lina Zhou[1], Lili Huang[2], Jeffrey C. Fink[3], Güneş Koru[1] and Youfa Wang[4]

[1]*University of Maryland, Baltimore County, 1000 Hilltop Circle, Baltimore, MD 21250, USA*

[2]*Jilin University, Department of Medical Informatics, Changchun, China*

[3]*University of Maryland, School of Medicine, Baltimore, Baltimore, MD 21250, USA*

[4]*University at Buffalo, The State University of New York, Buffalo, New York, USA*

ABSTRACT

With emerging new technologies and growing interests in patient-centered healthcare, the role of patients in healthcare is shifting from a passive recipient of care to an active information seeker and collaborator. It becomes crucial to provide patients with ubiquitous, secure access to their electronic health records (EHR) and personalized healthcare services such as patient education. Such capabilities are highly limited in most existing healthcare IT systems. The researchers in this study designed, developed, and evaluated an mHealth information system that enables patients or authorized others to access patients' EHR, to navigate personalized patient education material, and to view patients' emergency contact information in case of an emergency through their mobile phones at anywhere and anytime while addressing patient identification and data privacy problems through a QR-code based patient identification mechanism. The results of a user evaluation study reveal that participants generally favor the proposed system and report a high level of perceived usefulness and intention to use the system.

KEYWORDS

QR-code, Mobile Health Information Systems, Medical Information Access, Personalized Patient Education, Mobile Health

1. INTRODUCTION

Nowadays, most patients and health service providers lack sufficient and timely access to patients' electronic health records (EHR) (Franczak, 2014), causing difficulty for them to keep track of patients' health and to consult other physicians. With emerging new technologies and growing interests in patient-centered healthcare, the role of patients in medical treatments and healthcare is shifting from a passive recipient of care to an active information seeker and collaborator. To support this shift, it is crucial to provide patients with secure, ubiquitous access to their EHR and with on-demand, personalized patient education. There are many situations in which ubiquitous, real-time access to patients' EHR can be helpful. For example, a patient needs to access his/her medical history to identify the trends or sudden changes in his/her blood sugar/GFI levels, or when she is seeking the second opinion from another doctor. There are other situations where a third-party's access to a patient's critical medical information can be life-saving, such as when a patient collapses on the street and loses consciousness.

Patient education is another important component in patient-centered care. Effective patient education can improve patients' compliance to treatment plans and medication adherence (Lowry et al, 2014; Wu et al, 2015). Currently, most patient education systems are one-size-fits-all, meaning that the identical educational material is provided to all patients. In reality, patients differ from one another in many aspects. Therefore, driven by patient-centered care, patient education tailored to specific individuals can help patients communicate with healthcare providers more effectively and adopt healthy lifestyle. Therefore, patient education should be customized to meet specific needs and medical conditions of individual patients.

Mobile technologies have become a cost-effective way for supporting patient-centered care by providing ubiquitous and real-time access to patient EHR and personalized patient education. The portability, ubiquity, and pervasiveness of mobile phones offer unprecedented potentials in transforming health IT. There have been growing interests in developing and deploying mobile health applications. For example, there have been studies on text-messaging based mobile interventions (Cornelius, 2012); mobile health monitoring systems (Bourouis et al, 2012; Walker et al, 2009); mobile telemedicine (Zisser, 2010); mobile interventions for weight control (Liu et al, 2015), and mobile sleep management (Potter, 2011). However, to date, there has been little research that explores technical feasibility and user acceptance of mHealth systems that provide ubiquitous patient medical information access and personalized patient education.

To fill the void, this research designed, developed, and evaluated a Quick Response Code (QR-code) based mHealth system that enables ubiquitous access to patients' health records and personalized education material. To achieve this goal, patient identification is one of the key challenges. In our system, we used a QR-code bracelet with an embedded unique URL to access patient-specific information stored on a web server, which enables cost-effective, accurate patient identification. Our design has taken into consideration different groups of users with different levels of access privileges. We have explored the technical feasibility of the system and evaluated user perceptions of the system using the survey methodology.

The rest of the paper is organized as follows. We first introduce the background and related work, then present the design and development of a QR-code based mHealth system, followed by the description of a user survey study. Next, we report and discuss results of the survey. Finally, we conclude the paper with a summary of major findings and limitations of this research.

2. BACKGROUND AND RELATED WORK

2.1 Patient Identification

Accurate patient identification is essential for EHR access. The U.S Joint Commission on Accreditation of Healthcare Organizations (JCAHO, 2005) has proposed several guidelines to improve the accuracy of patient identification. There are several patient identification methods used in healthcare settings, including verbal and visual identification, chart-based identification, hand-written wristbands, barcode identification, and more advanced identification technology (Aguilar, 2006). Each method has its pros and cons. With verbal identification, patients may not be able or willing to speak out their identity in a public environment; identifying patients based on visual identification is not reliable because the visual appearance of patients may change over time (Vidal, 2003); for chart-based identification, some errors may occur due to misplaced or wrongly referenced medical charts (Kohn et al, 2000); for hand-written wristbands, illegible hand writing and limited information that can be put on a wristband cause problems; the main limitations of barcode identification include that the information embedded in a barcode is limited. Advanced identification technologies including radio frequency identification, smart cards, and biometrics can provide more advanced services for identifying patients. However, they are often more costly and difficult to deploy and use, which prohibits their wide adoption.

2.2 QR-codes

A QR-code (Figure 1) can be generated and printed as easily as a barcode (Denso, 2012), but contain much more information in diverse formats (Soon, 2008; HKHA, 2010). A QR-code can hold 7,089 characters for a numeric code or 4,296 characters for an alphanumeric code. It can contain information in diverse formats, such as letters and numbers. Non-alphanumeric characters, such as Chinese and Japanese, can also be stored. A QR-code is presented as a matrix because it contains rows and columns.

QR-codes are emerging as an attractive alternative for patient identification (Avidan et al, 2015; Dixon et al, 2013). The QR-code based technology integrated with smartphones offers advanced features such as high data storage capacity, technical simplicity, low implementation cost, and ample availability of free software for data encoding and decoding. Therefore, QR-codes are promising for unambiguous and ubiquitous patient identification (García-Betances and Huerta, 2012). Although QR-codes have been increasingly used in hospitals, little research has explored their use in ubiquitous access to patients' electronic health records.

2.3 Patient Education

Health literacy is defined as “a shared function of social and individual factors, which emerges from the interaction of the skills of individuals and the demands of social systems" (WDCTNA, 2004). Health literacy plays a huge role in improving health and compliance of patients with chronic diseases (Sarkar et al, 2010; Fang et al, 2006). Patients’ lack of health information and knowledge related to their diseases and treatment processes is one of the most significant problems in healthcare (Tait et al, 2009). The level of health literacy of patients can influence their decisions and behavior (Wagner et al, 2007), which will in turn have key impacts on management and prevention of chronic diseases (DeWalt, 2009; Berkman et al, 2007). In addition, health literacy can improve communication between patients and health care providers. Health service providers need to deliver educational material to patients in ways that patients can easily understand and benefit (FitzGerald and Poureslami, 2014). This problem contributes to poor treatment compliance and reluctance of medication adherence of patients (Wu et al, 2015). However, there has been relatively little research on personalized patient education through mobile devices using a QR-code.

2.4 Access to Patients’ Electronic Health Records

If patients request to access their health records, in many cases, they would receive paper copies from their health service providers. Those paper copies are difficult to maintain, share, and analyze. An earlier study showed that providing patients with online access to their EHR appeared to be useful (Cimino et al, 2000). Another recent study proposed a cloud-based system architecture to enable patients to access their health records (Coats and Acharya, 2014). However, those systems require a software program installed on a desktop or a laptop computer. There has been little research on ubiquitous health record access through mobile devices regardless of time and location. Mobile access can provide benefits to not only patients by enabling them to keep track of their own health, but also healthcare providers, especially those non-primary care providers, by allowing them to access patients’ health and medical history easily when necessary.

To reduce the risks of compromising patient privacy and data security, several different methods for access controls on EHR have been proposed. They can be categorized into discretionary access control, mandatory access control, and role-based access control. Discretionary access control is a way to restrict access to objects based on the identity of subjects (Lampson, 1971). Mandatory access control specifies access control based on a central authority’s decision, not based on the owner of data (Denning, 1976). The owner cannot change access rights. A role-based access control is based on the roles of individual users in an organization (Osborn et al., 2000).

3. RESEARCH METHODOLOGY

This study is carried out in two stages. In stage 1, we designed and developed a prototype of QR-code based MHealth system called QRM to support ubiquitous, secure, and privacy-preserving access to health information and personalized patient education through mobile phones. In stage 2, we conducted a survey study with 20 participants to evaluate user perceptions and acceptance of the system.

3.1 Stage 1: Design and Implementation of QRM

3.1.1 The Design of QRM

QRM consists of three key components: (a) QR-code patient identification, (b) personalized patient education, and (c) ubiquitous and multi-level health record access. QR-code patient identification is a gateway for accessing patients’ EHR. Coupled with traditional user name and password protection, a QR-code with a URL printed on a patient’s medical bracelet or on an ID card helps improve patient data security and privacy protection while reducing potential errors. Once a user is identified, he/she can either access a patient’s health records, if he/she has the access privilege, or navigate educational material customized for the patient on her/his mobile phone whenever necessary.

QR-code based Patient Identification

To design a reliable patient identification method for ubiquitous health information access, we need to consider at least three factors: usability, security, and privacy protection. Ideally, patients and their health service providers should be able to access patients' health information at any time, any place. Because patient health information may contain not only patients' demographic information such as age and gender, but also detailed personal health information such as symptoms, diseases, laboratory test results, and other medical histories, the design of an mHealth system needs to take data privacy and security into consideration. In addition, the system needs to have high usability so that users can use it effortlessly.

To achieve privacy protection, QRM uses a QR-code printed on a medical bracelet (or on an ID card) for patient identification, as shown in Figure 1. The patient ID and the URL of a web server that stores patients' EHR are embedded in a QR code. A patient needs to install a free QR-code reader application on his/her smartphone. When a user (e.g., a patient or a doctor) attempts to access a patient's EHR, he/she first scans the QR-code using his/her phone. A query such as "http://[proxy web server IP]/qr code?i=[encryped user ID]" will be sent to the web server. The patient ID is encrypted with a customized MD5 message-digest algorithm. After the server receives a user request, it prompts the user to enter his/her password associated with the scanned patient ID for authentication. Once the user is authenticated, he/she can start browsing health records. Otherwise, the user would only be able to view emergency contact information.

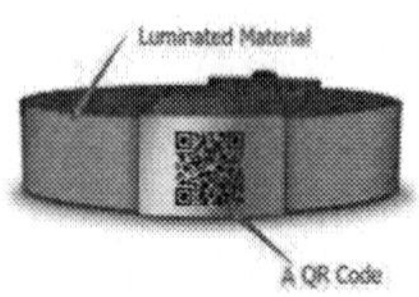

Figure 1. A medical bracelet with a QR-code

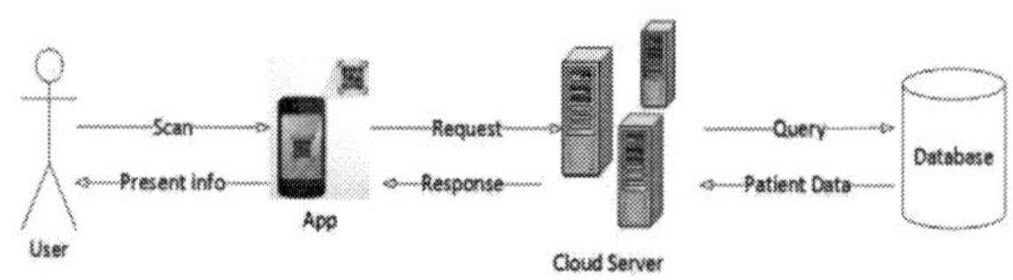

Figure 2. The Architecture of QRM

Personalized Patient Education

QRM supports personalized patient education through mobile phones. In comparison to traditional patient education methods such as face-to-face education, printed material, or computer-based education programs, QRM offers several unique advantages, including:

a) personalized patient education, in which education material is customized for individual patients. Unlike most existing patient education systems that use a one-size-fits-all design, after a patient is identified through his QR-code medical bracelet, QRM can deliver customized educational content to his phone based on his specific disease, medical needs, health condition, and personal preferences. For example, for two patients with depression, patient A may receive educational material related to healthy diet and physical exercises because his depression is largely caused by type 2 diabetes, while patient B receives education of anti-depression drugs and their side effects. In this study, we use information about diseases, health conditions, and wellness collected from MedlinePlus of the National Library of Medicine as the educational material resource. Such information is tailored based on individual patients' profiles on the server before being delivered to patients' mobile devices.

b) anytime, anywhere, on-demand delivery of education material to users' mobile phones. Users can access and navigate electronic educational material through their mobile phones whenever they need, even on the move, instead of being restricted to desktop computers at home or in office. As a matter of fact, nurses and doctors in an increasing number of hospitals are provided with mobile devices by their hospitals as tools to access and display patients' health information and make notes when they see patients; and

c) low cost. A QR-code bracelet only costs as little as 20 cents (e.g., http://www.alibaba.com/showroom/qr-code-bracelet.html), which is affordable to everyone.

Ubiquitous and Multi-level Health Record Access

To ensure the security and privacy of patients' health information, our system uses discretionary access control. Recognizing that there are different types of users who may need to access a patients' EHR through their mobile phones, our mHealth system allows patients to set up different levels of EHR access privileges for different users. A patient may grant the full mobile access to her EHR to her primary doctor, but only partial access to other users (e.g., emergency contact information only).

3.1.2 System Development and System Architecture

We have implemented a prototype system of QRM on Android phones based on the above design, mainly to explore its technical feasibility. Figure 2 presents the system architecture. To use it, users need to install it and a QR-code reader on their smartphones. Currently, QRM deals with three types of user roles: patients, health service providers, and third parties, which can be easily extended. The first two types of users need to go through a two-step authentication process, which is not required for third-party users who can view some non-sensitive information set by a QR-code owner after they scan the QR-code. The web server authenticates a user, forwards inquires to a back-end EHR database to retrieve a patient's records, and returns them to the user's mobile phone in an encrypted manner. Finally, those records are decrypted and presented to the user.

QRM enables a patient to access his/her HER in the following way. First, the patient needs to enter his/her user name and password to log in the system. After successful authentication, the patient can view personalized medical suggestions, navigate tailored educational material, edit emergency contact information, and/or set access control of their medical records for other potential users. To protect privacy and ensure data security, a patient needs to first scan her/his QR-code on her/his bracelet or a card using his/her smartphone, and then enter the login password again for user authentication before retrieving health records. The dual authentication design increases the security of patients' health information. For a health care provider, once he successfully logs into this system, he can scan the QR-code on a patients' bracelets and use a QR-code reader on his smartphone to review the patient's medical records if he has been granted the full access. Otherwise, she/he would only be able to view the emergency contact information of patients. A third-party user would only be able to view the emergency contact information of a patient after scanning the patient's QR-code. This function could come in handy for emergency situations.

We tested the functions of the prototype system through simulations of different users. The results showed accurate user authentication and appropriate retrieval of EHR and educational material with 100% accuracy, demonstrating the technical feasibility of QRM.

3.2 User Evaluation

The second objective of this study is to evaluate the design of QRM in terms of user perceptions and intention to use. We have conducted a survey to collect user perceptions, acceptance, and feedback about the QRM system, aiming to further refine the design of the proposed solution.

We recruited 20 university students in the information systems major from an east coast university in the United States to participate in this survey because they are one of the major user groups of smartphones and mobile applications. All participants indicated that they owned a smartphone. Among participants, 11 were female; 13 were between 21 to 30 years old; 5 were between 31 to 40 years old, and 2 were over 40 years old; 2 were undergraduate students, 4 were master students, and 14 were doctoral students.

We prepared a 7-minute video to introduce the QRM system that we have developed. The introduction covered the motivations of the system design, a demo that introduced main functions of the system and how they worked, and system workflows for different groups of users. The participants watched the video after signing a consent form. They also played with the prototype system to gain some first-hand experience. Then, they completed a survey.

The survey focused on two main research constructs: intention to use and perceived usefulness. The former asked for participants' general feelings about intention to use this system. The latter solicited participants' perceptions of the utility of this system. The survey questions were developed based on existing instruments (Davis et al, 1989) and adapted to the context of this study. Those survey questions used a 7-point Likert scale, with 1 and 7 representing "strongly disagree" and "strongly agree", respectively, and 4 being 'neutral'. Additionally, there were three open-ended questions asking for participants' feedback on benefits, limitations, and suggestions for future improvements of the QRM system.

4. RESULTS AND DISCUSSION

We first tested the internal consistency of the survey items using Cronbach's alpha. All of Cronbach's α values are well above the accepted level of 0.7 (Table 1), indicating good internal validity of our instruments.

Table 1. Internal validity of research constructs

Perceived Usefulness	**Cronbach's alpha**
Health information self-management	0.938
Personalized health education	0.962
Intention to use the system	
Medical emergency information access	0.882
Personalized health education	0.962
Health information self-management	0.902

Table 2 presents descriptive statistics of participants' perceived usefulness and intention to use the mHealth system for patient education and health information self-management. Results show that participants in general felt the QRM system useful for health information access and patient education, and reported a high level of intention to use it. We also examined the potential differences in perceived usefulness and intention to use across different genders and ages but did not find any significant difference.

Table 2.Means and standard deviations of research constructs (mean [standard deviation])

Research constructs	**Perceived usefulness (1~7)**	**Intention to use (1~7)**
Medical Emergency information access	6.40 [0.88]	5.58 [0.990]
Personalized health education	5.77 [0.83]	5.33 [1.139]
Health information self-management	5.89 [0.915]	5.35 [1.023]

Reflected by the responses to the open-ended questions, most participants felt that QMR was convenient and easy to use for EHR access and patient education. In addition, the participants expected that providing access to patients' emergency contact information should improve the efficiency and accuracy of patient-to-physician communication, which could save lives. The participants also commented that the system would be very helpful for patients to adhere to treatment routines by providing personalized education content whenever and wherever they need it. Some participants were particularly interested in the function of QR-code based user authentication, which they believed to be crucial for secured access to patient information.

One participant was concerned about potential risks if patients lose their QR-codes. Another participant expressed a concern about the security of wireless data communication. In addition, three participants identified the accessibility of the system as a concern because elderly patients may not use a smartphone. The participants also made a few constructive suggestions in their feedback for improving the current QME system, such as proactively pushing recommendations of new educational material to patients and customizing the design of QR-code medical bracelets for individual patients.

5. CONCLUSION

In this study, we designed and evaluated a QR-code based mHealth system to provide patients with ubiquitous access to EHR through their mobile phones in an on-demand manner. A QR-code is used as an essential part of user identification to enable secured health information access. Additionally, this system also provides patient-centric education material based on medical needs and health conditions of authenticated users. In addition to investigating the technical feasibility of a prototype system, we also investigated the participants' perceptions and acceptability of the system through a survey. The findings of the survey showed that the participants perceived the proposed mHealth system to be useful for accessing their health information and personalized health education material for their own use. Moreover, the participants would like to adopt this system for self-management of health information and improving patient education.

This research makes several contributions to research and practice. First, it addresses the problem of secured and ubiquitous access to patients' EHR by combining a QR-code and a smartphone. Second, the proposed solution is cost-effective and has great potential scaling and adapting to various health applications.

Third, this QR-code based mHealth system enables multi-level access to patients' EHR and delivery of personalized patient education and feedback. Furthermore, the findings of this study demonstrate that users perceived the system to be useful and would like to adopt it. QMR can be extended to other health care services that require accurate patient identification and ubiquitous patient information access.

The developed mHealth system offers significant implications and benefits for patients, particularly those with chronic diseases. There has been increasing prevalence of chronic diseases, such as cardiovascular disease, diabetes, and cancers. Chronic diseases need long-term care and patients' active efforts, including receiving related treatments and making lifestyle changes for good health outcomes. Patients with chronic diseases face many challenges during their treatments and recoveries, especially in medical information access and patient education. This mHealth system can facilitate the treatment and recovery of these patients, and help reduce health care cost since it can enhance medical information access and patient education.

This research has two limitations that present future research opportunities. First, we did not use real patients in our evaluation. Although university students are a major group of mobile device users, they may not fully represent patient population. We plan to conduct a field study with real patients in future to validate the findings of this study. While a number of legal, economical, and organizational challenges remain to be addressed for effective patient-centered care by the larger society, the evidence from this study about technical feasibility and user acceptance can be immediately useful to decision makers at various levels and to those advocating or facilitating the adoption of QR-code based technologies in healthcare settings.

REFERENCES

Aguilar A., Van Der Putten W, Kirrane F., 2006. Positive patient identification using RFID and wireless networks. *In HISI 11th Annual Conference and Scientific Symposium*.

Avidan A., Weissman C., Levin P.D., 2015. Integration of QR codes into an anesthesia information management system for resident case log management. *International Journal of Medical Informatics*.

Berkman N.D., Sheridan S.L., Lohr K.N., Lux L., Sutton S.F., Swinson T. Bonito A.J., 2007. Literacy and Health Outcomes: Evidence Report/Technology Assessment. *In Literacy and Health Outcomes: Evidence Report/Technology Assessment Agency for Healthcare Research and Quality*.

Bourouis A., Feham M., Bouchachia A., 2012. A new architecture of a ubiquitous health monitoring system: a prototype of cloud mobile health monitoring system. *International Journal of Computer Science Issues*, 9(2), pp. 434-438.

Cimino J.J., Li J., Mendonça E.A., Sengupta S., Patel V.L., Kushniruk A.W., 2000. An evaluation of patient access to their electronic medical records via the World Wide Web. *In Proceedings of the AMIA Symposium*.

Cornelius J., Lawrence J., Howard J., Shah D., Poka A., McDonald D., White A., 2012. Adolescents' perceptions of mobile cell phone text messaging-enhanced intervention and development of a mobile cell phone-based HIV prevention intervention. *Journal for Specialists in Pediatric Nursing*, 17(1), pp. 61-69.

Coats B., Acharya S., 2014. Leveraging the cloud for electronic health record access. *Perspectives in Health Information Management*.

Davis F.D., Bagozzi R.P., Warshaw P.R., 1989. User acceptance of computer technology: a comparison of two theoretical models. *Management science*, 35(8), pp. 982-1003.

Denso W., 2012. QR code features. Archived from the original on 2012-09-15. Retrieved 8 March 2015.

Denning, D. E., 1976. A lattice model of secure information flow. *Commun. ACM* 19, 2, 236–243.

DeWalt D.A., Hink A., 2009. Health literacy and child health outcomes: a systematic review of the literature. *Pediatrics*, 124 (Supplement 3), S265-S274.

Dixon J.L., Smythe W.R., Momsen L.S., Jupiter D., Papaconstantinou H.T., 2013. Quick response codes for surgical safety: a prospective pilot study. *Journal of surgical research*, 184(1), pp. 157-163.

Fang M.C., Machtinger E.L., Wang F., Schillinger D., 2006. Health literacy and anticoagulation-related outcomes among patients taking warfarin. *J Gen Intern Med*.

Franczak M.J., et al., 2014 In emergency departments, radiologists' access to EHRs may influence interpretations and medical management. *Health Affairs*;33(5):800–806.

FitzGerald J.M., Poureslami I., 2014. Chronic disease management: a proving ground for health literacy. *Population health management*, 17(6), pp.321-323.

García-Betances R.I., Huerta M.K., 2012. A review of automatic patient identification options for public health care centers with restricted budgets. *Online journal of public health informatics*, 4(1).

Hong Kong Hospital Authority (HKHA), 2010. HA Quality & Risk Management Annual Report. *Patient Safety and Risk Management Department*.

JCAHO, 2005. 'JCAHO: Guidelines for patient safety at hospitals', *Joint Commission on Accreditation of Healthcare Organisations*.

Kohn L., Corrigan J., Donaldson M.K., McAndrew M.H., 2000. To err is human: building a safer health system. Committee on quality of health care in America, Institute of Medicine.

Lampson, B. 1971. Protection. *In Proceedings of the 5th Symposium on Information Sciences and Systems*. 437–443.

Liu F., Kong X., Cao J., Chen S., Li C., Huang J., Kelly T.N., 2015. Mobile phone intervention and weight loss among overweight and obese adults: a meta-analysis of randomized controlled trials. American journal of epidemiology, 181(5), pp. 337-348.

Lowry P., Zhang D., Wu D., 2014. Understanding patients' compliance behavior in a mobile healthcare system: the role of trust and planned behavior. *International Conference on Information Systems (ICIS 2014).*

Osborn, S., Sandhu, R., & Munawer, Q., 2000. Configuring role-based access control to enforce mandatory and discretionary access control policies. *ACM Transactions on Information and System Security (TISSEC)*, 3(2), 85-106.

Potter V., 2011. Better sleep through technology: Zeo sleep manager. *Mobile ComputerWorld.com*.

Sarkar U., Karter A.J., Liu J.Y., Moffet H.H., Adler N.E., Schillinger D., 2010. Hypoglycemia is more common among type 2 diabetes patients with limited health literacy: the Diabetes Study of Northern California (DISTANCE). *J Gen Intern Med*.

Soon T.J., 2008. QR code. Synthesis Journal, section 3.

Tait A.R., Voepel-Lewis T., Moscucci M., Brennan-Martinez CM, Levine R., 2009. Patient comprehension of an interactive, computer-based information program for cardiac catheterization: a comparison with standard information, *Archives of Internal Medicine*, pp. 1907-1914.

Vidal Y., 2003. 101 ways to prevent medical errors. Medical Management, Lara Publications.

Washington DC: The National Academies (WDCTNA), 2004. Institute of Medicine: Health literacy: a prescription to end confusion.

Walker W., Aroul A.L., Bhatia D., 2009. Mobile Health Monitoring Systems, *31st Annual International Conference of the IEEE EMBS.*

Wagner V.C., Knight K., Steptoe A., Wardle J., 2007. Functional health literacy and health-promoting behavior in a national sample of British adults. *Journal of epidemiology and community health*, 61(12), pp. 1086-1090.

Wu D., Lowry P., Zhang D., 2015. Investigating treatment compliance behavior of patients supported by a mobile healthcare education system. *Hawaii International Conference on Systems Sciences (HICSS 2015).*

Zisser H., 2010. The omnipod insulin management system: the latest innovation in insulin pump therapy. Springer Healthcare, 1(1), pp. 10-24.

A COLLABORATIVE SITUATION-AWARE MODEL TO SUPPORT INFORMATION EXCHANGE AMONG MEDICAL TEAMS

Vinícius Tocantins Marques[1,2], Cristiano André da Costa[1],
Jorge Luís Victória Barbosa[1] and Rodrigo da Rosa Righi[1]
[1]*Applied Computing Graduate Program, Universidade do Vale do Rio dos Sinos (Unisinos), São Leopoldo, RS, Brazil*
[2]*Federal Institute of Education, Science and Technology of Roraima (IFRR), Boa Vista, RR, Brazil*

ABSTRACT

The ubiquitous computing and the situation awareness are evolving elements for computer applications in hospitals. Specifically, the application that is able to correlate data from heterogeneous networks to improve the success of healthcare, produces a wide collaboration network. In this context, this article proposes the development of Doctor Collab, a collaborative model that supports the exchange of information between physicians medical teams using the situation awareness. The model aims to use ubiquitous computing resources to improve the inclusion of relevant data in the application, as well as optimize the data output on mobile devices. As scientific contribution, the proposed model employs computational inferences by analyzing different situations in order to improve medical decision-making and support collaboration between medical teams. Evaluations show that the Doctor Collab reached an average of 86.9% acceptance using the *Technical Architecture Modeling* model to check the assent of application to the attending physicians.

KEYWORDS

Situation Awareness, Collaborative Computing, Medical Emergency, Ubiquitous Computing, Activity-Based Computing

1. INTRODUCTION

The creation of solutions that help physicians is critical to the medical effectiveness. The decision-making process has always been one of the main pillars targeted by institutions that seek quality in their work, and in the health area is no different. This criterion becomes crucial to aid medical teams seeking satisfactory solutions to everyday problems, with an appropriate response in a timely manner, especially in situations in which requires Task Management in multi-level (Li, 2014). One of the interesting features in the aid decision-making in multilevel is the possibility of working with heterogeneous groups, due to the challenge of integrating a variety of different networks. It is necessary to ensure the exchange of information without errors between medical teams. Intercommunicate these networks will create a system more efficient in high stress work environments (Li, 2014).

In the case of applying the structure, a cloud-based model computer can be defined as a ubiquitous on-demand access to a set of computing resources (Mell & Tim 2010). This model demonstrate to be a satisfactory alternative to working with collaborative data base. This structure besides being safe and unified, can boost the dissemination of information to several other communities and universal formats (Sultan, 2014). After the cloud stored data is organized, we can work with a large volume of information in high-scale schemes, thereby producing more accurate decisions based on the quality of information to be searched, filtered and presented to the physicians team.

In this article we present the model Doctor Collab targeting at supporting information exchange among medical teams. The main research challenge is the use of collaborative software for emergency medical environments, and we focus on answering the following question: *How would a computer model to support collaboration and exchange information among medical staff in areas of emergencies, using situation awareness?*

In this model, cloud computing (Mell & Grance, 2010) is a structure that gives doctors access to various information related to the patient quickly and transparently in order to group a set of computational knowledge stored remotely, aiming to optimize the medical inferences within the Doctor Collab. The external collaboration is another important point, as in emergency environments where it is of great importance that applications offer support for professional experts who are not physically in attendance place to collaborate in the best possible way, for the well being of patient. This collaboration will take place both in order to encourage mating time and space derailment.

As the main scientific contribution, the proposed model uses computational inferences using contextual levels present in an ontological basis (Chen *et al,* 2003) in order to improve medical decision-making and support collaboration between healthcare teams. The model has a set of modules that allow distributed functionalities to encourage better access to medical records data. In this context, the model employs situation awareness (Endsley & Garland, 2000), by using inferences in ontology. Doctor Collab should manage activities among users who may be physically distant and be able to store important informations for patient care according to established standards.

This article is organized as follows. In section 2 we describe related work. The proposed model is presented in section 3, along with implementation details in section 4. Evaluation aspects are described in section 5. Finally, section 6 presents the conclusions of the work and some directions for future works.

2. RELATED WORK

This section lists some of the most relevant studies and important in search of the state of the art on Situation Awareness and Activity-Based Computing focused on collaboration and use of ubiquity.

Bardram (2005) presents a solid overview of the Activity-Based Computing study and how the concept works with human activities. The framework presents: i) support the management of human tasks using computer; ii) mobility support and distribution activities across heterogeneous environments; iii) support for asynchronous collaboration, allowing in this way that many other people can participate; iv) support synchronous collaboration, thus creating collaborative environments in real time, such as video conferencing.

The study also shows the three-dimensional Activity-Based Computing, they are: i) task and material where the tests will be included; ii) time and space, where they can be controlled status information (started, suspended, ready and finished) as well as support the work multitasking; and iii) users, where it is possible to provide collaboration between system people.

The article by Juan Li et al (2014) sought to address how they can work with a community-based collaborative system for local classified as emergency, like tsunamis, floods and epidemics. In these circumstances it is very important to work with a well-organized system, there is a high level of stress and any information failure organization could result in big problems.

In another study, Bardram (2012) presents an analysis of smart spaces by using Computer Based on activity support collaboration using mobile devices. The work focuses on support for: i) unify interaction between applications using the ReticUI; ii) the management of complex tasks between users and displays, iii) the use or remote location of the services provided; and iv) collaboration among both local users and remote users.

The Fouzi Lezzar study (2013) presents an analysis of the use of collaborative mobile devices in favor of improving the planning focused health tasks. The platform was developed in Android system providing the framework necessary for the implementation of collaborative experiments using mobile devices. For this, Lezzar developed a synchronous grouping of Android mobile devices in order to enable a real-time collaboration where members of these groups may be geographically separated, but still manage to use the system.

The last related work (Abbas *et al*, 2014) used the Utility Theory of multiple attributes to aid in comparison with other different systems that is based on the recommendation and planning for health issues, an important technique for analyzing decisions. The model allows the use of heterogeneous data. For planning information for each data was used to structure cloud DaaS (Data as a Service). The model uses the Centroid Rank Method - ROC (Solymosi & Dombi, 1986) for efficiency testing and ranking of the planning processes.

Table 1. Comparison among related works

Features	Activity-based computing (2015)	Community-based collaborative information (2014)	ReticularSpaces (2012)	Mobile Collaborative Tasks Planning (2013)	A cloud based health insurance plan recommendation system (2014)
Activity-Based Computing	Yes	No	Yes	No	Yes
Multi Level Decision	Yes	Yes	No	Yes	Yes
Emergency Management	No	Yes	No	No	No
Cloud computing	No	No	No	No	Yes
Ontology	No	Yes	No	No	Yes
Collaboration	synchronous / asynchronous	sharing information for community	synchronous / asynchronous	Mobile Collaboration (synchronous)	Yes (potential)
Ubiquitous computing	Yes	No	No	No	No
Context	Activity as context	Model Activity W3C	Adaptive context - Activity Roaming	Medical Context	No

3. DOCTOR COLLAB MODEL

The proposed solution involves the development of a model to assist in the collaborative activities of a medical emergency in order to facilitate the exchange of information among duty physicians. For this idea, some assumptions were established in order to contribute to the development of the model: a) Support collaboration in the application layer: With collaboration, doctors may perform a richest form of patient care through collaborations throughout the evolution of the patient's health status or in real time, b) Computing inferences: Data as contexts and tasks are stored aiming to contribute to the situation awareness proposed in this model, c) Activity Management with a focus on collaboration: Doctor Collab model systematize data traffic, which helps the exchange of information and collaboration.

Figure 1 shows the architecture of Doctor Collab. One of the main features of this structure is its standard-based paradigm Model View Controller - MVC, using concepts of reuse and interaction between each. The architecture's packages were created in order to provide better control of the information trafficked during the exchange of medical shifts. Its components can be detailed in order to optimize the understanding of architecture structure, they are: a) Context Access; b) Activity Management; c) Inference Situation; d) Knowledge Base; e) Activity Database; and f) Collaborative Management.

To protect application data, the Doctor Collab model uses SSL protocol in the security layer. This protocol will be part of an HTTPS connection with data to be transmitted through an encrypted connection. This type of security is necessary for the patient data can be transmitted within the Doctor Collab without the information is seen by other unauthorized persons, thus creating a secure communication channel and an insecure network.

The situation awareness within the Doctor Collab is presented as a solution to improve the perception of the elements found in a medical emergency in order to optimize the medical diagnosis of the future. For this, the model implements three levels of perceptions, based on the concepts of Endsley (1999): i) Level 1 - perception of Emergency Medical elements: period that analyzes the elements of the hospital environment, their status, and dynamic attributes of the elements; ii) Level 2 - Understanding the Current Situation: this understanding is by summary of level 1 items. This level that analyzes the importance of the elements in favor of a specific goal; and iii) Level 3 - Projection of future states: this level is intended to project future actions of the environmental features faster. For this to be possible, it is necessary to have insight and understanding of the elements of a medical environment.

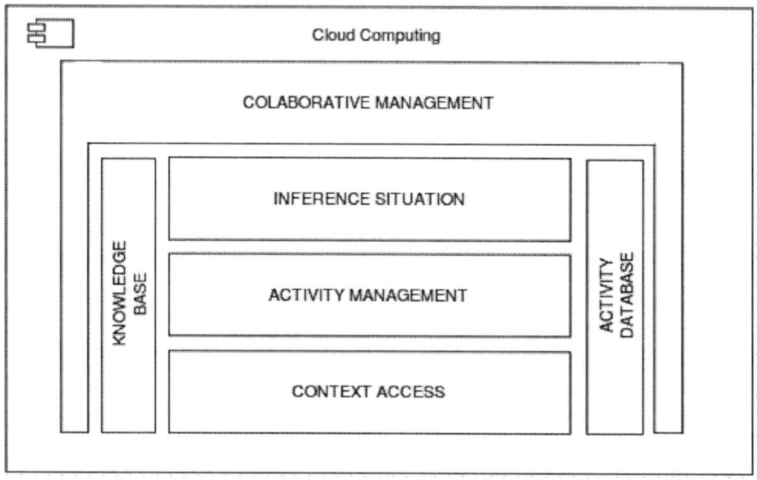

Figure 1. Doctor Collab Architecture

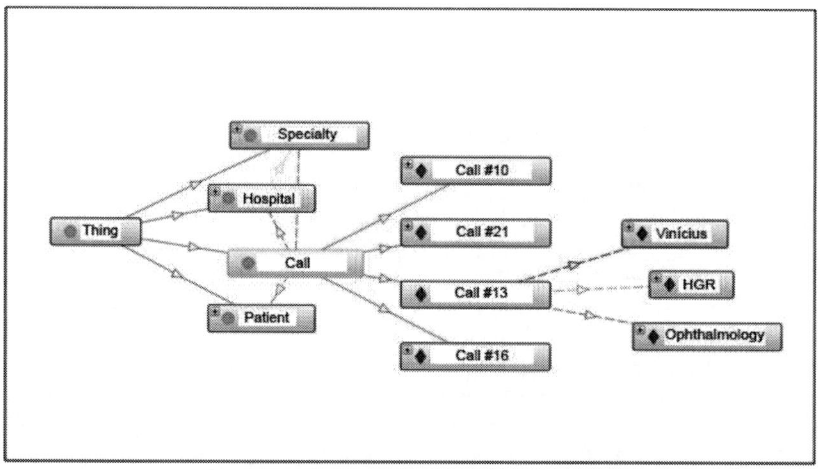

Figure 2. Doctor Collab Ontology

An ontology is used to define situations in this model. With the ontological structure, the model is able to answer the following questions: a) What is the risk classification of the patient's health?; b) What kind of medication available in the hospital would be the most indicated as patient history to be served?; and c) What doctor, even physically far from the hospital, could benefit clinical improvement of a patient?

Ontology Doctor Collab has relations based on object properties (Figure 2). The first relationship is represented by lines, and is between the classes Service (Domain) and patient (range). The property in question is Call -> Meets -> Patient. Still on the relationships that can happen during a call in an emergency medical environment have the Customer class that interacts with the need class through the relationship Customer -> NecessityToSpecialty -> Necessity.

The Reasoner incorporates optimizations through a table of decisions in several areas to highlight: i) Awareness Verification; ii) satisfaction; iii) Classification; and iv) Realization. This topic calculates the different aspects of each individual.

4. IMPLEMENTATION

To evaluate the model, we developed a prototype that meets the collaboration issues within medical settings. In general the Doctor Collab model sought to maintain the minimum structure required to answer the research question. For the production of Doctor Collab model some tools were used. It was used initially the vector drawing tool of Draw.io Web environment. For the design of UML diagrams was used the Astah software design tool in its free version (Community). For the design of the ontological structure was used the Protègè tool, available free from Stanford University. The encoding occurs with Java programming language. The information storage was accomplished by Stardog knowledge base, a Bank of semantic data. This information storage style is given by the need to generate computational inferences and Web Semantics information by Jena Apache Framework.

Some screenshoots of the developed prototype are presented in Figure 3. The interface was designed using the concepts of responsiveness web (Mohorovicic, 2013), so that the screens can adapt to different sizes of devices. Soon after user authentication, the application shows the number of patients within the medical emergency categorized by color. The application gives the possibility of registering attendance beyond the hospital capacity. On the home page is a summary of the number of patients within the medical emergency and categorized by color, red for high risk life, yellow for moderate and green for patients risk of low life. Another important screen to be shown in Figure 3 with regard to the success of service registration and the computational inference. The information is added to the Semantic Stardog database according to the model of RDF triples. In addition, the medical necessity in the requested attendance register is inferred within the Ontological file to check availability of care necessity.

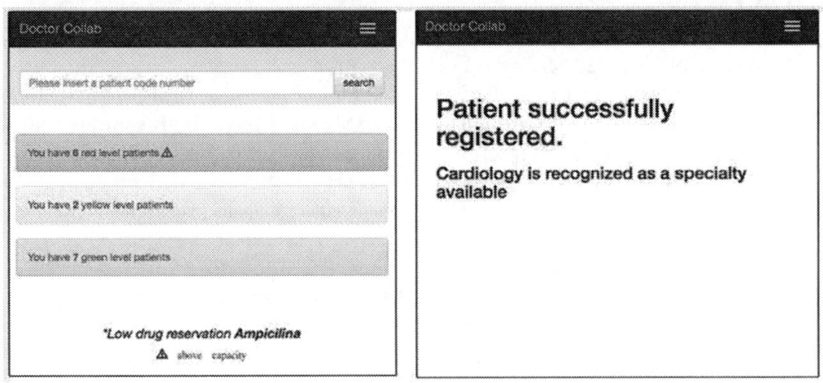

Figure 3. Doctor Collab Interfaces

In Doctor Collab, the detection of situations was modeled in Stardog semantic database, database according to the model of RDF triples. Users can request the attendance register and infer situations within the Ontological file to check availability of care necessity. The records are stored in triple format within Stardog knowledge base and it can be monitored through the Web Information manager Stardog. Computational situations can be understood as an abstraction in high-level settings and information from the application of knowledge bases. This information is also available to improve the level of application intelligence. Figure 4 shows the modeling of a situation. The schema model is defined by the file "DoctorCollabOntology" and the database as "DoctorCollabData". The *executeInference()* method uses the *InfoModel.contains* function of the Jena framework to relate the reasoner with application data, thus informing whether a particular fact is contained in the system. The situation is modeled by inference that is based on sub inheritance classes ontological schema, recognizing instances, like the medical specialties available in the service registration form, inferring that way if the specialty is or is not available in this doctor on duty.

```java
public String executeInference(String tipoEspecialidade) {

    org.apache.log4j.BasicConfigurator.configure(new NullAppender());

  Model schema = FileManager.get().loadModel("/Users/infomac/Downloads"
        + "/doctor-collab-ontologies-owl-REVISION-27/TestOntology.owl");
  Model data = FileManager.get().loadModel("/Users/infomac/Downloads"
       + "/doctor-collab-ontologies-owl-REVISION-27/teste-owlDemoData.rdf");
   Reasoner reasoner = ReasonerRegistry.getOWLReasoner();
   reasoner = reasoner.bindSchema(schema);
   InfModel infmodel = ModelFactory.createInfModel(reasoner, data);

   Resource hospital = infmodel.getResource("urn:x-hp:eg/Hospital");
   Resource especialidade = infmodel.getResource("urn:x-hp:eg/"
           + tipoEspecialidade);

   System.out.println("o valor de especialidade é: "+ tipoEspecialidade);

   if (infmodel.contains(especialidade, RDF.type, hospital)) {
      return "Cardiologia é reconhecido como uma especialidade disponível.";
   } else {
      return "Falha no reconhecimento de uma especialidade disponível.";
   }

}
```

Figure 4. Doctor Collab Inference

5. EVALUATION

To evaluate Doctor Collab, we performed a qualitative assessment using the usability verification methodology. For this we used the TAM (Technical Modeling Architecture) proposed by Davis (1989). For the evaluation of this work were incorporated some variables and have the meanings following: **Ease of use** is intended to prove how easily the user can complete the task in the first contact with the Doctor Collab or how fast user performance is improved. **Satisfaction** analyzes the user will proceed to use the application again. **Utility** intended to analyze how the application solves a specific problem in question presented during search.

The Following assumptions for the proposed TAM have been identified:

- H1: The ease of use positively influences the application of the utility;
- H2: The satisfaction positively influences the implementation of the utility.

The first stage of the evaluation was the choice of participants for field experiments. It were selected 20 medical volunteers from 1 to 6 years of emergency medical experience within the Emergency sector at Roraima General Hospital and participants of the Emergency League of Roraima, both in Brazil, chosen for convenience and in a controlled environment. First the doctors were encouraged to use the Doctor Collab application and then fill out the forms of care of hospitalized patients in the emergency department, thus creating a support collaborative environment of activities and medical conditions in that place.

After using the Doctor Collab, we applied a survey containing 8 statements and the evaluators used the Likert scale (Likert, 1932) of five points to agree or disagree. The survey aimed at evaluating Doctor Collab regarding collaboration and situation awareness. This scale provides five choices in a range that starts at point 1 (strongly disagree) to point 5 (strongly agree). After obtained the results, we used statistical techniques for data analysis. The reliability of the form is shown from the use of Cronbach's alpha (Cronbach, 1951) thus allowing to estimate clearly the correlation between responses and respondents. Cronbach's alpha value of this research has reached the approximate value of 0.83 indicating that the questionnaire is reliable to be above 0.7.

Figure 5 shows the positive responses of respondents regarding the use of Collab Doctor in medical emergencies and the high regularity of type responses strongly agree and agree, as well as the higher incidence on the issue 5. Notes also that the issue was one that generated a greater difference in responses, with a high degree of disagreement referring to the statement, this is due to the fact that users disagree with the question stated that users experienced difficulty in using the application.

Many of the comments related to the usefulness of Doctor Collab were positive, thus confirming the information provided in this study. Many stressed the high importance of resources to enhance collaboration between medical teams. According to one user: "Having an application like this in our department would be very good, we lost a lot of time passing the information to the next team." Another reviewer said: "It is great to see that such a platform could be available in public hospitals in Brazil, it would improve greatly the search for information and communication between doctors."

As worst result, it was noted that in the issue number 7, which addresses the user satisfaction, 20% of respondents were indifferent or had no opinion that Doctor Collab application would promote greater interest to the medical management activities within the hospital. This is due to the fact that the natural resistance to professional changes in a bureaucratic process. The question 8 was one of the largest medical acceptance values, 90% positively answered the question that examines whether the assessed application facilitates the work of medical team. It shows the hope of health professionals to join the computer world facilities with health problems of the world. One of the doctors who evaluated positive answered: "We know Information Technology solutions that have been well used in other areas such as law and engineering, and every time that we see health IT solutions, we get motivated, even more solutions for our labor sector as the emergency. Informatics is a reality, we all have to adapt."

Taking into account the results presented in this topic, it was possible to confirm the hypotheses H1 and H2, as shown in Table 2. Thus it can be confirmed that the proposed model is consistent with the identified assumptions.

Table 2. Comparison between the related work

Hypotheses		Analysis
H1	The ease of use positively influences the application of the utility	Confirmed
H2	The satisfaction positively influences the implementation of the utility	Confirmed

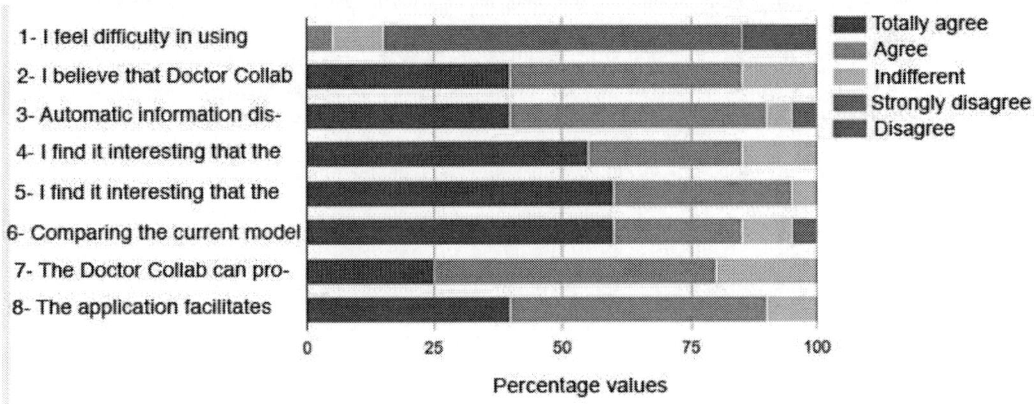

Figure 5. Doctor Collab results

6. CONCLUSION

This article addressed the design of a model to support collaboration and exchange of information through the use of situation awareness on medical inference. Doctor Collab proposes a solution that encourages collaboration between medical teams to improve the exchange of information in the shift change in emergency environments. In this way, the main scientific contribution of this article is a model with an ontology structure and inferences of medical situations.

In order to assess the viability of Doctor Collab model we developed a prototype and evaluated with physicians. For 95% of respondents, the use of an application that uses medical inference is a good solution to improve the passage of information between health professionals. Reinforcing this information, 90% of respondents believe that the Doctor Collab facilitates the work of medical team. Doctor Collab had an average acceptance of 86.9%. Within the evaluation of this study were not analyzed topics such as scalability and efficiency, these issues are suggested for future work.

The current version of the model presents some opportunities for future works. In the field of collaboration, we suggest a deepening on how topics like the coupling of time and space derailment influence the exchange of information between medical teams. With regard to medical inferences, we can provide more rules enabling different situations. We foresee also a need of a performance evaluation and of how the model behaves in an everyday real situation. Finally, further studies related to security to the mechanisms of interaction among medical emergency teams.

ACKNOWLEDGMENTS

The authors would like to thank to CAPES, CNPq and FAPERGS for partially funding this research.

REFERENCES

ABBAS, Assad et al, 2014. A cloud based health insurance plan recommendation system: A user centered approach. *Future Generation Computer Systems*, [S.l.], v. 43, p. 99- 109.

BARDRAM, Jakob et al, 2012 ReticularSpaces: activity-based computing support for physically distributed and collaborative smart spaces. *Proceedings of the SIGCHI Conference on Human Factors in Computing Systems.* ACM, Paris - France, p. 2845-2854.

CHEN, Harry; FININ, Tim; JOSHI, Anupam, 2003. An ontology for context-aware pervasive computing environments. *The Knowledge Engineering Review*, [S.l.], v. 18, n. 03, p. 197-207.

DAVIS, Fred D, 1989. Perceived usefulness, perceived ease of use, and user acceptance of information technology. *MIS quarterly*, Minnesota, p. 319-340.

ENDSLEY, Mica R.; GARLAND, Daniel J, 2000 Situation awareness analysis and measurement. *CRC Press*, [S.l.].

LEZZAR, Fouzi; ZIDANI, Abdelmadjid; CHORFI, Atef, 2013. Using A Mobile Collaborative Approach To Improve Healthcare Tasks Planning. *International Journal of Multimedia and Ubiquitous Engineering*, [S.l.], v. 8, n. 3, p. 407-420.

LI, Juan et al, 2014. Community-based collaborative information system for emergency management. *Computers & Operations Research*, [S.l.], v. 42, p. 116-124.

LIKERT, Rensis, 1932. A technique for the measurement of attitudes. *Archives of psychology*, New York – USA, p. 1-55.

MELL, Peter; GRANCE, Tim, 2010. The NIST definition of cloud computing. *Communications of the ACM*, [S.l.], v. 53, n. 6, p. 50.

MOHOROVICIC, S, 2013. Implementing responsive web design for enhanced web presence. *Information & Communication Technology Electronics & Microelectronics* (MIPRO), 2013 36th International Convention on. IEEE, Opatija – Croatia, p. 1206- 1210.

NOY, Natalya F, 2001. Ontology Development 101: A Guide to Creating Your First Ontology: Knowldege Systems Laboratory, Stanford University. *Stanford Knowledge Systems Laboratory Technical Report KSL-01-05 and Stanford Medical Informatics Technical Report SMI-2001-0880*, Stanford – USA.

SATYANARAYANAN, Mahadev, 2010. Mobile computing: the next decade. *Proceedings of the 1st ACM workshop on mobile cloud computing & services: social networks and beyond*. ACM, San Francisco - USA, p. 5. APA.

SOLYMOSI, Tamás; DOMBI, Jozsef, 1986. A method for determining the weights of criteria: the centralized weights. *European Journal of Operational Research*, [S.l.], v. 26, n. 1, p. 35-41.

SULTAN, Nabil, 2014. Making use of cloud computing for healthcare provision: Opportunities and challenges. *International Journal of Information Management*, [S.l.], v. 34, n. 2, p. 177-184.

ZAUPA, D.; COSTA, C.; SILVA, J, 2012. Implementing a spontaneous social network for managing ubiquitous interactions. *Computer Systems (WSCAD-SSC), 2012 13th Symposium on*, Petropolís – Brazil, p. 163-170.

A UBIQUITOUS MODEL FOR HEART MONITORING BASED ON SITUATION AWARENESS

Cristofe Coelho Lopes da Rocha[1,2], Cristiano André da Costa[1] and Rodrigo da Rosa Righi[1]
[1]*Applied Computing Graduate Program, Universidade do Vale do Rio dos Sinos (Unisinos), São Leopoldo, RS, Brazil*
[2]*Federal Institute of Education, Science and Technology of Roraima (IFRR), Boa Vista, RR, Brazil*

ABSTRACT

Patients with heart failure and without daily medical monitoring may have their heart physiological signs compromised, causing them many health problems. This recurring scenario reduces the patient's life quality, resulting in new hospital admissions, thus becoming a cost to the health system. We consider that the use of ubiquitous healthcare, by using sensor and wearables, may improve this process by reducing the number of hospital admissions. In this context, this article proposes a model named UbHeart, which employs situation awareness to identify possible cardiac problems. As a scientific contribution, the model provides monitoring of degradation of the vital signs of the patient's heart through detection of situations of cardiac complications. Health parameters established by the Brazilian Society of Cardiology were used. Thus, the evaluation of UbHeart was made using physiological sings and developed prototype and showed promising results.

KEYWORDS

E-Health, Heartbeat, Blood pressure, Ubiquitous Computing, Situation awareness

1. INTRODUCTION

Readmissions in hospital systems have been significantly increasing in the latest years. Despite the advancements in healthcare for patients with health failure (HF), results after hospitalization are not getting any better (Chaudhry et al. 2013). This pathology is considered one of the main medical challenges of our time (Ukena et al. 2012). Without daily medical monitoring, the patients' physiological signs could be compromised and hospitalization becomes inevitable. This recurring scenario reduces the patient's life quality and results in return to the hospital, thus becoming a cost to the health system.

Factors associated with the increase of the rates of hospital admissions include noncompliance with the medication, failure to seek immediate medical treatment when the symptoms are exacerbated, and self-medication (Anker, 2011). A promising strategy is telemonitoring, which consists in observing the patient's physiological signs so that health care practitioners may intervene earlier in case there is evidence of clinical deterioration (Chaundhry et al. 2013).

The evolution of mobile and ubiquitous computing has favored the development of solutions that use sensors and mobile applications in benefit of human beings. The situation awareness allows to correlate logically aggregated contexts in order to determine a user's involvement in a given more complex scenario (Anagnostopoulos et al. 2007). Particularly, smartphones have significant context detection and user interaction capabilities, which may be explored in order to build powerful applications in the area of health care (Scott et al. 2015). Within this context, the area of ubiquitous health allows to use mobile and ubiquitous computing for monitoring the patient's health anywhere and at any time, with no need for the person to be in a clinic or hospital. The purpose of keeping medical care ubiquitously, which has been called ubiquitous healthcare, is to provide the patients with a convenient service, facilitating diagnosis of clinical conditions (Gelogo et al. 2013).

Considering ubiquitous healthcare, this work is particularly focused on heart failure and proposes a model named UbHeart. First, a previous diagnosis is made by using information acquired through sensors. When a situation of risk is identified, an alert is sent to the patient, also being possible to be communicated to the people responsible for the patient as well as to the hospital, which calls the doctor.

The main scientific contribution of UbHeart is the possibility of recognizing information that may identify possible physiological degradations and combine them in order to characterize a situation of heart risk to the patient. To this moment, no paper that uses situation awareness applied to monitoring of vital signals of patients with heart failure was found. During the research, the study highlighted as important the monitoring of the patient's progress over time and the need for analyzing the sorting order of measurements in order to help the doctor regarding the degree of investigation (Kashem et al. 2008; Mulvaney et al. 2012). Some papers listed point out that the measurements performed by the sensors were associated with the questions that the doctor asked the patient, and color codes informed in the system (Kashem et al. 2008).

This work is divided into five sections. Section 2 describes the related work. Section 3 describes the UbHeart model. Section 4 describes the model implementation. An evaluation based on a case study is presented in section 5. Finally, section 6 presents the conclusions.

2. RELATED WORK

The models analyzed during the study used features of ubiquitous computing and context awareness. The paper describes a model of use of a wireless sensor network to identify measurements and provide indices to analyze tendencies and send possible complication alert to the patient. The measurements of glucose, blood pressure, temperature and breathing were acquired through sensors and sent to the clinic through a mobile device. A communication layer provides transfer of information to the remote doctor and the clinic. The study points out the importance of tendency analysis for monitoring the patient's progress over time and thus determine the patient's situation and may give anticipated alerts of possible complications that might develop.

Kashem et al. (2008) propose a model applied to telemedicine that uses information on weight, blood pressure, and heartbeat, in order to find possible situations of risk to patients. The processing operation is performed on a server and the patient's clinic condition is defined by using measurements that the patients inform manually. The proposed system is divided into three parts: patients, domain providers and server, and it allows the patients to send data directly from the database and receive diagnoses provided by a doctor. Although the paper highlights the relevance of the patient's health situation, the model describes the situation qualification by means of analysis of measurements related to questions the patients are asked during the telephone call made by the nurse.

The model proposed by Winkler et al. (2011) allows for the acquisition of physiological signs by using portable medical equipment of electrocardiogram, blood pressure, body weight, and self-assessment measurements that are processed on a remote server. The measurements are classified individually by using a color code and received generating events according to the rules of medical prioritization to initiate a review process guided by workflow in the system and a more detailed assessment by the medical practitioners. The model allows to change the order of visualization of the data processed in the medical center according to its critical level and interaction by the patient, who makes their self-assessment by using a scale of a color code.

The model proposed by Suh (2011) makes an analysis of linear regression, in addition to checking the absence of a necessary piece of information and its integrity, in order to define the patient's health.

In general, the studied models demonstrated that the processing operation and situation analysis were performed asynchronously by the cardiologist physician. They indicated the need for monitoring the vital signs degradation of the patient over time. Furthermore, they showed the need to analyze the order of the measurements. Contexts are analyzed individually without monitoring evolution. The situation analysis applied in this way may hinder quick intervention in order to prevent degradation of the patient's physiological signs. Many false positives may also be generated based on an analysis over isolated contexts.

3. UBHEART MODEL

The proposed model allows monitoring vital signals by using medical equipments, wearables, interconnected through a Bluetooth network, which allow the acquisition of physiological signs in a way that is more convenient to the patient in residential environment, as it can be seen in Figure 1a. The patient's smartphone informs the patient's profile to the system, which through sensors, acquires the physiological signs and builds a health history, which is sent to the hospital through the Internet. The information base sent by the smartphone to a service on the cloud allows the system to analyze the health situation based on a risk classification, relating the patient's profile to the acquired contexts. The health history sent to the hospital allows the physicians responsible for the patient to know how health is in a short period of time, assuring quick assistance and thus preventing new hospitalizations.

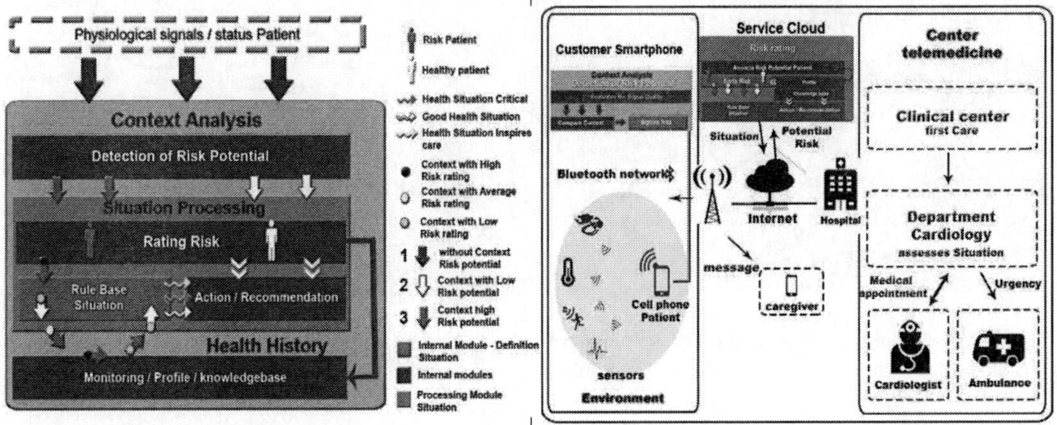

(a) (b)

Figure 1. UbHeart proposal: (a) Overview of the general solution; (b) UbHeart architectural model

The clinic center takes the first care measures by passing information to the patient through recommendation made by the system. In case the health condition needs specialized assistance, an appointment with the cardiologist is made, just as, in case it is urgent, an ambulance may be sent to the place. Health changes are informed to the caregiver by cellphone messages. The patient receives several recommendations of how to proceed in order to improve their health indices or how to act to prevent worsening of their health condition upon immediate need. We can notice that the model proposes various features in order to prevent the patient from lacking medical care and prevent their physiological signs to go down to degrading levels, as it can be seen in Figure 1b.

The model of the service running on the patient's smartphone is presented in Figure 2a. The physiological signs and the patient's status are acquired by the system (arrow 1 in the Figure). The Situation Processing component gathers modules for classification of the risk, rules and actions of the system, definition of the health situation, and these are processed by a service on a computational cloud. This service receives the contexts from an analysis made by the module of risk potential detection on the patient's smartphone. This service is responsible for detection of the patient's risk potential. On this service, the model indicates the risk potential based on the context information and the norms of the Brazilian Society of Cardiology[1].

Contexts are acquired based on the patient's physiological signs (arrow 1 in Figure 2a). The *evaluate quality of sign* function checks whether the physiological sign detection was successful or features any abnormality, and in case it does, the sign is disregarded. Once this stage is completed, the context is sent to the *compare context* function, which is responsible for comparing the acquired values with the ones established by the Brazilian Society of Cardiology in issues related to age and pathology.

Each context is compared individually according to the patient's profile at the time it is acquired, and then the *indicate risk* function is activated. In case the context value is out of the one established by the standards, a risk potential is indicated with colors (arrows 2 and 3). It is appropriate to highlight that the identification of potentiality does not determines the risk, but it is exactly extremely important for determining its classification and later the situation, in addition to contributing to modeling the knowledge. This module is based on the context analysis and therefore does not correlate the contexts, but identifies them individually, passing it through to the UbHeart service on the cloud.

The cloud service classifies the patient's risk and is presented on Figure 2b. According to the previous classification of risk potential and the contexts of risk identified, the *associate risk potential with the patient*

[1] http://publicacoes.cardiol.br/2014/diretrizes.asp

function makes a query to a knowledge base. There are two possible analyses, which are: (i) compare the contexts with risk potential indication and the patient's profile with the knowledge base; in case the patient's profile is not found, (ii) the model actuates the *classify risk* function, which is responsible for classifying the risk, associating it with the guidelines of the Brazilian society of cardiology.

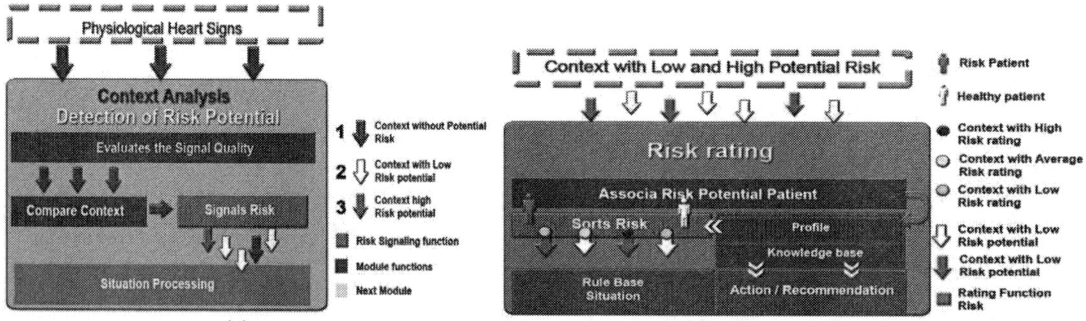

(a) (b)

Figure 2. Risk analysis in UbHeart: (a) Risk Potential Detection Service on smartphone; (b) UbHeart Risk Classification through Situation Awareness

The risk classification is performed in three levels: black, yellow, and green, representing respectively high, medium, and low risk. Then it sends the contexts to the module that analyses the situation based on rules. This module perform actions based on various context associations. The information from the physiological signs identified with risk potential are associated with the contexts of the patient's profile and from the calculations made and the standards determined by the Brazilian Society of Cardiology, it classifies the risk in which the patient may be involved.

We are using rules to enable situation awareness.. The rules are defined according to the determined functions, which are: (i) Degradation – responsible for executing the activities *select the patient's profile* and *check the classification level* of the physiological sign; (ii) Monitoring – Started by an event sent by the rule of degradation, it is responsible for monitoring the evolution of degradation of the patient's vital sign, besides monitoring related contexts, whether from sensors or according to the patient's profile; (iii) Determining of the situation – this rule determines in which situation the patient is, correlating the values acquired by the *track the gradation evolution* rule based on the guidelines of heart care, in a period of time, to the contexts of location and profile. The results may converge into a situation that, although identified with potential and classification of low risk, may represent situations of imminent risk, depending on the location and context of the patient's profile, and vice-versa. The *action rules* are actuated according to the classification of the situation. They may be: (i) No action, in case there is no history for the rule or even because it is not a situation of risk; (ii) Recommend, situation with classification of low risk, it actuates the rule that sends guiding information to the patient's smartphone; (iii) Call caregiver, situations with medium and high classifications, which are reported to the patient's caregiver and finally to the center of telemedicine.

4. IMPLEMENTATION

The development of the prototype involves the implementation of three modules: the module for analysis of risk potential, located on the patient's smartphone, the module for processing the situation, and the module of action rules and inference in the Knowledge Base. We implemented a prototype for mobile devices, in order to make it possible to evaluate representing the contexts, which are used as requirements for situation analysis. We also implemented, in the cloud computing module, the algorithms for processing the situation analysis.

For implementation of the module for analysis of risk potential, the Android system was used with the SQL Lite database. The module of action rules and inference in the knowledge were programmed in Python.

Figure 3 describes the input data, processing and output of the algorithm for situation analysis in variations of hue of the colors gray, red and green, respectively, according to the proximity to the end of the processing operation. In this stage, calculations of standard and index of degradation and compromising rate were made, and they consubstantiated the algorithm decision regarding the degree of the patient's engagement concerning the health situation.

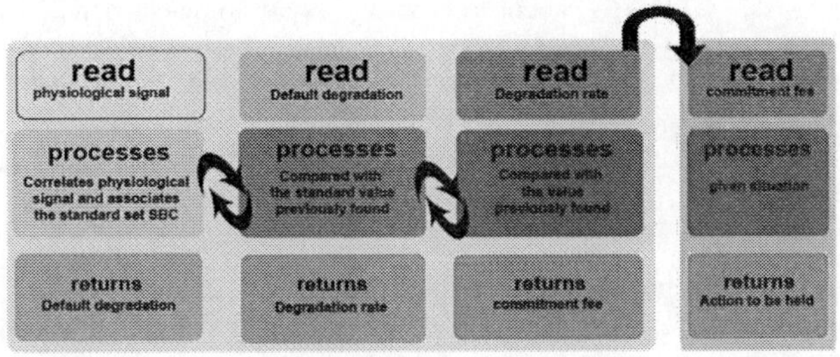

Figure 3. Calculation of the standard, index of degradation and compromising rate

Figure 3 shows the processing of events according to their output: (i) The first processing operation extracts the average difference of the physiological signs with relation to the patient's profile from the ones established by the standards; (ii) The second stage reads the standard value of degradation and compares it with the previous one. The difference between these values may be equal to, less or greater than zero. This stage informs the degradation index, which is responsible for identifying the evolution of degradation of the patient's physiological sign. In case it is greater than zero, it means that clinic deterioration of the patient is occurring; if negative, the patient is getting better over time; (iii) The third stage analyzes the uniformity of the degradation index regarding the occurrences. This stage informs the compromising rate of the patient concerning the situation. It analyzes the index of degradation, so that it does not undergo changes that hinder its uniformity, since the patient who is sensitively improving their index must show negative values, tending to zero. In case their health state is getting worse, they must show positive values or zero, and never alternated values between negative and positive in the analyzed interval.

5. EVALUATION AND DISCUSSION

The scientific community has used scenarios for evaluation of ubiquitous applications and context-aware systems (Satyanarayanan, 2011). From this strategy, a scenario was defined for evaluating UbHeart model. The objective is to evaluate health risk indication. This consisted in checking the operation of the model during analysis of the contexts and situation awareness from a set of physiological signs.

We created a database to represent heartbeats and blood pressure, complying with the measuring intervals established by the Brazilian Society of Cardiology. The simulation methodology by means of a database and development of ubiquitous algorithms is used by the scientific community for heart health applications, which perform context analysis and have been showing satisfactory results (Sarkar, 2011; Landolina, 2012). The database created contained 100 physiological signs obtained from typical values of patients according to their age, varying from 18 to 65. There were modeled heartbeats in the range between 60 and 100. Regarding blood pressure, Table 1 describes the values assumed.

Table 1. Values established for the testing base

Classification	Systolic pressure (mmHg)	Diastolic pressure (mmHg)
Sleep	~110	~70
Optimal	<120	<80
Normal	<130	<85
Limitary	130	85-89
Hypertension stage 1	130-139	90-99
Hypertension stage 2	140-159	100-109

The generic rule was actuated for values out of the ranges established for the heartbeats and the limitary classification for the systolic and diastolic blood pressure described in Table 1. For patients above the age range, specific rules were used based on the normal classification and heartbeat range 60-90. The physiological signs were filled in manually, where the generic and specific rules were actuated for monitoring the patients with features described in Table 2.

Table 2. Patient with change in physiological signs

Classification	Heartbeat	D/S diastolic / systolic pressure
72-year-old elder	96	15/80
23-year-old youngster	100	14/80

During the monitoring, 100 physiological signs from each context in five intervals were selected, in sequence, where the standard of degradation, index of degradation and compromising rate were calculated, determining the degree of certainty that we assert for involvement of the patient with the situation of risk. A chart of heartbeat, presented in Figure 4, was used to analyse the results. The vertical axis represents the oscillation for heartbeats and blood pressure, and the horizontal axis represents the physiological signs that occurred. The lines in blue show the beginning of the monitoring that occurs when the physiological signs are found outside the acceptable limits.

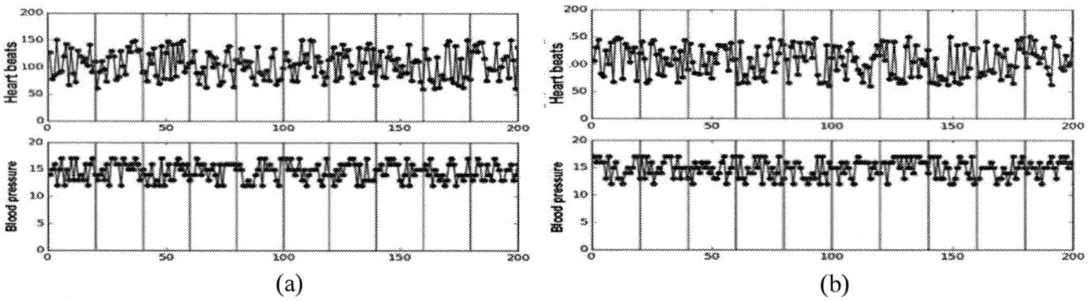

Figure 4. Heartbeat physiological sign and systolic blood pressure of (a) elderly patient and (b) young patient

By making an analysis for the elderly patient in Figure 4a, in the first stage of monitoring of heartbeats and blood pressure, we may notice that although the elder features some physiological signs within the limits established in Table 1, most of the other signs are out of the limit, and this occurrence is determining for the degradation analysis. The chart demonstrates that there is an evolution of the degradation of the physiological signs, whose calculation is made based on the average found, according to the red line in Figure 4a.

Regarding the young patient, the results are different, because the average was below their limit, according to the green line in Figure 4b. Therefore, the values out and within the range have their tendency analyzed and are considered for the calculations of situation analysis. During the monitoring intervals, the physiological signs oscillated, making it difficult for a visual conclusion of the patient's real health situation. After obtaining the average of the values in the interval, it was possible to indicate the health risk. However, the statement of possible health compromising based on the average of the values may not demonstrate the real situation; therefore, it is necessary to calculate the compromising rate of the indication of risk based on all the intervals.

The correlation between the various contexts related to heart health was analyzed associatively, once specific rules were adapted to each patient's profile. Patients with different physical features, which inspired health care, were represented without any difficulty. In practice, an elderly patient features physiological signs with different limits due to their age. Moreover, some of the absolute values of the contexts have representation, as they actuate the monitoring rules.

Nevertheless, the other contexts acquired in the interval must be considered for determining the real health situation, because the lack of a sufficient amount of contexts may compromise the indication of risk. The calculation of the compromising rate accomplishes the comprehension of the acquired physiological signs, logically aggregating them in order to analyze the patient's degree of involvement with the situation of risk based on situation awareness.

5.1 Situation Awareness Evaluation

Two approaches were used for the situation awareness evaluation, and they allowed for more accurate results, without need for other invasive methods of acquisition of physiological signs. The first consists in calculating the compromising rate based on the average of the physiological signs (TxM) found in the intervals. Therefore, we obtained five average values that serve as the basis for calculating degradation for each of them comparing to the one before it. The index of degradation, difference of the degradation found with relation to the previous one, may represent an ascending sequence for evolution of degradation, descending for the patient's improvement, or stable in case none of the previous ones occur. The TxM is calculated based on deduction of 20% for the values of the index of degradation, which does not follow the sequence, since five reference values are used. The second form is to calculate the average of the compromising rates based on the logic (TxL) of the physiological signs found in each interval. The physiological signs were analyzed in the interval and may feature a sequence of ascending values for the evolution of degradation, descending for the patient's improvement, or stable, in case none of the previous ones occurs.

At the end of 20 physiological sings, the compromising rate of the interval was calculated, where each physiological sign that is out of the logical sequence had a discount of 5%. The TxL represents the average of all the rates of the five intervals. In Table 3, the TxM column describes the compromising rate based on the average values of the physiological signs. The variation of the degradation standard (DS) showed an improvement in the patient's clinic condition. In the case of the young patient, results that describe up to the third value to the right were found, discounting only 20% in the case of the value of 4.75, which switches to increase of the degradation. Then we obtained the TxM with value of 8% and so for the other patients, according to Table 3. The values of the column TxL demonstrate a low compromising rate.

Table 3. Average of the physiological signs (TxM) and average of the compromising rates (TxL)

Patient	Heartbeats	Standard (DS)	Index (ID)	TxM	TxL
72-year-old elder	108.3 /108.9 /97.15 /108.9 /97.1	10.83 < 10.89 > 7.15 < 10.89 > 7.10	0.06 | -3.74 | 3.74 | -3.79	80%	50%
23-year-old youngster	115.25 /109.8 / 106.35 104.0 / 104.75	15.25 > 9.8 > 6.35 > 4.0 < 4.75	5.45 | 3.45 | 2.35 |-1.75	80%	20%

The occurrence indicates that a significant amount of physiological signs was deducted from the found logic. The analysis demonstrated that despite having an indication of evolution of degradation for the elder and improvement for the youngster, this assertion was not accurate, because some of the acquired physiological signs in the interval compromised the assertion and, therefore, they were deducted. For further analysis, the physiological signs were grouped five times, each group containing 25 physiological signs. Although a physiological sign may show, in insolation, health problems, when analyzed based on the degradation standard, that is, the difference between the one before and the one after it, there is a reconsideration of the isolate analysis, because they are grouped.

The degradation standard demonstrated that the features associated with the physiological sign do not represent imminent risk, as the history associated with the occurrence of the context and the rule generated by the monitoring actuated by this sign will or will not determine the evolution of degradation of the physiological sign. During the evaluation, we observed two perspectives for comprehension of the situation, in order to issue the compromising rate. Both perspectives have distinct possibilities to comprehend the relation between the values of the contexts logically aligned and determine the patient's degree of involvement regarding the health situation. However, the possibility of considering the logical sequence of the physiological signs represented a considerable difference with relation to the average obtained in the intervals.

With these results, we observed that one context does not determine the situation that the patient is in and its absolute value combined with a physiological profile may raise doubts regarding the situation analysis. The UbHeart model considered that a degraded physiological sign may feature low compromising of the patient regarding the health situation, due to the absence of contexts in the very same interval or low health risk, if the degradation standard associated with it decreases. Furthermore, the assertions made by the system regarding health risk were analyzed based on a compromising rate, which by means of the situation awareness determines the degree of reliability of the assertion.

6. CONCLUSION

Heart failure is considered one of the main medical challenges of our time. Medical specialists use heart physiological data and correlate them with information from the patient's profile in order to diagnose their health. In this context, this work proposed UbHeart. The main scientific contribution of this work was the possibility of recognizing information that may identify possible physiological degradations and logically group them in order to understand their relations. Furthermore, the model was able to determine each patient's degree of compromising with a situation of cardiac risk, evaluating the evolution of the degradation of the physiological signs and representing an aid in medical care for preventing hospital readmissions. As results, we observe that a part of the context was taken into consideration to determine the situation, since the occurrence was not disregarded. However, when aggregated logically, its history and relation with other signs previously and posteriorly acquired were also evaluated.

For future work, we intend to carry out definitions of risk situations admitting the absence of contexts used for the analysis of the evolution of degradation and the location of the patient.

ACKNOWLEDGMENTS

The authors would like to thank to CAPES, CNPq and FAPERGS for partially funding this research.

REFERENCES

Anagnostopoulos, C. B., Ntarladimas, Y., & Hadjiefthymiades, S. (2007). Situational computing: An innovative architecture with imprecise reasoning. Journal of Systems and Software, 80(12), 1993-2014.

Anker, S. D., Koehler, F., and Abraham, W. T. (2011). Telemedicine and remote management of patients with heart failure. The Lancet, 378(9792), 731-739.

Chaudhry, S. I et al. (2010). Telemonitoring in patients with heart failure. New England Journal of Medicine, 363(24), 2301-2309.

Endsley, M. R. (1995). Toward a theory of situation awareness in dynamic systems. Human Factors: The Journal of the Human Factors and Ergonomics Society, 37(1), 32-64.

Gelogo, Y. E., and Kim, H. K. (2013). Unified Ubiquitous Healthcare System Architecture with Collaborative Model. International Journal of Multimedia and Ubiquitous Engineering, 8(3).

Kashem, A., Droogan, M. T., Santamore, W. P., Wald, J. W., and Bove, A. A. (2008). Managing heart failure care using an internet-based telemedicine system. Journal of Cardiac Failure, 14(2), 121-126.

Landolina, M., Perego, G. B., Lunati, M., Curnis, A., Guenzati, G., Vicentini, A., ... & Marzegalli, M. (2012). Remote Monitoring Reduces Healthcare Use and Improves Quality of Care in Heart Failure Patients With Implantable Defibrillators The Evolution of Management Strategies of Heart Failure Patients With Implantable Defibrillators (EVOLVO) Study. Circulation, 125(24), 2985-2992.

Mulvaney, D., Woodward, B., Datta, S., Harvey, P., Vyas, A., Thakker, B., and Istepanian, R. (2012). Monitoring heart disease and diabetes with mobile internet communications. Int. Journal of telemedicine and applications, 2012, 12.

Sarkar, S., Hettrick, D. A., Koehler, J., Rogers, T., Grinberg, Y., Yu, C. M., ... & Tang, W. W. (2011). Improved algorithm to detect fluid accumulation via intrathoracic impedance monitoring in heart failure patients with implantable devices. Journal of cardiac failure, 17(7), 569-576.

Satyanarayanan, M. (2011). Mobile computing: the next decade. ACM SIGMOBILE Mobile Computing and Communications Review, 15(2), 2-10.

Scott, R. E., Mars, M., Scott, R. E., and Mars, M. (2015). Telehealth in the developing world: current status and future prospects. OncoTargets and Therapy, 8, 289-294.

Suh, M. K., Chen, C. A., Woodbridge, J., Tu, M. K., Kim, J. I., Nahapetian, A., ... & Sarrafzadeh, M. (2011). A remote patient monitoring system for congestive heart failure. Journal of medical systems, 35(5), 1165-1179.

Ukena, C., and Böhm, M. (2013). Management of heart failure: are specialists really needed? European heart journal, 34(6), 416-418.

Winkler, S., Schieber, M., Lücke, S., Heinze, P., Schweizer, T., Wegertseder, D., ... & Anker, S. D. (2011). A new telemonitoring system intended for chronic heart failure patients using mobile telephone technology—feasibility study. International Journal of Cardiology, 153(1), 55-58.

REFOCUS: CURRENT & FUTURE SEARCH INTERFACE REQUIREMENTS FOR GERMAN-SPEAKING USERS

Maximilian Speicher[1], Andreas Both and Martin Gaedke[1]
[1]*Technische Universität Chemnitz, 09111 Chemnitz*

ABSTRACT

While smartphones are widely used for web browsing, also other novel devices like Smart TVs become increasingly popular. Yet, current interfaces do not cater for the newly available devices beyond touch and small screens, if at all for the latter. Particularly search engines—today's entry points of the WWW—must ensure their interfaces are easy to use on any web-enabled device. We report on a survey that investigated (1) users' perception and usage of current search interfaces, and (2) their expectations towards current and future search interfaces. Users are mostly satisfied with desktop and mobile search, but seem to be skeptical towards web search with novel devices and input modalities. Hence, we derive *REFOCUS*—a novel set of requirements for current and future search interfaces, which shall address the demand for improvement of novel web search and has been validated by 12 dedicated experts.

KEYWORDS

Empirical Study, Interfaces, Novel Devices, Requirements, Search Engines, User Research

1. INTRODUCTION

By the end of 2014, the number of mobile users exceeded the number of those using desktop PCs.[1] Moreover, the sales numbers of web-enabled novel devices total over 300 million units.[2] Hence, there is a strong shift towards devices beyond desktop PCs that provide options to browse the web, which include smart phones, tablet PCs, video game consoles and smart glasses, to name only a few. These *novel devices* introduce a new variety of input (touch, gestures, speech etc.) and output modalities (dominated by images, video, speech, 3D etc.) that go beyond what is possible with traditional keyboard, mouse and mid-sized computer screens[3]. This trend calls for novel, cutting-edge approaches towards web interfaces to adapt to the new circumstances and opportunities. However, from own observations we know that in today's industry, focus is still often on desktop PCs alone.

Search engines have become *the* main entry point to the WWW for many users. Particularly, three search engines are ranked among the top five *Alexa top sites*[4]. Also, the default start pages of web browsers on all modern devices feature prominent search boxes. This has led to users more and more "us[ing] web search engines as a replacement for web page bookmarking" (Weber and Jaimes, 2011). Also, Weber and Jaimes (2011) found that "the most frequent queries are navigational where the user might just as well type the query in the browser's address bar to re-find a URL from his browsing history". Hence, for the user, URLs are only a mere intermediate step, which makes it highly necessary to provide usable search interfaces for the whole range of web-enabled devices that are available nowadays.

In this paper, we present—to the best of our knowledge—the first empirical study that results in a *requirements specification for both, current and future search interfaces*. The study was intended as *exploratory* research, which means that we do not try to answer a specific research question, but rather want to "get a feel for" users' perceptions of and expectations towards current and future search engines. Our ten

[1] http://www.businessinsider.com/mobile-will-eclipse-desktop-by-2014-2012-6 (July 20, 2016).
[2] http://goo.gl/bKshhP (July 20, 2016).
[3] In the context of this paper, we define the term NOVEL DEVICE as follows: *All types of devices that go beyond desktop PCs, laptops and commonly used smart phones and tablet PCs. The latter refers to the tier of devices that is currently represented by* iPhone, iPad *and alike. Examples for novel devices are smart TVs, cutting-edge video game consoles and tabletops.*
[4] http://www.alexa.com/topsites (July 20, 2016).

key findings show that users are generally satisfied with search experience on desktop PCs and mobile devices. Yet, they are rather skeptical towards novel devices and input modalities beyond touch. Users prefer input via regular keyboards and touch while tendentially disapproving speech recognition and motion-sensing techniques for web search. From our findings, we derived eleven requirements for any existing or future search interface to support developers and designers. These requirements have been reviewed and verified by 12 dedicated experts. Since the underlying survey was conducted almost exclusively with German-speaking users, the key findings and requirements are only valid for that specific group, as cultural differences have to be considered.

In the following, we describe a representative selection of related research (Sec. 2) and introduce the underlying survey (Sec. 3), the findings of which are described in Sec. 4. Sec. 5 defines and validates REFOCUS, our new requirements specification, before giving concluding remarks in Sec. 6.

2. RELATED WORK

Purcell et al. (2012) have conducted a large-scale study with 2,253 participants to investigate general web search. Among their most significant results are the facts that 65% are against using information from previous searches for search result ranking, 73% are against personalized search results and 68% are against targeted advertising. Furthermore, 91% stated they always or most of the time find their desired information, search engines are perceived as an unbiased source of information by 66% and more than half of the participants said that search results had gotten better over time. Also, positive search experience is more common than negative, although 38% stated that they have had the experience of feeling overwhelmed.

Each year, the *Consortium of Public Broadcasters in Germany* carries out a representative survey on Internet usage. The main findings of the 2014 edition (ARD/ZDF, 2014) are that in Germany, the fraction of people who go online (at least occasionally) has grown to 79.1% among those aged 14 and older and that it is mainly used by male users between 14 and 49 years. Moreover, usage duration per day has been increasing to 166 minutes in 2014 with mobile surfing and video consumption gaining importance. They also report that nowadays novel devices such as video game consoles or TVs are becoming considerable access points to the Internet. Some more detailed findings of this survey will be given along our own results.

While there has already been a considerable amount of research on mobile search (e.g., Carrascal and Church, 2015; Church and Oliver, 2011; Cui and Roto, 2008; Kamvar et al., 2009), the field of web search on novel devices is still in the early stages of development. For example, using a current search engine with novel input devices such as a video game controller still requires the use of an on-screen keyboard, which is highly cumbersome. Rather, interfaces should be provided that are tailored to the available input modalities, e.g., motion-sensing cameras or methods for voice recognition. Particularly *Apple* and *Google* have taken significant steps into the direction of leveraging speech as a new input modality for web search[5]. Other research has focused on the usage of Microsoft's *Kinect* (Liebling and Morris, 2012; Nebeling et al., 2014), 3D interfaces (Wiza et al., 2004), graspable interfaces (Keck et al., 2014) and image input (Both et al., 2014). Moreover, Wilson et al. (2010) evaluated existing search systems and provide a taxonomy intended for developers of future search interfaces.

Hearst (2011) points out four important trends that will drive future search interfaces. First, voice input will gain importance, as speaking is a more natural input technique than typing. Second, queries will become more natural language–like. Third, consumption of video content will increase, as it is less mentally demanding compared to reading. Fourth, social and collaborative search will gain importance and will be facilitated even across devices by frameworks. In general, Hearst predicts that search interfaces will become more natural.

All of these are promising research approaches with respect to the development of future search interfaces. Yet, a thorough investigation of the *user's perspective* is still missing. Also, there exist no *general requirements* that cover both, current *and* future search interfaces. For instance, Purcell et al. (2012) perform an empirical analysis of general web search but do not focus on different kinds of devices or interfaces while Wilson et al. (2010)—in their taxonomy for developers of future search interfaces—do not focus on an empirical analysis of users' perceptions and usage of current search systems.

[5] http://www.apple.com/ios/siri/, https://www.google.com/search/about/features/01 (July 20, 2016).

3. SURVEY

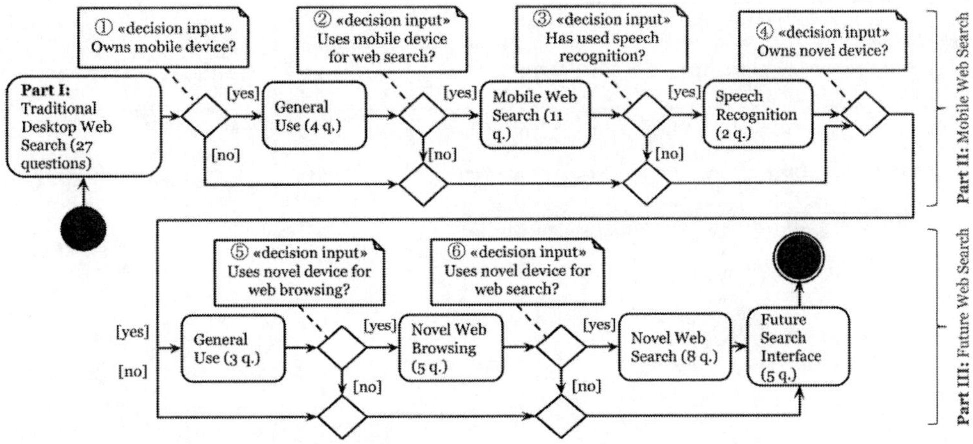

Figure 1. Flow chart of the survey with its different decision nodes. Questions for "no" answerers and demographic questions are omitted for simplicity

Our survey consisted of three main parts—*traditional desktop, mobile* and *future* web search—and a fourth part containing standard demographic questions (Fig. 1). This was necessary as we intend to provide a *general* set of requirements that spans the whole range from validating and revising existing search interfaces to supporting the development of new, "futuristic" ones. For answers expressing a frequency, likeliness or agreement with a given statement, we used 5-point Likert scales. We also posed a number of yes/no, multiple choice and open-ended questions. In total, the survey featured 98 questions of which 20 were optional.

The survey was prepared as a *Google Form* in German and English. Before publishing, it was revised by five experts from the search engine industry (one back-end developer, one front-end developer, one designer, one PhD student and one product manager). Participants were recruited through internal and external mailing lists, social networks and personal contact. Each participant who finished the survey received a thank-you gift in terms of a coupon worth 50 Euros for booking a trip on a German travel website. The complete survey and translated results are available via our online appendix at https://github.com/maxspeicher/ search-interface-requirements.

4. RESULTS

Overall, we collected 118 valid data sets. The participants (57.6% male, 42.4% female) had an average age of 29.8 years (σ=8.1) and were mainly German (N=103, 87.3%). Only seven participants (5.9%) stated they were not living in Germany. Furthermore, 114 participants (96.6%) stated they live in a German-speaking country. Hence, w.l.o.g. we assume that our results *refer to search interfaces for German-speaking users*. 23.7% of the participants were students, 55.1% had a formal qualification in computer science and 16.1% had one in web design (whereas only 1.7% stated they have a formal qualification in web design but none in computer science). 28.9% of the participants stated their work or studies are concerned with search engines. Due to the demographic structure of our test participants, ARD/ZDF (2014) will be the main source of comparison for our results (we consider the weighted average of the age groups 14–29 and 30–49), although it has to be considered that our audience was *more proficient than average*, which is reflected by the results. In general, our participants surfed the web for *more than 240 minutes (4 hours)* per day [ARD/ZDF (2014): 197 minutes], mainly for work (97.5%), news [75.4%, ARD/ZDF (2014): 55.2%], social networks (61.9%), shopping [41.5%, ARD/ZDF (2014): 18.6%] and videos [34.7%, ARD/ZDF (2014): 45.6%]. In the following, due to limited space, we are not able to provide in-depth results, but describe the ten key findings derived from participants' answers to our survey. From these findings we then derive the requirements specification that is the main contribution of this paper in Sec. 5. All results and qualitative feedback can be found in our online appendix.

Table 1. Main demographic properties of other studies we refer to

	Purcell et al. (2012)	ARD/ZDF (2014)	Church and Oliver (2011)	Our study
N	1,729*	1,814	18	118
Countries considered	U.S.	Germany	Multiple (Europe)	Multiple**
Languages	English, Spanish	German	English	German, English
Average age	n/a***	n/a***	29 (σ=7.7)	29.8 (σ=8.1)

* Internet users; ** 96.6% German-speaking; *** representative studies

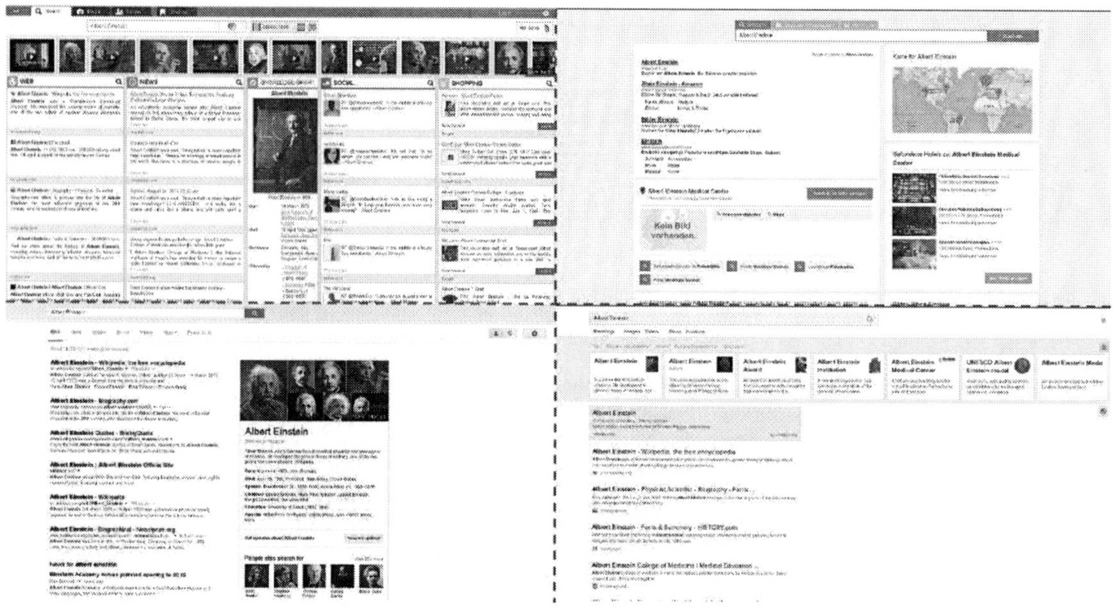

Figure 2. Clockwise from top left: *Qwant*, an experimental, non-public interface, *DuckDuckGo,* and *Google*

Finding 1. NUMBER OF CONSIDERED RESULTS PAGES. From two multiple-choice questions (I.10., I.11.)[6] we learned that in contrast to earlier research (e.g., Silverstein et al., 1998), users usually *do* consider pages beyond the first page of search results. If they still cannot find what they are looking for, they refine their search query rather than trying another search engine.

Finding 2. ADVERTISEMENTS. The results of six multiple-choice questions (I.4.–I.9.) show that users tolerate ads on SERPs if they are displayed in an unobtrusive way. Also, almost half of the users click on ads if they are helpful for their search. Our results indicate that acceptable numbers of ads are *two* above the search results and *five* elsewhere.

Finding 3. RESULTS PRESENTATION. From qualitative and quantitative assessments of different search engines (Fig. 2) by all 118 participants (I.13.–I.27), we found that users appreciate a clearly structured look & feel with a carefully balanced information density. They see advantages in the presentation of results from different domains, if they are relevant to their search query and not *just might* be of interest. Ditto for info boxes that answer queries directly on a SERP. Users tend to dislike scanning for information in two spatial dimensions at once (cf. Qwant.com).

Finding 4. MOBILE BROWSING. From 11 multiple-choice questions (II.5.–II.15.), we learned that mobile devices are widely accepted for web browsing and search. Also, users like to use familiar interfaces across devices, e.g., the Google *website* on mobile rather than a native app.

Finding 5. SPEECH RECOGNITION. Five multiple-choice questions (II.16.–II.20.) and additional qualitative feedback from 55 participants (46.6%) showed that in general, users are rather negative about speech recognition. Those who already used it are undecided about the importance of speech recognition in the

[6] These numbers refer to questions from our survey, which can be looked up at http://goo.gl/u7YvCv.

future. Those who have not yet used it primarily feel uncomfortable talking to a device (particularly in public) and have strong privacy concerns.

Finding 6. NOVEL BROWSING. Based on six multiple-choice questions and qualitative feedback (III.5.–III.8., III.21.–III.24.) from 53 participants (44.9%), we found that using a novel device for web browsing is not very common among users, which seems to be mainly due to the different use cases. Also, users are not satisfied with the available input modalities. Currently, there seems to be no alternative that can cope with the efficiency of regular keyboard input.

Finding 7. USE CASES. Qualitative feedback from 77 participants (65.3%) indicated that particularly, the majority of users see no reason for mixing different use cases. This is in line with ARD/ZDF (2014), who found that all-in-one devices are far from being the norm. About 30% of our participants owned at least three web-enabled devices. ARD/ZDF (2014) report an average of 5.4 web-enabled devices per household, of which, however, only 2.8 are used.

Finding 8. CREATURES OF HABIT. A total of 27 multiple-choice questions (e.g., II.7., II.22., III.18., III.21.) as well as qualitative feedback from 113 participants (95.8%) indicated that users prefer to use systems they already know. This accounts for interfaces (e.g., Google) as well as devices (e.g., keyboards, touchscreens).

Finding 9. POTENTIAL OF NOVEL SEARCH. From 22 multiple-choice questions and qualitative feedback (III.2.–III.28.) from 77 participants (65.3%), we learned that users generally acknowledge the potential of mobile and novel devices and input modalities for web search (and vice versa). Although our participants were generally satisfied with mobile search experience, they noticed plenty of room for improvement concerning search interfaces beyond desktop PCs. The latter particularly applies to interfaces for novel devices.

Finding 10. Based on qualitative feedback from 30 participants (25.4%), A FUTURE SEARCH INTERFACE realized in the midterm would involve *touch interaction*, *speech recognition* and *familiar technology* that is deployed *across devices*. For example, the Google search, running on a Smart TV that accepts gesture and keyboard input from an iPad. At home, the distributed search interface would be augmented with optional voice input. In public, the interface would be available via a single mobile device.

5. REFOCUS: REQUIREMENTS SPECIFICATION

In the following, we present a first draft of *REFOCUS*—our novel set of general requirements, which is directly inferred from the findings of the exploratory study above. Yet, to guarantee the generality of the proposed requirements (w.r.t. German-speaking users) as well as their validity for current and future search interfaces, we had them reviewed by 12 experts working in the search engine industry. This happened following the *find–fix–verify* pattern by Bernstein et al. (2010), however, with a combined *fix–verify* phase.

5.1 Intermediate Results (*Find* Phase)

Current and future search interfaces for German-speaking users should (information in square brackets refers to the validation from Sec. 5.2):

1. *Finding 1* → provide adequate ranking also for results beyond the initial viewports. If the user cannot find what they are looking for, proper related search inputs should be proposed. [*U*niversally valid]
2. *Finding 2* → provide ads in a subtle way. They should accompany the search results rather than demanding their space in the initial viewport. If ads are placed above results, their number should not exceed *two*; if they are placed elsewhere, their number should not exceed *five*. [*C*urrent search interfaces]
3. *Finding 3* → above all ensure that all displayed information is relevant to the search query. The most relevant piece of information should be immediately identifiable, as form follows function. If applicable, semantic results should answer the query directly in the initial viewport. [*U*]
4. *Findings 3, 8* → not require the user to scan information in more than one spatial dimension simultaneously. Different categories of results should be selectable rather than displaying all information at once. [*U*]

5. *Findings 3, 9* → make proper use of the available space, particularly with respect to increasing display sizes. [*U*]
6. *Findings 4, 6, 8* → leverage the advantages of interfaces familiar to the user. Transition to radically new concepts should happen in small steps. Fallback functionality for legacy input/output modalities should be provided. [*U*]
7. *Findings 5, 6, 8* → always provide an easily reachable alternative to voice input. Users should be properly informed about privacy issues and where it is unproblematic to use speech recognition. [*U*]
8. *Findings 6, 7* → be tailored to the target audience of the devices they run on. For instance, a web-enabled video game console should provide a search interface that focuses on finding games and information relevant to those. Furthermore, it must be optimized for efficient input with the same device as is used for playing. [*U*]
9. *Findings 9, 10* → support cross-device interaction, i.e., the search interface is distributed and input/output can optionally happen on different devices. [*F*uture search interfaces]
10. *Findings 9, 10* → be ubiquitous, thus focusing on devices users carry around most of the time. These include, but are not restricted to, mobile devices, devices like Google Glass and fitness bracelets. [*F*]
11. *Finding 10* → consider input/output formats other than text, such as images, music, gestures, 3D visualizations and image-based zoomable user interfaces. [*F*]

5.2 Reviewed & Validated Requirements (*Fix–Verify* Phase)

The above intermediate results were given to 12 dedicated experts in fields related to the development of search engines and corresponding interfaces. Nine of them worked in academia, two worked in industry and one in both. Four considered themselves to be a practitioner, one to be a researcher and seven said "half/half". 11 were male (one female) at an average age of 29.7 (σ=3.70), with 11 coming from Germany and one from Spain (but living in Germany). Seven experts owned a Master's, one a Bachelor's and one a PhD degree; three said "other" (e.g., the German *Diplom,* which is equal to a Master's degree).

Table 2. Experts' ratings of the set of requirements concerning their validity for different types of search interfaces

Requirement	Universally valid	Current search only	Future search only
R1	11	0	1
R2	6	6	0
R3	10	1	1
R4	9	2	1
R5	10	0	2
R6	10	2	0
R7	7	1	4
R8	7	3	2
R9	6	0	6
R10	3	1	8
R11	5	0	7

They were first instructed to thoroughly read the detailed results of the empirical study as well as the ten key findings. After that, each expert was asked to review the set of requirements and for each one indicate whether it is (1) universally valid, (2) valid only for current search interfaces or (3) valid only for future search interfaces. Also, they had to indicate whether the requirement should be removed, should stay in its current form or needs adjustments. If they indicated the requirement should be altered, they had to state how.

The experts found seven requirements to be universally valid (*U*), one to be valid only for current search interfaces (*C*) and three to be valid only for future search interfaces (*F*). This was determined by majority vote (>6) and is summarized in Tab. 2 and moreover indicated in the list above in square brackets. In the cases of R2 and R9, six votes sufficed for "current search only" and "future search only", respectively, because votes for "universally valid" implicitly count towards those as well.

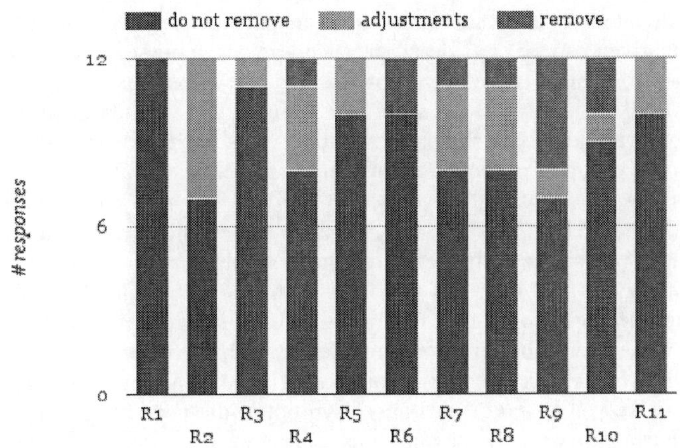

Figure 3. Experts' votes concerning whether requirements should be adjusted or not

As for the adjustment of requirements, we defined the following rule beforehand: If the majority of experts (>6) vote for revising a requirement and at least two experts propose the same adjustment, the requirement will be changed accordingly. Yet, the number of votes for "adjustments" did not exceed the threshold of six for any of the requirements. Besides, regarding the adjustments that were proposed, none was requested by more than one expert. Hence, the set of requirements named REFOCUS can be considered valid in their current form w.r.t. the respective type(s) of interface(s)—universal, current or future.

When looking at the final set of requirements, one could argue that they are formulated in a rather vague way and contain recommendations that are well-known and have been long established. At this point, we want to note that the intention of our *exploratory* study was to provide a set of requirements that are of a *general* nature and *agnostic* w.r.t. devices and input/output modalities. This implies that our requirements have to be formulated in a non-specific way. Hence, they should be seen as a mixture of existing (which are re-validated by our study) and novel findings (which pave the path towards future search interfaces).

The complete survey and detailed results for the above follow-up expert study can be found in our online appendix.

6. DISCUSSION & CONCLUSIONS

We have reported on the results of an exploratory user study involving 118 participants. The underlying survey was—to the best of our knowledge—the first to be concerned with use and perception of and expectations towards current *and* future search interfaces. Our results show that users are generally satisfied with the current state of desktop and mobile search, but are skeptical towards novel devices beyond mobile when it comes to web search. Also, keyboard and touch input are preferred over new input modalities such as speech recognition and motion-sensing technology. This is mainly due to users sticking to interfaces and technologies they are familiar with. From our ten key findings, we were able to deduce *REFOCUS*—a novel 11-point *requirements specification for current and future search interfaces for German-speaking users*, which is particularly intended for search engine developers and designers and in an additional step has been reviewed and validated by 12 experts.

The results of our exploratory study give a good impression of how users perceive current search interfaces as well as established and emerging technologies for web browsing. During analysis, it turned out that results became more and more *qualitative* as the survey progressed from the "Traditional Desktop Web Search" to the "Future Web Search" part. This was the case due to the investigated technologies becoming more and more advanced, which meant that the corresponding questions were applicable only to a thinning fraction of our participants. On the one hand, a main reason for this was the relatively small size of our overall sample (N=118). Yet, our audience shows demographic structures that are partly similar to established surveys (e.g., ARD/ZDF, 2014). On the other hand, it reflects the fact that novel technologies for web search have not yet arrived to take their place at the center of society. Also, this gave us the opportunity to more thoroughly review individual opinions regarding novel technologies and approaches to web search.

This has proven valuable for understanding users' expectations towards future search interfaces. The qualitative statements given can be considered profound as our audience was *more proficient* in web design and search technology than the average user. However, as part of our future work, we intend to carry out the survey with a larger audience at a later point in time to investigate trends in web browsing/search on novel devices. Moreover, we want to extend the part on future web search and consider it in isolation with an even more specifically chosen group of participants for a more quantitative analysis.

To conclude this paper, we want to give a *vision of the future of search interfaces*. In an open-ended question, we asked the participants of our study to share their visions of a potential search interface of the future. Combining their responses, a future search interface realized in the long term would be *ubiquitous*, involving *devices such as Google Glass* as well as *eye tracking*. Interfaces would be directly projected into the user's field of view. *Image input* (e.g., Both et al., 2014) would be possible by simply focusing things. Optimally, such interfaces would be further augmented by *brain–computer* interaction technology (cf. del R. Millan, 2006). Imagine yourself lying on your couch wearing your augmented reality glasses. On TV you see an interesting building, so you look at the "Pause" symbol in the top-left corner of your field of view. Your TV stops and by focusing it, your glasses automatically perform a search for more information about the building. The results are visualized in 3D right in your living room. They are sorted by date on the X axis, by popularity on the Y axis and by type (image, news, blog etc.) on the Z axis. By focusing different parts of the visualization you zoom into and explore the results and finally learn that the interesting building is the famous Sagrada Família in Barcelona, which has to be completed yet.

ACKNOWLEDGEMENT

Many thanks go to all survey participants! We also thank F. Funke, C. Lemke, S. Nitsch, M. Röder and S. Schattenberg for their help with creating the survey. This work has been supported by the ESF and the Free State of Saxony.

Gefördert aus Mitteln der Europäischen Union

Europa fördert Sachsen.
ESF
Europäischer Sozialfonds

REFERENCES

ARD/ZDF, 2014. *ARD/ZDF-Onlinestudie 2014 [Survey on Internet Usage in 2014 by ARD/ZDF]*. http://www.ard-zdf-onlinestudie.de/ (accessed September 19, 2014).

Bernstein, M. S. et al., 2010. Soylent: A Word Processor with a Crowd Inside. *Proc. UIST.*

Both, A. et al., 2014. Get Inspired: A Visual Divide and Conquer Approach for Motive-based Search Scenarios. *Proc. 13th Intl. Conf. WWW/Internet.*

Carrascal, J. P. and Church, K., 2015. An In-Situ Study of Mobile App & Mobile Search Interactions. *Proc. CHI.*

Church, K. and Oliver, N., 2011. Understanding Mobile Web and Mobile Search Use in Today's Dynamic Mobile Landscape. *Proc. MobileHCI.*

Cui, Y. and Roto, V., 2008. How People Use the Web on Mobile Devices. *Proc. WWW.*

Hearst, M. A., 2011. 'Natural' Search User Interfaces. *In Commun. ACM,* Vol. 54, No. 11, pp. 60–67.

Kamvar, M. et al., 2009. Computers and iPhones and Mobile Phones, oh my! A logs-based comparison of search users on different devices. *Proc. WWW.*

Keck, M. et al., 2014. Revisiting Graspable User Interfaces. *Proc. DUXU.*

Liebling, D. and Morris, M. R. (2012). Kinected Browser: Depth Camera Interaction for the Web. *Proc. ITS.*

del R. Millán, J., 2006. Brain-computer Interaction. *Proc. UIST.*

Nebeling, M. et al., 2014. XDKinect: Development Framework for Cross-device Interaction Using Kinect. *Proc. EICS.*

Purcell, K. et al., 2012. *Search Engine Use 2012.* http://www.pewinternet.org/2012/03/09/search-engine-use-2012/ (accessed March 11, 2016).

Silverstein, C. et al., 1998. *Analysis of a Very Large AltaVista Query Log*. Technical report 1998-014, Systems Research Center, Compaq Computer Corporation.

Weber, I. and Jaimes, A., 2011. Who Uses Web Search for What? And How? *Proc. WSDM.*

Wilson, M. L. et al., 2010. From Keyword Search to Exploration: Designing Future Search Interfaces for the Web. *In Found. Trends Web Sci.,* Vol. 2, No. 1, pp. 1–97.

MICROSCOPIC APPROACH FOR EXPERIMENTAL ANALYSIS OF MULTIPATH TCP THROUGHPUT UNDER INSUFFICIENT SEND/RECEIVE SOCKET BUFFERS

Toshihiko Kato[1) 2)], Masaaki Tenjin[1)], Ryo Yamamoto[1)], Satoshi Ohzahata[1)] and Hiroyuki Shinbo[2)]
[1)] *University of Electro-Communications, 1-5-1, Chofugaoka, Chofu, Tokyo 182-8585, Japan*
[2)] *Advanced Telecommunications Research Institute International, 2-2-2 Hikaridai Seika-cho, Sorakugun, Kyoto 619-0288, Japan*

ABSTRACT

Recently, the multipath transport protocol such as Multipath TCP becomes increasingly important. It allows more than one subflow TCP connections via different paths to compose one multipath connection. However, it has some problems when subflows are established with different delays. Especially, the limited buffer space at either sender or receiver may degrade the throughput due to head-of-line blocking. Although there are several studies focusing on the Multipath TCP under insufficient buffer size, they only use macroscopic performance metrics, such as average throughput, and they mainly focus on receiver side buffer. This paper shows the results of detailed microscopic analysis on how insufficient send/receive socket buffers give impacts on Multipath TCP throughput. The results indicate that insufficient send buffer reduces the throughput more than the receive buffer by introducing time gaps caused by retransmissions.

KEYWORDS

Multipath TCP, Send/Receive Socket Buffer, Head-of-Line Blocking, Opportunistic Retransmission

1. INTRODUCTION

Resulting from the wide spread of multi-homed devices, the multipath transport protocols become increasingly important. They use multiple connectivity with the Internet and provide high performance data transfer and flexibility of connecting points to the Internet. Among them, Multipath TCP (MPTCP) is widely recognized and installed in personal computers and smart phones/tablets. MPTCP is defined in three RFC documents by Internet Engineering Task Force. RFC 6182 [Ford, A., et al., 2011] outlines architecture guidelines for developing MPTCP protocols, by discussing the high level design decisions on selecting the protocol functions from multiple candidates. RFC 6824 [Ford, A., et al., 2013] presents the details of extensions to the traditional TCP to support multipath operation. It defines the MPTCP control information realized as new TCP options, and the MPTCP protocol procedures for the initiation and association of subflows (TCP connections associated with an MPTCP connection), the data transfer and acknowledgment over multiple subflows, and the closing MPTCP connection. RFC 6356 [Raiciu, C., et al., 2011] presents a congestion control algorithm that couples the congestion control algorithms running on different subflows.

MPTCP has some problems when subflows are established over heterogeneous paths with different delays, such as Wireless LAN and 3G/4G mobile network. Such a heterogeneous network environment will be more critical in the future 5G mobile network where multiple communication paths provided multiple network operators are commonly involved [NGMN Alliance, 2015]. The acknowledgment from a path with longer delay returns later than that from a shorter delay, and this causes a head-of-line (HoL) blocking, in which a data segment over a longer delay subflow blocks the window sliding while waiting for the acknowledgment [Scharf, M. and Kiesel, S., 2006]. In order to avoid it, MPTCP uses the subflow penalization [Raiciu, C., et al., 2012] which decreases the congestion window for a subflow with long delay, and the increasing of out-of-order buffer in a receiver side. This means that the HoL blocking becomes worse if a receiver has a limited size of receive socket buffer. There are several reports on the impacts of the receive socket buffer on the throughput of MPTCP [Raiciu, C., et al., 2012], [Paasch, C., et al., 2013], [Ferlin, S., et al., 2014].

Besides them, it is mentioned that the MPTCP throughput is also affected by the scheduler which decides how to transfer data over multiple subflows. The default scheduler of the current version of MPTCP, called *minRTT*, is based on round-trip time (RTT) [Paasch, O., et al., 2014]. It uses a subflow with the lowest RTT continuously until filling its congestion window. When one of the subflows blocks the data transfer due to the HoL blocking, minRTT scheduler retransmits the blocked segments over the lowest RTT subflow and penalizes the higher RTT subflow causing the blocking. The results of performance evaluation are shown for the minRTT, round robin based, and random based schedulers [Paasch, O., et al., 2014], [Arzani, B., et al., 2014]. There is a proposal of a new scheduler called BLEST (BLocking ESTimation based scheduler), which estimates whether a subflow will cause HoL blocking and dynamically adapts scheduling to prevent blocking [Ferlin, S., et al., 2016].

Although those studies give new findings and proposals, they have some flaws from the viewpoint of performance evaluation. First, all of them use only macroscopic performance metrics. For example, they use the average goodput for a file transfer, or the completion time for a web access. They do not discuss the detailed performance analysis. Secondly, they mainly focus only on the receive socket buffer size. But the send socket buffer size also gives impacts on the TCP throughput. While a few papers discuss on the impacts of the send socket buffer size [Arzani, B., et al., 2014], [Ferlin, S., et al., 2016], [Yang, F., and Amer, P., 2013], we believe that more discussions are necessary.

Based on these considerations, this paper presents the results of detailed microscopic analysis on experiments where two hosts are connected via two links with heterogeneous delay and either send or receive socket buffer size is limited. We analyze the data transfer not only over individual TCP subflows but also over an MPTCP connection. As a microscopic analysis, we conduct two kind of performance evaluations. One is to check the time variation of performance metrics such as the throughput for individual subflows. The other is to analyze the sequence and acknowledgment numbers used in both subflows and MPTCP connections. As a result, we point out that insufficient send socket buffer degrades the MPTCP throughput more than insufficient receive socket buffer.

The rest of this paper consists of the following sections. Section 2 introduces the overview of MPTCP. Section 3 describes the experimental settings. Section 4 describes the detailed results of the performance evaluations. In the end, Section 5 gives the conclusions of this paper.

2. OVERVIEW OF MULTIPATH TCP

2.1 MPTCP Connections and Subflows

As described in Figure 1, the MPTCP module is located on top of TCP. MPTCP is designed so that the conventional applications do not need to care about the existence of MPTCP. MPTCP establishes an *MPTCP connection* which is associated with two or more regular TCP connections called *subflows*. The management and data transfer over an MPTCP connection is done by newly introduced TCP options for MPTCP operation.

Figure 2 shows an example of MPTCP connection establishment where host A with two network interfaces invokes this sequence for host B with one network interface. In the beginning, host A sends a SYN segment to host B with a *Multipath Capable (MP_CAPABLE)* TCP option. This option indicates that the initiator supports the MPTCP functions and requests to use them in this TCP connection. It contains host A's *Key* (64 bits) used by this MPTCP connection. Then, host B replies a SYN+ACK segment with MP_CAPABLE option with host B's Key. This reply means that host B accepts the use of MPTCP functions. In the end, host A sends an ACK segment with MP_CAPABLE option including both A's and B's Keys. Through this three-way handshake procedure, the first subflow and the MPTCP connection are established.

Next, host A tries to establish the second subflow through another network interface. In the first SYN segment in this try, another TCP option called a *Join Connection (MP_JOIN)* option is used. An MP_JOIN option contains the receiver's *Token* (32 bits) and the sender's *Nonce* (random number, 32 bit length). A Token is an information to identify the MPTCP connection to be joined. It is obtained by taking the most significant 32 bits from the SHA-1 hash value for the receiver's Key (host B's Key in this example). Then, host B replies a SYN+ACK segment with MP_JOIN option. In this case, MP_JOIN option contains the random number of host B and the leftmost 64 bits of the Hash-based Message Authentication Code (HMAC). An HMAC value is calculated for the nonces generated by hosts A and B using the Keys of A and B. In the third ACK segment, host A sends an MP_JOIN option containing host A's full HMAC value (160 bits). In the end, host B acknowledges the third ACK segment. Using these sequence, the newly established subflow is associated with the MPTCP connection.

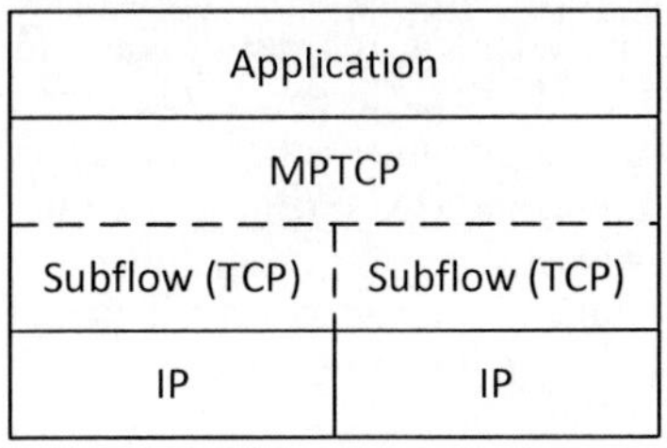

Figure 1. Layer structure for MPTCP

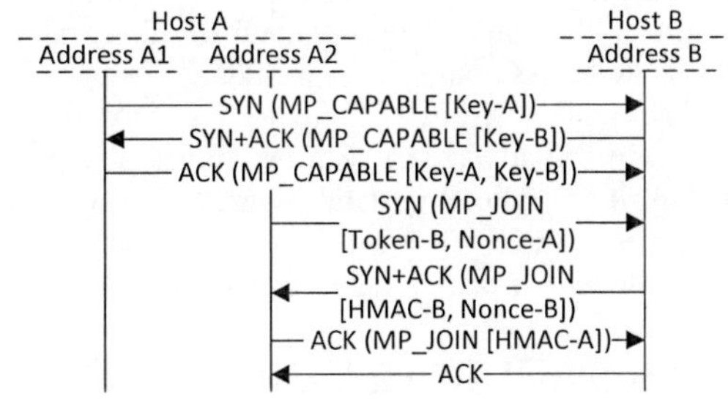

Figure 2. Example of MPTCP connection establishment

2.2 Data Transfer

An MPTCP implementation will take one input data stream from an application, and split it into one or more subflows, with sufficient control information to allow it to be reassembled and delivered reliably and in order to the receiver side application. The MPTCP connection level maintains the *data sequence number* independent of the subflow level sequence numbers. The data and ACK segments used in a subflow may contain a *Data Sequence Signal (DSS)* option depicted in Figure 3.

The data sequence number and data ACK is 4 or 8 byte long, depending on the flags in the option. The number is assigned on a byte-by-byte basis similarly with the TCP sequence number. The value of data sequence number is the number assigned to the first byte conveyed in that TCP segment. The data sequence number, subflow sequence number (relative value) and data-level length define the mapping between the MPTCP connection level and the subflow level. The data ACK is analogous to the behavior of the standard TCP cumulative ACK. It specifies the next data sequence number a sender expects to receive.

We need to say that there is no window size field in the DSS option. Instead, the window size contained in the TCP header is used for the flow control in MPTCP. That is, the flow control is performed for the data sequence number at the MPTCP connection level as well as the subflow level. The control for the data sequence number is done in a way that the data sequence number is not more than the data ACK plus the window size. It is also required that the upper window edge in the MPTCP connection level (the data ACK plus the window size) does not shrink.

In order to fully utilize the capacity of all subflows, a receiver needs to provide enough buffer space so that a sender can keep all subflows fully utilized, even in the event of reordering due to delay differences or packet losses. MPTCP recommends that the receive socket buffer size is :

$$\text{Buffer size} = \sum_{i}^{n} bw_i \times RTT_{max} \times 2 \qquad (1)$$

where n is the number of subflows, $bw_i$is the bandwidth of subflow i, and $RTT_{max}$is the highest RTT among all subflows. This formula means that an MPTCP connection can send data segments at full speed during the highest RTT, even if a loss event occurs.

Kind (= 30)	Length	Subtype (= 2)	Flags
Data ACK (4 or 8 octets, depending on flags)			
Data sequence number (4 or 8 octets, depending on flags)			
Subflow sequence number (4 octets)			
Data-level length (2 octets)		Checksum (2 octets)	

Figure 3. Data Sequence Signal option

As mentioned above, multiple schedulers are implemented or proposed. The current version of MPTCP implementation for Linux operating system (MPTCP v0.90 Release) supports the default scheduler, minRTT, and the round robin scheduler [icteam, 2016]. The minRTT scheduler will first send data on subflows with the lowest RTT until their congestion window is full. Then, it will start transmitting on the subflows with the next higher RTT. The round robin scheduler will transmit traffic in a round-robin fashion.

As also stated above, the minRTT scheduler adopts the opportunistic retransmission and penalization mechanism [Raiciu, C., et al., 2012] in order to compensate for delay differences. Consider the situation where a subflow has sufficient congestion window to send more data segments but where there is no more space in the advertised window and it is required to wait for the acknowledgment for sent data in order to transmit the following data segments. The opportunistic retransmission re-sends some unacknowledged data segments which were sent over higher RTT using a subflow with the lowest RTT. At the same time, the subflow which occurred a HoL blocking is punished by halving its congestion window.

2.3 Related Work on MPTCP Performance Evaluation

As mentioned in Section 1, the papers on MPTCP performance evaluation use only the *macroscopic* metrics such as an average throughput during 60 second bulk data transfer. This trend might come from the work by C. Paasch, et al. which applied the *experimental design* approach to MPTCP performance evaluation [Paasch, C., et al., 2013]. The experimental design is an approach for complex systems influenced by controllable and uncontrollable factors. They say that the performance of MPTCP is influenced by various factors, such as bandwidth limitation, delay, packet losses and memory constraints. So they conducted many experiment runs by changing values of factors and checked the average and distribution of obtained macroscopic metrics.

We believe that, however, MPTCP has the clearly defined protocol rules and heuristics. Although they are complicated, it is possible to follow the MPTCP connection level sequence by tracing the data sequence number and data ACK, and to estimate the MPTCP scheduling by maintaining the mapping between data sequence number and subflow TCP sequence number. In this paper, we apply a detailed *microscopic* approach to the MPTCP performance evaluation.

3. EXPERIMENTAL SETTINGS

In this paper, we focus on the influence of insufficient send/receive socket buffer on MPTCP throughput. In the case of single TCP connection, the send and receive buffers effect the TCP throughput independently, and so we designed the following experimental setting.

- Data sender and receiver connected through two path, one of which provides larger propagation delay.
- The sizes of send and receive socket buffers are set independently.
- In order to avoid the effect of congestion control, no transmission errors are inserted.

Figure 4 shows the configuration of our experiment. Two hosts running the Linux operating system, data sender and receiver, are connected together through two 1Gbps Ethernet links. The private IP addresses are assigned as shown in the figure. In one Ethernet link, a network emulator is inserted in order to 25 msec propagation delay in both directions. So, RTT of the path between 192.168.2.2 and 192.168.2.1 is around 50 msec. Although the physical data rate is 1Gbps, the frame transmission speed is limited to 100 Mbps using Linux traffic control (`tc`) command. The sender and receiver run MPTCP Linux implementation version 0.90 release. We establish one MPTCP connection between two hosts with two subflows, one between 192.168.2.2 and 192.168.2.1 (we call *slow subflow*) and the other between 192.168.1.2 and 192.168.1.1 (we call *fast subflow*). The scheduler is the default one, minRTT.

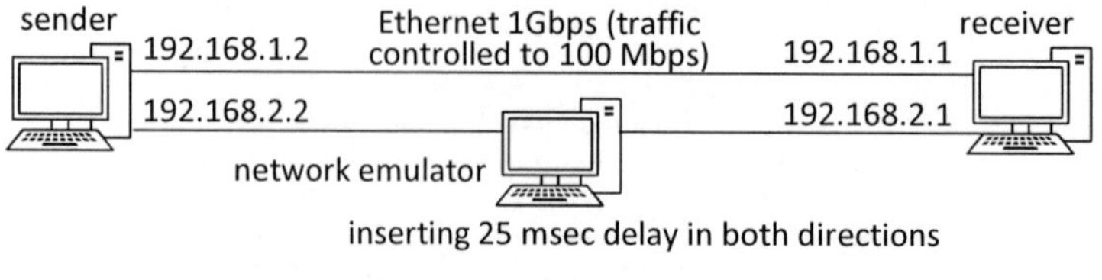

Figure 4. Configuration of experiment

In the performance evaluation, iperf is used in both hosts and bulk data transfer is executed for 10 seconds. During the bulk data transfer, packet traces are collected at the sender side by use of tcpdump. Those traces are examined in detail with Wireshark [Wireshark, 2016], a network protocol analyzer whose version 1.7.1 and after can analyze the MPTCP options.

In the experiments, we change the send socket buffer size at the sender and the receive socket buffer size at the receiver separately, as shown in Table. 1. In the evaluation by changing the send buffer size, 200 Kbyte, 400 Kbyte, 800 Kbyte and 1.6 Mbyte are used as the size of send socket buffer at the sender. At the receiver, the default socket buffer size is used. In the evaluation by changing the receive buffer, the send socket buffer at the sender takes the default setting, and the receive socket buffer at the receiver takes 200 Kbyte, 400 Kbyte, 800 Kbyte and 1.6 Mbyte. It should be noted that the recommended buffer size in our experiment setting is 2.5 Mbyte, which is calculated using Formula (1).

In TCP, the send/receive socket buffer size is managed by the auto tuning [Fisk, M. and Feng, W., 2001]. That is, the socket buffer size is dynamically changed according to the network bandwidth, RTT and so on. In order to set the socket buffer size to a specific value in our experiment, the Linux `sysctl` command is used for setting `net.ipv4.tcp_wmem/rmem` and `net.core.wmem/rmem` variables to that value.

Table 1. Setting of send/receive socket buffers

(a) Changing send buffer size

Send buf at sender	200KB	400KB	800KB	1.6MB
Recv buf at receiver	default			

(b) Changing receive buffer size

Send buf at sender	default			
Recv buf at receiver	200KB	400KB	800KB	1.6MB

4. RESULTS OF PERFORMANCE EVALUATION

4.1 Overall Results

Table 2 shows the results of measuring the bulk data transfer throughput at the MPTCP connection level. Table 2(a) shows the results when we change the send socket buffer size at the sender, and (b) shows the results for changing the receive socket buffer size at the receiver. From the results, insufficient send and receive socket buffers give different impacts on the MPTCP connection level throughput. Specifically, when the send socket buffer size is small at the sender, such as 200 Kbyte and 400 Kbyte, the throughput is around 100 Mbps, which corresponds to the bandwidth of the fast subflow. When the send socket buffer size increasesr, such as 800 Kbyte, the MPTCP connection level throughput decreases. After that, as the send socket buffer size becomes much larger, such as 1.6 Mbyte, the MPTCP connection level throughput recovers again. It should be mentioned that the send and receive socket buffer sizes are in the default setting, the measured MPTCP connection level throughput is 193 Mbps, which fully utilizes the total capacity of two subflows. On the other hand, when the receive socket buffer size increases from 200 Kbyte to 1.6 Mbyte, the MPTCP connection level throughput also increases. When the receive socket buffer size is 200 Kbyte or 400 Kbyte, the throughput is smaller than the case that the same buffer size setting is applied to the send socket buffer. When the buffer is size is 800 Kbyte or 1.6 Mbyte, however, the throughput when we change the receive buffer size increasesr than the case for changing the send buffer size.

Table 2. Results of MPTCP connection level throughput

(a) Changing send buffer size

Send buf size	200KB	400KB	800KB	1.6MB
Average throughput	99.2 Mbps	99.4 Mbps	49.8 Mbps	98.5 Mbps

(b) Changing receive buffer size

Recv buf size	200KB	400KB	800KB	1.6MB
Average throughput	74.0 Mbps	88.6 Mbps	103.0 Mbps	153.1 Mbps

4.2 Microscopic Analysis based on TCP/MPTCP Protocols

4.2.1 Time Variation of TCP throughput

Figure 5 shows the time variation of MPTCP connection level throughput, the throughput of the slow subflow, and that of the fast subflow, when we change the send socket buffer size at the sender. When the send buffer size is 200 Kbyte (Figure 5(a)), there is no data traffic over the slow subflow, and instead, the fast subflow utilizes its full capacity. The result is the same for the case that the send buffer size is 400 Kbyte. On the other hand, when the send buffer size is 800 Kbyte or 1.6 Mbyte (Figure 5(b) and (c)), the throughput of two subflows becomes similar. Especially, in the case of 800 Kbyte, the total is smaller than the bandwidth of one subflow.

Figure 6 shows the time variation of MPTCP throughput when changing the receive socket buffer size at the receiver. When the receive buffer size is 200 Kbyte (Figure 6(a)), there is no traffic over the slow subflow, and the throughput of the fast subflow is smaller than its bandwidth. The result is similar for the case of 400 Kbyte. When the receive buffer size is 800 Kbyte (Figure 6(b)), the fast subflow utilizes its capacity and there is a little data traffic over the slow subflow. When the receive buffer size is 1.6 Mbyte, the fast subflow fully utilizes its capacity and there is some data traffic over the slow subflow. From those results, we can suppose that, in the case of insufficient receive socket buffer size, the sender side MPTCP tries to transmit data segments over a faster subflow (lower delay in our case) with the limitation of advertised window, and if the faster subflow reaches its capacity, MPTCP uses a slower subflow for the rest of data traffic.

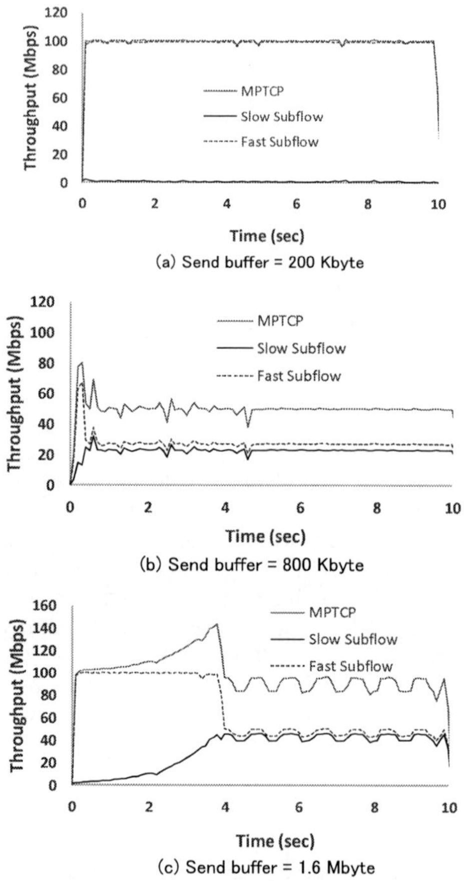

Figure 5. Time variation of throughput when changing send buffer size at sender

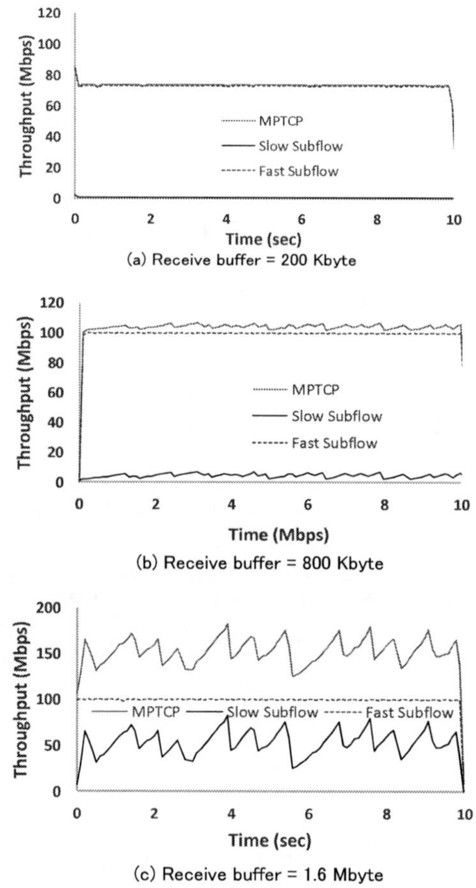

Figure 6. Time variation of throughput when changing receive buffer size at receiver

4.2.2 Analysis of Subflow Sequence Number and Data Sequence Number

Next, we examine closely what happens in the TCP and MPTCP protocols. We pick up the case that the send and receive socket buffer is set to 1.6 Mbyte respectively. From Figures 5(c) and 6(c), we select one second period from 4 sec to 5 sec, because we decide this period will represent a typical behavior in individual communication. Figure 7 shows the time variation of the data sequence number and the subflow TCP sequence numbers when the send socket buffer size is set to 1.6 Mbyte at the sender. The value of the data sequence number given in Figure 7(a) is obtained by Wireshark for two subflows and calculated as a relative number from the start of MPTCP connection. The subflow TCP sequence numbers given in Figure 7(b) are also relative values from the start of individual subflows. This figure says that the data transfer is intermittent in both the fast and slow subflows, and that the data retransmission is performed constantly at the MPTCP connection level, although there are no retransmissions at the subflow level. Figure 7 shows the time variation of the sequence numbers when the receive socket buffer size is 1.6 Mbyte at the receiver In this case, on the contrast with the insufficient send buffer case, the data transfer over the fast subflow is performed continuously while that over the slow subflow is intermittent. Besides, the number of retransmissions at the MPTCP connection level is much smaller than the insufficient send buffer case. During one second from 4 sec to 5 sec, the retransmissions occur only twice. From those figures, we can conclude that, in the case of insufficient send socket buffer, the fast and slow subflows provide similar throughput due to the intermittent data transfer. On the other hand, in the case of insufficient receive socket buffer, the fast subflows utilizes its capacity fully, but the throughput of the slow subflow is limited due to the intermittent data transfer.

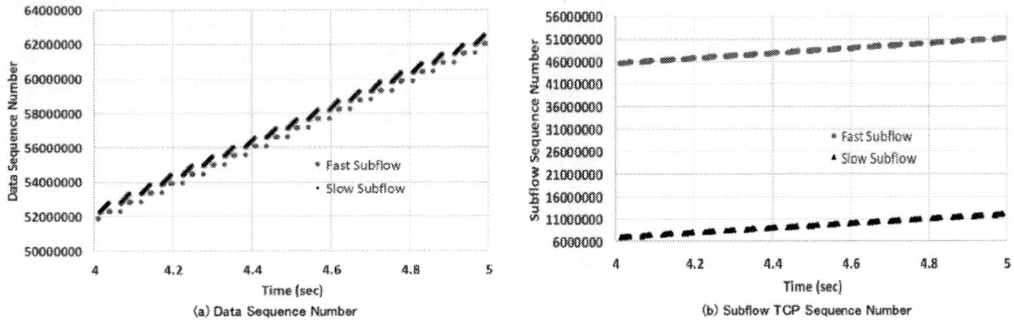

Figure 7. Time variation of data and subflow sequence numbers when send buffer size is 1.6 Mbyte at sender

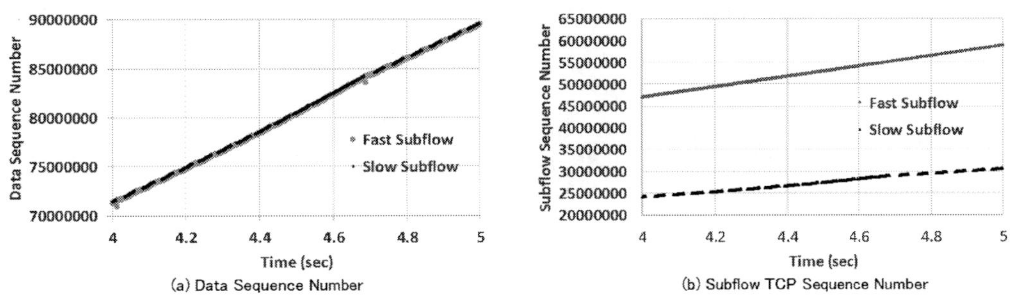

Figure 8. Time variation of data and subflow sequence numbers when receive buffer size is 1.6 Mbyte at receiver

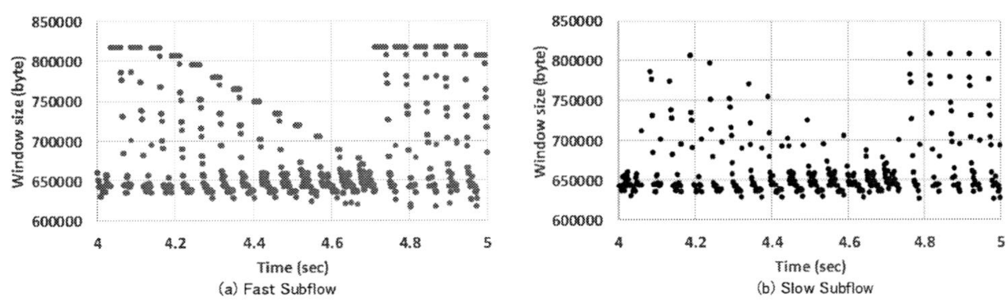

Figure 9. Time variation of window size when receive buffer size is 1.6 Mbyte at receiver

Figure 9 shows the time variation of the advertised window in the case of insufficient receive buffer size. Figures 9(a) and 9(b) show the window size in the TCP header of the fast and slow subflows, respectively. Both of them take a value between 600 Kbyte and 850 Kbyte. In this case, the receiver sets its receive socket buffer size to 1.6 Mbyte, and the number of subflows is two. As described in Subsection 2.2, the upper window edge in the MPTCP connection level must not shrink. So, the window sizes advertised by the fast and slow subflows need to share evenly this socket buffer. As a result, it is considered that the advertised window sizes are around half of 1.6 Mbyte. On the other hand, in the case of insufficient send socket buffer size, the advertised window size takes a value between 2.56 Mbyte and 2.59 Mbyte for both the fast and slow subflows. It should be noted this value corresponds to the recommended value we mentioned in Section 3.

In order to examine the retransmission at the MPTCP connection level, we analyze the behavior between 4.0 sec and 4.1 sec, in more detail. Figure 10 shows the correspondence between the MPTCP level data sequence number and data ACK used in the fast and slow subflows. In this figure, the gray circle and gray triangle indicate the data sequence number and the data ACK in the fast subflow, respectively. The black dash line and black triangle are for the slow subflow. As shown in Figure 10(a), there is a time gap (from 4.036 sec to 4.066 sec) in both fast and slow subflows for the case of insufficient send socket buffer. Just before this time gap, the fast subflow retransmits several data segments. Those segments were not sent over the fast subflow but sent over the slow subflow. In this sense, this retransmission seems to be an opportunistic retransmission. After the time gap, the transmission restarts by the retransmission over the fast subflow. This is also the retransmission of data segments sent over the slow subflow. The time gaps in both fast and slow subflows are repeated regularly from 4.0 sec to the end of data transfer, and become the reason for the throughput degradation.

On the other hand, in the case of insufficient receive socket buffer, the data transfer over the fast subflow continues without any time gaps, although there is one retransmission over the fast subflow (Figure 10(b)). The retransmitted data segment here was originally sent over the slow subflow, and so this is also an opportunistic retransmission. But in this case, the number of retransmissions is small and it seems that the retransmission does not impact on the throughput.

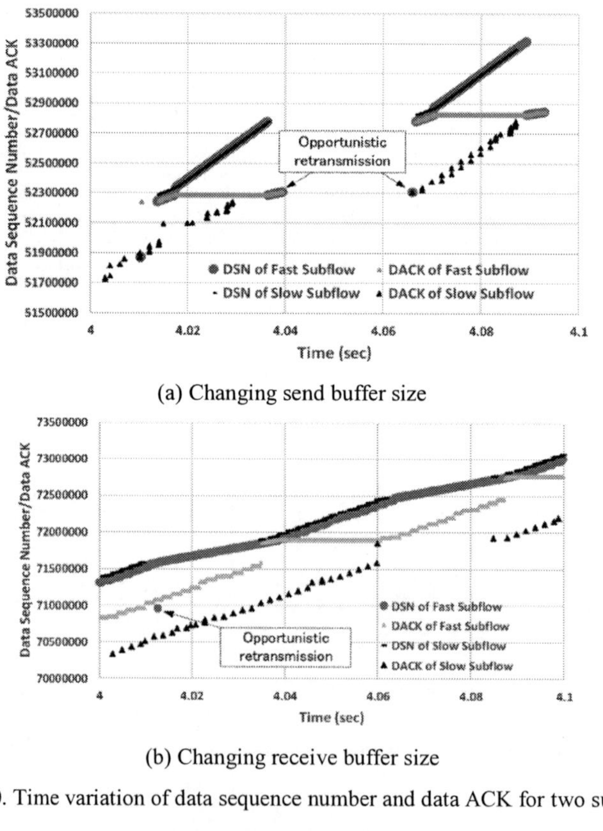

Figure 10. Time variation of data sequence number and data ACK for two subflows

In summary, when the receive socket buffer is limited at a receiver, the buffer size is shared among subflows and advertised to a sender by use of the TCP header. The sender will respond to this insufficient window size and try to provide as high throughput as possible. However, when the send socket buffer is limited and the window size is large, the sender might assign traffic evenly to fast and slow subflows.

5. CONCLUSIONS

This paper describes the results of analyzing how insufficient send and receive socket buffers give impacts to the MPTCP throughput. We conducted an experiment using two subflows with different delays and examined the collected packet traces by analyzing the parameters of TCP and MPTCP. We evaluated the time variation of subflow level throughput, and analyzed the sequence numbers of subflow level and MPTCP connection level. The results indicate that the MPTCP throughput is different for the cases of insufficient send and receive socket buffer. In the case of insufficient send buffer, the MPTCP level retransmissions occur repeatedly and they introduce intermittent data transfer. As a result, the throughput degradation is worse than the case of insufficient receive buffer. In order to point out the reason of these retransmissions, we need to investigation of MPTCP source program.

ACKNOWLEDGEMENT

This research was performed under the research contract of "Research and Development on control schemes for utilizations of multiple mobile communication networks," for the Ministry of Internal Affairs and Communications, Japan.

REFERENCES

Ford, A., et al., 2011. *Architectural Guidelines for Multipath TCP Development*. RFC 6182, IETF.

Ford, A., et al., 2013. *TCP Extensions for Multipath Operation with Multiple Addresses*. RFC 6824, IETF.

Raiciu, C., et al., 2011. *Coupled Congestion Control for Multipath Transport Protocols*. RFC 6356, IETF.

NGNM Alliance, 2015. *5G White Paper*. https://www.ngmn.org/uploads/media/NGMN_5G_White_Paper_V1_0.pdf, accessed Sept. 2016.

Scharf, M. and Kiesel, S., 2006. Head-of-Line Blocking in TCP and SCTP: Analysis and Measurements. *Proc. of IEEE GLOBECOM '06*, pp.1-5.

Raiciu, C., et al., 2012. How Hard Can It Be? Designing and Implementing a Deployable Multipath TCP. *Proc. of 9th USENIX Symposium on Networked Systems Design and Implementation (NSDI '12)*, pp.1-14.

Paasch, C., et al., 2013. On the Benefits of Applying Experimental Design to Improve Multipath TCP. *Proc. of 9th ACM Conference on Emerging Networking Experiments and Technologies (CoNEXT '13)*, pp.393-398.

Ferlin, S., et al., 2014. Multi-Path Transport over Heterogeneous Wireless Networks: Does it really pay off? *Proc. of IEEE GLOBECOM 2014, Wireless Networking Symposium*, pp.4807-4813.

Paasch, O., et al., 2014. Experimental Evaluation of Multipath TCP Schedulers. *Proc. of 2014 SIGCOMM Workshop on Capacity Sharing Workshop (CSWS '14)*, pp.27-32,

Arzani, B., et al., 2014. Impact of Path Characteristics and Scheduling Policies on MPTCP Performance. *Proc. of 28th International Conference on Advanced Information Networking and Applications Workshops*, pp.743-748,

Ferlin, S., et al., 2016. BLEST: Blocking Estimation-based MPTCP Scheduler for Heterogeneous Networks. *Proc. of IEEE IFIP Networking 2016*, pp.431-439.

Yang, F., and Amer, P., 2013. Non-Renegable Selective Acknowledgments (NR-SACKs) for MPTCP. *Proc. of 27th International Conference on Advanced Information Networking and Applications Workshops*, pp.1113-1118,

icteam, 2016. *MultiPath TCP –Linux Kernel implementation*. http://www.multipath-tcp.org/, accessed: July 2016.

Wireshark, 2016. *About Wireshark*. https://www.wireshark.org/, accessed: July 2016.

Fisk, M. and Feng, W., 2001. Dynamic Right-Sizing in TCP. *Proc. of Los Alamos Computer Science Institute Symposium*, pp.1-7.

STRATEGIES FOR ZERO-DOWNTIME RELEASES: A COMPARATIVE STUDY

Diego Quirino Silva, Everton Gomede and Rodolfo Miranda Barros
Universidade Estadual de Londrina
Londrina, Parana, Brazil

ABSTRACT

Adopting continuous delivery means facing new challenges: it requires, as one of the conditions, to manage continuous deployment of new versions or bug corrections. However, lack of planning may cause the system or service to be temporarily unavailable, and because of that approaches on how to decrease risks (or manage zero risk) are needed. This study presents a comparative analysis on the advantages and disadvantages of possible strategies, as well as a description of an approach believed to solve the unavailability problem.

KEYWORDS

Zero downtime, continuous delivery, virtualization

1. INTRODUCTION

The software development process includes several stages. The most critical is the delivery stage, from which the software truly begins to deliver value for the client.

However, by adopting the continuous delivery approach, which is the ability of delivering reliable and quality software at any time (Humble and Farley 2010), new challenges arise. One of them is related to the moment of providing users with the new application or update. This is usually a moment when errors can be made (even assuming tests were performed in previous steps) causing the application to be unavailable for minutes or even hours (worst scenario).

In a continuous delivery environment (Humble and Farley 2010) in which the application can be deployed several times a day, it would be acceptable to risk having it unavailable for the same number of times.

Such unavailability is known as downtime. An unavailable system or service, for whatever the reason, will impact on the corporation and its clients: in risk operation environments this can only be acceptable under SLA (Humble and Farley 2010), and it could still cause losses (Oracle 2015; Silva et al. 2009). According to (Humble and Farley 2010), zero downtime in continuous delivery is the ability to drive users between versions in an almost instantaneous way.

This study aims to present a comparative analysis on the strategies of migration downtime in the shortest possible time, or time equals zero. The transition from the previous to the latest version must be managed with minimal impact, and must be imperceptible to users, because when they face service unavailability the trust rating decreases ultimately resulting on giving up using the system.

The means to solve this problem include mitigation or elimination – the possible strategies are: blue-green deployment, canary release or, in last case, rollback (Humble and Farley 2010). Adopting one or more strategies may provide the corporations with the essential competitive differentiation.

This study is divided as: in Section 2 a theoretical foundation takes place in order to present the concepts; in Section 3 the approaches and possible strategies are described; in Section 4 the results of the comparative analysis and the strategies limitations are reported; and lastly, in Section 5, the conclusion and possibilities for future studies are presented.

2. THEORETICAL FOUNDATION AND RELATED STUDIES

Continuous delivery is the ability to create value from an internal or external idea, which means, in other words, having the software working in the shortest possible time (Akerele et al. 2013).

Continuous delivery brings many visible and tangible benefits. Authors (Neely and Stolt 2013; Chen 2015) stress that even in corporations working with an adequate software process structure, continuous delivery allows improvements.

Achieving continuous delivery demands more than the adoption of suggested practices and techniques – it requires an effort towards architecture planning and projecting, as well as understanding related costs. Once the project is defined, the environment becomes ready to continuous deployment, which must be a quality attribute (Bellomo et al 2014). Defining tactics in order to achieve this attribute is supported by (Bellomo et al 2014), who stresses that tactics must allow continuous integration, enable test automation, enable fast and solid operation deployment, and allow flexible and syncable environments.

Downtime sources: lack of control over changes in the production environment (Humble and Farley 2010), software aging causing degradation of the application over time, resulting in unavailability (Silva et al. 2009; Thein et al. 2008; Shetty et al. 2008).

Regarding the cons of downtime, a qualitative research conducted by (Oracle 2015) shares the following findings: 50% impact in interruption of IT businesses and services, 37% decrease in productivity, 34% negative impact on IT corporations, and 24% negative impact on businesses.

Hardware and/or software replication is one of the techniques applied in attempting to avoid downtime in high-availability environments; the way it is performed vary among the authors (Gavrilovska et al. 2002; Silva et al 2009; Thein et al. 2008; Shetty et al. 2008), but replication is always stated as the chosen method.

While choosing the strategy to mitigate downtime, it is necessary to consider the TCO (Total Cost Ownership) in order to define the best solution. This scale measures all the costs involved in software resources and the corporative infrastructure, from purchasing to disposal.

MTTR (Mean Time to Repair) is another indicator related to the time spent in order to repair something – an error or service unavailability. It is obtained by the total duration of failures divided by the total number of failures. E.g. MTTR = 180 min / 6 failures = 30 minutes (Agarwal et al. 2010).

The SLA (Service Level Agreement) is used to determine (in a contract) the level of obligation by which a service should remain available. It is mostly used in cloud computing, but it is not restricted to that, also being associated with telecommunication services, web services, or any other in which the client requires functioning assurance in a specified period of time (Stamou et al. 2013; Shu and Meina 2010).

TCO, MTTR, and SLA are extremely important because they allow the selection of the strategy to be adopted, as well as verify whether the results achieved meet what was initially planned.

2.1 ITIL

In order to be successful, corporations must make efforts and provide resources towards optimization. However, this is not a reality in all corporations, especially regarding the IT – which is underestimated and misunderstood, considered to be expensive and not a profitable activity.

This is due to the apparent detachment between IT and corporative goals, because many times the IT is not able to properly communicate the benefits of adopting a specific technology or the implementation of a new approach for given problems or market opportunities. This gives space for misunderstanding, or lack of understanding of those charged with the responsibility to carry out new plans.

In this context, the OGC (Office of Government Commerce) developed, in the 1980s, the first version of ITIL, which continued to be improved in the next few years, coming to its latest version (3) in 2007 (Esmaili et al. 2010).

ITIL (Information Technology Infrastructure Library) is a framework consisting of a collection of guidelines to design, implement, and maintain IT services. From the third version on, ITIL included 5 books that are core and cover the service lifecycle from beginning to end (Esmaili et al. 2010). The books are divided as: service strategy, service design, service transition, service operation, and continual service improvement.

The implementation of ITIL in a corporation allows the alignment of IT and the corporative strategic objectives (Esmaili et al. 2010), supporting high-level performance. Nevertheless, it is not an easy process, because even though ITIL provides the corporation with suitable guidelines, it does not present practical solutions – that being responsibility of each corporation.

2.1.1 Service Transition

From all ITIL framework books, service transition is the most suitable for the understanding of this study. Corporations seek to meet market requirements, which means transforming opportunities in profitable activities, while keeping regular users safe. Thus, it is important to define the basic procedures so that both opportunity and risk decrease come safely and effectively.

The service transition process accurately covers the aspects of status change from development to delivery (Eikebrokk and Iden 2012). This is important because most of the software products are considered to be services – some are essential – and they cannot stop working. Besides that, the service transition combines elements such as the release management and the project risk management, placing them in the context of service management.

With continuous delivery, improvement flows continuously as well as the transition between service versions, and adopting processes to make this technique successful becomes a necessity.

The basic processes for service transition, as described in ITIL framework are:

Transition planning and support: this process aims to plan and coordinate resources to assure the new function will meet what was pre-established in terms of cost, quality, and time; and ensure standardization of a reusable framework and provide comprehensible planning in order to clarify the plans of service transition (Service transition 2007).

Change management: aims to ensure the changes will be recorded and validated, authorized, prioritized, planned, tested, implemented, documented, and reviewed in order to be controlled (Service transition 2007).

Service asset and configuration management: defines and controls infrastructure service components and properly maintains configuration information (Service transition 2007).

Release and deployment management: allows the planning of deployment and release to be easily understood so that both clients and businesses can be aware of such changes; successfully reaches build, installation, and testing in the target environment according to the deadline; assures the deployed change is able to meet agreed requirements; assures minimal impact in actions of service, operation and support to the corporation; and assures clients, users, and the service management team are satisfied with the service transition (Service transition 2007).

Service validation and testing: aims to assure the release process will be trustful in the sense that new services reach results that meet the desired cost, capacity, and restriction values; aims to guarantee the delivered service meets expected performance levels; and to confirm the defined requirements of users and stakeholders are met, in order to avoid having corrections on deployed services (Service transition 2007).

Evaluation: aims to guarantee the intended changes in the service will meet agreed levels of corporative capacity, resources, and restrictions provided; provides good outcomes so that the change management can decide to approve and start performing the change (Service transition 2007).

3. ZERO-DOWNTIME STRATEGIES

For many corporations, the software is more than a service – it is the very condition of their existence, for instance: Netflix®, Google Doc®, and Home Broker of financial institutions. These corporations cannot face unavailability, because having a service interrupted can cause the satisfaction level of clients to decrease, as well as result in harmful financial trials.

As long as the failures take place in controlled environments, such as development or homologation, it is not a matter of concern. However, when these affect the client they must be reduced or eliminated, because it may decrease the user trust level.

Most of users hardly take service unavailability easily, because in same cases the services are fundamental, such as in financial or health care situations.

In order to mitigate or eliminate the service unavailability there are some strategies, such as the blue-green deployment and the canary release.

3.1 Blue-green Deployment

The blue-green strategy works with the commutation concept between production environments, namely blue and green, being that the new version is deployed in one of these environments, and the users' requests are redirected to them (Humble and Farley 2010), as shown in Figure 1.

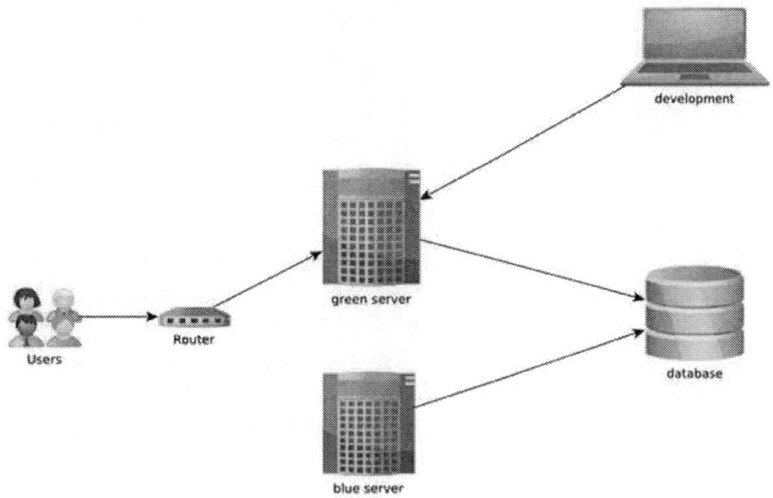

Figure 1. Blue-green deployment

During the deployment of the new version, failures do not affect clients, who will be in a different environment and protected from any side effect of the new version. Thus, the service is not interrupted, allowing the error source to be detected and corrected.

If the deployment happens as expected and does not face any obstacle, the clients are commuted to the new version through the router configuration, being able to start using it.

It is true that some errors can only be perceived in cases of system overload. In that case, if any service instability or degradation is reported after the clients' commutation to the blue environment, the switching process should be reverted to the previous version, avoiding the complete unavailability of the application.

Even in corporations with few resources this can be performed simply by setting the application to run (at the same time and independently) in the same server, using virtualization technologies, with no need for a real distribution environment. Corporations enjoying more resources may use the same strategy, adding a real distributed server system.

It is important to mention, also, that the database used by the application may be the source of the service interruption or instability, meaning that precautions must be taken. Firstly, the reason for the new deployment must be defined, whether it is an update of the application or data change.

The application update – assuming the database would be the same for any version of the running application – will not affect the clients. However, in case of changes in the data scheme, they should be performed prior to the application interaction starts, through refactoring the database that supports both previous and new versions (Fowler 2010).

3.2 Canary Release

Canary release is a technique by which only a small pre-selected group of users is granted access to the new version, as seen in Figure 2, minimizing deployment-associated risks (Humble and Farley 2010; Sato 2014).

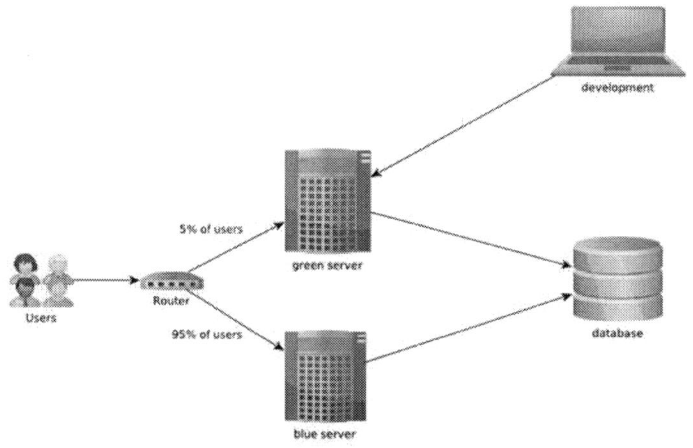

Figure 2. Canary release

Having only a single version of the application brings benefits such as better bug correction management and infrastructure, but it may also have side effects. This is true in the sense that bugs would only show up while the application runs in the production environment (Humble and Farley 2010).

This technique allows zero downtime by subjecting only a small group of users to possible errors.

The benefit of canary release is that at any sign of problem – related to inadequate functioning of a new application functionality, or below expected performance – it will only affect a small and more tolerant group of users, which differs from the aforementioned strategy where all users could suffer. It also gives the possibility to rate the most used functions and discontinue the ones that are not being used (this technique is known as A/B test). This technique keeps developers from performing useless tasks, allowing them to work with more important functionalities (Humble and Farley 2010).

This strategy requires much more hard working with the chosen architecture, because it demands specific configurations so that only a small group of users is granted access to the new functionality.

3.3 Lightweight Virtualization

The aforementioned strategies require means of performing deployment, and one of the possibilities is through virtualization. Virtualization is the technology used in the main cloud computing services, for it allows the best use of available resources. A new virtualization method, which is important to mention, is known as lightweight virtualization.

This technology was developed to work as a type of virtualization, but focused on smoothness and speed. In the same sense of conventional virtualization, it tends to have a lower TCO for the users. The major difference between the techniques is that lightweight virtualization does not use virtual machine monitor, redundant operating system kernel, and libraries – all of which makes it lighter (Morabito and Komu 2015).

The container technology became popular with the development of Linux special versions. A container is a repository of several resources, such as CPU, network input and output, and host machine RAM memory. Some of the products available are: LxC, Docker, Linux V-Server, among others (Morabito and Komu 2015).

The technology also includes some application models, some of which are specifically designed for delivery strategies, having an interface that communicates with the containers in a service level. The containers' ability to isolate from others helps testing and development, and can be used jointly with the continuous integration process (Morabito and Komu 2015).

Although there are advantages, the technology still faces some limitations, as presented by (Morabito and Komu 2015), such as lack of interoperability in cases of difference between the container operating system and the host operating system; and safety issues, given that the kernel system is shared by all containers.

4. COMPARATIVE ANALYSIS DISCUSSION

The possible approaches for downtime mitigation may include the following strategies: Blue-green and lightweight virtualization (Morabito and Komu 2015), Blue-green and virtualization (Silva et al. 2009; Thein et al. 2008; Shetty et al. 2008), Canary and lightweight virtualization, and Canary and virtualization. Both the blue-green and the canary release strategies may have to deal with issues of distributed infrastructure, which would demand from the corporation (aiming to improve its availability) to increase resource investment, and this may not always be the case.

Corporations do not usually have idle servers (because of the cost) to apply a distributed blue-green strategy, and on the other hand there may be servers unable to operate with all the available hardware resources. By using lightweight virtualization or virtualization technologies both problems could be avoided at once.

Virtualization is a tested and supported technique associated with environments hosting high-availability services. Virtualization provides capacity, for instance, for a server to create several virtual resources (Thein et al. 2008; Sagana 2013), allowing the corporation to perform tasks in a single server. E.g. running several levels of a web server, each having their own networking, but sharing the server's RAM memory (Vaughan-Nichols 2006).

Blue-Green and lightweight virtualization

Advantages: low cost – does not require new equipment purchase; better performance – considering the lightweight virtualization technology works with less software layers, it achieves better processing (Vaughan-Nichols 2006).

Disadvantages: high complexity for installation and management of the lightweight virtualization, because it is a new technology (Vaughan-Nichols 2006); requires specialized labor – deployment and management of virtualized environments require high-level knowledge; and it may cause impact on some users in case the new deploy presents problems regarding new functionalities (not included on previous versions).

Blue-Green and virtualization

Advantages: easy to implement – it only requires the replication of the automation and production environments in order to commute them to each new deploy, or defining permissions so that someone can be in charge of performing the tasks; low cost – does not require new equipment purchase; lower installation complexity compared to lightweight virtualization.

Disadvantages: requires specialized labor – deployment and management of virtualized environments require high-level knowledge; and it may cause impact on some users in case the new deploy presents problems.

Canary and lightweight virtualization

Advantages: low impact on users, because only a small and more tolerant group of users will be affected; low cost – does not require new equipment purchase.

Disadvantages: requires specialized labor – deployment and management of virtualized environments require high-level knowledge; high complexity – requires configuration of both the virtualization technology and the network, in order to select the users who will have access to the new version.

Canary and virtualization

Advantages: low impact on users, because only a small and more tolerant group of users will be affected; low cost – does not require new equipment purchase; better performance – the container technology operates with a layer less of software.

Disadvantages: average complexity – requires higher network configuration so that only a restricted group of users has access to the new version.

Table 1 and Table 2 present the advantages and disadvantages of each of the combinations described. A more detailed description of the tables is presented below.

Table 1. Combined approaches advantages

	Blue-green & Virtualization	Bue-green & Lightweight Virtualization	Canary & Virtualization	Canary & Lightweight Virtualization
Low cost	•	•	•	•
Clear for the user			•	•
Low complexity	•			
Performance		•		•

Table 2. Combined approaches disadvantages

	Blue-green & Virtualization	Bue-green & Lightweight Virtualization	Canary & Virtualization	Canary & Lightweight Virtualization
Specialized labor	•	•	•	•
High complexity		•	•	•
Impact on users	•	•		•

Tables 1 and 2 detailed description:

Advantages:

1. Low cost – None of the combinations require new equipment purchase;
1. Better performance in Blue-green/Canary & Lightweigh Virtualization cases, because the container technology works with a layer less of software and has better processing performance (Vaughan-Nichols 2006) ;
2. Easy implementation in Blue-green/Canary & Virtualization – it only requires the replication of automation and production environments in order to commute each new deploy;
3. Low complexity of installation in Blue-green/Canary & Virtualization compared to lightweight. The lightweight virtualization technology is more recent (Vaughan-Nichols 2006) when compared to the standard virtualization;
4. Low impact on users in Canary & Virtualization/Lightweight Virtualization – only a small and more tolerant group of users will be affected;

Disadvantages:

1. High complexity in Blue-green/Canary & Lightweight Virtualization, because the lightweight virtualization technology is more recent (Vaughan-Nichols 2006);
2. Requires specialized labor – all the cases require high-level knowledge in order to use virtualization;
3. Blue-green & Virtualization/Lightweight Virtualization – can impact on some users in case the new deploy presents errors regarding new functionalities (not included on previous versions);
4. High complexity in Canary & Virtualization/Lightweight Virtualization – it requires higher network configuration so that only a small group of users is granted access, besides the complexity of lightweight virtualization itself.

Such approaches are – theoretically – efficient because the virtualization brings several benefits and can be combined with the last stage of continuous delivery.

Figure 3 shows the steps after the new functionality commits in the control system of the version, using one of the possible approaches:

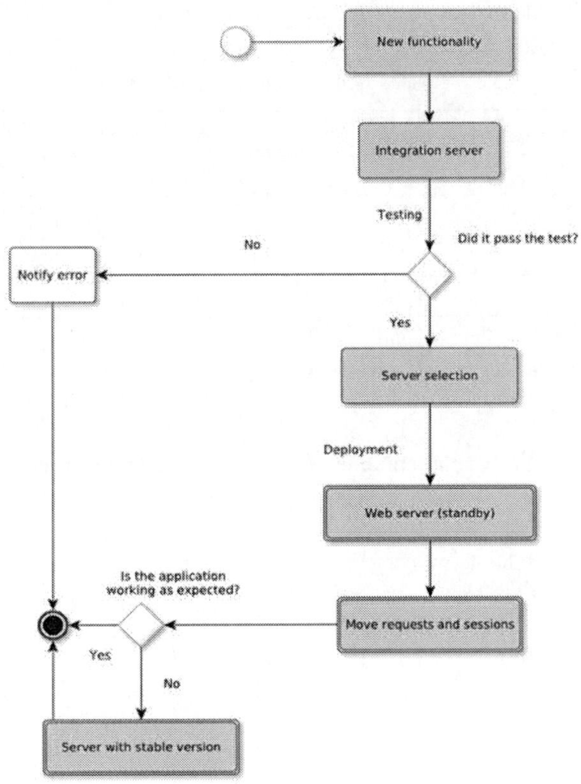

Figure 3. Activity diagram

The virtualization approach described by (Silva et al. 2009) brings solid results and the description matches with the blue-green strategy – the benefits include achieving goals and objectives.

The virtualized environment described by (Silva et al. 2009) consists of three environments:

The first virtualized resource is the load balancer, which is responsible for detecting performance problems and errors that could only be perceived in a production environment with full access by the users – problems that could not be detected in previous testing or in the homologation environment. This component is responsible for moving the clients from one environment to another in the described situations, but in order to answer continuous delivery effectively it must also work such that when a new deployment occurs, the clients would be moved automatically to the new version, and not just in case of failures.

The second and third virtualized resources would lie inside the production environment itself, playing the role of blue and green environments. These components are where the application server is installed. Because it is a virtualized environment, servers from any producers can be adopted.

This approach brings several benefits, such as:

The virtualized resources could be described in script language in order to run through automatized processes – as suggested by (Humble and Farley 2010) – and, thus, work together with the version control system.

Given that the environment is a result of virtualization, there would be no need to purchase new hardware, subsequently decreasing the TCO.

The environment would be properly instrumentalized – as described by (Silva et al. 2009). Once the software stopped meeting defined performance requirements or detected log failures, the clients would be moved back to the previous steady version.

This approach is supported by the results shown in authors' (Silva et al. 2009; Thein et al. 2008; Shetty et al. 2008) studies, which demonstrate a virtualized environment that provides high-level availability, and even though they focus on the software aging issue, it can be applied to continuous delivery and adapted to the blue-green strategy. Table 3 presents criteria for selecting this approach.

All achieved goals are aligned to unavailability risk minimization and can be adapted to the blue-green strategy.

Table 3. Related studies comparative of virtualization use

Criteria	(Silva et al. 2009)	(Thein et al. 2008)	(Shetty et al. 2008)
Self-recovery	•	•	•
Applicable on any server	•		
MTTR decrease	•		
Virtualization	•	•	•
No loss of requests or sessions	•	•	
Manageable in just one computer	•	•	•

The last topic to stress is that the combined approaches described previously present adhesion points between them and the ITIL framework – especially the service transition steps. The adhesion topics are shown in Table 4:

Table 4. Adhesion between trasition service and aprroaches

Processes	Blue-Green/Canary & Virtualization/Lightweight virtualization
Transition planning and support	
Change management	
Service asset and configuration management	•
Release and deployment management	•
Service validation and testing	•
Evaluation	•

The adhesion between framework and approaches is described as follows:

Service asset and configuration management: according to (Humble and Farley 2010), when it comes to virtualized environments, all the configurations and specifications of the used environments can be described in script language, and stored in version control systems, so that every and any modification will be recorded – and can be undone. The modifications will also be properly documented.

Release and deployment management: in virtualized environments, release and deployment tasks can be performed by automatized services, with the only need to define permission preferences to select who will be able to perform these tasks and who will not.

Service validation and testing: all the testing and validation steps are clearly defined in the continuous delivery process described by (Humble and Farley 2010) in the pipeline. Prior to arriving at the release and deployment stages, several tests are performed and only if they are successful the service can move to the next stages.

Evaluation: after the deployment in the selected environment, stress tests can be performed in order to confirm whether it meets pre-defined requirements – only if it passes the tests the commutation between virtualized environments is performed. In more specific situations, the commutation stage can be performed manually, but only after the responsible for release approves it.

Processes not adherent to approaches:

Transition planning and support, and change management: These are not included in the approaches because they escape their scope – both processes focus on activities that are prior to the deployment of a new service.

This approach is more suitable to corporations with available equipment and at least a few initial resources, but it is not restricted to them.

4.1 Limitations

There are some limitations and disadvantages related to the proposed approach, which needs proper attention.

First, even tough it does not require new material resources, it demands human resources with high-level knowledge in virtualization, so that it can work adequately and as expected.

Second, if the clients using new functionalities are moved to the previous version due to some error, they may face unavailability, because the new functionality is not included in the previous version. Therefore, the session or request will not be re-established, causing them to lose in-progress work.

Third, failures occurring in the single server with virtualized environments will cause service unavailability anyways.

Forth, the issues related to the database are not mentioned in the described approaches. Thus, this is a question yet to be solved in this context.

5. CONCLUSION AND FUTURE STUDIES

This study attempted to provide a comparative analysis between the possible solutions related to the unavailability problem, as well as suggest means of dealing with downtime – we believe the described technique is a possible path to follow. In general, the described approaches succeed in helping corporations with few available resources meet their clients' expectations. Finally, it is important to mention this is a theoretical study that needs to be tested in order to provide solid results for possible users.

REFERENCES

Agarwal, B., Tayal, S., and Gupta, M. (2010). *Software Engineering and Testing*. Computer science series. Jones & Bartlett Learning. Pages: 110-112.

Akerele, O., Ramachandran, M., and Dixon, M. (2013). System dynamics modeling of agile continuous delivery process. *In Proceedings - AGILE 2013.*

Bellomo, S., Ernst, N., Nord, R., and Kazman, R. (2014). Toward design decisions to enable deployability: Empirical study of three projects reaching for the continuous delivery holy grail. *In Proceedings of the International Conference on Dependable Systems and Networks*.

Chen, L. (2015). Continuous Delivery: Huge Benefits, but Challenges Too. *IEEE Software,* 32(2):50–54.

Eikebrokk, T. R. and Iden, J. (2012). ITIL Implementation: The Role of ITIL Software and Project Quality. *In 2012 23rd International Workshop on Database and Expert Systems Applications* , number January, pages 60–64. IEEE.

Fowler, M. (2010). Blue-green deployment. Available at: http://martinfowler.com/bliki/BlueGreenDeployment.html. (Accessed on 06/28/2016).

Gavrilovska, A., Schwan, K., and Oleson, V. (2002). A practical approach for 'zero' downtime in an operational information system. *In Proceedings 22nd International Conference on Distributed Computing Systems*, pages 345–352. EEE Comput. Soc.

Esmaili, H. B., Gardesh, H., and Sikari, S. S. (2010). Strategic alignment: ITIL perspective. *In 2010 2nd International Conference on Computer Technology and Development*, number Icctd, pages 550–555. IEEE.

Humble, J. and Farley, D. (2010). *Continuous Delivery: Reliable Software Releases through Build, Test, and Deployment Automation*. Addison Wesley Signature Series (Fowler). Pearson Education.

Morabito, R., Kjallman, J., and Komu, M. (2015). Hypervisors vs. Lightweight Virtualization: A Performance Comparison. In 2015 IEEE International Conference on Cloud Engineering , pages 386–393. IEEE.

Neely, S. and Stolt, S. (2013). Continuous delivery? Easy! Just change everything (well, maybe it is not that easy). I*n Proceedings - AGILE 2013.*

Oracle (2015). Zero downtime database upgrade using oracle goldengate. Available at: <http://www.oracle.com/technetwork/middleware/goldengate/overview/ggzerodowntimedatabaseupgrades-174928.pdf> (Accessed on 06/28/2016).

Sagana, C., Geetha, M., and Suganthe, R. C. (2013). Performance enhancement in live migration for cloud computing environments. *In 2013 International Conference on Information Communication and Embedded Systems (ICICES)*, pages 361–366. IEEE.

Sato, D. (2014). Canary release. Available at: http://martinfowler.com/bliki/CanaryRelease.html. (Accessed on 06/28/2016).

Service transition (2007). *Service transition IT infrastructure library.* Stationery Office, 2007. pages 42-84.

Shetty, H., Nambiar, M., and Kalita, H. (2008). Analysis and application of conditional software rejuvenation — A new approach. *In 2008 IEEE International Conference on Software Reliability Engineering Workshops (ISSRE Wksp)*, pages 1–5. IEEE.

Shu, Z. and Meina, S. (2010). An architecture design of life cycle based sla management. *In Advanced Communication Technology (ICACT), 2010 The 12th International Conference on*, volume 2, pages 1351–1355.

Silva, L. M., Alonso, J., and Torres, J. (2009). Using Virtualization to Improve Software Rejuvenation. *IEEE Transactions on Computers*, 58(11):1525–1538.

Stamou, K., Kantere, V., and Morin, J.-h. (2013). SLA data management criteria. *In 2013 IEEE International Conference on Big Data*, pages 34–42. IEEE.

Thein, T., Chi, S.-d., and Park, J. S. (2008). Improving Fault Tolerance by Virtualization and Software Rejuvenation. *In 2008 Second Asia International Conference on Modelling & Simulation (AMS)*, pages 855–860. IEEE.

Vaughan-Nichols, S. (2006). New Approach to Virtualization Is a Lightweight. *Computer*, 39(11):12–14.

A DYNAMIC PERSONAL HEALTH RECORD WITH SEMANTIC INTEROPERABILITY SUPPORT

Vitor Secretti Bertoncello, Cristiano André da Costa and Rodrigo da Rosa Righi
Applied Computing Graduate Program, Universidade do Vale do Rio dos Sinos (Unisinos), São Leopoldo, RS, Brazil

ABSTRACT

The constant growth of life expectancy brought to the focus a challenge for the healthcare systems. The increased longevity of the population directly results in an increased registration of chronic diseases, rising the demand for healthcare. Overcoming this challenge is to change the healthcare model, whose goal is to insert patients as active members in the care of their own health. This new model has generated demand for new information and communication technology solutions that must be able to satisfactorily meet the patient, as solutions in mobile and ubiquitous computing. In this context, this article proposes a model called AllHealthcare, consisting of a Personal Health Record (PHR) solution where patients are able to build a Dynamic Accompanying Profile (DAP) for their healthcare. The profile is defined according to their needs, and changed as either new demands or focus are considered. This dynamism in building a custom profile is achieved because the proposed model is based on openEHR standard archetypes, which also provides the feature of semantic interoperability to this proposal. In a review research focusing on PHR, most of the solutions are designed and focused for treatment of a particular disease or their models do not fulfill a number of important and current operational requirements, such as healthcare mobility and semantic interoperability of information. Finally, to evaluate AllHealthcare , we designed two use case scenarios based on a developed prototype.

KEYWORDS

e-Health. Web Semantics. Mobile Computing. Health Records. Ubiquitous Healthcare

1. INTRODUCTION

Information technology solutions and health-oriented communication have gained strategic strength to combat the rising of health costs at North America and European healthcare systems (Fan and Sui, 2016). Health Information and Communications Technology (ICT) force a change in people's healthcare model, making the patient an active member in the care of own health by making use of software tools, especially in the prevention of diseases (Moraes et al., 2013). Nowadays, the goal of preventive health care is to make people maintain a healthier lifestyle, preventing the occurrence or recurrence of diseases, mainly the chronic diseases, because given their long duration, they require a long-term and systematic approach to treatment; health services must integrate the response to these diseases. More commons chronic diseases are cardiovascular diseases, mainly heart disease and stroke; cancer; chronic respiratory diseases; and diabetes (Lähteenmäki et al., 2015).

The advancements in ubiquitous computing technologies enable better healthcare model, with the patient as an active member in their own health care, which encompasses the use of smartphones, tablets, sensors, which can explore connectivity advantages (Kumar et al., 2013). This scenario makes possible the availability of health care anywhere and anytime with these devices (Hansmann et al., 2001). Therefore, ICT applications in health have become important factor to empower the patient as an agent in their own healthcare. (Gençtürk, 2015).

It is widely accepted that patients with access to their own health status increase control over the care of the body. But the simplicity of the tools and methodologies are factors that can contribute significantly in the patient's level of involvement with the application. In addition to access to your health information, the inclusion of routine data in a PHR, the patient makes it an active member in the care of own health and provides an important step for reducing costs and better health care quality (Gençtürk, 2015).

Some initiatives for integration between PHR and Electronic Health Record (EHR) have been conducted, but, the medical records of patients still in majority, are kept in separate, closed systems, generating medical records sharing difficulties between hospitals, laboratories, PHRs, among others (Belyaev et al., 2013). In order to overcome these difficulties, international standards have been developed for representation of clinical information to enable the sharing of health information of patients between different health service providers. Among these standardizations that promote interoperability of information, it highlights the openEHR[1] and Health Level Seven[2] (HL7). Generally, PHR solutions are using static fragments these standardization in order to offer care to a specific disease. This format is valid, but remains plastered to new possibilities for healthcare or even an improvement in the treatment of a disease.

The use of standardization for clinical knowledge representation favors interoperability between different systems. Interoperability is the ability of two or more systems and components to exchange information and use them (IEEE, 1991). In a study of PHRs led by Bastianen (2015), in 68 analyzed PHRs, only one was integration with EHRs, the most held their own and closed structure without communication with other means, which according Bastianen (2015), is a reality of the situation of systems for available PHRs.

Therefore, we are presenting in this article a model called AllHealthcare model, which is a PHR model that enables the development of DAP for specific healthcare for each user. The profile is compatible with mobile devices, in addition to supporting semantic interoperability, which is the most advanced level of sharing of information between health care providers (Walker et al., 2005). This model is based on openEHR standard, which has a medical and information technology community working on archetypes structures, capable of carrying clinical knowledge of each existing concept in medicine. The main scientific contribution of this work is two-folded: (i) combining the ability for users to build their health care profile in their own PHR, and; (ii) to enable semantic interoperability. The construction of the DAP will have the clinical knowledge base of openEHR standard, as well as interoperability will be based on the same standard. Health standards are gaining adepts by their use's flexibility (Lin et al., 2016).

This article is organized as follows: section 2 will be presented related work and their characteristics; Section 3 will present the proposed model by this work; Section 4 will present implementation aspects; in section 5 will be described the evaluation model through its prototype and finally, in section 6, the final considerations.

2. RELATED WORK

In researching by contributions from studies in PHRs area, six studies stood out because they are concerned about proposals interoperability for sharing information and thus used standardizations for representation of clinical information. Table 1 shows these six studies which were analyzed in relation the standard used, the tool implemented platform and also focused on the particular disease or set of information.

Table 1. Characteristics of related work

Property	(Brugués et al., 2015)	(Peng, 2013)	(Gençtürk, 2015)	(Franz et al., 2015)	(Song et al., 2015)	(Moraes et al., 2014)
Standard	HL7	HL7	HL7	HL7	HL7	OpenEHR
Platform	Mobile (Android) and Web	Desktop	Web	Mobile (Android)	Mobile (Android)	Not specified
Disease and specific care	Diabetes	Diabetes	Rheumatism	Cardiac and vital signs	A limited data group	Only read sensors

Analyzing the options for each study on the use of standardization, HL7 was predominantly more used. This behavior can be explained because of the HL7 be more widespread. The openEHR standard is improving and recently has been integrated as a valid option, especially for having the distinction of clinical knowledge database in archetypes format.

[1] http://www.openehr.org
[2] http://www.hl7.org

Referring to the platform used, the majority of studies has developed in mobile devices or for web. When applicable to mobile devices, the Android Operating System was the choice for all related works. This option was justified by the quantity by the authors because includes most existent mobile devices. The availability of the PHR through mobile devices has been contemplated as one of the requirements that a PHR should provide users according research conducted (Vitaletti and Puglia, 2014). The third examined characteristic is directly related to the main contribution presented in this paper. It indicates the object of PHR tool of the analyzed work. All works propose a specific healthcare to a particular disease or monitoring pre-determined specific data.

Unlike this, not having a disease or treatment as a specific focus, this paper proposes the DAP to healthcare, which consist in a process of construction adding the clinical concepts. Clinical concepts of interest to the user or to help in a specific healthcare situation. Clinical concept refers to a medication or perception of the body such as temperature, weight, heart rate, blood pressure and many others. Thus, this PHR model intends to be the unique PHR solution for any healthcare. Beyond, the model consider too other important resources that a PHR solution needs, like health information's integration with health institutions and the mobile devices compatibility.

3. PROPOSED MODEL

The AllHealthcare model is a PHR solution that utilizes openEHR standard like supplier of clinical knowledge. The openEHR standard contains two main layers, called reference model and archetype model. The archetype model has numerous structures called archetypes where each structure defines a clinical concept containing all the details of possibilities. Are created, reviewed and maintained by an open medical community, the openEHR Foundation, that has an archetype repository, called Clinical Knowledge Manager (CKM). In the purpose model, the archetypes are used by PHR users build their own healthcare profile, only containing important concepts for itself.

The archetypes adoption to the construction of a dynamic PHR is proposed innovation of model. Different from majority of PHR solutions, the objective is not care a particular disease or finite set of information with a static tool. The model was thought to be flexible and adaptable over time, ever supporting the demand of each user or a medical novelty, beyond support for mobile devices and interoperability between different healthcare providers. Interoperability between health institutions is not a novelty, but do it from a dynamic PHR is complex.

The openEHR adoption helps in that problem because the archetype too have the data structure and terminology information, required for data integration. The logic of openEHR for interoperability between different systems is avail the same data structure used, i.e., the same archetypes in both sides of data integration. Figure 1 shows the software architecture proposed by the AllHealthcare model.

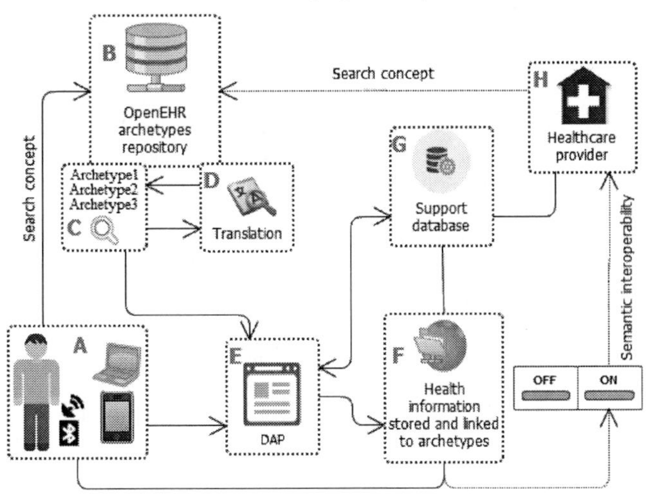

Figure 1. AllHealthcare software architecture model

Explaining the model in Figure 1, initially, to build the DAP the user enters a keyword for the desired clinical concept to the accompanying in the PHR. Sample keywords are "weight", "respiration", "pressure" and "temperature". For each clinical concept informed, a search is performed on the openEHR archetypes repository (B). The research in archetypes repository applies a scan on file archetype available (C), exploring its information represented in formal language Archetype Definition Language (ADL) or Extensible Markup Language (XML). The scan process explores the following fields of the file structure, in this exact sequence: keywords, purpose and use. Figure 2 illustrates the search being performed successfully, with the clinical concept "fever".

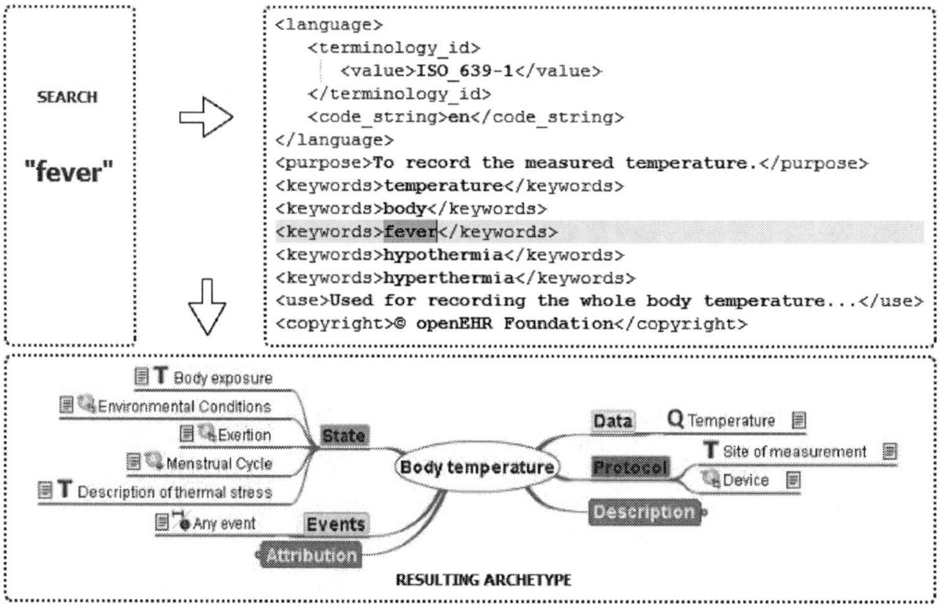

Figure 2. Archetype search in AllHealthcare demonstration

In the search process, if a clinical concept entered by user is not found, the search term is translated from the user's origin language to English (D), and the search is performed again (C). The translation is necessary because most of the openEHR archetypes are in english language. In the proposed model, the translation uses an Application Programming Interface (API), like Google Translate API. The resultant archetypes that corresponded to the user search are send back to the user. If there is no result that matches the search, even after translation, then nonexistence is informed to user.

After adding all the desired clinical concepts, the user can customize them, removing data fields from each archetype in according to their needs. Initially, the archetypes have several detailed fields, that can exceed information needs of their users. The body weight archetype, for example, currently presents seven fields for their clinical representation, but only one is required. Thus, for customization of an archetype, the model purposed uses the archetypes, especially the section containing the data fields description. This section specifies all the fields of personalized archetype, including which ones are mandatory and which are optional, also including possible measurement units for each attribute.

The proposed model allows that the healthcare provider (H) performs the DAP construction. This feature has been thought to be easy to use for elderly people. The DAP construction from by the health provider is not a mandatory option in the model, thus, in the Figure 1, this bind is show by dotted line.

The health information entered by the user in the PHR are stored using a specific database (F). The support database stores the utilized archetypes, personalization made in the archetypes and connection details from PHR with the health institutions for integration of information PHR-EHR within an interoperability scenario. The interoperability proposed by this model, showed in Figure 1, perform the sharing of patient's information with healthcare institutions (M) without losing any semantic meaning of the data, enabling the destination institution immediately use the information. In an environment of semantic interoperability between different systems, communication occurs through structured and coded messages, standardized data, causing the system to exchange information with the same vocabulary.

Utilizing openEHR in both sides for data integration, the messages are transmitted in same vocabulary, the use terms and expressions are equals, shared and pre-established. In this format translation or interpretation is not necessary. In the proposed model, the user can PHR utilize without data integration, thus, in the Figure 1, this resource is showed with dotted line.

4. IMPLEMENTATION ASPECTS

The implementation of the prototype to represent the model aims to demonstrate the main contributions proposed in this article, as the construction of DAP along with the integration of health information PHR with an EHR on a mobile platform for the PHR user. The prototype implementation was divided into three modules: client module, service module in a cloud computing, and a health institution module, that is an EHR also based openEHR for integrate health information, through interoperability.

In the client module has been adopted PhoneGap technology, by Adobe, to allows the application to be developed with web solutions such as Hypertext Markup Language (HTML), JavaScript (JS) and Cascading Style Sheets (CSS) and resulting a app compatible with several operating systems available for mobile devices. In the application use, all interactions are performed through web requests, requiring a web server to meet these requests. Figure 3 shows the user interfaces proposed, starting in PAD construction, with search of clinical concepts, personalization, removing fields in necessary cases and information insertion.

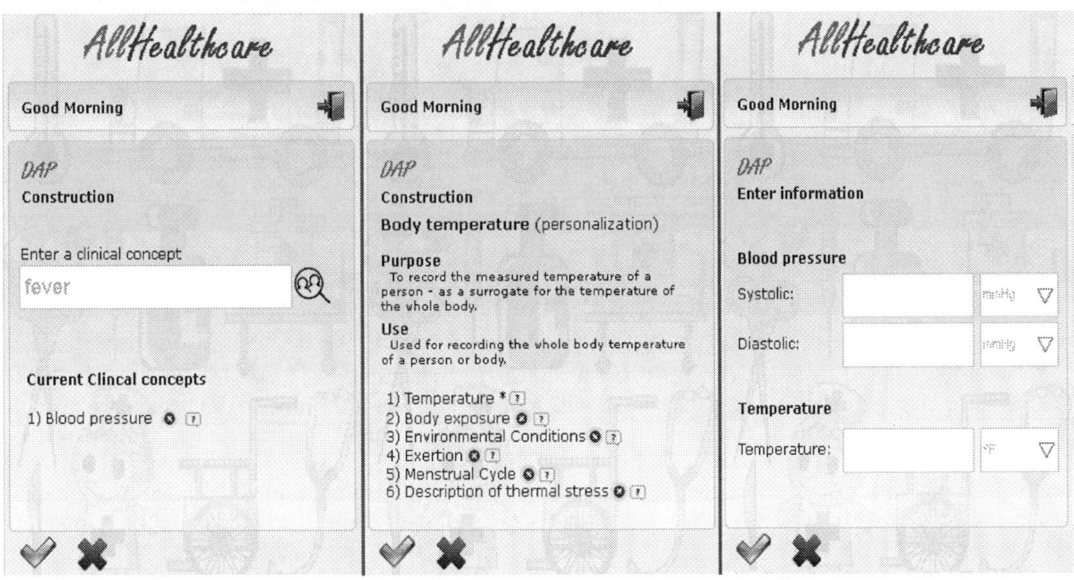

Figure 3. Prototype user interfaces

The cloud computing module contains most of the services because receives e send back requests from client module. Also, perform searches for DAP construction and handles all resources. This module have a web server Apache with PHP to answer the requests, handling files, archetypes, databases, translation API and web services for interoperability of health records with a health institutions.

In the DAP build, this module receives the search term of a clinical concept and run the search algorithm, which may involve calling the translation API, trying to find archetypes containing its description in the local language of the user. Contextualizing the three modules, the Figure 4 shows the content of each and the transitions between them.

The data persistence uses two database management systems, each with different structures e characteristics. The first is a MongoDB database that has a NoSQL structure and is used to register user's health information. This structure has advantages for handling large volumes of data quickly. NoSQL databases have no relational structure, but provide better results for speed and scalability. The second is a PostgreSQL database, that has a relational structure and is used to store user's access data, personalized DAP and interoperability settings. Ever that user to start the PHR app to insert information, a requisition is performed in this database to mount the constructed profile and updated. Both database management systems choices were considered by being open source and have extensive documentation available.

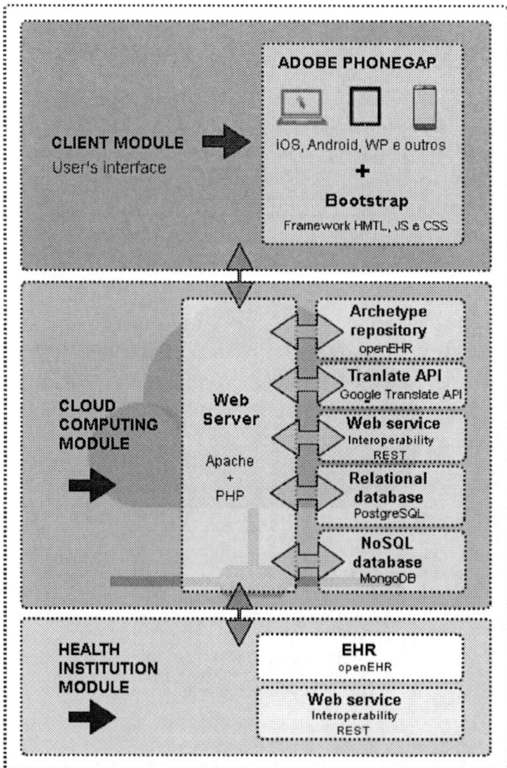

Figure 4. The three modules of the model and their relations

The integration of data between PHR and healthcare providers occurs through web services REST type connection. Due the data leaving the cloud service module and be transmitted to the healthcare provider, the PHR's user do not need to be continuously connected to the Internet. The data are transmitted as according availability of necessary resources. In addition, this integration of health records only occurs with the user's consent. From this, a web service can be configured in the health institution module, pointing to the EHR for transmission of user's health information stored in the NoSQL database in the cloud computing module.

5. EVALUATION AND RESULTS

This section describes the evaluation of AllHealthcare model, in order to assess the proposed PHR using the DAP with interoperability for sharing of health semantic information. The evaluation using scenarios has been adopted by the scientific community on mobile and ubiquitous solutions (Satyanarayanan, 2010; Costa et al, 2015), therefore, a scenario was modeled for evaluation, adding demands that this solution proposed to solve. Two scenarios were proposed.

The first scenario is described as follows: "Lucas started to use PHR application on his smartphone, which allows the creation of a Dynamic Accompanying Profile of several health factors, as needed. To better monitor the progress of his body with the beginning of a routine physical activities, he has created a initial profile. After a few days, and with the constant lack of air during the physical activities, Lucas decided to improve his profile by entering the accompaniment of smoking, to try to reduce the use of cigarettes. Even with the reduction of smoking, their air lacks persisted and he decided to seek help from a physician. Through the PHR application, he authorized the transfer of all the information to the healthcare institution database, facilitating the diagnosis."

The described scenario and the prototype was performed by a person with expertise on smartphone utilization. The PAD construction was analyzed step by step. The user initially searched by two clinical concepts: “weight” and “mass”. These two clinical concepts resulted in two archetypes: body weight and body mass index. In the personalization step, the user kept the fields weight and state of dress for the body weight archetype and for the body mass index archetype the user kept only the index field. To add tobacco accompaniment, the user searched by "cigarette". This term resulted the tobacco use archetype. In the personalization, the user kept the follow fields: specified day, tobacco use and form, which specifies the cigarette type. Thus, to execution this first proposed scenario, the prototype achieved openEHR archetypes with clinical knowledge to support the accompaniment requested by the user, including maintenance to add one more clinical concept on time later. The returned archetypes were analyzed as to content quality. The keyword list formation contained six words and the use and purpose fields contained a long description, justifying the search success.

The second scenario explores a different situation, as follow: “Marie has seventeen years old and has headache frequently. In the doctor's appointment, she was recommended monitoring their blood pressure (ever in sit position) and sharing this information with the hospital. The doctor requested the patient return a month later”. The second scenario was performed by a young person with basic expertise on smartphones. The user handled the prototype, starting by the DAP construction. The search clinical concept was "pressure". The returned archetype by the prototype was Blood Pressure. The user has accepted and went to the next step, the personalization step. The user has removed some data fields, keeping the data fields diastolic, systolic (mandatory) e keeping too the fields position and sleep status. Has attending for doctor's request, the user does authorization to the blood pressure information sharing with health institution. Thus, the PHR information form, personalized by the user stood with four data fields to shared entries with medical institution for patient's accompaniment e monitoring.

Analyzing the PHR prototype's behavior in this scenario, it was returned the Blood Pressure archetype for user. The search found two correspondent keywords in this archetype's description: mean arterial pressure and pulse pressure. Moreover, the personalization allowed the user to highlight the position for obtaining the blood pressure, in accordance with physician's request. Therefore, the evaluation was considered positive because the user achieved the proposed goals without difficulties. More than dynamic profile construction, the clinical knowledge transported from the openEHR archetypes to the DAP helps user on an unknown area for it, that is the clinical area. The information sharing with healthcare institution met the expectations because the user easily found the sharing resource for authorization. Finally, these evaluated scenarios with PHR prototype's use showed how the solution proposed behaves on a different, but specific user profiles. Another evaluation is planned, which will consist of the prototype free use for ten different users.

6. CONCLUSION

This article proposed a PHR model called AllHealthcare, which enables the user to create a Dynamic Accompanying Profile to healthcare, utilizing the openEHR standard to accomplish this. The openEHR uses archetypes to represent clinical knowledge which were created to improve the interoperability level between different healthcare information systems.

The main scientific contribution of AllHealthcare is combining the ability for users to build their health care profile in their own PHR, also enabling semantic interoperability. In the researched literature, we did not find examples of exploitation of archetype's descriptive content. The majority of PHR solutions are focused in specific diseases treatment. The DAP to healthcare enables user to utilize PHR for their personal and momentary necessity. Beyond the DAP, the model also offers support the semantic interoperability, turning possible to share PHR information with other healthcare institutions, such as hospitals, clinics and laboratories, without the need for data mapping or any kind of conversion.

Considering the evaluation, two scenarios were modeled to define some use situations. Through the implemented prototype, we could execute the two proposed scenarios. The result was satisfactory because the user achieves the proposed goals without difficulties in execution. As future works, we aim at suggesting clinical concepts based in user's choices. We also plan to assess the prototype with real users and different types of chronical diseases.

ACKNOWLEDGMENTS

The authors would like to thank to CAPES, CNPq and FAPERGS for partially funding this research.

REFERENCES

Bastianen, S., 2015. *Towards an architecture for the support of integrated Personal Health Records.* Eindhoven, Nederlands.

Belyaev, K. et al, 2013. Personal health record storage on privacy preserving green clouds. *9th International Conference on Collaborative Computing: Networking, Applications and Worksharing.* Austin, USA, pp. 448-457.

Brugués, A. et al, 2015. Providing interoperability to a pervasive healthcare system through the HL7 CDA standard. *Proceedings of 15th International HL7 Interoperability Conference.* Prague, Czech Republic, pp. 5-12.

Costa, CD. et al, 2015. A spontaneous social network based on mobile devices. *Social Networks Analysis and Mining.*Vol. 4 No. 1 *, pp 1-13.*

Fan, J and Sui, Y., 2016. An Empirical Study on Personal Health Records System based on Individual and Environmental Features. *WHICEB 2016 Proceedings.*Wuhan, China, pp. 160-166.

Franz, B. 2015. Applying FHIR in an Integrated Health Monitoring System. *EJBI.* Vol. 11. No. 2. pp. 51-56.

Gençtürk, M., 2015. *Self Management of Patients With Ankylosing Spondylitis Through a Personal Health System.* Ankara, Turkey.

Hansmann, U. et al, 2001. Home Services. *Pervasive Computing Handbook.* pp. 363-370.

International Organization For Standardization - ISO/TR 20514, 2005. Available in: < http://www.iso.org/iso/iso_catalogue/catalogue_tc/catalogue_detail.htm?csnumber=39525>

Kumar, S. et al, 2013. Mobile Health: Revolutionizing Healthcare Through Transdisciplinary Research. *Computer*, Vol. 46, No. 1. pp. 28-35.

Lähteenmäki, J. et al, 2015. *Online electronic services for preventive and customer-centric healthcare.* VTT Technology 232, Finland.

Lin, C, et al., 2016. An exploratory study using an openEHR 2-level modeling approach to represent common data elements. *Journal of the American Medical Informatics Association.* Vol. 23, No. 4.

Moraes, J. et al, 2013. A novel architecture for message exchange in Pervasive Healthcare based on the use of Intelligent Agents. *Computer Systems and Applications (AICCSA), 2013 ACS International Conference on.* Ifrane. Marocco, pp. 1-8.

Peng, C., 2013. *A Hybrid Cloud Approach for Sharing Health Information in Chronic Disease Self-Management.* School of Computing - Blekinge Institute of Technology, Karlskrona, Sweden.

Satyanarayanan, M., 2010 Mobile computing: the next decade. *ACM SIGMOBILE Mobile Computing and Communications Review*, Vol. 15, No. 2, pp. 2-10.

Song, Y. et al, 2015. Empowering patients using cloud based personal health record system. *Software Engineering, Artificial Intelligence, Networking and Parallel/Distributed Computing (SNPD), 2015 16th IEEE/ACIS International Conference on.* Takamatsu, Japan, pp. 1-6.

Vitaletti, A. and Puglia, S., System Overview of Next-Generation Remote Healthcare. *Systems Design for Remote Healthcare,* pp. 31-53.

Walker, J. et al, 2005. The Value Of Health Care Information Exchange And Interoperability. *Health affairs.* Vol. 24. No. W5. pp. 5-18.

USING SELECTION ATTRIBUTE ALGORITHMS FROM DATA MINING TO COMPLEMENT THE REP-INDEX

Gláucio R. Vivian[1], Cristiano R. Cervi[2] and Diogo N. Rovadosky[2]
[1]*University of Passo Fundo - UPF / IFFar FW*
[2]*University of Passo Fundo - UPF*

ABSTRACT

In this paper we propose a complement to the Rep-Index reputation metric for researchers, using data mining techniques specific for selecting a subset of the most relevant elements to Rep-Index. We redid the experiments with the original author's data and found the best algorithm. At the end we propose the new weights for classification of researchers with correct classification rate higher than the original Rep-Index. For Computer Science the best selection attribute is InfoGain. The Spearman's correlation is 0.5520 against 0.3932 for Rep-Index with original weights. The results show that Rep-Index is adaptable, flexible and the approach proposal complements the original index to offer better classification for researchers.

KEYWORDS

Data Mining, Researchers Reputation, Rep-Index, Selection Algorithms, Scientometrics

1. INTRODUCTION

Currently, the management of science, technology and innovation goes through a qualification process that seeks to increasingly meet the researcher's needs and their activities in order to correct the direction in their research, plan recommendations and proper guidance for application of resources that generate opportunities. Development agencies, research centers and most of the universities feel the need to get information on the scientific production and the activities developed by the researchers in order to support decision making. Thus, the development agencies would be able to channel resources to proven competency groups in specific areas of knowledge, stimulate the development of science and technology and seek competitive advantages and academic excellence.

Despite the efforts of the academic community to develop strategies to identify the reputation of researchers defining scientific metrics, the vast majority of works based on their contribution are citations of articles from researchers. However, these forms of evaluation do not consider the trajectory of the researcher, even the stage where there are inserted. The citations of articles should be only one element to be analyzed and not the only element.

The search for profile templates of researchers and demand for quality evaluation criteria in the academic is increasing. This has been the focus of studies over the last decade. This growth arises from the pursuit of excellence in key areas of research. It is also motivated by other factors, such as competition for scholarships and grants which are available resources for development agencies. High competition in such a scenario requires that the quality criteria are objectively defined, preferably using an approach that can be easily reproduced.

In this context, in the Scientometrics and Bibliometrics there are several metrics to analyze scientific production and determine the reputation of researchers. In essence, they are divided into two major groups. The first originates in the h-index and all proposals for improvement as g-index, AR-index, e-index, hg-index, h'-index, H_I-index, etc. The second large group builds on the success of Google's PageRank algorithm. In this group, we can cite the PageRank modified, weighted PageRank, PaperRank and CITEX. The rep-Index is a new proposal that seeks to incorporate other elements present in the academic life and in the research. It has five categories: identification of education degree, advisory, examining board, membership and production.

In Brazil the researchers have a specific platform to publish their curriculum. This is called Platform Lattes[1] and it is developed by National Council for Scientific and Technological Development (CNPq)[2]. The CNPq classify the researchers in levels. There are 1A, 1B, 1C, 1D, 2 levels (in descending order). Each level has the specific criteria, in these are include scientific production, formation of new researchers, innovation, coordination or participation in research project, participation in reviewer of journals and conference committee coordinator.

In the data analyses area there are several technologies to auxiliary in decision making and knowledge discovery. The Data Mining is one of the most important. It performs analysis of large volumes of data and can discover interesting frequent patterns in data. According to Witten and Frank (2005), in Data Mining there is the problem of high-dimensional datasets, the computational complexity of classification increased with number of attributes (elements of Rep-Index). In this way there are two options. First, improve more sophisticates methods to classification. The experience shows what this approach is dangerous, because raises the complexity and use more computational resources. The best solution is algorithms for filter the elements with more relevancy to CNPq level. The selection attribute algorithms are a good option for this work.

The main objective of this work is complementing the Rep-Index metric. In the original proposal, the authors of Rep-Index use weights equals for all areas of research. However, there are relevance differences between each area. The idea is find the best weights for all elements presents in Rep-Index. For this we study data mining algorithms specifics for selection of subset the elements. The experiments are made with original data from Brazilian researchers of Computer Science area. For this area we analysis the best algorithm and find the specific weights.

The paper was organized in the followings sections: section 2 presents the study about works with relevance for our purpose. Section 3 proposes the approach, dataset and how the experiments are made. Section 4 presents the experiments and results of the proposal. Finally, section 5 shows the discoveries of this work. The future works are presents in this section, too.

2. RELATED WORKS

Hirsch (2005) defines the h-index as: "the amount of papers (quantity) with number of citations (quality or visibility) greater than or equal to h for each paper". Through a simple single number, it is possible to evaluate and compare the citations and the scientific publications. The total number of citations is always greater than h^2 because papers may not have the minimum amount of h citations.

Egghe (2006) presents the g-index to improve the h-index. The fact is that the g-index does not consider the amount of citations that an article has, in other words, working with high amount of citations represents an indication of quality and therefore their relevance should be considered. The definition is: "For a set of articles, in descending order of citations, the g-index is the largest number such that the top g articles received (added together) at least g^2 citations". From this definition it is already clear that $g \geq h$. Despite the g-index being an evolution of the h-index, we still have some limitations. The impact of the publication, self-citation, getting the entire production/citations and comparisons between different areas. A single highly cited work can also generate a false index, putting the researcher far above average performance. In the work of Costas and Bordons (2008) the g-index is analyzed as compared with the h-index. This study shows that the g-index is more sensitive than the h-index for the assessment of selective scientists.

Jin et al. (2007) propose the AR-index to complement the h-index. It is defined by: the square of the sum of the mean of citations per year in the h-core. The follow equation shows the AR-index.

$$AR = \sqrt{\sum_{j=1}^{h} \frac{cit_j}{a_j}} \qquad (1)$$

[1] http://lattes.cnpq.br
[2] http://cnpq.br

Where h is h-index, cit is the quantity of citations and a is the number of years since the publication of the paper. The great contribution of AR-index is the use of the year of publication to compute the complement to the h-index. This allows for a more comprehensive behavior for the researchers.

Beel and Gipp (2009) propose the i10-index to Google Scholar[3] site. The standard version is a quantity of papers with 10 citations. There is another version of this metric, but computed from the last five years. Another feature of Google Scholar site is the h-index.

Zhang (2009) presents the e-index aiming to approach the two h-index problems. The first is to avoid the loss of citations less than h-core. Another limitation is the low resolution; this is due to the use of integers numbers to represent the index. Thus the author proposes the use of real numbers. The e-index is defined by the following equation:

$$e^2 = \sum_{j=1}^{h} (cit_j - h) = \sum_{j=1}^{h} (cit_j - h^2) \tag{2}$$

Where cit_j are the citations received by the jth paper and e^2 denotes the excess citations within the h - *core*. This index shows a fundamental complement to evaluate authors with high amounts of quotes. It also enables the comparison of researchers where the h-index is tied.

The Alonso et al. (2009) presents the hg-index. It is the combination of h-index and g-index metrics. The idea is to combine the benefits of both a single and an improved metric, seeking to eliminate the disadvantages with the combination. The hg-index is calculated by the geometric mean of the two indexes as the following equation: hg = $\sqrt{h.g}$. The authors demonstrated that $h \leq hg \leq g$ and $hg - h \leq g - hg$. This metric provides a more balanced view of the scientific production.

Zhang (2013) proposed the h'-index to improve the h-index by combining the h-index, e-index and publications that are below the h-core (also known as h-tail or t-index). The combination of these three papers charts of the areas with citations allow for a complete analysis of all production and citations. Thus, there is no loss of information in the calculation of h'-index. The index in question is calculated by the following equation.

$$h' = rh = \frac{eh}{t} \tag{3}$$

Where e, h and t are the e-index h-index and t-index, respectively. At end of the work, the authors claimed that h'-index is a real number for evaluating a scientific output in a way that it is fairer and more reasonable.

Zhai et al. (2014) purposed the h_l-index to improve the h-index based on the quality of the citing papers. In order to analyze the quality a citation network among academic papers was built. The definition is: "The h_l-index of a set of articles is h meaning that h is the biggest integer such that the set of articles has at least h articles satisfying that the in-lobby index is no less than h". The analysis on the properties of the h_l-index demonstrates that: $0 \leq \text{hl} - \text{index} \leq \text{h} - \text{index}$.

The success of PageRank algorithm by Page et al. (1999), points out many proposals to for use in metrics to analyze scientific production and determine the reputation of researchers. Chen et al. (2007) compare the original PageRank and weighted PageRank with the citation ranking, h-index, and centrality measures. In order to make this comparative they selected 108 of the most highly cited authors in the information retrieval area from the 1970s to 2008. The damping factor ranging from 0.05 to 0.95. To check the results, the Spearman Correlation was used. The main conclusion is then citation rank is similar to PageRank to author co-citation network.

In the work of Du et al. (2009) the authors mention the similarity between web and scientific citation networks. It is proposed a PaperRank extension to the PageRank model proposed by Page et al. (1999), and HITS proposed by Kleinberg (1999), to measure the scientific publications. The idea is to measure relativities between papers, to compute the indirect citation relationship between papers used the Dijkstra's algorithm. The results are stored in the relativity matrix R. The matrix R is used to compute co-citation and co-reference matrix. The association matrix is built by measuring the relativity of associating direct and indirect relationships between two papers. The next step is to compute de transition probability matrix. Finally, the

---

[3] http://scholar.google.com.br

ranking scores are calculated. The experimental results show that PaperRank can find more authoritative papers than the other methods.

According to the authors Pal and Ruj (2015), Citex gives normalized scores to authors and papers to determine their rankings. The problem is modeled with a publication and citations graphs, when authors and papers are nodes, an undirected edge between two nodes is when the authors have written a paper (publication graph). A directed edge from a paper to another paper is a citation (citation graph). The goal of this work is to compute scores with a specify algorithm. The values are stored in two columns of vector (one for the authors and the other for papers). At the end, the scores are normalized by dividing the author/paper scores by the sum of the authors/papers scores, so that each score lies between 0 and 1, and the sum of the scores is 1. The limitation of this work was assuming that all authors have contributed equally to a paper.

2.1 Rep-Model and Rep-Index

Cervi et al. (2013a,b) propose the Rep-Index as, an index to classify metric of the researchers with other criteria besides the paper and citations. In paper the education degree, advisory, examining board, membership and production are included. The metric is a positive integer between 1 and 5 (in ascending order). The great differential of the others metrics is weigh weighed, wide scope and adaptability. The Rep-Index is based in a specific profile to researches, named Rep-Model. It is a set of elements that represents the academic and scientific behavior of researchers. This elements that focus not only in bibliometry. In the Table 1 you can view the category, elements, acronym and weights.

Table 1. Categories and Elements for Rep-Model with the respective weights in the Rep-Index

Category			Element		
	Acronym	Weight		Acronym	Weight
Identification	ID	15	Education Degree	ED	15
Advisory	ADV	15	Postdoctoral Advisor	PA	6
			PhD Thesis Advisor	PTA	5
			Master Dissertation Advisor	MDA	4
Examining Board	EB	10	Participation in Examination Boards PhD Thesis	PEBPT	6
			Participation in Examination Boards Master Dissertation	PEBMD	4
Membership	MS	10	Editorial Board Member	EBM	5
			Reviewer of Journals	RJ	3
			Conference Committee Coordinator	CCC	1
			Conference Committee Member	CCM	1
Production	PROD	50	Articles in Scientific Journals	ASJ	15
			Books Published	BP	8
			Book Chapter Published	BCP	5
			Complete Work Published in Conference Proceedings	CWPCP	8
			H-Index	HI	7
			Network Co-authorship	NC	3
			Research Projects	RP	2
			Software	SOFT	2
		100			100

The decimal value from Rep-Index is computed for equation 4.

$$Rep-Index_{(R)} = \sum_{i=1}^{c}\left(\sum_{j=1}^{e_i}\frac{(v_j.w_j)}{max(v_j)}\right) \tag{4}$$

When R refers to the researcher whose reputation one wants to find out, c represents the total number of categories, i represents the range of 1 up to the total number of categories (c), e_i represents the total elements in each category, j refers the range of 1 up to the total number of elements (e_i), v represents the value of the element, w_j refers to the weight element, $max(v_j)$ represents the higher value of the element. To compute the integer value to Rep-Index, use the equation 5.

$$Rep-Index_{(R)} = \begin{cases} 1 & Rep-Index_{(R)} \geq 0 \wedge < 20 \\ 2 & Rep-Index_{(R)} \geq 20 \wedge < 40 \\ 3 & Rep-Index_{(R)} \geq 40 \wedge < 60 \\ 4 & Rep-Index_{(R)} \geq 60 \wedge < 80 \\ 5 & Rep-Index_{(R)} \geq 80 \wedge \leq 100 \end{cases} \quad (5)$$

This equation classifies the reputation of researchers in five levels. Level 1 is the initial level and 5 is the final level. The idea is that beginner researchers take initial levels and the more advanced ones take the highest levels.

3. MATERIALS AND METHODS

For this work we use the originals dataset from Rep-Index authors. In this dataset there are data for 404 Brazilian researchers of Computer Science. The data of the researchers was collected from Lattes Platform and h-index from Publish or Perish tool[4]. Figure 1 presents the number of CNPq researchers in each level.

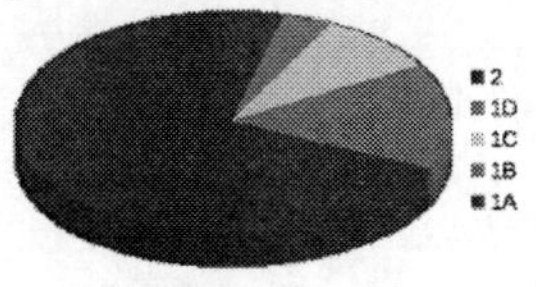

Figure 1. Graphic of researchers from Dataset in each level of CNPq

It is observed that there are more researchers in the initials levels (2, 1D and 1C). In the dataset there are values for all elements of Rep-Index.

With the Weka tool by Hall et al. (2009), we analyzed the dataset to attribute evaluation algorithms. There are several algorithms for the selection attribute in the science literature. In this proposal we chose five for this study. According to Witten and Frank (2005) there are: *i)* ChiSquared: method evaluates elements by computing the chi-squared statistic regarding the CNPq level. *ii)* GainRatio: evaluates elements by measuring their gain ratio regarding the CNPq level. *iii)* SymmetricalUncert: evaluates an attribute by measuring its symmetrical uncertainty regarding the CNPq level. *iv)* ReliefF: is instance-based: It samples instances randomly and checks neighboring instances of the same and different elements. It operates on discrete and continuous CNPq level data. *v)* InfoGain: evaluates elements by measuring their information gain regarding the CNPq level. It discretizes numeric elements first using the MDL-based discretization method. The results of scores are used to define new weights for Rep-Index. This calculation is made by the follow equation.

$$w_i = \frac{score_i.100}{\sum_{j=1}^{n}(score_j)} \quad (6)$$

When w is the new weight for the i element and n is the number of elements in the Rep-Index. With this weights, we computed the Rep-Index for each result. The next step is checking the best weights option. For this, we used the following correlations coefficients: Pearson, Spearman and Kendall. In the work of Kozak and Bornmann (2012) the Spearman rank correlation was used to evaluate a family of cumulative indexes for to measure scientific performance of researchers.

This correlations are computed with levels of CNPq in numerical values and integer value of Rep-Index. To convert the level of CNPq we adopt the following rules: level 2 value 1, level 1D value 2, level 1C value 3, level 1B value 4 and level 1A value 5. In addition to the correlations, we used scatter plots to visually evaluate the results. This plot is made with statistical software R[5]. In this graph type, the x-axis represents the level of CNPq and the y-axis the value of Rep-Index subjected to testing. The green line is a linear regression to the data. The inside ellipse contains 5% of the items, the external ellipse contains 95% of the graphic elements. The blue line represents the ideal situation, where there is maximum correlation between five levels of CNPq and five levels of Rep-Index. In this situation the *intercept* = 0 and *slope* = 1 to line equation: $f(x) = (slope * x) + intercept$.

[4] http://www.harzing.com/pop.htm

[5] https://www.R-project.org/

4. RESULTS AND DISCUSSION

In this section, we analyzed the dataset with a methodology defined in Materials and Methods section. The data were subjected to the attribute selection algorithms. From the values obtained in the selection of elements, we calculated the weight of each item present in Rep-Index. In Table 2 you can view the scores and weights proposed by selection attributes algorithms.

Table 2. Scores and Calculated Weights for Dataset

	InfoGain		**ChiSquare**		**SymmetricalUncert**		**GainRatio**		**ReliefF**	
Element	Score	Weigth	Score	Weigth	Score	Weigth	Score	Weigth	Score	Weigth
ASJ	0.415	23.87	217.086	22.33	0.258	19.24	0.237	12.70	0.041	7.69
BCP	0.072	4.15	38.394	3.95	0.059	4.39	0.073	3.92	0.017	3.20
BP	0.063	3.64	34.631	3.56	0.052	3.87	0.065	3.49	0.011	2.08
CCC									0.012	2.26
CCM									0.023	4.25
CWPCP	0.141	8.10	99.330	10.22	0.143	10.69	0.284	15.18	0.028	5.24
EBM	0.088	5.07	74.191	7.63	0.103	7.69	0.366	19.62	0.022	4.10
ED								0.00	0.057	10.63
HI	0.136	7,83	75.640	7.78	0.112	8.35	0.141	7.56	0.059	10.91
MDA	0.177	10.20	95.033	9.78	0.119	8.85	0.117	6.25	0.043	7.92
NC	0.168	9.66	87.362	8.99	0.115	8.59	0.116	6.21	0.036	6.62
PA	0.069	3.94	41.950	4.32	0.063	4.70	0.097	5.18	0.018	3.28
PEBMD								0.00	0.034	6.38
PEBPT	0.149	8.58	86.052	8.85	0.106	7.88	0.110	5.90	0.030	5.54
PTA	0.260	14.96	122.335	12.59	0.211	15.75	0.262	14.00	0.056	10.38
RJ									0.020	3.69
RP									0.024	4.51
SOFT									0.007	1.31
	1.738	100	972.002	100	1.340	100	1.868	100	0.539	100

It is observed that various elements were weightless. This occurs when the algorithm considers that the criterion is irrelevant for the final result, in the order that the key drivers were selected to decrease the number of variables included in the calculation. After we obtained a set of weights, we performed the calculation of the Rep-index using, and we applied the correlations in order to validate the results. In this process we used the integer value of Rep-Index in conjunction with the classification of CNPq for each researcher. In Figure 2 you can view the results.

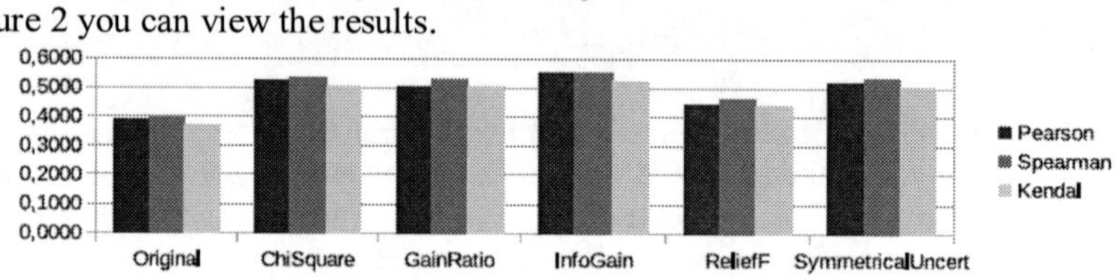

Figure 2. Correlations results for Computer Science

We observe then Pearson, Spearman and Kendall correlations have practically the same values and ranking. The technique that got the biggest hit is the InfoGain with 0.5523 for Pearson, 0.5520 for Spearman and 0.5233 for Kendall. Due to the worker of Kozak and Bornmann (2012) will opt for the Spearman correlation to make comparisons. The value of Spearman's correlation for Computer Science is 0.5520 (InfoGain) against 0.3932 for the Rep-Index with the original weights. These values show that despite the slight increase, we can complement the Rep-Index metric in this work. In the original Rep-Index there was 18 elements. After selection attribute algorithms, it is observed that the Computer Science have 11 elements with weights. In the Figure 3 is presented the scatter plots for Rep-Index original, ChiSquared, GainRatio, InfoGain, ReliefF and SymmetricalUncert.

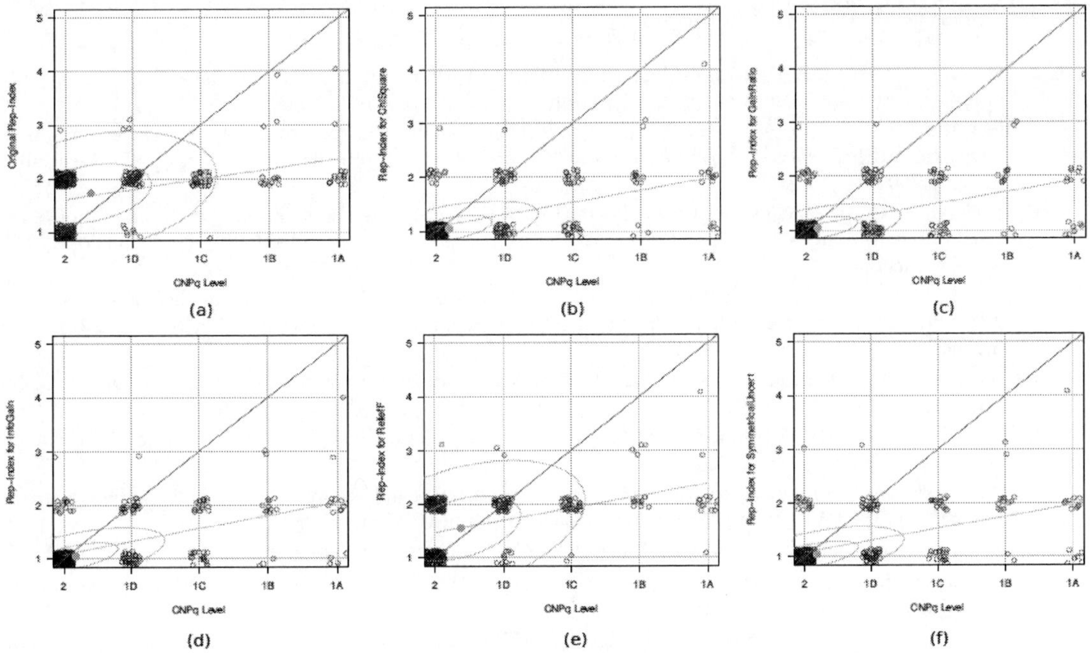

Figure 3. Evaluation for Rep-Index to Computer Science

Observing the scatter plots, it can be noted that Figure 3 shows the linear regression line (green) closer to the ideal situation considered (blue). The data distribution histogram also approximates the original CNPq distribution. The Figure 3 (d) has the best results with InfoGain Algorithm.

5. CONCLUSION

In this study, we proposed a complement to Rep-Index. The objective was to change the original weights for Rep-Index with five different selection attributes algorithms from Data Mining. For experiments, the data for Brazilian Researchers of Computer Science was used. The experiments are compared with three correlations. At the end, we observed that the Rep-Index is very flexible and adaptable. The methodology for calculating the weights makes it possible to apply the index in several areas of knowledge. Opting for the technique that results in better results in relation to the main group of researchers in the field (CNPq) we obtained the best possible set of weights to classify other researchers. Thus, we have the possibility of doing performance comparisons between researchers from different areas and with specific focus in their academic career.

It sees in the future further studies are more up to date and comprehensive data, including at least one area of research for each of the following areas of expertise: Agricultural Sciences, Biological Sciences, Exact and Earth Sciences, Humanities, Applied Social Sciences, Health Sciences, Engineering, Linguistics, Letter and Arts.

ACKNOWLEDGEMENT

This work is partially supported by PIIQP-BE, PIIQP-AM and PIIQP-AD programs from IFFar.

REFERENCES

S. Alonso, F. Cabrerizo, E. Herrera-Viedma, and F. Herrera. hg-index: A new index to characterize the scientific output of researchers based on the h-and g-indices. Scientometrics, 82(2):391–400, 2009.

J. Beel and B. Gipp. Google scholar's ranking algorithm: an introductory overview. In Proceedings of the 12th International Conference on Scientometrics and Informetrics (ISSI'09), volume 1, pages 230–241. Rio de Janeiro (Brazil), 2009.

C. R. Cervi, R. Galante, and J. P. M. d. Oliveira. Comparing the reputation of researchers using a profile model and scientific metrics. in: XIII IEEE International Conference on Computer and Information Technology(CIT), 2013a. Sydney, Australia.

C. R. Cervi, R. Galante, and J. P. M. d. Oliveira. Application of scientific metrics to evaluate academic reputation in different research areas. in: XXXIV International Conference on Computational Science(ICCS) 2013, 2013b. Bali, Indonesia.

P. Chen, H. Xie, S. Maslov, and S. Redner. Finding scientific gems with google's pagerank algorithm. Journal of Informetrics, 1(1):8–15, 2007.

R. Costas and M. Bordons. Is g-index better than h-index? an exploratory study at the individual level. Scientometrics, 77 (2):267–288, 2008.

M. Du, F. Bai, and Y. Liu. Paperrank: a ranking model for scientific publications. In Computer Science and Information Engineering, 2009 WRI World Congress on, volume 4, pages 277–281. IEEE, 2009.

L. Egghe. An improvement of the h-index: The g-index. ISSI newsletter, 2(1):8–9, 2006.

M. Hall, E. Frank, G. Holmes, B. Pfahringer, P. Reutemann, and I. H. Witten. The weka data mining software: an update. ACM SIGKDD explorations newsletter, 11(1):10–18, 2009.

J. E. Hirsch. An index to quantify an individual's scientific research output. Proceedings of the National academy of Sciences of the United States of America, 102(46):16569–16572, 2005.

B. Jin, L. Liang, R. Rousseau, and L. Egghe. The r-and ar-indices: Complementing the h-index. Chinese science bulletin, 52(6):855–863, 2007.

J. M. Kleinberg. Authoritative sources in a hyperlinked environment. Journal of the ACM (JACM), 46(5):604–632, 1999.

M. Kozak and L. Bornmann. A new family of cumulative indexes for measuring scientific performance. PloS one, 7(10): e47679, 2012.

L. Page, S. Brin, R. Motwani, and T.Winograd. The pagerank citation ranking: bringing order to the web. Stanford InfoLab, 1999.

A. Pal and S. Ruj. Citex: A new citation index to measure the relative importance of authors and papers in scientific publications. In Communications (ICC), 2015 IEEE International Conference on, pages 1256–1261. IEEE, 2015.

I. H. Witten and E. Frank. Data Mining: Practical machine learning tools and techniques. Morgan Kaufmann, 2005.

L. Zhai, X. Yan, and B. Zhu. The h l-index: improvement of h-index based on quality of citing papers. Scientometrics, 98 (2):1021–1031, 2014.

C.-T. Zhang. The e-index, complementing the h-index for excess citations. PLoS One, 4(5):e5429, 2009.

C.-T. Zhang. The h'-index, effectively improving the h-index based on the citation distribution. PloS one, 8(4):e59912, 2013.

Short Papers

USING QUALITY FACTORS TO FIND "GOOD" RESOURCES ON THE GEOGEBRA MATERIALS SHARING PLATFORM

Markus Hohenwarter[1] and Cristian Hedes[2]
[1]*Johannes Kepler University Linz, Austria*
[2]*Babeş-Bolyai University of Cluj-Napoca, Romania*

ABSTRACT

The GeoGebra Materials sharing platform offers nearly half a million interactive worksheets and books for learning and teaching mathematics and science. These open educational resources have been created and publicly shared by students and teachers from around the world, in many different languages and for all levels of education. This paper addresses the question how to find "good" materials within this very large number of interactive learning objects. It describes a first attempt to extend the previous text-based search algorithm of the GeoGebra Materials platform in order to sort materials based on quality factors for materials, authors and searching users.

KEYWORDS

Open educational resources, search, quality, mathematics

1. INTRODUCTION

The large number of open educational resources for learning and teaching mathematics and science offered by sharing platforms like LearningApps (2016) or GeoGebra Materials (2016) makes it difficult for users to quickly find appropriate resources (Trgalova et.al., 2011). The problem of inconsistent quality particularly appears on platforms with user-generated educational resources that aren't supported by an editorial team (Camilleri et.al., 2014).

For the GeoGebra Materials platform, Kimeswenger (2016) addresses the issue of quality aspects of dynamic materials by investigating possible quality criteria for dynamic materials based on the opinion of experts who describe their views on educationally valuable use. It seems impossible to decide in general, whether a specific resource is of "high quality" as a given resource can be good in one context and poor in another. Nevertheless, there seem to be certain strategies that users apply when searching for "good" dynamic materials. For example, expert users of the GeoGebra platform indicated that they tend to search for materials of already known "high-quality authors", which they expect to produce "good" dynamic materials according to their own standards of quality.

Thus, the possibility to follow certain authors and get notified about their new creations was recently added to the GeoGebra platform. In addition, several other quality measures have been suggested by expert users and literature (Kimeswenger, 2016; Ott & Hielscher, 2015). In this paper, we describe how we have tried to include these quality factors based on existing parameters available in the database of the GeoGebra Materials platform. This has allowed us to improve the previous text-only search into a direction where now both relevant text descriptions as well as certain quality factors are considered when a user enters a search term on this platform.

2. QUALITY FACTORS

Previously, the GeoGebra Materials platform used a search algorithm based on textual relevance, i.e. the classic Xapian search with the BM25 weighting formula (Xapian, 2016). The goal was now to improve this approach by not only looking at texts (i.e. titles, descriptions, and worksheet content) but to also include quality factors concerning the material, its author and the user who has entered a specific search term (see Fig. 1).

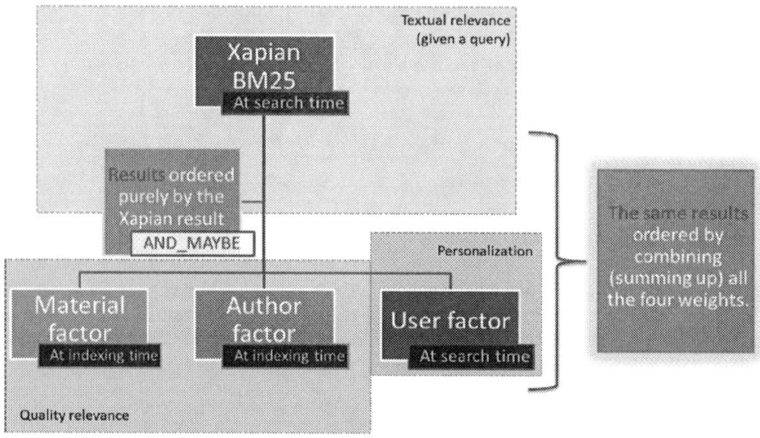

Figure 1. Combining Xapian Search with Quality factors

Based on the qualitative interviews with expert users of Kimeswenger (2016), we have tried to identify and use already existing meta-data of the GeoGebra Materials platform where we think that they could help us to quantify the quality of materials using certain factors. We have defined three factors relating to the material itself, to the author of a material, and to the user searching for good materials which are described in the following sections.

2.1 Material Factor

The material factor tries to measure the activity happening around a certain material, i.e. how much it is being used, copied and favorited. The following parameters are used for the materials factor:

- featured: materials that have been featured by the GeoGebra team should have higher priority
- type: books (collections of worksheets) should have higher priority than single worksheets
- derived: materials with many copies should have higher priority
- groups: materials used by many groups should have higher priority
- books: materials used in many books (collections) should have higher priority
- favorites: materials that have been favorited by many users should have higher priority
- views per day: materials that are viewed more often should have higher priority

2.2 Author Factor

The author factor should reflect the expertise and relevance of a material's author in the GeoGebra community. Materials of people with many followers or many published materials should have higher priority in the search results. The following parameters are combined into the author factor:

- followers: materials of author's with many followers should have higher priority
- community: materials of authors with GeoGebra community badges should have higher priority
- public materials: materials of authors with many public materials should have higher priority
- teacher: materials of teachers should have slightly higher priority than materials of other users

2.3 User Factor

The user factor is a measure available only at search time and depends exclusively on the current user who has entered a search term. This personalized factor currently only uses two parameters:

- language: materials in the same language as the user's language should have higher priority
- userID: the materials of the searching user should have higher priority than materials from other users

3. NORMALIZING AND WEIGHING THE QUALITY FACTORS

In order to use the described quality factors for sorting search results on the GeoGebra Materials platform together with the classic Xapian weights, it was necessary to normalize their parameters and weigh the factors themselves. Firstly, we had a look at the different parameter values of materials for the most popular search terms, i.e. for '3d', 'parabola', 'graph', 'pythagoras', and 'transformation'. We computed all the values of the abovementioned parameters of our quality factors for all materials listed as results of these search terms. Using a spreadsheet, we analyzed and compared the different parameter values with the standard Xapian weights for text search.

We have asked a small group of expert users to manually rank the Xapian search results for the search term '3d' by "quality", i.e. according to their own subject quality criteria. These rankings of expert users have helped us to choose weights and weighing functions as described in the following paragraphs. We are aware that these weights and functions are only a first experimental attempt and that they can and should be tuned based on further user testing in the future.

For example, while the Xapian weights for the most popular search term '3d' was in the range [0, 9.69], the 'public materials' values ranged from 0 to 15611. Thus, we decided to normalize all the different parameters to a range of [0, 10]. For this reason, we used functions such as LOG10, LN, and SQRT based on an overview of the data behavior in comparison with the Xapian classic weight. Experimentation led us to the normalization functions shown in Tables 1 and 2 which we are now using for the parameters of our three quality factors.

Table 1. Material factor: normalization functions

ATTRIBUTE	min value	max value	normalization function	min normalized	max normalized
featured	0	1	10*	0	10
type	1	255	LN	0	5,541263545
derived	0	13	SQRT	0	3,605551275
groups	0	2	SQRT	0	1,414213562
books	0	80	LN	0	4,394449155
favorites	0	14	LN(#+1)	0	2,708050201
views per day	0	4,76	*LN(1+(1+views_count)/days_passed)*	0	4,76
				MAX TOTAL	32,42352774

Table 2. Author factor: normalization functions

ATTRIBUTE	min value	max value	normalization function	min normalized	max normalized
followers	0	7	SQRT	0	2,828427125
community	0	5	SQRT	0	2,236067977
public_materials	0	15611	LOG10(#+1)	0	4,193458543
teacher	0	1	-	0	1
				MAX TOTAL	10,25795364

These normalized parameter values are now combined to quality factors by simply computing their sums. Considering the results obtained for the factors we still observed that some quality factors seemed to influence the final search weight more than they should. In order to decide what weights to use when combining the individual quality factors, we have asked a small group of GeoGebra expert users to do a manual ranking by quality of selected materials. For this little experiment, 3 combinations of surveys were created, each of them consisting of four sets of 5 materials from a total of 60, plus an extra set consisting of the best materials from each of the previous sets. Based on this heuristic approach, we were able to compare the expert rankings with different quality factor weights.

This has led us to choose the following weighted quality factors in relation to the classic Xapian weight:

- Material Factor = 0.5 * (featured + type + books + favorites + groups + derived + views per day)
- Author Factor = 0.3 * (followers + community + public materials + teacher)
- User Factor = 6 * material language + 100 * userID
- New Search Weight = Classic Xapian Weight + Materials Factor + Author Factor + User Factor

This new search weight is now being used on the GeoGebra Materials platform for each material search query. During our experiments we also tried to use factor weights depending on the Xapian weight for a specific search term. However, we finally decided to compute the weights for the Material and the Author factors a priori in order to get faster search times.

4. CONCLUSION

The described new material ranking approach of the GeoGebra Materials sharing platform combines the classic Xapian text-relevance search with quality factors for materials, authors and users. We have chosen normalization functions and weighing factors based on analyzing top search results and a small set of materials that were manually ranked by expert users.

We see plenty of room for future improvements, both in the way that weights are chosen as well as for further parameters to be included. For example, the user factor could include more personalized parameters like whether this user is following the author of a material or what favorite materials this user already has. The current algorithm makes it difficult to find materials of new users as they have no followers and only a small number of public materials. Thus, it will be necessary to find a way how we can make materials of new users more visible to others. So continued work is definitely needed and planned. We would very much welcome any suggestions from the research community on how to improve and test our approach for finding "good" materials in the future.

REFERENCES

Camilleri, A. F. et.al., 2014. State of the Art Review of Quality Issues related to Open Educational Resources (OER). Luxembourg: Publications Office of the European Union.

GeoGebra Materials, 2016. Platform. www.geogebra.org/materials, retrieved on 2016-07-25.

I2Geo, 2016. Platform. http://i2geo.net, retrieved on 2016-07-25.

Kimeswenger, B., 2016. Addressing Quality Aspects of Dynamic Mathematics Materials. Proceedings of 13th International Congress on Mathematical Education (ICME 13). Hamburg, Germany.

LearningApps, 2016. Platform. http://learningapps.org/, retrieved on 2016-07-25.

Ott, M., & Hielscher, M., 2015. Kriterien für die automatisierte Bewertung von user-generated educational Microcontent. In E-Learning Fachtagung Informatik. Proceedings Series of the Gesellschaft für Informatik, Vol. P-233, pp. 73–84.

Trgalova, J. et. al., 2011. Quality assessment process for dynamic geometry resources in Intergeo project. ZDM - International Journal on Mathematics Education, 43, 337–351.

Xapian, 2016. The BM25 Weighting Scheme. https://xapian.org/docs/bm25.html, retrieved on 2016-07-25.

CONNECTCITY: A COLLABORATIVE E-GOVERNMENT APPROACH TO REPORT CITY INCIDENTS

Amanda Carolina Pistolato and Wladmir Cardoso Brandão
Department of Computer Science - Pontifical Catholic University of Minas Gerais

ABSTRACT

Governments around the world fail in effectively identify and classify incidents in public areas, as well as in rout them to the right government agent responsible to address the problem. In particular, several incidents take long time to be solved by the fact that the agent does not know their existence, generating financial losses and frustration to society. In this article, we propose a collaborative e-government approach to report city incidents and perform usability evaluation using think aloud method and SURE questionnaire. The proposed approach is simple and effective, and different from others related works it can be used to report several categories of city incidents.

KEYWORDS

E-government, collaborative technologies, social media, crowdsensing, social networks

1. INTRODUCTION

The Brazilian urbanization process increased in a disorderly and accelerated way, especially after 70's, counting, in most cases, with an ineffectively involvement and commitment of state and civil society in organization of urban space, resulting in several problems, such as traffic incidents - one of the major causes of urban deaths. Indices related to the number of traffic incidents are increasingly worrying, as they are responsible for financial losses and immeasurable loss, the human costs. (Ferreira & Freitas). Additionally, other minor incidents, such as holes, water leaks, fallen trees, tall grass, and garbage scattered in roads occur frequently. In this scenario, it is hard for city administrators to quickly identify and classify incidents without the support of the society. Similarly, it is hard for citizens to choose the right channel to report incidents. Therefore, the development of collaborative technologies that reduce the communication gap between government and society is paramount to increase government effectiveness on incident solution.

In this article, we propose ConnectCity, a collaborative e-government approach to report city incidents. Our approach offers an easy and simple interface for citizens to register and classify incidents, as well as a routing mechanism to deliver information on incidents to the right government agent responsible for the solution. In addition, we evaluate our prototype by using the SURE methodology (Wangenheim et al. 2014). Experimental results show that our prototype: i) is error tolerant by avoiding users to commit errors and helping them to correct those committed; ii) generates user engagement by providing a pleasant and useful interface which satisfies user needs; iii) is easy to learn by being consistent and predictable with functions and information where users expect to find them; iv) is efficient by requiring a minimum number of user interactions and time to complete a task and; v) is effective by allowing users to easily find relevant information and functions to complete tasks. The key contributions of this article can be summarized as follows: i) we propose a collaborative e-government approach to report city incidents. The proposed approach is simple, effective and can be used to report different categories of city incidents; ii) we perform usability evaluation of our prototype, highlighting its strengths and weaknesses.

The remainder of this article is organized as follows: Section 2 reviews the related literature on collaborative technologies and e-government. Section 3 presents related tools reported on literature. Section 4 describes ConnectCity, including its architecture and main components. Section 5 describes the setup and results of the experimental evaluation. Finally, Section 6 provides a summary of the contributions and the conclusions made throughout the other sections, presenting directions for future research.

2. BACKGROUND

E-government is a way to improve governance and reduce communication gaps between citizens and government using information and communication technologies (ICT). In the context of cities, e-government approaches provide communication bridges between the city government administration and its citizens by introducing ICT in every day urban life (Giffinger et al. 2007).

Crowdsensing mobile applications, are applications used to share data and extract information collected from computing devices in order to measure and map phenomena of common interest . Infrastructure crowdsensing is used to measure public infrastructures, such as road conditions or broken traffic lights. There are two ways to collect data, participatory way and opportunistic way. Participatory manner requires user action taking a picture or reporting incident for example. Opportunistic requires minimal involvement of the user, information is sent almost autonomously (Ganti et al. 2011).

Collaboration is a process in which two or more agents work together to achieves shared goals. The increasing use of ICT by society is transforming the way citizens interact with governments and how government conducts their daily operations and tasks. As part of this movement, citizens and governments are looking for transparency, accountability and performance, which require information sharing and collaboration for effective management and provision of government services. The ICT driven collaboration environments, such as social networks, focused on government challenges are referred to as collaborative e-government.

Social networks (SN) are Internet-based platforms that connect persons through their interests. They allow users to create personal profiles and develop social structures for content sharing. In addition, SN users can start relationships, create and disseminate events, express opinions and organize social interventions, dictating trends to other users.

3. RELATED WORK

In this section, we present related tools, including a comparative analysis of the related tools to demonstrate the differences between them and ConnectCity, showing the novel functions and features of our approach.

Gainey (2003) proposed a web application for creating, maintaining and analyzing incident reports from anywhere in the world. The application, according to a user level, allows creating a report, searching for a report, listing all reports, creating a text report and creating a graphical report.

Colab.re[1] is a social network geared towards citizenship that aims to connect citizens and government entities with a focus on problem solving, project discussion and evaluation of public services. The structure of Colab.re is formed by an environment of interaction between users, using web or smartphone applications, and a second administrative environment in which a government entity can manage the demands of citizens. To use the tool users should access the website of the developer company or download the application on a phone and complete the registration form. Login and registered password provide to users access to register inspections, proposals and evaluation directed to entities responsible, monitor the progress of their inspections, proposals and evaluation, interact with the responsible entity for the provision of public services, comment and evaluate inspections, proposals and evaluations of other users, and participate in surveys.

Urbotip[2] is an application that helps citizens to share issues in their cities with the world, trying to show authorities the right places where to act.

Cidade Legal[3] is a collaborative application to map cities incidents. Objective is the creation of a shared communication mechanism between citizens and the government. Users are citizens who want to report an incident in a particular area of the city. Users don't need to create an account.

Different from the related tools aforementioned, ConnectCity maps city incidents and improves communication between citizens and government entities, covering potential problems in a city, whether it be related to health (dengue fever, noise), infrastructure (holes in the roads, broken signpost), urban planning (traffic, flooding), crime (sexual harassment, assault), natural disaster (floods, landslides), or human disaster

[1] http://www.colab.re
[2] http://www.urbotip.com
[3] http://cidadelegal.com

(car accidents, industrial fires, river contamination). The related tools have limitations covered by ConnectCity. They are most focused in one problem – infrastructure. One of the related applications don't have user identification, allowing fake information and most of them don't work related to social networks. Some applications don't allow users to see all local incidents and it is necessary because that way user could check if a specific region has, for example, many assaults or floods, avoiding possible incidents. Besides that, in ConnectCity, when users report an incident, it became a kind of event, and other users could open it to explore and insert additional information.

4. THE CONNECTCITY APPROACH

ConnectCity is a collaborative e-government approach with a citizen to government relationship, where citizens create social relations to report city incidents in a collaborative way, helping the government to improve governance in their cities. With a common objective, show where government must act, users inserted in this social structure could help increasing the number of data about each incident, including comments, more pictures or supporting incidents that were created by other citizens.

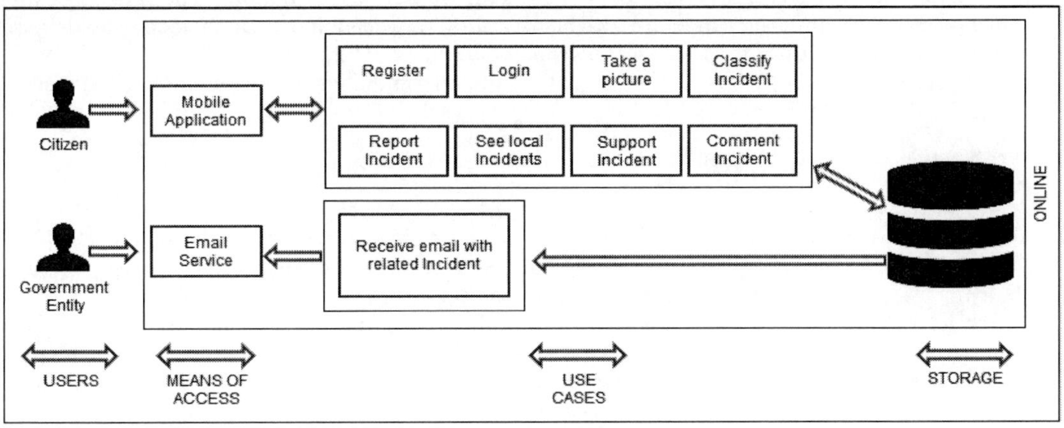

Figure 1. ConnectCity Architecture

Figure 1 shows that ConnectCity have two means of access, citizens could access using the mobile application and Government Entity receives notifications about related incidents in a pre-registered email. A citizen must register in application to be able to use it. Registration primarily consists of entering name, CPF (Brazilian national identification number) and email address. After registration, citizens insert email and password in order to access the application. Afterwards, a page with incidents near to the citizen will appear with the identification of the citizen that created the incident. Citizens are allowed to take a picture to be used in the report, for that, they must enable GPS on cell phone, that way, GPS coordinates will be used to show a map with location before citizen report the incident and could be used to assure the reliability of the incident reported to the government. After that, citizen choose incident type in a list, insert a title, description and decides if will report incident as anonymous or not. Then, a map with location will appear and citizen could select report or cancel, if citizen select cancel, application will return to local incidents page. Citizens can also see a map with local incidents, enter in an incident and support, comment or add a picture.

5. RESULTS

To evaluate our collaborative e-government approach, we evaluate its usability by using the SURE methodology (Wangenheim et al. 2014). Particularly, in this section we answer the following research questions:

1. How error tolerant is ConnectCity?
2. How easy to learn is ConnectCity?
3. How ConnectCity performs to provide user engagement?
4. How efficient and effective are ConnectCity?

5.1 Experimental Setup

To assess the effectiveness of our collaborative e-government prototype, we use the think aloud method and SURE (Smartphone Usability questionnaire), a questionnaire and scale to evaluate smartphones applications usability after usability test (Wangenheim et al. 2014). Potential users of our approach answered a set of questions and the answers are used to validate its usability. The set is composed by 31 questions and the answers are divided into 4 items in a Likert scale: i) strongly disagree; ii) disagree; iii) agree; iv) strongly agree.

We select the user sample, people with age between 25 and 34 years old, by relying on (TIC 2014), which demonstrates that the majority of citizens in Brazil that use Internet to contact government because of public transport or other urban services, such as cleaning and maintenance of roads, have between 25 and 34 years old. Additionally, we consider 10 users for our research, with 10 users, the lowest percentage of problems revealed by any one set was increased to 80% (Faulkner 2003), when think aloud method is used, 9 users are needed to detect 80% of usability problems (Hwang & Salvendy 2010).

After distributing tasks to the 10 probably users and perform the test using the think aloud method, was given the SURE questionnaire.

5.2 Experimental Results

In this section, we present the results of the experiments we have carried out to evaluate our collaborative e-government approach. In particular, we address the four research questions stated previously, evaluating its usability by using the SURE questionnaire (Wangenheim et al. 2014).

Error tolerant approaches avoid user errors while help users to solve committed errors. Considering answers in SURE that point to error tolerance topics, 50 percent of users did not consider the help and tips given by our approach useful. However, 90 percent strongly agree that it is easy to fix a mistake. Taking into account user answers, we can observe that users did not consider the help and tips given by our approach useful because users think help and tips are not necessary. ConnectCity does not unduly penalize user errors, when an user make a mistake, it keep working and give options and tips for users to fix their mistakes without the user has to think a lot.

An easy to learn approach is consistent, predictable, behaving always in the same way, and presents functions and information where users expect. Considering answers that point to learning facility topic, we can observe that 40 percent of users disagree that symbols and icons are clear and intuitive in our approach. It is because of an icon that aimed to return to the main application page. To avoid this situation the icon was changed. This was the only question that received a disagree answer. Therefore, according to the users, ConnectCity is easy to learn.

An engaging approach is useful, pleasant and satisfies the user information needs. Considering answers in SURE that point to user engagement topics, we observe that all users strongly agree with the fact that they felt confident and in command using ConnectCity. None of users disagreed with any of engaging questions. According to the users, ConnectCity promotes user engagement.

While Efficiency is related with how quickly a task can be completed, effectiveness considers how well the work is done (Quesenbery 2001). Considering answers in SURE that point to user efficiency, 90 percent of users strongly agree that the time to complete tasks using our approach was suitable, while 80 percent agree that even in a hurry they could perform the tasks using our approach. According to users, the prototype has proved to be efficient. In conformity to answers that point to effectiveness topic, we found a problem in the map view page that shows all incidents, the map was not showing any incident, only the predefined markup, but that was not user fault and, from what we can see, didn't influenced users. Despite of the problem with the map, users are satisfied with the effectiveness of ConnectCity.

6. CONCLUSION

In this article we propose ConnectCity, a collaborative e-government approach to report city incidents. Our approach offers an easy and simple interface for citizens to register and classify incidents, as well as routing mechanism to deliver information on incidents to the right government agent responsible for the solution. Additionally, we conduct usability experiments showing that our approach is error tolerant, easy to learn, efficient, effective, and generates user engagement. Moreover, it is simple and can be used to report different categories of city incidents. ConnectCity can be used by city administrators to reduce the communication gap between government and society, decreasing the time to solve problems and avoiding financial losses.

For future work, we plan to deploy and assess the efficiency of other functionalities, such as posting videos and comments on incidents, sharing incidents in external social network, and predicting the occurrence of critical incidents. Another plan is to adapt the proposed approaches to work with other mobile operating systems and languages besides Brazilian Portuguese.

ACKNOWLEDGEMENTS

We thank the partial support given by FAPEMIG, PUC Minas (grant FIP 2015/9396-S1), and CNPq Grant 444156/2014-3 (Wladmir C. Brandão).

REFERENCES

Faulkner, L., 2003. Beyond the five-user assumption: Benefits of increased sample sizes in usability testing, *Behavior Research Methods, Instruments, & Computers*, vol. 35, no. 3, pp. 379–383.

Ferreira, D.L. and Freitas, M.P., 2010. Acidentes de Trânsito no Brasil e em Uberlândia (MG): Análise do Comportamento e a Forma de Utilização deste Indicador para a Gestão da Mobilidade Urbana, *Observatorium: Eletronic magazine of geography,* Vol. 2, No.5, pp.114-133.

Gainey, P.M., 2003. System and method for recording and using incident report data. US 2003/0023476 A1.

Ganti, R.K. et al., 2011. Mobile Crowdsensing: Current state and future challenges, *IEEE Communication Magazine*, Vol.49, No.11, pp.32-39.

Giffinger, R. et al., 2007. Smart cities-ranking of european medium-sized cities. *Centre of Regional Science, Vienna University of Technology*, Vienna, Austria, pp.1–28.

Hwang, W. and Salvendy, G., 2010. Number of people required for usability evaluation: the 10±2 rule, *Communications of the ACM Magazine,* Vol.53, No.5, pp.130-133.

Quesenbery, W., 2001, What does usability mean: Looking beyond ease of use. *Proceedings of the 48th Annual Conference, Society for Technical Communication*. Chicago, United States, pp. 432–436.

TIC, 2014. *TIC Domicílios e usuários*." [Online] Available at: http://data.cetic.br/cetic/explore?idPesquisa=TIC_DOM&idUnidadeAnalise=Usuarios&ano=2014 [Accessed November 2015].

Wangenheim, C.G. et al. , 2014. Sure: uma proposta de questionário e escala para avaliar a usabilidade de aplicações para smartphones pós-teste de usabilidade. *Proceedings of Conferencia Lationamericana de Diseño de Interacción*. Buenos Aires, Argentina, pp. 1–8.

SMART-READER FOR A BETTER E-LEARNING

Ilmi Yoon[1], Imram Alavi[1], Selman Kahya[2], Joshua Lee[3] and Ji Won Shin[4]
[1]Computer Science, San Francisco State Univ., 1600 Holloway Ave. SF, CA94132
[2]Yahoo Inc.
[3]Dougherty Valley High School
[4]Princeton Univ.

ABSTRACT

E-Book readers are changing the way people read books in many ways. Unlike traditional books, E-Book Reader (Kindle, iBook etc.) can produce very valuable assessment and information of reading habits from the natural reading activity in a natural environment. It is possible to track minutes per page to understand reading behavior for individual readers and to find the most popular pages among books across several readers as well. Words that readers look up while reading a book can be collected and analyzed. We believe that this data can be effectively used for assessment of reading levels as well as the source for possible educational and fun activities. By processing the data, many valuable services could be provided back to readers, parents (teachers), authors, and publishers. This paper introduces the Smart Reader project whose ultimate goal is to develop a reading model to understand various readers' reading comprehension and their learning experience. We attempt to analyze readers' natural reading behavior and study their reading patterns along with developing new tools to aid the readers.

KEYWORDS

E-book, epub, tracking reading behavior, reading behavior visualization

1. INTRODUCTION

An electronic book (variously: e-book, eBook, e-Book, e-book, digital book, or even e-edition) is a book-length publication in digital form, consisting of text, images, or both, readable on computers or other electronic devices. There are several advantages that e-Books offer that people prefer compared tor traditional books. To buy a book, you had to go to a bookstore or order online and wait until it gets delivered. However, with digitization of the books, it would take couple of clicks to buy, download and start reading. Also, instead of carrying the books or having storage to keep them all, it is relatively easy to have a device with couple of gigs of memory. Modern E-Book readers have the capacity to store thousands of books. It is also possible to read books online without first saving them on the device. Consequently, e-books are getting more popular and it seems likely that, at least in the short term, e-book sale will settle between 10% and 20% of the total market (Milliot 2014).

Emerge of e-book opens a new possibility of tracking, assessing, and quantitatively measuring of reading behavior. Reading is critical to future academic and vocational opportunities as a foundational skill for learning (Lesnick, Gorerge, Smithgall, & Gwynne, 2010). However, with traditional books, understanding reader's natural reading and consequential comprehension have not been studied before. Unlike traditional books, e-book readers can produce very valuable data from the natural reading activity. For example, time-spent on each page can be tracked. When a book is given as a reading assignment, instructor cannot verify if a student has actually read a book or not if it is a traditional book. Instructor may verify using reading comprehension questions. With e-book, time-spent on each page provides a better indication if the student actually read it. Comparison to other students' reading charts of time-spent on each page, it is easy to assess if the student has read the book with sincere effort or just skimmed through it. If students have read with sincere effort like majority of other readers but still fail the reading comprehension question, then it implies that students need different support or the book is beyond the students' reading level. Also, most of the popular e-book readers provide word look-up functionality that helps users to look up the definition of unfamiliar vocabulary while reading. However, word look-up data is rarely used to offer additional services to readers. In this paper, we present various approaches to utilize the power of e-book in learning especially when a community of readers exist.

Since the emergence of ebooks, there has been active research on reading comprehension. Although the page presentation looks similar to traditional books, these ebooks offer integrated multimedia features such as animations, music, narrations, illustrations, and sound effects (de Jong & Bus, 2003; Labbo & Kuhn, 2000). Johnson et al. (2011) predicted and emphasized the significance of the mobility of hand held devices and ebooks' influence on teaching and learning. Significantly, the presentation of new information utilizing ebooks may reduce the extraneous cognitive load that weakens problem solving (Srivastava & Gray, 2012; van Merriënboer & Sweller, 2005) as learning new information must be processed in working memory, which is affected by load not necessary to learning (extraneous cognitive load) (van Merriënboer & Sweller, 2005). Rosenfield (2011), Benedetto (2013), Harris (2013), and Conlon (2011) found that for shorter reading sessions that require less cognitive effort, the optical qualities of an LCD computer screen are sufficient, which may explain why many people have abandoned print newspapers and magazines in favor of the greater convenience of on-line editions. However, the non-illuminated displays of e-paper and print books are better suited to reading longer, more challenging texts.

This research mostly focuses on delivery of information and reading comprehension comparison with tradition book reading. We shift the focus on tracking data from reading behavior that can be effectively used for assessment of reading level and by processing the data, many valuable services could be provided back to readers, parents (teachers), authors, and publisher. To readers, list of words that were looked up can be used to create flash cards or word games. Parents or teachers can receive assessment results compared to similar reading level kids. To authors and publishers, the pages that majority readers stayed longest or frequent words for look-up can provide valuable data for the next edition. It can effectively help students' critical reading study or professional text book reading (by providing extra level word look-up for technical terms).

In the next section, we present the technical design and implementation to be able to produce the necessary tracking data. In section 3, we present the tracking data that are collected from various users.

2. DESIGN AND IMPLEMENTATION

Design objective is implementing a possible and plausible solution to create a prototype of tracking and presenting user reading activity by creating new services from the assessment. We aim to study ways to interpret or understand readers' comprehension of the book by analyzing reading behaviors; track minutes per page to assess reading comprehension level for individual reader and to find the most popular pages among books across many readers as well. Parents can be provided with the average minutes per page for specific book, statistics from kids with comparable reading level and the words that their child looked up while reading.

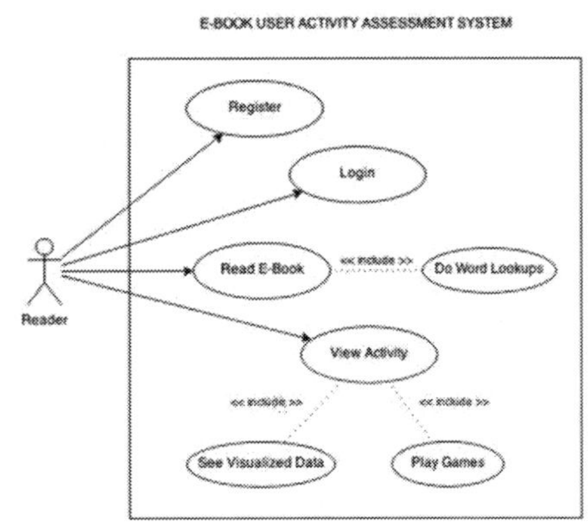

Figure 1. Use Case Diagram

This project would have been ideally tested if implemented on kindle, the most widely spread e-book reader, but the kindle is a closed platform where a plug-in API is not available. As an alternative, we simulate an environment that can similarly demonstrate the user experience with available technologies such as ePub,

JavaScript, AJAX, PHP, MySQL, and mobile app development. Our current solution is an extension to an existing e-Book reader for the Chrome browser. In that way, we do not have to develop an e-Book reader from scratch, and instead we could spend more time on thinking how to analyze and present tracking data. We used the popular Readium project that provides an open source implementation for handling EPUB documents. It has an API that makes it easy to upload, view and develop EPUB content. We were able to merge our project with the Readium E-book Reader. One of the problems that we encountered was the ability to understand when to start tracking user activity. Obviously, users may be using the Chrome browser for other purposes than just reading e-books. To solve this problem, we thought of adding a "Start Tracking" button as can be seen in the picture. Then there was another problem. In order us to process each activity on the back-end, users have to register and have a unique user id. However, since the extensions do not allow having a complex UI, we were not able to create a registration page within the extension. We discovered that if we were to develop a Chrome extension, we might also have to create a web application that users can visit to register and see their activity which would increase the scope of the project as well as the complexity of the overall design. We decided to create a Chrome Packaged Application by using AngularJS - JavaScript MVC Framework - which allowed us to develop all the required features as separate modules and have both a tracking script and user interface for registration and viewing activity in a single platform. So, in our app, user can register, login, load and read E-Book while doing word-lookups (Figure 1). Users can also view their activity such as viewing visualized data or play word games using the words that user looked up while reading. The application runs on chrome browsers on Windows and Android tablets. On the server side, we designed a RESTful API that handles incoming requests from the Chrome application. Tracking data is stored in a MySQL database. The back-end is responsible for making complex tracking analysis while the application is only responsible for presenting the given data (Figure 2).

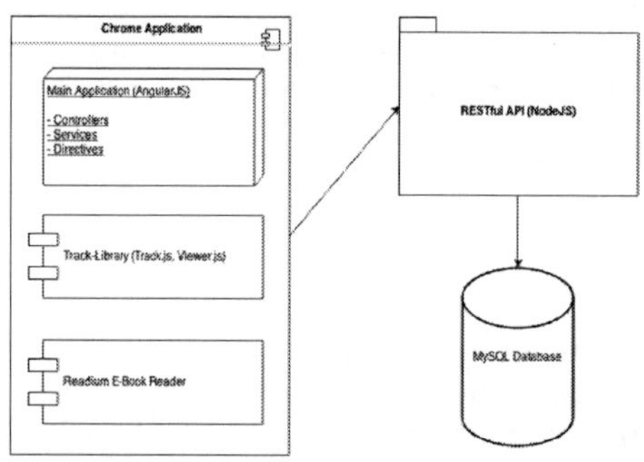

Figure 2. System Design Diagram

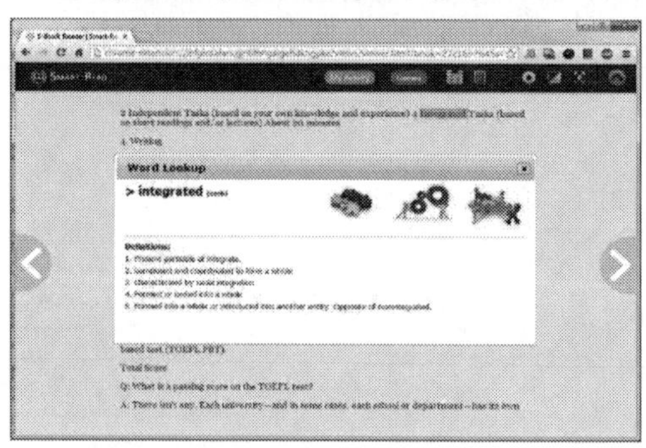

Figure 3. System Design Diagram

We noticed all e-book word look-ups are showing only text description while images can explain and depict the definition as well as increase the memorization of the word. So, we added images when user clicks for word-lookup using Google Image Search API (Figure 3). We also utilized these images for word game later: a definition is shown first, and then user tries to guess the word. If user cannot guess the word, s/he can ask for a hint. In that case, our application will show four relevant pictures to the user. We mark the word as quiz_taken and quiz_result_successful if the answer is correct. User also has 'skip question' option.

User can see their activity data using the "My Activity" page where user can see the list of words that were looked up while reading and other statistics of activities (Figure 4 & Figure 5).

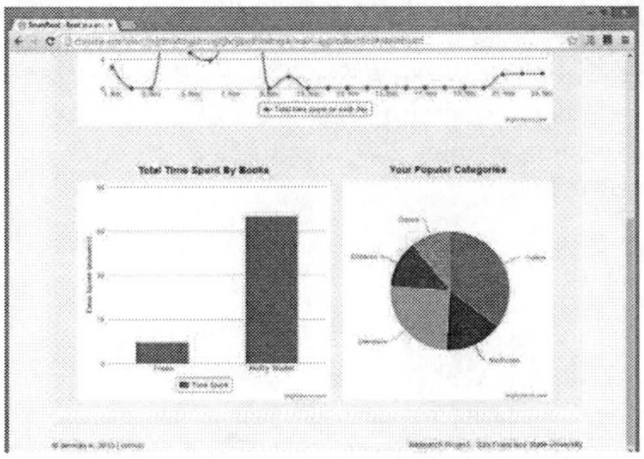

Figure 4. Visualization of user activity – total time spent on each day chart, time spent by books and the time spent on each categories

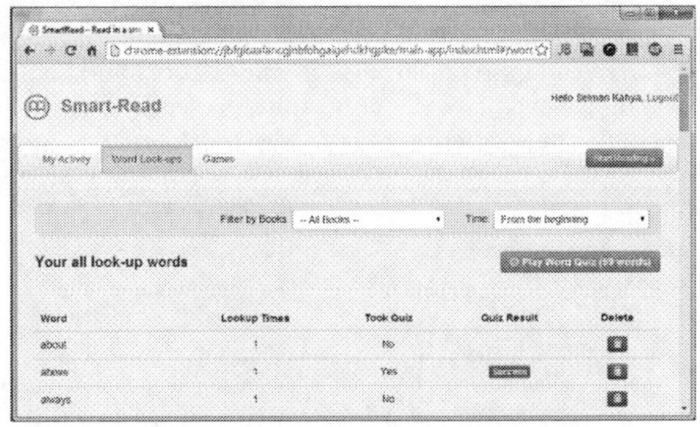

Figure 5. Word look-up report where user can play word game. We can create Flash cards using these words and the images

3. RESULTS

We are currently working with two types of results. First group is a focus group (6 computer science students) to understand the reading behaviors clearly and then apply the findings or patterns to the general audience in the second group. Focus group were given two books. The first book used in the focus group was a custom book that one of co-author created about software design patterns more specifically Observable and the MVC patterns as a Computer Science course supplementary material. There is a pattern in reading this book and most readers stay with the pattern while one or two students are off from the pattern (Figure 6). Through the interview with students, it is clear that students who stay within the pattern had a better understanding of the material. Students who were not showing the similar pattern seemed having problems in understanding the material. The word-lookup were also showing similar patterns. Students who were showing similar pattern also looked up most of words that the group of students in the same pattern looked up.

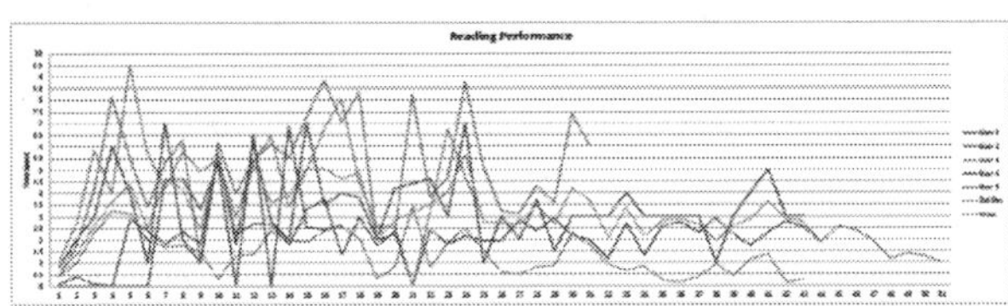

Figure 6. Data for six adults while reading Design Patterns. The users in this research are students of Computer Science

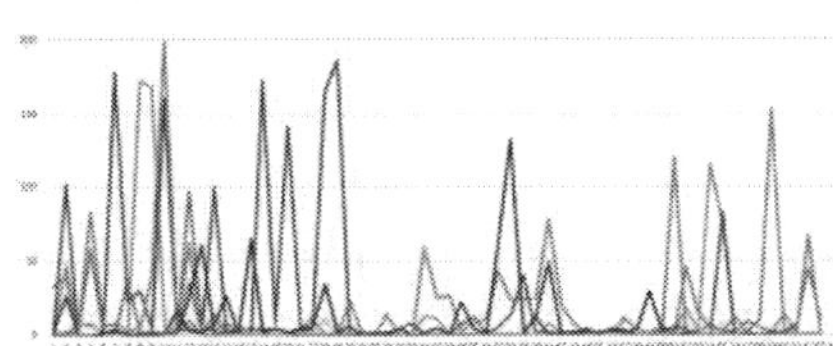

Figure 7. Time spent on each page collected from 8 readers reading, "The legend of Sleepy Hollow"

The second group is the general audience who downloaded our app from Google Chrome web store and provided anonymous tracking data while they are reading. Over 16000 readers downloaded our app and used our app to read any book they want to read in natural reading style. There are 268 books that were read by more than one user. There are 511 users who read more than one book. One of users read 133 different books. The general audience group data was unexpected benefit from posting the app at the Google Chrome web store, however we do not know who these readers are (gender, age etc) as these are anonymous. We are currently working on finding reading patterns from this data. From these readers, we found that time spent on each page exceeding 3 minutes usually represents break, not deeply delving in the contents. By comparing across multiple readers, pages multiple readers seem reading deeply still didn't exceed 3 minutes while there are random spikes exceeding 3 minutes. We removed page that user spent more than 200 seconds and plotted chart (Figure 7). Some readers tend to have frequent habitual breaks across all books that they read while some readers read through a whole book with only a few breaks. Figure 8 shows two individual reader reading several books (each line presents different book read by same reader). Chart-in-chart shows the original data before removing the breaks (page reader spent longer than 200 seconds). Even after removing the breaks, each reader creates unique reading patterns shown at figure 8.

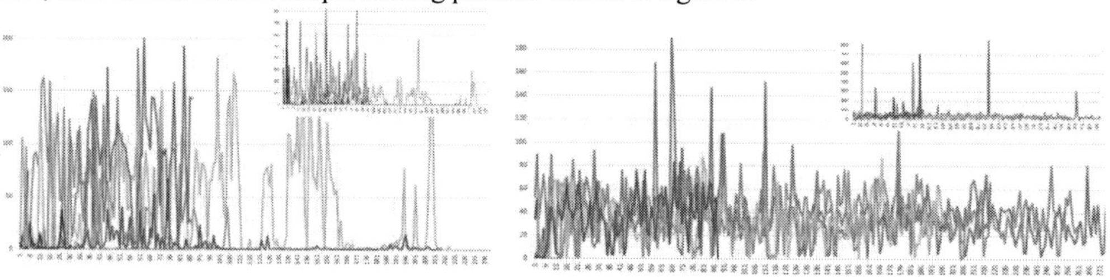

Figure 8. Different reading pattern from two different readers. X axis represents page number, y axis is time in second. Each colored-plot represents one book read by same reader

4. CONCLUSION

Our paper presents an approach to track reader's natural reading behavior and its possible applications such as vocabulary flashcards or word games as well as personal reading behavior analysis and visualization. Most significantly, we are working on mining the data obtained from a community of readers with the same reading levels. We also have tried with highly professional material to see the need of support for technical terms for word-lookup as the general description for technical terms is not sufficient. Time spent on each page collected from community of readers produced interesting data, but there are too many variables across readers. In the future, we like to collect reader information (gender, age group, favorite genre) to study homogeneous characteristics of each group. We are extending the team to include data mining experts and contents experts to understand and develop reading model more accurately.

REFERENCES

Benedetto, S., Drai-Zerbib, V., Pedrotti, M., Tissier, G., & Baccino, T. (2013). E-readers and visual fatigue. PLoS ONE 8(12). doi:10.1371/journal.pone.0083676

Conlon, E. & Sanders, M. (2011). The reading rate and comprehension of adults with impaired reading skills or visual discomfort. Journal of Research in Reading 34(2), 205-209. doi:10.1111/j.1467-9817.2009.01421.x

Harris, A. (2011). How effective are print-based comprehension models for reading and assessing multimodal texts? Literacy Learning: The Middle Years, 19(3), 19-32. Retrieved from http://go.galegroup.com/ps/i.do?id=GALE%7CA 269531647&v=2.1&u=vic_liberty&it=r&p=AONE&sw=w&asid=4f806a13ac4b7 fccdab331de56a106a9

Labbo, L. D., & Kuhn, M. R. (2000). Weaving chains of affect and cognition: A young child's understanding of CD-ROM talking books. Journal of Literacy Research, 32(2), 187 - 210. doi: 10.1080/10862960009548073

Lesnick, J., Gorerge, R., Smithgall, C., & Gwynne, J. (2010). Reading on grade level in third grade: How is it related to high school performance and college enrollment. Chicago, IL: University of Chicago.

Milliot, Jim (2014, April). Print, digital book sales settle down. Publishers Weekly. Retrieved from http://www.publishersweekly.com/pw/by-topic/industrynews/publisher-news/article/62031-print-digital-settle-down.html

Reinking, David, and Schreiner Robert. "The Effects of Computer-Mediated Text on Measures of Reading Comprehension and Reading Behavior."*Reading Research Quarterly* 20, no. 5 (1985): 536-52.

Rosenfield, M. (2011). Computer vision syndrome: A review of ocular causes and potential treatments. Ophthalmic and Physiological Optics 31(5). doi:10.1111/j.1475-1313.2011.00834.x

Van Merriënboer, J. J. G., & Sweller, J. (2005). Cognitive load theory and complex learning: Recent developments and future directions. Educational Psychology Review, 17(2), 147-178. doi: 10.1007/s10648-005-3951-0

ACADEMIC ADVISING BUSINESS PROCESS REMODELING IN EGYPTIAN EDUCATIONAL INSTITUTIONS

Lamiaa Mostafa[1], Nermin Khalifa[1], Rami M. Ayoubi[2] and Andrew Thomas[3]
[1]Arab Academy for Science and Technology and Maritime Transport, Alexandria, Egypt
[2]International Development Team and School of Management, Cardiff Met University
[3]School of Management, Cardiff Met University

ABSTRACT

The academic advising is a crucial process for a student's career path. The manual process is challenging since the student are advised to register specific courses that might affect his career path taking into consideration regulations imposed by school and knowledge and expertise of advisor. Therefore, there are several limitations in the manual academic advising process that could be managed by enhancing the process of the advising using business process remodeling. The paper aims to remodel the advising process using an information technology tool that can enhance the education process and automate the advising process. The paper will use multi-methodological approaches that combine case study, focus group, system implementation and questionnaire. The case study will depends on many evidences: interview with advisors and students, manual process observation to detect deficiency of existing advising process, archival documents reviews to get content of sample courses and transfer it into interrelated concepts. The paper will use concept-related data to feed and develop system that automate this service providing to deliver enhance educational service. The paper will refer as well to expect system outcome and ensure that remodeling process provide better and optimized service for students and academic institution using a questionnaire filled by academic advisors.

KEYWORDS

Educational Service; Academic advising; Business process remodeling

1. INTRODUCTION

Business process management is a new trend to manage the business processes and to enhance the quality of the business output. One of the educational services in universities is the academic advising. Academic advising is the process of selecting courses to register by the student. The courses to be register follow the curriculum of the student's major. The selection of the courses to be register depends on the academic advisor of the student and his knowledge.Business process remodelling aim is changing the actual processes in business to enhance the output. Academic advising has drawbacks as advisor knowledge, complex cases, time consumption, curriculum requirements, and unavailable advisor (Schomaker, 2015).

The aim of this research is to enhance the academic advising process, and proposing an advising process remodeled to solve the academic advising problems. An information technology tool will be implemented (E-Advisor) to reduce advisors unavailability compared to huge number of students, advisor limited knowledge, complication of the transfer between majors and universities. The aim of this research is helping the academic advisor to choose the suitable major of the student based on his history and the curriculum of each major. The research is Case study in the Arab Academy for Science and Technology University in Egypt. The process of transfer was a manual step in the university, so the researcher implemented an online tool to enhance the quality of the advising process.

The paper is organized as follows. The first section is the problem identification. Second section is the literature review of the academic advising process, business process management and knowledge sharing. The third section is the advising process remodeling description; the fourth section is the results. The last section includes the advantages of the proposed process and the directions for future work.

2. LITERATURE REVIEW

The following subsections will define these ideas: academic advising, and business process remodeling.

2.1 Academic Advising

Academic advising is process guiding students to select courses to register in each semester and fulfil the degree requirement. Academic advising is a process in student' educational life. Each semester, there should be a face-to-face meeting between the academic advisor and the student to guide student for registration and courses selection process (Ahmar, 2011).The expertise of the academic advisor can effect the student academic path by choosing courses in the advising process that may delay the student to graduate, one of the main problems in the advising process is the academic advisor knowledge (Schomaker, 2015) ,(Henning, 2007)and (Pokrajac and Rasamny, 2006).Academic advising affect educational development in college or university (Kalamkarian and Karp, 2015; Keston and Goodridge, 2015; Yanosky, 2014; Bettinger& Baker, 2014; Mohamed, 2015).

Sharing the knowledge of different academic advisor is important for the purpose of automating this step, since the academic advising categorizes the student's transcripts into groups that share the same advising document also data mining techniques as artificial neural network (Henning, 2007), rule-based reasoning (Schomaker, 2015), (Zhou and Yu, 2008),(Deorah et al., 2010), and classification (Romero et al., 2008). For the importance of knowledge sharing in educational institutions, (Deorah et al., 2010)shows the interaction between data systems and educational institutions, this model discusses how schools and other educational institution can collect better data and learn how to transform that data so that the information held within can be effectively shared among all stakeholders.

Manual academic advising has many drawbacks related labor intensive, time consumption, human advisors use their accrued knowledge and the large number of students compared to the number of advisors (Chinta et al., 2016; Aghajari, 2010).An Automated Course Advising System (ACAS) is implemented in Electrical Engineering Department of the United Arab Emirates University (UAEU). The system is developed to help student register the academic courses. Students in Engineering department face the following problems: lack of experience of advisers, inappropriate advising time schedules, selecting unnecessary and incorrect courses, and missing out suitable courses for registration (Laghari, 2014).Quality Academic Advising requires committed staff to be accessible to handle the assignment. Money related requirements regularly make it unfeasible to contract staff exclusively to advise and henceforth existing staff are generally allocated for this additional work, making their general obligations labour intensive (Tarí and Dick, 2016;Belhaj et al., 2013;Binh et al., 2008;Keston and Goodridge, 2015).

2.2 Business Process Remodeling

Business Process Management is a systematic approach with aim of reaching organization's objectives by restructuring the business process (Crowe et al., 2002). Critical Success factors (CSF) is one of the important topics of the BPR implementation. The success of BPR depends on how it meets predetermined goals within the project scope and over a longer period of time. The six factors that affect the success of BPM approach include strategic alignment, governance, BPM methods, IT, people and culture (Rosemann and Broke, 2010). Other factors are process analysis, process metrics, process performers, process infrastructure and process (Harmon, 2010). Example of BPR output are: reduction in process time, cost reduction, enhance service quality, enhance process (Albadvi et al., 2007).

3. PROPOSED ADVISING PROCESS REMODEL

Advising Process Remodelling that uses the E-advisor is validated using the following quality attributes: service tangibility, service responsiveness, service reliability, service empathy, service assurance (Mostafa et al., 2014). The business process management is validated using two of the critical success factors: people and organizational culture.

Tangibles attribute represented as the physical facilities (Haveckin, 2012). Responsiveness is the process of helping customers and providing service, reliability is the process of providing service accurately Haveckin, 2012). Assurance is the aim of manager to spread trust between the employees (Haveckin, 2012). Empathy is defined as customizing each service or product for each customer (Daniel and Berinyuy, 2010).Salimifard et al.(2010) listed critical success factors as: people, organizational culuture, business needs ,business process and IT tools.Business process remodelling involves understanding how business processes currently operate, and the aim of the BPR is to redesign these processes to eliminate the wasted effort and improve efficiency and quality. BPR assist the organization to gain competitive advantage and enhance the relationship with its customer. BPR support organizations goals by maintaining tasks, managing people or redesigning IT systems. In this research the process of the advising process is described in details and the enhanced advising process that is remodelled is defined.

The advising process has 3 main actors: student, academic advisor and registration department. The student starts the process by asking for enrollment in one of the available colleges or majors. The required document for the enrollment process is the student information document, student previous (external transcript).

The student information document contains the personal information of the student and the previous educational profile. Educational profile is the history of the student if he was enrolled in previous university, or in the same university with different college. The second document is the student's external transcript. The transcript will contain the courses finished and the grade of each course taken by the student.

The student will handle the two documents to the academic advisor. This will start the decision of accepting the documents or not. The academic advisor will check the information of the student and his documents for any missing detail. If the documents are rejected this will end the process and the student must start from the beginning by the required documents. The academic advisor will compare the name of the courses in the student external transcript and with the AAST courses list document. The process of comparing courses is a manual process that depends mainly on the experience of the academic advisor, advisor availability and the complexity of the student case.The selection of courses to be transferred is a vital process that will define the student academic path and number of courses to be taken, and graduation year. The aim of this research is to enhance the efficiency of this process by redesigning this process to be automated using IT tools.

Each academic advisor has his experience and working tasks, so if the student academic path and graduation year depends on these criteria's, it should take more attention from the university management.

Many student cases are delayed in their academic years, lose their interest in their major based on the decision of major selection and transferred courses decision.The process of advising as described in the previous section should be enhanced. The factors that affect the quality advising process are: knowledge of the advisor, student satisfaction and the time. The aim of the enhanced advising process is to modify the quality of the process and eliminating the waste of time, effort.

The main actors in enhanced process are student, academic advisors and E-advisors. E-advisor is a website to help the academic advisor in the advising process. This research design and implement the E-advisor tool.

The enhanced advising process is divided into six modules. The student asks for enrollment while providing the following documents: student external transcript, student information document and the description of the courses taken in the previous university. The academic advisor receives the three documents from the student and at the same time he opens the E-advisor to check whether the details of the student's previous university is stored in the E-advisor or not.

The case study started with the research observation. In order to translate the research observation and findings, a group of academic advisors were interviewed. The result of the observation and the interview was translated into a list of tasks. The researcher designed the advising process to be implemented. A focus group is also established for the purpose of defining the importance of keywords on courses. The advising process is implemented for the purpose of overcoming the manual advising process drawbacks.E-advisor is an online tool that help the advisors in the advising process. The link of the E-adviosr is http://www.aast-advisor.com/. The webpage starts with a login page either the user is an administrative or academic advisor. When the academic advisors enters the authentication information the list of universities, departments and courses are available. The academic advisors chooses the suitable courses that is finished by the student and the E-advisor proposes a specific major for the student to enrol in.

4. ADVISING PROCESS REMODELING EVALUATION

After implementing and testing the remodelled Advising process, it is important to understand the feedback and the perception the academic advisors. For this reason the questionnaire was designed and spreaded to be filled with the academic advisor working in the Arab Academy for Science and Technology and Maritime Transport university, College of Management , Business Information System Department. Questionnaire was filled by 160 academic advisors. The statistical package of social sciences (SPSS) was used to analyze the collected data. Several techniques were used to reach the results and the findings of this paper.

First, a frequency analysis was conducted to ensure the consistency of the various items in each instrument used in the questionnaire. Second a correlation was undertaken to measure the strength and the direction of the relationship between the service quality, people , organizational culture on the advising quality.

The frequency analysis is defined as "the number of times various subcategories of a certain phenomenon occur from which the percentage and the cumulative percentage to their occurrence can be easily calculated"(Sekaran,2003, p.395).Service Quality frequency table reveals that 91.2% (agree) and 8.8% (disagree) of the academic advising convinced that the service quality affected the advising process quality.

People frequency tables reveal that 84.4% (agree) and 15.6% (disagree) of the academic advising convinced that the people factor affected the advising process quality. Organizational culture frequency tables reveal that 89.4% (agree) and 10.6% (disagree) of the academic advising convinced that the organizational culture affected the advising process quality.

In order to test the proposed model, Pearson correlation analysis was used to measure the relationship between the variables under investigation. Pearson correlation analysis indicates the strength, direction, and significance of the relationship between only two variables at a time, then it is used to test the paper hypotheses (Sekaran, 2003). If P is between 1 and 0.5 then the strength of the relationship is strong, when p is between 0.5 and 0.3 then the relationship is moderate, while when p is between 0.3 and 0.1 the relationship is weak and finally when p is less than 0.1 the relationship is very weak (Sekaran, 2003).

The correlation analysis shows a strong positive relationship between the service quality and the advising process quality. Advising process quality increases when service quality increases. The correlation analysis shows a strong positive relationship between the people participation and the Advising process quality. The Advising process quality increases when the people participation increases.The correlation analysis shows a moderate positive relationship between the organizational culture and the advising process quality.

5. CONCLUSION

The paper provides a proposed model to enhance the academic advising process using business process remodelling. An automated tool (E-Advisor) is used to execute the advising process remodelling.

A questionnaire was spread and filled in by academic advisors to evaluate the proposed advising process remodelling. The analysis of the questionnaire had shown that 91.2% of academic advisor agreed that service quality affected the advising process quality.84.4% of the academic advisor agreed that of the academic advisors accepted that people factor affected the advising process quality. 89.4% of academic advisor convinced that organizational culture affected the advising process quality.

The limitation of this research can be defined in the following points: This research focuses on remodeling the advising process so as the advising process is better quality, accurate and less time consumption; however any research still has a list of limitations. First limitation is the case study, the case study was made in one university which is the Arab Academy for Science and Technology. Since the researcher works in College of Management and Technology (CMT) so the participators of all case study evidence were from the CMT. The participant of the survey were hundred and sixty academic advisors whose available for advising process. All the academic advisors are faculty members so they were so busy working to advice students and prepare their teaching materials and also they were trying the system.Advising process remodeling uses an IT tool (E-advisor), the database used in the E-advisor is limited to three universities: Arab Academy for Science and Technology,Pharos University and Alexandria University.

REFERENCES

Henning M., 2007.*Students' Motivation to Learn, Academic Achievement, and Academic Advising*,AUT University.

Zhou Q., Yu F.,2008. Knowledge-Based Major Choosing Decision making for remote students. *International Conference on Computer Science and Software Engineering,IEEE.*

Deorah S., Sridharan S., Goel S., 2010.SAES- Expert System for Advising Academic Major, *IEEE.*

Romero C., Ventura C., Garcıa E.,2008. Data mining in course management systems: Moodle case study and tutorial", *Computers & Education 51. 368–384,Elsevier.*

Aghajari N.,2010.Comparison of Knowledge Management Technologies in Academic environment, *In Proceedings of International Conference on Education and Management Technology (ICEMT 2010).*

Binh N.,Duong H., Hieu T., Nhuan N., Son N.,2008. An integrated approach for an academic advising system in adaptive credit-based learning environment, *VNU Journal of Science, Natural Sciences and Technology 110-121.*

Ahmar, M.,2011.A Prototype Student Advising Expert System Supported with an Object-Oriented Database. *International Journal of Advanced Computer Science and Applications,Special Issue on Artificial Intelligence,(IJACSA).*

Pokrajac D., Rasamny M.,2006. Interactive Virtual Expert System for Advising (InVEStA). *36th ASEE/IEEE Frontiers in Education Conference, October 28 – 31, San Diego, CA, IEEE.*

Laghari,M.,2014.Automated Course Advising System. International Journal of Machine Learning and Computing, *Vol. 4, No. 1, February 2014.*

Crowe,J., Fong P.and Zayas-Castro J., 2002. Quantitative risk level estimation of business process reengineering efforts. *Business Process Management Journal, 8(5): 490-511.*

Rosemann, M., Brocke, J., 2010.The six core elements of business process management, *higher education journal.*

Rosemann (eds.), *Handbook on business process management*, vol. 1, Springer, Heidelberg, pp. 3–16.

Harmon, P. ,2010.The scope and evolution of business process management, in J vom Brocke and M Rosemann (eds.), *Handbook on business process management, vol. 1, Springer, Heidelberg, pp. 37–81*

Albadvi, A, Keramati, A & Razmi, J., 2007.Assessing the impact of information technology on firm performance considering the role of intervening variables: organizational infrastructures and business processes reengineering', *International Journal of Production Research, vol. 45, pp. 2697–2734.*

Daniel,C., Berinyuy L.,2010.Using the SERVQUAL Model to assess Service Quality and Customer Satisfaction.An Empirical study of grocery stores in Umea.*Master Thesis.UMEA University.*

Mostafa,L.,Oately,G.,Khalifa,N. and Rabie,W.,2014.A Case based Reasoning System for Academic Advising in Egyptian Educational Institutions,*2nd International Conference on Research in Science, Engineering and Technology (ICRSET'2014), March 21-22, 2014 Dubai (UAE).*

Haveckin B.,2012. Information Technology outsourcing by large Australian organisations , *Faculty of Business and Law Victoria University, Australia, 2012.*

Salimifard, K., Abbaszadeh,M. and Ghorbanpur, A.,2010. Interpretive structural modeling of critical success factors in banking process re-engineering. *International Review of Business Research Papers, 6(2): 95-103.*

Sekaran,U.,2003.Research methods for business:A skill building approach,*6 edn,John Wiley and Sons, Inc.*

Keston, L., Goodridge, W. (2015).AdviseMe: An Intelligent Web-Based Application for Academic Advising. *International Journal of Advanced Computer Science and Applications, 6(8).*

Kalamkarian,H. and Karp, M.2015. Student Attitudes Toward Technology-Mediated Advising Systems. *Community College Research Center Teachers College, Columbia University ,CCRC Working Paper No. 82.*

Yanosky, R. 2014. Integrated planning and advising services: A benchmarking study. Louisville, *CO: EDUCAUSE Center for Analysis and Research.*

Bettinger, E., Baker, R. 2014. The effects of student coaching: An evaluation of a randomized experiment in student advising. *Educational Evaluation and Policy Analysis, 36(1), 3–19. doi: 10.3102/0162373713500523.*

Mohamed, A. 2015. A decision support model for long-term course planning. *Decision Support Systems, 74, pp.33-45.*

Belhaj F. ,Ayed O. & Kammoun,R. (2013).Student perception of higher education quality in Tunisian business schools. Journal of Applied Research in Higher Education, Vol. 5 Iss 1 pp. 5 – 16.

Tarí J. ,Dick G. (2016),"Trends in quality management research in higher education institutions", Journal of Service Theory and Practice, Vol. 26 Iss 3 pp. 273 – 296.

Schomaker,R. (2015),"Accreditation and quality assurance in the Egyptian higher education system", Quality Assurance in Education, Vol. 23 Iss 2 pp. 149 – 165

Chinta R., Kebritchi,M. & Ellias ,J. (2016).A conceptual framework for evaluating higher education institutions. International Journal of Educational Management, Vol. 30 Iss 6 pp. 989 – 1002.

AN ONTOLOGY-BASED APPROACH TO USE REQUIREMENTS ENGINEERING IN PORTALS OF TRANSPARENCY

Tainara Lucateli Bernardi, Roberto dos Santos Rabello and Cristiano Roberto Cervi
University of Passo Fundo
BR 285, São José, Passo Fundo/RS, Brazil

ABSTRACT

For information technology professionals can develop systems that assist in governance and in meeting the obligations given by the legislation, they need to understand the conceptual basis involved in the complex areas of the problems experienced by local governments. The lack of standardized concepts complicates the process and elicitation of validation requirements for the development of new software systems. Given this reality, we present an ontology for bids and administrative contracts and propose a form of application of this ontology in the activities of Requirements Engineering. Through the specified process, we expect to achieve a significant improvement in the elicitation process and validation of software requirements.

KEYWORDS

Administrative Contracts; Requirements Engineering; Bids; Ontology; Public Transparency

1. INTRODUCTION

One of the biggest challenges faced by software developers to the government area is the complex and non-standard structures. This reality makes it difficult to understand and build the necessary knowledge to solve government problems. With the aim to facilitate the software development process and enable the understanding, sharing and exchange of information between people, devices and computers, we understand how important the definition of conceptual and structural patterns. From this standardization, requirements engineers can minimize the difficulties encountered in the process of knowledge of the problem domain, as they will have access to an organized and documented conceptual framework that will facilitate the understanding of definitions and concepts presented by professionals in the government area.

In this context, with the goal of facilitate the activities of requirements engineering in the government context, we present a domain ontology for bids and administrative contracts. This ontology aims to standardize the structure of the information, which is essential and necessary for the understanding of the domain and the process for defining software requirements in the municipal area. The application of ontology in requirements engineering activities allow verification, analysis and the formulation of suggestions for improvements in search of a definition of requirements concise and consistent with the real needs and interests of the government and the population.

This paper is organized as follows. Section 2 and 3 presents the theoretical framework and related work. Section 4 describes the materials and methods used to build the ontology and for the definition of the application process engineering requirements. The final considerations are presented in Section 5.

2. THEORETICAL BACKGROUND

As provided for in the Federal Constitution (Brasil, 1988) and Supplementary Law number 131, published in May 2009, also known as the Transparency Law, the right of every citizen to have access to government information, as is the obligations of the State ensure this access through objective and timely, transparent, clear and easy to understand language. Therefore, the creation of the Transparency Portal was one of the solutions defined by the Brazilian government to improve the state of relations with citizens, with enterprises and among government bodies (Araújo & Aguiar, 2014). Because transparency portals may contain content from different government databases, there is the concern with understanding the information published, which need to be organized so that users understand its syntax and semantics. Much of the government data is difficult to interpret for lay users and professionals in the computer area that use them as a base for the development of information systems.

To cater the principles of transparency, a semantic organization of data is required. In order for this to become reality, international government agencies have sought to define standards to mitigate data integration issues published. One of the policies proposed by the Brazilian government on e-government interoperability standards shows that: to facilitate the crossing of data from different sources of information, when its use by other member organizations of public administration, by civil society or by citizen, they should be used resources such as controlled vocabularies, taxonomies, ontologies and other methods of organization and information retrieval (Brasil, 2015).

According to the W3C Consortium (W3C, 2015) ontology is understood as "the definition of the terms used in the description and representation of an area of knowledge." Briefly, ontologies should provide descriptions for the types of classes of concepts / things in various fields of interest, relationships between these classes / things, as well as properties / attributes that these classes / things must have (Breitman, 2005). Yet, the ontology is defined as an explicit specification of a conceptualization, which is a simplified view of a knowledge domain (Corrêa et al., 2015). Ontologies have been developed to facilitate the sharing and reuse of information (Breitman & Leite, 2004), in addition to clarifying the structure of knowledge, promoting a shared understanding of the area in question.

Use ontologies in the process of knowledge and understanding of the problem domain is a way to minimize excessive effort demanded in activities of the engineering requirements. In this case, the ontology is used as a means of standardized presentation of clear and scope accosted, avoiding the erroneous setting requirements for lack of knowledge of the context.

3. RELATED WORKS

In the governmental area, domain ontologies are used as a form of standardization and presentation of a problem domain. In Requirement Engineering domain ontologies establish a common understanding between the parties involved, allowing better communication in the pursuit of elicitation and most complete analysis possible for the requirements of the systems (Zapata et al., 2010).

In 2006 (Kaiya & Saeki, 2006) presented a method of requirements gathering called ORE (Ontology-based Requirements Elicitation), which suggests that ontologies are used in the field of knowledge they contain semantic rules that give meaning to requirements of sentences . Thus, when using rules of inference can find out what requirements must be added or deleted to ensure completeness and consistency. In this method, the concepts and relationships modeled in the domain ontology allow, through an analysis formula, check the quality of elicited requirements outside his correctitude, completeness, consistency and ambiguity.

Recently (Amina Adadi, 2015) presented an ontology related to public administration domain, called WebGov. The same is intended to provide a global knowledge model of implementation of the administrative services provided by the government, in order that it be used in the development of electronic services.

In 2007 Zong-Yong et al. (2007) proposed a framework based on KADS knowledge modeling (Knowledge Aided Design System), which uses multiple ontologies for lifting requirements. The structure combines foundational ontologies, domain ontology and task ontology in a metamodel to organize and standardize the assessment process requirements.

Given the above, the existence of a domain ontology to be used in the engineering of transparency portals requirements or other systems related to procurement and administrative contracts is a way to minimize human efforts.

4. MATERIALS AND METHODS

We divided the study in three phases, each with specific activities involving studies, research, ontology construction and definition of ontology application process engineering of government transparency portals requirements. The Following are each work phases.

4.1 Ontology Construction

The activities developed in the first phase of work sought to understand the complexity of the information used in the context of public management, directing the focus of study for the area of procurement and administrative contracts. The choice of this area considered the complexity of the concepts involved, the lack of structural standardization of information and the importance of these topics to society, considering that they are part of municipal financial management.

After the study and construction of the necessary knowledge about the problem domain, the process of verification and search of information to be modeled as concepts, properties and relationships in the ontology started. This activity considered the recommended transparency standards by the Brazilian government and the requirements presented in the current legislation in the country.

In sequence started the second phase of work. The definition of the methodology to be used in the construction of ontology, the choice of language and editing tool, the conceptual definition and relationship to be modeled in addition to the actual construction and documentation of the domain ontology. The first step of this stage was the study of the methodologies, in order to identify the most appropriate method to be used in this work. Upon completion of the analysis, it was decided to use the Ontology Development 101 methodology. The choice was based on its simplicity and the details presented for each work step. As (Isotani & Bittencourt, 2015), the method presents an iterative approach and describes in detail the steps that guide the work of those involved.

Further, there was the choice of tool to be used. Second (Isotani & Bittencourt, 2015) the most popular are: Apollo, OntoStudio, Protégé and TopBraid Composer, among others. Analyzed the editors, the Protégé is one of the most known and used by the international community, is open source and free. Also, another important and decisive factor in choosing the editor is the fact that the Ontology Development 101 method has a close relationship with the tool (Noy & McGuinness, 2001).

The choice of implementation language complete the requirements needed to start construction of the ontology. Among the languages recommended by W3C (W3C, 2015), the OWL is recommended because it is suitable for situations where information needs to be processed and interpreted by the machine, as well as having easy to express meanings and semantics.

After defining the concepts, properties, relationships and semantic rules to be modeled in the ontology, has started the process of building it in the Protégé tool. During the modeling process, it was emphasized the inclusion of details and descriptions of each concept, attribute and relationship, thereby building documentation. This documentation will be important for understanding and building the knowledge base represented by domain ontology. Figure 1 shows one form of graphical display of the modeled ontology classes.

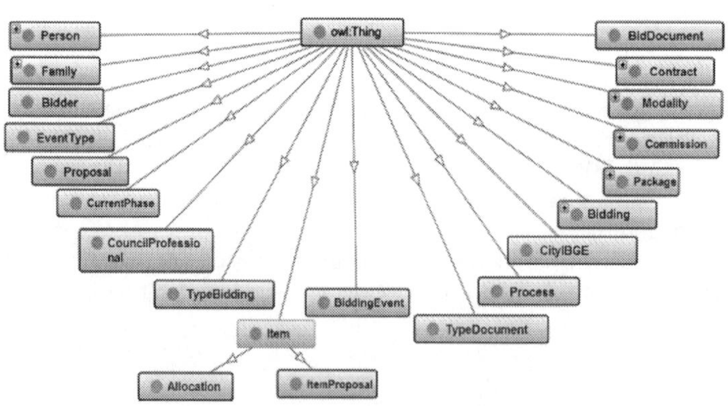

Figure 1. Ontology for bids and administrative contracts

4.2 Application of Ontology

Ontology proposal will be applied as exemplification process of its use in the elicitation activities and validation requirements. The modeling and documentation will be used as a means of standardizing knowledge, providing professional computing area the understanding necessary to maintain clear communication with stakeholders.

Based on the concepts and the submitted information, software engineers will make the process for defining a new system requirements (Figure 2 - Process 1). They should relate each requirement to one or more concepts in the ontology, as the similarity between them. Through the process relationships, it will be possible to identify the concepts that are not covered by the requirements set, indicating that they may be incomplete, or even the need to define new requirements for the system. On the other hand, the existence of concepts that have many relationships can alert ambiguities. The ontology will allow requirements engineers make these assessments, because not always the application of elicitation techniques such as interviews, questionnaires, meetings are sufficient to capture all the conditions required for the development of a good information system.

Through the process of comparison made between the terms of ontology and the requirements already elicited in order to validate them (Figure 2 - Process 2), we seek to ensure that the portal of transparency meets the needs of citizens and obligatoriness under the laws. The process of using the ontology engineering requirements should submit suggestions for improvements to be made in the requirements. As an example, the existence of terms that are mandatory in the field and are not covered by the requirements set; the presence of ambiguous requirements, which can directly affect the quality of the information provided; the existence of confusing definitions and wrong relationships between requirements; and enables engineers to make other analysis using the structure modeled by the ontology. The comparison of terms proposed in the first instance, be performed manually using the graphical visualization of the ontology to relate the concepts and elicited requirements.

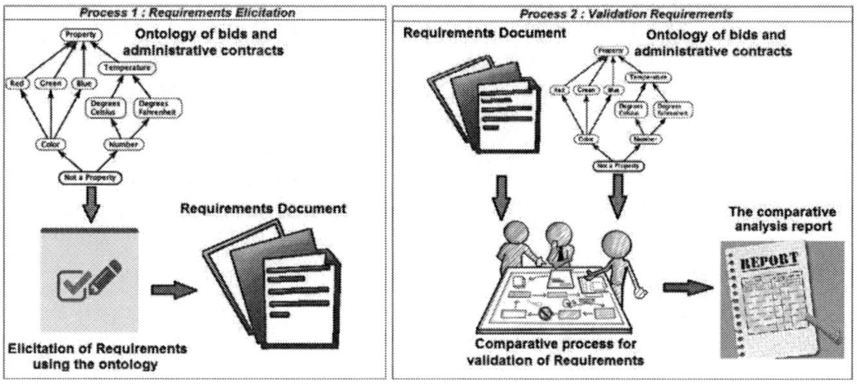

Figure 2. Ontology application in elicitation and validation requirements

With the completion of the use of ontology engineering requirements, a report with the test results and the suggestions for improvement given the document of official requirements of the new system will be developed. The application processes the ontology elicitation and validation requirements are shown in Figure 2.

To confirm the expectations of the proposed process, a software development team must implement the modules of bids and administrative contracts a portal of municipal transparency. During this development, the team will report all experienced situations, and at the end of the process, must present a descriptive report with the observations made during the execution of each of the activities of engineering requirements. This report will present evidence to confirm the benefits observed during the ontology application process.

5. FINAL CONSIDERATIONS

This work presents an ontology-based approach to the elicitation of requirements on transparency portals. With the use of the proposed approach is expected to confirm expectations that the ontology will solve many of the problems faced by professionals in the Requirements Engineering area. They will have the opportunity to meet the modeling domain, facilitating the activities of elicitation and validation requirements for the development of municipal transparency portals or other useful software for public management.

Ontology has presented a standardization and semantic organization of information of bids and administrative contracts, which will enable interoperability of transparency portals with other information systems and other government databases. The built ontology will be available in specific libraries, allowing other professionals to reuse, enhance or complement.

This project does not end with the approach proposed in this work, because our goal is that the ontology can add new concepts, as well as the development of new ontologies that include other areas related to public transparency.

REFERENCES

Amina Adadi, M.B.D.C., 2015. Ontology based composition of e-Government services using AI Planning. In *2015 10th International Conference on Intelligent Systems: Theories and Applications (SITA)*. Rabat, 2015. IEEE.

Araújo, D.B. & Aguiar, E.L., 2014. Dados governamentais abertos como ferramenta de participação social e aproximação entre governo e sociedade. In *CONSAD - Congresso Brasileiro de Gestão Pública*. Brasília, 2014.

Brasil, P.d.R., 1988. *Constituição da República Federativa do Brasil de 1988*. [Online] Available at: http://www.planalto.gov.br/ccivil_03/Constituicao/Constituicao.htm [Accessed 02 Junho 2015].

Brasil, M.d.P.O.e.G., 2015. *Padrões de Interoperabilidade de Governo Eletrônico - ePING - Versão 2015*. [Online] Available at: http://eping.governoeletronico.gov.br/ [Accessed 25 Junho 2015].

Breitman, K.K., 2005. *Web semântica: a internet do futuro*. Rio de Janeiro: LCT.

Breitman, K.K. & Leite, J.C.S.d.P., 2004. Ontologias - Como e porque criá-las. In *Anais do SBC*. Rio de Janeiro, 2004.

Corrêa, A.S., Borba, C., Silva, D.L.D. & Corrêa, P., 2015. A Fuzzy Ontology-Driven Approach to Semantic Interoperability in e-Government Big Data. *International Journal of Social Science and Humanity*, 5(2), pp.178-81.

Isotani, S. & Bittencourt, I.I., 2015. *Dados Abertos Conectados*. São Paulo: Novatec.

Kaiya, H. & Saeki, M., 2006. Using Domain Ontology as Domain Knowledge for Requirements Elicitation. In *4th IEEE International Requirements Engineering Conference*., 2006.

Noy, N.F. & McGuinness, D.L., 2001. Ontology Development 101. Available at: http://protegewiki.stanford.edu/wiki/Ontology101 [Accessed 25 Abril 2015].

Zapata, C.M., Giraldo, G.L. & Mesa, J.E., 2010. Una Propuesta de Metaontología para la Educción de Requisitos. *Ingeniare. Revista chilena de ingeniería*, 18(1), pp.26-37.

Zong-Yong, L. et al., 2007. Towards a Multiple Ontology Framework for Requirements Elicitation and Reuse. In *31st Annual International Computer Software and Applications Conference(COMPSAC 2007)*., 2007. IEEE Computer Society.

EVALUATION OF REST INTERFACES FOR RELIABLE INVOCATION SEMANTICS

Ricardo Filipe and Filipe Araujo
CISUC, Dept. of Informatics Engineering, University of Coimbra
Coimbra, Portugal

ABSTRACT

Nowadays, the REpresentational State Transfer (REST) architectural style plays a central role in distributed software. All major web and cloud providers, such as Facebook, Dropbox, Google, Instagram, Amazon, among many others, expose public REST interfaces for web, mobile and stand-alone clients. This raises the question of knowing the reliability of these REST services, as they run over the network, thus being inevitably prone to failures. While some of these failures might be harmless, and others might be overcome with a simple repetition of the same request, a few others, e.g., payments, need a much more careful treatment. In these cases, repeating the same request might not be an option, because duplicate executions might be worse than no execution at all.

To answer this question, and determine the reliability of top-tier REST interfaces, we evaluated three real services, from leading web and cloud providers. We repeatedly invoked their REST functions for several days, to count the number of unsuccessful interactions. Despite running smoothly for most of the time, our initial results show that all these services suffered perturbations during the course of our experiment. This observation supports a straightforward conclusion: if even at this level we observe this number of problems, then, developers must definitely provide additional logic on the client and server, to ensure reliable interactions in the presence of faults. This experiment is part of a larger effort, to provide clear guidelines for reliable invocation semantics in web pages.

KEYWORDS

REST, Reliability, Invocation semantics

1. INTRODUCTION

REpresentational State Transfer (REST), first defined by Fielding in his PhD thesis in 2000 (Fielding (2000)), has become a major standard for services provided over the Internet. The power of REST comes from the versatility of interfaces that simultaneously support the presentation layer of web pages developed in JavaScript, mobile applications that are native for Android or iOS, and interaction with third-party providers, most notably for the sake of authentication, but by no means limited to it. The modern computing infrastructure, including the cloud, heavily relies on REST services as these became ubiquitous. The number and names of web site providers using REST and making their REST interfaces available for programmers is huge: Facebook, Twitter, Instagram, Amazon, Microsoft, Google, YouTube and countless others.

In spite of this success, critical web interactions still pose a major challenge for developers, whenever operations fail to execute properly. Services involving reservation of some resource, payments, or other business-oriented interactions cannot easily tolerate requests with error responses or no responses at all.

This is neither new, nor specific to REST, as the effect of faults in distributed systems is a well understood topic that deserved thorough attention for decades. However, the extreme popularity of the running REST interfaces, the sheer number of available operations and the always increasing number of users they support, provide us new opportunities to evaluate the reliability of real, highly relevant distributed systems. In particular, we would like to know exactly how likely is it for an operation requiring an exactly-once semantics to fail without providing adequate information to the client.

To achieve this goal, we ran an experiment using successive HTTP invocations to REST services of three major providers of video and file storing and sharing. We did this for several days, keeping notice of response times, unanswered requests, HTTP status of the responses and HTTP headers. To avoid disclosing sensitive information regarding these services, we keep them anonymous and refer to them by the letters A, B and C.

The results are noteworthy: even major providers cannot avoid a significant number of errors in the access to their REST resources and a wide disparity of response times. While some of these problems come from the network, the provider itself is also to blame in many cases. Although small in relative numbers, errors do not only exist, but exist in large amounts, when we consider the vast utilization of these services. Hence, we can clearly conclude that, to build reliable distributed systems, developers must use mechanisms that take connectivity, availability and performance problems into account. The results of this paper aim to motivate developers for the central problem of achieving reliable invocation of services over the network. If it is true that abundant theory exists about the problem (Spector (1982)), it is also true that developers have no widespread guidelines that can help them to properly protect their programs against invocation failures. The solutions we are aware of are ad hoc, error-prone and subject to memory leaks.

2. EXPERIMENTAL SETTINGS AND RESULTS

To evaluate the reliability of online REST services, we ran a client that regularly requested operations from three well-known service providers. All three providers reside in the west coast of the United States, whereas the client is in Portugal, around 9,000 Kms away. We used the crontab scheduler on a Linux machine, to run the cURL command, which invoked the same REST resource during several days, with intervals of 4 seconds. We accessed two file sharing providers (A and B) and a video sharing provider (C). In the file sharing providers, we did a REST request to get the contents of the home directory of a user account; in the video sharing provider, we did a REST request to get the 50 most popular videos. To access data from provider A, we had to use the HTTP POST method; from the other two providers, we used the GET method. Note that according to the HTTP protocol (Fielding and Reschke (2014)), the POST method is non-idempotent. Repeating an invocation might thus have an unintended effect.

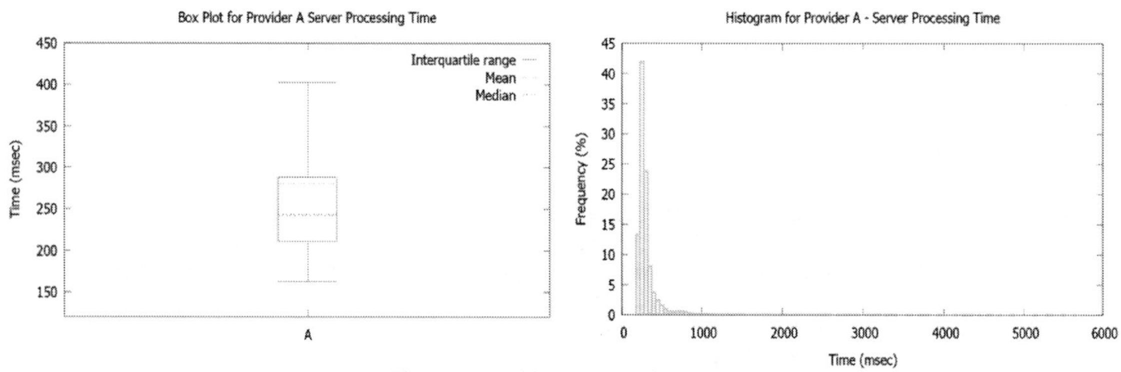

Figure 1. Provider A server time statistics

We also gathered a specific HTTP extension header from provider A, which stated the time that the server took to answer the request. This extension allowed us to determine server-side times, regardless of network performance. In Figure 1-left, we show the box plot associated with the server response time, while on the right side, we show the histogram of the same samples, distributed by the time it took to answer the request (x axis) and the number of times each time interval occurred (y axis). Looking at both plots, we can observe that the servers of provider A take around 250 *ms* to reply to the majority of requests, once they arrive. However, as we can see in the box plot, the actual times vary a lot. Additionally, if we take a closer look to the histogram, we verify that sometimes the server responses take as much as 6000 *ms*. These response times (plus the network latency) may be treated as a timeout by the client software or users, which might be tempted to reload or resubmit forms several times during this interval.

Concerning the network time between our client and the servers of providers A, B and C, in Figure 2 we show a box plot for the server+network times of our samples. Service invocations will necessarily involve large network latencies, as light takes around 60 *ms* to cover the round-trip (in vacuum). Interestingly, provider C presents a very stable connectivity, having very short interquartile ranges and a mean similar to the median. The results of provider C are truly remarkable, suggesting, not only, that providers A and B take long internal times to fulfill the service, but also that such times have a large variance (i.e., they cannot be attributed to the network). These differences might result from the nature of the services involved. It might be simpler to prepare the response to a request for the most popular 50 videos in store, than it is to provide the list of files in the home directory of a specific user. The precise reasons, however, are difficult to discern, without knowing the internal details of these providers. Furthermore, as far as we could tell, the requests we did to provider C were not served by any cache.

The comparison of Figures 1 and 2 also suggests that the total internal server time of provider A is larger than what we see in Figure 1. Furthermore, since variances for providers A and B are somewhat large, they might pose some problems for client-side software, especially if developers want to wait for (outlier) responses taking more than the 75 percentile to arrive.

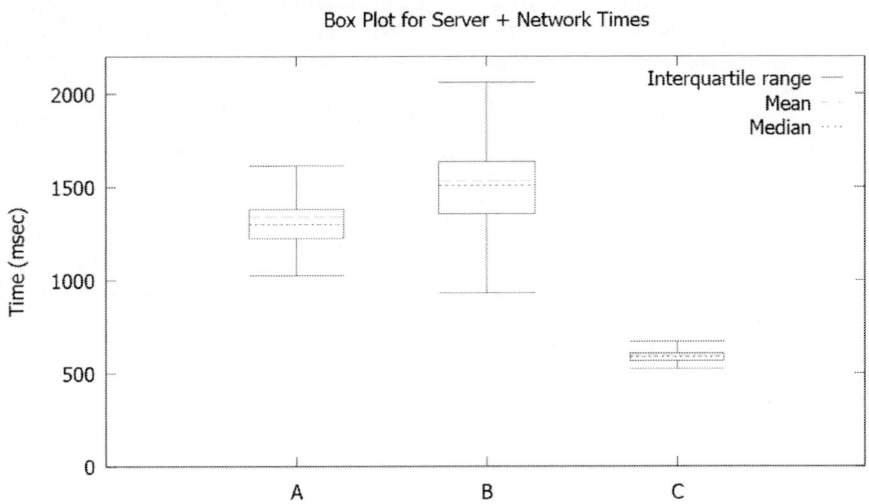

Figure 2. Server + Network time statistics for the distinct providers

Table 1. Number of errors

	Provider A	Provider B	Provider C
Connection setup errors	104 (0.057%)	43 (0.018%)	6 (0.005%)
Connection crashes	5 (0.003%)	28 (0.012%)	7 (0.005%)
Provider errors	38 (0.02%)	3 (0.0012%)	0 (0%)

Our next step was to count the errors in response to our requests (refer to Table 1). We divide errors as seen by clients in three different classes: network errors related to the connection setup phase (first line), network errors occurring *after* the connection is setup (second line), and application errors (third line). Network errors include connection timeouts, connection crashes, read timeouts, or unreachable hosts. Application errors occur when the client gets an HTTP error in the ranges 4xx or 5xx (we only got 5xx, since we kept using a limited list of addresses in our requests). We can see that the number of failed requests is quite relevant, especially when one accounts for the intensive utilization of these services. Most errors are due to the network interaction, whereas only a few occur in the application, caused by some temporary server overload, for example.

While service providers can invest in resources and software to improve their network and the response of the application, connection setup errors and connection crashes might be out of their control, as they mostly depend on third party providers. On the other hand, for developers, the most difficult problems to overcome are connection crashes and provider errors, because applications can hardly be sure about the outcome of the REST invocation, when these happen. This situation might be even worse for mobile clients, as intermittent connections will certainly cause more errors, thus raising the importance of tolerating ambiguous, absent or erroneous responses.

3. DISCUSSION AND CONCLUSION

We are by no means the first ones to evaluate or benchmark online services. For example, Palma et al. (2014), made a study to identify the lack of REST patterns in major operators. In Laranjeiro et al. (2009), authors evaluated the robustness of web services, using invalid call parameters, to observe programming or design errors. Although we also care for web services, our main concern is on the reliability of invocations, like in Ivaki et al. (2015) or Shegalov et al. (2002). Indeed, we are not aware of other work comparing distinct providers in terms of error counting, request response times, and their distribution.

The importance of knowing the normal behavior and the frequency of errors in online services comes from the paramount importance of ensuring that non-idempotent REST requests execute at most once. However, when the user receives an error and risks to resubmit the request, s(he) will be left without knowing whether the request was executed zero, one or more times. This is an inevitable source of mistrust about the service provider and ultimately contributes to the degradation of the provider's reputation.

Although we recognize the need for collecting additional information from other top web providers, the evidence we collected so far strongly supports the idea that developers need to employ fault-tolerance techniques, if they use non-idempotent services. Depending on the provider, the fraction of invocations that fail with ambiguous results might be as large as 0.02 percent. Unfortunately, despite being a well-known problem, we are not aware of any widespread technique that can result in a standard implementation of the at-most-once or (in certain conditions) exactly-once execution semantics in HTTP.

From previous interactions with web site developers, we realized that one common technique they use, to ensure that all operations are idempotent, is to include a unique identifier with the request, and provide the same identifier on subsequent submissions of the same request. The difficulty of this approach concerns the timely deletion of old responses from the server cache. Another possibility would be te use the HTTP Header *If-Unmodified-Since* with the date of the last (supposed) update. The server would either respond with success, if the resource was not modified after the date, or respond with an *HTTP 412 PreCondition Failed* otherwise. However, this mechanism is not ensured by most providers; furthermore, this approach would force the server to associate a date to each resource.

As a final remark, we can say that 1) we showed in this paper that problems in non-idempotent REST invocations occur frequently, and 2) there is no ready-to-use reliable invocation solution for web developers. This motivates us to work on such a proposal, based on our own review of all protocols that might ensure at-most-once and exactly-once invocations (Ivaki et al. (2015)).

REFERENCES

Fielding, R. & Reschke, J., (2014), *Hypertext transfer protocol (http/1.1): Message syntax and routing*, RFC 7230, RFC Editor. http://www.rfc-editor.org/rfc/rfc7230.txt.

Fielding, R. T. (2000), *REST: Architectural Styles and the Design of Network-based Software Architectures*, Doctoral dissertation, University of California, Irvine.

Ivaki, N. et al, (2015), A taxonomy of reliable request-response protocols, *in Proceedings of the 30th Annual ACM Symposium on Applied Computing*, New York, USA, pp. 456–463

Laranjeiro, N. et al, (2009), Improving web services robustness, *in 'Web Services, 2009. ICWS 2009. IEEE International Conference'*, Los Angeles, USA, pp. 397–404.

Palma, F. et al, (2014), Detection of REST Patterns and Antipatterns: A Heuristics-Based Approach, *Service-Oriented Computing: 12th International Conference, ICSOC 2014*, Paris, France, pp. 230–244.

Shegalov, G. et al, (2002), Eos: Exactly-once e-service middleware, *in 'Proceedings of the 28th International Conference on Very Large Data Bases', VLDB '02*, Hong Kong, China, pp. 1043–1046.

Spector, A. Z. (1982), *'Performing remote operations efficiently on a local computer network'*, Communications of the ACM 25(4), 246–260.

A CHANNEL ALLOCATION MECHANISM FOR VANET BASED ON NODE BEHAVIOR

Roni Francis Shigueta[1], Mauro Fonseca[2] and Aline Carneiro Viana[3]
[1]*PUC-PR – Pontifical Catholic University of Parana, Curitiba, Brazil*
[2]*UTFPR – Federal Technological University of Parana , Curitiba, Brazil*
[3]*INRIA , Palaiseau, France*

ABSTRACT

This article presents a mechanism for channel allocation in Vehicular Ad-hoc Networks (VANETs). The proposed mechanism uses a distributed approach to access dynamically the IEEE 802.11p spectrum. Our main contribution is to propose the node behavior to guide the channel allocation process in order to respond quickly to change in the network topology. In our work, the node behavior is represented by the association of parameters as mobility, traffic history, and node degree. Our performance evaluation shows that using the node behavior as a decision criterion leads to better results when compared with a simple channel and random allocation.

KEYWORDS

Dynamic Spectrum Access, Distributed Channel Allocation, IEEE 802.11p

1. INTRODUCTION

Vehicular Ad-hoc Network (VANET) is an extension of Mobile Ad-hoc Network (MANET) and it aims to provide services that result in higher road safety (reducing the number of accidents) and greater comfort for the vehicle user. Despite having some similar characteristics of MANET, vehicular networks present major challenges such as the frequency of connections/disconnections between vehicles and rapid changes in the network topology.

In addition to the intermittency problems, the available frequency spectrum for VANETs is limited (e.g., IEEE 802.11p standard offers only six service channels and one control channel). Thus, it is necessary new mechanisms for optimizing the use of the frequency spectrum in vehicular networks.

In this context, this paper presents a mechanism to optimize the channel allocation process in VANETs that use the frequency spectrum of the IEEE 802.11p standard. A distributed approach based on node behavior is adopted to quickly respond to changes in the network topology.

The paper is organized as follows. Section 2 presents a background about VANET and the channels of IEEE 802.11p standard. Section 3 addresses related work. Section 4 presents the network, interference, and mobility models. Section 5 details the channel allocation mechanism. The vehicular network scenario used for performance evaluation and the corresponding results are presented in Section 6. Finally, Section 7 concludes the paper.

2. BACKGROUND

VANET is a vehicular network which has an architecture consisting of three components (Liang et al. 2015): Road Side Unit (RSU), On Board Unit (OBU), and Application Unit (AU). RSU is a device fixed along the roadside or in dedicated locations equipped with one network device based on IEEE 802.11p standard or other network devices for communication within the network infrastructure. OBU is a device mounted onboard in a vehicle, used to exchange information with RSUs or other OBUs. AU is the device within the vehicle that runs the applications and uses the communication capabilities of the OBU.

Vehicle to Vehicle communication (V2V) is performed between OBUs, and Vehicle to Infrastructure (V2I) communication is performed between OBU and RSU. In our work, we consider V2V communications.

VANETs can use different wireless access technologies such as (Al-Sultan et al. 2014): 3G, IEEE 802.11p, Wi-Fi, Wi-Max, LTE, and so on. Each technology has different characteristics and communication ranges. In this, work we address the 802.11p standard that uses the frequency spectrum reserved by Federal Communications Commission (FCC) for vehicular networks and allows a transmission range up to 1 km. In the IEEE 802.11p standard, the 75 MHz spectrum (between 5.850 GHz and 5.925 GHz) is divided into seven channels (from 172 to 184) (Miao et al. 2012). The capacity of each channel is 10 MHz and Channel 178 is a control channel (CCH) used for safety communications. The other six channels (SCH) can be used for both safety and non-safety applications.

3. RELATED WORK

In the literature, several authors address the channel allocation in VANETs using IEEE 802.11p standard. In (Chu et al. 2012) the authors propose a channel allocation mechanism (DCAS) using IEEE 802.11p standard considering a highway scenario. The control channel interval is divided into two periods, one for the channel reservation and other for the dissemination of control messages and security. DCAS is based in TDMA and to avoid interference among links are selected different time slots for links with 2-hops away.

In (Park et al. 2013), the authors present a mechanism (DSCA) for service channel allocation in a vehicular network. The objective is to assign a service channel (SCH) for each vehicle using access categories to improve the network throughput. The mechanism uses the historical of service announcement messages sent by vehicles. Before a vehicle to announce a service (and its corresponding channel), it calculates the capacity in each channel (based on a current number of users) and selects the highest capacity channel.

In (Frigau et al. 2015) the author presents an adaptive multi-channel allocation mechanism that selects opportunistically a service channel among all six service channels. The channel selection is based on the channel status. This status is obtained through the periodic exchange of beacons messages on the control channel. The beacon message allows a vehicle to know if a channel is busy and how many vehicles are accessing a channel. Our work differs from previous ones because we do not use a TDMA-based channel allocation scheme. In previous work using a single network interface requires time synchronization for use of the interface as control or data interface. In our approach, we used two network interfaces, one for control operations and other to transmit/receive data. In addition, we consider the profile of mobility, traffic history, and node degree to allocate the channel, and not only the number of users or messages on the control channel.

4. NETWORK, INTERFERENCE AND MOBILITY MODELS

The network model is an urban vehicular ad-hoc network, represented by nodes in a communication graph. The model uses two network interfaces: control and data interfaces. Control interface (CCC) exchanges information about nodes (like routing, mobility, and channels) and data interface sends data packets and changes the channel according to channel allocation algorithm. We use channel 172 as a control channel. Channel 178 is reserved exclusively for safety applications. The others channels are used as a data channel. We use a 2-hops interference model that considers two links interfering if they are exactly 2-hops away from each other and uses the same channel. We use this model to prevent close links using the same channel generate interference on each other. Thus, the goal of the algorithm is to allocate different channels to links that are 2-hops away from each other. As urban mobility model, we use Manhattan Grid model.

5. THE CHANNEL ALLOCATION MECHANISM

The channel allocation mechanism uses Hello Messages for exchanging information about available channels and mobility of the nodes. A node receives a Hello Message, extracts the list of available channels from the message and makes an intersection between that list and the local channel list. The resulting set of channels is ordered according to channel quality (the quality is higher if the channel is not interfering with 2-hops neighbors). The links of the node are then ordered according to link priority. This priority (in a future time window (Δ)) is given by:

$$p_k(t+\Delta) = 1 - (\propto * T_k(t) + \beta * M_k(t+\Delta) + \gamma * D_k(t)) \tag{1}$$

$$\text{s.t.} \begin{cases} 0 \leq \propto \leq 1 \\ 0 \leq \beta \leq 1 \\ 0 \leq \gamma \leq 1 \\ \propto + \beta + \gamma = 1 \end{cases}$$

Where α, β, γ are weights applied in each of the parameters and depend on the network scenario, and T_k, M_k, and D_k are the normalized traffic, mobility, and node degree, respectively. The traffic parameter is the amount of bytes transmitted by the link. Mobility parameter corresponds to the Euclidean distance between the nodes of the link. Node degree is the amount of direct neighbors of the node. After ordered the links, the algorithm associates each ordered channel for each ordered link. This association is only a channel allocation proposal. In sequence, the mechanism calculates the node priority. The node priority $P(t+\Delta)$ for n links is given by:

$$P(t+\Delta) = \frac{\sum_{k=1}^{n} p_k(t+\Delta)}{n} \qquad s.t. \quad n > 0 \tag{2}$$

The channels proposed for each link and the node priority are sent to neighboring nodes through Interaction Message. A node receives the Interaction Message and compares the priority (contained in the message) with its local priority. If the priority of Interaction Message is higher, the local node accepts the channel proposed for the link that received the message and recalculates the channel (looking for a different channel of the 2-hops neighbors) in the others links. If the priority of Interaction Message is lower, the message is discarded.

6. PERFORMANCE EVALUATION

The evaluation scenario corresponds to a network simulation consisting of 40 vehicles distributed in an area of $600m^2$ with a transmission range of 120 m. The road topology is composed of 6 blocks in the x and y-axis of a Cartesian plane. Vehicle speed varies from 1 m/s to 5 m/s. The probability of the vehicle to change its direction is 0.3. The distribution and mobility of the vehicles are determined by Manhattan grid mobility model.

We use the NS-3 simulator and 100 simulations were performed. In each simulation, the results of the current proposal, identified as NBCA (Node Behavior-aware Channel Allocation), are compared with two other methods: single channel (SC) assignment and RANDOM assignment. We compare our method with RANDOM because many RSUs and OBUs allocate channels to advertise their services using a random allocation method. In the simulation, four CBR data flows were generated (each having 3000 packets) during 12 seconds with the pair source and destination determined randomly, following a uniform distribution. The packet size used was 1000 bytes and the simulation time was 72 seconds. We used the evaluation metrics of aggregated throughput, packet delivery rate, and end-to-end delay. The aggregated throughput is the sum of packets delivered to all network nodes per unit of time. The packet delivery rate is the number of packets received in relation to the number of packets sent. The end-to-end delay is the time interval that a packet takes to reach its destination. Figure 1 illustrates the simulation results.

Figure 1(a) shows the aggregated throughput according to the number of channels.

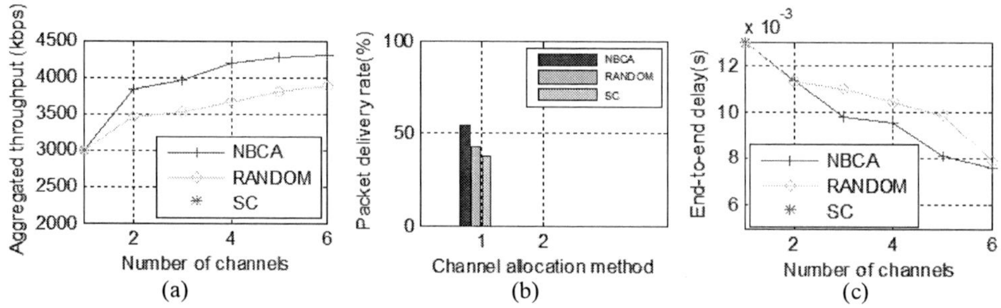

Figure 1. Simulation results

NBCA algorithm presented a throughput about 11% and 28% higher (considering 2 channels) compared with RANDOM and SC, respectively. SC is represented in Figure 1(a) as a point on the y-axis (and not a row, as NBCA and RANDOM). As the number of channels increases, the NBCA algorithm maintained the same performance (around 11% for 6 channels) compared with RANDOM. Regarding the SC, NBCA obtained an increase of 43% (considering 6 channels). The higher performance of NBCA algorithm occurred due to the fact that the channel assignment priority occurs in links with closer neighbors, allocating a different channel for links that are 2-hops away. Figure 1(b) illustrates the comparison of the average packet delivery rate among NBCA, RANDOM, and SC allocation methods. NBCA presented the highest packet delivery rate corresponding to 54.4%, while RANDOM and SC presented 42.85% and 37.71%, respectively.

Figure 1(c) illustrates the average end-to-end delay. NBCA and RANDOM allocation methods presented very close values in the order of 11.4 ms (for 2 channels) and 7.8 ms (for 6 channels). SC has an end-to-end delay value in the order of 13 ms. The end-to-end delay is higher with few channels, due to the contention process to generate waiting time in the transmission buffer. As the number of channels increases, decreases the number of contentions and the delay to send a packet.

7. CONCLUSIONS

In this paper, we propose a distributed channel allocation method for VANETs. The main contribution of this work is in the use of mobility, traffic history, and node degree parameters as a criterion for decision-making in the allocation of channels. Results show that our method (NBCA) presents values for aggregated throughput and packet delivery rate greater than RANDOM and SC allocation methods. Furthermore, the end- to-end delay is lower (for 3, 4 and 5 channels) for NBCA. This proposal also opens perspectives for future works. Examples of possible future works have: incorporation of quality metrics of service (as buffer size, packet priority), analyzes the impact of the distribution of weights of the link priority function for different scenarios and simulations with others mobility models.

REFERENCES

Al-Sultan S. et al, 2014. A Comprehensive Survey on Vehicular Ad hoc Network. *In Journal of Network and Computer Applications*, Vol. 37, No. 1, pp 380-392.

Chu, I. et al, 2012. An IEEE 802.11p based Distributed Channel Assignment Scheme Considering Emergency Message Dissemination. *Vehicular Technology Conference (VTC Spring)*. Yokohama, Japan, pp. 1-5.

Frigau, M. et al, 2015. Social-based Forwarding in Multi-channel Vehicular Networks. *IEEE International Workshop on Smart City and Ubiquitous Computing Applications*. Larnaca, Cyprus, pp. 166-173.

Liang W. et al, 2015. Vehicular ad hoc Networks: Architecture, Research Issues, Methodologies, Challenges, and Trends. *In International Journal of Distributed Sensor Networks*, Vol. 2015, No. 1, pp 1-11.

Miao L. et al, 2012. Evaluation and Enhancement of IEEE 802.11p Standard: A Survey. *In Mobile Computing*, Vol. 2, No. 1, pp 15-30.

Park, S. et al, 2013. Dynamic Service-channels Allocation (DSCA) in Vehicular Ad hoc Networks. *IEEE Consumer Communications and Networking Conference*. Las Vegas, EUA, pp. 11-14.

VIDEO QUALITY COMPARISON IN VIDEO STREAM OVER WIRELESS NETWORKS

Luiz Teixeira[1], Reinaldo Gomes[1], Luciana Gomes[2] and Anderson Costa[3]
[1]*Federal University of Campina Grande*
[2]*State University of Paraiba*
[3]*Federal Institute of Education Science and Technology of Paraiba*

ABSTRACT

The use of streaming services has grown in the past few years. The videos are streamed in real time anywhere in the world and since many users of these services have wireless networks in their homes, it is possible that the video has a degenerated image quality due to the presence of the wireless network. In this paper, we compare the quality of video transmitted and received via streaming to verify if there is a decrease in quality and the best format for compression among the ones chosen (HEVC, H.264 and MPEG-4). Through the data obtained using the experimental approach, we see that the videos suffer with the presence of the wireless network and the HEVC loses less quality in the video received.

KEYWORDS

Video, stream, HEVC, H.264, MPEG-4

1. INTRODUCTION

A computer network consists of one or more computers (or mobile devices) capable of exchanging information and / or share resources, interconnected by a communication sub- system, in other words, a network exists when we have at least two computers (or mobile devices) interconnected so that they can share physical and / or logical resources such as data, printers, scanners, emails, among others. A network can use cables or the air (wireless) to communicate. The most known and used network is the Internet.

A video is a technology for signal processing, analog or digital, to capture, store, transmit or display a set of images with the impression of movement. The main application of the video appeared on television with all its numerous applications (entertainment, education, engineering, science, defense, etc...). The video displayed on computers is just a digital compressed video using a specific format.

Video streaming is a technology in which the video is constantly transmitted, received and displayed by the user while being delivered by a provider. You can begin by showing the video without having the whole video; that is, it is displayed as it is transmitted.

Wireless networks tend to suffer more interference from external sources because they use air as the propagation medium, that is, the network will compete with any networks at the same frequency or even our household appliances (microwaves, cordless phones, etc.), besides suffering a lot with signal attenuation.

Nowadays, more and more users use systems for streaming videos like Netflix, Hulu and YouTube. These systems make the stream via Internet (which is mostly wired). But what happens when those data start to traffic on a wireless network? It is quite common to have Wi-Fi routers at users' homes, especially with the ease and mobility that this kind of network gives us to connect various devices (laptops, tablets, smartphones, etc.). Will these videos be affected by the wireless network? The results of our experiments show us that this happens and also show us that there is a difference in the compression format used.

2. METHODOLOGY

2.1 Objective and Research Questions

The objective of this study is to compare the quality of videos received via streaming in different compression formats through a wireless medium. To this end, we consider the following questions:

- Is the quality of the received video affected by wireless transmission?
- Is there a difference between the qualities of videos received using different compression formats?
- If there is a difference, what is the best compression format?
- Does the video content affect the video quality?

2.2 Design of Experiments

2.2.1 Independent Variable

Since we want to compare the quality of videos received in different compression formats, we need to choose a few. The ones chosen were HEVC, H.264 and MPEG-4 formats because of their fairly widespread use and their high quality images in the compressed videos.

2.2.2 Dependent Variable

As dependent variable we have the SSIM (Structural Similarity), which measures the similarity in the structure of the frames of videos. This variable is calculated by comparing the original video and the video received to represent video degradation. When SSIM obtained between two videos is equal to 1, we know that the videos are identical, so we wish to obtain the closest possible value of 1. Also, we use PSNR (Peak Signal-to-Noise Ratio), which measures the ratio between the maximum possible power of a signal and the power of corrupting noise that affects the fidelity of its representation.

3. PRESENTATION AND ANALYSIS OF THE RESULTS

3.1 Video Quality Metrics

To evaluate the data obtained from the experiments and try to answer the research questions, graphics of confidence intervals regarding video quality metrics were generated.

According to the graphs shown in Figures 1 and 3, we can conclude that all codecs suffered with the transmission problems existent in wireless environments, since all of them presented some degradation in the received videos. However, HEVC presented a better adaptation than the other evaluated codecs, obtaining best values in any chosen metrics. Regarding H.264 and MPEG-4, both obtained similar results, as can be seen by their confidence intervals, but H.264 presented a tendency of better adapting to wireless environment than MPEG-4.

When considering video types (Figures 2 and 4), it's possible to note that videos with rapid movements always presented a higher degradation than the other two types of video. This is expected because videos with more movement need more and bigger packets to be transmitted, and when any information is discarded it will compromise video quality. Slow and moderate movement videos experienced much better quality than rapid one in all metrics, being very close to the value 1, which means that no could be noted in the received video when comparing with the transmitted one. However, slow movement videos reached values a little better than moderate movement videos, indicating, as expected, that simpler videos are less affected by transmission characteristics present in wireless communication environments.

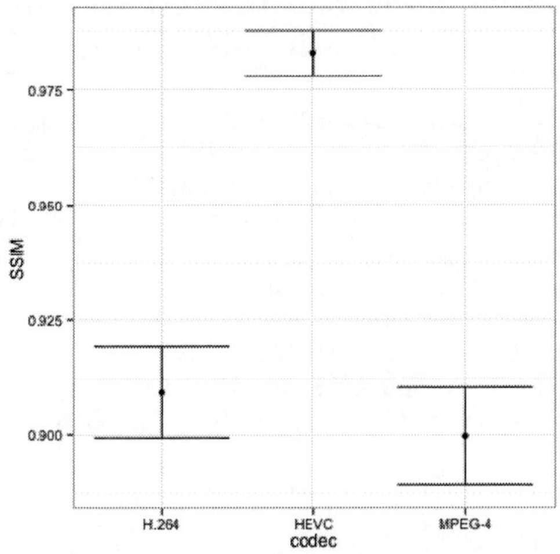

Figure 1. Confidence intervals with alpha=0.05 for SSIM for HEVC, H.264 and MPEG-4 formats

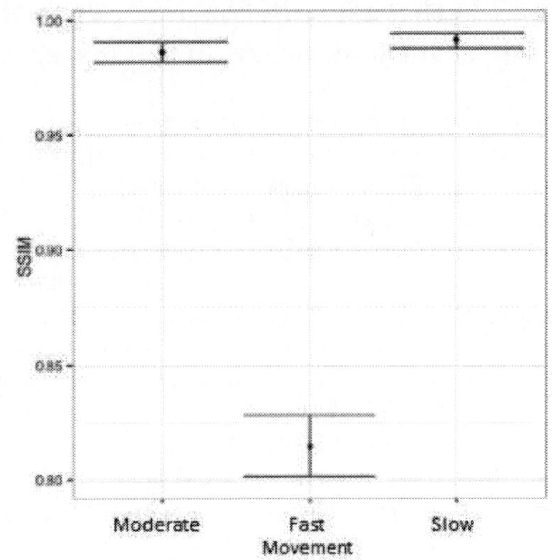

Figure 2. Confidence intervals with alpha = 0.05 for SSIM with the three types of the videos

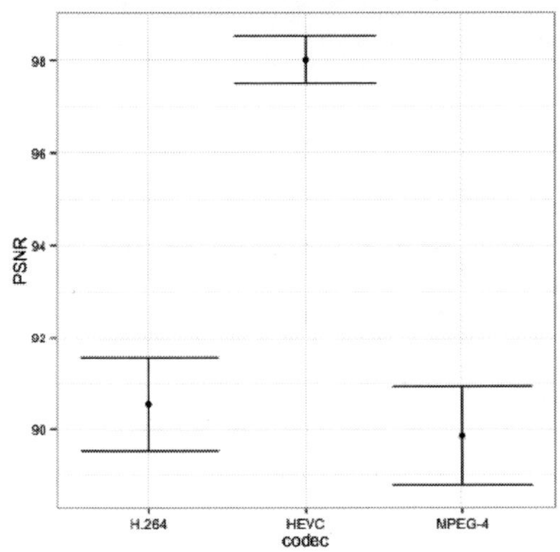

Figure 3. Confidence intervals with alpha=0.05 for PSNR for HEVC, H.264 and MPEG-4 formats

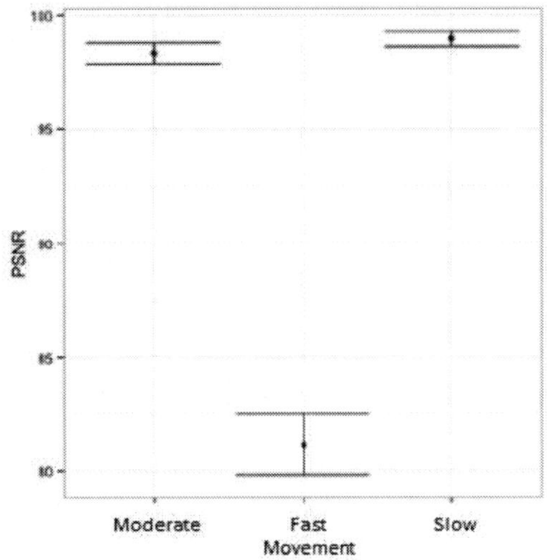

Figure 4. Confidence intervals with alpha = 0.05 for PSNR with the three types of the videos

3.2 Is the Quality of the Received Video Affected by Wireless Transmission?

To verify if the received video had its quality affected, we must observe the metric for video quality evaluation. These metrics might have some standardized values to indicate that no losses were found in the received videos. SSIM maximum average must be 1 to indicate that no degradation happened in the video, while PSNR varies from 0 to 100.

As can be seen in Figures 1 and 3, none of the codecs reached the higher possible value in any of the metrics indicating that some degradation has identified. This happens because videos do not have exactly the same content in all received frames and hence their qualities were affected by transmission over a wireless environment.

3.3 Is there a Difference between the Qualities of the Videos Received using Different Compression Formats?

To verify if there is a difference in quality between two videos received by the formats, we applied the Pairwise-Wilcoxon test. It is a nonparametric test applied to more than two groups. This test performs paired tests until it has compared all the possibilities, checking the equality of the means of samples.

With the test run, we obtained p-values to all tests among the three codecs indicating that the mean of all of them are different from each other to SSIM and PSNR.

To find the best compression format is, we need to identify the format that has the highest average. To this end, we used a Mann-Whitney Wilcoxon test.

When performing the test, we obtain a p-values that indicate that HEVC obtained best similarity between transmitted and received videos, proving that this codec could adapt better to wireless communication restrictions. HEVC was followed by H.264 and MPEG-4 respectively, reinforcing the differences among them in wireless environments.

3.4 Does the Video Content affect the Video Quality?

To answer this question, we also used the Pairwise-Wilcoxon test for the metrics SSIM and PSNR.

Based on the obtained values videos with rapid movement presented the higher degradation among the evaluated ones. For videos of slow movement and moderate movement, it was also possible to note statistical difference between obtained results, demonstrating that slow movement videos reached better values in video quality metrics. Thus, we conclude that the video content affects its quality.

4. CONCLUSIONS AND FUTURE WORK

Through this work it was possible to prove that video transmitted via a wireless network tend to lose quality. The loss in quality was observed in tests with the data obtained for HEVC, H.264 and MPEG-4 format. It was also possible to observe that there is difference in quality when comparing the received videos in the three formats and furthermore, we perceive that the HEVC can maintain a higher quality, but H.264 presented less influence in network metrics perspective.

As it is a simple work, its greatest contribution is the range of future works which it generates. Among them we can mention:

- Comparison of several existing protocols for streaming and types of content of videos;
- Verification of the cause of loss of video quality in a transmission via wireless networks. What is the factor that influences the most? Packet loss?
- Addition of metrics for video quality evaluation and network communication evaluation.

REFERENCES

[1] J. Chan, K. Zeng, P. Mohapatra, S.-J. Lee, and S. Banerjee, 2005, "Mpeg- 4 video streaming quality evaluation in ieee 802.11e wlans," IEEE International Conference on Image Processing, vol. 1, pp. 197–200.

[2] D. Gao, J. Cai, and Z. H. Paul Bao, 2010, "Metrics for evaluating video streaming quality in lossy ieee 802.11 wireless networks," Proceedings IEEE INFOCOM, pp. 1–9.

[3] D. C. Begazo, D. Z. Rodriguez, and M. A. Ramírez, 2011, "Avaliação de qualidade de vídeo sobre uma rede ip usando métricas objetivas," Revista Iberoamericana de Sistemas, Cibernética e Informática, vol. 8, pp. 25–29.

[4] K. Choi, J. kyun Choi, J. H. Hong, G. J. Min, and J. Lee, 2008, "Comparison of video streaming quality measurement methodologies," 10th International Conference on Advanced Communication Technology, vol. 2, pp. 993– 996.

[5] "Soekris net5501 single board computer," http://soekris.com/products/ net5501.html.

[6] "Ffmpeg," http://www.ffmpeg.org/.

[7] "Evalvid - framework to evaluate video quality," http://www.tkn.tu-berlin. de/menue/research/evalvid/.

IQUIKWRITING - AN IWATCH VIRTUAL KEYBOARD

Gláucio R. Vivian[1], Cristiano R. Cervi[2] and Willingthon Pavan[2]
[1]*University of Passo Fundo - UPF / IFFar FW*
[2]*University of Passo Fundo - UPF*

ABSTRACT

The Human-Computer Interaction area seeks to create accessible and at the same time fast, wearable, easy to learn interfaces. Keyboard development for mobile devices is a research field of the human-computer interface area. The Apple iWatch does not have a feature for this purpose. This paper aims to adapt the QuikWriting method for writing small texts on it. Improvements were conducted in order to reduce the number of movements for Portuguese Language. The experiments showed that this approach reduced in 347,835 movements to typing the full Holy Bible.

KEYWORDS

Human-computer interaction, iWatch, QuikWriting, user interface, virtual keyboard

1. INTRODUCTION

Mobile computers are more and more presents in our lives. Apple Computers has innovated the concept of mobility with the new iWatch. This new device is not a simple watch, it is an extension of iPhone applications. The Fource Touch technology is the key of this interface. It makes it possible to access other options of iWatch menu by pressing firmly in the screen. The words entered, are exclusively with the personal assistant for iPhone called Siri. This approach use the built-in microphone to process the user natural language. This is interesting technology, however there are moments in which the user is not able to talk (e.g. noise pollution, sensitive data, fraud voice recordings and others situations).

This paper aims to present a solution to allow iWatch users to type direct on the screen without using the iPhone or Siri. The main goal of this paper is to make a keyboard with QuikWriting method (adapted to Portuguese Language) improved with deterministic finite automaton. The language optimization is performed by new layout proposed from the analysis of relative frequency of characters (percentage of frequency for one character by totals characters).

The paper was organized into following sections: section 2 presents the study about human-computer interface for small devices. Section 3 proposes the approach to build a new interface specific to Portuguese Language. Section 4 presents the experiments and results of the proposal. Finally, section 5 shows the conclusions.

2. RELATED WORKS

Proposals of keyboard for devices with restrict dimension are often found in literature and conference of Human-computer interaction and user interface, as ACM SIGACCESS conference on Computers and accessibility (ASSETS), International Conference on Human-Computer Interaction with Mobile Devices and Services (MobileHCI), ACM symposium on User interface software and technology, Nordic conference on Humancomputer interaction, ACM Conference on Human Factors in Computing Systems, SIGCHI conference on Human factors in computing systems.

The QuikWriting method was proposed by Perlin (1998). Perlin propose to divide the writing area in nine parts with three rows and three columns. The writing always starts and ends in the central area. From the offset to the underlying areas, the user performs the character encoding. Thus, it is possible to encode one character from 2 to 4 movements. The method has four maps, representing lowercase, uppercase, numbers and symbols. Guimbretiére andWinograd (2000) proposed the FlowMenu, it is the addition of application menus to QuikWriting. Later Isokoski and Raisamo (2004) conducted a longitudinal study on user performance. In this study 20 people used stylus and joystick.

Mankoff and Abowd (1998) developed the Cirrin. It is a circular keyboard format with an empty central area and the edges filled with characters. From the movement between these areas, the user performs the typing of characters. The authors perform an experiment with a person using a layout designed not optimized heuristically. The user has obtained the speed of 20 words per minute (wpm). In the work of Partridge et al. (2002) was proposed the TiltType. The proposal to use four keys to first select the character set, then pressing the desired option, the device presents on the screen nine options of characters, sorted in alphabetical order, each with an arrow pointing in one direction. The choice for the desired character is performed by moving the device in the direction of the arrow, this move is detected by the accelerometer. The authors not performed experiments or optimizations of layout. MacKenzie et al. (2011) presents the H4-Writer. This method uses four areas arranged one on each edge of the screen. The combinations are coded according to a ranking established using Huffaman code. In a longitudinal study with six participants, an average text entry speed of 20.4 wpm was observed in the 10th session. In work of Kristensson and Vertanen (2014) was formulated the inviscid text entry rate. The conclusion was that it is necessary around 67 wpm for user to use satisfactorily mobile devices. Grossman et al. (2015) present the optimized SwipeZone. It is a keyboard to glass. The layout is similar to QUERTY, but was modified the locations of "P" and "L". The modification resulted in 8.73 wpm. Leiva et al. (2015) improved the ZoomBoard (a QUERTY keyboard with zoom). The proposal was callout-based soft keyboard and ZShift (visual feedback through a zoomed callout). The limitation of work is not implementing the error corrector.

3. IMPLEMENTATION OVERVIEW

To build a keyboard with QuikWriting to iWatch, we used the deterministic finite automaton. This approach is different from the original QuikWriting implementation. However, we believe they are more efficient to future improvements mentioned in the final section of this paper. The idea is encoding the movements per areas of QuikWriting in numbers from 1 to 9. After this, the sequences of this numbers are submitted to automaton with the objective of recognizing the valid movements. There are 32 movements valid for a matrix of 3x3. Each valid movement corresponding to an index between 0 and 31. This index is used to localize the final value in tables of characters. In Table 1 it is show the possible values and index to deterministic finite automaton.

Table 1. Valid movement corresponding to an index

Sequence	Index	Sequence	Index	Sequence	Index	Sequence	Index	Sequence	Index
5,1,2,3,5	**0**	5,2,5	**7**	5,4,5	**14**	5,7,5	**21**	5,9,6,3,5	**28**
5,1,2,5	**1**	5,3,2,1,5	**8**	5,4,7,5	**15**	5,7,8,5	**22**	5,9,6,5	**29**
5,1,4,5	**2**	5,3,2,5	**9**	5,6,3,5	**16**	5,7,8,9,5	**23**	5,9,8,5	**30**
5,1,4,7,5	**3**	5,3,5	**10**	5,6,5	**17**	5,8,5	**24**	5,9,8,7,5	**31**
5,1,5	**4**	5,3,6,5	**11**	5,6,9,5	**18**	5,8,7,5	**25**		
5,2,1,5	**5**	5,3,6,9,5	**12**	5,7,4,1,5	**19**	5,8,9,5	**26**		
5,2,3,5	**6**	5,4,1,5	**13**	5,7,4,5	**20**	5,9,5	**27**		

It is possible make specifics maps of characters to other languages, by codifying the most used letters with fewer movements. In this work, we make a new map to Portuguese Language. Initially, we obtained the frequency of characters in the specific language. To make this study, Quaresma (2008) was analyzed 141 texts, from 47 authors, with a counting of 11,133,372 letters and 2,400,295 words. In Figure 1 is presented the relative frequency.

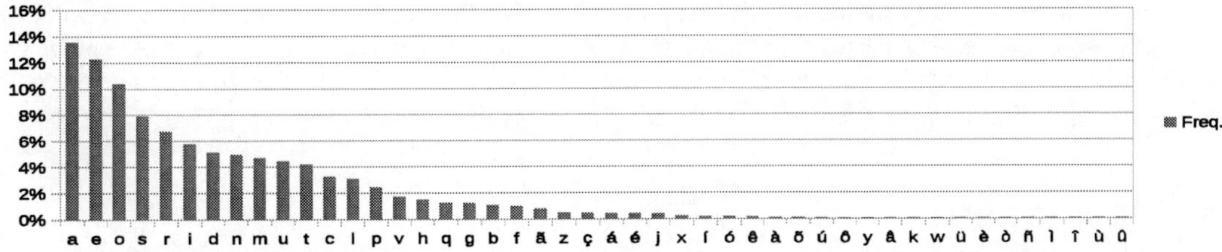

Figure 1. Relative frequency of characters to Portuguese Language (Adapted from Quaresma (2008))

The QuikWriting has 8 movements with 3 zones, 16 movements with 4 zones and 8 movements with 5 zones. To propose a new layout to QuikWriting in Portuguese Language we changed the less possible in the original layout. The characters with more frequency are positioned in movements with 3 zones and with less frequency in movements with 5 zones. In Figure 2 the original layout and specific to Portuguese Language is presented. The red characters are the changes proposed in layout to Portuguese Language.

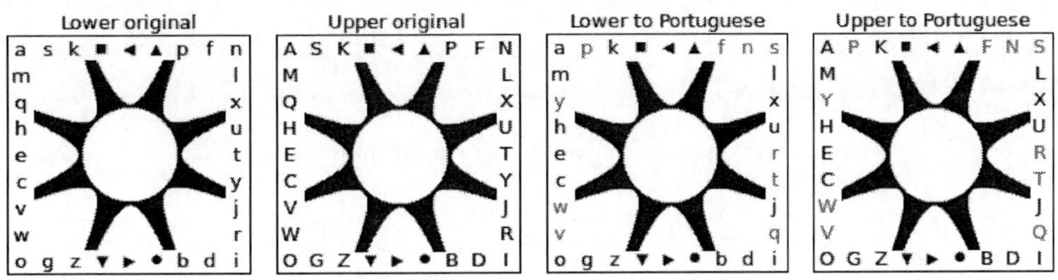

Figure 2. Layout to QuikWriting to Portuguese Language

The interface was built in XCode IDE with Swift language. We use nine buttons in 3x3 matrix configuration. Each button represents one number. The sliding in button sends to automaton your number. When automaton find one sequence of valid characters, the value is stored in actual characters table is sent to memory buffer. This buffer can are an active application or iPhone.

4. EXPERIMENTS AND RESULTS

To evaluate our proposal, we have compared the quantity of movements to type the full Holy Bible with original QuikWriting and Portuguese layout. The text of the Holy Bible is very trusty to the Portuguese grammar, that is why we have adopted it to this experiment. We have obtained the translation in Bíblia Livre Project by Santos et al. (2016). This translation was based on the 1819's edition, wrote by João Ferreira de Almeida (in public domain). In order to make this comparison, a simple class in Java Language was built. There are 3,869,021 characters (lowercase and uppercase), typing with original QuikWriting was encoded with 9,405,756 movements, against 9,057,921 movements to Portuguese Layout. This results in 347,835 fewer movements to our proposal. In Figure 3, the relative frequency of characters for the Holly Bible is presented.

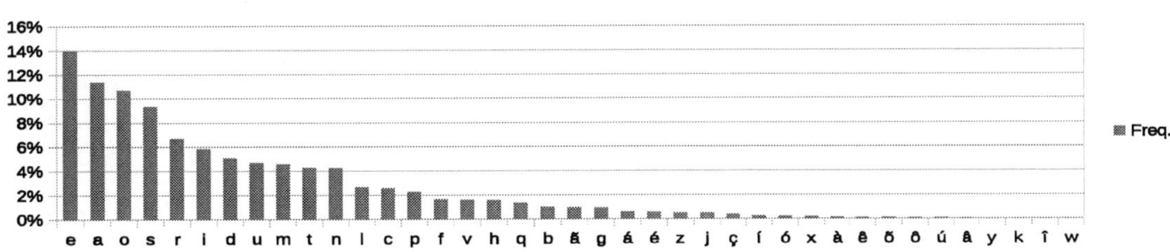

Figure 3. Relative frequency of characters to the Holy Bible

The comparative of the relative frequency of characters for the Holly Bible (Figure 3) with relative frequency of characters for Portuguese Language (Figure 1) show differences. Then, we try the new layout to QuikWriting with relative frequency of Holy Bible. However, just one single change in character "g" by "f" has occurred.

5. CONCLUSION

In this paper, we propose a new user interface to iWatch with the aim of writing a text direct to the screen of this device. The QuikWriting implemented in iWatch showed that it is possible to write small texts direct to the screen of this device. The optimized keyboard layout increased the writing speed by reducing the number of movements to codify the characters with more frequency. There are many possibilities to improving this application. It is possible to use a dictionary of words to auto complete the text, therefore, accelerating the typing and reducing the errors. Other possibility too, is to build a component to XCode IDE, making it possible to build others full applications to run directly in the iWatch without use of iPhone.

ACKNOWLEDGEMENT

This work is partially supported by PIIQP-BE, PIIQP-AM and PIIQP-AD programs from IFFar.

REFERENCES

R. Black. The PhonicStick - A joystick to generate novel words using phonics. The proceedings of the 13th international ACM SIGACCESS conference on Computers and accessibility - ASSETS '11, page 325, 2011. doi: 10.1145/2049536.2049630.

T. Grossman, X. A. Chen, and G. Fitzmaurice. Typing on Glasses. Proceedings of the 17th International Conference on Human-Computer Interaction with Mobile Devices and Services - MobileHCI '15, pages 144–152, 2015. doi: 10.1145/2785830.2785867.

F. Guimbretiére and T.Winograd. Flowmenu: combining command, text, and data entry. In Proceedings of the 13th annual ACM symposium on User interface software and technology, pages 213–216. ACM, 2000.

P. Isokoski and R. Raisamo. Quikwriting as a multi-device text entry method. In Proceedings of the third Nordic conference on Human-computer interaction, pages 105–108. ACM, 2004.

P. O. Kristensson and K. Vertanen. The Inviscid Text Entry Rate and its Application as a Grand Goal for Mobile Text Entry. Proceedings of the 16th international conference on Human-computer interaction with mobile devices & services - MobileHCI '14, pages 335–338, 2014. doi: 10.1145/2628363.2628405.

L. A. Leiva, A. Sahami, A. Catalá, N. Henze, and A. Schmidt. Text Entry on Tiny QWERTY Soft Keyboards. CHI '15 Proceedings of the 33rd Annual ACM Conference on Human Factors in Computing Systems, pages 669–678, 2015. doi: 10.1145/2702123.2702388.

I. S. MacKenzie, R. W. Soukoreff, and J. Helga. 1 thumb, 4 buttons, 20 words per minute: Design and evaluation of h4-writer. In Proceedings of the 24th annual ACM symposium on User interface software and technology, pages 471–480. ACM, 2011.

J. Mankoff and G. D. Abowd. Cirrin: a word-level unistroke keyboard for pen input. In Proceedings of the 11th annual ACM symposium on User interface software and technology, pages 213–214. ACM, 1998.

K. Partridge, S. Chatterjee, V. Sazawal, G. Borriello, and R. Want. Tilttype: accelerometer-supported text entry for very small devices. In Proceedings of the 15th annual ACM symposium on User interface software and technology, pages 201–204. ACM, 2002.

K. Perlin. Quikwriting: continuous stylus-based text entry. In Proceedings of the SIGCHI conference on Human factors in computing systems, pages 215–216. ACM, 1998.

P. Quaresma. Frequency analysis of the portuguese language. Technical report, University of Coimbra, Department of Mathematics, 3001-454 Coimbra, Portugal, July 2008. ISSN 0874-338X.

D. R. d. Santos, M. S. d. S. Figueira, and M. A. T. d. Costa. Bíblia Livre. GitHub, 2016. URL https://github.com/blivre/BibliaLivre. Accessed in 04/06/2016.

DESIGNING ACCESSIBLE WEB SYSTEMS FOR USERS WITH VISUAL IMPAIRMENT

Vinicius Diehl de Franceschi and Marcos Alexandre Rose Silva
Colégio Politécnico, Federal University of Santa Maria. Avenida Roraima, nº100, Santa Maria, RS, Brazil.

ABSTRACT

Nowadays, Web has been used in many daily activities as researching, shopping, among others. On the other hand, a considerable part of people, particularly who have special needs, have some difficulties to access and use Web for these and others activities. In this context, we describe here two important strategies for accessibility, one called WCAG which is internationally known and another called eMag, which was defined considering WCAG and others accessible strategies and guidelines. Taking these two strategies into consideration a web site was developed and used by some people with visual impairments. After observation of the use of it and others sites, new guidelines were identified. As result, this paper also presents these new guidelines to be used as WCAG and eMag complement.

KEYWORDS

Accessibility. Web. Technology. Visual Impairment

1. INTRODUCTION

The access to information technologies significantly changed the way people relate to each other and the world. For example, the way people perform the tasks of daily life, trade, work, as well as, teaching and learning processes. Every day, the web becomes more important in various sectors of society. It is used by people to provide and receive information in addition to be a mean of interaction with society. Because of that, an accessible web to all people, including those that have some kind of special need, is really important. All people have to be able to use the potential of information technology and web in their activities. This paper aims to investigate Human-Computer Interaction (HCI) strategies related to accessibility to support accessible interface design, and to observe users with disabilities using web sites in order to collect information about their experiences. Considering this context, the paper is organized as follows: Section 2 reports the percentage of people with disabilities in the world; Section 3 provides a brief reasoning about HCI strategies which are guidelines to support accessible web design; Section 4 presents the first version of the site using guidelines; Section 5 reports user tests; Section 6 presents the new guidelines considering guidelines researching and user tests results; Section 7 presents the second version of the site with the new guidelines and, finally, there are the final considerations and future work.

2. THE DEFICIENCY IN THE WORLD

Over a billion people (or about 15% of the world´s population) live with disability. According to the World Health Survey about 110 million and according to Global Burden of Disease about 190 million people have significant difficulties in functioning. Approximately 314 million people have visual impairment and 45 million of them are blind (World Health Organization, 2011). In a lot of countries, there are more people with visual impairment than others kinds of deficiency.

For example, in Brazil, according to the data from the Brazilian Institute of Geography and Statistics (IBGE), more than 45.6 million Brazilians declare having some kind of disability, representing almost 24% of the Brazilian population. Of all the disabilities, the Population Census Data indicate that visual impairment has reached 35.7 million people (IBGE, 2010).

This huge number of people with disabilities, especially with visual impairment, shows how important of accessibility in the world is. Considering the digital world, it shows the necessity of researchers, etc., related to improve the interaction between people with disabilities and computer in order to facilitate it, i.e., without or with less obstacles, allowing easy access to information (Halbach, 2015). One of these researches is represented by guidelines which describe rules or recommended practice to design accessible web sites.

3. GUIDELINES

WCAG (Accessibility Guidelines for Web Content) and eMag (Model Accessibility in Electronic Government) are guidelines considering rules, technical standards to design accessible site for everyone.

- WCAG came from World Wide Web (W3C), an international group community where member organizations, the public and organizations around the world work together to develop Web standards, describing also Web guidelines and techniques (W3C, 2015). In this context, there are Web Content Accessibility Guidelines (WCAG) to provide standard for web content accessibility, i.e., WCAG describe how to make web content more accessible to people with disabilities (WCAG, 2015).
- eMag came from Brazilian government. It considers WCAG and others countries examples, with guidelines or reports related to web content accessibility. eMag contains guidelines explaining standards to be followed to develop computational systems and sites for Brazilian government. It intends to support professionals during development in order to make systems/sites where a lot of people with different characteristics and necessities can use it, including people with disabilities.

4. THE FIRST WEBSITE VERSION

After accessibility guidelines investigation, the first version of a site was created. Figure 1 represents it. Each part of the site is explained below, considering WCAG and eMag guidelines.

1.7 – The main menu has an orderly guide rule. This technique aims to provide a logical tab order to read through links, form control and objects. The tab order can be specified in order to follow the content of the relationship without following the order of code elements. In this site, the sequence is Música (music), Novelas (soap opera), Artesanato (handicraft) and Times (soccer teams) (WCAG: Criterion of success 2.4.3 (Technique H4 – Creating a logical tab order through links, form controls, and objects); eMag: Recommendation 1.4 – Sort a logical form and intuitive reading and tab).

1.8 –The division of content into blocks is the base for the use of shortcuts, facilitating a quick access to the desired content block by user. This technique consists in dividing the areas of information into manageable groups. The most common divisions are: top, content, menu and footer, which make the structure more organized. In this site, there are menus (first 1.8) and the content (second 1.8) divisions (WCAG: Criterion of success 3.2.3(Technique G61 - Presenting repeated components in the same relative order each time they appear); eMag: Recommendation 1.8 – Divide the areas of information).

3.5 – A link that allows the user to explore more about the information described. This option, added to the end of paragraph, is clicked when the user accesses a short block of text and wants to know more about it. These links help to use the Tab key to move through links to make it easier for visually impaired users to explore the context of each the link. In this site, there is Leia mais.. (read more) link (WCAG: Criteria of success 2.4.4 and 2.4.9; eMag: Recommendation 3.5 – Describe clearly and succinctly links).

3.6 –The purpose of this technique is to provide a text alternative to describe the images shown on the site, using the alt attribute. However, there is no character limit for the alt attribute. It is recommended to describe the image in a few words or a short phrase making it clear to the user. In this site, there are alternative texts in each image, for example, in the first image with Grêmio word, the alternative text is "logo from Grêmio soccer team" (WCAG: Criterion of success 1.1.1(Technique H2 – Combining adjacent image and text links for the same resource); eMag: Recommendation 3.6 – Provide alternative text for images of the site).

4.1 – In the Accessibility menu, the contrast technique was implemented to help users who are color blindness or low vision in reading the texts. Its purpose is to provide enough contrast between text and background so that the text can be more readable. In this site, there are two options: the first called cor (color) makes black background and white text; the second Padrão (default) makes white background and black text (WCAG: Criterion of success 1.4.3; eMag: Recommendation 4.1 - Offer minimal contrast between the background in the foreground).

4.3 –The page must remain legible and functional even when resized up to 200%. To ensure that the page content does not suffer change in content, causing overlapping images and texts (WCAG: Criterion of success 1.4.4; eMag: Recommendation 4.3 - Allow resizing without loss of functionality).

4.4 – This feature provides an operating mode in which the keyboard focus can be visually identified. By default, links and form elements already have a highlighted border to receive the keyboard focus. In this site, all short blocks of text are highlighted considering keyboard focus (WCAG: Criterion of success 2.4.7; eMag: Recommendation 4.4 - Enabling the element with the focus is visually evident).

Some guidelines are not shown in Figure 1, but they have been implemented. For example, the page can be resized without losing functionality (4.3) and keyboard focus can be identified (4.4).

5. USER TEST

Comprehension test and Key test were applied in order to observe users from an association called ACDV, for people with visual impairment, interacting with this site (Krug, S. 2014). Comprehension test means users interacting with a site or a system to observe their comprehension of it, i.e., goal and tasks understanding. In this case, users were also asked about what they think about it, what they think they can do through it, etc. Key test means interacting with a site or system to execute specific tasks. A task was to identify and read a chapter of a soup opera. Users' behavior and interaction were analyzed to identify difficulties and facilities. Tests were applied with 3 blind users, two men and one woman. They interacted with the site using a screen reader called NVDA (NVDA, 2015).

One man knew how to interact with internet to read e-mails, chat, skype, work and games, as well as, he uses screen readers as DosVox (DosVox, 2015), NVDA (NVDA, 2015) and Virtual Vision (Virtual Vision, 2015). He had no difficulties with comprehension and task.

Another man user has little computing knowledge. He was starting a course typing and it was his first interaction with a web site. Because of that, he did not identify easily some key from keyboard as "tab", "enter", "←", "→", etc. He had difficulties with comprehension and task.

The woman user knew how to interact with computer to access internet for e-mail and news reading, as well as, she uses screen readers as Jaws (Jaws, 2015) and NVDA (NVDA, 2015). She had no difficulties with comprehension and task.

In summary, one user did not realize the goal of the site and the page with a chapter of soap opera was not found by him. His main difficult was to use keyboard. In the end of the test, users reported some problems during interaction through NVDA.

1 – NVDA read in a random way some menus and links, i.e., Tabindex was not considered some times.

2 – NVDA can read alternative text of options when user presses "tab" to find an option. On the other hand, it did not read when user presses some keys as "←", "→". For example, considering some options related with font size as "increase font" and "decrease font" represented by symbols "A+" and "A-", NVDA read the alternative text increase and decrease font after pressing "Tab", but after pressing "→", it just read "A" for all options which symbol contains "A".

3 – Because of problem 2, users did not figure out the meaning of these options

4 – Users did not know how to use AccessKey.

6. NEW GUIDELINES

Some improvements were identified after user tests, described above, and observation of others ten user with visual impairment, from ACDV, using others sites as Facebook.com, Gmail.com, among others sites related to news. These improvements were described as guidelines. There are five guidelines.

It is important to say that these ten users from ACDV did not interact with the site, because they could not attended ACVD when it was under analyzed, i.e., when users were interacting with.

1. **Play the sound when the page is loaded:** One of the difficulties, reported by users, was about no idea if the page was loaded completely or not. An audible warning to alert page loaded ready for use was implemented.
2. **Describe the accessibility buttons**: In tests, users could not identify the meaning of the buttons of accessibility (A+, A-, color, default), which are used to increase the text font and change the contrast. Because of that, the functions of buttons were described, for example, from A+ to "increase text", from A- to "decrease text", from A to "normal text", from color to "contrast", from default to "original colors".
3. **Menus in alphabetical order**: Users identified difficulty navigating the menu because its organization was difficult to remember. The suggested alternative was to organize the menu items in alphabetical order to facilitate the memorizing of the items. A person from ACDV said that this alphabetical order allow him to navigate through menus, because if he wants a menu which starts with "A", he will use Tab to go to beginning of the menu, i.e., he will not need to navigate through all menu to identify where this option is.
4. **Contrast:** After changing the contrast, it will be kept on every page of the site, to avoid the user having to adjust the contrast for each new page. This problem was also identified during others sites navigation at user tests, because users needed to select the option "contrast", which means black background and white text, in each page every time. After clicking in this option, this setting must keep in all pages.
5. **Category:** There was a suggestion related to category definition to improve the interaction. For example, many soap opera names were in one page, after clicking in soap opera menu. Because of that, user needs to navigate through all names to identify one he wants. This task can be harder considering the number of names; therefore, this navigation can be easier through categories, i.e., in this case, the names of soap opera could be organized considering the television channel which shows them. Using this example, after clicking in soap opera menu, users could see a page with television channels and then, after choosing one, user could see a list of soap opera related to this channel.

7. THE SECOND WEBSITE VERSION

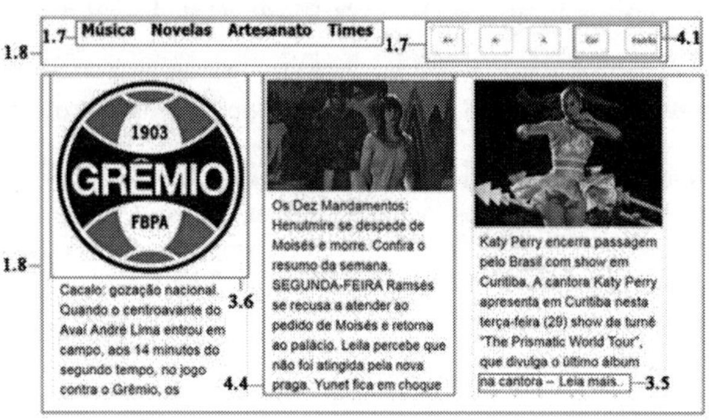

Figure 1. The First Website Version.

Figure 2. Second Website Version.

Figure1 shows the first Website version and Figure 2 presents a site with new accessibility guidelines and others characteristics explained below.

1.7 – The main menu and accessible menu were changed. Alphabetical order was implemented at main menu and a logical tab order to read through links was changed at accessible menu. Blind people do not need to access these options through Tab, because bigger or smaller texts, as well as, contrast do not make any difference for them, so the tab was hidden to avoid confusing users who do not need to access this menu. For example, if they press Tab, they will navigate through main menu and then the tab focus will be at content. In this case, there are less options to navigate, improving the interactions, because user do not need press tab for all main and accessible menu.

3.5 – A link that allows the user to explore more about the information described was changed. In the first version there was a read more link, but it does not have a useful mean for users. They cannot figure out what kind of information they will access, because the screen reader read just "read more" using tab, so now there is a complete sentence "read more about Katy Perry in Brazil", i.e., read more and the title of the news.

3.6 – The purpose of this technique is to provide an alternative to describe the images shown on the site using the alt attribute to facilitate understanding of the text with an image. However, there is no character limit for the alt attribute. It is recommended to describe the image in a few words or a short phrase making it clear to the user (WCAG: Criterion of success 1.1.1(Technique H2 – Combining adjacent image and text links for the same resource);eMag: Recommendation 3.6 – Provide alternative text for images of the site).

4.1 – The accessibility buttons were described and a preview was implemented at Auto Contraste (Contrast) and Cores Originais (Original Colors) buttons to allow user see what they will visualize after clicking in these buttons, e.g., Contrast buttons has black background and white text, because the site will be in this way after clicking in it. The same idea for Original colors button. After choosing any option from accessible menu, the whole site will be presented at same way, i.e., same colors, size, etc. Users do not need to repeat these choices at all pages as before.

Others new guidelines are not shown in Figure 2, but they were implemented. For example, there is an audio to alert when the page is loaded.

8. FINAL CONSIDERATIONS AND FUTURE WORK

Considering data from World Health Organization and IBGE, the number of people with disabilities, in special visual impairments, is increasing. Because of that, it is important to investigate and discuss about improvements and what can be done to support people with disabilities computer interaction.

Each guideline described here can make difference to support this interaction. All of them came from observation and users opinions, as well as, they did not identified in others documents as WCAG or eMag. In other words, these guidelines can be used as a complement of these documents.

As future work, a new version of site, considering these guidelines, will be available for new user tests and, others researches and observations with different sites will be done in order to identify and apply improvements to support people with disabilities computer interaction.

REFERENCES

DosVox. Available in: http://intervox.nce.ufrj.br/dosvox/. Last Visit: November, 2015.

eMag (Electronic Government Accessibility Model). Available: http://www.governoeletronico.gov.br/acoes-e-projetos/e-MAG. Last Visit: March, 2016 .

Halbach, T. Lyszkiewicz, W. 2015. *Accessibility checkers for the web: how reliable are they, actually?*. In Proceedings of the IADIS International Conference WWW/Internet. Greater Dublin, Ireland.

IBGE (Brazilian Institute of Geography and Statistics). Available in: http://g1.globo.com/brasil/noticia/2012/04/239-dos-brasileiros-declaram-ter-alguma-deficiencia-diz-ibge.html. Last Visit: October 2015.

Jaws. Available in: http://www.freedomscientific.com/Products/Blindness/JAWS. Last Visit: October 2015.

Krug, S. 2014 . *Don't make me think: A Common Sense Approach to Web Usability*. New Riders Publisher, Rio de Janeiro, Brazil.

NVDA (Official Site). Available in: http://www.nvda-project.org/. Last Visit: November, 2015.

Virtual Vision. Available in: http://www.virtualvision.com.br/. Last Visit: December, 2015.

W3C (The World Wide Web Consortium). Available in: https://www.w3.org/Consortium/. Last Visit: December 2015.

WCAG (Web Content Accessibility Guidelines). Available in: https://www.w3.org/WAI/intro/wcag. Last Visit: December 2015.

Mariotti. Silva. P. 2011. *World Health Organization. Global Data On Visual Impairments*. Available in: http://www.who.int/blindness/GLOBALDATAFINALforweb.pdf. Last Visit: March, 2016.

World Health Organization, 2011. *World report on disability*. Available in: http://www.who.int/disabilities/world_report/2011/report.pdf. Last Visit: March, 2016.

EVALUATING VM LIVE MIGRATION OVERHEAD WITH XEN HYPERVISOR

Petrônio Bezerra[*§], Gustavo Martins[*], César Rocha[*§], Reinaldo Gomes[*] and Fellype Cavalcante[*]
[*] *Federal University of Campina Grande (UFCG) – Paraíba – Brazil*
[§] *Federal Institute of Education, Science and Technology of Paraiba (IFPB) – Campina Grande – Paraíba – Brazil*

ABSTRACT

There has been a growing interest within the networking community to look into the potential of virtualization. Existing research efforts have addressed the overhead of virtualization in challenging scenarios. Yet, there are important research challenges to be addressed. One of them is the overhead that occurs due to the VM live migration process. Commonly, this overhead is perceived on the client's side by a decrease in performance over services deployed in these VMs. In this paper, we made a preliminary statistical analysis of the overhead caused by the VM live migration process using both real and virtual environments. Our evaluation, which has been conducted through a series of measurements with Xen hypervisor, has shown that the VM live migration process significantly affects the normal operation of primary client's services (e.g., database operations and Web services).

KEYWORDS

Migration, Xen, Cassandra, ab, overhead

1. INTRODUCTION

Cloud computing is a technology that brings many benefits but also many challenges. A great benefit is to provide computational structure that can be rented with molded service features according to customer needs. Thus, customers pay for the time and resources they use. In return, these companies offer many benefits such as high availability of services, scalability, security, cost reduction, etc. As highlighted in Ramachandran (2016), a US spending projection in cloud computing between 2010-2015, estimates an annual growth of around 40%, reaching an investment of USD 7 billion. In line with this trend, the scientific community has deposited a lot of effort in this area of great technological interest. Virtualization is a technology easily found by cloud computing providers. This approach involves a software layer, located between the hardware and Operating System (OS), which is called a Virtual Machine Monitor (VMM) or hypervisor (Bezerra, 2014). This technology allows different Virtual Machines (VM) to run with its own OS, despite being different from each other, in the same physical machine and at the same time.

An essential feature that it is possible to perform with VMs is VM migration, which consists of changing a VM from one host to another. One interesting way of doing this is by using live migration, a procedure that can be performed with little or no downtime of the service deployed on the virtualized server. There are many benefits obtained with the process of live migration. We can cite the VM remapping procedure that allows better utilization of physical servers, saving resources and maximizing profit. Despite these benefits, there is a negative point, which is the overhead generated by the virtualization layer.

In this work, we conducted a preliminary statistical analysis of the sampled data to observe and quantify the overhead caused by a VM live migration process. In a second direction, we plan to investigate the factors that have more influence on the overhead caused by a VM live migration process. In particular, we want to identify the effect perceived by a client host when accessing some services, such as web server and DBMS, which are deployed on a virtual server during a VM live migration process.

In order to achieve this, a set of experiments with Xen[1] hypervisor was performed. Xen is an open source hypervisor that allows the use of both full virtualization and paravirtualization techniques. Xen was chosen

[1] www.xenproject.org

because it is commonly adopted in the investigations into live migration (Li, 2013 and Padalla, 2007). Most current research on virtualization overhead adopted a benchmark that runs on the server side, therefore, only checking overload effect on the server side. The performance analysis has been a major subject of these investigations. Most of the articles apply the strategy of use a series of benchmark software to compare hypervisors by testing a wide range of system devices, for example I/O, disk, memory and processors (Li, 2013). Many of the studies did not consider performance evaluation of a specific application running on VM.

The performance evaluation of services running on VMs has previously been investigated in standalone environments (Padala, 2007), and more recently in cloud computing scenarios (Galloway, 2015). In Martins (2015), a study was conducted to evaluate performance of different databases using hypervisors. However, the authors did not analyze the impact of the VM migration process.

Considering existing works lacks, this paper brings a preliminary statistical analysis to evaluates migration process in a different perspective of most of previous investigations which can help researchers and cloud computing administrators to better understand the live migration effects and the main factors that contribute to the overhead process from the client's perspective. The tests did not run within the server itself, but from a customer, simulating the utilization of the services provided. Thus, it is possible to measure the perception of service from the client's perspective.

2. EXPERIMENT SETUP

Some experiments were conducted to identify the migration impact in two distinct scenarios: Scenario I comprised by virtual hosts (Figure 1) and Scenario II, comprised only by physical hosts.

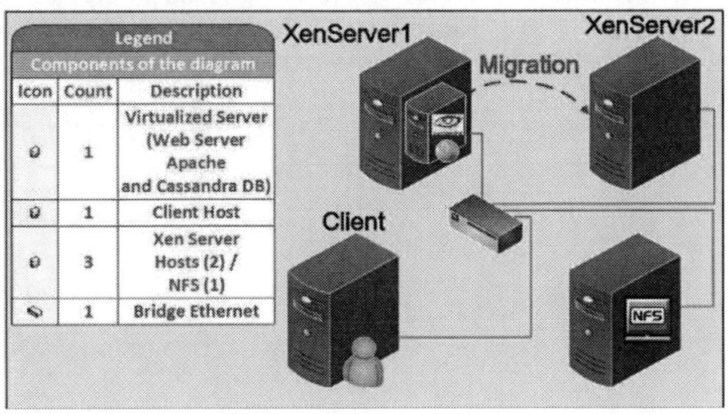

Figure 1. Environment totally with virtualized machines

In Scenario I, the environment consisted of one real machine which contained all the virtualized hosts. This host contained four VMs: XenServer1, XenServer2, Client, the Network File System (NFS) Server and a Virtual Ethernet Switch. These VMs were virtualized by the VMware Workstation Player[2] free hypervisor. To evaluate the overhead from the client's perspective of a service deployed on the virtual server during the occurrence of a live migration event of that server, two widely used services were provided. The Apache[3] Web Service™ and the Apache[4] Cassandra™ a Database Management System (DBMS) were installed on the same server, which was called WebServer and was virtualized by Xen. Xen was installed on two servers (XenServer1 and 2) that were used for live migration of the WebServer host. The live migration process is highlighted in red in Figure 1. The real machine was configured with 16 GB RAM, Intel® Core™ i7-4790 3.60GHz 64 bits and 680 GB of disk. This CPU was the same used at all virtualized hosts. All the machines (real and virtual) used on two scenarios of the experiment had Ubuntu 14.04 Desktop OS, except the Web Server host, which had Ubuntu 14.04 Server.

Scenario II consisted of four real machines with one virtualized host that migrated between XenServers1 and 2 using the same organization presented in Figure 1. The real hosts were: XenServer1, XenServer2,

[2] http://www.vmware.com/br/products/workstation
[3] http://www.apache.org
[4] http://cassandra.apache.org/

Client, the NFS and an Ethernet Switch. The Apache Web Server and DBMS Cassandra were installed on the same server, which was called WebServer and was virtualized by Xen. Hypervisor Xen was installed on two servers (XenServer1 and 2) that were used for migration of the WebServer host. The real environment used the same machine configurations as presented on virtual environment.

Two benchmarks, running on client's side, were used in our experiments to fulfill a series of performance tests. One of them was the *ab*[5] – Apache HTTP Server Benchmarking tool that was the workload to Web Server. With this benchmark it was measured the mean number of request per seconds. To test the database, the Yahoo! Cloud Serving Benchmark[6] was used. With this benchmark it was measured the number of operations per seconds using the Workload A option, which makes 50% of load operations and 50% of select and update operations. Ten repetitions in each environment with each benchmark were made, with and without VM live migration. In total, we had 8 samples of 10 observations.

3. RESULTS AND ANALISYS

Before deciding which way to go to start the analysis of the collected data, some considerations must be made. We wanted to find the treatment that has major impact on the services deployed on virtual server, from a client's perspective, when the virtual server passes through a live migration. To do this, we began evaluating the data, seeking statistical normality, because many statistical techniques assume the data are normally distributed. First, with all results (YCSB on virtual and real environment with and without live migration, and the same to *ab*) the distances between the mean and median were analyzed. If this distance is large, the normality assumption is probably false. Among our data, the lowest value (equal to 3) was found in the difference of the data set from *ab* on VM with live migration. In the other cases, that difference was bigger than 19. This is a great difference, which suggests that the data sets were not normally distributed. The range of coefficient of variation was from 2,3% up to 11,1%.

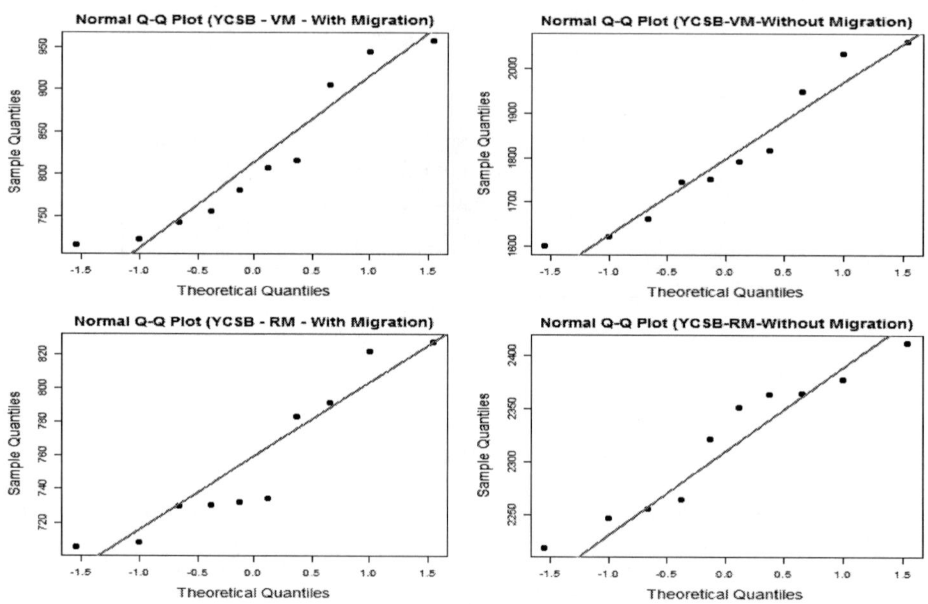

a)

[5] https://httpd.apache.org/docs/2.4/programs/ab.html
[6] https://github.com/brianfrankcooper/YCSB/wiki

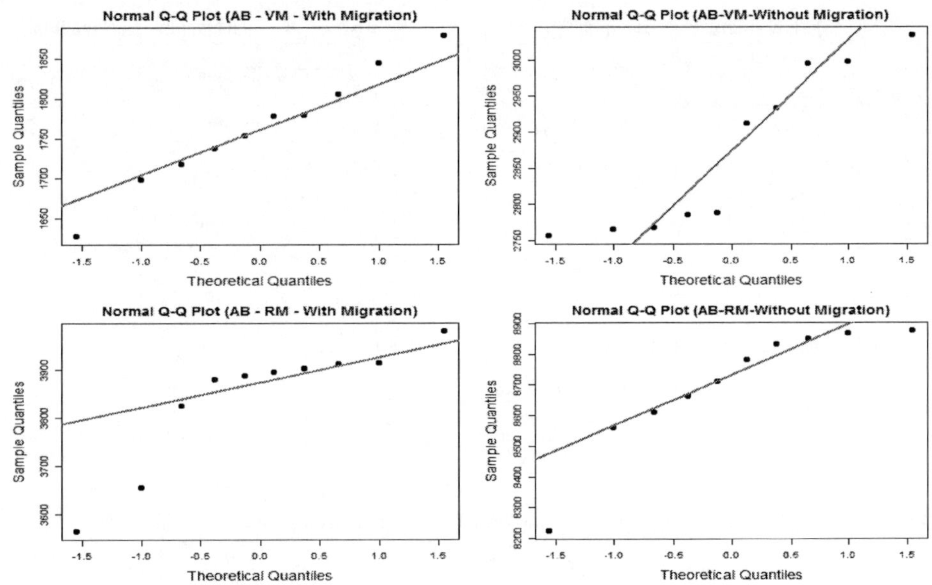

b)

Figure 2. *a)* Normal Q-Q plots for YCSB benchmark and *b)* Normal Q-Q plots for *ab* benchmark.

To confirm those assumptions, statistical tests were performed to confirm if the sample data comes from a normal distribution. The Shapiro-Wilk test (whose parameter is W) was chosen and in almost all results the null hypothesis was refuted. P-values less 0.05 with $W < 1.0$ were found. As the p-value was less than the 0.05 significance level, and $W < 1.0$ we reject the null hypothesis. The only test with a p-value=0.9963 (>0.05) and W very close to 1.0 (W=0.9896) was that with *ab* on VM and with live migration. This result is in agreement with the chart of Figure 2*b)* upper left, where it is possible to see the most points fall along on straight line.

Other information perceived from the box plots of Figure 3 is that the samples are independent, they seem come from distinct populations and the samples do not affect each other. As we want to compare the performance of a service deployed on VM during the occurrence or not of a VM live migration, it is important to check that the data comes from different samples. Doing that, it is possible to measure the impact of the VM live migration on the service, perceived by a client.

Another result that is possible to see through Figure 3*a* and 3*b*, comparing real and virtual environments, is that on real environment the performance (analyzing the mean number of request per seconds or number of operations per seconds) was better than on virtual.

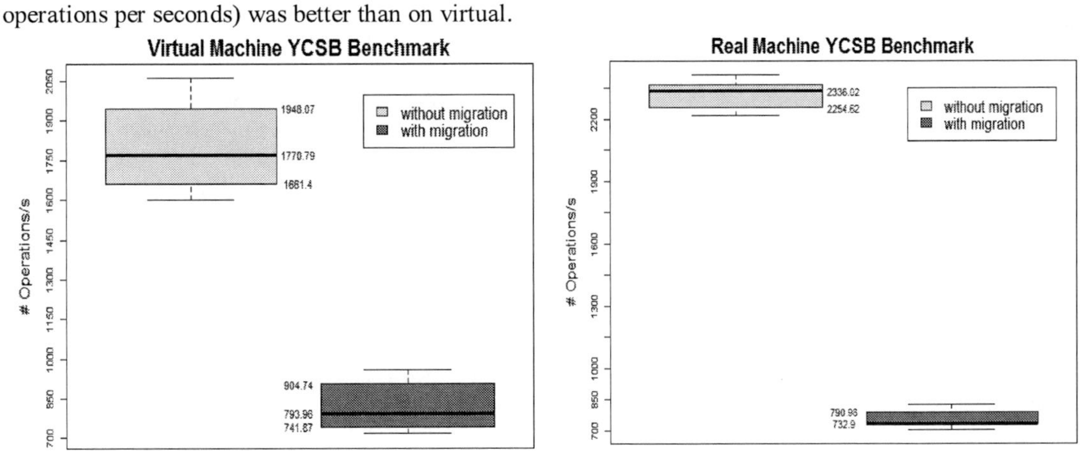

a)

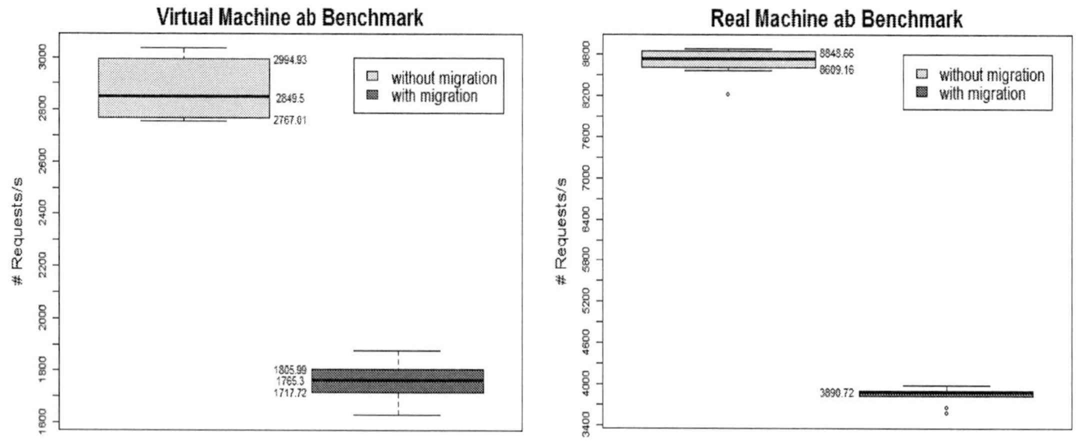

b)

Figure 3. *a)* YCSB and *b) ab* benchmarks on virtual and real environments, with and without live migration

The preliminary results, based on graphs and in statistical test analysis of the data obtained in this experiment, lead to the decision to use non-parametric statistical tests for continuation of the work. From the analysis made, we can conclude that the most appropriate test for these samples is the Mann-Whitney-Wilcoxon Test, a non-parametric test, which can decide whether the population distributions are identical without assuming them to follow the normal distribution. We intend to use this test in the sequence of this work.

4. CONCLUSION

In this paper, we have presented a preliminary statistical analysis of an experimental study that uses Xen hypervisor, to analyzing the impact of VM live migration overhead on service operations running on virtual servers, from the client's perspective. Furthermore, early results showed that VM live migration process using a real environment had better performance when compared to a completely virtual testbed. In a second direction, however, we plan to quantify the effects concerning factors that more increases the overhead. To do so, a $2^k r$ experimental design will be used, moreover, we will try to find which service deployed on VM accommodates better and in which environment.

REFERENCES

Bezerra, P. C. and Gomes, R. C. M., 2014. Comparing Performance Overhead of Virtual Machine Monitors. *In: IADIS 11th International Conference on Applied Computing, 2014, Porto - Portugal.* Proceedings of the IADIS International Conference on Applied Computing. pp. 206-213.

Galloway, M. et al., 2015. Performance Metrics of Virtual Machine Live Migration. In 2015 IEEE 8th International Conference on Cloud Computing. IEEE, 2015. pp. 637-644.

Jain, R. 1990. The art of computer systems performance analysis: techniques for experimental design, measurement, simulation, and modeling. John Wiley & Sons, New York, USA.

Li, J., 2013. Performance overhead among three hypervisors: An experimental study using hadoop benchmarks. *In 2013 IEEE International Congress on Big Data*. pp. 9-16. IEEE.

Martins, G. et al., 2015. Evaluating performance degradation in NoSQL databases generated by virtualization. *In Network Operations and Management Symposium (LANOMS)*, 2015 Latin American, pp.84-91.

Padala, Pradeep, et al., 2007. Performance evaluation of virtualization technologies for server consolidation. *HP Labs Tec. Report.*

Ramachandran, M. and Chang, V., 2016. Towards performance evaluation of cloud service providers for cloud data security. *International Journal of Information Management*, 36(4), pp.618-625.

PROPOSAL FOR A NEW BASIC INFORMATION CARRIER ON THE INTERNET: URL PLUS NUMBER SEQUENCE

Wolfgang Orthuber[1] and Wilhelm Hasselbring[2]
[1]*UKSH, Kiel University, Arnold-Heller-Straße 3, D-24105 Kiel, Germany*
[2]*Software Engineering Group, Kiel University, Christian-Albrechts-Platz 4, D-24118 Kiel, Germany*

ABSTRACT

A new searchable data structure on the Internet is presented, which can be defined with maximized information density for maximal efficiency of information transport. For this purpose, the new basic information carrier "URL (of standardized online definition) plus number sequence" is introduced. It is called "Domain Vector" (DV). The online definition defines a "Domain Space" (DS) in a standardized (machine-readable) way. This DS is a metric space whose elements are the DVs. A DV can precisely represent any definable information, from a simple word to complex multidimensional information, e.g., in science, medicine, industry, or economy. DVs may be defined by anybody, and the definition can be optimized as required by the application. If the length of the URL is minimized (e.g. using a short local substitute), DVs contain only necessary data (numbers) to enable maximal information density. They are internationally uniformly defined and identified (by the URL), and searchable according to user-defined criteria. This way, the proposed data structure fulfills the intended requirements. The online implementation http://numericsearch.com demonstrates examples and shows searchability.

KEYWORDS

Online definition, domain space, domain vector, Internet standard

1. INTRODUCTION

There have been many proposals to improve the data structure resp. information representation (the basic digital coding of information) on the Internet [Auer 2016, Guha 2016]. However, we noticed that e.g. user defined quantitative (numeric) data are not searchable on the Web. This deficit motivated us to study in more detail the existing shortcomings to derive the most important requirements that an approach to data on the Internet should fulfill: The data structure should allow efficient information transport. This can be quantified in several ways, e.g. by the information density D = I / (number of bits used for information transport). At this "I" quantifies the communicated information [Kolmogorov 1968, Section 1]. D should be maximized to minimize cost of information transport. This means that the number of bits used for transport of certain information (the length of information representation) should be minimized.

Information always describes a selection from a set of possibilities or a "domain" [Shannon 2001]. Thus, a well defined domain is precondition for precise digital information. The domain should have an online definition with unique URL to be efficiently accessible and well known by all participants of a conversation. The domain should be ordered and its definition should be standardized, machine readable and complete, such that for information transfer only the URL of the definition and (as information resp. data) a sequence of numbers (for description of the selection within the domain) is necessary. The URL of the definition is also identifier of a certain kind of data. This is important e.g. for search. Due to completeness of the online definition the data (numbers which describe a selection) do not need to contain parts of the definition. The software can download all necessary details for user-friendly representing, editing, comparing and searching the data from the online definition.

After describing the requirements, we show an example for the current data structure on the Internet. Figure 1 shows an RDF example [W3C 2016], which contains 3 variables (patientnumber, date, bodytemperature):

```
<?xml version="1.0"?>
<rdf:RDF
xmlns:rdf="http://www.w3.org/1999/02/22-rdf-syntax-ns#"
xmlns: cd="http://www.example.ns/cd#">
<rdf:Description
rdf:about="http://www.example.ns/cd/bodytemperature measured">
   <cd:patientnumber>987654</cd:patientnumber>
   <cd:date>2015-02-28</cd:date>
   <cd:bodytemperature_celsius>37.01</cd:bodytemperature_celsius>
</rdf:Description>
</rdf:RDF>
```

Figure 1. Modification from http://www.w3schools.com/Xml/xml_rdf.asp to code the observation of body temperature. There is no Link to a standardized definition of the variables

We did not found in RDF (Figure 1) and not in similar approaches a link to a complete standardized online definition (see e.g. Figure 3) of the variables. However, this is a basic requirement. After detailed study of existing approaches (e.g. schema. org [Khalili 2013], RDF [W3C 2016, Quilitz 2008], HL7 [Benson 2012, Pedersen 2004], FHIR [Smits 2015]) for machine-readable data on the Internet [Orthuber 2015, Section 1.2], we noticed that the above requirements are not yet fulfilled. Before providing a solution, we first define more precisely the used term "URL".

Definition 1 (URL): By "URL" we mean an (internationally) unique resource locator (literally speaking). It can be e.g. the uniform resource locator defined in [W3C 2016]. It can also be a shorter locally defined substitute, e.g. a number (index) which points into a locally stored table with conventional external URLs. If the table contains u external URLs, not more than $\lceil \log_2 u \rceil$ bits are necessary for the local substitute of the (external) URL. In the future, external URLs can be shortened (e.g. replaced by hierarchical number sequences). A short modified start of data (with meaning "SameURLAsBefore") can make repetition of defining URLs superfluous.

2. DESCRIPTION OF THE APPROACH

A new explicit definition of the basic data structure is proposed [Orthuber 2016] that represents digital information as bit sequences. A bit sequence is also a number sequence (like 0 and 1). We prefer the term "number sequence" as carrier of digital information because it can be used more universally to clarify a possible order in the digital information that later can be used for similarity search or as pointer within a set. For example, text can be coded as numbers which each point to a certain character within a coding system such as Unicode, or as numbers that point into an ordered set of words. It depends on the intention whether we see a large data file, a word or only a bit as carrier of information. In every case the digital representation of information is a number sequence (with variable length). It always describes a selection within a set resp. domain. Central requirement of Section 1 is a link to the definition of the numbers. Therefore, additionally to the usual (by context defined) information carrier **"number sequence" (1)** we propose the combination **"URL (of standardized online definition) plus number sequence" (2)** as new basic information carrier on the Internet. It is called "domain vector" (DV) [Orthuber 2015] and is element of a set called "domain space" (DS) which is defined by the online definition. Therefore, the online definition can be also called "DS definition". A DS contains all DVs with the same URL and is a metric space to allow similarity search [Kriegel 2010, Zezula 2005]. The URL makes (2) longer than (1). To minimize this disadvantage, the URL is defined according to Definition 1. This means that it can be replaced by a local substitute, e.g. by a short number. If the length of the number sequence is variable, (2) must also contain information (e.g. an additional number) which specifies the actual length.

The DV resp. (2) has substantial advantages compared to (1). For programmers or designers of databases this may be obvious, because any number can be globally optimized for a certain application. A well-defined domain is precondition of precise information transfer. Therefore, the URL of the online definition is important and (2) can be used as general carrier of information on the Internet, which fulfils all requirements listed in Section 1.

Figure 2 shows the structure of a DS definition. The main content is an ordered sequence of dimension definitions. To allow access to dimension definitions, besides the full DS definition every dimension definition is also addressable by a URL. Figure 3 shows a short syntax example of a DS definition. At the given URL it exists *once on the web* and defines all DVs of this DS. Figure 4 shows a possible text form of a DV.

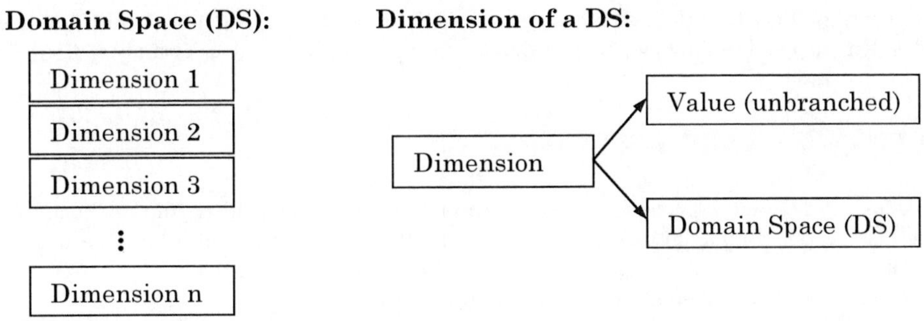

Figure 2. Structure of a DS and DS dimension. The DS and every of its dimensions have a URL. Every dimension of a DS represents an unbranched value (number) or again a DS. This can be used for nesting DS definitions

```
<?xml version="1.0"?>
<DS>
  <v>1</v>
  <kw>BodyTemperature</kw>
  <dim>
    <kw>Patientnumber</kw>
    <co>patient number in data collection xx</co>
    <type>int</type>
  </dim>
  <dim>
    <kw>Date</kw>
    <type>yyyy-mm-dd</type>
  </dim>
  <dim>
    <kw>Body-Temperature-Morning</kw>
    <co>Body temperature at morning directly after stand up</co>
    <unit>degree Celsius</unit>
    <type>float</type>
  </dim>
</DS>
```

Figure 3. XML example of a (not nested) three-dimensional DS definition. Its DVs represent the same data as Figure 1. The keyword (kw) of every dimension must be unique in the DS and can also be used for building a URL of every dimension definition. Thus, every dimension definition can also be accessed as DS definition of a one-dimensional DS

```
<v http://numericsearch.com/patbt.xml; 987654; 2015-02-28; 37.01>clickable text</v>
```

Figure 4. Exemplary syntax of a DV in text form (e.g. for insertion into HTML) which represents the same data as Figure 1, using the DS definition of Figure 3. Still more abbreviation is possible by using a binary form

The DV in Figure 4 contains the same numeric data as the RDF example in Figure 1. In the DV it is not even tried to provide a (partial) definition together with the data. The DV contains only the (numeric) data and the URL of its definition, this way it is much shorter. Nevertheless, it contains useful additional information: the clickable text is e.g. necessary for integration into HTML and the URL is necessary for identification of the data *and* for providing a link to the definition (Figure 3), which can contain much more information than Figure 1. According to Definition 1, the URL can be abbreviated as a number. Still more abbreviation is possible by direct binary coding of the DV, and of the DS definition (Figure 3). Using the DS definition DVs can be user friendly edited using e.g. an appropriately designed table (Figure 5).

0	987654	Patientnumber
1	2015-02-28	Date | yyyy-mm-dd
2	37.01	Body-Temperature-Morning | degree Celsius

Figure 5. Tabular representation of a DV in our implementation [Orthuber 2012], which can be used for editing the DV

Such a table (Figure 5) is a basic possibility for viewing and editing data. In the DS definition, more sophisticated (e.g. graphical) possibilities can also be defined. As already introduced [Orthuber 2015], search of DVs is possible according to criteria defined by users in the DS definition. This includes similarity search [Zezula 2005] and is demonstrated [Orthuber 2012]. A detailed description is available [Orthuber 2016].

3. EVALUATION, EXAMPLES, SCOPE

The approach includes several new aspects for possible evaluation, which depend on the application, for instance, the exact increase of information density D (Section 1). Because users can adapt the DS definition to the application and repetition of defining context is no longer necessary, relevant improvement of information density can be expected (compare e.g. Figure 1 and Figure 4).

Evaluation of searchability is of particular interest. We programmed an implementation [Orthuber 2012] with a new scalable "synchronized index". The evaluation [Orthuber 2012, Section 4] showed that this index allows a posteriori combination of DS dimensions for search. This is important especially in case of high dimensional DSs or if later dimensions from different DSs need to be combined for multidimensional search.

We now provide an example of a typical application: Combination of searchable data with a resource (e.g. a picture) or its URL. Subsequently the name of a DS starts with "DS..". Let DS_gps contain (two-dimensional DVs with) GPS coordinates (latitude, longitude) and DS_map contain (rectangular, west east oriented) maps in jpg form. Let DS_gps_midpoint contain (DVs with) GPS coordinates of the map's midpoint, let DS_date contain a dimension with dates, let DS_kwmap contain DVs which each represent an index within a table of appropriate keywords (e.g. city, satellite, air-pollution, weather, ...), let DS_km_westeast and DS_km_northsouth contain dimensions of the map in km. According to Figure 2, we can combine these definitions in the definition of a new DS_map_searchable in the order DS_gps_midpoint, DS_date, DS_kwmap, DS_km_westeast, DS_km_northsouth, DS_map. Figure 6 shows the definition in our implementation [Orthuber_2012].

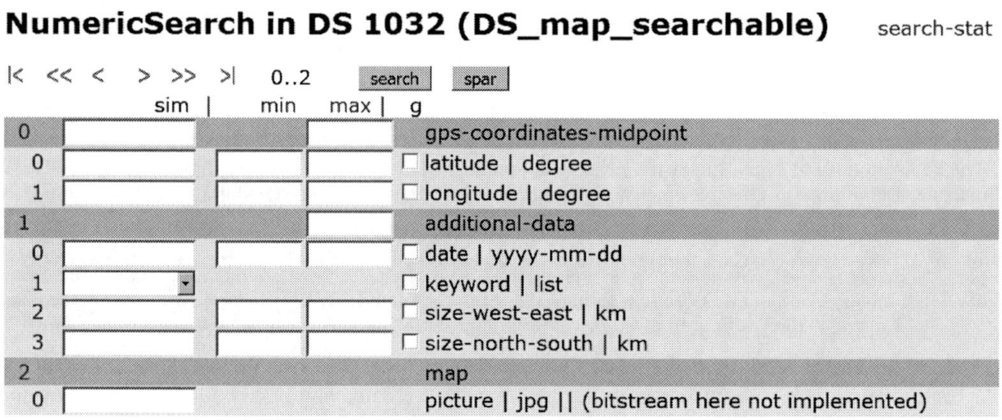

Figure 6. Definition of DS_map_searchable, except DS_map (long bitstream)

Because long bitstream (DS_map) is not defined precisely, it is not suitable for meaningful similarity search. But the other data (numbers) of DS_map_searchable are precisely searchable.

DVs with partial content are possible, e.g. with placeholders instead of numbers at omitted positions. We can also allow definitions of DSs with variable length. A DV with variable length can contain any kind of binary data ("bitstream"), e.g. those which are currently stored as files with certain ending (zip, pdf, jpg, doc, docx, mp3, mp4 ...) or also text with certain meaning (xml, txt, cpp, jsp, ...). This includes URLs. One advantage is that such data can be identified more precisely than with current approaches. For example, a DV can be defined as bitstream in jpg form with additional comment "passport photo" and numbers with specific measurements for such a photo. Further applications are nesting (combination of DS definitions, see Figure 2). In healthcare grouping of dimensions about anamnesis, therapy and result is useful for decision support [Orthuber 2016 August, Pedersen 2004, Haas 2005]. The global validity of DS definitions facilitates a large data collection and is important for interoperability [Orthuber 2012]. Global validity is even useful for zero dimensional DSs. A zero-dimensional DS contains only one DV with the URL of the DS definition. Such a

DV can e.g. represent a globally well-defined (partial) meaning of a word or a phrase. A multilingual DS definition can contain many translations of this representation. If needed, dimensions with additional numeric data can be added.

DSs can be freely defined on the web. Our implementation [Orthuber 2012] for demonstration purposes shows some exemplary definitions of DSs to certain topics, e.g. ride, my-location, real-estate, car, cupboard, diode, screw, opinion-about-xx, climate-fluctuations, meeting, traffic-accident etc.. On the Internet much more data are available and all DS definitions can be reused in other DS definitions. Therefore, published DS definitions should be freely usable and restrictions e.g. by patents or copyright are counterproductive. Combination of existing definitions is possible also a posteriori by using algebraic equations. For example, a simple proportionality factor could be used to connect definitions with different units. Hereby, worldwide search and comparison over multiple online defined (dimensions of) DSs becomes feasible.

Complex applications are feasible also by integration into programming systems, e.g. by automatic creation of DS definitions from classes of well known programming languages like Java or C++. This can be useful (especially in open source applications) if a certain task can be only solved by automatic exchange of (a limited amount of) specific data between many local systems. If the data are only temporarily used and not published on the Internet, local usage of temporary DS definitions can be an option.

4. DISCUSSION

After considering existing well-known concepts [W3C 2016, Quilitz 2008, Smits 2015, Benson 2012] for machine-readable data on the Internet, we decided for our approach - to achieve the requirements mentioned in Section 1. We list some possible issues and answer to them:

- Without (online) DS definition the data of the DS are no longer readable.
  Answer: This can be solved by periodical reliable data storage (backup) of published DS definitions.
- How is separation of subject, predicate and object (as in RDF) possible?
  This separation is only a special case. By nesting DS definitions (see Figure 2) groups of dimensions can be separated like subject, predicate and object or used for building more complex sentences, or grouped for other purposes (Section 3).
- Data are not self-contained.
  Answer: To get self-contained data, DS definitions may automatically be downloaded together with DVs. This has to be done *only once* for the same DS (kind of data). If definitions are mixed with data (Figure 1), these are repeatedly downloaded also during repetition of the same kind of data. (Remark: currently many data are not self-contained due to not standardized or not locatable or missing definition by context. This approach provides a systematic solution.)
- There will be many DS definitions for the same thing, such that an unclear situation can result.
  Answer: Up to now **(1)** is defined by context (see Section 2) which (e.g. free text) is even for the same thing *very* variable. By **(2)** we get a systematic approach to solve resulting problems. Existing DSs definitions can be searched before and during creation of a new DS definition. New definitions can be connected (e.g. by "sameAs") with or derived from existing definitions (by using algebraic expressions).
- The length of the URL makes **(2)** longer than **(1)**.
  Answer: Usually the length of a URL is much shorter than the length of the information provided at a URL. Furthermore, the URL can be abbreviated, see Definition 1. Additionally, it is an identifier.

We made the experience that even experts initially often underestimate the range and potential of **(2)**. It is important to recall that also today numbers are basic carriers of all information on the Internet and despite of a short URL, the online DS definition can be very sophisticated and optimized for individual applications.

5. CONCLUSION AND FUTURE WORK

The DV data structure "URL (of standardized online definition) plus number sequence" is searchable and enables the combination of maximal competence (online definition by all Internet users) and maximal efficiency (number sequence). Therefore, it has high potential as general carrier of digital information.

As future work, we intend to investigate and optimize binary coding of data and definitions, as well as the process of defining interoperability standards in our setting [Grimson 2000, Hasselbring 2000, Hasselbring 2002, Niemann 2002].

REFERENCES

[Auer 2016] Auer, S., Heath, T., Bizer, C., Berners-Lee, T. 2016. LDOW2016: 9th Workshop on Linked Data on the Web. In Proceedings of the 25th International Conference Companion on World Wide Web (pp. 1039-1040).

[Benson 2012] Benson, T. 2012. *Principles of health interoperability HL7 and SNOMED.* Springer-Verlag.

[Grimson 2000] Grimson, J., Grimson, W., Hasselbring. W. 2000. The SI challenge in health care. *Communications of the ACM* 43 (6), 48-55.

[Guha 2016] Guha, R. V., Brickley, D., Macbeth, S. 2016. Schema.org: Evolution of structured data on the web. *Communications of the ACM*, 59(2), 44-51.

[Guyon 2006] Guyon, I., Gunn, S., Nikravesh, M., Zadeh, L. 2006. *Feature Extraction, Foundations and Applications. Studies in Fuzziness and Soft Computing*. Springer, Berlin, Heidelberg.

[Haas 2005] Haas, P. 2005. Medizinische Informationssysteme und Elektronische Krankenakten. Springer-Verlag.

[Hasselbring 2000] Hasselbring, W. 2000, The Role of Standards for Interoperating Information Systems. *In Information technology standards and standardization: A global perspective,* IGI Global. Pp. 116-130.

[Hasselbring 2002] Hasselbring, W. 2002. Web data integration for e-commerce applications. *IEEE Multimedia* 9 (1), 16-25

[Khalili 2013] Khalili, A., Auer, S. 2013. Wysiwym authoring of structured content based on schema. org. *In International Conference on Web Information Systems Engineering.* pp. 425-438. Springer Berlin Heidelberg.

[Kolmogorov 1968] Kolmogorov, A. N. 1968. Three approaches to the quantitative definition of information. *Problems of information transmission,* 1(1), 1-7.

[Kriegel 2010] Kriegel, H.P., Kröger, P., Renz, M., Schubert, M. 2010. Metric spaces in data mining: applications to clustering. SIGSPATIAL Special Volume 2 Issue 2, 36-39.

[Niemann 2002] Niemann, H., Hasselbring, W., Wendt, T., Winter, A., Meierhofer, M. 2002. Kopplungsstrategien für Anwendungssysteme im Krankenhaus, *Wirtschaftsinformatik* 44 (5), 425-434

[Orthuber 2010] Orthuber, W., Dietze, S. 2010. Towards Standardized Vectorial Resource Descriptors on the Web. *In Lecture Notes in Informatics, Service Science - Neue Perspektiven für die Informatik*. Band 2 pp. 453-458.

[Orthuber 2012] Orthuber, W. 2012. Online implementation of vectorial description and numeric search. *http://numericsearch.com*. and http://numericsearch.com/intro.pdf

[Orthuber 2015] Orthuber, W. 2015. How to make quantitative data on the web searchable and interoperable part of the common vocabulary. *Lecture Notes in Informatics (LNI), Gesellschaft für Informatik*, Bonn

[Orthuber 2016] Orthuber, W. 2016. Uniform definition of comparable and searchable information on the web. *arXiv preprint arXiv:1406.1065*. http://arxiv.org/abs/1406.1065.

[Orthuber 2016 August] Orthuber, W. 2016. August. Collection of Medical Original Data with Search Engine for Decision Support. *Studies in health technology and informatics 228,* 257.

[Pedersen 2003] Pedersen, S. und Hasselbring, W. 2003. Structuring and combining domain-specific standards for interoperability in health care. *In: Proceedings of EFIS 2003*, Coventry, UK.

[Pedersen 2004] Pedersen, S. und Hasselbring, W. 2004. Interoperabilität für Informationssysteme im Gesundheitswesen. In *Informatik Forschung und Entwicklung*. pp. 174-188. DOI 10.1007/s00450-004-0146-8.

[Shannon 2001] Shannon, C. E. 2001. A mathematical theory of communication. *ACM SIGMOBILE Mobile Computing and Communications Review*, 5(1), 3-55.

[Quilitz 2008] Quilitz, B., Leser, U. 2008. Querying distributed RDF data sources with SPARQL. In *European Semantic Web Conference* (pp. 524-538). Springer-Verlag

[Smits 2015] Smits, M. et al, 2015. A comparison of two Detailed Clinical Model representations: FHIR and CDA. *EJBI*, 11(2), 2015.

[W3C 2016] W3C RDF Examples, http://www.w3schools.com/xml/xml_rdf.asp , viewed January 2016.

[Zezula 2005] Zezula, P. et al. 2005. The Metric Space Approach. *Series: Advances in Database Systems*, Vol. 32., Springer, Berlin, Heidelberg.

CAN PERSONAL HEALTH RECORDS SUPPORT THE PRACTICE IN SPEECH AND LANGUAGE THERAPY?

Alexandra Queirós[1] and Nelson Pacheco Rocha[2]
[1]Health Siences School/ IEETA, University of Aveiro
[2]Clinical Sciences Department/ IEETA, University of Aveiro
Campo Universitário de Santiago, 3810-199 Aveiro, Portugal

ABSTRACT

The study reported in this paper aimed to evaluate if Personal Health Records (PHR) can contribute for the communicating and sharing of clinical information between patients, their informal caregivers, and speech and language therapy (SLT) professionals. Questionnaires were passed out to SLT professionals of different domains (ie, assessments of dysphagia, aphasia and language disorders, and language interventions with children) in order to identify their information requirements. Afterwards, using the Unified Modelling Language (UML), Electronic Health Records (EHR) information models were defined and a deeper analysis was performed in order to determine the type of information that patients, their informal caregivers, and SLT professionals need to communicate and share. The results suggest the importance of the PHR to complement EHR and, therefore, to support the clinical practice in the studied SLT domains.

KEYWORDS

Speech and language therapy; personal health record; electronic health record.

1. INTRODUCTION

The use of information technologies to support the practice in Speech and Language Therapy (SLT) is not new and it is generally accepted that they can improve efficiency and efficacy of the services being provided (Luz and Kane, 2016). SLT comprises different care domains, each one with specific requirements, vocabularies and stakeholders such as therapists, physicians, pathologists or teachers, besides the patients and their informal caregivers (eg, the parents of a child or the relatives of a person with mental or cognitive disability).

Throughout the rehabilitation processes one of the most important tasks is to collect data related to the clinical history, including problems already identified, and past diagnoses and interventions (Cornett, 2006). Furthermore, it is essential that there should be an easy access to the available information of the patients, not only to support clinical decisions, but also to guarantee the correctness of the follow-ups, and robust mechanisms to communicate and share this information between the involved stakeholders (Gomes, Queirós and Rocha, 2015). The digital recording of assessments and interventions facilitates the diagnoses, optimizes the definition of the baseline interventions, and sustains legal issues (American Speech-Language-Hearing Association, 2003).

Häyrinen and colleagues (Häyrinen, Saranto and Nykänen, 2008) demonstrated the impact of Electronic Health Records (EHR) on the quality of the clinical information: completeness and accuracy (eg, using EHR leads to a more complete documentation by health care professionals); reliability (eg, information from EHR is more reliable when compared to paper records); and user satisfaction (eg, EHR present the ability to retrieve information that satisfies the needs of their users).

Additionally, nowadays, EHR are seen as powerful tools to communicate and share information among the multidisciplinary teams involved in the rehabilitation processes (Robles-Bykbaeva et al., 2015). For that, is essential the existence of EHR promoting high quality clinical information as well as the systematization of concepts among professionals (Robles-Bykbaeva et al., 2015; Adler-Milstein & Bates, 2010).

On the other hand, Ahmadi and colleagues (Ahmadi, et al., 2012) refer that some relevant information may be lost, ignored or never registered in the EHR, and that the use of Personal Health Records (PHR), defined as electronic tools managed by the patients and their informal caregivers for communicating and sharing their clinical information to whom they authorize (Tang et al., 2006), may complement the information provided by EHR.

SLT professionals follow the patient-centered paradigm which means that the patients and their informal caregivers are strongly involved in the care providing processes (Snyder and Engström, 2016). In addition, information about home activities of the patients, namely rehabilitation exercises, is considered extremely relevant (Gomes, Queirós and Rocha, 2015). In this context, the PHR may support the patient-centered paradigm allowing the empowerment of the patients and their informal caregivers, promoting self-care and shared decision-making, and providing new ways to measure the clinical outcomes (Pagliari, Detmer and Singleton, 2007).

Therefore, assuming that PHR may complement EHR, the study reported in this paper aimed to evaluate if PHR can contribute for the communicating and sharing of clinical information between patients, their informal caregivers, and SLT professionals.

2. REQUIREMENTS ANALYSIS

To achieve the formulated research objective, the authors developed EHR information models for four SLT domains with different contexts: dysphagia and aphasia assessments performed in hospital settings, language disorder assessments performed in educational settings, and language interventions with children performed in outpatient clinical settings.

To support the requirements analysis of these SLT domains questionnaires were passed out to 54 speech therapists, each one with several years of training and work experience (Henriques, 2009; Figueiredo, 2010; Cardoso and Queirós, 2012; Gomes, Queirós and Rocha, 2015).

The results of the questionnaire allowed the definition of detailed information models using the Unified Modelling Language (UML). The required packages (ie, mechanisms to organize elements semantically related into groups to provide a better structure for system models) to aggregate the functional requirements, identified in all the four studied SLT domains, were the following: Assessment, Attendance, Planning, Intervention and Patient/Caregiver.

The Assessment package includes the functional requirements related to the assessment of patients, from the anamneses to the re-assessments. On the other hand, all the functional requirements related to the care plans as well as all the required resources to perform the interventions are included in the Planning package, which depends on the Assessment package. The Attendance package depends on the Planning package and includes the administrative tasks performed by SLT professionals such as scheduling therapeutic sessions or meetings between professionals. The execution of the care plan is included in the Intervention package that allows SLT professionals to report the results of the interventions and to register the evolution of the patients. This package allows editing and updating the data included in the Assessment package and, consequently, modifying the care plans. Finally, the Patient/Caregivers package represents all the functional requirements of the patients and their informal caregivers.

The EHR packages to support SLT practice together with the respective UML diagrams were the basis for the analysis of the relevance of PHR and the systematization of their attributes.

The Patient/Caregivers package considers different types of actions so that the patients and their informal caregivers can provide relevant information that may influence the interventions. The information related to patients is composed of: demographic data (eg, name, address, birthday or support network) and instructions to the patients or their informal caregivers, including care procedures or strategies that may or shall be performed at home. Therefore, mechanisms to edit or append pieces of data were considered.

Only the requirements analysis performed considering the educational context does not report the need of accessing information related to instructions. SLT domains related to hospital settings, besides the patient's clinical information, also require information related to the professionals, namely timetables and fees. Information about daily events and indirect intervention (eg, when part of the intervention is performed by another professional, such as a teacher) is present in the SLT domains of language disorder assessments and language interventions with children. In all the four studied SLT domains, there are requirements of accessing information recorded during the interventions (eg, assessment reports or session plans).

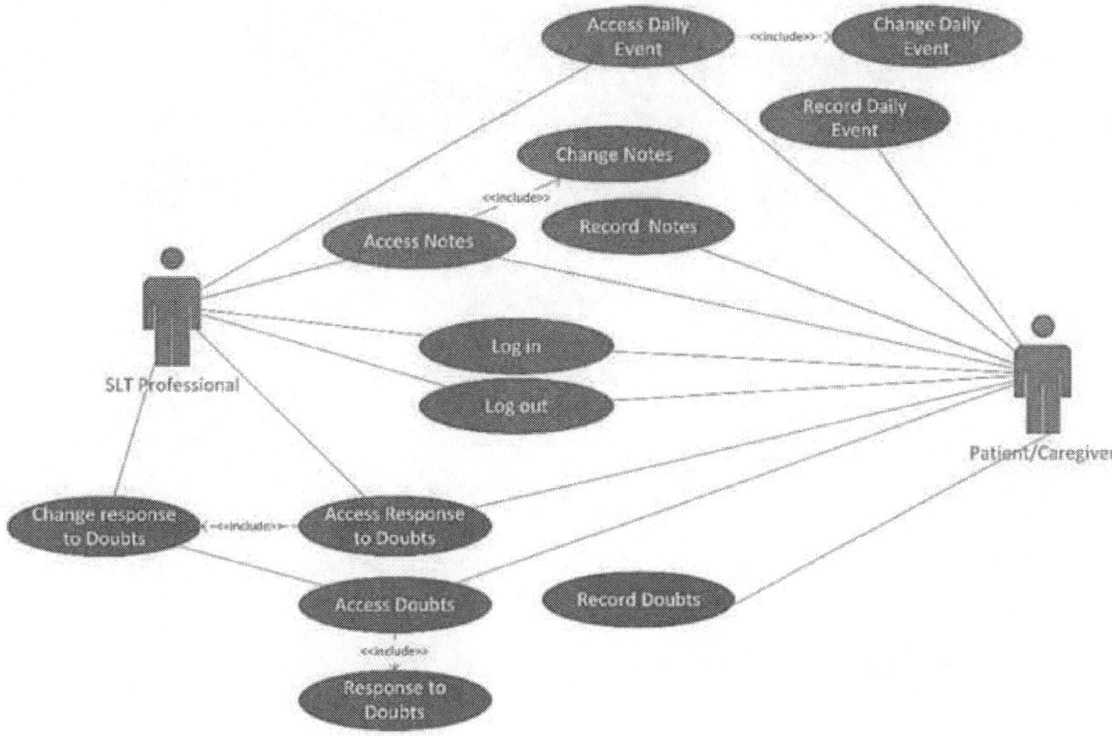

Figure 1. Use case diagram of the Patient/Caregiver according to the perspective of personal records stored in the PHR

Considering the results of the analysis of the four studied SLT domains, there are no references to the need of PHR (Henriques, 2009; Figueiredo, 2010; Cardoso and Queirós, 2012; Gomes, Queirós and Rocha, 2015). However, there are evidences related to the need of specific modules that should be accessed both by SLT professionals, patients and their informal caregivers, which may indicate that exist the need of interaction between the SLT professional and patients that can be satisfied with the use of PHR.

For a better legibility, three views of the UML use case diagrams were created (Figures 1 to 3).

Figure 1 presents the use case diagram of the Patients/Caregivers package according to the perspective of personal information stored in the PHR. It shows the functions that patients and their informal caregivers may perform namely daily events, notes or doubts. The daily events are reports of situations that occur during the daily activities that may be important for the rehabilitation processes (eg, in the morning the patient cannot talk or the patient eats a specific food choke). Notes are pieces of information that the patients and their informal caregivers want to register (eg, during a specific period of time there was a pain relief). Finally, doubts are related to specific questions that the patients and their informal caregivers need to clarify or to share with SLT professionals.

The use case diagrams of Figures 2 and 3 show that patients, their informal caregivers and SLT professionals need to communicate and share information.

Figure 2 presents the use case diagram related to the functional requirements of the patients and their informal caregivers in terms of the information that they can manage but that must be registered in the EHR. For instance, they can update demographic information which should be transmitted to the EHR. Other examples are the rescheduling of a session or the communication of the results of rehabilitation exercises performed at home that must be registered in the EHR in order to be analyzed by SLT professionals.

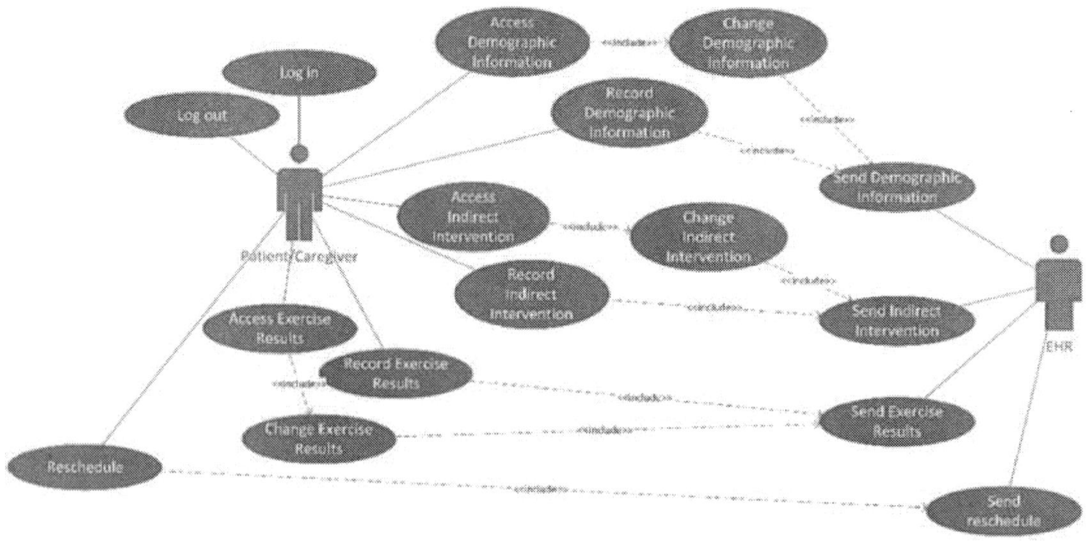

Figure 2. Use case diagram that represents the functional requirements of the patients and their informal caregivers according to the perspective of the information that should be sent to the EHR

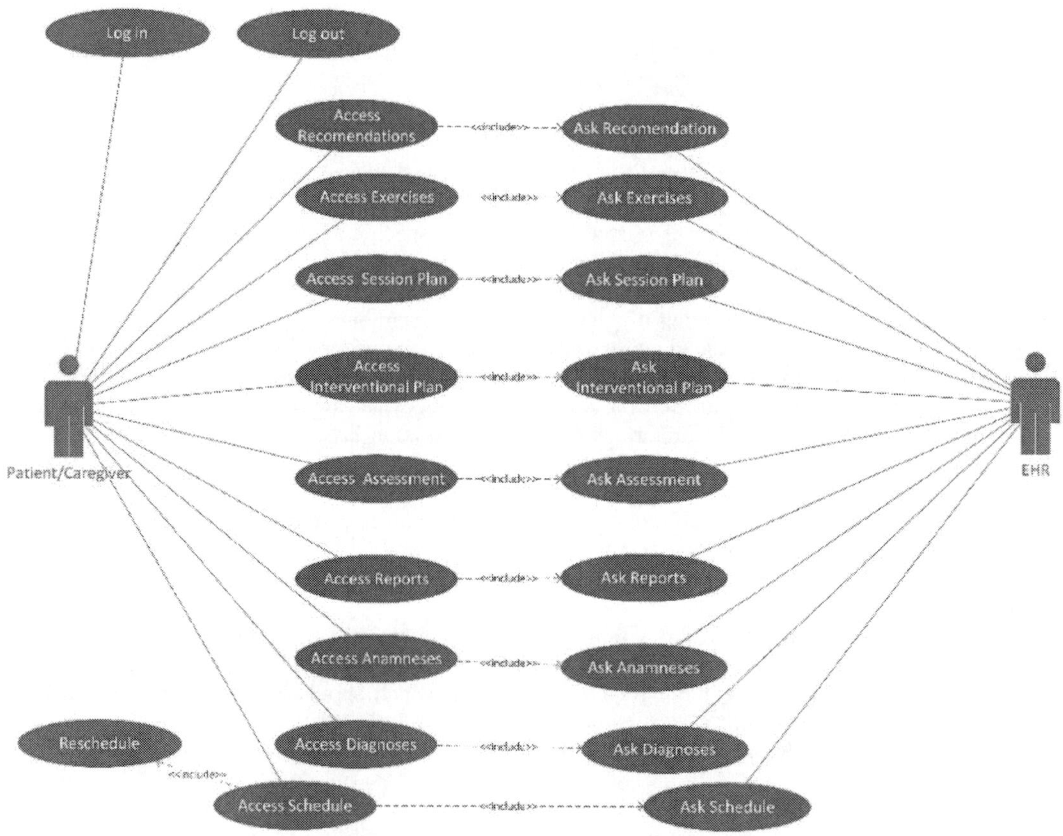

Figure 3. Use case diagram that represents the functional requirements of the patients and their informal caregivers according to the perspective of the information that should be received from the EHR

The use case diagram of Figure 3 presents the information managed by SLT professionals, registered in the EHR, and that should be shared with patients and their informal caregivers. This information is related to the results of the various interventions performed during the rehabilitation processes, managed by SLT professionals and registered in the EHR, such as interventions and session plans, anamnesis, diagnoses, schedule of the sessions or recommendations.

3. DISCUSSION AND CONCLUSION

In all the four studied SLT domains, the performed analysis identified that there is a need for communication and sharing information between patients, their informal caregivers, and SLT professional. This is in line with the recognition that more informed and active patients and respective informal caregivers can bring added value to the provision of health care services, in general (Pagliari, Detmer and Singleton, 2007, Ahmadi et al., 2012), and to the SLT practice (Cornett, 2006), in particular.

The results also show that the access to specific information produced and managed by SLT professionals is not the only requirement. Information produced and managed by the patients or their informal caregivers is also important for SLT professionals, which is in line with other studies (Snyder and Engström, 2016; Pagliari, Detmer and Singleton, 2007). Another important finding is the definition of the functions that PHR should present to support the daily clinical activities of SLT professionals. Clearly, PHR should follow a connected model (Tang et al., 2006), which means that there are connections that are required between PHR and EHR (Figures 2 and 3).

Curiously, the analysis of the four studied SLT domains refer the need of specific modules for the patients and their informal caregivers, but didn't refer the need of a PHR. Probably this occurs because, in Portugal, EHR to support SLT practice are still in a developing phase and, therefore, are the main priority for the professionals.

Ahmadi and colleagues (Ahmadi et al., 2012) investigate the differences between different countries in terms of PHR, comparing their characteristics and identifying the main features.

From the 16 items available in various PHR (Ahmadi et al., 2012), the present study points seven of them: i) possibility of confidential exchange of messages of persons/patients with the provider; ii) possibility of appointment timing; iii) ability of automated data transfer from electronic health record; iv) ability of automated data transfer to electronic health record; v) ability of tracing and administration of health plans; vi) possibility of adding data generated by the person himself; and vii) possibility of exchange of information throughout the health system.

Furthermore, two other items are partially required (only for demographic data): i) possibility of editing and adding data in the future; and ii) possibility of editing and adding data at present.

Finally, seven items identified by Ahmadi and colleagues (Ahmadi et al., 2012) were not referred: i) possibility of survey of person/ patient's health data by himself; ii) offering and use of knowledge bases for support; iii) offering and use of knowledge bases for sending reminders and warnings; iv) containing important health information of individuals throughout their lives; v) containing information from all health care providers; vi) owner's supervision on access of other people to his medical information; and vii) possibility of exchange of recorded information through the internet.

This may indicate that the main requirements are satisfied by existing PHR. The fact that some of the items of existing PHR were not identify in the information requirements doesn't mean they are not relevant in SLT practice, but only means that considering the analysis of the questionnaires passed out to SLT professionals there was no evidence that these attributes were required by these specific professionals.

According the conclusions achieved through the analysis of EHR information models developed for the practice in four different SLT domains, the patients or their informal caregivers need to communicate and share information with SLT professionals and, as a consequence, PHR can be used for that purpose. Therefore, considering the research question that has been formulated for the study reported in this paper, the authors conclude that PHR might satisfy the needs of communicating and sharing information within different SLT domains.

Since only four specific SLT domains were considered, a limitation of this study is that further work is required to verify if the results can be generalized to other SLT domains. Another limitation is related to the fact that the objective of the study was to understand if PHR are relevant for SLT professionals and not to conceptualize information models for PHR. Therefore, the basis of this study were the requirements and opinions of the SLT professionals, which mean that further studies are required to collect the requirements and opinions of patients and their informal caregivers.

As future work it is planned to validate the attributes proposed and conceptualize a PHR information model to support SLT practice. For that, patients and their informal caregivers will be involve, as well as experts and experienced professionals in different SLT domains.

REFERENCES

Adler-Milstein J, Bates DW, 2010. Paperless healthcare: Progress and challenges of an IT-enabled healthcare system. *Business Horizons*. Vol. 53, No. 2, pp 119-30.

Ahmadi M, Jeddi F, Gohari M et al., 2012. A review of the personal health records in selected countries and Iran. *Journal of medical systems*. Vol. 36, No. 2, pp 371-82.

American Speech-Language-Hearing Association, 2003. Code of Ethics (revised). *The ASHA Leader*, Vol. 6, No. 23, pp 2.

Cardoso F, Queirós A, 2012. Electronic health record in the assessment of aphasia post CVA. *7th Iberian Conference on Information Systems and Technologies, CISTI 2012*. Madrid, Spain.

Cornett S, 2006. Clinical documentation in speech-language pathology: Essential information for successful practice. *The ASHA leader*. Vol. 11, No. 12, pp 8-25.

Figueiredo T, 2010. *Registo de saúde electrónico na avaliação da linguagem em crianças*. University of Aveiro, Aveiro.

Gomes D, Queirós A, Rocha NP, 2015. Electronic health record for clinical intervention in children with language disorders. *10th Iberian Conference on Information Systems and Technologies, CISTI 2015*. Aveiro, Portugal.

Henriques R, 2009. *O registo clínico electrónico na avaliação da disfagia em adultos*. University of Aveiro, Aveiro.

Häyrinen K, Saranto K, Nykänen P, 2008. Definition, structure, content, use and impacts of electronic health records: a review of the research literature. *International journal of medical informatics*, Vol. 77, No. 5, pp 291-304.

Luz S, Kane B, 2016. Perspectives on Intelligent Systems Support for Multidisciplinary Medical Teams. *2016 AAAI Spring Symposium Series*. Stanford, USA.

Pagliari C, Detmer D, Singleton P, 2007. Potential of electronic personal health records. *British Medical Journal*, No. 335, pp 330.

Robles-Bykbaeva V, López-Noresb M, Pazos-Ariasb J et al., 2015. An Ecosystem of Intelligent ICT tools for speech-language therapy based on a formal knowledge model. *MEDINFO 2015: eHealth-enabled Health*. São Paulo, Brazil, pp 50-54.

Snyder H, Engström J, 2016. The antecedents, forms and consequences of patient involvement: A narrative review of the literature. *International journal of nursing studies*, No. 53, pp 351-78.

Tang P, Ash J, Bates D et al., 2006. Personal health records: definitions, benefits, and strategies for overcoming barriers to adoption. *Journal of the American Medical Informatics Association*, Vol. 13, No. 2, pp 121-6.

FHIR HEALTHCARE DIRECTORIES: ADOPTING SHARED INTERFACES TO ACHIEVE ARCHITECTURE INDEPENDENCE

Timothy Tyndall and Ayami Tyndall
RAIN Live Oak Technology

ABSTRACT

Motivation: Healthcare directories are a key tool for achieving interoperability among medical service providers and technology vendors, but past efforts at standardizing directory services have failed to find traction. Current implementations are often overly strict, incompatible with legacy databases, and cumbersome for discovering complex datasets. An architecture-independent system is needed to enable directory services across organizational boundaries.
Objective: Develop and deploy a healthcare directory service platform implementing FHIR access to enable discovery of healthcare services by HIE and EHR information systems. A directory backend supports a dataset and a FHIR API provides an abstracted, interoperable query model. Shortcomings of past directory efforts need to be addressed, including the ability to map hierarchical data resources and to enable interoperability by delivering exchange endpoint information.
Design: A directory-oriented dataset will be designed using FHIR as a guideline, while also adapting the dataset to meet organizational requirements and to support management of the database outside a FHIR environment. By abstracting the backend to be mapped to FHIR data elements we can provide standardized directory access to a variety of database systems (SQL, LDAP, document-oriented, etc.). Database flexibility enables integration with existing systems while maintaining interoperability through a standardized FHIR API.
Conclusion: FHIR is a powerful asset in the development of new healthcare directory services. Its rich data set enables reliable record delivery, while abstracted data mapping allows health information systems to use their choice of underlying databases. FHIR's query specification enables intuitive data retrieval and automatic grouping of related resources into a single response document.
By focusing on how data is represented without dictating how it must be stored and managed we can improve exchange and facilitate directory use on a national level through the implementation of open source, fully interoperable tools.

KEYWORDS

FHIR, Healthcare Provider Directories, Health Information Exchange, Interoperability

1. INTRODUCTION

Health information is increasingly available through electronic medical records (EHR) with a growing number of EHR systems connected through health information exchange (HIE) networks, but these services only provide meaningful improvement when made available to a wide range of trusted exchange partners. The greater the number of inter-connected systems, and the wider the geographic area they serve, the greater the benefit from directory services providing exchange access information such as security, certificate and chain-of-trust records for listed endpoints. [1]

Two of the greatest barriers to effective health record exchange are (1) the need to accurately discover a partner system's access information, and (2) the need for shared data standards to enable systems to exchange documents and correctly interpret them. Numerous solutions to these challenges have been proposed but many fall prey to their own strictness; rigorous, exact communication specifications enforce compatibility and guarantee security but also limit usability by setting such concrete architectural requirements that the specifications become incompatible with the information systems of potential implementers. Even the best exchange protocol becomes unappealing if its use requires overhauling an established data model.

The need for efficient document exchange has spurred the development of directory services for the health information industry. The goal of these efforts has been to provide a unified protocol to enable the discovery of healthcare organizations, practitioners, and the Health Information Exchange endpoints they have available. These directories carry data profile and security specifications for endpoints to enable automated connectivity even if a given pair of systems have never previously exchanged records. The forerunner among such service standards has been Healthcare Provider Directories (HPD), an IHE (Integrating the Healthcare Enterprise) standard defining the use of LDAP (Lightweight Directory Access Protocol) to deliver directory information. HPD was designed for the needs of the healthcare industry but was unable to find the traction hoped for, as evidenced by the loss of support for HPD by major vendors during the past two years. The need remains, however: a rapidly expanding health information exchange ecosystem necessitates a protocol for the discovery of access endpoints to reduce data isolation. [2]

The new focus in health information development is a transition toward shared interface standards to enable exchange. This design methodology increases usability by defining the document structure returned from a query without dictating the underlying system design. Shared application programming interfaces (APIs) are used to enable data retrieval regardless of design of participating systems. At the forefront of this change is FHIR (Fast Healthcare Interoperability Resources), a project from HL7 (Health Level-7) defining a set of data resources and APIs for accessing them. FHIR improves flexibility over previous exchange protocols by introducing a higher level of abstraction, allowing data to be represented in a unified format independent of the underlying data architecture used by the health system implementing the API. [5]

Health information stakeholders have expressed agreement that healthcare directories are a valuable resource to enable discovery of exchange endpoints but interoperability has not yet been achieved. This paper describes an alternative approach, as support decreases for HPD, which we are exploring using FHIR to deliver directory services and to address the shortcomings of previous efforts. [2]

2. BODY OF PAPER

2.1 Objectives

The goal of healthcare directory services is to store information on medical organizations, practitioners and services, and to enable authorized individuals and organizations to search the records. Data must be accessible in a predictable format, must contain information relevant for health information exchange, and must be reasonably assured to be authoritative and up-to-date. These needs are reflected in the technical requirements of many health information systems, with directories having the unique characteristics of not directly carrying protected health information (PHI) and being focused on the discovery and establishment of connectivity to services outside the directory itself. To advance the adoption of Health Information Exchange technology RAIN Live Oak Technology has begun development of a FHIR-enabled Directory Service project to deliver a new healthcare directory solution.

One of this paper's authors, Ayami Tyndall, has been closely involved in the development of the IHE HPD (Healthcare Provider Directory) standard, including work on the addition of a federation option to the specification and participation in drafting of a regional extension to the specification. This directory service project is being developed as a successor to HPD, incorporating strengths of previous efforts and building on lessons learned from earlier directory projects. By implementing the open FHIR standards this project will deliver entity and service discovery compatible with established APIs and able to be implemented as an access gateway to various types of systems. [7]

The goal of RAIN Live Oak's FHIR-enabled Directory Service project is to demonstrate the application of FHIR as an abstracted access layer to retrieve records from an underlying database with a data model not directly mirroring the FHIR data set. Rather than using a restrictive data set, as some past efforts attempted in order to ensure interoperability, we are implementing FHIR at the access-layer so that directory records can be presented in a unified format without limiting the design of the underlying database. FHIR's use throughout the medical industry and its rich data set make it an ideal choice for a modern directory API. By applying these new models we will develop a more robust directory system which can be easily extended and integrated with a variety of database/data-storage architectures.

The use case addressed in this paper is the discovery of electronic exchange endpoint information based on the organization and/or practitioner whose health system is accessible through it (*see Figure 1*). Using FHIR-compliant queries, a user will be able to search for an organization/practitioner based on a variety of criteria (address, specialty, affiliation, etc.) and retrieve a list of associated electronic services, including the type of service (patient lookup, document exchange, prescription, etc.) and the specific data profile and protocols used by the system.

Primary shortcomings of previous healthcare directory systems which this project will address are limitations on data storage and the complexity of queries. Previous directory specifications tied data to a specific storage protocol such as LDAP, making implementation effort-intensive for health systems not already supporting the required protocols. This had the effect of requiring additional investment and development, the duplication of data in a directory-specific storage system, or the decision by the implementer to abandon the service entirely. By employing a more abstracted data model we will develop a directory service which offers a unified data set without dictating the underlying storage scheme, enabling a wider range of systems to employ such a service. [3]

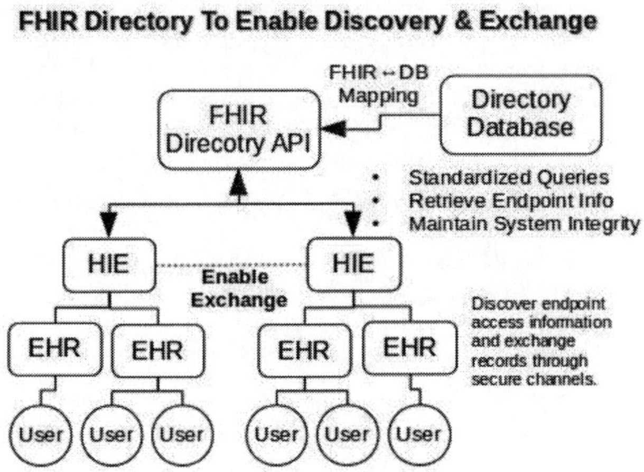

Figure 1. FHIR-Enabled Directory Interoperability

Previous healthcare directory services were also hampered by poor query performance. HPD was tied directly to LDAP, which, while optimized for simple directory lookups, was cumbersome and required multiple verbose queries to retrieve a relatively small data set with elements directly related to one another. Adopting FHIR's RESTful API not only simplifies queries, facilitating faster integration, but also reduces the number of queries required to retrieve a relevant collection of resources. The use of an architecture independent query API will enable interoperability between systems regardless of how they store and structure their internal data.

The final outcome of this development will be a modern, standards-based healthcare directory service which will enable discovery of organizations, practitioners and services through a uniform query structure which can be added as a new access layer compatible with existing health systems. Such a system will allow health organizations to either add a compliant directory API to their existing records system, or to easily deploy a new directory service using their choice of database architectures.

2.2 Design

To achieve our objectives we have designed a directory service accessible through a FHIR API. A key factor of this design is that the FHIR data set applies only to the returned record: responses to queries are in a FHIR-compliant format, but this is abstracted from the underlying database, using intermediate serialization to map arbitrary directory data to FHIR resources. This allows a variety of database back-ends to be employed while maintaining a unified FHIR API and response data format for maximum interoperability. [4]

The FHIR Directory Service consists of an underlying database populated with directory records and a FHIR API to provide query-based access. The primary FHIR resources made available in the directory are Organization, Practitioner and Endpoint (for electronic exchange services). Additional resources are used to represent additional layers of information about these resources and the relationships between them, such as the Role resource to represent a Practitioner's role within an Organization. These resources represent a similar data set to past healthcare directory efforts, which also focused on organizations, providers and services, allowing for a logical mapping of FHIR elements to commonly used directory information.

The complex dataset outlined by FHIR does not dictate the underlying data structure used by the system backend. Instead, FHIR allows data to be serialized from a variety of sources to form conformant response documents. For this project we are using an SQL relational database system to store data. However, a FHIR directory could use other data storage types by adjusting mapping to serialize directory entries as FHIR records. Such alternative options for storage include document-oriented databases, object databases, directory access protocols such as LDAP, or simple flat-file storage. This flexibility allows a FHIR-enabled directory to integrate with a variety of systems and gives engineers the option to choose the storage scheme which best fits their use case and scaling requirements without losing interoperability. [6]

For this project's relational database approach, FHIR resources are modeled as primary resource tables (Organization, Practitioner, Endpoint) with foreign keys referencing subsets of data in secondary tables (*see Figure 2*). These secondary tables are effectively layered underneath the primary resource tables and will not be directly accessed. Common elements, such as physical addresses and contact information, shares a format across resources and so a single table can be used for all resources referencing that sub-set of data. The relational tables need not be structured as FHIR resources as long as all the required elements are available within the database. Conformance with FHIR is achieved when the data is retrieved and serialized as JSON or XML, structuring it according to the FHIR standards and abstracting the underlying database. In many cases a single FHIR resource will actually be built from multiple tables.

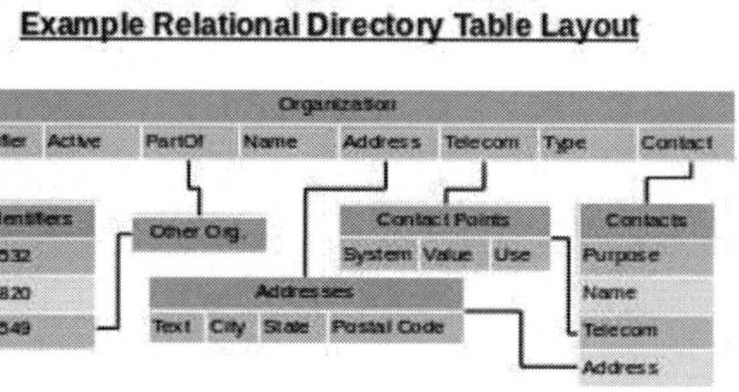

Figure 2. Example SQL Structure

We have developed a new database structure designed to meet the needs of a dedicated directory service, but the flexibility of this project's approach to data mapping would allow it to instead use an existing data schema, such as one established in a health information system. In such a case the data mapping would be adjusted to serialize any arbitrary data set as FHIR resources to be returned through the API. The underlying data structure would not require alteration and existing methods for creating and managing directory entries would continue to be used. The only change would be the introduction of a FHIR API as an additional access tool.

Acting as an API, FHIR allows systems with differing internal data structures to seamlessly exchange records. It is this shared interface approach—emphasizing how data is represented rather than the underlying database model—that allows us to achieve architecture independence while maintaining a unified exchange protocol. The directory's FHIR resources are made accessible through an HTTP RESTful interface to enable the queries specified by the FHIR standard. Once a query is received, the directory service takes the appropriate actions to model the search parameters as a query to the internal directory database. In the case of SQL and an object-oriented programming language, this will involve the use of an object-relational mapping engine to access database tables as manipulatable objects. These object's properties, representing the database record attributes, are mapped to FHIR resource elements to be viewed as JSON or XML. There is no defined specification for mapping between FHIR and SQL, and so two organizations might both use SQL directories but employ different schemas for the relational tables. Each organization would employ significantly different database structures but remain able to return matching records by mapping internal data to FHIR resources. [9]

This separation of interface from architecture allows health information systems to achieve FHIR compliance for directory interoperability while employing a database model that meets their organizational requirements. This approach also allows for much smoother integration with existing systems: a FHIR interface can be added as a new access point to an existing system, mapping directory records to FHIR resources even if the underlying directory predates FHIR entirely. This creates opportunities for more organizations to deploy healthcare directories at a lower cost and without major expansion to their IT footprint. The use of shared interfaces ensures interoperability without dictating management practices or requiring compliance with a rigid data model. [5]

3. CONCLUSION

The relational database directory schema we have developed is inspired by FHIR and draws on our experience with healthcare provider directories but it is just one possible design for a medical service directory. The FHIR interface being developed turns an internal directory—useful but limited in scope—into a tool to achieve interoperability and broaden data exchange. By mapping directory data to FHIR resource elements we expose a standardized API to enable queries following open standards. The FHIR standard unifies disparate directories into a shared resource to facilitate interoperability and exchange.

As more FHIR-compliant directory services become available we will be able to explore opportunities for federation, enabling multi-directory queries across organizational boundaries to further enhance the wealth of data made available. By employing such directories for endpoint discovery, HIEs can establish new exchange connections without compromising the data requirements of individual repositories. Resources already defined in FHIR—especially Organization, Practitioner and Endpoint—carry the same range of data elements as past directory specifications while remaining fully compatible with the wider body of FHIR standards. Uncoupling a FHIR interface from the underlying database allows organizations to implement a data model that meets their needs and enables better compatibility with existing systems. The shared API provided by FHIR allows participating healthcare organizations to query for and share directory information without refactoring their internal systems or implementing a sub-system solely to provide directory services. Healthcare directories are a valuable resource to enable discovery of healthcare organizations, providers and services, and our current implementation of FHIR directory services facilitates more health systems making their information available to healthcare partners, building a culture of interoperability and exchange. [8]

Standardized APIs will create accessible directories from existing data repositories without requiring the creation of directory-specific services. Emphasizing how data is represented rather than the underlying database model allows us to achieve architecture independence while maintaining a unified exchange protocol.

REFERENCES

[1] Bequette, Terry. February 2016. ONC-SIM Health IT Resource Center State Health IT Modular Functions for Value-Based Payment Strategic Implementation Guide - Provider Directories

[2] California Trust Framework Pilot Phase 1: Federated Provider Directory Policy: https://www.healthit.gov/sites/default/files/appendix7_caonboardingrequirementsfortfpilot.pdf.

[3] Suranga, K., Burke, M., Harsha, K., Grahame, G., & Paul, B. (2015). *Enabling Better Interoperability for HealthCare: Lessons in Developing a Standards Based Application Programing Interface for Electronic Medical Record Systems. Journal of Medical Systems*, 39(11), 1-8.

[4] Nikolaos Beredimas ; Lab. of Med. Inf., Aristotle Univ. of Thessaloniki, Thessaloniki, Greece ; Vassilis Kilintzis ; Ioanna Chouvarda ; Nicos Maglaveras - *A reusable ontology for primitive and complex HL7 FHIR data types* - 2015 37th Annual International Conference of the IEEE Engineering in Medicine and Biology Society (EMBC) - ISSN : 1094-687X - INSPEC Accession Number: 15584935 DOI: 10.1109/EMBC.2015.7318911 Publisher: IEEE

[5] Bender, Duane, P.Eng and Sartipi Kamran, PhD, P.Eng, 2015. *HL7 FHIR: An Agile and RESTful Approach to Healthcare Information Exchange*. IEEE , ISBN: 978-1-4799-1053-3 D.O.I. 10.1109/CBMS.2013.6627810

[6] Qadeer, M.A., Salim. M. , Akhtar, M.S., 2015,. *Profile Management and Authentication Using LDAP. IEEE, ISBN:978-1-4244-3334-6, D.O.I. 10.1109/ICCET.2009.126.*

[7] Cluet, Sophie, Kapitskaia, Olga, Srivastava, Divesh, 1999. *Using LDAP directory caches.* ACM, ISBN: 1-58113-062-7, D.O.I.: 10.1145/303976.304003

[8] Connecting Health and Care for the Nation A Shared Nationwide Interoperability Roadmap DRAFT Version 1.0, ONC

[9] Leroux, Hugo, Metke-Jimenez, Alejandro, Lawley, Michael J., `ODM on FHIR: Towards Achieving Semantic Interoperability of Clinical Study Data. The Australian E-Health Research Centre, Health and Biosecurity, CSIRO.

Reflection Papers

BENEFITS AND DRAWBACKS OF SYNCHRONOUS ONLINE CONFERENCING

Iris Wunder
PhD Student, Lancaster University
Centre for Technology Enhanced Learning
Educational Research Department
Lancaster University
Lancaster. LA1 4YD

ABSTRACT

The study explores the benefits and drawbacks experienced when using synchronous online conferences. The use of virtual learning environments has become more or less standard at universities; however, the current literature falls short specifically investigating synchronous online sessions in virtual classrooms. Given the increased popularity of using synchronous elements for audio/video-conferencing, this work is concerned with addressing possible benefits and drawbacks of using virtual classrooms. Grounded Theory is employed to combine Glaser's (2012) approach with Strauss and Corbin's (1990) ideas, where three forms of coding are used to analyse the data further. Data are gathered through semi-structured interviews with three purposefully selected individuals, who teach at universities offering courses with a blended-learning approach in Germany and the UK. In this paper I present the core category, communication, and its relationship with the categories technology, social interaction and learning in synchronous online conferences. To summarise, all participants see more benefits than drawbacks of using a virtual classroom to meet synchronously both for the purpose of sharing and constructing knowledge and creating common visions. However, the results were controversial regarding the use of webcams in and the recording of virtual classroom sessions.

1. INTRODUCTION

The rapid progress of technology significantly influences computer-based learning in distance education. Due to its pedagogical impact, one of the most important aspects is interactivity which has three main components: student-student interaction, student-instructor interaction, and student-content interaction (Moore, 1989). Distance-education technology has moved toward multimedia-oriented systems which allow an effective synergy of synchronous and asynchronous interaction in so-called virtual classrooms.

These are designed to provide the opportunity for participants to interact with each other in real time (synchronously). They can talk to each other via microphone, use a chat facility, express their current feelings with the use of emoticons and, depending on the setting, use a video camera to transmit real-time pictures of themselves. Furthermore, the moderator can split the participants into groups and send them into breakout rooms, where they can perform group activities on their own. The virtual classroom also offers an integrated white board, where one can upload Microsoft (MS) PowerPoint slides, which participants can write and draw onto.

2. CURRENT RESEARCH

The study explores the benefits and drawbacks experienced when using synchronous online conferences. Data was gathered through semi-structured interviews using Skype, as two of the participants were in Great Britain and one of them in Northern Germany, whilst I live in the South of Germany. Thus it was easier than meeting them personally. The participants were all teaching at universities in courses with a blended-learning or online-only approach. I used Grounded Theory and combined Glaser's (2012) with Strauss and Corbin's

(1990) ideas and used three forms of coding to analyse the data further. In this paper, I reflect on the core category I found for both the benefits and the drawbacks, communication, and its relationship to other categories that emerged from the analysis.

3. BENEFITS OF USING SYNCHRONOUS ONLINE CONFERENCES

3.1 Relationship between Communication and Technology

This relationship exists as the technology of the virtual classroom offers a wide range of functionality for communicating, such as the chat, the microphone and the emoticons, for example. Participant 3, a 38-year old University lecturer, who teaches at a British Law School pointed out: *"You can see exactly who is in the room. You get students holding up their hand, etc."* Additionally, the use of a webcam is beneficial for a more natural interaction and offers the possibility of interpreting facial expressions and gestures, which enriches communication. According to Participant 2, a 34-year old research fellow, who teaches at a German University, students appreciate the use of webcams: *"I know from the participants...that they really like to use the camera and to see the faces and all of the reactions".*

A study by Martin et al. (2012, p. 249) reveals the same results with students stating "that the visual presence of the instructor was beneficial". Guichon (2010) and Wang (2004) come to the same conclusion, as well. Bullingham and Vasconcelos (2013) go even one step further and argue that not using a webcam supports the risk of students providing an identity that reproduces only part of their offline identity. Furthermore, recording can be used to communicate what happened in the session to students who were not able to attend or who want to listen to it a second time.

3.2 Relationship between Communication and Learning

As the location does not matter, courses which use a virtual classroom attract people from all over the world. Their variety of experiences enhances the group's learning. Participant 3 argues, that *"it enables students who are in different time zones to attend. And I think, that can make the tutorial much richer because indeed, the student experiences will be different."* As students are speaking with their teacher and peers it is possible to ask questions for better understanding. Furthermore, those questions will help other students, too, even if the session is provided in lecture style. Participant 2 adds, that *"...even when there wasn't interaction with the participants planned, more questions to the teachers, we had the effect that they could learn from the questions of the others."*

Falloon's (2011) study of a postgraduate course using a virtual classroom at the University of Waikato revealed similar results, as the students said it was easy to ask questions, for example. The course concepts can be discussed in the virtual classroom but also applied in the workplace later, so communication and learning both continue after the sessions. Participant 1, a 46-year old University lecturer, who teachers at a British Business School, points out that one benefit is *"that it can be used for supporting people's learning".*

This confirms Schullo et al.'s (2007, p.2) findings, who state that synchronous interaction of students and teachers in distance education programmes provides "deep and meaningful learning opportunities" and "builds learning communities".

3.3 Relationship between Communication and Social Interaction

In the virtual classroom, students from all over the world meet and talk. Thus, they get familiar with each other and their teacher, which imitates the situation in a face-to-face classroom and as pointed out by Participant 2, *"...after a deadline, they come together and have a little party to say, great we made it."* Participant 1 adds that *"students really enjoy the opportunity to be able to communicate with each other...those that turn up definitely appreciate that opportunity to be able to interact with each other."*

This is confirmed in a study by Chou (2002), which showed that social-emotional interactions happened more frequently in synchronous online sessions than in asynchronous forum chats.

Socialising is enhanced when a webcam is used as the mimic and gestures of the one who is seen help getting to know each other and the background might also offer some information about the participant. According to Participant 2, *"this helps a lot for social interaction...because if you recognise the book that is in your shelf as well, or if you like a picture you see on the wall."*

Following Collis (1996), using synchronous tools in distance learning improves the motivation and engagement of students and supports group identity and the formation of community, which confirms these results. Martin et al. (2013) add, that another advantage of using synchronous technology is increased social interaction. Furthermore, according to Lu et al. (2013) social capital can be produced virtually through social interactions and thus will have a positive effect on learning outcomes.

4. DRAWBACKS OF USING SYNCHRONOUS ONLINE CONFERENCES

4.1 Relationship between Communication and Technology

The greatest hindrance in communication is a weak Internet connectivity, as this leads to delayed transmission of speech and in worst case, it excludes participants from taking part in virtual classroom sessions, e.g. if webcams are used. As Participant 3 argues, *"it means you need more bandwidth, so it would eliminate some students from attending if they are on an Army base in the middle of nowhere or somewhere in Africa."*

Paige et al. (2011) also state that a high speed Internet connection was very important for the synchronous virtual classrooms to function efficiently. The virtual classroom is also an artificial environment with limitations of how many people can speak at the same time, for example. Additionally, using a webcam can cause distractions as Participant 2 confirms: *"I know participants who say they don't like the camera and that it's a distraction and that they can't focus."*

If the technology does not work, students or the teacher can be ejected of the session without the participants knowing what happened. As Participant 3 points out, *"if some students or I get thrown out, I can't keep communicating with them saying: Something has happened to my Internet, give me two minutes, I'll log back on."* In their study of using a virtual classroom at a South-eastern university in the United States, Martin et al. (2013) also argue that it is difficult to react when students or instructors are facing technical difficulties.

4.2 Relationship between Communication and Interaction

Without using a webcam, the participants miss out on mimic and gestures and thus both student-student and student-teacher interaction might be less powerful. Participant 3 argues: *"So, I can't see if any of my students are totally going blank."* This is confirmed by Martin et al. (2013) who found that it is difficult to read the students and change instructional strategies during a session, as the teacher is not able to see if there is confusion by reading facial expressions. Paige et al. (2011) also explained that the powerlessness to help students when they get disconnected was frustrating for teachers.

Moreover, when communication takes place in the chat at the same time as the teacher and/or the other students are speaking it can be very interactive but also very difficult for the teacher to follow. Participant 3 states that *"even if it is lecture type, you can't just give your lecture because there's so much chat going on, so you need to wait half an hour, keep track of that as well."* Kear et al. (2011, p. 954) elaborate further and state that "the need to split attention among auditory, textual and visual material ...can result in cognitive overload." Finally, if virtual classroom meetings are organised by the students themselves, they rarely make breaks and thus social interaction is missing, as Participant 2 explains: *"Students do not plan breaks, they want to be efficient and therefore there is less social interaction in the virtual classroom."*

5. CONCLUSION

The results of the entire study indicate that teachers experience more benefits than drawbacks when using a virtual classroom for synchronous online conferences.

Interestingly, the participants provided various reasons for not using a webcam (e.g. distraction) but on the other hand were missing the possibilities of using facial expressions to interpret how students feel and to inspire them with their own mimic and gestures. However, the main reason seems that the bandwidth needed for a functional use of the webcam is not yet existent in every location. These controversial statements can be found in the existing literature, too (for example, Guichon, 2010, Wang, 2004). The same controversy existed in the use of recordings. Although the benefits, such as availability for students who could not join the session or wanted to listen to it again were highlighted, it seems that the nature of recording had an immense negative effect on the communication and possibly even on the attendance.

However, the results seem to confirm Daniel et al.´s (2003) argument, that virtual classroom sessions can be used to form a virtual learning community with its five components individuals, content, shared purpose, social protocols and communication. Furthermore, social capital can be developed as collaboration takes place when working on common tasks (Daniel et al., 2003).

REFERENCES

Bullingham, L., Vasconcelos, A.C., 2013. "The presentation of self in the online world": Goffman and the study of online identities. J. Inf. Sci. 39, 101–112. doi:10.1177/0165551512470051

Chou, C.C., 2002. A comparative content analysis of student interaction in synchronous and asynchronous learning networks, in: Proceedings of the 35th Annual Hawaii International Conference on System Sciences, 2002. HICSS. Presented at the Proceedings of the 35th Annual Hawaii International Conference on System Sciences, 2002. HICSS, pp. 1795–1803. doi:10.1109/HICSS.2002.994093

Collis, B., 1996. Tele-learning in a digital world: The future of distance learning. Thompson Computer Press, London.

Daniel, B., Schwier, R.A., McCalla, G., 2003. Social Capital in Virtual Learning Communities and Distributed Communities of Practice. Can. J. Learn. Technol. Rev. Can. L'apprentissage Technol. 29.

Falloon, G., 2011. Falloon, G. (2011). Making the Connection: Moore's Theory of Transactional Distance and Its Relevance to the Use of a Virtual Classroom in Postgraduate Online Teacher Education. J. Res. Technol. Educ. 43(3), 187–209.

Glaser, G., 2012. Stop. Write! Writing Grounded Theory | Grounded Theory Review.

Guichon, N., 2010. Preparatory study for the design of a desktop videoconferencing platform for synchronous language teaching. Guichon N 2010 Prep. Study Des. Deskt. Videoconferencing Platf. F Comput. Assist. Lang. Learn. 171–184.

Kear, K., Chetwynd, F., Williams, J., Donelan, H., 2012. Web conferencing for synchronous online tutorials: Perspectives of tutors using a new medium. Comput. Educ. 58, 953–963. doi:10.1016/j.compedu.2011.10.015

Lu, J., Yang, J., Yu, C.-S., 2013. Is social capital effective for online learning? Inf. Manage. 50, 507–522. doi:10.1016/j.im.2013.07.009

Martin, F., Parker, M.A., Deale, D.F., 2012. Examining interactivity in synchronous virtual classrooms. Int. Rev. Res. Open Distrib. Learn. 13, 228–261.

Martin, F., Parker, M.A., Oyarzun, B., 2013. A Case Study on the Adoption and use of Synchronous Virtual Classrooms.

Moore, M.G., 1989. Editorial: Three types of interaction. Am. J. Distance Educ. 3, 1–7. doi:10.1080/08923648909526659

Paige, G.A., Fierstein, M., Sturm, C., Pauli, J., 2011. Faculty Adoption of Technology: The Use of Elluminate Live. Technol. Teach. Educ. Annu. 2606–2614.

Schullo, S., Hilbelink, A., Barron, A., Venable, M., 2007. Selecting a Virtual Classroom System: Elluminate Live vs. Macromedia Breeze (Adobe Acrobat Connect Professional) [WWW Document]. URL http://jolt.merlot.org/vol3no4/hilbelink.htm (accessed 9.4.16).

Strauss, A. & Corbin, J., 1990. Basics of Qualitative Research. Sage, London.

Wang, Y., 2004. LLT Vol8Num3: SUPPORTING SYNCHRONOUS DISTANCE LANGUAGE LEARNING WITH DESKTOP VIDEOCONFERENCING [WWW Document]. URL http://llt.msu.edu/vol8num3/wang/default.html (accessed 9.4.16).

OPPORTUNITY OR CHALLENGE? WHEN DESIGNING MHEALTH APPLICATIONS FOR UNDERSERVED POPULATION: A CASE STUDY ON MIGRANT WORKERS IN CHINA

Shijuan Li[1], Lingmiao Yao[1], Zhixing Liu[1] and Tianyuan Liu[2]

[1]*Department of Information Management, Peking University, No.5 Yiheyuan Road, Haidian District, Beijing, China 100871*

[2]*Institute of Computer Science and Technology, Changchun University of Science and Technology, No. 7089, Weixing Road, Changchun, China 130022*

ABSTRACT

This study particularly examines if mHealth applications can contribute to providing more opportunity for the underserved population, i.e. migrant workers, to access to improved healthcare. A qualitative study was conducted to examine the migrant workers' attitude, behavior and habit towards mHealth applications, which involves the users in the early stages of designing of a health behavior change system. The findings from the interviews include: the migrant workers are familiar with smart phones though they are lack of health information literacy; they seek health information mainly from mass medias, such as TV, news etc.; they tend to accept health information passively, i.e. via information pushing, and believe in it immediately without any verification. Then a mobile application was prototyped to examine the feasibility to satisfy the migrant workers' needs and habit.

KEYWORDS

mHealth, Migrant workers, Mobile applications, Underserved population

1. INTRODUCTION

Rural migrant workers constitute an important part of the working class in China. In 2015, according to the National Bureau of Statistics of China, there were approximately 277 million rural migrant workers working in Chinese cities (National Bureau of Statistics of China, 2016). They mainly work in the manufacturing industry, construction business, wholesale and retail trade etc.; in total composing nearly 65% of the work force (National Bureau of Statistics of China, 2016). However, only 17.6% of the migrant workers have medical insurance, with the lowest rate in the highly risky construction business, which restricted their access to local healthcare system (National Bureau of Statistics of China, 2016). Fu and Zhou indicate when the migrant workers left their farmland and started their jobs in the cities, their health status might get worse (Fu, 2011, Zhou, 2010). Thus, migrant workers remain as the majority of underserved population for healthcare.

mHealth as defined by the World Health Organization (WHO), is an area of electronic health (eHealth) that provides health services and information via mobile technologies such as mobile phones and PDAs. Goel et. al. note that mHealth can support the performance of healthcare by dissemination of clinical updates, learning materials, and reminders, particularly in underserved rural locations in low and middle-income countries (Goel, 2013). Nevertheless, studies regarding underserved populations', such as migrant workers, health information literacy, attitude and health information behaviors etc. towards mHealth applications haven't been investigated widely, which have significant impacts on the success of designing, development and implementation of an mHealth program.

This study particularly examines if mHealth applications can contribute to providing more opportunity for the underserved population, i.e. migrant workers, to access to improved healthcare. The core questions are designed include: If migrant workers are ready for mHealth applications? What factors influence positively or negatively their acceptance and use of mHealth applications? How these affect the design of an mHealth application for migrant workers? The rest of the paper is organized as follows: a qualitative study examining the migrant workers' attitude, behavior and habit towards mHealth applications, which involves the users in the early stages of designing of a health behavior change system; followed by the development of a prototype and a summary of designing guidelines for migrant workers; end with a discussion.

2. METHODS AND MATERIALS

In order to gain insight information from rural migrant workers on their attitudes towards mHealth applications, health beliefs and health information behaviors etc., a semi-structured interview were conducted to collect qualitative data and to involve them in the early stages of an application design at the same time. Then, a mobile health prototype particular for migrant workers was proposed and the design guidelines were summarized.

2.1 Involvement of Underserved Users in Early Stages of Designing of an mHealth Application

The participants were approached and interviewed via telephone while they were working in different Chinese cities, which provided the possibility of reflecting diverse issues widely. Their hometown dialogue was used to interview the participants to increase the fluency of the process since they were originated from the same province (Hunan province). Then the recorded data were translated into mandarin by one of the team and analyzed utilizing content analysis methods. The participants' information is summarized in Table 1.

Table 1. Participants information summary

Feature	Brief statistics	
Age	18-30: 50%	30+: 50%
Sex	Female: 50%	Male: 50%
Apps experience	Yes: 75%	No: 25%
Smartphone experience	Yes: 100%	No: Nil
Health issues	Back pain (50%); edema (25%); respiratory issues (25%); diabetes mellitus (25%)	
Health information acquisition	TV (25%); Apps (25%); Internet (25%); friend and family (25%); news (50%)	

The preliminary findings are: First, the most frequently used information media is mobile phone, then followed by pc. All of the participants have experiences using smart phones. Second, the participants are suffering from various chronic conditions, including back pain, edema, respiratory issues, diabetes mellitus etc, which have a relation with their job or health habit. Third, they admitted that mass media is the health information source for them, along with family or friends. Fourth, they tend to playing games rather than manage their own condition or acquire health information via mobile phones, since they were aware of little information on health applications either from the hospitals or commercial suppliers. Last but not least, they tend to read and immediately believe in the information pushed to their phones rather than searching health information themselves.

2.2 Designing an mHealth Prototype for Migrant Workers

An mHealth prototype was proposed and prototyped utilizing JustInMind^{R} which is a tool for mobile prototype development. Figure 2 shows the snapshots of the selected interfaces and functionalities: information push, information organization and hometown forum etc. Considering their health literacy, health habit and healthcare insurance status, the following design guidelines are summarized and proposed. Basic functionalities such as search engine, information push, hometown forum was deliberately designed, as they are the particularly preferred by the migrant workers. The search engine provides a convenient approach to satisfy the users' particular information needs. Information pushing is arguably effective for those who used to access health information passively. Online forum is believed as particularly effective for those who originated from the same area, as they were sharing similar healthcare insurance and reimbursements policy. And personalization option is a desired function which can facilitate their chronic condition management and health status for different individuals.

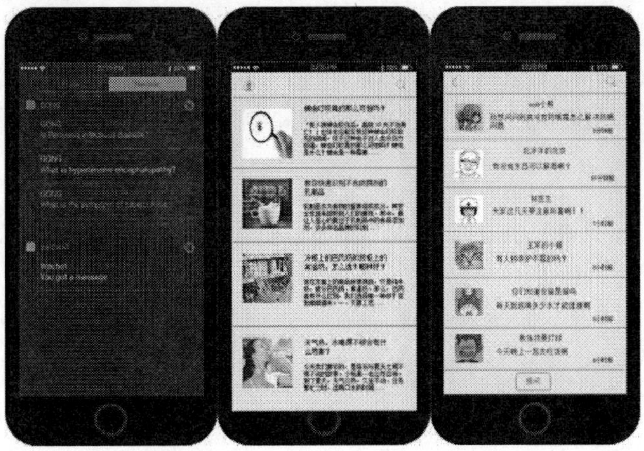

Figure 2. A proposed mHealh application: interfaces and functionalities

3. DISCUSSIONS

In 2009, the WHO Global Observatory launched a survey among the member states as sought to determine the status of mHealth in the participated member states. The majority of member states (83%) reported offering at least one type of mHealth service (World Health Organization, 2011). In China, the hospitals have been utilizing mobile applications, WeChat (a Chinese popular social media software), and self-service machines to supplement their self-service networks for registration appointments, medical expenses charge, examination reports look-up etc. According to the Statistical Report on the Development of the Thirty-sixth China Internet Network, there are 668 million (48.8% population) Internet users in 2015; among the new Internet users, 48% were from rural area. Moreover, mobile phone was the main Internet access device (69.2%), and it is believed that using mobile phones to access to the Internet will remain the main driving force in the upcoming years. (National Internet Network Information Center of China, 2015). The rapid development of mHealth applications and devices bring the underserved population a promising future to access to better healthcare. Nevertheless, the mHealth applications are mainly pilot-scale projects and lack of evaluations. Evaluation is part of the process that can determine cost-effectiveness. It involves educating the public about the benefits of mHealth and leads to the creation of government policy, though these factors were reported as among the most persistent barriers to mHealth adoption. Moreover, the assessment and examination of underserved population's attitude, health behavior and habits are desired.

REFERENCES

China Internet Network Information Center. 2016. The 36th report on the status and statistics of China Internet Development. Retrieved on 20th June 2016, from http://www.cnnic.net.cn/hlwfzyj/hlwxzbg/hlwtjbg/201507/P020150723549500667087.pdf. In Chinese. 中国互联网络信息中心. 第 36 次中国互联网发展状况统计报告 [EB/OL]. 2016.

Fu, Y., 2011. An empirical study on health demand and its influencing factors of migrant workers in the construction industry in Taiyuan. Master thesis. Shanxi Medical University. In Chinese. 付瑜. 太原市建筑业农民工健康需求及其影响因素的实证研究. 山西: 山西医科大学, 2011.

Goel, S., et al., 2013. Bridging the Human Resource Gap in Primary Health Care Delivery Systems of Developing Countries With mHealth: Narrative Literature Review. JMIR mHealth and uHealth, 15, e25.

National Bureau of Statistics of China, 2016. *Report on monitoring of migrant workers*. Retrieved on 21st July 2016, from http://www.stats.gov.cn/tjsj/zxfb/201604/t20160428_1349713.html. In Chinese. 中国国家统计局. 2016 年全国农民工监测调查报告 [EB/OL]. 2016.

World Health Organization, 2011. mHealth: new horizons for health through mobile technologies. *Social Indicators Research*, Vol. 64, No. 7,pp 471-493.

Zhou, F., 2010. An empirical study on the health needs of migrant workers in Hangzhou. Master thesis, Zhejiang University. In Chinese. 周菲. 杭州市农民工健康需求的实证研究. 浙江：浙江大学，2010.

Posters

PROTOTYPING AN INNOVATIVE COOPERATIVE CAMPUS SYSTEM

Herbert Neuendorf
Duale Hochschule Baden Württemberg Mosbach
Department of Business Information Systems
Lohrtalweg 10, D74821 Mosbach

ABSTRACT

The applicability of cooperative social computing has been investigated for the community of students, faculty and university staff and a webbased mobile cooperative IT system has been prototyped. A site-specific cooperation scenario and system concept have been developed. Core functions have been implemented that can be used to organize cooperative projects and tasks, to demand for individual services and establish open innovation activities. The crowd of students, faculty and staff may demand for services and fulfill services. To ensure a balance of demand and supply, a social virtual currency has been defined and integrated into the system. The system also appeals to social engagement. It intends to initiate and support personal interaction and cooperation in real life projects and activities. Overall, a new site-specific channel for communication, coordination and cooperation has been developed.

KEYWORDS

Cooperative System, Social Computing, Crowdsourcing

1. INTRODUCTION

Social Computing deals with the design and development of socio-technical information systems that support social interaction and cooperation. We focus on prototypical design and implementation of an intermediary cooperative IT system (based on student research projects), that may serve as a platform for the coordination of cooperation. The system enables to call for participants in cooperative projects and single tasks, to ask for individual services and to establish open innovation activities at the university campus – adressing primarily students, faculty and stuff as users and "crowd" (Howe 2009). The system attempts to mediate the social context and the activities of its users (Gross 2013) and intends to enable (but also drive) social interaction and awareness (Dourish 1992). This contribution follows the design research and engineering approach (Hevner 2004, Österle 2010) that focuses on user-centered development of socio-technical systems.

2. SYSTEM DESIGN AND IMPLEMENTATION

2.1 Semantic System Design

To exert a participatory system design process, potential system users (students, faculty and staff) were interviewed to determine main use cases and success factors.

The system potentially addresses all members of the campus community. Thus, the overall system should not be organized hierarchically but should show a peer to peer character concerning its users and use cases. The clearly-defined local carrier and user group may stimulate reasonable user interest and trust. The focus of the system is not conventional social networking or the establishment of a virtual campus (like established learning management systems) (Karacapilidis 2010) but to catalyze real interaction and cooperation within a trusted local organization. The system intends to enhance and coordinate real life engagement in social activities and organizational tasks at the campus and to act as a driver and enabler of those local activities. Primary concern are the coordination of services by students for students and collective activities (Open Day etc.) as well as support for innovation requests and proposals. The system might etablish a new channel for cooperation, coordination, communication and innovation – thus intensifying and supporting collective activities and interaction within the community.

To make the system work consistently, mechanisms for control, incentive and feedback are needed. This implies the confirmation and registration of task fulfillment. The system also addresses ethical aspects. It represents a call for activity and social commitment, stimulating social emergence. A balance of hedonistic and altruistic user impetus had to be established. This was achieved by a Social Credit Point currency system that operates as a reciprocal feedback mechanism and manifestation of social capital (Bourdieu 1983).

2.2 Implementation

2.2.1 Use Cases

Main use cases of the system have already been implemented:

Requested tasks and services are described by the requesting consumer and displayed in the system. Potential providers of services may apply for jobs and have to be accepted or rejected by the consumer. Fulfillment of tasks is confirmed by the consumer. Tasks are categorized and tagged (task type, required qualification of providers, number of participants, expected duration, time frame, location, complexity). Search and history functions have been implemented based on task category and tagging. Calls for cooperative problem solving and innovation proposals may be submitted.

Participation requires a personal system account using a minimum of personal data. In the context of the system, the provision of services for the real life campus community is much more important than personal profiling. The virtual identity of system users thus recedes behind their socio-functional identity as members of the real community at the campus (Bakardjieva 2012). When a user deletes her account, personal data is erased (quick goodbye pattern (Schümmer 2007)). There is a role concept which defines three different user groups and authorizations (administrators / students / faculty and staff). Basic functions and use cases mentioned are accessible to all roles.

2.2.2 Technology

A running prototype was implemented as a three tier multi user client server system. The system uses a responsive mobile frontend and is run on a statelessly operating web/application server and a relational DB6 database. The system is based on SAP NetWeaver Application Server 7.30 (ABAP) (running on Linux) and its integrated Internet Communication Framework (ICF). The system is hosted at a SAP University Competence Center (UCC TU Magdeburg). Development and testing were carried out remotely from our DHBW campus via SAPGUI. The system uses stateless SAP ABAP Business Server Pages and SAP's UI5 responsive JavaScript frontend framework in its open source version OPENUI5. The crypto-js framework is used to encode passwords. The system was implemented based on SAP technology to evaluate SAP's web based development and programming models. Nevertheless the project primarily focuses on semantics and the system could also be realized using standard Java EE frameworks for example.

Due to its responsive frontend the system may be used by various mobile devices. Because the crowd of students in particular should be addressed, mobile usability is an important success factor.

2.3 Social Credit Point Currency System

As a reciprocal feedback component and serious game feature (Gibson 2015) a Social Credit Point (SCP) mechanism has been integrated into the system: SCPs are transferred from service consumers to service providers. SCPs are accumulated to request new services. SCPs thus ensure a balance of demand and supply of services. They mediate between hedonistic and altruistic motivations of system users (Schulz 2015). Following Ernst (et al. 2013) an ethically dual system was created.

SCPs represent a social virtual currency (social capital). This social currency requires regulatory functions that were integrated into the system. New users obtain a SCP account with an initial credit. Requesting services based on SCP transfer is only possible with a laid SCP account that must not be overdrawn. SCPs are only transferred after confirmation of service fulfillment. Only users defined by a special role (faculty and staff) have an unlimited amount of SCPs at their disposal. The system administrator is able to check the total amount of circulating SCPs. However, social activities should be encouraged by the SCP system and not obstructed. So it is also possible to request for services, activities etc. without SCP compensation.

3. CONCLUSION

The prototype is work in progress and will be enhanced by further student research projects. Yet unsolved issues are the conversion of SCPs in material or immaterial goods and the appropriateness of digital badges based on accumulated SCPs and their presentation within the system ("Hall of Social Fame").

The system has the transformative potential to catalyze the coordination of local cooperation via system mediated activities and to act as enabler and driver of social emergence and social awareness ("Awareness is an understanding of the activities of others, which provides a context for your own activity." (Dourish 1992)).

This intermediary cooperative system innovatively addresses and integrates different semantic aspects of social computing (Crowdsourcing, Open Innovation, Serious Games, Social Capital) in a dynamic environment based on current mobile technologies.

REFERENCES

Bakardjieva, M. and Gaden, G., 2012. Web 2.0 Technologies of the Self. *Philos. Technol.* 25, pp 399-413.

Bourdieu, P. (1983). Ökonomisches Kapital, kulturelles Kapital, soziales Kapital. In: Reinhard Kreckel (Ed.): *Soziale Ungleichheiten. Soziale Welt.* Sonderband 2, pp 183 - 198.

Dourish, P. and Bellotti, V. (1992). Awareness and coordination in shared workspaces. *Conference proceedings on Computer-supported cooperative work*, pp 107-114.

Ernst, C-P., et al. (2013). Hedonic and Utilitarian Motivations of Social Network Site Adoption. *Working Papers in Information Systems and Business Administration*, 01/2013, Johannes Gutenberg-University Mainz, Department of Information Systems and Business Administration.

Gibson, D. et al. (2015). Digital badges in education. *Educ. Inf. Technol.* 20, pp 403-410.

Gross, T. (2013). Supporting Effortless Coordination: 25 Years of Awareness Research. *Computer Supported Cooperative Work*, 22(4-6), pp 425-474.

Hevner, A. R. et al. (2004). Design science in Information Systems research. *MIS quarterly*, 28(1), pp 75-105.

Howe, J. (2009). *Crowdsourcing*. Three Rivers Press, New York, USA.

Karacapilidis, N. (2010). Novel Developments in Web-Based Learning Technologies. Information Science Reference, Hershey, New York.

Österle, H. et al. (2010). Memorandum zur gestaltungsorientierten Wirtschaftsinformatik. *Zeitschrift für betriebswirtschaftliche Forschung* 6, pp 664-672.

Schümmer,T and Lukosch, S. (2007). *Patterns for Computer-Mediated Interaction*. Wiley, Chichester, West Sussex, England.

Schulz, M. et al. (2015). How Idea Creativity and Hedonic Value Influence Project Success in Crowdfunding. *12th International Conference on Wirtschaftsinformatik*, Osnabrück, Germany, pp 948-962.

EXPLORING YOUNG PEOPLE'S PERCEPTION ON THE ASSESSMENT OF THE CREDIBILITY OF ONLINE HEALTH INFORMATION: A CASE STUDY ON UNIVERSITY STUDENTS IN CHINA

Beidi Yu and Shijuan Li *
Department of Information Management, Peking University
No.5 Yiheyuan Road, Haidian District, Beijing, P.R.China

ABSTRACT

The assessment of online health information, i.e. its credibility, trustworthiness, etc., influences the users greatly in their judging and health behavior change process. Related works haven't come to a consensus on the framework of trust formation process. Nor much attention has been paid to one of the most active groups of online health information users, the youth. This study examines the young people's perception and judgment towards online health information, utilizing searching experiment, followed by an interview. To test the design and reveal deficiencies of the study and procedure before time and resources are expended on large scale studies, a pilot study was designed and conducted. The preliminary findings include: young people pay more attention to well-known healthcare providers; they neglect the content or design of health information; their take-for-granted trust on the experts decides the youth's choices.

KEYWORDS

Information credibility, information trustworthiness, information literacy, youth, health information seeking

1. INTRODUCTION

Young people have been recognized as one of the most active groups of the Internet users (China Internet Network Information Center, 2016). According to China Internet Network Information Center (CNNIC), in 2015, there were approximately 688 million Internet users in China, among which 36.4% (around 224 million) were young people (aged between 10 to 24). Though they are supposed to have comprehensive surfing skills, they still have difficulty in evaluating the quality of the online information, especially with online health information (Gray et al., 2005, Dobransky and Hargittai, 2012). Assessment of information's credibility influences users' trust judgement and health behaviour change eventually. Related work considered credibility as a key impact factor of trust formation (Everard and Galletta, 2005, Rowley et al., 2015). Other work indicated that trust and credibility are two concepts overlapped, since they share same sub-domains, i.e. brand, content, usefulness, style, while considering constructing an assessment framework (Fogg et al., 2003, Rowley et al., 2015). This work tries to explore the factors that may affect young people's judgement when assessing the credibility of online health information, which then will help to understand users' health information behaviour.

2. METHODS

Young people's perception and judgment towards online health information are investigated utilizing searching experiment and interviews. Twenty participants (aged below 25) are approached within the Peking University to take part in the investigation. The participant first attends a half-hour session to search for

* corresponding author

information within a given health field. Each participant should provide concurrent, oral "think aloud" protocols as they search the Internet for health information. Meanwhile, a numerical scale, from one to ten, will be provided to them to score the credibility of the searching results. Then a brief interview is followed to explore the rational on how they allocate scores for the credibility of each result.

3. ANALYSIS OF A PILOT STUDY

A pilot study was designed and conducted to reveal deficiencies in the design of the study and procedure before time and resources are expended on large scale studies. Questions that were not answered as expected were re-worded or re-scaled; time that taken to complete the session was recorded to decide whether it is reasonable; ambiguities in questions were identified and clarified. The participant was a 3rd-year undergraduate who was interviewed about basic information about online health information search and credibility judgement. He searched health information online once health issues happened. The preliminary results of the pilot study were analyzed utilizing content based analysis as shown in table 1 in greater details.

Table 1. Analysis of the pilot study

Code	Theme	Explanation	Quote
IS	Credible information source	Health websites, hospital websites, question and answer community	The most credible website is hospital website.
IP	Credible information provider	Large public hospitals, doctors from famous hospitals	Large hospitals hired these doctors have verified their professionalism.
CI	Credible information	Disease symptoms, appointment information, hospital and department ranks, misunderstands of information	That information is provided by professional doctors and it can't impact my health.
NI	Not credible information	Recommended medicine, recommended therapy	If I suffer from health problems which I can't solve with common sense, I must go to the hospital. I don't trust commercial recommendations.
NF	Not credible factor	Advertisement	Heavy advertisements are for profit only. They may exaggerate the issues.
AA	Active acquisition	Hospitals and departments	I use Internet to search what the disease is and which hospital and department I should go to.
PA	Passive acquisition	Pushing articles	I read these articles carefully because they are filtered by editors who should be responsible.
TF	Information trust formation	Information from authority consistently	When I browse the information I get from search engine, all of them are consistent.

4. DISCUSSION

Sillence et al. (2007) noted design and content of information were major impact factors within the dimension that users utilized to assess the credibility of online health information. In the pilot study, we found that the participant payed more attention to the trustworthy information providers, i.e. leading hospitals, doctors and web editors, which contribute to the credibility of health information. The take-for-granted trust on experts and large public hospitals arguably affects young people's assessment of credibility of online health information, and excludes other information sources such as private sectors. Nerveless, the lack of provision of health information from well-known organizations and consumers' deficiency in health information literacy restricts the health information seeking and utilizing behavior. The reason of this difference between our pilot study and previous studies will be explored in future large scale studies. In addition, the result of pilot study indicated that when conducting searching experiment the task should be set about the symptom of an uncommon disease which young people are more likely to suffer from. The active acquisition and passive acquisition should be also considered when improve the research method.

REFERENCES

China Internet Network Information Center, 2016, Statistical Report on Internet Development in China. < http://www1.cnnic.cn/IDR/ReportDownloads/201604/P020160419390562421055.pdf>.

Dobransky, K. and Hargittai, E., 2012, Inquiring Minds Acquiring Wellness: Uses of Online and Offline Sources for Health Information. *Health Communication,* Vol. 27 No. 4, pp. 331-343.

Everard, A. and Galletta, D. F., 2005, How Presentation Flaws Affect Perceived Site Quality, Trust, and Intention to Purchase from an Online Store. *Journal of Management Information Systems,* Vol. 22 No. 3, pp. 55-95.

Fogg, B. J. et al, 2003, How Do Users Evaluate the Credibility of Web Sites? A Study with Over 2,500 Participants. Proceedings of the 2003 conference on designing for user experiences, San Francisco, California, pp. 1-15.

Gray, N. J. et al, 2005, Health information-seeking behaviour in adolescence: the place of the internet. *Social Science & Medicine,* Vol. 60 No. 7, pp. 1467-1478.

Rowley, J. et al, 2015, Students' trust judgements in online health information seeking. *Health Informatics Journal,* Vol. 21 No. 4, pp. 316-327.

Sillence, E. et al, 2007, How do patients evaluate and make use of online health information? *Social Science & Medicine,* Vol. 64 No. 9, pp. 1853-1862.

APPLICATIONS OF CLASSIFICATION ALGORITHMS FOR ANALYSIS OF FACTORS WHICH INFLUENCE THE PREDICTION OF THE IMPACT FACTOR ON SOCIAL NETWORKS

Marco Aurélio Schünke[1] and Dante Augusto Couto Barone[2]
[1]*Instituto de Informática Universidade Federal do Rio Grande do Sul (UFRGS), Porto Alegre. RS - Brazil*
[2]*Universidade Federal do Rio Grande do Sul, Instituto de Informática, Departamento de Informática Aplicada. Porto Alegre. RS - Brazil*

ABSTRACT

The dissemination of advertisements on social networks has grown tremendously in recent years, but is not always possible to evaluate factors that influence the impact of interactions through advertising. Companies as Google and Facebook are on the list of the largest companies in the world. Investment on advertising and pages creation for dissemination of advertisements and brands has led Facebook to an outstanding position in this scenario. In this context, this study aims to analyze and predict the number of interactions in news published in five fan pages, which are the most accessed at the Facebook social network in Brazil. As a contribution is proposed to determine the impact factor of publications, considering the average of three mentioned features, the number of likes, the number of comments and the number of times that the news was shared. Results of different techniques of classification will be evaluated, beyond the influence of characteristics related to words and more frequent terms.

KEYWORDS

Prediction, Data Mining, Social Networks

1. INTRODUCTION

Social networks were used only as an entertainment for some enthusiastic users and nowadays are used for many purposes, as for example, disclose travel, products, companies, photos, videos, links, stories, events, promote education and even broadcast news that can drive major changes in society, according to (BUZA, 2012) as the revolutions in the Islamic world, or US presidential election.

2. METHODOLOGY

The data processed in this study were obtained from fan pages, which were relevant, according to the site (Tecmundo, 2016). According to (Renan Hamann December 16, 2016 - 10 am 58). The selected pages are among the ten most accessed and liked on Facebook by Brazilian users as the following list.

Another subfield of artificial intelligence applied to the work is the Natural Language Processing (NLP) which aims to study automatic understanding problems of human language, in other words, seeks for transform stored information in databases into language understandable to humans (Jurafsky , 1999).

- Guaraná Antarctica (35.938 milhões)
- Coca-Cola (35,750 milhões)
- Skol (32,935 milhões)
- Hotel Urbano (19,299 milhões)
- Garoto (19,104 milhões)
- Lacta (17,281 milhões)
- L`Oreal (16,430 milhões)
- Itaú (16,427 milhões)
- Halls (16,086 milhões)
- Netshoes (16,039 milhões)

The data were collected between 2010 to 2016 from public pages of companies which own the following brands: Guaraná Antarctica, Coca-Cola, Hotel Urbano, Garoto and Lacta.

To perform the task of getting the data from a fan page of Facebook social network, we used the Facebook SDK that provides a set of features that allows to access API calls from the Facebook server. In order to facilitate the extraction of information in this task we identified the stream table that makes possible to obtain 44 attributes of a fan page.

2.1 Classification of Attributes

According to Rezende (2003) The prediction is the generalization of examples (classification, regression). That is, by classifying it is possible to determine to which class an object belongs, given the values of a set of object attributes. For example, this study proposes the impact factor which consists of the average of interactions of a Facebook fan page. This impact factor was established and classified according to the following classes, High Impact Factor, Medium and Low Impact Factor.

Below is shown an example of the classification used in the corpus obtained from Guarana Antarctica Fan Page as the formula.

$$Fi = \sum (cu\ co\ cm) / 3$$

At where,

Fi Impact factor

cu Number of likes

co Number of comments of a message

cm Number of Shares of a message

Once calculated the limits of classes the message classification is done.

IF (Fi >= Fa)

High Impact Factor class

IF ((Fi >= Fm) && (Fi < Fa))

Middle Impact Factor class

IF (Fi < Fm)

Low Impact Factor class

2.2 Application of Prediction Algorithms

For the application of the algorithms responsible for prediction, was used the Weka software, acronym (Waikato Environment for Knowledge Analysis), a data mining tool that provides a collection of algorithms of machine learning art, and preprocessing algorithms.

For the prediction task are listed the algorithms used at work according to the following roll.

- ✓ NaiveBayes
- ✓ J48
- ✓ AdaBoostM1
- ✓ DecisionTable
- ✓ RandomTree
- ✓ AttributeSelectedClassifier
- ✓ LWL

2.3 Attributes influencing the Impact Factor

In this step to statistically analyze the relative frequency where FRI is the quotient between the absolute frequency value of the event and the total number of events, as represented by the formula:

FRI = fi/n

At where:

n It represents the total number of events;

fi is the number of times that the value of particular event occurs

The results are demonstrated through experiments with mined data from five pages more accessible fans in Brazil in order to answer the questions you want this job.

3. CONCLUSION

This study application analysis for ranking algorithms of the factors that influence the prediction of the impact factor in social networks through experiments conducted here, in particular, identifies that among the classification technique with better results in the task of predicting factor impact the J48 algorithm presented a rate prediction 91.9324% correct classification instances to news published in the Guarana Antarctica fan page and also a 86.0963% prediction rate of correct classification instances to news published on page fans of Lacta.

With these results the task of analyzing and predicting the number of interactions on news disseminated on social networks was answered as expectations of work and also that among the employed algorithms though the J48 algorithm presented an excellent result in predicting the impact factor the DecisionTable algorithm presented a very good result in most corpora used.

Another contribution of this work was to define the impact factor, consisting of the average of the three interactions, identified as number of likes, commented and shared stories, and thereby enabled the exploration of the use of machine learning algorithms to predict the attribute impact factor in corpora fan pages in Facebook social network meeting the expectations of this work and the use of natural language processing techniques and Knowledge Discovery in Data base.

In addition, then another expected result is to reveal what are the factors that influence to a published news has an impact of greater interactions on the social network.

The results indicate that among the five corpus of messages classified with greater High Impact factor have on average 11 words in the messages, while the 5 messages classified less Impact Factor Low have on average 33 words in each message, revealing it the amount of words in a news posted on a fan page is a pattern that influences the classification of impact factor. In other words, the size of the message from a news reader influence one community in a social network in motivating interactions of both positively and negatively.

It identified also that the degree of influence of the High Impact Factor in news released by months of the year, may be related to the months that have holidays for dissemination of news providing a wave propagation of information through interactions enjoy, comment and share.

It is also revealed that the afternoon shift is the most promising for achieving high impact factor, interactions.

Another factor influencing Fi in the fact that there is the presence of photos or images that contributes to the motivation of Internet users interact with threads and this interaction spread the news through the relationships of friends circles.

More details on all the experiments are available in LUME, digital repository of the Federal University of Rio Grande do Sul (LUME, 2016).

The findings also allow an orientation for Brazilian companies to promote their products through more accurate news with an opportunity to achieve a Greater Impact for the dissemination of news, announcements and brands, since the information is a new economic asset class such as a coin or gold.

REFERENCES

Buza. K. *Feedback Prediction for Blogs*. The 36th Annual Conference of the German Classification Society on Data Analysis, Machine Learning and Knowledge Discovery. Hildesheim, Germany. August 1-3, 2012.

Jurafsky, D.l S. (Daniel Saul) *Speech and Langauge Processing / Daniel Jurafsky*, James H. Martin. p. cm., 1999.

LUME UFRGS. *Aplicação de algoritmos de classificação para análise dos fatores que influenciam na predição do fator de impacto nas redes sociais*. Disponível em: <http://hdl.handle.net/10183/134588>. Acesso em: 10 set. 2016.

Rezende, S. O.; Pugliese, J. B.; Melanda, E. A.; Paula, M. F., *Mineração de Dados*, in REZENDE, S. O. (Eds.), Sistemas Inteligentes. Editora Mnoela Ltda., p.307-335.2003.

Tecmundo, Disponível em: <http://www.tecmundo.com.br/facebook/48147-as-10-paginas-mais-populares-do-facebook-2013-.htm> Acesso em 01/06/2013.

AUTHOR INDEX